Catholic Intellectuals
and the Challenge of Democracy

CATHOLIC INTELLECTUALS

AND THE

CHALLENGE OF DEMOCRACY

JAY P. CORRIN

UNIVERSITY OF NOTRE DAME PRESS

Notre Dame, Indiana

Copyright © 2002
University of Notre Dame
Notre Dame, Indiana 46556
All Rights Reserved
http://www.undpress.nd.edu

Manufactured in the United States of America

Library of Congress Cataloging-in-Publication Data
Corrin, Jay P., 1943–
    Catholic intellectuals and the challenge of democracy / Jay P. Corrin.
      p.   cm.
    Includes bibliographical references and index.
    ISBN 0-268-02271-2 (cloth : alk. paper)
      1. Christianity and politics—Catholic Church—History—19th
century.   2. Democracy—Religious aspects—Catholic Church—
History—19th century.   3. Christianity and politics—Catholic
Church—History—20th century.   4. Democracy—Religious aspects—
Catholic Church—History—20th century.   I. Title.
BX1793 .C57   2002
261.7'088'22—dc21
    2002006418

∞ *This book is printed on acid-free paper.*

This book is dedicated
to the memory
of my mother

PATRICIA

my first and best teacher

Contents

Acknowledgments

I wish to extend my gratitude to those who have offered encouragement and provided thoughtful criticism in the making of this book. I am especially indebted to Rev. Robert A. Krieg, C.S.C., Professor of Theology at the University of Notre Dame, and to James R. Langford, former director of the University of Notre Dame Press, for the enthusiastic support they gave my project. Professors José Sanchez and Gordon Zahn read large portions of the early manuscript and offered valuable, insightful advice. My good friend Professor John Gagliardo of Boston University, whose command of German is legendary, was instrumental in illuminating difficult German colloquialisms in the letters of H. A. Reinhold and Waldemar Gurian. Discussions with Professor Stephen Collins of Babson College helped sharpen the focus of this study, placing it more clearly within the context of the historical issues central to modernization.

I am very appreciative of the assistance given by a number of archivists who went beyond the call of duty to help me in the research for this book. Special thanks to John Atteberry, Senior Reference Librarian at Bapst Library, Boston College; Nicholas Scheetz, Manuscripts Librarian, Special Collections Division, Georgetown University; and Lyle Dorsett, former director of the Marion E. Wade Center, Wheaton College, Illinois.

Throughout years of teaching at Boston University's College of General Studies my research and writing were supported by our late dean, Brendan Gilbane. His successor, Linda Wells, has continued this generosity and understanding. I thank them both.

Portions of this book have appeared in *The Chesterton Review, The Catholic Historical Review,* and the *Records of the American*

Catholic Historical Society of Philadelphia. I thank their editors for granting me permission to reprint parts of these articles in the present revised form.

I have had the good fortune of the steady hand of a perceptive editor, whose close reading and demanding standards immeasurably improved whatever qualities this book might possess. Thank you, Rebecca DeBoer, for guiding this manuscript to publication. Finally, I wish to acknowledge the unflagging support of Barbara Storella, whose efficiency of labor, charm, and all-around good cheer have made the Division of Social Science at Boston University's College of General Studies such a pleasant place to work. I also wish to thank my wife, Nancy, for everything she has had to put up with as I have labored to finish this project. Lamentably, despite all this help, whatever faults one finds in this book are my very own.

Jay P. Corrin
Bass Harbor, Maine

Introduction

This book describes the struggles of progressive and reactionary Catholic intellectuals to adjust their religious views to the dynamics of social change, from the French Revolution to the rise of the twentieth-century dictators. Those who tried to accommodate their faith with political and social democracy were the true precursors of what Pope John XXIII referred to as *aggiornamento*, the task of bringing the Church up to date with the times.

The Second Vatican Council (1962–1965), convened by Pope John XXIII, called upon Catholics to broaden their historical perspectives, move beyond a static theology fixed to the past, and embrace the kinds of changes that would allow the Church to be more in step with contemporary society. Its invocations were not without pain and serious divisiveness, for many saw the dangers of taking the Church down the perilous paths of modernity.[1] Part of the problem, it has been argued, was that the Church had to move too quickly through uncharted waters. The challenge of resolving the conflicting demands of religion and modernity by *aggiornamento* was forced on a community whose intellectual and spiritual bearing had become rigidified by tradition.

Protestantism, on the other hand, had centuries of experience trying to accommodate itself to the culture of modernity. In the words of theologian Langdon Gilkey, Protestants had the good fortune to study the interaction of Christianity and modernity slowly over a period of some two hundred years, their theological structures having developed out of the very economic and political matrix that propelled modern social change in the first place:

Catholicism . . . has really for the first time tried to absorb the effects of this whole vast modern development from the Enlightenment to the present in the short period between 1963 and 1973! Thus *all* the spiritual, social, and technological forces that had structured and transformed the modern history of the West have suddenly, and without much preparation, impinged forcefully on her life, and they have had to be comprehended, reinterpreted, and dealt with by Catholicism in one frantic decade.[2]

Gilkey's assessment, however, is not entirely accurate, for it draws on the conventional view that the Catholic Church has always been the servant of right-wing reaction, fervently resisting change by virtue of its authoritarian structures and traditionalist theology.[3] His judgment has certain validity when applied to the Vatican Curia, a good number of the Roman Catholic episcopacy, and conservative, even reactionary, Catholic intellectuals. Although it was indeed a challenge for the Catholic masses and tradition-bound clerics to embrace John XXIII's call for change in a single decade, a Catholic liberal, democratic tradition had already been in place for over two hundred years. In fact, the corpus of such thought not only prepared the ground for *aggiornamento* but also made it possible to implement the changes recommended by Vatican Council II.[4]

The antecedents of *aggiornamento* are rooted in an imaginative, progressive, and carefully reasoned Catholic response to the various social, economic, and political revolutions of the nineteenth century. This rich but unappreciated legacy reveals that the Church could not only accommodate itself to democratic culture but could even transform it in ways suitable to the needs of all social classes. This "liberal" Catholic response to modernity has gone largely unrecognized by historians of our own day.[5]

The so-called Catholic "third way," an alternative to the extremes of socialist collectivism and unfettered capitalism, was initially laid down in the writings of the Frenchman Frédéric Ozanam, of Bishop Wilhelm von Ketteler of Germany, and of England's Cardinal Henry Edward Manning. Their insights concerning Catholicism and industrial society informed the seminal social and political encyclicals of Pope Leo XIII.

Yet from the beginning of the Church's efforts to address social change, there were contrary strains in Catholic thinking that worked against accommodation with democratic institutions. The liberal-minded, pluralistic positions articulated by Ozanam, Ketteler, and Manning were offset by those of reactionary, "integralist" Catholics, who, rather than finding common ground with political and social revolution, sought a return to a hierarchical age of paternalistic authoritarianism.[6] This antidemocratic tradition, for a time, was largely overshadowed by the impetus given Catholic social action through the publication of Pope Leo XIII's encyclicals.

In the English-speaking world, the Leonine social and political encyclicals matured most fully in the Distributist movement inspired by G. K. Chesterton and Hilaire Belloc. Contrary to the views of many historians, Distributism was not an oddity, out of step with modern culture, nor was it the mere whimsical infatuation of two clever publicists. In my view it represented the single most important synthesis of Catholic social and political thinking to emerge in the English-speaking community in the early twentieth century, and its values had a telling impact on Catholic intellectuals in Britain and America.

The more radical, democratic dimensions of Catholic social teaching were illustrated by the response of the Chesterton brothers, Belloc, and their followers to the labor unrest that beset England in the turbulent decade before World War I. Labor's struggle against what Belloc called the "Servile State" brought together a number of disparate groups (radical liberals, anarchists, guild socialists, and Marxists) who recognized the need to unite against the drift towards monopoly capitalism as well as collectivism and, in the process, to prepare the ground for a new social order responsive to the needs of individuals. The battle against the Servile State played a seminal role in the development of anti-statist thinking in Great Britain, which in turn shaped various political movements on the left, from anarcho-syndicalism to guild socialism. In all, the struggle of the Chestertons and Hilaire Belloc against both big business and big government reveals the progressive, even radical lengths to which Catholic social teaching could be applied to modern economic and political problems.

The thinking of the Chestertons, Belloc, and the Distributist movement was also conditioned by Hilaire Belloc's encounters with Parliament and Britain's governing establishment. His bitter experiences as a muckraking journalist and parliamentarian and his sense of being spurned as an academic pushed Belloc to the fringe, from liberalism to views akin to the antidemocratic positions of the continental integralist Catholics. Belloc's unfortunate encounters with what he called the "money powers," whom he believed controlled the political process, moved him to search for a man on a white horse, a strong heroic figure who could lead Christendom out of the swamp of greed and decadence to new heights of glory. Belloc found such men in Mussolini and Franco and essentially embraced their variants of fascism as acceptable alternatives to the danger of communism.

G. K. Chesterton's vision, on the other hand, remained comparatively liberal and pluralistic, revealing its roots in the democratic traditions set down by Ozanam, Ketteler, and Manning. His untimely passing, however, combined with the growing Catholic preoccupation with the threat of international communism and the considerable influence of Hilaire Belloc, had the effect of splitting the Distributist movement and ultimately moving the journals that claimed its legacy into the camp of political reactionaries.

The fate of the Distributist movement in Britain was a mirror image of events for Catholic intellectuals in America. Like Belloc and company (whose influence among American Catholics was paramount), numerous eminent Catholics in the United States became obsessed with the spread of communism and enamored of Latin dictators. These sentiments created an atmosphere that offered little tolerance for free or critical thinking, largely ignored the message of the papal social encyclicals, and ultimately alienated the American labor movement and the liberal intellectual community from Catholic social teachings.[7]

Those who fought to keep the pluralistic traditions of the social encyclicals at the forefront of Catholic action were a distinct minority by the late 1930s, constantly besieged by their co-religionists on the political right who endeavored to present a monolithic image of Catholic conservatism to the outside world. Yet it was this liberal group of Catholic intellectuals who were the true upholders of the

Distributist vision originally formulated by Chesterton and Belloc. One individual who seemed to best represent the liberal legacies of Ozanam, Ketteler, and Manning during the upheavals of the inter-war years was the German refugee priest, Father Hans A. Reinhold. Reinhold and his friends (Virgil Michel, O.S.B., Don Luigi Sturzo, Waldemar Gurian, George Shuster, and Jacques Maritain, among others) managed to see through the smoke screen of fascist corporatism that so beguiled conservative Catholics, and their analyses of the various programs of the dictators revealed how much such initiatives deviated from Catholic social teachings.

Although Father Reinhold's social views may have been a model of Chestertonian-style Distributism (and I would assert that his connections with the liturgical movement and Dorothy Day's Catholic Worker group represented the clearest application of Distributist teachings to America), the persecution he endured as a critic of totalitarian social and political ideas symbolized, on a personal level, the failure of Catholicism to engage the modern age. In the end, the liberal, pluralistic calls to economic and political reform first expressed by Ozanam and others were drowned out by the voices of reactionary Catholics who found guides in Hilaire Belloc and his circle.

A critical chapter in the ongoing struggle between "integralist" and liberal Catholicism was played out in the Spanish Civil War. I maintain that the Catholic response in Britain and America to the tragedy of Spain was largely defined by Hilaire Belloc and his followers. From the outset Belloc declared the conflict a religious crusade against atheistic communism, one in which General Franco played the role of a latter-day El Cid holding back a wave of barbarism from engulfing Christendom. The Spanish Civil War was far more complex than the Catholic defenders of Franco claimed, but it soon became difficult, if not impossible, for liberal Catholics to suggest other ways of viewing the war. In the end the Bellocian line prevailed. Any reasoned, dispassionate discussion among Catholics of the real social, political, and economic issues that wracked Spain was precluded once the struggle had been defined as a holy war.

The failure of Catholics in the 1920s and 1930s to speak out with a united voice on the evils of fascism and the procrustean definition of the Spanish Civil War as a holy crusade have contributed significantly to the judgment that Catholicism is an agent of reaction, highly suspicious of democracy, liberalism, and state-directed social reform.[8] The Catholic Church, of course, has always provided a tent large enough to accommodate a myriad of traditions and contentious ways of thinking about the secular world. It is therefore important to realize that during the era of the twentieth-century dictators a distinct Catholic tradition of pluralistic political thought also existed, which championed radical social and economic reform and which, if given more institutional support during the interwar years, might have altered the one-dimensional, simplistic picture of Catholicism as socially conservative and inherently authoritarian.

What follows is a study of political Catholicism. My purpose is not to explore the theological and spiritual dimension of this religion. The focus is rather political and sociological. I intend to both analyze and explicate how religion shaped the consciousness of a group of seminal Catholic thinkers as they responded to the process of modernization, that is, to the forces for change unleashed by the combined experiences of social and political revolution that were the legacy of 1789 France, as well as of industrialism, capitalism, socialism, Marxism, and fascism. In this sense, the subject of the book moves beyond Catholicism itself, for it addresses a broader issue: religion as a vehicle for engaging in a positive and creative fashion the modern culture of the West. The views of liberal Catholics described here stand in sharp contrast both to a certain strain of conservativism, which essentially rejects modernity in favor of ways of living that arguably have limited practical application in the present world, and to postmodernism, which seems to deny the reality of modernization itself.

I have chosen to focus on that influential man of letters, Hilaire Belloc, as the emblem of right-wing Catholicism in the English-speaking world. Belloc and his circle demonstrate why Catholicism is seen by historians as a force for political and cultural reaction. Hilaire Belloc also assumes a prominent profile in this study because of the enormous influence he had on British and American Catholic political thought, a phenomenon relatively unnoticed by contemporary historians. Belloc and those who fell under his influence revealed a deep-seated revulsion against liberalism, cultural secularization, and parliamentary democracy. As an alternative, they essentially called for a return to medieval cultural values and found much to their liking in the syndicalist, authoritarian offerings of fascist-style political movements.

The career of Father H. A. Reinhold, in juxtaposition to that of Hilaire Belloc, represents in this study the liberal side of the Catholic tradition. Unfortunately, Father Reinhold, much like the legacy of liberal Catholicism itself, never garnered the high public profile of a Hilaire Belloc and the reactionary positions that he represented. Yet Reinhold's liberal stands were firmly rooted in Catholic social and political teachings. Reinhold was typical of those few Catholic intellectuals whose voices of protest against tyranny and social injustice resisted the tide of tribal, reactionary politics. These were the Catholics who refused to either sit on the sidelines of history, as Guenter Lewy and others have claimed the Vatican itself did,[9] or join the armies of Catholic militants, some of whom were political pragmatists who saw gains to be made from supporting authoritarian regimes. The vast majority of these people had entered the marketplace of political advocacy, lost sight of Catholic moral doctrine, and essentially committed their own *trahison des clercs* by failing to judge fascism according to the dictates of natural law.[10] The reluctance of such Catholics to follow the logic of their own moral tradition was frequently recognized and remarked upon by non-Catholics. The journalist Walter Lippmann, for instance, appreciated the frankness of Don Luigi Sturzo's critique of fascism, because, unlike so many other of his co-religionists, Sturzo realized that as a political creed the Italian *totalitaro* was a violation of Catholic political principles.[11]

In short, Catholic thinkers in the early decades of the twentieth century had access to a rich pluralistic religious tradition which could be drawn upon to address the challenges of modernity. Moreover, as the assaults against the Church increased throughout the twentieth century, many Catholics discovered in practice that even the legacy of political liberalism had something to offer in the battle against tyranny. Some recognized a certain symmetry between Catholicism and liberal philosophy, each capable of complementing and giving strength to the other.[12] This was the legacy to which the Vatican eventually gave its imprimatur after World War II. Prior to this, it must be emphasized, there was no doctrinal bias that precluded Catholics from accepting democratic, socially and economically progressive ideas. Nor were Catholics ever limited by religious teachings from joining movements or parties with progressive or even radical agendas. Indeed, there were sufficient ways to legitimize such approaches through the broad corpus of Catholic social writings. Many influential conservative Catholics argued otherwise, but they had no official theological sanction to substantiate the claim. Putting it another way, there was nothing intrinsic to Catholicism itself that precluded support for a liberal, democratic world order.[13]

The main objective of this study is to give voice to those Catholics of the period under study who drew from their religious traditions a liberal and progressive approach to the problems of modern social change. This position has too often been unheard and therefore unappreciated and undervalued because of the more strident claims of Catholics on the political right. The telling of their story may help to modify the prevailing historical judgment of Catholicism as a force for social and political reaction.

CHAPTER 1

European Catholics Confront Revolution

T he nineteenth century, a "Century of Revolution," inaugurated an era of unprecedented economic expansion. By emancipating individuals and social classes from paternalistic political orders, it became a golden age for European civilization. Yet the historical forces behind such change—the disintegration of the medieval order brought on by the accumulated blows of the Renaissance, Reformation, and Enlightenment culminating in the French Revolution—generated painful conflicts in values and social relationships. No institution was more directly challenged by these forces than that which had shaped the cultural ethos out of which European civilization had emerged: the Roman Catholic Church. The consciousness of nineteenth-century Europe had become transformed and, in the process, disenchanted and earth-bound. The "Modern Mind," wrote Peter Wust, "was secularized, the world stripped of its sacred meaning, the Church ruled out of public affairs, God dethroned in the soul of man."[1]

The cultural configuration of this new industrial age was shaped by the ascendancy of the bourgeoisie, a social class whose driving purpose was business and the amassment of material wealth. Theirs was a world where religion and spiritual values, presumably old-fashioned sentiments that had no relevance to the marketplace, were relegated to drawing rooms or the Sunday musings of one's private life. Most significantly, the era was defined by the power of the state, a social institution that, beginning with the age of absolute monarchy and then finely-tuned by Robespierre and the Jacobins, had come to dominate cultural and economic life. By the nineteenth century this institution was falling swiftly under the control of the middle classes, a new elite that both legitimated and rationalized its position through the canonization of capitalism.

The nineteenth-century capitalist-driven economy reposed on the principle of individual freedom; its central belief was that each person must be free to pursue his own self-interest unfettered by governments or the prerogatives of privilege. The word "liberty," enshrined as religion, was the core idea of liberalism, the political philosophy of the bourgeoisie that made the practice of capitalism possible. The central premise of liberalism was that humans were benign, rational creatures who, if given freedom, could achieve self-perfection by following the dictates of reason.

Closely allied to liberalism was the creed of nationalism. Where liberalism fought against all domestic constraints that mitigated individual self-enhancement, nationalism demanded liberty for the group, asserting that the sovereignty of the people (popular democracy), freed from the compulsions of other foreign powers, would assure the self-fulfillment and ultimate perfection of the nation-state. Both nationalism and liberalism were legacies of the French Revolution. Furthermore, given the punishing anticlericalism that accompanied the overthrow of the old regime in France, the French Revolution also appeared to present a formidable opposition to the traditions of the Roman Catholic Church.

Not surprisingly, many Catholic laymen and Church prelates were not prepared to endorse the cultural tendencies of the nineteenth century and had made common cause with aristocratic and monarchist elements in defense of dogma and privilege. Many of these conservative Catholics were also deeply troubled by the social problems brought on by the revolution in industry and politics, but they approached these issues from assumptions that were increasingly irrelevant. The solution they advocated for the excessive individualism that had left people at the mercy of the state and of industry was to resurrect a Church-dominated organic social order along medieval lines. For these Catholics the problem was mono-causal and moral: the secularization of society had led to a permanent separation of politics and economics from religion. Their approach to resolving the challenges of modernity has been called *Sozial-reform* by German scholars of Catholic social and political history.[2]

The French Church tended to be sympathetic to these sentiments, in particular the Gallican wing, which was nationalistic (that
is, loyal to the old regime), monarchistic, aristocratic, and opposed
to the rational legacies of the Enlightenment. This group was challenged by "liberal" French Catholics, essentially proponents of
Sozialpolitik, meaning that they were prepared to recognize the gains
of the French Revolution and reconcile the Church with democratic
values. These Catholics were "ultramontane," prepared to go "beyond
the mountain" to Rome; they appealed to papal authority in their
struggle against conservative monarchist sympathizers within the
French Catholic hierarchy. Liberal Catholics with *Sozialpolitik* leanings recognized that the chief sacramental mission of the Church,
the salvation of souls, required entering the temporal world as it was
currently constituted. This was a demanding challenge, but many
argued that the Church's mission could be more easily pursued
within the democratic liberal state than under the inflexible absolutist regimes of the past.[3]

The liberal nineteenth-century European Catholics also emphasized the Church's tradition of "social deaconry," a recognition that
clergy, in addition to their sacramental responsibilities, also had an
obligation to perform supplementary welfare work to improve the
social life of the community.[4] There was no necessary conflict between saving souls and engaging in social work, since the Church
historically had been a central part of both the spiritual and temporal realms. Yet since the mundane world, that which St. Augustine called the "City of Man," was by its very nature flawed and
imbued with sin, social deaconry could not be expected to achieve
the perfection associated with the sacral community. Social deaconry should be guided by the ideals of Christian living but should
direct its action toward present needs and be prepared to shift tactics according to the requirements of the day. To such Catholics,
the emergence of the liberal state was a historical reality with which
the Church had a social responsibility to engage and contend.
Rather than fleeing back into the past (*Sozialreform*), liberal Catholics were more interested in working with what might be salvaged
in the present. In the words of the French Catholic Frédéric Ozanam, the Church needed

to search out in the human heart all the secret cords which can lead it back to Christianity, to reawaken in it the love of the true, the good, and the beautiful, and finally to show in revealed faith the ideal of these three things to which every soul aspires; to regain, in short, the strayed spirits, and to increase the number of Christians.[5]

Ozanam, a devout Catholic layman and renowned scholar, was one of those who hoped to rekindle the social deaconry of the Church.[6] At the age of eighteen, in 1840, he published a pamphlet entitled *Reflections on the Doctrine of Saint-Simon,* a response to socialists who challenged Catholics to match words with deeds, in which he called upon his co-religionists to apply the message of the Gospels to ameliorate the conditions of the working poor. Church-men, he wrote, must not only preach the truth of Christ but work for a "speedy improvement in the moral and physical condition of the most numerous class. . . ."[7] Ozanam singled out economic liberalism as the source of labor's misery. Its doctrines, he asserted, dehumanized the laborer by relegating his value to the impersonal laws of supply and demand, thereby transforming his person into a mere commodity of the marketplace. Ozanam went beyond criticism to action after witnessing an armed revolt of weavers at Lyons in 1831. In 1833, while still a university student, he established the Society of St. Vincent de Paul, whose mission was to work for the welfare of the laboring classes in Paris.

Many of Ozanam's contemporaries who shared this spirit of "Catholicism in action" recognized the importance of becoming directly involved with the needs of the working classes, lest they be lost to the Church by falling prey to the rising voices of radical social revolution. A number of liberal Catholics in France became active in the labor movement, aiding the working classes in efforts to develop the solidarity necessary to defend themselves against the claims of capitalism.

French liberal Catholics moved against their conservative adversaries in November 1831 when their leading spokesman, Félicité de Lamennais, made a pilgrimage to Rome and appealed directly to Pope Gregory XVI to support the reformist position. Gregory's response was swift and disappointing: his encyclical *Mirai vos,* issued on 15 August 1832, condemned Catholic liberal attempts to compromise with the age. The Pope denied that the Church had any need to regenerate itself or modernize, and he rejected the notion that liberty of conscience and freedom of the press were unqualified rights. This was a particularly crushing blow to Lamennais, whose profound disappointment eventually led to his repudiation of Catholicism.

Despite Gregory's rejection of the principles of the liberal state, Catholic liberals continued their efforts to come to grips with the political issues of the day, especially as they concerned Church-state relations and the interplay between faith and reason. French liberals such as Count Charles de Montalembert, for instance, persistently dismissed the notion that Catholics had anything to fear from freedom of ideas and liberty of conscience, since the Church had always held its own in the intellectual give-and-take that was part of the evolution of Western culture. Montalembert pointed out to his fellow Catholics that the recent resurgence of the faith in Belgium, for example, was directly due to "liberty, nothing but liberty, and the struggle made possible by liberty." Political freedom, he asserted, "has been the safeguard and the instument of Catholic revival in Europe."[8]

Mirai vos in fact had little effect on the continued growth of nineteenth-century Catholic social action. None worked more diligently to apply Christian teaching to labor problems than Frédéric Ozanam, who, along with Bishop Wilhelm Emmanuel von Ketteler of Germany, established the groundwork for the Catholic social movement and was a major inspiration for Pope Leo XIII's great labor encyclical, *Rerum Novarum* (1891). Ozanam's Society of St. Vincent de Paul, whose "Conferences" eventually spread throughout Europe and became one the the world's largest organizations for the relief of poverty, had a purpose beyond simply alleviating the suffering of the poor. The Society was a means to an end: "our true aim," wrote Ozanam, "was to preserve intact in ourselves the Catholic faith in all its purity and to communicate it to others through the channel of charity. We wished to be able to answer those who, in the words of the Psalmist, asked of us: *Ubi est Deus eorum?*" (Where is their God?).[9]

Ozanam modeled his society on the worldwide organization of the Sisters of Charity, founded by Vincent de Paul in 1617; however,

Ozanam's organization aimed to draw into its rank young men, mainly university students. The conferences of the Society of Vincent de Paul became the training ground for Catholicism's next generation of social activists. In the words of Albert de Mun, they "were the great school of experience in which we first learned to serve the cause of the people. Out of them sprang the whole Catholic Social Movement of the nineteenth century."[10]

Ozanam had begun his analysis of labor and capital in response to the socialist followers of Saint-Simon, who had demanded to know how Catholicism could do anything positive to improve the lives of the working poor. His subsequent writings on the labor question went far beyond the analyses of the Saint-Simonians and reveal a level of sophistication and moral insight that compare more closely with Marx's critique of capitalism. It should be noted that Ozanam's early criticisms in *Reflections on the Doctrine of Saint-Simon,* emerging fully in his university lectures after becoming a professor of literature at the Sorbonne, predated by some eight years the publication of Marx and Engels' *Communist Manifesto,* which appeared in February 1848.[11]

Like Marx, Ozanam had recognized that the ethos of unbridled capitalism, buttressed by the classical liberal ideas of influential economic philosophers such as Adam Smith, Thomas Malthus, David Ricardo, and Frédéric Bastiat, was a powerful tool used to justify the rapacity of the economically strong. In Ozanam's view, the equally destructive and misguided socialist alternative to such exploitation, was, however, a logical response to the excesses of capitalism. Socialism, said Ozanam, simply was reaping the harvest of the transgressions of liberalism.

Ozanam, of course, condemned the debasement of labor brought on by the wage slavery of industrial capitalism. Such degradation, however, was not in itself a unique occurrence. Labor had been degraded in the ancient world, where the tasks of production had been relegated to helots and slaves. A special virtue of Christianity (symbolized in the divine artisanry of Joseph and Jesus) was that it resurrected labor to the dignified position it deserved as the source of humankind's creative capacity. Ozanam, like Marx, recognized that capitalism had bifurcated the laboring process, that is, separated the cerebral dimension of work from its natural physical counter-part. This was an inevitable outcome of the wage system. Labor, however, was of many kinds—physical, intellectual, and moral—and the evil of capitalism was that it had destroyed the unity of this natural productive process. Unlike Marx, Ozanam believed that the traditions of Catholicism could resuscitate the solidarity of the laboring process, much as it had existed in the guild society of the Middle Ages. What this demanded in the industrial era, asserted Ozanam, was just compensation to all those who produced. Capitalism rewarded unfairly those with economic and intellectual power at the expense of the numerous classes who provided physical labor. The worker, Ozanam insisted, was entitled to a "just wage" that would provide for a decent living and the education of his children.

Ozanam believed that adequate compensation was denied the worker because he lacked the ability to organize (since it was forbidden by the liberal state as a restraint of trade) and, at the same time, because he was being exploited by the owners of capital.[12] Employers, he pointed out, had not considered "the worker as an associate and an auxiliary, but as a tool from which to derive as much service as possible at the least possible expense."[13] The use of humans as tools of production—which Marx would later identify as the objectification of the laboring process—had profound moral implications, for it ultimately eroded the home and family. All this, said Ozanam, was the logical outcome of the liberal laissez-faire assumptions regarding political and economic affairs.

What was to be done? Ozanam found the answer by embracing the most pervasive product of modernization: he turned to the power of the state. The government had both a moral and a social obligation to shape the economic order, since the absolute liberty of capital led to exploitation of labor and spawned conditions for violent social revolution. This was a revolutionary proposal in an era that ana-thematized the idea of state intervention. But unlike conservative Catholic philosophers who longed for the return of absolutist forms of government, Ozanam saw no role for a paternalistic state. Command economies of the past had only constricted industry and commerce, and for this reason Ozanam rejected not only mercantilist economics but also socialism as solutions to the modern industrial problem. He proposed, instead, a balanced approach, a middle way between the requirements of freedom and authority, undertaken by a government that would carefully weigh the needs of both management and labor before taking action and would act only when the common welfare required it. Ozanam's solution to the excesses of laissez-faire liberalism presaged the position articulated by John Stuart Mill's *On Liberty*, which did not appear until 1859 and is recognized today as the classic justification for the interventionist state in the Anglo-Saxon liberal tradition.

In the final analysis, however, Ozanam did not regard the problems of modernity as primarily economic or political in origin. The age lacked charity and economic justice, but the latter could never be restored without universal goodwill and brotherly love. Ozanam provided an important message to his fellow Catholics: charity required taking an active role in relieving the social problem. He put the issues most succinctly in a letter to his friend Lallier in 1836:

> The question which agitates the world to-day is not a question of *political forms*, but a *social* question; if it be the struggle of those who have nothing with those who have too much, if it be the violent shock of opulence and poverty which is making the ground tremble under our feet, our duty, as Christians, is to throw ourselves between these irreconcilable enemies, and to induce one side to give in order to fulfill the law, and the other to receive as a benefit; to make one side cease to exact, and the other to refuse; to render equality as general as it is possible amongst men; to make voluntary community of possession replace taxation and forced loans; to make charity accomplish what justice and law alone can never do.[14]

The above passage displays Ozanam's prescient sociological analysis as well as his faith in charity. At least a decade before the appearance of the *Communist Manifesto* (1848), Ozamam recognized that divisions between men were linked to economic disparities and warned of class war unless social programs were initiated to mitigate such inequities.

The approach to social amelioration suggested by Ozanam required that Catholics—those with any measure of power or privilege—make a fundamental political reorientation. This would mean "passing over to the barbarians," as he put it, that is, embracing the causes of the majority of the people in order to draw them into the Church. Catholics must occupy themselves with those "whose rights are too few," who justifiably cry out for a share in public affairs, and who require guarantees for work and protection from distress. Ozanam's call to embrace the struggle of the masses anticipated what Marx described as the historical mission of the "liberated" bourgeoise to join the revolutionary cause of the proletariat.

Ozanam's call for Catholic action demanded courage and commitment, something Ozanam himself possessed in abundance. He never let a day pass without taking time from his schedule of teaching, scholarship, and journalistic endeavors to work among the poor for the Society of St. Vincent de Paul. Catholics had nothing to fear from the calling of the social deaconry: "Do not be frightened when the wicked rich, irritated by your pleading, treat you as communists. They treated St. Bernard as a fanatic and a fool. Remember that your fathers, the French priests of the eleventh and twelfth centuries, saved Europe by the Crusades; save her once more by the crusade of Charity, and, as it involves no bloodshed, be you its first soldiers."[15]

For Ozanam, however, "crossing over to the people" meant embracing certain political forms, in particular, democratic participatory government, which offended conservative Catholics. In the context of his own times, this arrangement was best represented in republicanism. Ozanam saw no inherent incompatibility between liberty and Christianity, and, for this reason, he labored to effect a reconciliation between the two; the one was a force for social and intellectual dynamism, the other a bonding agent creating the unity that would allow society to govern itself. Until the end of his life, even during the storm of working-class unrest in the French Revolution of 1848, Ozanam was convinced that a republic was the best form of government, indeed, the one toward which all enlightened nations were tending; and since the people were to become sovereign, it was all the more important that they be reconciled with Christianity. Ozanam believed that freedom was complementary to both the republic and the Church. Political liberty was necessary for developing the full creative powers of the individual citizen, and freedom for the Church, liberated from the bondage of the state, would allow her to provide the teaching, guidance, and the requisite moral rules for the spiritual happiness of the community. "My knowledge of history," said Ozanam, "leads me to the conclusion that in the nature of mankind democracy is in the final stage in the development of political progress, and that God leads the world in that direction."[16]

Ozanam's historical theory of governmental evolution and his progressive views on politics and the social deaconry of the Church drew him into an ongoing battle on two fronts, which he waged with indomitable courage until the end of his life. On the one hand, his devout Catholicism rendered his position at the Sorbonne a difficult one, that institution having been aggressively anti-Christian, for half a century. By the time he arrived at the Sorbonne, Ozanam, through his careful scholarship, was well aware of the enormous debt that Western civilization had owed the Catholic Church. In his courses he unabashedly focused on the Christian background to European political and literary development. But Ozanam's Christian forbearance and toleration toward those who opposed his Catholicism, combined with his pro-republicanism, brought down upon him the wrath of conservative Catholics. The battle against Catholic monarchists became particularly heated during the Revolution of 1848, which Ozanam recognized as fundamentally a social revolution and part of the historical evolution to republican democracy.

In order to counteract the enormous influence of such Catholic conservative publications as the *Univers* and provide a forum for more advanced social and political views, Ozanam and Jean Baptiste Henri Dominique Lacordaire founded the newspaper *L'Ere Nouvelle* ("The New Era") in April 1848. The publication's chief objective was to show how Catholicism could be reconciled with republicanism and thereby wean the increasingly revolutionary working classes from radical socialism to Christianity. Ozanam's articles pleaded with clergy and the rich to "seek the justice of God and the welfare of the Country" by searching out the poor and preaching the gospel; he also called on Christians to become more actively engaged in the political process by standing for election to the National Assembly. The current danger with labor unrest could have been avoided, he argued, if Catholics had been more responsible about the social question in the first place. As Ozanam wrote his brother, "If a greater number of Christians, and above all priests, had but occupied themselves with the working class these last ten years, we should be more secure of the future, and all our hopes rest on that little that has been done in this direction up to the present."[17]

When it became clear that the French Republic would collapse by the spring of 1849, and after unceasing vituperative attacks from the *Univers* (which called Ozanam's paper "L'Erreur Nouvelle") and other conservative Catholic quarters, Ozanam's journalistic efforts for a Christian Republic came to a close. In April 1849, a year after it was founded, *L'Ere Nouvelle* ceased publication. With the support of the archbishop of Paris, Ozanam's supporters founded another journal, *Moniteur Religieux,* but Ozanam was in ill health and unable to contribute to their efforts. Frédéric Ozanam's brilliant career ended prematurely in 1853 when he died at the age of forty.

I I

Another nineteenth-century pioneer of modern Catholic social action was Baron Wilhelm Emmanuel von Ketteler, Bishop of Mainz.[18] Ketteler responded to the political and industrial issues of his day by advocating what he called "true communism." This was intended to be an alternative to the most radical synthesis of nineteenth-century socialism: Marx and Engels' *Communist Manifesto*. Ketteler condemned many of the same evils as had Marx and Engels and, in a fashion similar to their critique of capitalism, identified the economic causes of poverty and the exploitation of labor. But Ketteler argued that these social ills were derivative of a larger problem that socialists ignored, the evil of sin:

> The most fatal error of our time is the delusion that mankind can be made happy without religion and Christianity. There are certain truths which cling together like the links of a chain: they cannot be torn asunder because God has joined them. Among these truths are the following:

There is no true morality without God, no right knowledge of God without Christ, no real Christ without his Church. Where the Church is not, there true knowledge of God perishes. Where true knowledge of God is not, there morality succumbs in the struggle with sin, with selfishness and sensuality, with the lust of the eyes, the lust of the flesh, and the pride of life. But where morality is not, there is no means left of making people happy and prosperous. In such a state men are ruled by their passions. They are the slaves of the tyrants of avarice and lust, in whose service the powerful oppress the weak, and the weak in their turn rise up against the powerful, and if they conquer, become the willing tools of the self-same tyrants, their passions. War without end will be waged between the rich and the poor; peace on earth among them is impossible. Intimately, inseparable, is the welfare of the people bound up with religion and morality.[19]

From his early years as a priest, Ketteler had been absorbed by the problems of poverty among the working class and had given considerable sums from his family inheritance to charitable causes. His reputation, however, quickly became that of a social reformer. As Europe was torn apart by revolutions in 1848, Ketteler, at the time parish priest of Hopsten, was elected unanimously by both Catholics and Protestants in his district to the Frankfurt National Assembly. This body had the task of drawing up plans for unification of the German states. As a member of the Assembly, Ketteler showed an aggressiveness on social and industrial issues that brought blushes to the faces of conventional bourgeois Catholic representatives.

Kettler made his reputation as a voice for "revolution" and, at the same time, gave birth to the Catholic social movement in Germany by a series of six sermons he delivered at Mainz during Advent, 1848, entitled "The Great Social Question of Our Time." The purpose of these sermons was to awaken Catholics to the problems of Germany's new industrial society. Rather than focusing on artisans, journeymen, and the semi-skilled workers of pre-industrial society as had Catholic Romantics and traditionalists, Ketteler initiated a new approach to the social problem by addressing the needs of the urban proletariat. He urged Catholic thinkers to look beyond obsolete medieval guild approaches to social dynamics and seek new paths that would have practical application to an industrial setting. This would require forsaking the old alliance with political reaction and establishing, instead, a new working relationship with progressive social forces. Along with Ozanam, Ketteler was one of the few men of his day to recognize the full significance of the working-class movement that was beginning to break out across Europe, and much of his writing on the subject was directed to the radical challenge of capitalism posed by the *Communist Manifesto*.

Ketteler pursued his study of the social problem with an openmindedness that was far beyond the appreciation of his Catholic peers or his liberal and socialist adversaries. He drew extensively from Engels' studies on the conditions of the laboring classes, corresponded lengthily with the socialist Ferdinand Lassalle, whose ideas on workers' cooperatives were of great interest to him, and sought advice on Church-state relations from Protestant and conservative social philosophers.

The opening salvo of Ketteler's famous Mainz sermons was aimed at liberalism's laissez-faire doctrine of unlimited competition and its position regarding the absolute rights of private property. His ideas on the social problem were developed more fully in a major book published in 1864, *The Labor Question and Christianity*. At this point, Ketteler had become Bishop of Mainz, and since it was a novelty for a bishop to write on labor issues, the book itself became quite a sensation, going through three editions in the first year of publication alone.

The Labor Question and Christianity attacked the liberal sacred cows of economic competition and unrestricted rights to property by drawing on principles set down by St. Thomas Aquinas. Arguing along lines established by the great scholastic theologian some six hundred years earlier, Ketteler asserted that the liberal concept of property as an exclusive right was a perversion of the Christian tradition of proprietorship, a crime against nature, since property and all the creatures of the earth ultimately belonged to God alone. Man's use of property could never be unrestricted; indeed, in such circumstances "property is theft," said Ketteler, because man has an obligation to God to utilize ownership responsibly. In effect, all property rights are derived from God and those who possess it have the burden of usufruct, an obligation to use it for the sustenance of the entire community. This is what Ketteler meant by "true communism," as opposed to the materialist version advocated by Marx and Engels. As St. Thomas established in *Summa Theologica* (II–II, 66, 1 and 2), the fruits of private property are not exclusive; they are the common property of all and thus should be shared with others according to their needs.

Ketteler also opposed the political agenda of liberalism because, in his view, it was simply a new form of absolutism[20] cloaked in the robes of the goddess of liberty. Modern liberals, like their Jacobin predecessors, justified legislative intrusions into the lives of ordinary citizens and their invasion of clerical jurisdiction by invoking Rousseauistic ideas about the "general will," sovereignty of "the people," and the legitimacy of popular elections. In fact, argued Ketteler, this was a disguise, a ploy to exercise absolute political power, made easier by manipulating public opinion and the power of the ballot box. Liberals talk about the sanctity of the vote, wrote Ketteler, but what this means is "going to the voting booth every couple of years for a few minutes to scratch a name on the ballot; in other words, to elect one's own taskmaster. Thereafter the taskmaster acts in the name of the people. . . ."[21] Ketteler's antidote to this "false Liberalism" and its handmaiden, the omnipotent state, was a government of laws, one which guaranteed the basic liberties of the natural corporate bodies (such as merchant classes, professional groups, workers, academicians, and churches) that provide the essential services upon which society depends.

Ketteler's criticism of the liberal position on private ownership and government, however, was balanced by a powerful condemnation of socialism. Nineteenth-century socialism was not only atheistic but, like liberalism, tended toward absolutism in its quest for control of the state; its purpose was to impose collectivist uniformity in the interests of a single group that would deny liberty to its class enemies. In many respects, liberalism and socialism were simply opposite sides of a coin. Both sought the power of state not to advance the commonweal but to promote the interests of their particular constituents. As Ketteler put it: "liberalism laughed at eternity and said the socialists laughed with them, declaring 'we laugh with you, but if this life is all there is, why should ninety per-cent be excluded from enjoying what the ten percent possess?'"[22]

Although Ketteler criticized the excesses of liberal concepts and practices concerning proprietorship, he appreciated the importance of individual ownership of property: it brought personal security, encouraged responsibility, good management, and pride in work-manship, and was the source of mankind's creativeness. For these reasons, Ketteler objected to the economic programs of radical socialists like Marx and Engels. He agreed with their desires to restore labor's rightful dignity and true value as the central factor in the productive process. But Ketteler strongly opposed socialist means to this end, namely, the forcible confiscation of property and the transfer of ownership of the means of production to the state. Ketteler knew that coercive measures to destroy the instruments of exploitation also would eliminate the very freedom that was at the source of labor's creativity. As for himself, Ketteler wrote that "Even if all the Utopian dreams of the Socialists were realized and every one was fed to his heart's content in this universal labor State, I should, for all that, prefer to eat in peace the potatoes that I grow myself, and to clothe myself with the skins of animals reared by me, and *be free*—than to live in the slavery of the labor State and fare sumptuously." This is what made socialism so dangerous and loath-some. Collectivist theory, in practice, would bring slavery back to life again. The collectivist state, warned Ketteler, is "an assemblage of slaves without personal liberty."[23]

In order to deal with modern social problems effectively, Ket-teler argued, it was necessary to examine carefully the two ways in which people have created social solidarity. One way is to structure society mechanically. In such an arrangement the unifying force is external, binding people together on a pragmatic or utilitarian basis. However, said Ketteler, this method lacks enduring internal prin-ciples. The other alternative is to bring order organically, allowing the practice of convention and communitarian traditions (social organisms) to form the bonding agents for solidarity. Such a pro-cess comes about through natural growth (*naturwuchsig*), develop-ing out of the nature of things, that is, out of the character of the customs and experience of time. Organic unity, Ketteler insisted, is less transitory than that brought about by mechanical, impersonal structures, for it represents a higher plane of existence; natural organisms have within them an inner and personal unifying force that nurtures and binds all parts of a community into one "overriding *individuum*."

It was Ketteler's conviction that political order based on corporations (modeled on the medieval guilds) corresponded closely to organic solidarity. Therefore he recommended the creation of a corporative political structure. The personal, intimate, and economically purposive ways in which it functioned as a *Volksgemeinschaft* (the nation as community) offered the best opportunities for individual political representation and better self-government: "Corporate bodies seem to me to be like living bodies and life organisms that are structures according to the natural order of things whose bond is not merely external, transient and accidental, but internal and natural."[24] On the other hand, political forms recommended by liberals and democratic socialists, in particular constitutional government and representative bodies that would bring delegates together on the basis of geographical regions, corresponded closely to mechanical solidarity, and were potentially less stable, since they tried to create solidarity by forcing natural groups into an artificial union (the state) and, most importantly, tended to encourage partisan interests.

The efforts to create order through rational mechanisms had led to the dissolution of "natural organizations," such as the guilds, and no group suffered more from this than the laboring classes. The medieval corporations, Ketteler argued, had given them protection through an organizing principle that allowed for the full development of personality. But with the growth of industrialism, accompanied by the liberal concept of laissez-faire economics, the workers, without wealth and structures of association, were at the mercy of capitalists and the naked power of the state. Consumed by his helplessness, "the workman is only too ready to join any and every movement that promises to help him, and to throw himself into the arms of every fool or lying demagogue."[25]

For these reasons, Ketteler advocated a reorganization of the prevailing industrial system based on cooperative production associations under the ownership and management of the workers themselves. What Ketteler had in mind was a corporative industrial scheme that had many of the characteristics of the medieval guilds. Although the old guild system had its faults and abuses, owing largely to its failure to adapt to the emergence of a market economy, Ketteler believed that its positive attributes—the integration of the worker into the productive order, giving him dignity and status— could be modified and incorporated into the new industrial order. What had been lost in the destruction of the guilds was any guarantee of security for the individual worker. Hence modern wage earners were organizing for united action to make their just claims against the owners of capital. Ketteler supported these efforts and insisted that the Church must wholeheartedly sanction the process. Christianity, said Ketteler, possessed certain truths that could impart the vigor and bonding necessary for workingmen's associations:

> When men combine in a Christian spirit, there subsists among them, independently of the direct purpose of their association, a nobler bond which, like a beneficent sun, pours out its light and warmth over all. Faith and charity are for them the source of life and light and vigor. Before they came together to attain a material object, they were already united in this tree of life planted by God on earth; it is this spiritual union that gives life to their social union. In a word, Christian associations are living organisms; the associations founded under the auspices of modern Liberalism are nothing but agglomerations of individuals held together solely by the hope of present mutual profit or usefulness.
>
> The future of unionism belongs to Christianity. The ancient Christian corporations have been dissolved and men are still zealously at work trying to remove the last remnants, the last stone, of this splendid edifice; a new building is to replace it. But this is only a wretched hut—built upon sand. Christianity must raise a new structure on the old foundations and thus give back to the workingmen's associations their real significance and their real usefulness.[26]

Along with his proposals for the creation of a corporativist industrial order, Ketteler took a strong public stand in support of labor's demand for higher wages. This was justified in the face of economic liberalism's degradation of labor to the level of a commodity and its tendency to look "on man himself, with his capacity for work, simply as a machine bought as cheaply as possible and driven until it will go no more."[27] Although a living wage was a basic necessity for labor, Ketteler was aware that the worker needed more than mere wages for his economic well-being. In this respect, Ketteler had been swayed by Ferdinand Lassalle's "iron law of wages," which stated that those who rely exclusively on wages are inevitably driven by competition to the level of bare subsistence. Ketteler recognized the need to transform the workers into owners. This could not be done through "self-help," as the liberals had argued, because the mass of workers were too poor to generate the necessary capital to achieve and maintain ownership as individuals. The workers would need the unity of numbers to reach this goal; Ketteler advocated the restoration of a guild order because he believed it had the greatest potential to provide workers with the opportunity of ownership, a responsibility they ultimately could share with management.

Bishop Ketteler was far ahead of his episcopal cohorts in advocating the application of social deaconry to the issues of modern society. He played an active and seminal role in organizing skilled workers in the Catholic Workers League, forerunner of the later Christian Trade Union movement. Ketteler saw no reason why the Catholic Church should stand apart from labor's efforts to unionize simply because the drive was being promoted by anti-Christians:

> It would be a great folly on our part if we kept aloof from this movement merely because it happens at the present time to be promoted chiefly by men who are hostile to Christianity. The air remains God's air though breathed by an atheist, and the bread we eat is no less the nourishment provided for us by God though kneaded by an unbeliever. It is the same with unionism: it is an idea that rests on the divine order of things and is essentially Christian, though the men who favor it most do not recognize the finger of God in it and often even turn it to a wicked use.[28]

In addition to his proposals for reforming the industrial order, Ketteler's most important contribution to the growth of Catholic social action was his insistence that the Church make an effort to train clergy more effectively to meet the needs of the working classes. Churchmen, he insisted, had to be informed about the social and economic conditions of the laboring poor, educated in economics and sociological theory, and acquainted with welfare policies and programs:

> The labor question cannot be ignored any longer in the courses of Philosophy and Pastoral Theology in our seminaries. It would be an important step in the right direction if a certain number of ecclesiastics could be induced to make a special study of political economy. They would have to be provided with traveling allowances to enable them to study labor conditions on the spot and to gain personal knowledge of the welfare institutions already in existence. The results of their investigation and observations would be communicated to their brethren in the ministry to periodic conferences established for the purpose.[29]

The German bishops meeting at the Fulda Conference in 1869 formally accepted Ketteler's recommendations on the social question, and the Twentieth Catholic Congress, meeting at Dusseldorf at the same time, unanimously accepted these principles and reform proposals, adopting them as the basis for all subsequent German Catholic social action.

By the end of an eminent career which had earned him the appellations "Bishop of the Workingman" and "The Fighting Bishop," Ketteler had come to the conclusion that although a reconstructed industrial order had to be morally guided by the social deaconry of the Church, and its redistribution of property undertaken only if there were a society-wide "interior regeneration of the heart,"[30] it could be put into the flesh only with the intervention of the state. In particular, governments must assume the task of giving legal protection to labor's struggle to create corporative enterprises. Ketteler's ideas on labor associations were rooted in the medieval notion of "estates," where each profession and productive unit— corporation—was self-governing and participated equally in the creation of national policy. He was convinced that these would mitigate the class divisiveness encouraged by Marxists. Ketteler outlined five conditions vital for a guild order based on vocations: "They must be natural growths, not simply creations of the State; they must be for economic ends and avoid political entanglements; they must have a moral basis and develop a corporate conscience; they must include all the members of the same class (vocation); and they must combine self-government and legal regulation in reasonable proportions."[31]

In 1873 Ketteler published a Christian political program for the German Center Party which appeared under the title *The Catholics in the German Empire*. Here he outlined a number of tasks the state should undertake which included, among other things, developing laws to protect worker's cooperatives, compensation for the disabled, prohibitions against child labor in factories, legal regulation of working hours, and government inspection of factories.

In the spirit of the Christian guild society of old, Ketteler also reminded laborers that they had mutual obligations to owners of capital. The workers must moderate their demands, and

> if they are to escape the danger of becoming mere tools in the hands of ambitious and unscrupulous demagogues, if they wish to keep clear of the inordinate selfishness which they condemn so severely in the capitalist, they must be filled with a lofty moral sense, their ranks must be made up of courageous, Christian, religious men. The power of money without religion is just as great an evil. Both lead to destruction.[32]

Ketteler's revolutionary social teachings were a major target in the *Kulturkampf* initiated by Chancellor Otto von Bismarck in an effort to subordinate the Catholic Church to the will of the newly formed German national state, a battle which contemporary observers viewed as a struggle between two opposing cultures. Ketteler was accused by Bismarck of creating what the chancellor called "political dualism," that is, of setting up a "State within a State" by forcing Catholics to follow the dictates of the "Papist" German Center Party. The autocratic Bismarck made these claims in order to discredit the patriotism of a powerful interest group that could challenge his imperious political agenda. In fact, Ketteler's concern was that Catholic rights not be destroyed by the new powers of a

German imperial government. His answer to such threats was a recommendation that Catholics organize through a strong political
party, for only then would the imperial authorities listen to Catholic ideas on political and social reform: "We must organize in such
a manner that every Catholic, whether burgher or peasant, will be
perfectly acquainted with our demands and ready to champion them
boldly and resolutely in his own particular sphere of activity. In
this way alone can we hope to gain the influence to which we are
entitled."[33]

Ketteler, however, was not proposing an exclusive Catholic program; he insisted that his principles spoke for all religious bodies
that required protection under the law. The sociopolitical positions
to which Bismarck referred were outlined in Ketteler's *The Catholics in the German Empire*. This treatise actually was written near the
end of the Franco-Prussian War of 1870 and was unknown to the
Center Party until it was published in the spring of 1873, proving,
of course, that the program was not drafted by Center Party politicians. An analysis of its contents reveals that Ketteler was simply
proposing a set of guidelines that would protect the basic democratic
rights of all Christian religious groups, guarantee public laws, assure
the principles of federalism, and safeguard individual and corporate
liberty against the potentially statist claims of the German Empire.

These guidelines were laid out in the spirit of political pluralism, Ketteler having carefully spelled out the need to guarantee the
autonomy of a multitude of interest groups in a society that had
become increasingly infatuated with the powers of "blood and iron"
political techniques. In this context Ketteler saw an extremely dangerous situation developing: the increasing powers of the state
"vested in a bureaucratic officialdom," on the one hand, and the
atomization of society caused by the breakdown of rural, closely-
knit community life due to rapid urbanization and industrialization,
on the other hand, had created a condition in which isolated individuals were engaged in unbridled competition under the sole control of industrial capitalists, an absolute monarch, or an equally
absolute parliamentary government. Throughout this process, "the
worker was isolated and left to his individual resources while the
money power . . . was centralized. The working class was atomized

into individual particles, so to speak, with each individual powerless by himself."[34] It was imperative, in Ketteler's mind, that the German working and peasant classes organize into self-governing corporations to protect their own interests.

These advanced proposals for sociopolitical reform were put forth when Germany's socialist movement was still in its infancy (the Social Democratic Party was not formed until May 1875), and Ketteler's recommendations were so progressive that they seemed foreign to the thoughts of average Catholics. Ketteler appreciated the unlikelihood that his programs would be given serious consideration by the state, and he knew his ideas were probably even too radical for most bourgeois German Catholics:

> We do not expect our program to be accepted on the spot, or even in the near future; our actions, however, are not governed by the passing needs of the hour and the fluctuations of the *Zeit-geist*, but by eternal principles, upon which alone the peace and happiness of nations are based and which, after seasons of revolutionary upheaval, always rise to the surface again.[35]

The accommodation of Catholics to political reality initiated by Ketteler—that is to say, acceptance of capitalism and the modern state (*Sozialpolitik*)—was brought to fruition by his disciple, Father Franz Hitze. Although Hitze was a distinguished professor at the University of Muenster and later a monsignor, his real love was the rough-and-tumble world of politics, where as a member of the Center Party he became a powerful advocate for labor in the German Reichstag.

Hitze was converted to the cause of social deaconry and practical social reform after witnessing firsthand the injustice and grinding poverty of the working class while serving as a young chaplain in the industrial town of Muenchen-Gladbach. Like Ketteler, Hitze came to appreciate the strengths of Germany's secular and Protestant traditions and, given the minority status of Catholicism, the impossibility of reconstructing modern society along clerical lines. He therefore focused his energies on a pragmatic approach to the problems, trying everything permissible within the spirit of the

Gospels to forge the best deal possible for labor within the social and political conditions of the day.

Hitze narrowed his goal to that which was possible. He created educational opportunities for Catholic workers by helping to establish the "Volksverein fuer das katholische Deutschland," and he encouraged Catholic labor action by involving workers in the broader-based, interconfessional Christian Social Workmen's Associations, of which he became the chief inspiration and organizer in 1882. Out of this grouping was formed the Federation of Christian Trade Unions, which worked for constructive social reforms well into the era of the Weimar Republic. The significance of Hitze's career is that he was successful in encouraging Catholics to become integrated into an ever-changing capitalist world order. By doing so he assured that German Catholics would not be marginalized from mainstream society, and he helped provide them with realistic opportunities to shape their social and political environment according to Christian principles.

Solving the "social question," in Hitze's mind, required an economic system that was adaptive to modern methods of production and integrated with modern values. Like his mentor Ketteler, Hitze rejected liberal capitalism, where the powerful preyed upon the weak; a distrust of bureaucracy and centralization also led him to deny the efficacy of state socialism. "Guild socialism," claimed Hitze, was the best solution to the modern social question. By this he meant the application of a modified medieval guild system to industrial production. Such a system would be more broadly based economically and far more democratic than that of the Middle Ages. However, a partial or voluntary application of the guild program would not be sufficient; it would be a feeble weapon for breaking through the "iron law" of wages. Hitze insisted that the guilds would have to be compulsory for all industries, trades, professions, and areas of agricultural production. Hitze's proclamation of the principle of "society reform through social policies"—the principle that the political parties must work for social improvement in tandem with the people, government, and prevailing economic conditions—represented the logical culmination of Ketteler's melioristic, pragmatic *Sozialpolitik* in action.[36]

Ketteler had been the first to articulate German Catholic opposition to capitalism and what could be called classical political liberalism (that which embraced the principles of laissez-faire, laissez-aller, and utilitarian individualism). Karl von Vogelsang, whose romantic and conservative ideas informed the so-called "Vienna School" of the Christian Social Movement, escalated this resistance to an exaggerated and uncompromising level.[37] Vogelsang was a personal friend of Ketteler's, having converted to Catholicism under his influence. But unlike Ketteler and Ozanam, Vogelsang believed it necessary to reject totally three historical products of modernity: democracy, capitalism, and socialism. Ketteler and Ozanam believed the excesses of capitalism resulted from economic and social developments that were a natural part of the historical process (the rise of industrial society) and thus were amenable to reform. Vogelsang, however, regarded modernization as an exclusively moral problem produced by the Protestant Reformation, an event which in his mind represented a perversion of Christianity. Consequently, capitalism and liberalism, integral components of that process of change, were beyond rehabilitation. Rather than reform such evils, Catholics must expurgate them from contemporary culture. For all these reasons, Vogelsang has been recognized as the "father of *Sozialreform*."[38]

Vogelsang descended from an aristocratic Prussian family, studied in German universities, and served for a time in the Prussian civil service. Eventually settling in Vienna, he became the most eminent of all the German Catholic publicists. Vogelsang joined the editorial board of the conservative paper *Das Vaterland* and in 1879 founded his own monthly, *Monatsschrift fuer christliche Sozialreform*. These publications became his platforms for attacking Austrian liberalism and working out his own *Sozialreform* version of Christian action. In Vienna Vogelsang found a fertile environment for the germination of his ideas. He enjoyed support from Catholic romantics and conservatives who shared his idealization of the Middle Ages and his opposition to liberal free enterprise and political democracy.

The Christian Social Movement which Vogelsang came to dominate, labeled by its critics "the Feudal Austrian School," had its origins in court circles. Among his supporters was a group of impor-

tant Viennese noblemen that included Prince Aloysius von Liechtenstein, Count Egbert Belcredi, and Prince Karl zu Löwenstein.
The feudal values of Austria's aristocrats were especially threatened
by the rapid social changes brought by industrialization. Independently, the nineteenth-century economic expansion had led to the
advancement of Austrian Jews, some of whom were well positioned
in finance and industry. By the early 1860s prohibitions against Jewish ownership of land were lifted throughout the Austro-Hungar-
ian Empire, and within a short while a number of wealthy Jews had
been able to accumulate considerable holdings in Galacia, Bohemia,
and Hungary. Not surprisingly, many Austrians came to associate
the disruptions of capitalism with Jewish influence. Catholic aristocrats, partly as a counteraction to capitalism's successful assault
on the feudal order, reasserted their traditional leadership roles by
taking on the defense of labor. Their tirades against capitalist social
and economic oppression, anticlericalism, and the corrosive materialistic values of liberal philosophy, a campaign which took on the
tones of an aristocratic populism, became at times violently anti-
Semitic.[39]

In the harsh polemical style that was his journalistic trademark,
Vogelsang asserted that the only antidote to the disease of modern
life was the resurrection of a corporatist sociopolitical order. But
unlike Ketteler's rights-centered state, his corporate state was to be
solidified by an authoritarian social structure designed after medieval precepts and under the political control of strong monarchy.
As part of their refusal to integrate with modern political and economic reality, the Austrian social Catholics who gathered around
Vogelsang called for an exclusively Catholic labor movement (something Ketteler had rejected) and a clerical political party. Vogelsang's
circle assumed the existence of a specific "Catholic" social, political,
and economic order that had formed the "integral" core of Western civilization and that stood in defiant opposition to the deviant
institutional forms appearing since the dissolution of the Middle
Ages. The rise of liberalism, capitalism, and the powers of finance
had been responsible for the destruction of the guilds, eliminating
the system of rules that protected those who produced from the rav-
ages of greed and, in the process, fundamentally transforming the

fabric of European culture: "Gin and the Jewish press," wrote Vogel-sang, "that is to say, drunken stupor and obscenities, manage to kill the remaining memories of a Christian past in these unfortunate victims."[40]

For those who embraced romantic notions of an integral Catho-licism that defined European culture, it became ideologically impos-sible to make accommodations with nineteenth-century social and political life. Vogelsang, for his part, simply accused anyone who dis-agreed with his views on the subject of being "liberal," meaning, in this case, un-Catholic.[41] The narrow confessionalism of the "inte-gralists" and their efforts to subordinate social life to clericalism estranged many Catholics from the vital realities of the day and failed to attract the working classes to Catholic sociopolitical positions.

Vogelsang's reactionary, anti-liberal ideas had an enduring in-fluence on later developments in Austrian Catholic social and politi-cal thought. The demagogic, anti-Semitic politician Karl Lueger, whose movement gained control of both Vienna and the Austrian countryside, was tutored by Vogelsang. Lueger became a champion of Vogelsang's corporative social monarchy ideas. This approach gave wide scope to the power of the state. Vogelsang believed that the evil consequences of liberalism (the destruction of family life and the guilds, increasing crime, the exploitation of labor, and pandemic urban poverty) were so deep and pervasive that only strict state control over the social order could provide the needed remedies.[42] Vogelsang's *Sozialreform* program was initially designed to appeal to the lower middle classes, artisans, and peasants, whose economic positions were seriously threatened by competing social groups that emerged from the growth of industrialism.

The integralist Catholics of *Sozialreform* were persistent critics of more liberal-minded Catholics who followed the melioristic *So-zialpolitik* approaches championed by Hitze. The latter collaborated with secular forces and were willing to make political compromises. Integralist criticisms, as a contemporary Catholic scholar has argued, revealed a fundamental misunderstanding of social deaconry, a prag-matic tradition never intended to be more than a supplementary ser-vice to ameliorate conditions in the material world. The integralist confusion of the social mission of the Church with the sacramental goals of the clergy, combined with their belief in an exclusive Catholic political and economic order, resulted in a rigid "clericalization" of social life and unrealistic theological theories underlying the practice of government and the organization of society.[43]

The nineteenth-century alliance between Catholic social reform and reactionary politics flourished in France as well as in Austria. In the aftermath of the French Revolution, for instance, one of France's most distinguished Catholic historians, Joseph de Maistre, in his condemnation of Jacobinism, developed an influential counter-revolutionary political philosophy that coupled monarchism with the teachings of the social gospel. Following the violence and anarchy of the Revolution of 1848, de Maistre's ideas gained a wide audience once again. The euphoria that had accompanied the publication of Lacordaire's and Ozanam's *The New Era*, which recognized the two basic principles upon which the Catholic social movement could be built—the need to improve the conditions of the laboring classes and the acceptance of political democracy as the instrument for doing so—quickly dissipated as the democratic energies behind the Revolution of 1848 turned to violence.

When Louis Napoleon transformed the Second Republic into the Second Empire in 1852, he put into place a republican form of government that in practice functioned as a monarchy. Under Louis Napoleon, the Church, at least during the early years of his reign, was treated favorably by the government. Many liberal Catholics saw no political threat from imperial government and, in practice, no impending conflict between monarchy and democracy. Catholic democratic philosophies and movements seemed increasingly irrelevant, and by the mid-1860s many of the leaders of these movements were dead. Furthermore, the political instability and working-class violence that followed the Revolution of 1848 discredited democratic political ideas and made many Frenchmen regard socialism as destructive and dangerous. Meanwhile, the French labor movement after 1848 became progressively more anticlerical, owing to the workers' bitter resentment of the Church's comfortable relationship with Louis Napoleon's absolutist regime. It was during the Second Empire that revolutionary Marxism began to make inroads into French working-class movements. Since the anti-religious Marx was of Jewish background, as were many European intellectuals who identified with their brand of socialism, there emerged in the minds of many Frenchmen a close connection between Jews, communism, and atheism.

An economist who perhaps best expressed the sentiment of most Catholics on the social question during this post-Ozanam era was Frédéric Le Play. Although he found much to his dislike in the social order of the Second Empire, Le Play did not believe that reform should come through social legislation or by working-class organization. In principle, he opposed governmental intervention, arguing that the state should retreat from social involvement and support the action of enlightened capitalists to improve conditions. Real social reform, said Le Play, must come from private quarters, starting with the family, and be carried into fruition by the voluntary action of employers and large landowners.

The significance of Le Play's views is that they helped reverse the direction established by Ozanam's circle and served as a transition to an even more reactionary school of Catholic social thought in the latter part of the century. Le Play repudiated political democracy as a means for social reform, emphasizing instead the voluntary, paternalistic efforts of the upper classes. He argued that moral reform was more significant than political or economic change, and he discussed ways that a modern monarchy could serve the needs of Catholicism.[44]

The cause of democracy and socialism was further discredited among Catholics with the popular uprising that led to the creation of the Paris Commune in the spring of 1871, following the surrender of France in the Franco-Prussian War. The insurrection was eventually put down by government troops in May, but only after the Communards, some of whom appeared to be under the influence of radical socialist ideas, had massacred the archbishop of Paris and a number of priests and had wreaked considerable damage on Church property. The violent episode convinced many French Catholics of the importance of becoming actively involved in social reform, but it also made it appear that socialism was now the enemy not merely of property but also of religion.

The excesses of the Paris Commune prepared the ground for an aggressive Catholic movement for social change under the direction of two aristocratic army officers, Count Albert de Mun and the Marquis René de La Tour du Pin. Albert de Mun had been initiated into the world of Catholic action when, as a soldier, he became an active member of the Clermont-Ferrand Conference of the St. Vincent de Paul Society. He and René de La Tour du Pin had shared a prison cell after the two were captured by Germans in the 1870 Metz campaign. A turning point in de Mun's life was his assignment to Paris in the spring of 1871 to help suppress the Communard uprising. He was appalled by the bloodshed but equally disturbed by the bourgeoisie's indifference to the fate of the workers. Soon after the end of the uprising, de Mun and a few others, including La Tour du Pin, formed a "Committee for the Foundation of Catholic Workingmen's Clubs."[45] Their aim in encouraging French workers to join Christian associations was to bring them closer to Catholic teachings and thus "inoculate" them against subversive and dangerous sociopolitical doctrines. The Committee mounted a nationwide campaign to induce upper-class Catholics to take an active role in social reform by patronizing the workingmen's clubs. By 1875 de Mun's Association of Catholic Workingmen's Clubs could claim 150 branches with eighteen thousand members. It grew to some sixty thousand members by 1900.[46] De Mun's mission, however, was decidedly different from Ozanam's. He was roused to action not by the spirit of democracy but by the perceived danger of revolution, the same fear which shaped the ideas of de Maistre and Le Play. Appropriately, de Mun's cohorts, the founders of the Workingmen's Clubs, called themselves "Soldiers of the Counter-Revolution."[47] They identified the "Counter-Revolution" with patriotism, France's military traditions, and aristocratic social leadership, and they viewed monarchy as the embodiment of French political culture.

The political ideas of the Soldiers of the Counter-Revolution were fertilized by a close association with the Austrian integralist Catholics. In the 1870s René de La Tour du Pin had served as French military attaché to Vienna, where he made the acquaintance of Catholics associated with the Vogelsang school. La Tour du Pin became particularly impressed with the group's advanced corporatist ideas, their "Christian economics" being far more sophisticated than anything he had found in France. A close link was established between the Vogelsang Catholics and the followers of de Mun and La Tour du Pin in France.[48] The reemergence of republicanism in France after 1875, accompanied by a rapid rise in anticlericalism, brought conservative Catholics to the barricades. In the summer of 1876 de Mun was elected on a clerical and antirevolutionary platform to the Chamber of Deputies, where he launched bold attacks on republicanism. Within a few years he felt confident enough to campaign actively for the restoration of monarchy, arguing that it alone could balance the excesses of liberty with firm paternal authority. De Mun and his allies criticized the Republican government's reluctance to undertake social reform. The government had failed to pass legislation allowing working-class association and refused to initiate state regulation of working hours on the grounds that it would upset the laws of the market and open the door to socialism. De Mun and the clerical-monarchists assailed the republicans as puppets of the selfish bourgeoisie who had forsaken the bonds that had traditionally tied leaders to the people.

A major source of labor's insecurity, asserted de Mun and his Catholic colleagues, was the "law of 1791," which allowed the Revolution to abolish the guilds. The law had made all organizations of workers illegal, giving complete economic control to those who owned the means of production. Count de Mun, whose Workingmen's Clubs stood for the principle that all classes had the right of association, became the spokesman for the Legitimist pretender to the French throne, the Count de Chambord, who claimed that monarchy had always been the defender of labor's right to organize.

The burden of acting as the pretender's interpreter required de Mun to develop and clarify his thinking more fully, and by 1882 he presented a plan for the application of guilds, modeled along medieval lines, to industrial production. His program called for self-governing associations of workers and managers, *syndicats mixtes,* held together by the bonds of Christian confraternity (involving reciprocal duties) and the common interest of enterprise. The "great social necessity of our time," said de Mun, is that which existed in the old guild institutions: "personal contact, conciliation of interest, appeasement, which cannot be had except by the reconstruction of the industrial family."[49] The guilds that de Mun envisioned would not only guarantee labor's basic rights (providing health insurance, regulating hours of work, maintaining living wages, and so on) but also give them a share in the management of industry, thus providing a greater sense of responsibility by restoring their interests and pride in the products of production. De Mun speculated that the guilds might someday become the vehicle for representing labor's political interests in government.

De Mun's social Catholicism was inspired by his predecessor, Frédéric Le Play. However, though he owed much to his master, it is obvious that de Mun developed a program more radical than Le Play's. Whereas the latter had eschewed statism in any form and advocated the voluntary creation of Christian guilds, de Mun's association eventually endorsed obligatory state action to create a guild social order. The founders of the Catholic Workingmen's Clubs were in close everyday contact with the problems of labor, and since they were committed to action, it was only natural that they would sacrifice some of their idealism as they struggled to bring social and economic improvement for the working classes.

La Tour du Pin had convinced the Association of Workingmen's Clubs to establish a special school to study social economics in 1872, and this "Council of Studies" worked out specific doctrines for establishing a new guild order along Christian lines. The council's ideas were published in it's review, *L'Association catholique,* and drew heavily from the Austrian integralist Catholics. The corporative system that La Tour du Pin and the council advanced was not only economic but religious, cultural, and political as well. In a series of reports that appeared between 1881 and 1883, the council concluded that the influence of liberal political economics had become so injurious to social relationships that the government had not merely a right but a duty to intervene. The council's report *Avis No. V* made specific recommendations for state action, suggesting a program of labor legislation which recalled that put forth by Ketteler a decade earlier in Germany.[50] Indeed, articles in *L'Association catholique* acknowledged Ketteler as the one who had blazed the path and provided the logic for their ambitious guild campaign. La Tour du Pin claimed that it was the German school which made them appreciate the intervention of state authority.

In the face of the challenges of the "Century of Revolution," a number of Catholic intellectuals managed to put forth needed socioeconomic programs suggesting that the Catholic Church was capable of dealing with modern social problems. In many respects, these nineteenth-century Catholic social analyses were economically and politically progressive. They articulated a critique of industrial capitalism and advocated reform programs as advanced as those urged by secular socialist movements in France and Germany. Yet Catholic critics of capitalism, notwithstanding La Tour du Pin's acknowledged debt to Ketteler, were divided in their analysis of the social problem and, more seriously, in fundamental disagreement about how to repair the social order. The melioristic, intellectually pragmatic group was willing to embrace the democratic values and political realities of the day; the "integralist" school was unalterably opposed to compromises with the bourgeois age and drafted plans for an alternative order that was politically and socially reactionary.

These two approaches would divide Catholic intellectuals well into the first half of the twentieth century.

CHAPTER 2

The Development of Catholic Social Action in Nineteenth-Century England

Although liberal Catholicism's first defenders emerged in France and Germany, perhaps its most intellectually illustrious champion was an English convert, John Henry Newman.[1] Newman had been the heart and soul of the Oxford-based Tractarian movement, which included the powerful minds and personalities of Richard Hurrell Froude, Edward Pusey, John Keble, and W. G. Ward. The name "Tractarians" derived from a series of pamphlets, *Tracts for the Times,* challenging the shallow, rationalistic, and latitudinarian tendencies of the Anglican clergy. The pamphlets revealed a yearning for a higher religious experience that would bring holiness, a presence of the divine, into everyday life. The Tractarians aimed to rekindle the religious *esprit de corps* of Britain's secularized clergy. The last of the series, *Tract No. 90,* published by Newman in 1841, appealed for an undivided, pre-Reformation Church. It was promptly condemned by the heads of the Oxford colleges. Newman thereafter went into seclusion and in 1845 joined the Roman Catholic Church.

Most Tractarians declined to follow Newman's path to Rome, but their mission to recharge the spirituality of the Church of England brought many of them close to the Vatican's theological positions. Their major criticism was that the Anglican Church had been taken over by liberalism, a result of its capture by secular forces that sprang from the Reformation. However, what the Oxford

41

movement meant by liberalism was essentially distilled Jacobin secularism. Liberalism represented, for them, "the tendencies of modern thought to destroy the basis of revealed religion, and ultimately
all that can be called religion at all." For Newman, "the combating
of liberalism" was his life work.[2]

Especially troubling to Newman was the steady intrusion of the
state into religious affairs, which in Britain had virtually turned the
Anglican Church into a department of the government. Newman's
later writings show that he ultimately realized that any practical
resolution of Church-state relations would require an accommodation with the modern state, and he seems to have accepted "liberal principles" along the lines of political pluralism as the best
means to this end.[3]

Newman, however, was primarily a thinker and a scholar. For
him, like those Tractarians who remained in the Anglican fold, the
Church's mission was the saving of souls. He was largely uncon-
cerned with social issues. The Oxford movement was quintessen-
tially academic, restricting its teaching to the educated classes.
Moreover, its outlook was not progressive but rather, in reaction
against the cold rationalism of the eighteenth and nineteenth centuries, was backward-looking and romantically medieval. As Pusey
said, it was "to the old times and the old paths" that the movement
wished to lead Christians, back to an age of mystery and emotion.
That time for the Tractarians was the Middle Ages.[4] It was not until
the end of his life that Newman recognized a connection between
faith and the social problems of the industrial age.[5]

The Anglican Church discovered its social deaconry chiefly
through the prodding of Frederick Denison Maurice, who abhorred
the Oxford movement. The Tractarians had made a serious error,
wrote Maurice, "in opposing to the spirit of the present age the spirit
of a former age, instead of the ever-living and active Spirit of God."[6]
Maurice had a seminal influence on the so-called second generation
of the Oxford movement, the contributors to *Lux Mundi,* a book of
essays published in 1889 by High Anglicans championing the application of Christian teaching to social problems of the industrial age.

The importance of Newman's conversion to Roman Catholicism was not the impetus he gave to social deaconry but the fact that
he inspired British Catholics, "a race that shunned the light," as he

put it, to assume a more active role for their religion in national life.[7] Whereas Newman diagnosed the spiritual ills of his age, it was a younger Oxford convert, Henry Edward Manning, a pragmatist with an activist bent, who showed British Catholics how their religion could be a tool for social change. In his later years as Cardinal Archbishop of Westminster, Manning was the Church's best-known and most influential advocate of Catholic social action, serving, in the words of one of his biographers, as the "leading social guru to European Catholics."[8]

Manning had been attracted to the high-minded spiritual principles of the Tractarians while the Anglican rector of Lavington. There he began an active correspondence with Newman. The two men became warm friends, though in later years differences concerning papal authority and Catholic education as well as personality issues led to antagonisms between them.

As was the case with Ozanam, the young Manning had been profoundly disturbed by capitalism's exploitation of the laboring poor. At Lavington and as the archdeacon of Chichester, he had been surrounded by the poverty of industrial and agricultural workers and frequently vented his anger on those complacent owners of capital who felt no responsibility to their laborers once wages were paid. "The dense masses of our manufacturing towns, the poor families of our agricultural villages, are each of them related, by the bond of labour and wages to some employer, and on him they have a claim for alms, both of body and soul."[9] But unlike Le Play in France, Manning was not content with mere charity and goodwill from the wealthier classes as a remedy to the social problem. As early as 1831 he saw the need of a living wage for labor as the best means of ameliorating poverty, and as archdeacon he regularly chastised capitalists for their economic theories: "It is a high sin in the sight of Heaven for a man to wring his wealth out of thews and sinews of his fellows, and to think that when he has paid them their wages he has paid them all he owes."[10]

Manning's liberal political tendencies can also be traced back to his earlier years when, as a university student, he became involved with his friend William E. Gladstone as a debater at the Oxford Union. It seems that the future Archbishop of Westminster was a good deal more progressive than his friend. In reflecting back on those years, Manning said that Gladstone had begun as a "Church-and-State Tory," whereas his own Tory sympathies were more short-lived, the product of a callow admiration of George Canning, and that early on he developed into a "Mosaic Radical." By this Manning meant a radical in the tradition of Moses, one who recognized the inseparability of morality and politics. This apparently was also what Manning meant when he told the young Hilaire Belloc, upon whose impressionable mind he had an indelible political influence, that "all human conflict is ultimately theological."[11] Belloc claimed this remark remained for him the single most important political insight: "it came to possess for me a universal meaning so profound that it reached to the very roots of political action; so extended that it covered the whole."[12]

Debating at the Oxford Union was exhilarating, and after regular visits to the House of Commons, Manning seriously considered a career in politics as a match for his driving ambition to improve the world. He never lost his passion for politics, but the family's economic situation suggested that Manning consider a profession more financially secure. In addition, it appears that Manning felt something vaguely troubling about his political ambitions, as if they sprang from a personal vanity which perhaps required mortification. Shortly after leaving Oxford, Manning made the acquaintance of his close friend's sister, Miss Favell Lee Bevan, whose family, like Manning's, had been steeped in the Anglican Evangelical tradition. The two studied Scripture together, had long spiritual discussions, and soon thereafter Manning announced his decision to prepare for the Anglican priesthood. As mentioned earlier, while serving at Lavington he fell under the influence of the Tractarians, and of Newman in particular, who asserted that Evangelical enthusiasm, especially in a day where individualism was running amok, was insufficient without the moorings of a fixed dogma.

Following the lead of the Tractarians, Manning read the Church fathers and undertook a careful study of the apostolic succession; and, like Newman, he concluded that Christian tradition had to be the chief authority for faith. The issue soon brought him to comparisons between Anglicanism and Roman Catholicism as the authentic repository of Christian teachings. Once Newman made his own decision on the issue, it was simply a matter of time, though much personal anguish, before Manning would follow the logic of *Tract 90* and also convert to the side of Rome.

The conversion of a person of Manning's energies and singular devotion to social action had a far-reaching impact on English Catholicism. The Catholic community in Britain had long ceased to play a significant role in social and cultural life. Since the Elizabethan Settlement, English Catholics had found that it was safer to withdraw from public notice and practice their religious beliefs behind closed doors. Leadership of the Roman Church fell to a number of old northern aristocratic families. These proud households, whose predecessors were martyrs for the cause, had kept the faith alive but had done so in isolation. They sent their sons to the continent for schooling, gave up any claim to national political leadership or pretensions to great intellectual achievement, and, for the most part, were content to blend into the English rural landscape as contented country squires. Those few Catholics who became politically involved in the last quarter of the nineteenth century (Lord Ripon and the Duke of Norfolk, for example) had little success in furthering the interests of their co-religionists. In the words of Dermot Quinn, their endeavors only brought "misplaced hopes and disappointed enthusiasms," for the political parties, both Whig and Tory, largely ignored the concerns of their constituencies.[13] Not only had these Catholics turned away from English political life, they had also developed a Gallican suspicion of Rome. Centuries in the theological wilderness, following the brave battles against the anti-Papist Elizabeth I and her successors, had bred a fierce strain of religious independence. Further, in the absence of a diocesan system, the old Catholic squirarchies were able to dominate their clergy almost as if they were bishops themselves.

Their numbers, however, remained small. In the eighteenth century Catholics probably numbered no more than sixty thousand in England, roughly one percent of the population. This demographic pattern began to shift dramatically by the mid-nineteenth century, owing to the influx of some half million Irish, the vast majority of whom were Catholic. Irish immigrants in flight from grinding rural poverty settled in the industrial towns of northern England where jobs could be found in manufacturing. The "Old Catholics" did not welcome this addition to their numbers, since the Irish were working class, often economically destitute, and, in the eyes of the Catholic squirarchy, culturally impoverished. The Tractarian convert Frederick Faber captured such sentiments when he complained that at the London Oratory the working poor produced "immovable *belts* of stink" which chased away Catholics from the washing classes. These types were "so plentiful in bugs that they walk about our surplices and take possession of gentleman's hats."[14]

However, this rapid growth of Catholics meant that the Vatican would have to reestablish England as an ecclesiastical province of the Roman Church.[15] This had long been the objective of certain Catholics at the Vatican, in particular, the titular bishop in England, Nicholas Wiseman, who himself was of Irish descent. The English Catholic hierarchy was restored in 1852 and Wiseman became the first Archbishop of Westminster and Metropolitan of the new Province. However good for the growth of Catholicism in England, these were inauspicious events for the Old Catholics, who now saw lay control of the English Catholic Church slipping into the hands of ultramontaine forces and, more particularly, of what was considered a rough Irish connection. The resistance of the Old Catholics was fortified by the fear that Wiseman, an alien and aggressive "Irishman," would encourage a backlash of anti-Catholic sentiment and legislation. As it was, the announcement of Rome's establishment of the hierarchy in England provoked outbursts of vitriolic criticism in the press and protests in the streets, where crowds burned effigies of Wiseman.

The Old Catholics were also threatened by the large number of converts who followed Newman into the Church, many of whom were aggressive about their newly discovered faith and appeared to Old Catholics as intellectually arrogant. Wiseman went out of his way to accommodate the Tractarian converts, appreciating that their religious zeal could provide the impetus for a Catholic revival in England. His penchant for promoting them to high posts and offices created hostility among the Old Catholics, who felt that the newcomers were being given advantages at the expense of "cradle" Catholics.

All this explains the resentment at Manning's early promotion within the English hierarchy. The former archdeacon's administrative and political talents clearly qualified him for episcopal office, and it would have been a profligate waste of talent for a man of Manning's abilities to waste away in the catacombs, as it were, in a life-style that appealed to far too many of the Old Catholics. Manning, for his part, was highly critical of the squirearchy's aloofness from social issues and their insularity from both national political life and the spirit of Rome. All the great works of charity, social reform movements, and efforts to ameliorate labor abuses in England, noted Manning, were initiated outside the Catholic Church. He advised his new co-religionists to learn something from the Protestants, in particular, from the deeds of General Booth and the Salvation Army. After all, he pointed out, the Holy Scriptures had not been placed on the Index.[16]

Despite the Old Catholics disagreements with Manning's evangelical style and ultramontaine views, they rallied to the papal colors and threw their support behind Manning when in 1865 Rome made him Wiseman's successor as Archbishop of Westminster (he was given the Cardinal's Hat in 1875). Meanwhile, Manning continued to prod the Catholic establishment to ally itself more closely with the masses. Catholic aloofness was not a deliberate attempt to avoid responsibility but rather a combination of ignorance and ingrained social prejudice, the spawn of benighted insularity, or, as Manning put it, a matter of being "unconscious that Lazarus lies at their gate full of sores."[17] But now, said Manning, it was time for Catholics to partake "in the trade winds of the nineteenth century." Seize this world, he urged, "meet it intellect to intellect, culture to culture, science to science."[18]

As Metropolitan and Cardinal Archbishop of Westminster, Manning concentrated his considerable political skill and concern for the poor on a variety of fronts, almost as if he were trying to compensate for the retarded social action of his fellow Catholics. He used his friendship with the Radical social reformer, Sir Charles Dilke, for instance, to obtain government assistance to build better housing in severely overcrowded and unhealthy working-class ghettos.[19] Manning's reputation as a social activist was such that in 1884 he was the first person invited to serve on the newly created Royal Commission on the Housing of the Working Classes. There he surprised his distinguished co-panelists with what Dilke called unrealistic and "revolutionary" suggestions for urban planning, one of which was to remove polluting factories from cities into the less populated countryside. Manning felt that the commission's final report was inadequate to the needs of the laboring classes. In any case, its recommendations were largely ignored. Although disappointed with the government's failure to enact the recommendations of the Royal Commission on Housing, Manning immediately threw himself into the cause of improving local government, where he did find considerable success in 1888 with the establishment of the London County Council.

Although Manning never despaired of democracy, his experiences with the tawdry side of English politics produced a dim view of the party system and Parliament. His bias against these would color the attitudes of certain key figures among the next generation of English Catholic intellectuals, upon whom Manning had so telling an influence. A note written in his later years shows Manning describing Whig and Tory as "two forms of class selfishness," well-to-do selfishness, the other aristocratic selfishness. He had contempt for their politics (defining his own as "social politics") and for what he called that "Talking Mill at Westminster."[20]

Early in his career Manning had come to despise the practical results of what he called the "heartless and headless" notions of laissez-faire liberalism. The first tenet of his own visceral political philosophy was that Christian statesmen had a responsibility to provide for the needs of the working population, the claims of the poor being far more important than profit generated by the maintenance of a self-serving open market. Like Ozanam and Ketteler, Manning's adherence to democratic political principles, and his urging of the Church to embrace them, made him an unabashed advocate of the interventionist state for the rights of labor. When an economist writing in the *Manchester Guardian* eulogized the unrestricted free market as the best mechanism for maximizing employment and the production of surplus value, since the so-called "law of accumulation" would surely create job opportunities, Manning asked the logical question of what would happen during those cycles of the market where there were no surpluses. "Theories of the gradual accumulation of surplus will not feed hungry men, women and children; and hunger cannot be sent to Jupiter or Saturn."[21]

Manning publicly identified himself as a labor activist in December 1872 when, presiding over a meeting at Exeter Hall in the midst of widespread dissatisfaction among farm workers, he proposed a motion of support for the newly formed Agricultural Union. This was the first time that a high-ranking Roman Catholic prelate in Britain had committed himself openly to the cause of labor, and his words brought cries of protest from many of his fellow Catholic and Tory conservatives who labeled him an "agrarian agitator." Manning replied that he was proud to be associated with such worthy efforts. The experience prompted a letter to Manning's old friend, Prime Minister Gladstone.

> I remember your saying to me many years ago that the next conflict would be between the masters and the workmen. I had been so much out of England then that I did not know how far this reached. I found last week that even my Irish hodmen are organized. I have also lately had means of knowing what the agricultural unionists are. As yet they are not political. They do not coalesce with the London men, but the London men will soon make capital of them if others do not interpose. The consequence of this would be disastrous. My belief is that some energetic and sympathetic act on the part of the Government would avert great dangers. Could not a Royal Commission be issued to take the evidence of men who are now appealing to public opinion for help? If they have a case, it could be dealt with. If they have none, it would be exposed.[22]

A short while later Manning again wrote Gladstone calling for more specific governmental action. The old Poor Law, he pointed out, had saved the working poor for over a century, but the 1832 Poor Law, inspired by the Manchester School, was not functioning as a safety net. The government had to do something about it and the continuing grinding down of the laboring classes:

> Why cannot you do these things for the labourer? Prohibit the labour of children under a certain age. Compel payments of wages in money. Regulate the number of dwellings according to the population of parishes. Establish tribunals of arbitration

in counties for questions between labour and land. If our unions were like the guilds, which created the City of London, I should not fear them. But the *soul* is not there.[23]

As part of his role as a clerical revolutionary (Bishop Ullathorne at the time claimed that Manning was "revolutionizing the country"),[24] Manning waged relentless warfare from the pulpit and in newspapers against what he called "the Plutocracy," a money-hungry clique of power brokers who had shown no compassion or justice for labor. Other Catholic prelates generally remained silent or, on the rare occasions when they did speak out, talked about the "duties" of the working class. In contrast, Manning called attention to labor's rights as a natural and important component of capital: "I claim for Labour, and the skill which is always acquired by Labour," voiced Manning in a lecture at the Leeds Mechanics' Institute in 1874, "the rights of Capital. It is Capital in its truest sense."[25] By arguing along such lines, Manning established the principle that property was inherent in labor itself. Labor, he said, was the most personal and fundamental form of capital that humans could possess. "The strength and skill that are in a man are as much his own as his life-blood; and that skill and strength which he has as his personal property no man can control. . . . He can buy with it, and he can sell it. He can set a price on it."[26]

In the same Leeds lecture Manning came out in full support of labor's efforts to organize trade unions, a natural right in accord with what he called "the higher jurisprudence." "What a man can do for himself," said Manning, "the State shall not do for him. And the converse if good. Therefore Self-help under limitation. Self-help is collective. Therefore Union."[27] Since labor was, in Manning's words, "Live Capital" (as opposed to money, which he called "Dead Capital") and hence private property, the worker had a natural freedom to associate with his own kind and had the liberty to decide for whom he would work and at what rate of remuneration. This logically carried with it the right to determine what constituted subsistence wages. The trade union movement, which Manning was one of the first high-ranking clergyman to support, was linked in his mind to the medieval guild tradition, in that it was an effort to create a society for common protection and mutual benefit.

Manning concluded his famous lecture at the Leeds Mechanics Institute (which was published under the title *The Rights and Dignity of Labour*, 1874) with an emotional appeal for a more equitable and just distribution of wealth. No Christian commonwealth could rest on the accumulation of wealth "like mountains" in the hands of classes or individuals if the moral and economic wounds of England's poor were to be healed.

In the following years, as British agriculture and industry came under increasing competition from Germany and America, triggering domestic unrest and labor agitation, Manning made numerous public appeals in the pages of *The Times* urging the government to provide relief work and provisions for the future that would mitigate sufferings produced by the inevitable cycles of capitalism. "Necessity has no law," Manning insisted, "nor has present distress, except a claim for prompt relief."[28] The revenues to support such measures, he argued, could come from temporary hearth taxes. Perhaps his most far-reaching defense of the worker came in an article in the *American Quarterly Review* (1887), in which he asserted that people had a natural right to subsistence that prevailed over the rights of property. A starving man committed no theft, said the Cardinal, if he took what he needed from his neighbor to sustain his own life. *The Times* deemed Manning's statement "a wild proposition," but he defended it by drawing on the teachings of Duns Scotus.[29]

Such outspoken ideas brought upon Manning the charge of being a socialist ("I would call it Christianity," said he).[30] The Cardinal neither rejected nor accepted the label, simply saying that it was a vague, politically charged word that no one really understood. In his opinion "Socialism" had the currency of a "party cry" that reactionaries used to discredit the ideas of those who advocated change.[31]

Although Cardinal Manning called upon Gladstone and other leading politicians of the day to initiate government intervention on behalf of the less fortunate, he never believed nor advocated state control of the market or the workplace. He rather envisioned a limited role for the state, like that of a physician who is called in only when the patient is ill and who removes himself when good health returns. The point to be emphasized was that the restoration of good social health required some careful doctoring. Anything more than a pragmatic, limited intervention could produce the opposite sickness and then certain disaster, "an exaggeration of the worst danger in politics—namely, exaggerated centralization."[32]

Up to this juncture, Manning had established a notable profile as a high-ranking Churchman who spoke out for the interest of the laboring poor. Increasing labor unrest and economic uncertainty, however, contributed to the Cardinal's becoming much more than a mere spokesman for workers. The threat of a working-class uprising against the capitalist system and the possibility of class war in England roused Manning to assume a national leadership role as mediator between the claims of the working class and the barons of industry.

By the decade of the 1880s, the boom and bust cycles of English capitalism had created chronic insecurity and hardship among the working classes. Their frustrations led to frequent outbreaks of violence, the most serious of which occurred on 13 November 1887, an episode known as "Bloody Sunday," when police attacked working-class demonstrators in Trafalgar Square. However, the horror of Bloody Sunday paled compared to the cataclysm threatened by the great London dock strike of 1889. Problems concerning pay scales, methods of labor remuneration, and irregularity of employment produced a wholesale work stoppage on the London docks and all along the Thames River when lightermen, firemen, riggers, engineers, and others joined striking dock laborers. The action was unusual in that it was one of the first times in England that skilled laborers combined and cooperated with unskilled workers. As the unrest continued, the possibility of a general strike rose, a move that would have brought all Britain to a standstill.

The threat of broader action was partly the result of the failure of England's leaders to take the situation seriously. Parliament had adjourned without even referring to the strike, and the Home Secretary, the Lord Mayor of London, and the chief of the London police had blithely left London for their summer holiday. Although Cardinal Manning was now at the advanced age of eighty-two, he rose to the occasion by quickly moving into the leadership vacuum. Even before the strike, the Cardinal had developed regular contacts with labor officials, in particular with Ben Tillett, the trade union leader who had been trying to organize unskilled workers in the London docks. Thus, he was well informed of the conditions on the waterfront and the men's grievances.

Manning's personal intervention (he, of course, never took holidays) led to negotiations between the dock directors and representatives of labor. The eventual settlement was largely the result of his skillful arbitration between the opposing sides. The final stage of negotiations required the old Cardinal to plead and cajole for over four long hours with the most recalcitrant and angriest workers. When a compromise agreement was ultimately reached, Manning delivered the terms to the joint committee of dock directors, since they refused to deal with anyone else. It took three additional days of tough negotiations to convince the owners to accept a settlement.[33]

The conclusion of the London dock strike brought Manning popular adulation and international fame. Workers were so appreciative of the Cardinal's performance that in 1890 his portrait was carried beside that of Karl Marx in their May Day commemorations, and for the rest of his days Manning was able to exercise considerable influence on the labor movement. One important result of the strike was that it revealed the efficacy of arbitration as a mechanism for settling differences that was far less costly than strikes or lockouts. Soon after the strike, Conciliation Boards, with equal representation of labor and management and with a neutral chairman, were set up in London and other cities. Manning, who can be considered the father of the concept, was invited to participate in one of the first such boards created by the London Chamber of Commerce.

Although Manning tried to play the part of disinterested intermediary in labor matters, his close contacts with influential trade union leaders, such as John Burns, Tom Mann, and Tillett, and Manning's own letters themselves suggest that his heart was with the workers. To Lord Buxton he confessed in December 1889:

> I have been turning over the strike matters, and the more I think the more I am on the side of Labour. Labour and skill are Capital as much as gold and silver. Labour and skill can produce

without gold and silver. Gold and silver are dependent *in limine*. The union of the two Capitals demands participation in the product. Wages are a minimized money representation of shares in product—that is, in profits. Silvertown gives 15 percent to its share holders and denies halfpence and farthings to its workers. This is more or less the state of the labour market at large. No strike is worth making except for a twofold share in the profits of a twofold Capital.[34]

Not only did the workers deserve a fairer share of the products of production, it was clear to Manning that the strike was a legitimate means for getting them. "A strike is like a war. If for just cause a strike is a right inevitable, it is a healthy constraint imposed upon the despotism of capital. It is the only power in the hands of the working men."[35]

Another significant result of Manning's intervention in the London dock strike was the advancement of social Catholicism. His example established in the eyes of the industrialized world that the Roman Catholic Church had an interest in resolving social problems in terms satisfactory to the working class. Manning had labored long in his clerical vineyard to establish this point. Moreover, Cardinal Manning's direct influence in such matters went well beyond Britain. Manning carried on a regular correspondence with Ketteler, with Cardinal Mermillod, Bishop of Geneva, and with Pope Leo XIII, which allowed Manning to play a seminal role in the drafting of *Rerum Novarum*. He had also developed a crucial relationship with Cardinal James Gibbons of Baltimore. Gibbons was an ardent disciple of Manning's, and through Gibbons Manning even made a significant contribution to the cause of nineteenth-century American Catholic social action.

Cardinal Gibbons sought to duplicate Manning's mission in England, namely, to convince the wealthier Catholics to become more responsible in social and political matters and to link the American Church more closely to the workers and immigrant communities. In seeking these goals, Gibbons threw his support to the trade union movement, including an American working-class organization known as the Order of the Knights of Labor.

Initially, the Knights of Labor had a small membership, and in order to preserve itself in an environment hostile to the idea of working-class association, it borrowed many of the practices of European secret societies (special handshakes, elaborate initiation ceremonies, vows of secrecy, and so forth). All this had an unfortunate parallel with continental Freemasonry. During the intellectual struggles that grew out of the Enlightenment, the Masons had sworn to overturn the influence of the Catholic Church. Rome, in a response of self-preservation, had banned Catholics from joining the Freemason societies in Europe.

The Knights of Labor became a problem for Gibbons and other clerical supporters of trade unionism in America when its membership expanded greatly in the late 1870s, owing largely to the influx of immigrant Catholic workers into its ranks. Matters became particularly troublesome after a Catholic, Terence V. Powderly, became leader of the Order. Under Powderly, Catholics came to make up two-thirds of the membership of the Knights of Labor. A devout Catholic himself, Powderly worked hard to get the American hierarchy's approval of the Order. He pointed out that their secrecy was ceremonial and no threat to government or religion, and he managed to have much of the ritual abolished.

Cardinal Gibbons gave active encouragement to Powderly's organization. The members of the Knights of Labor by this time were primarily unskilled workers, and they were flushed with the glow of victory after a successful strike against New York's streetcar lines. But the Archbishop of Quebec, Elzear-Alexandre Taschereau, and the Jesuits and Redemptorists in America, raising the specters of "socialism" and Free Masonry, disapproved of the Knights and planned to petition Rome to condemn the Order. This would have been a disaster for Gibbon's efforts to attach Catholic workers closely to the Church, since it was estimated that at least five hundred thousand American Roman Catholics were members of the Knights of Labor.

Manning intervened to settle the matter by openly committing himself to Gibbons' position. The Order represented trade unionism, pure and simple, said Manning, and he reminded the Roman authorities that trade unions originated in the Collegia of Rome, out of which they passed into Christian law: "In the Church of Santa Maria dell' Orto every chapel belongs to, and is maintained by, some college or *universitas* of various trades."[36] Given his stature as an expert on labor-Church relations, and his close ties to key influential ecclesiastics in Rome, Manning was able to arrange a favorable decision for Gibbons on the Knights of Labor as a legitimate organization representing the interests of Catholic workers.

The verdict was probably decisive in preventing massive alienation of American workers from the Catholic Church. Manning followed up on these behind-the-scenes efforts by publishing a letter in the London *Tablet* fully supporting the Knights of Labor and pointing out their link with the English trade union movement as part of a common and justifiable democratic struggle for securing the rights of labor. The letter was translated and republished in Catholic papers throughout the European continent. Cardinal Gibbons remained forever grateful for Manning's decisive intervention. Years later he wrote: "I can never forget the anxiety and distress of mind of those days. If the Knights of Labour were not condemned by the Church, then the Church ran the risk of combining against herself every element of wealth and power. . . . But if the Church did not protect the working men she would have been false to her whole history."[37]

The final and most advanced articulation of Manning's social program was outlined in an important letter to Monsignor Doutreloux, Bishop of Liege, who invited the Cardinal to address a session of the all-important International Social Work Congress at Liege in 1890. Although Manning was too old to make the journey, the reading of his letter created a great sensation among the bishops in attendance. His letter was described as "a trumpet call to change. It roused the majority to enthusiasm while it angered those who were more conservative than Catholic."[38]

In addition to advocating the principle that social justice demanded the intervention of the state (since the power of capitalism was so great that the competition with labor was unequal), Manning in his address to the Liege Congress also criticized liberal political economy for its narrow focus on value and exchange in absence of human considerations. Labor, the source of all value, was a "social function and not a commodity" and therefore had to be factored into all economic calculation. This social dimension of labor meant that individual workers should be given adequate time to meet their own personal and domestic needs. Therefore, the length of the working day and rates of remuneration had to be reevaluated in light of such requirements: "To make labour and wage pass before the necessities of human and domestic life means the destruction of that order established by God and nature, and the ruin of human society in its original principle."[39] The economy of industrial society must be held to a higher moral authority.

Two important consequences followed from Manning's social theory of labor: limitations should be placed on the length of the work day; and, since labor was a social function, a worker's wages should be decided not on the basis of supply and demand but according to the importance of the social function he served. The practical program that Manning suggested from these principles called for, among other things, an eight-hour day for heavy labor, a tenhour day for lighter work, limitation on hours of labor for women and children, rest on Sundays, "a just and suitable standard regulating profits and salary," free contracts between capital and labor, and a fixed minimum wage.[40]

These were bold proposals, and although they received a sympathetic hearing from most of those at the Liege Congress, many conservative Catholics found Manning's platform radical to the extreme. A number who were disturbed at the "excesses" of the Liege Congress withdrew and established a rival congress recommending more moderate reforms and a program that was not so perilously close to dreaded socialism.

Cardinal Manning's career marked the culmination of a nineteenth-century tradition of social deaconry. As Thomas Bokenkotter has observed, in his efforts to advance the cause of social justice Manning carried on the work of Ozanam and Ketteler.[41] This liberal Catholic response to the emergence of modern industrial society was not fully accepted by many Catholics, especially by those who preferred to continue the traditional alliance between throne and altar. However, the writings and works of these liberal Catholics established a body of social and economic theory that was rooted in Catholic tradition, yet fully in step with the cultural realities of the modern industrial age. It called for Catholics to reaffirm their commitment to the Gospels by what Ozanam had called "passing over to the barbarians." "God forbid," wrote Cardinal Manning, that "we should be looked upon as servants of plutocracy, instead of the guides and guardians of the poor."[42] This would entail a willingness to embrace democracy and support labor's struggles to create solidarity and economic power through trade unionism. The social activism of the liberal Catholics also required that the Church accept a working relationship with the modern state. There were many forces within the various national Catholic churches and in the highest quarters of the hierarchy in Rome itself that resisted these calls for accommodations with modernity. The potential for drafting a coherent, systematic program of social action for all Catholics to follow suddenly became possible with the ascension of Joachim Pecci, Archbishop of Perugia, as Pope Leo XIII.

CHAPTER 3

Leo XIII and the Principles of *Rerum Novarum*

T he pontificate of Pope Leo XIII (1878–1903) was a watershed in Catholic history, for it redefined the Church's relationship to the modern world, establishing intellectual, socioeconomic and political principles that Catholics could use as guides for meeting the challenges of an ever-changing industrial society.

Leo XIII's encyclicals laid the foundations for the modern European political movement known as Christian Democracy. Its ideas were first articulated in the 1901 encyclical *Graves de Communi*. Here Leo committed the Church to the religious, moral, and economic development of the working classes. This initial pledge to serve the common people opened the door for more dynamic action, especially by Catholic laymen who wished to address political, economic, and social problems in the light of Christian values. Many of these Catholics ultimately concluded that the promises of the social gospel could best be realized through political democracy, worker participation in the management of industry, and the liberation of individual energies from the confines of a patriarchal society.[1]

Joachim Pecci, the future Pope Leo XIII, was the product of a rigorous Jesuit education and thus well prepared to engage the secular world on its own terms. Although his early duties brought him into archconservative circles at the Vatican, Pecci's appointment as papal nuncio to the Kingdom of Belgium at the impressionable age of thirty-three exposed him to the world of liberal politics and the social problems brought on by industrialization.

Belgium served as a magnet for European capitalist investment and was one of the first countries on the continent to undergo heavy industrial development. The noisy steam engines of spinning mills and gigantic metallurgical factories belching noxious gases over once serene pasturelands shattered the rhythms of rural existence. Those who had supported themselves in handicraft endeavors or agricultural labor were thrown out of work by the expansion of mechanized production and obliged to accept meager hourly wages that in many cases were inadequate for subsistence. Workers who found factory jobs were herded into cramped, squalid, and unhealthy slums where they labored gruesomely long hours in adjoining factories and died young. During Pecci's nunciatore (1843–45) it was estimated that fully half the population of Bruges was destitute; a third of Brussels had to be supported by public welfare. These were circumstances shockingly different from the stable agricultural society that Pecci had known in Italy. The economic revolution that was uprooting Western Europe's social order, sinking many Catholics like stones into the ranks of a destitute, exploited proletariat, created breeding grounds for radical, anti-Christian movements that ranged from anarcho-syndicalism to Marxian socialism.

In Brussels Pecci also encountered a new state that functioned far differently from the absolutist monarchical systems he knew in southern Europe. Belgium and neighboring England, France, and the German Rhineland had experimented with various forms of liberal democratic institutions that depended on popular participation in political and legislative decision-making. Pecci quickly realized that Catholicism in these democratic, industrialized states was evolving to meet changing circumstances in ways that made the religion different from that which prevailed in the more conservative Mediterranean parts of Europe. The Church in Western Europe faced new challenges but also was given new opportunities. To meet these effectively the Church needed imaginative leadership on the part of Rome, one that could forge a pact between religion and modern secular culture so as to offer Catholics greater opportunities to find alternatives to socialism and radical liberal political ideology.

It was after his experiences in Belgium that Pecci began to study Catholic writings on the social and economic challenges of industrial society, especially those of Bishop Ketteler, who had argued that Catholicism had a central role to play in transforming modern culture along humanitarian and Christian lines. The archbishop of

Mainz had also recognized that the Church must collaborate with the state to effect such changes.

By the time Pecci became archbishop of Perugia (1846–1877), he was well-versed in Catholic social theory, and his diocesan efforts in the cause of social deaconry suggest that the liberal Catholic theorists had a significant influence on him. As archbishop, Pecci's major priority was the improvement of the intellectual and spiritual training of the clergy, but most of his time and thoughts were devoted to the pastoral care of Perugia's working population.

Archbishop Pecci was part of a group of Catholic scholars and ecclesiastics, spearheaded by Italian Jesuits, who believed they had discovered the mechanics for creating a working compact between the Church and modern civilization in the works of the great thirteenth-century Dominican scholar, St. Thomas Aquinas. As archbishop of Perugia, Pecci promoted the restoration of Thomistic teachings (as he would for all Catholics when he became Pope Leo XIII) as the core program of study in seminary curricula and in all diocesan schools. Those Catholics who were behind the revival of Thomism were convinced that the Dominican scholar's analytical system and especially his brilliant synthesis of faith and reason as sources of knowledge were readily applicable to the problems of modern civilization.

In the minds of Catholic scholars there were serious errors in modern secular philosophy and scientific thinking. Many believed that Thomas's system could be used to point out the moral flaws in contemporary thought, protect Christianity from the results of such error, and, at the same time, demonstrate that there was no inherent conflict between Catholic teachings and modern science. Most importantly, St. Thomas had shown that fundamental principles of Christian morality were a prerequisite for the solidarity of any sociopolitical order. As such, these principles were exactly the formulae for bringing coherence to the modern condition, where individualism and the collectivist claims of radical socialist movements were running amok.

Archbishop Pecci, like Ozanam and Ketteler before him, labored to show that the Church was not intrinsically opposed to the historical forces of modern times. In a famous Lenten pastoral letter of 1877, Pecci asserted that the nineteenth-century infatuation with the idea of progress, especially regarding economic and technological improvement, could be shared by Catholics:

> Society, then, being composed of men essentially capable of improvement, cannot stand still; it advances and perfects itself. One age inherits the inventions, discoveries and improvements achieved by the preceding one, and thus the sum of physical, moral and political blessings can increase marvelously.[2]

When Archbishop Pecci succeeded Pius IX as Pope Leo XIII on 20 February 1878, the Church throughout Europe was besieged by liberal extremism and a hostile nationalism. Catholicism in Germany was under the pressure of Bismarck's *Kulturkampf,* and in France and Italy nationalism had combined with a ferocious anticlericalism in an all-out effort to eliminate Church influence in politics and culture. Leo's predecessor, Pius IX, had managed to heighten tensions by anathematizing the modern age. Leo XIII made rapid progress defusing these issues and securing a leadership role for the Church, because he combined firmness with temperance and displayed a spirit of compromise for the sake of political dialogue.

Within two months of his elevation to the papacy, Leo XIII began to issue a series of encyclicals on a broad front of modern problems.[3] In contrast to many of his predecessors, whose vision was constricted by the parochialism of Vatican politics, Leo XIII was especially well-informed about contemporary issues. He drew on the thoughts of a variety of advisers and Vatican economic and political specialists, studied carefully both Christian and nonreligious literature on social questions, and regularly read all the major newspapers of the day. Leo XIII's active interest in current events and his firm grasp of Church social and economic teachings prompted the plethora of encyclicals issued under his name. Taken as a whole, these remain the most complete Catholic statement on social, economic, and political issues ever delivered by a single Roman pontiff. Moreover, these encyclicals were largely the product of Leo's own thoughts and language.[4]

The central purpose behind Leo XIII's major political encyclicals was to show that Christianity was not at odds with the core of modern civilization and thereby to revive the Church's position as the central moral force in society.[5] These concerns underlined one of the most serious challenges to Leo's papacy: the need to arrange a *modus vivendi* between the Republic and Catholicism in France. The strength of the extremists—unyielding Catholic antidemocratic royalists on the one side, and Rousseauistic, Jacobin liberals on the other—exacerbated the conflict.

By the 1880s the French Church's persistent association with aristocratic and conservative interests had managed to alienate not only the urban working classes but even large numbers of the peasantry from Catholicism. Catholic intellectuals also were growing impatient with the Church's reactionary political and social posturing.

Beginning in 1879 the Republican government decided to break the Catholic-royalist alliance by attacking the Church's monopoly of education. Declaring his intention to "organize society without either God or King,"[6] Jules Ferry, Minister of Public Instruction, sought to establish a completely secularized national public school system in France. In the positivist spirit of his friend Auguste Comte, Ferry viewed education as the key to social engineering. Thus the laicization of education was the central great reform, claimed Ferry, "which contains within itself all other reforms," a prerequisite for all who believed "in the natural rectitude of the human mind, in the definitive triumph of good over evil, in reason, in democracy."[7]

Leo XIII joined the French bishops in protest against such extreme legislation (in France all education was under the control of the Church), but he discouraged Count Albert de Mun from establishing a confessional political party to battle liberalism along lines pioneered by the German Center Party. Instead, he hoped to break the Church's dangerous association with social and political reaction by reconciling French Catholics to the Republic and convincing them to concentrate not on revolution but on reform from within the legitimate political structures. Known as the *Ralliement,* this program endeavored to bring together Catholics and moderate Republicans in a common cause; its goal was to reintegrate Catholics into national political life in order to work for a Christian society.

Many of Leo XIII's political encyclicals had the French situation as their background. In the long run, the *Ralliement* was successful in convincing the vast majority of Catholics to support the Republic.

Most of the hierarchy and especially the younger clergy rallied to the pope's appeals; Catholic public opinion also seemed to become more sensitive to France's pressing social problems. However, the Catholic radicals on the fringe, extreme monarchists whose religious principles were frequently compromised for political agendas, continued to resist the Republic and in fact attacked the *Ralliement* as foolhardy. Their reactionary opposition later took on the unpleasant odor of anti-Semitism, an unsavory accompaniment of the controversy surrounding the Dreyfus case, and this continued to do much harm to the Church's efforts to reconcile itself with moderate Republicanism and win support from the working class.

One of the most significant points that Leo XIII established in his political encyclicals was that democratic forms of government were perfectly compatible with Christian moral teaching. This had special relevance to the political struggle in France, since the royalists had asserted that monarchical government naturally complemented the hierarchical structure of the Church and Catholic theology in general and therefore should be the model for all civil order. Leo rejected this argument, pointing out that the state was the product of historical evolution, had taken on various forms because of differing cultural experiences, and hence could not be expected to conform to an absolute political paradigm. Regarding governments, there were a few basic criteria that should concern Catholics:

> Of the various forms of government, the Church does not reject any that are fitted to procure the welfare of the subjects; she wishes only—and this nature herself requires—that they should be constituted without involving wrong to anyone, and especially without violating the rights of the Church.[8]

The encyclicals *Diuturnum* (1881) and *Immortale Dei* (1885) rejected the notion that the papal monarchy could be the only suitable model for good political governance. Instead, a number of political forms were permissible for Catholics, provided they were capable of ensuring the welfare of the community. Leo XIII went even further, remarking that in some forms of polity it may even be

obligatory for Christians to actively participate in their own governance: "Neither is it blameworthy in itself, in any manner, for the
people to have a share, greater or less, in the government; for at
certain times, and under certain laws, such participation may not
only be of benefit to the citizens, but may even be of obligation."[9]
Although Leo did not claim that the democratic state was the only
form or even the best for just governance, the fact that he only insisted
that a government should conform to Christian moral teaching created a framework for resolving the conflict between the Republic
and Catholicism in France.

The pope was more specific about what types of government
conflicted with Christian morality, and it was in this context that he
confronted the theoretical basis of the continental liberal state. Leo
XIII's condemnation of "liberalism" would reverberate through
Catholic intellectual circles and become a central feature of conservative Catholic political writing well into the twentieth century.
But it must be emphasized that his commentaries concerned "continental" liberalism, that which had evolved out of the Jacobin tradition of the French Revolution with Rousseau as its guide. Leo's
political encyclicals failed to make a distinction between this form
of liberalism, which indeed had proven itself to be an enemy of the
Church, and that which developed in England and migrated to
America, the "Anglo-Saxon" or Lockean variety that accepted the
existence of natural law and fundamental God-given human rights
and denied absolute power to the state.[10]

A crucial difference between these two kinds of liberalism was
that the continental form, inspired by Rousseau's *Social Contract,*
asserted that all rights derived from the state; thus there could be no
rights outside the new revolutionary social compact. This fateful
premise was adumbrated in the famous *Declaration of the Rights of
Man and of the Citizen* (1789), a document far different from the
American Declaration of Independence that partly inspired it (the
American document speaks of natural rights "above" the state). This
premise allowed the Jacobins to affirm that nothing could restrict
the so-called "general will." Two key articles from the French
Declaration illustrate this lethal point. Article 3 posits that "The
source of all sovereignty resides essentially in the nation: no group,

no individual may exercise authority not emanating expressively therefrom." Article 6 further elaborates on this sovereignty: "Law is the expression of the general will; all citizens have the right to concur, either personally, or by their representatives in its formation. It should be the same to all, whether it protects or punishes. . . ."[11]

In practice these claims meant that the authority of the revolutionary government, emanating from the "will of the nation," could not be limited in any fashion. Those who opposed such force were outside nature, that is, beyond the nation and hence bereft of any natural rights. The logical consequence of such thinking made it possible for Louis de Saint-Just and Robespierre, the grand Jacobin interpreters of the general will, to assert that the killing of Louis XVI was no crime, for the King had set himself in opposition to the nation. As the historian Conor Cruise O'Brien has observed, Robespierre could say that "Louis Capet (*ci-devant* Louis XVI) was *hors nature*, a monster; so that cutting off his head didn't even amount to manslaughter."[12]

This Revolutionary redefinition of sovereignty, from that which reposed on the concrete person of the king whose governance was limited by God's laws, to the abstract, collective person of an indivisible general will which recognized no law higher than itself, was at the basis of Leo XIII's condemnation of continental liberalism. In effect, not only had Rousseauistic notions of national sovereignty replaced monarchs, but a democratic state legitimated by the general will had also taken the place of God. The significance of this was noted by the German philosopher Hegel, who observed that the new state was "the walk of God on earth."[13]

Rousseau's influence on the French *Declaration of the Rights of Man and of the Citizen* was largely the result of the involvement of an uncritical admirer, Emmanuel-Joseph Sieyès, an influential clergyman and member of the National Assembly who published one of the early important documents that established the direction of the Revolution. Rousseau's murky notion of the "general will" first made its appearance in Sieyès' seminal pamphlet, "What is the Third Estate?", one of the earliest and most influential efforts to redefine the basis of modern sovereignty. Here we find the Revolution's first attempt to identify the people—the nation—with what

Rousseau meant by the general will: "The third estate therefore includes everything that belongs to the nation; and everything that is not the third estate cannot be regarded as being of the nation. What is the third estate: Everything."[14] Sieyès introduced this concept of power into the final drafting of the *Declaration,* after having raised objections to what he called "conventional" American ideas that had inspired the writing of the French document up to that point: The American declaration, Sieyès claimed, had "clung to an old image of power and its limitations, an image unacceptable to a 'people resuming its full sovereignty.... There is only *one* power, only *one* authority.'"[15]

Under the hand of Sieyès, the final draft of the *Declaration* played down any limitations on civil authority and instead celebrated power for the state with a vengeance. It was the Rousseauistic version of sovereignty, accepted uncritically by many supporters of the nineteenth-century liberal state, that Leo XIII directly challenged in the encyclical *Diuturnum Illud* (1881). This document established the general foundations upon which Leo could later erect an entire doctrine on government.

The initial proposition of Leontine political reasoning was that all civil authority came from God, not from any arbitrary human contrivances concerning social contracts.[16] This is supported by the premise that man is by nature a social animal and must live with and depend upon others to develop his personality and to survive. But the requisite social order itself cannot achieve solidarity without someone having the authority to rule. The ultimate sanction for such authority comes not from the people whom the ruler serves but from God. The counterclaim that the people were the ultimate source of sovereignty was, in Leo's mind, one of the great errors of the century, for it placed "authority on too weak and unstable a foundation. For the popular passions, incited and goaded on by these opinions, will break out more insolently; and, with great harm to the common weal, descend headlong by an easy and smooth road to revolts and to open rebellion."[17] This is not to suggest that the people cannot designate their ruler through whatever means proves effective, but only that the conferral of authority to rule comes from a higher source. In this sense the exercise of popular sovereignty means that the people determine the manner or mode of expressing rulership, but the authority for governance, that is to say, the right to exercise power, can be conferred only through God.

Since society must be orderly for individuals to reach their potential and fulfill their purposes, it is necessary, argued Pope Leo XIII, for citizens to obey political authority whatever its mode of designation since it is of divine origin.[18] A central purpose of Leo's political encyclicals was to ensure the stability of civil order, since social gains rarely compensated for the pain and turmoil of revolutions. It was in the context of such considerations that Leo confronted the errors of the social contract of Rousseau.

In Catholic political thinking, the people or the "general will" could never be the source of power. Therefore the people do not have the authority to unmake rulers, for only God had such powers: "But no man has in himself or of himself the power of constraining the free will of others by fetters of authority of this kind. This power resides solely in God. . . . There is but one law giver and judge, who is able to destroy and deliver."[19] Leo denied the legitimacy of a revolution against established rule. His justification for taking this line of argumentation came from the Pauline Epistles, for Christ and the apostles themselves were obliged to live under the authority of repugnant governors.

However, since governors hold their right to rule from God, they have a duty to exercise power responsibly and according to the dictates of natural law. If they fail to do so, the people do not have an obligation to obey. Numerous martyrs throughout history have chosen the course of disobedience. But disobedience is not the same as the deployment of force to overturn government. Repulsive regimes may be resisted, and Catholics have the right to seek the substitution of a corrupt governance for one that conforms to natural law. However, the pope refused to countenance the use of brute force, advising instead the Christian virtue of patience against political tyranny. Leo emphasized the efficacy of Christians pressuring their rulers to make timely reforms as the best remedy against revolution, but in no single passage of his voluminous writing on the subject of Church-state relations did he ever see revolution as an answer to political oppression.[20]

The political encyclicals clarified Catholic approaches to the modern state. Pope Leo XIII's most celebrated encyclical, *Rerum Novarum* (1891), laid out the general framework for addressing the most serious social issues of the industrial age. In many respects, the social problems created by industrialism were a far greater threat to the Church than the political struggles with republicanism, for the potential for class warfare went well beyond the borders of France. By the last two decades of the nineteenth century much of Europe faced the specter of working-class insurrection. A rising tide of fury was becoming more focused through the aggressive ideologies of Marxism and anarcho-syndicalism. Both advocated the violent destruction of capitalism and its cultural bulwark, organized Christianity.

In order to fight these battles, Pope Leo XIII had already revealed his willingness to draw on the rich tradition of Catholic social writing. Meanwhile, however, Catholic social reformers were failing to attract the working classes to their positions and, at the same time, found themselves isolated within the Catholic community. Regarded as a fringe element tainted by the odor of socialism, they had become a distinct but largely uninfluential minority among mainstream Catholics. The reformers were in desperate need of help from any quarter. Thus, Pope Leo XIII's active interest and eventual support was of momentous importance; in the view of Rev. Joseph N. Moody, it was comparable to the "capture of the Papacy by the reforming elements in the eleventh century."[21]

On a number of occasions Pope Leo had made public statements encouraging workers to form associations to improve their laboring and living conditions. He also had gone out of his way to welcome several workers' pilgrimages to the Vatican. These laborers came to discuss their social and economic concerns with the pontiff. In addition, the pope had supported Gibbons' and Manning's arguments in defense of the American Knights of Labor.

By the early 1880s Leo XIII had apparently decided that the challenges of industrialism required a thorough and systematic analysis from the Catholic perspective. He urged the formation of a special study group to undertake the analysis. The resulting Roman Committee of Social Studies was headed by Bishop Mermillod of

Germany, but its membership was recruited primarily from the Roman aristocracy. Its purpose was to undertake a detailed examination of social problems, particularly as they concerned the lives of the laboring classes, with the intention of drafting a program for action that would satisfy Catholic moral principles.

This Rome-centered organization soon spread its communication links throughout Europe, due to the urging of La Tour du Pin. His experience with the French Workingmen's Clubs had convinced him of the importance of establishing an umbrella organization to unite all European Catholics who were studying social problems. Born in 1884 in Bishop Mermillod's library in Freibourg, the so-called Freibourg Union was composed primarily of socially-minded lay Catholic upper-class intellectuals whose purpose was to study the social and industrial issues from an international perspective and to present their findings to the Vatican in the hope of inspiring some official action.

Mermillod was president of the Union. Major leadership roles were taken by Austria's Counts Blome and Kuefstein and by the Liechtenstein brothers (Alfred and Aloys), as well as by La Tour du Pin and Albert de Mun of France. With the exception of Mermillod, most of its leading lights were ardent disciples of the feudalist Karl von Vogelsang. Given the different economic and political situations within the various countries represented in the Freibourg Union, the organization was never able to speak with one voice regarding the ways in which the Church should address social problems. The democratic leanings of Manning and the followers of Ketteler, for example, did not mesh easily with the paternalism of the Vogelsang School. There also were serious differences regarding the role of the state in reforming the industrial order.

Charles Perin and Frédéric Le Play of France interpreted the contemporary social problems not as the product of institutional failings but rather as the outcome of endemic moral turpitude. In their eyes social evil was rooted in the hedonistic spirit of laissez-faire capitalism. They were convinced that genuine social reform could come about only through the universal application of Christian charity. For them, the enactment of social legislation by an activist government in the absence of society-wide moral regeneration would be much like trying to construct a house from the roof down.

Such a project defied the laws of logic and was doomed to failure. They and their followers dissented vigorously from the interventionist policies of the Congress of Liege, under the direction of Bishop Doutreloux, which, following the advice of Cardinal Manning, had called for the state to take an active role in social and economic reform. To Perin and his followers, this was heading down the perilous path to socialism. They seceded from the Social Work Congress of Liege in 1890 and established their own anti-interventionist association.

There were other disagreements among those who did not accept the need for action by the state. Those affiliated with the *Frei Vereinigung* (Free Association), a group of German and Austrian social reformers including Counts Blome and Kuefstein, were committed to the abolition of wages as well as the system of credit upon which capitalism operated. To these reformers capitalism itself was the source of all social evil. It was a system driven by the relentless quest for self-gratification. It was rooted in an ethic that allowed the exploitation of labor through wages and usurious credit schemes (in the hands of the Jews), keeping the majority of men in thrall to the few. Therefore they recommended that the Church work toward the abolition of capitalism with its replacement by a corporative system modeled along medieval lines.

Another influential group of Catholic reformers urged a less radical and more realistic alternative. They believed that it was possible to reform the capitalist system from within. Archbishops Jacobini and Mermillod, both leaders in the Roman Committee of Social Studies formed by Leo XIII, asserted that labor itself was a key factor of production and could therefore demand a fair price in the marketplace. They recognized the worker as one of the three components required for industrial output (along with the entrepreneur, or manager, and the capitalist) and argued that it was possible to create an environment in which all three "partners" could share equally in the profits of production. Not only could the current economic system be made to work better, but, they pointed out, the capitalist system of credit served a crucial function. It lubricated the gears of the economy and assured the accumulation of the profits in which all three "partners" should share.

Although the Catholic voices of reform took on a cacophonous tone, there was a certain continuity of purpose that tied together the work of the various study associations, the workers' pilgrimages to Rome, Gibbons' defense of the Knights of Labor, and especially Manning's program for settling the London docker's strike of 1889. What was needed was a synthesis of such thinking and a sharply focused program for Christian action on contemporary social problems that could bring together all varieties of concerned Catholics. This was the central challenge for Pope Leo XIII, and he aptly met it in the encyclical *Rerum Novarum*.

All those Catholics who sought a public forum for their social and economic ideas were given a careful reading before Leo drafted his most important encyclical. *Rerum Novarum* proved to be a brilliant synthesis of Catholic social thought, incorporating the ideas of Ozanam, Ketteler, de Mun, Manning, and Gibbons, among others. Of course, almost all Catholic activists claimed that the encyclical was a vindication of their own particular platforms and concerns. However, *Rerum Novarum* did not endorse specific approaches to resolving social problems, since the historical process is dynamic and there are cultural differences from one country to another. Thus *Rerum Novarum* made no effort to define a single Christian culture or program, but instead laid out broad general principles upon which a consensus for reconstruction might take place. In the end this was the best approach: it avoided disappointing particularistic interests and prevented a liberal/working class backlash, since many of the special programs advocated by the Austrian-Vogelsang School were too amorphous, paternalistic, and economically regressive to win the support of either labor or moderate bourgeois opinion in the Western parts of Europe. The significance of *Rerum Novarum* was that it constituted an official Catholic, Vatican-led alternative for social action at a time when the extremes of free-wheeling capitalism and Marxian socialism had arrogated to themselves the right to define the parameters of the industrial age. As such it offered a "third way," a path of compromise for dealing with the socioeconomic dilemmas of modernity. It avoided the radical alternatives of either an uncontrolled, predatory market system or authoritarian collectivism. Yet there was nothing fanciful or backward-looking about *Rerum Novarum*. In the spirit of social deaconry, the encyclical demanded that Catholics look at the world realistically.

Like the influential *Communist Manifesto*, against which *Rerum Novarum* was meant to be compared, Leo's social encyclical began by focusing on the traumatic impact of industrial production on the condition of labor. The encyclical located the central problem in the class structure of industrial society, a dichotomy of owners and workers spawned by the liberal creed of individual self-aggrandizement. What set this age apart from the past was the radical polarization of employers who monopolized the means of production and those who owned nothing but their capacity for labor. With the passing of the guilds, the working classes were deprived of any corporate body that could protect them from the rapacity of their masters:

> by degrees it has come to pass that working men have been surrendered, isolated and helpless, to the hard-heartedness of employers and the greed of unchecked competition. . . . To this must be added that the hiring of labor and the conduct of trade are concentrated in the hand of comparatively few; so that a small number of very rich men have been able to lay a yoke little better than that of slavery itself.[22]

Rerum Novarum's socioeconomic analysis may have dovetailed with Marx's critique of capitalism, but there were unbridgeable differences in the ways in which they proposed to change the situation. Whereas Marx accepted class warfare as a key factor in an inevitable process of social liberation, Leo emphasized the necessity of mitigating the struggle for purposes of social harmony. Marx held that the social problem was produced by contradictions within the cultural institutions of bourgeois society. These would produce inexorable conflicts that would ultimately destroy the social and political order. Leo, on the other hand, believed that the problem was caused by the misuse of institutions and was convinced that the system could be reformed through moral leadership and a general society-wide commitment to change.

Pope Leo XIII disagreed with both liberal and Marxist economists who deemed labor to be the source of all value. Echoing an argument raised previously by Jacobini and Mermillod of the Roman Committee of Social Studies, the pope asserted that an alliance between the worker and capital was required to produce wealth. The idea that working men were destined by law to live in mutual conflict with management was based on a false reading of history and was thoroughly irrational. Capital and labor were rather mutually dependent. "Each needs the other; capital cannot do without labor, nor labor without capital."[23] Thus it would be unfair to destroy the power of the one simply because it abused the means of production.

Leo rejected the notion of an inevitable dialectic of struggle (part of what Marx called the law of history), which, taken to its logical conclusion, negated man's efforts to control his own destiny. He also pointed out the folly of trying to help the poor by transferring private property to the state. Instead of eliminating private ownership, Leo sought ways of preserving proprietorship in such a fashion that the privilege would be enjoyed by the greatest number of people. The pope's defense of property was drawn from the teachings of St. Thomas: proprietorship had a central social and economic function, namely, to provide security and freedom for individuals in their communal groups. To give the state sole monopoly over its use not only invited serious abuse of power but would constitute a violation of natural law. As two prominent interpreters of the labor encyclicals have pointed out, property was so intrinsically bound up with the rhythms of human life "that to abolish it would be a violation of human rights. To destroy this institution would be to impair fundamentally man's capacity for right living. Therefore it would be an act of gross immorality."[24]

Central to *Rerum Novarum* was the assertion that labor itself constituted private property. The individual worker had the right to sell this property—in effect, his labor power (the ability to produce value)—to the capitalist for payment of wages. The worker was motivated to enter this marketplace out of a natural desire to survive but also to enlarge his personal property, which he could do through the careful disposition of his wages:

> it is precisely in such power of disposal that ownership obtains, whether the property consists of lands or chattels. Socialists, therefore, by endeavoring to transfer the possessions of indi-

viduals to the community at large, strike at the interests of every wage-earner, since they would deprive him of the liberty of disposing of his wages, and thereby all hope and possibility of increasing his resources and bettering his condition of life.[25]

Socialism, however, was by no means the sole concern of *Rerum Novarum*. In very precise language, Leo XIII castigated the abuse of private property by capitalists. As he was quick to point out, "To exercise pressure upon the indigent and destitute for the sake of gain, and to gather one's profit out of the need of another is condemned by all laws, human and divine."[26] Furthermore, unbridled competition, fueled by economic liberalism's worship of individualism, failed to recognize the importance of man's need for security (which disappeared in the free-for-all of a pure market economy) and ultimately led to one of the most dangerous political situations: too much power in the hands of a few. Despite the potential for evil that accompanied the abuse of private proprietorship, which loomed as a chronic dark shadow in the market economy, Leo at no time advocated its abolition. Instead, *Rerum Novarum* appealed for a redistribution of property so even more people would have the opportunity for personal growth and independence. Laws favoring the widest possible ownership could diffuse the traditional source of civil conflict (the class problem), since the gulf would be narrowed between vast wealth and abject poverty. A more equitable distribution of property also might have the salutary economic effect of increasing productivity, since individuals labor more diligently on property that belongs to them personally.

As a means to this end, Leo XIII advocated an interventionist state (this was emphasized throughout the encyclical, thereby serving as an imprimatur of the programs of Ozanam, Ketteler, Manning, and others), though he advised that such power regarding property be used cautiously. The state's authority derived from nature, not man: "the State has the right to control its use in the interests of the public good alone, but by no means to absorb it altogether."[27] But it had no right to appropriate property to itself.

Although *Rerum Novarum* asserted the inviolability of private property, in adherence to the teachings of St. Thomas it emphasized that proprietorship was not an absolute right but one that required responsibility, a duty dictated by the "necessities of good living" for the community as a whole. The central issue was not ownership so much as proper use. In this respect property was a trust. Its owners were obliged to serve as stewards of the goods that God has provided for human betterment; they had a responsibility to serve the community. But nowhere in *Rerum Novarum*, or in any subsequent official writings, was it ever declared that such stewardship should be entrusted to the guardian of an elite.

What then was *Rerum Novarum's* program for social reform? Although he appreciated the importance of the Church's traditional reliance on charity, Leo realized that the gravity of the social problems caused by industrialization was well beyond the sway of individual actions and instead required a collective effort assisted by the state. However, all practical programs for reforming the social order had to be preceded by the recognition that what confronted modern society was a profound moral problem. At the core of *Rerum Novarum* was the recognition that the welfare of humanity must be the prime concern in all economic calculations. Man's inherent dignity, born of God's creation, needed to be reflected in all facets of society, no less the economic sector. Thus the science of economics was obliged to serve man's moral needs, an ethical imperative largely missing in the modern age.

Since the social problem was deemed to be the product of moral failure, not systemic institutional dysfunction—which Marxists believed required revolution—it became necessary to raise the spiritual consciousness of the entire community to undertake reforms: "since religion alone . . . can destroy the evil at its root, all men should rest persuaded that the main thing needful is to re-establish Christian morals apart from which all the plans and devices of the wise will prove of little avail."[28] This requisite society-wide moral commitment to action was a vast undertaking that must go beyond confessional lines. Therefore, Leo XIII appealed to all men and women of good will to participate in the effort: *Rerum Novarum* was addressed to the entire Western community, not just Catholics alone.

In the Apostolic tradition Leo XIII called upon his Catholic clergy to take the first step in providing the necessary moral leadership that would inspire action: each must "put his hand to the work," as Leo put it, so as to raise the social consciousness of the community. Ultimately, of course, the moral crusade would need the cooperation and hard labor of everyone, not simply lay and clerical Catholics.

Once the appropriate moral commitment had been established, *Rerum Novarum* spelled out what Catholic social doctrine required of the state. The encyclical broke cleanly with prevailing liberal laissez-faire policy by insisting that government had a responsibility not just to protect those of wealth, but to serve the common good. If this meant that certain elements of the community were suffering unfairly from the "cruelty of men of greed," the state must correct the situation through legislation in the interests of justice and for the prevention of social unrest. In addition, the state should protect private property, curb those who advocate public violence, and provide remedies to settle conflicts between labor and capital.

Although Leo XIII stressed the social responsibilities of the state, he cautioned that its powers should not be so extensive that they absorb those parts that are anterior to civil society, namely, the individual and the family. Both have rights and duties of their own that have a higher sanction than the prerogatives of government. Pope Leo insisted that the power of the state be guided by the principle of subsidiarity: government should provide auxiliary services to its citizens so as to supplement the efforts of individuals and their families. But direct state intervention into the lives of citizens should occur only when those basic agencies proved incapable of protecting themselves: "If a family finds itself in exceeding distress, utterly deprived of the counsel of friends, and without any prospect of extricating itself, it is right that extreme necessity be met by public aid, since each family is part of the commonwealth."[29]

The political powers of the modern state were so far-reaching that they had to be held to the strictest standards of control in order to prevent abuse. As a general guideline its powers should be used for "public well-being and private prosperity" and to "benefit every class."[30] The extent of its domestic intrusions should be decided "by the nature of the occasion which calls for the law's interference— the principle being this, that the law must not undertake more, nor go further, than is required for the remedy of the evil or the removal of the mischief."[31]

In the final analysis, *Rerum Novarum's* notions of social legislation were rooted in its Christian appreciation of the sacredness of the individual person: the state had a duty to interfere in economic affairs when human rights were threatened.

In combination with the state and Church, the third agency to which *Rerum Novarum* appealed in the effort to combat social problems was organized labor. Leo XIII's encyclical made the revolutionary declaration that workers had both the right and the responsibility to organize into cooperative associations—trade unions or guilds—to satisfy their basic human needs of protection and self-governance and, very importantly, to strengthen their hand in bargaining with management. Only by coordinating their desires through large-scale combinations could workers marshal sufficient strength against the weapons of capital. In order to augment this arsenal of defense, *Rerum Novarum* upheld the legitimacy of strike action when all reasonable negotiation failed. It was clear to Leo XIII that the worker had no power acting as an individual agent in a social environment controlled by the overwhelming forces of wealthy capitalists. A laborer's only recourse was to combine with his fellows in order to garner strength through numbers. A playing field governed by the rules of economic liberalism (which asserted that combinations of workers constituted a restraint of free trade) was grossly unfair to workers. The right to organize and to use the weapon of the strike would balance the contest by giving workers a more equitable chance to share in the fruits of production.

Rerum Novarum also supported the principle of association because it was a practical way to mitigate the mentality of class war. In order to form such unions individuals had to overcome their own differences and learn the art of cooperation. Once they were able to merge their interest and strengths into the ensemble of a larger federation, they would possess the collective power to defend their interests and also to demand further institutional reform.

The concept of federation was such an imperative of social change that Leo XIII and his successors urged other groups besides labor to organize as well. Professional people, civil servants, employers, farmers, indeed all those involved in producing goods and services could improve their position and facilitate the process of transforming society by joining together in their respective social units. In effect, Leo XIII was recommending the resurrection of a pluralistic corporative social and economic order. The medieval corporations had been destroyed by the onslaught of the Enlightenment and French and industrial revolutions. The result was the atomization of humanity: individuals, bereft of their traditional associative bodies, were at the prey of wealthy capitalists and the omnipotent state. A restoration of a corporative society would counter this problem by allowing individuals to maximize their economic strength through becoming members of a group. Standing alone, man was too weak to contend against the larger economic and political forces that engulfed him: "It is better that two should be together than one; for they have the advantage of their society. If one fall he shall be supported by the other. Woe to him that is alone, for when he falleth he hath none to lift him up."[32]

The natural impulse to gravitate toward private associations for self-protection bound individuals to the civil order. These smaller, "private" societies within the larger body politic had a natural right to existence as part of the "public" commonwealth; the state, Leo insisted, instead of legally prohibiting such associations (as was the case in countries under the sway of economic liberalism), was obliged to both guarantee access to these associations and protect their corporate integrity. Yet governments must be temperate in the exercise of such power: "The State should watch over these societies of citizens banded together in accordance with their rights, but it should not thrust itself into their peculiar concerns and their organizations, for things move and live by the spirit inspiring them, and may be killed by the rough grasp of a hand from without."[33]

Although *Rerum Novarum* avoided recommending specific political and economic programs, it was very precise about the fundamental rights of the working classes. In addition to the prerogatives of organizing into unions or guilds, these included the rights of access to accident and health insurance, a benevolent working environment, restrictions on the hours and conditions of employment, the observance of holidays, and, not the least, labor's right to a minimum wage. *Rerum Novarum* emphasized that "wages ought not be insufficient to support a frugal and well-behaved wage-earner."[34] This was crucial if workers were to be able to provide themselves and their families with the basic necessities of life. The just wage, however, was not a final goal, but only a minimum required for the laborer to embark on the more important objectives of owning his own property and gaining an equal share with management in the ownership and administration of the means of production.

Although *Rerum Novarum* made numerous references to medieval values, the document never called for a restoration of the corporate order of the Middle Ages. This was made clear on the issue of unions or guilds, in which the pope purposely avoided any mention of the form they should take: "We do not judge it possible to enter into minute particulars touching the subject of organization; this must depend on national character, on practice and experience, on the nature and aim of the work to be done, on the scope of the various trades and employments, and on other circumstances of fact and time—all of which must be carefully considered."[35]

It would seem obvious that Leo believed modern circumstances precluded a return to the guild order of medieval times. This may have proved disappointing to some conservative Catholic social thinkers affiliated with the Union of Freibourg, most of whom were monarchists favoring what were called "mixed corporations" consisting of employers and workingmen. The encyclical's more comprehensive approach, calling for associations "consisting either of workmen alone, or of workmen and employers together" acting independently of the state, showed that the pope was prepared to entertain modern programs for reconstruction. This prevented conservatives and doctrinaire social Catholics from combining their preferences for "reform from above" with medieval concepts of corporation and monarchy.[36] The broader suggestion for handling the social threat gave *Rerum Novarum* a strong appeal to modern workers. Permitting workers to form unions or guilds on their own, without the presence of employers or the involvement of the state—a position favored by Manning and Gibbons—was welcomed by labor in France and Italy, where there had been great suspicion of management's paternalistic intentions.[37]

It is unclear how much influence Manning and Gibbon had on the encyclical's comments on the rights of workers to form their own unions. However, there can be little doubt that Manning's ideas concerning strike settlements played a seminal role in the position taken by the pope on the issue of labor-management relations: in situations where both owners and workers believed their rights injured, "nothing would be more desirable than that a committee should be appointed, composed of reliable and capable members of the association, whose duty would be, conformably with the rules of the association, to settle the dispute."[38] This was precisely the concept of arbitration boards that Cardinal Manning had proposed for settling future industrial disputes in England. In the case of *Rerum Novarum*, Pope Leo XIII recognized the efficacy of its application to all of industrial society.

CHAPTER 4

The Appearance of the "Chesterbelloc"

S ince England was thoroughly saturated with Protestantism in both religion and culture, most Catholics considered it futile to try and influence public policy along Catholic lines. In the words of Christopher Hollis, nineteenth-century English Catholics "still had among them the memory of the catacombs"[1] and preferred to avoid attracting attention to themselves. Old fears and prepossessions die hard. Leslie Toke, one of the first laymen to advocate English Catholic social action, noted that the fact of having been cut off from active political participation for three centuries had effectively undermined the English Catholic community's habit of citizenship. Only slowly would this group shed its timidity and apathy.[2] English Catholics tended to support the conventional programs of the two political parties, over which they had little interest in providing either influence or leadership. In general, it can be said that English Catholics were essentially conservative, suspicious of trade unionism, leery of anything suggesting socialism, and critical of their co-religionists who were politically active.

These tendencies were mirrored in the Church's highest leadership. Herbert Vaughan was a man of far different timber from Cardinal Manning, whom he succeeded in 1892, and under his tutelage the Roman Catholic Church in England assumed a conservative political profile in stark contrast to what it had been under the "People's Cardinal." Although Manning had been Vaughan's friend and patron, as well as his own choice as heir apparent to the See of Westminster, the two men were of contrasting temperament. Vaughan came from one of England's oldest Catholic families, with a pedigree going back so far in time that it lost itself "in the twilight of fable,"[3] and thus was sufficiently steeped in the isolated gentry traditions that had so annoyed Manning. This heritage, along with his education in continental Catholic colleges, had bequeathed a distinct Tory paternalism that would always shadow Vaughan's social and political sentiments. Unlike his predecessor, Cardinal Vaughan was uncomfortable with England's fastest growing Catholic community, the immigrant, primarily working-class, Irish. England's Irish Catholics were grateful for Manning's tireless efforts on their behalf, which reached a climax when he boldly came to their defense during the London dock strike of 1889. Manning spoke with truth when he stated in 1887 that he spent his life "working for the Irish occupation of England."[4]

As Bishop of Salford, Vaughan had been both moved and shocked by what he saw of working-class life in the grimy industrial cities of the North; these experiences galvanized his commitment to pastoral and charitable missions among the poor, the "Crusades of Rescue," as he called them. Yet his socialization into a gentry world made it difficult for Vaughan to empathize with working-class culture. The Cardinal pitied the destitution of the workers and was saddened by the grisly procession of hearses through their ghettos, but he never fully understood their behavior and values. His candid views of them betrayed the enormous gap in England between aristocratic culture and the working class. To Vaughan the laboring men appeared to be "broad-backed powerful animals." With "words of the coarsest, foulest, and most degrading meaning," the workers "are flesh and blood, and they think and speak of nothing else."[5] A delegate from the National Committee of Organised Labour, who met with Vaughan to discuss his support for the group's pension scheme, related how the Cardinal was gracious, refined, and regal yet somehow out of touch with the world of workingmen: "He wanted to be sympathetic, but did not quite know how, and moved uneasily in dealing with our subject, as one who travels on unfamiliar ground."[6]

Cardinal Manning, whose expansive social activism left even radical politicians with their mouths agape, occasionally chided Vaughan for having the rigidity and aloofness of an aristocratic stuffed shirt: you are already a good Catholic, Manning once told him, and need only sit at the feet of General Booth to be a good Christian![7] Although Vaughan admitted a moral and intellectual debt to Manning (Manning was responsible for "the formation of my character"),[8] he had been slightly scandalized by his mentor's praise of the Salvation Army. He openly criticized what he considered Manning's overzealous public political activity, in particular, his role in the great London dock strike, and frankly disapproved of many of Manning's radical social policies. These Vaughan ascribed to "senile decay."[9] Reflecting the assumptions of the "old Catholic" traditions, Cardinal Vaughan preferred to address social problems through Catholic institutions under the direction of the official hierarchy, rather than to work for change through public organizations in cooperation with any who shared his objectives (even Protestants!), a modus operandi with which Manning had been perfectly comfortable.

One of Manning's driving objectives as archbishop of Westminster was to persuade Catholics to "come out from their traditional obscurity and take full part in the national life of the country,"[10] and this naturally meant developing a strong political position regarding social questions. For this reason Manning had urged Vaughan to cultivate wider interests and join causes that had no direct concern with sacramental work.[11] But Manning would have been disappointed by his successor's approach to social questions, which followed more conventional lines. Vaughan concluded that the application of the general principles for bringing social reform, that is, laboring in the trenches of the slums and pushing for change in the economic and political sphere, was better left to "experts" and "to the controlling influences of a more enlightened public opinion."[12] All this would take much time, but, unlike his predecessor, Cardinal Vaughan was in no hurry to force the pace.

Although Cardinal Vaughan discouraged Catholic political activism, he himself kept very busy making certain that what Catholics read about politics and their religion was responsibly conservative. To this end he purchased *The Tablet* and used its pages to wage battle against what he regarded as one of the scourges of the age: we are "opposed by every instinct and principle to the spurious Liberalism and irreligious revolution of the Continent, we shall denounce it in all its forms—especially when it manifests its influence among ourselves."[13] In striking contrast to Manning, Vaughan with his strong conservative inclinations and close connections to the English gentry, was also unsympathetic to Home Rule for Ireland. The *Tablet's* anti-Irish and Unionist bias made Vaughan highly unpopular among Irish working-class Catholics in England.

A vigorous effort to organize Catholics to take more responsibility for social reform did not occur until after the passing of Vaughan, and the inspiration for doing so came from laymen rather than high-ranking ecclesiastics. The progress was slow and confused. In 1893, for instance, a mildly reformist body called the Catholic Social Union was created, but it soon collapsed. The demise of this organization was due in no small part, claimed one disgruntled activist, to the fact that "its name was supposed in some occult manner to connect it with 'that dreadful Socialism.'"[14] This particular critic, Leslie Toke, published a somewhat angry essay in the *Downside Review* in 1907 which condemned both the apathy of well-educated and wealthy Catholics with respect to social problems and their antipathy to anything suggesting socialism. Widespread Catholic ignorance of papal social teachings could be seen, Toke noted, in the conspicuous absence of Catholic names on the membership roles of many reform societies in Britain. Toke wrote that the great majority of Catholics were "as completely unable to realize the fundamental change that has taken place in political, social and economic questions as were the French noblesse on the eve of the Revolution."[15] In fact, a good many Catholics had so little understanding of socialism that they made no distinction between the revolutionary writings of Karl Marx and the moderate musings of the Fabian Society. As a corrective to their ignorance, Toke recommended a scheme for spreading papal social teachings through special study groups and the publication of educational pamphlets.

Another voice for action along these lines came from Virginia M. Crawford, a close associate of Cardinal Manning's. Contributing money to charities might make wealthy Catholics feel good, but this was not enough, declared Crawford. She urged English Catholics to take their French counterparts (both she and Toke admired *Le Sillon*, a radical social democratic paper advocating dialogue with Marxists and Catholic solidarity with the working class) as well as the new English converts to the faith as models for more aggressive social action. Toke, Crawford, and a few others who spoke out on such issues prepared the ground for the creation of the Catholic Social Guild (CSG) in 1909. Taking *Rerum Novarum* as its charter, the Guild served to coordinate various individual efforts at social reform along Catholic lines. It established study clubs, sponsored lectures, and published books and pamphlets to diffuse Catholic social principles throughout Britain. One of the Guild's most important contributions was to publish an English translation of *Rerum Novarum*, thereby making it possible to introduce Leo XIII's social teachings to a working class audience.

From its beginnings and well into the next few decades of the twentieth century, the leaders of the Catholic Social Guild maintained a working relationship with other reform groups, in particular, with the Fabian Society, which had a considerable influence on the Guild's development. Virginia Crawford and Beatrice Webb, for instance, had been close friends since childhood and maintained a regular correspondence throughout their adult lives. The Guild's first president, Monsignor Henry Parkinson, greatly admired the work of the Fabians and recommended that his students at Oscott College join the society. The Guildsman most thoroughly imbued with Fabianism was Leslie Toke, who had become a member of the society as a student at Oxford in the 1890s. Toke urged Catholics inclined to social action to make contact with the Fabian Society and its academic progeny, the London School of Economics.[16] Taking its cue from the Fabian Society, the Catholic Social Guild viewed its chief function as pedagogical; it hoped "to permeate" the consciousness of the working classes through Catholic social teachings.

From the outset the CSG made it clear that it would assume a moderate course of action and make special efforts to avoid controversial political issues. According to its organizational statutes as revised in 1912, the Guild was not allowed to take part in party politics. The CSG's reading packages, the so-called "book boxes," contained an assortment of standard publications on sociology, trade unionism, wage questions, and the like, but works of "a purely political nature and those representing extreme viewpoints on the social questions are generally avoided."[17] This policy was extended to other organizations that grew out of the CSG as well. The Catholic Evidence Guild, for example, which was founded to teach the faith to non-Catholics, was forbidden to incorporate politics into its platform: "The rule is extended in practice to the avoidance of controversial questions of a social and economic nature, which though not strictly political yet might easily distract the meeting from its true aim, which is religious."[18] Manning would have been pleased with the Catholic Social Guild's efforts to move beyond confessional lines by cooperating with non-Catholics and with its willingness to work among the laboring poor in the cause of social deaconry. Yet the Catholic Social Guild probably would not have measured up fully to Manning's standards, for he himself was committed to political action in order to force the state to use its powers of legislation as a vehicle for social change. The Guild took little interest in politics and, though it made general references to *Rerum Novarum,* failed either to support particular pieces of legislation to ameliorate social problems or to articulate a distinctly Catholic alternative to the prevailing capitalist mentality of the governing elites. The Roman Catholic hierarchy in England also remained silent on issues that might have shaken the established order.

Cardinal Manning's liberal political enthusiasms and his espousal of state-sponsored programs for social reform were not matched in Catholic circles after the turn of the century. In many respects, however, his ideals were carried on by several Anglican social activists and, most importantly for the purposes of this study, by two writers who were soon to become some of Britain's leading men of letters: Hilaire Belloc and Gilbert Keith Chesterton. The powerful personalities and ideas of these two, whom George Bernard Shaw labeled the "Chesterbelloc," sparked a worldwide sociopolitical movement called Distributism. This movement, along with the two men's voluminous writings, became one of the most important influences on Roman Catholic opinion in the English-speaking world well into the first half of the twentieth century.[19] In 1969, for example, Adrian Cunningham remarked that in Distributism one finds "the maximum possible consciousness of the social Catholicism that immediately precedes our own time."[20] Although the Distributists were few in number, they had an enduring impact on the Catholic intellectual establishment. In the words of Cunningham:

> That influence is not just something 'there' which affects us, as it were externally; it was, and in some ways still is, an 'internal' phenomenon, part of the cultural apparatus through which British Catholics have established their idea of themselves and their role in society, it is part of our perception and self-consciousness.[21]

The irony of the Distributist movement is that its breeding ground was the turf of Anglicans and socialists rather than that of Roman Catholics. Most of the creative forces behind Distributism—Cecil and Gilbert Chesterton, A. J. Penty, Maurice Reckitt, Eric Gill, and others—had entered the political arena from the traditions of Christian and Guild Socialism. The early careers of these writers had been influenced by Christian Socialists, a group of activists from across denominations who, inspired by the work of F. D. Maurice, sought to apply the Gospels to Britain's social problems. Maurice had been a critic of the Victorian churches' narrow insistence on confining religion to personal morality and salvation. The "Kingdom of God," said Maurice, includes the whole of His creation, embracing man in all his parts, secular and religious. Like the continental Catholics who accepted the calling of social deaconry, Maurice, in the words of Bishop E. R. Wickham, had "earthed" the Gospel. [22]

The economic ideas of the early English Christian Socialists (notably J. M. Ludlow, the founder of the movement, and the novelist Charles Kingsley) derived from French Catholic socialists, some of whom were associated with Frédéric Ozanam. Ludlow had studied the teachings of the Catholic convert and socialist P.-J.-B. Buchez in Paris. Like Ozanam, Buchez had worked for a reconciliation between Catholicism and popular democracy. Buchez believed that a major mechanism for essentially "Christianizing" the forces unleashed by the French Revolution would be a clergy prepared in the traditions of social deaconry.[23] Buchez also was one of the first in France to recommend the creation of workers' cooperative associations that ultimately might take over ownership of the means of production. This would create the conditions for social- ism, which Buchez regarded as the ideal, divinely-intended model for society.

Charles Kingsley, on the other hand, fell under the sway of the liberal Catholic Félicité Lamennais, who labored to break the alliance between the French Catholic Church and monarchism. Lamennais' newspaper, *L'avenir*, championed a decentralized social and politi- cal order held together by workers' cooperatives under the leader- ship of the Catholic Church.

Buchez, Lamennais, and other French Catholic socialists preached that capitalism was parasitic and destructive of God's worldly design. However, they believed that human progress could be assured through proper social reform, since a benevolent God (in contrast to the vengeful, fire-breathing Deity of the British evangelicals and nonconformists) had endowed individuals with an innate sense of social morality that would naturally surface given the appropriate political conditions, namely, an environment that encouraged co- operation and democratic, participatory government.

The English Christian Socialists were convinced, however, that none of this could come to fruition while the working classes were alienated from religion. This alienation could be laid directly at the door of the Victorian churches, whose leaders, in the words of K. S. Inglis, cared less about the material and spiritual welfare of the work- ing classes than the workers were alleged to care about religion.[24]

A number of significant associations emerged from Christian Socialist circles. One of the first was Stewart Headlam's Anglo- Catholic Guild of St. Matthew, established in 1877. The guild had links to the earlier Oxford movement and the Fabian Society (Head- lam being on the "left wing" of that group). Headlam advocated what was called "sacramental socialism," arguing that the holy sacra- ments, especially the Mass, were expressions of a true Christian socialism. Those affiliated with the Guild of St. Matthew and the other socialist associations that grew out of it, the Christian Social Union and the Christian Socialist League, focused on the doctrine of the Incarnation, the role of Christ as man in the secular world, and his redemptive and sanctifying message for all men.

Much like Cardinal Manning, who condemned the old Catholics for their aloofness from the common man, those in the Guild of St. Matthew despaired of an Established Church that had distanced itself from the urban laboring masses, catering, instead, to Tory squires and the new captains of industry. The guild worked to bring the Church of England closer to the people and, at the same time, proposed a redistribution of wealth and expanded opportunities for the masses to participate more fully in the process of governance.

There were good practical reasons for the Guild of St. Matthew to be concerned with such matters. The general economic downturn that set in by the early 1880s had produced levels of unemployment on a scale far greater than ever before. Not only were the effects of unemployment uncomfortably visible to the prospering classes, but those affected by recession were no longer willing to stay quietly behind doors, patiently waiting for the trade cycle to revive as it so often had in the past. In the spring of 1886, for instance, unruly crowds of poor smashed the windows of fashionable clubs in London's West End and looted shops in Piccadilly. Capitalism seemed to be faltering, and the Guild of St. Matthew believed it was necessary to prepare Anglicans to apply the Gospels to the ensuing social and economic breakdown.

The real significance of Headlam's association was that it attracted a variety of bright and talented people dedicated to providing Christian social and political leadership. Initially laboring under the tutelage of the Guild of St. Matthew, many of them became the catalysts for more radical and influential movements such as Guild Socialism.

An important offspring of the Guild of St. Matthew was the Christian Social Union (CSU), founded during the London dock strike of 1889. The Union's birth was marked by the publication of a book of essays edited by Charles Gore called *Lux Mundi: A Series of Studies in the Religion of the Incarnation*. The book attempted to explain the centrality of the Christian faith for resolving the major moral and intellectual issues of the times. In addition, the authors emphasized the responsibility of owning private property, which, they insisted, must be recognized as a public trust involving explicitly social obligations. It was the book's insistence on applying

Christianity to political and social matters that led to the establishment of the Christian Social Union. This organization's main purpose was to study and publicize social and economic problems, and
its members were prepared to draw on Pope Leo XIII's writings to
make their points. The failure of the Anglican Church hierarchy to
take a lead in resolving the London dock strike was an embarrassment to its membership, and one of the Union's first tasks was to
counter the public's impression that only the Catholic leadership—
namely, Manning—was prepared to take up the cause of labor.

Borrowing techniques from the Fabian Society, of which many
of its associates were members, the CSU mounted a campaign to
educate the public about social problems. One prominent member,
F. L. Donaldson, gained notoriety by telling his followers that
"Christianity is the religion of which socialism is the practice"[25] and
insisting that a truly Christian state had the obligation to find employment for workers if the private sector failed to do so. The CSU
practiced what it preached through activist social programs. In 1893,
for instance, it published a "white list" of firms that supported trade-
union wages and recommended that its members patronize them.
Various Christian Social Union local branches initiated a Christian "buyers boycott" of companies that were anti-union, a policy
that would be copied by the Distributist League in the interwar
years. A special research committee of the CSU investigated the
problem of housing for the poor and the issue of drunkenness. Some
local branches of the Union undertook detailed studies of working
conditions and sent them to the press, the home secretary, and
members of Parliament. The Christian Social Union's influence in
the House of Commons played an important role in shaping the
Factory and Workshops Act of 1901 and the Trade Boards Act of
1909. Flushed with the confidence that comes with having influence,
one CSU member, Percy Dearmer, boasted that the association was
becoming "an informal committee of the English Church upon
social questions."[26]

Another issue that galvanized the energies of the Christian
Social Union was British imperialism, in particular, the South African
Boer War of 1899–1902. The two chief figures of the CSU, Charles
Gore and Scott Holland, were especially disturbed by the popular

jingoism that sustained Britain's overseas expansion. Their voices of protest were joined by several other young members of the Union, notably Conrad Noel, whose powerful sermons against munitions makers led to threats to blow up his church,[27] and Gilbert Keith Chesterton. These men believed that the Boer War was the product of a capitalist plot carried out by international mining interests: it was a classic example of what the journalist J. A. Hobson had called "economic imperialism" in search of new markets and investment opportunities.[28]

G. K. Chesterton's writings on the Boer War first brought him into the public spotlight. In 1899 he joined *The Speaker*, a radical Liberal publication that had been taken over by a group of Hilaire Belloc's Oxford friends who hoped to use the paper as a lever for moving the Liberal Party toward the cause of social justice. Under the direction of J. L. Hammond, E. C. Bentley, and others, *The Speaker* soon became a major voice of anti-imperialism, arguing that the war in South Africa was brought about by capitalist wire-pullers in quest of new economic opportunities. Chesterton articulated an ironic critique of the war: he said he supported the Boers because he himself was a good English nationalist. As opposed to the particularistic nationalism of Rudyard Kipling, which ignored the patriotism of others, Chesterton expressed a sympathy for the rights and customs of all ethnic groups. Thus he supported the Boers chiefly because they were willing to take to horse and ride in defense of their farms against intruders. Chesterton's concept of nationalism was simply incompatible with imperialism. True British patriots, said he, could never be imperialists, "for if they believed in nationality they could not really believe in empire, because the cosmopolitan idea tends to destroy the nationality of others."[29] Yet Chesterton was not necessarily pro-Boer; he opposed the war mainly because it was unjust and degraded the honor of England.

Chesterton quickly developed a reputation as the bête noire of the imperialist Fabians who rallied around George Bernard Shaw. Shaw defended the war on the grounds that it would serve to bring benighted savages into the mainstream of civilization via the British Empire. Chesterton considered this defense of imperialism the mortal enemy of patriotism and an affront to human dignity. He defined imperialism as an attempt by a European country to create a sham Europe which it could dominate, instead of the real Europe, which it could only share: "It is a love of living with one's inferiors."[30] Imperialism was the enemy of liberty, for it negated the deepest of democratic principles—it denied the equality of man by imposing "our standards" on another nation, yet learning nothing from them.[31] And, of course, it denied true liberty, which, Chesterton had come to believe, could be attained only within a defined sphere of activity and by wielding power over "small things."

The anti-imperialists of the Christian Social Union made headlines with their scathing criticism of the Boer War. They were less effective in bringing their social views to the English working classes. On the whole, the CSU's chief impact was on the hierarchy of the Church of England, where it managed to generate considerable sensitivity toward economic and social problems, including the plight of labor, and a recognition of Christian socialism as a possible remedy for such ills. For the radical members who wanted more than papers and speeches on social evils—men like G. K. Chesterton and Conrad Noel—this was not enough. Noel claimed that the Union lacked a clear dogma on theology and politics, that it had no "fixed standard" by which to direct or judge social reform.[32] Chesterton expressed his concerns in verse, in one instance suggesting how CSU speakers on the stump might appear to typical Nottingham tradesmen:

> The Christian Social Union here
> Was very much annoyed;
> It seems there is some duty
> Which we never should avoid,
> And so they sing a lot of hymns
> To help the Unemployed.
>
> Upon a platform at the end
> The speakers were displayed
> And Bishop Hoskins stood in front
> And hit a bell and said
> That Mr. Carter was to pray,
> And Mr. Carter prayed.

Then Bishop Gore of Birmingham
He stood upon one leg
And said he would be happier
If beggars didn't beg,
And that if they pinched his palace
It would take him down a peg.

He said that Unemployment
Was a horror and a blight,
He said that charities produced
Servility and spite,
And stood upon the other leg
And said it wasn't right.

And then a man named Chesterton
Got up and played with water,
He seemed to say that principles
Were nice and led to slaughter
And how we always compromised
And how we didn't orter.

Then Canon Holland fired ahead
Like fifty cannons firing,
We tried to find out what he meant
With infinite enquiring,
But the way he made the windows jump
We couldn't help admiring.

He said the human soul should be
ashamed of every sham,
He said a man should constantly
Ejaculate "I am"
. . . when he had done, I went outside
And got into a tram.[33]

The Christian Socialist League (CSL) was established in 1906
by those associated with the Guild of St. Matthew and the Chris-

tian Social Union who wanted a movement that was primarily devoted to socialist political action—therefore in touch with trade-union activities—and more liberal in religion. Membership would be open to persons of all faiths (thus assuring that the organization would be less homogeneous than the Anglo-Catholic, upper-class Guild of St. Matthew and the CSU) and to those who were willing to commit themselves to a democratic commonwealth founded on "economic socialism," in which wealth would be owned collectively by the community.

The members of the CSL varied widely in the radicalism of their political and social views and included such diverse people as George Lansbury, the future leader of the Labour Party, Conrad Noel, who would become known as the "red priest" of Thaxted, J. N. Figgis, the father of "political pluralism" and a major influence on the later development of Guild Socialism, and the brothers Cecil and G. K. Chesterton. The CSL soon became involved in the wave of working-class unrest that swept England in the years preceeding the outbreak of World War I. Conrad Noel, a close friend of the Chestertons and a stalwart warrior in many of the causes for which the brothers so ardently crusaded, was typical of the political militancy of the association when he wrote in 1912 that the main hope of the future was in "the revolt of the people against their 'leaders' as manifest in sympathetic strikes and the general labour unrest."[34] Noel's views were undergirded by Christian teaching. He claimed that he was an advocate of "Catholic Socialism," the seeds of which were found in the teachings of the early Church fathers, who he believed, were radical revolutionaries committed to the sharing of property and full-scale democracy.[35]

Perhaps the most radical member of the Christian Socialist Leaguers, a group whom the Anglican bishops called "dangerous men," was Cecil Chesterton. As leader of the League's militant wing, Chesterton vigorously opposed the association's dealings with the Liberal Party and urged that only candidates who were avowedly socialist should be given CSL support.[36]

One of these "dangerous men," Gilbert Keith Chesterton, had the greatest impact on modern English Catholicism.[37] G. K. C., as he was popularly known, was raised in a Unitarian family. In his early years Chesterton developed Anglican connections and quickly gained a reputation as a defender of Christian orthodoxy. In 1922 he converted to Catholicism, though many argued that he had been a Catholic long before then. One of his first books, *Heretics* (1905), was an attack on what he considered the great "errors" of his age. Its central argument was that Chesterton's contemporaries—Shaw, Wells, Kipling, and others—had fallen victim to the fad of progress, a mad worshipping of change and all things new in the unfounded belief that they would assure social improvement. None of these "heretics," claimed G. K. C., had established any ethical standards upon which to measure progress:

> Nobody has any business to use the word 'progress' unless he has a definite creed and a cast-iron code of morals. . . . For progress by its very name indicates a direction; and the moment we are the least doubtful about the direction, we become in the same degree doubtful about progress. Never perhaps since the beginning of the world has there been an age that had less right to use the word 'progress' than we.[38]

Chesterton announced his own solution to moral anarchy with the publication in 1908 of *Orthodoxy*. He too, he explained, had been a heretic, that is, he had sincerely tried to be original and struggled to find a "heresy of my own." However, when he prepared to put the final coat of paint on his worldview, he discovered it was orthodoxy. It was not that his new, painfully chiseled truths were false but only that they were not his: "When I fancied that I stood alone I was really in the ridiculous position of being backed up by all of Christendom."[39]

In *Orthodoxy* Chesterton asserted that Christian theology, as expressed in the Apostle's Creed, was the basis of sound ethics and the provider of a dual spiritual need, "the need for that mixture of the familiar and the unfamiliar which Christendom had rightly named romance. For the very word 'Romance' has in it the mystery and the ancient meaning of Rome."[40] Chesterton's answer to the heretics was a reaffirmation of traditional Christianity, which he discovered was the foundation from which his own liberal sympathies and orientations had evolved.

Orthodoxy was also a defence of Chesterton's belief in and commitment to liberal politics. Chesterton's liberalism rested on the idea that the individual could reach his fullest potential in a democratic environment of limited government ("the most terribly important things must be left to ordinary men themselves")[41] founded on Christian religious traditions. From his understanding of history and psychology, Chesterton regarded it as natural for man to search for religion: "Christianity seeks after God with the most elementary passion it can find, the craving for a father, the hunger that is as old as the hills."[42] Finally, for Chesterton, Christianity provided the only solid base from which democracy could be justified, for it asserted the twin dogmas that all men are made in the image of God (even the poor) and that all men are tainted with original sin (even the rich).[43]

Chesterton's spiritual resolution was based on his conviction that there was divine order in the world, a pattern revealed, as he said, in "the green architecture that builds itself without visible hands" yet follows a design already drawn in the air by an invisible finger.[44] The admission of such a plan brought with it the recognition that someone else, some strange and unseen force, had designed the universe.

As a young man Chesterton was keenly interested in politics, and his views on the subject evolved from moderate (he was a Christian socialist at the turn of the century) to radical (he supported anarcho-syndicalism on the eve of World War I). As early as 1900, however, he recognized a disturbing pattern in parliamentary politics: the parties tended to curb the views of their more unconventional members so as not to disturb the political establishment.[45] Nevertheless, always considering himself a "true Liberal," Chesterton supported the Liberal Party in the first few years of the century. He hoped that a dedicated group of reformers working within the system might be able to push the parties toward positive change. In 1902, for example, he joined Conrad Noel, C. F. G. Masterman, and others in establishing the "Patriot's Club," a group who wanted to force Liberal MPs to pay more attention to the living conditions of the poor.[46] It also was in the hopes of altering the Liberal Party's stand on imperialism that Chesterton had joined the *Speaker* group in opposition to the Boer War.

Chesterton's faith in the Liberal Party's ability to respond to such inside, reformist pressures was put to the test after the general election of 1905, which gave that party the opportunity to form a new government. When the leadership failed to carry out its campaign promises (among others, the promise to use state power to enforce wage contracts) and when Chesterton discovered that it prohibited certain Liberal MPs from speaking out on their convictions for the sake of political stability, his fears and suspicions of inter-party collusion in the interests of high finance were powerfully confirmed. The problem with government, he observed in the fall of 1905, was not serious disagreement between bitterly divided factions but the fact that the parties were essentially united as a single "governing class."[47]

Chesterton's disillusionment with the political system soon spread to the Liberal press as well. Prior to the 1905 election, the newspapers for which he wrote (Alfred Harmsworth's *Daily Mail*, the London *Times*, and George Cadbury's *Daily News*) had led the charge of corruption against the Conservative government. But once the Liberals were in power, articles critical of the government ceased to appear. When Chesterton's own essays were censored, he concluded that the press, like the political parties themselves, had fallen under the control of a few rich men who were dedicated to the preservation of the status quo.

During the first decade of the new century Chesterton also came to recognize another evil, even more insidious than the plutocratic corruption of party and press. This was the threat to individual liberties contained in socialism. If followed to its collectivist end, socialism would sacrifice the individual to the machinery of the state. This end was particularly evident in the programs of the Fabian Society, which aimed to centralize the political powers of the state, turning over governance to bureaucratic experts trained in the science of efficiency. The Fabian engineers could assure, in the words of Sidney Webb, that each individual would fulfill "in the best possible way, his humble function in the great social machine."[48] Beatrice and Sidney Webb, major forces behind the Fabian Society, had a lingering distaste for and suspicion of the laboring classes and felt it necessary to discipline them in order to maintain social order. For Sidney Webb, the masses were "apathetic, dense, unreceptive to any unfamiliar idea."[49] For this kind of socialist, revolution did not mean immersing oneself with and becoming part of the masses to bring on equality and justice; it meant rather a program of intellectual coercion which "we," the "clever ones," would impose upon "them," the lower orders.[50] This frame of mind was best typified by George Bernard Shaw, who envisioned the working classes as little more than children to be amused but disciplined. This was Shaw's advice to his fellow Fabians: "never give the people anything they want: give them something they ought to want and don't."[51]

G. K. Chesterton had contended that the Fabians were working not for a classless society but rather for a planned society via the introduction of a bureaucratic form of socialism. H. G. Wells, for example, had complained that Marx's notion of socialism was "unattractive to people who had any real knowledge of administration" and was grateful for the Fabian Society's converting "Revolutionary Socialism into Administrative Socialism."[52] This kind of thinking also betrayed a deep contempt for democracy, which threatened not only the freedoms of Englishmen but also those of the citizens of other lands. Shaw contended that "the world is to the big and powerful states by necessity, and the little ones must come within their border or be crushed out of existence." Sidney Webb, no less an imperialist zealot than Shaw, was convinced that the future would belong to "the great administrative nations, where the officials govern and the police keep order."[53] For the Fabians, the Victorian scramble for empire, raising its ugly head in the Boer Wars, was inspired by "love of one's country" and a natural part of the struggle for existence. It was denounced by G. K. Chesterton as a perversion of patriotism. What these people meant by the love of country, he claimed, "was not what a mystic might mean by the love of God" but more like what "a child might mean by a love of jam." Chesterton called for a "renaissance of true love" for one's native land, which could only be discovered and cultivated through a better understanding of history:

> What have we done, and where have we wandered, we that have produced sages who could have spoken with Socrates and poets who could walk with Dante, that we should talk as if we have never done anything more intelligent than found colonies and

kick niggers? We are the children of light, and it is we that sit in darkness. If we are judged, it will not be for the merely intellectual transgression of failing to appreciate other nations, but for the supreme spiritual transgression of failing to appreciate ourselves.[54]

Chesterton eventually turned his back on socialism for two reasons: it approached the problem of reform from the perspective of the state, not of the individual, and it depended on a false theory of human nature. Social reform imposed from above by the state could never be durable because it did not directly involve those whom it was deemed to benefit, namely, the common man. From a moral and pragmatic standpoint, Chesterton believed that people must participate individually in any programs that would affect their personal lives. Reform directed from above, outside the communities in which the individual associates, would also stifle democracy, since the state would be usurping initiative from the agents of primary socialization, namely the family, the workplace, and so forth. Chesterton clearly realized that the advocates of collectivism were building the engines of big government that potentially could wield totalitarian control over its citizens. In his view, the collectivist emphasis on efficiency and the rationalization of centralized planning were contrary to human nature. The collectivists' programs would strengthen the state at the expense of the basic social institution of the family, which he viewed as the wellspring of liberty and the source of creativity. Chesterton's analysis of the problems of socialism and his appreciation of the family as the basic unit of good living, the keystone of all social systems, followed very closely the principles upon which Pope Leo XIII had constructed *Rerum Novarum*.

II

The other half of that pantomime beast—the quadruped that Shaw had called the "Chesterbelloc"—that was Hilaire Belloc. Unlike the convert Chsterton, Belloc was born into the Catholic Church. As a young man, he fell under the influence of his family's friend, Cardinal Henry Edward Manning. While living in London before going up to Oxford, he visited Manning at every opportunity. Belloc recalled how much he admired the man for never having "admitted the possibility of compromise between Catholic and non-Catholic society. He perceived the necessary conflict and gloried in it."[55] (The young Belloc's enthusiasm probably fell short of endorsing his mentor's teachings on the evil of drink. Even Belloc's mother, a close friend of Manning's, parted with the good Cardinal on this issue: when he talked teetotalism, wrote Belloc, mother thought it "most unworthy of him to have anything to do with such vulgar rubbish.")[56]

If imitation is the best form of flattery, Belloc's early career would have made Manning proud. There were few in England more uncompromising than Belloc on matters of faith. Like the cardinal, Belloc's Catholicism was ultramontane and continental, and his dislike of the old English Catholic families, whom he considered insular and arrogant, was every bit as strong as Manning's. Indeed, Belloc was convinced that the old families were a major obstacle to the progress of the faith itself. As a group, he asserted, they were wedded to the Protestant establishment. This betrayal of the cause revealed itself in their tendencies to sympathize more with the American Puritan traditions than with those of the immigrant Irish, Poles, and Germans who represented a vigorous brand of Catholicism that threatened the complacency of the rich and comfortable.[57] The old Catholic families were "invariably ignorant" on all subjects of public importance: "They dislike all nations of Catholic culture; they detest the Irish; they loathe the French; and down to the smallest details they try to be as like the anti-Catholic atmosphere of our wealthy society as they can manage."[58]

Manning also became Belloc's political mentor, though, as was the case with Chesterton, it would take some hands-on political experience before Belloc fully accepted the Cardinal's positions. Manning was outspokenly contemptuous of the parliamentary party system, being convinced that party labels were nothing but camouflages for greed:

> Whig and Tory are names without equivalents. The Revolution of 1688 whipped them both out. The parliamentary title of the Crown equalises both. They survive as two forms of class

selfishness. The aristocratic selfishness and the well-to-do self-ishness. Liberal and Conservative are still more unmeaning. The law and constitution of England excludes all such political sections.[59]

It was only natural that Belloc would enter the political arena as a Liberal. He was a descendant of the radical philosopher and scientist Joseph Priestly and the grandson of Joseph Parkes, founder of the Reform Club and a major leader of the Liberal Party.[60] Belloc's mother, Bessie Parkes, followed closely her father's political inclinations. She had married Louis Belloc of La Celle Saint Cloud in France, where Hilaire was born and where he spent the early, impressionable years of his life. These were to be bittersweet memories, however, for the family's life at La Celle Saint Cloud was rudely interrupted by the Franco-Prussian War and the subsequent occupation of the village by Prussian troops. The Belloc family estate was looted and left in ruins. This episode had much to do with Belloc's life-long hatred of Germany, in his mind a truly evil empire which he persisted in calling "Prussia."

Belloc appreciated Cardinal Manning's love of democracy and his Christian-style socialism, which ultimately reached maturity in the "third way" of Leo XIII's *Rerum Novarum*. Belloc quickly recognized the wisdom of Manning's and Leo XIII's dual condemnation of both the callous rich who exploited the laboring poor and the equally distorted collectivist reaction to unfettered capitalism. Under the guidance of Manning, *Rerum Novarum* and especially its emphasis on the "duty of the state" to fight injustice and to "protect the poor and helpless" became the cornerstones for all of Belloc's subsequent sociopolitical and economic ideas.[61]

Belloc's youthful days in London, punctuated by memorable visits with Manning, constituted a heady, idealistic interlude before he encountered socialism and democracy as actually practiced in the English political system. At the age of nineteen, Belloc was swept up by enthusiasm for the great London dock strike, a classic confrontation between the capitalist bosses and the exploited workers freshly aroused by the sense of class consciousness. Along with mobs of workers, Belloc trekked through the streets of London to hear strike leaders like John Burns defy imprisonment for the sake of telling tales of a new and better world to come through the gospel of socialism. These were genuine passions, Belloc would later write, before the socialist creed was taken over by the politicians for the sham battles at Westminster:

> The leaders *did* desire, and *did* think they could achieve an England in which the poor should be poor no longer, and in which there should be sustenance and happiness for all. They *did* still believe the amazing proposition that what they called 'the community'—that is, in practice, the politicians—could own all we have and handle it with a superhuman justice. Great God! They believed it![62]

But through all this stress and storm nothing came: "The mill turned noisily enough, but it ground not corn."[63] This observation, however, was made with hindsight, after Belloc's own efforts in the political mill ground no corn.

The public career of Hilaire Belloc began auspiciously while he was a student at Oxford University. In 1894 he was one of the few Roman Catholics to have enrolled at Oxford following the 1871 act that opened English universities to Roman Catholics. Partly through his brilliant speeches at the Oxford Union, Belloc quickly developed a reputation as a militant Catholic, a defendant of all things French (he was the only undergraduate who could claim to have served in the French army before entering the university), and an unabashed advocate of democracy.

There may have been a touch of the exotic about Belloc, but, on the other hand, he was clearly an influential force on campus. The weight of his opinions can be measured by the publication of *Essays in Liberalism,* a collection of discourses by Belloc and several of his friends (F. Y. Eccles, J. S. Phillimore, J. L. Hammond, J. A. Simon, and F. W. Hirst) who later became the leading lights behind *The Speaker.* The book's introduction noted that the writers had been primarily inspired and guided by Belloc's political vision. Already, in this early collection of essays, Belloc revealed his concerns about the threat of state power to individual freedoms. The book's contributors recommended a return to the "fundamental principles of Liberalism" as an antidote to statist tendencies. Belloc's conception of Liberalism, however, reposed on the democratic principle that such a political system could be legitimized only if each member of the community played a part in the government he was to obey.[64] He also asserted that a truly free citizen must be politically and economically independent. In order to assure this independence, Belloc drew on the teachings of *Rerum Novarum* to advocate a wider distribution of private property. The sociopolitical positions set forth in *Essays in Liberalism* were so unorthodox that the Oxford undergraduate journal, *The Isis*, felt compelled to point out that they did not correspond to any recognized opinion within the parliamentary Liberal Party.

In addition to his unconventional ideas on Liberalism, a number of other positions and attitudes marked Belloc as a man on the fringes. The most troublesome were his views on Jews. Anti-Semitism was rife in turn-of-the-century English upper-class circles, but Belloc's views were more strident and systematic than most.

The roots of Belloc's thinking about Jews and of his antiliberalism, the latter of which emerged after his career as Member of Parliament, can be traced to the French Right. Belloc was exposed to this tradition while a young conscript in the French army, following which he became an avid reader of Charles Maurras, the anti-Semitic monarchist editor of *Action Française*.[65] As a young man in France, Belloc also had developed a close friendship with his neighbor, Paul Déroulède, and had joined his Lique de Patriotes.[66] A major purpose of the Lique de Patriotes, besides taking to the streets to pressure French politicians to recover the lost provinces of Alsace and Lorraine, was to attack the defenders of Alfred Dreyfus, a Jewish officer in the French army who was unjustly accused of spying for the Germans. Déroulède's Lique recruited men of the political right to oppose those who defended Dreyfus. Déroulède, a "Don Quixote in an Inverness cape," as Henri de Rochefort called him, was an ardent patriot and, like Belloc, an admirer of Jacobin Republicanism. But he was opposed to the Third Republic because of its financial corruption, parliamentary instability, and its pusillanimous policy toward Germany. The source of these problems, Déroulède believed, had much to do with the political and economic influence of Jews.

The Dreyfus affair was a major influence on Belloc's views concerning Jews. Like the ultra-patriotic French Right, he believed that a reexamination of Dreyfus's guilt could only hurt the French army and that the demand for a retrial was being engineered by a small group of Jewish financiers. Belloc's anger over the whole affair never abated, and he remained convinced that the vindication of Dreyfus destroyed the French Intelligence Bureau and was responsible for prolonging World War I. In Belloc's mind, the unfortunate Dreyfus episode shed light on a dark, dirty secret: the existence of a Jewish power bloc with enormous influence in international political and economic circles.

Belloc's militant Catholicism and his strident views on Jews and politics, combined with what must be called an overbearing personality, did not endear him to the Oxford academic establishment. These liabilities were responsible for his rejection as a Fellow, a blow from which he never fully recovered. It seems that many of Belloc's friends and mentors, in particular, Dr. Benjamin Jowett, had given him assurances that a fellowship was his for the asking. Belloc claimed that he based his career plans on that calculation, but that when the time arrived he was turned down for religious reasons. In particular, said Belloc, the dons objected to his historiography, which emphasized the effect of religion on behavior, and to the way in which Catholicism informed his public views.[67] Such ideas clashed with their own. One college after another turned him down, and in this way, claimed Belloc, he wasted the first critical years of his life: "It was too late to go to the Bar, and I had no capital upon which to live until briefs should come in. I went to London, and have had to earn my living since then as best I could."[68] In future there would be many literary skirmishes with Oxbridge dons, and Belloc seems to have relished the opportunity of tweaking their scholarly noses:

Hunting Dons is almost as much fun as establishing Roman roads. I know all the didges [dodges?] for making them break cover and just where to stand to shoot them in the thorax when they get out of the wood into the stubble. I never wing them, I always kill.[69]

Belloc also developed unorthodox views on Catholicism itself, which, when taken with his revisionistic ideas on English and European history, seemed downright revolutionary. He was convinced that European culture was fundamentally Catholic—that was what he meant by the controversial expression "Europe is the faith and the faith is Europe"—and that it would have to reject Protestantism or perish. Since Belloc viewed Catholicism as both religion and culture, for him a temporal loyalty and a spiritual loyalty to Rome were essentially inseparable. This kind of thinking, redolent of the views of continental "integralist" Catholics, provides a key for understanding Belloc's position on the issue of European imperialism and his condemnation of England's role in the Boer War. Belloc simply opposed anything that in his opinion served to destroy the unity of the Roman Church. With violent prejudice overruling historical integrity, he hated the Hohenzollerns because they brought Protestantism to Germany; he disdained the Jews because in defiance of the Christian corporate ethic they made money-making the *raison d'être* of life and work; he condemned the entire development of capitalism since it destroyed the legacy of imperial Rome as it was reborn in the cultural unity of medieval Christendom. Imperialism was simply an extension of the money-grubbing which had destroyed the medieval social and political order.

Belloc's identification of Catholicism as culture was similar to that of the French Restoration writers Joseph de Maistre, François René Chateaubrian, and Louis de Bonald (likely influences on Belloc's thinking, though he never admitted it), as well as the Vogelsang circle in Vienna. But unlike these Catholic reactionaries, Belloc welcomed the French Revolution. At first glance his political views appear contradictory: he was an advocate of monarchism and appreciated the strong hand of dictatorship, yet called himself a democrat and a republican. This paradox can be bridged by understanding Belloc as both Jacobite and Jacobin, a fusion symbolized in his romantic attachment to the medieval aristocratic order and simultaneous admiration for the revolutionary forces in France that purged the old order after it had become decadent.[70] As John P. McCarthy has shown, the Jacobin tendencies predominated in Belloc's early career, during the years of labor unrest before the Great War and while he tried to bring democratic change through the political system as Member of Parliament (1906–1910).[71] After Belloc became disillusioned with the possibility of bringing change through Britain's existing institutions, the Jacobite strain came to the surface and prevailed throughout his later years, when he identified himself as a monarchist. Yet his willingness to entertain the idea of revolution endured. When parliamentary democracy was under siege on the continent during the 1930s, Belloc wrote his American friend Hoffman Nickerson (no devotee of democracy himself) that when such institutional practices had gone beyond mending, "one's first duty is to get rid of it, there will always be something likely to take its place."[72]

Belloc's Jacobin attachments grew out of his admiration of Greco-Roman culture. The Romans civilized Europe by preserving the culture of Greece, and they brought political unity by extending throughout Europe their own language, laws, and civic institutions. The political genius of the Romans forged a variety of ethnic groups over disparate geographical areas into a single state. Just as the Roman Empire had kept alive the higher tradition of Greece, so, Belloc argued, the Church, in the face of barbarian and Islamic invasion, had preserved and revitalized the institutions of Rome. The civilization of Roman Catholic Europe reached its zenith in the High Middle Ages from the eleventh to the fourteenth century. This was a golden age in Belloc's mind, a world stabilized by the great guilds and a time in which the common man was approaching full economic freedom through the possession of private property. Belloc believed that the Stuart monarchs in England had fought to preserve these traditions against the Protestant ascendancy, a land-grabbing clique who stole monastic properties. The Protestant clique had prevailed and had replaced the old order (unlike eighteenth-century France, the English system at the time of the Stuarts was still vital and pure) with an oligarchy of special interests.

Belloc's vast historical writings elaborated on these basic themes and were designed to counter the Whig bias that prevailed in English academic circles. He disdained the Gibbon-Macaulay historiographical canons, which emphasized the development of parliamentary government and the curbing of monarchical prerogative, because they exalted the forces which had destroyed Catholic universalism and the social structure of the Middle Ages, and they eulogized an event (the abolition of the monasteries) that helped spawn a new class of predatory capitalists.[73] Belloc even went so far as to argue that this historiographical tradition was the single most important factor preventing England's return to the Catholic fold.[74] Coupled with Belloc's detestation of Whig historiography was an abhorrence of the rich. He disliked the wealthy primarily because they were corruptors of politics and exploiters of the poor. Belloc's loyalty to what he defined as Republicanism seems to have been related to his antipathy toward the rich and privileged.

Yet Belloc parted ways with most Catholic intellectuals who steadfastly supported the memory of the ancien régime. Belloc's defense of the French Revolution seems puzzling, given its attack on the Catholic Church. Belloc believed, however, that the Revolution was never the enemy of Catholicism as such, nor did he see any incompatibility between the Church and the democratic spirit behind the Revolution, since the Church by tradition was a defender of the poor and a proponent of social justice. The conflict between Catholicism and Revolution, according to Belloc, was part of a misunderstanding caused in large part by the corruption of the eighteenth-century Gallican Church. Isolated from Rome and co-opted by the privileged, the French Church had distanced itself from the common people and had fallen into a state of decay. Because of its identification with the excesses of the old regime—"the State wore Catholic clothes"[75]—the Church was the most visible object of attack for those who hoped to rejuvenate the community. As an official institution of absolutism, the French Catholic Church was but a portion of the world which the populace hated and which they thought it necessary to destroy. Nor could it be defended adequately. The religious orders were too devoid of spiritual energy, too far removed from the life of the nation, to rise in its defense. Those aristocrats who rallied to the Church's cause did so, not because they understood the faith, but because they viewed it as an integral part of the privileged order of which they were a part. However, the revolutionaries erred in thinking the institution moribund; their Civil Constitution of the Clergy had the effect of turning a small minority who were true Catholics in France against the Revolution.

Belloc always insisted that the Revolution was necessary. The old order had decayed to the point that radical surgery was required to restore the community to health. The organs of government "had become stiff with age, and had to be supplanted."[76] An admirer of Rousseau, Belloc interpreted the French Revolution as an expression of the "general will," the vehicle through which the communal spirit manifested itself. Yet Belloc did not believe that this will was always best expressed through representative government. After his bitter experiences with English politics, he concluded that parliamentary forms of government were simply mechanisms by which the wealthy could rule.[77] In his view, the principles of democracy and justice were best implemented through the forceful personality of an enlightened monarch, who could rise above petty politics, avoid the temptations of avarice, and guide the state in the best interest of the general will. It was on such ground that Belloc championed Napoleon as a savior of the French Revolution: his significance was the substitution of personal rule for oligarchy. Napoleon became the "incarnation of the community in one man" as against the plutocracy that was always the fruit of "representative government."[78]

Napoleon had succeeded in providing a force for integration that bound French society together in a corporate whole. Belloc believed that men in large numbers could not be so organized save under monarchy or a traditional governing class (an aristocracy) that won the loyalty of the masses. The Revolution had torn up France by the roots, having been triggered by the failure of the two traditional integrative mechanisms (monarchical and aristocratic) to command the loyalty of the people. Napoleon, for Belloc, represented an effort "to re-found" a new set of values that could bind the nation together. The noble experiment failed because Napoleon was defeated. Yet Belloc would never accept the proposition that the French Revolution had caused the crisis in modern politics. The real disaster, he claimed, was not the events of 1789 but rather a deep religious malignancy: "the Calvinist organisation which spread and strengthened itself, preventing spiritual unity from its origin to our day."[79]

Belloc played a small, controversial, but perhaps important role in modern English historiography in that he, like R. H. Tawney, convinced many to look more closely at religion as a motivating

force for historical change. Douglas Woodruff, the influential editor of the London *Tablet*, was a great admirer of Belloc because he
broke the convention of treating religion as strictly a personal matter.
As opposed to other historians who dismissed the faith as a causal
factor in public behavior and who therefore concealed historical
truth, said Woodruff, Belloc shed new light on the religious motives
behind historical events. He was simply ahead of his time, though,
as Woodruff argued in 1949, his positions had become much more
obvious with the rise of Lenin and Hitler and their war against the
Christian religion.[80]

Belloc's historiography was motivated not merely by a genuinely
felt need to correct what he regarded as the institutionalized bias
of Whig historians. He also intended to retaliate against the academics at Oxford whom he believed had conspired to prevent him
from exercising his talents as a historian. Belloc claimed that these
university-sanctioned propagandists deceived their readers through
a smoke screen of spurious footnotes and other such academic para-
phernalia, which upon close investigation could not support their
tendentious arguments.

Belloc's histories were lucidly written, but he wrote too much
and he did so with hurried hand. Privately Belloc admitted to these
faults, arguing that he was obliged to publish prolifically in order
to support his considerable family: "my children scream for caviar
and pearls."[81] Such mercenary labor, Belloc always insisted, was
necessitated by his having been turned down for a fellowship at All
Souls. These burdens were made all the greater because he had to
write for an audience that hated his faith. Unlike the books of writers like Lytton Strachey, "who copied me a great deal," claimed Belloc, there was no popular market for works like *Napoleon*. How
could American and English readers understand the idea of a hero
uniting Europe and resurrecting the Roman Empire?[82] After his
parliamentary experiences and controversial journalistic crusades,
Belloc was essentially shut out of the English popular press[83] and,
to earn a living, wrote increasingly for the American market.[84]

The necessity of drawing on an American audience was a considerable annoyance. It was "heart breaking work," Belloc wrote his
friend Lady Frances Phipps, stooping to "third-rate American Catholic papers" for subsistence. The readers were "completely unedu-

cated," making independent thought and the discussion of problems other than "the small clerical interests" impossible. It was for these reasons that Belloc so enjoyed writing articles for the far more sophisticated French market.[85]

Although Belloc's histories may have been thoroughly researched,[86] stylistic masterpieces, he defied the most important tenet of the historian's craft by dismissing the necessity of objectivity.[87] Belloc's chief purpose in writing history was to propagate a point of view. Did Belloc's books then speak the truth? The demands of the market make this a difficult question to answer. As he told an acquaintance who sought his advice on writing books, it is important to separate your work into two parts: "half for livelihood and half for telling the truth. Telling the truth will never provide a livelihood."[88]

Belloc clearly was not overly sensitive about accuracy in his historical studies. The Oxford historian Harold Fisher, who knew Belloc well, told Arnold Lunn that Belloc had absolutely no conscience as a historian, though his books were worth reading for their literary merits. Fisher related to Lunn a story about meeting Belloc one hot summer day at the Archives in Paris. Staggering beneath crushing loads of books, the director of the archives and his assistants were busily preparing a table where Belloc could examine documents, pamphlets, and other such materials of every description that he had requested. Upon spotting Fisher, Belloc invited him and the director, a very important man, to lunch. This afforded Belloc the opportunity to hold forth on his favorite theme, that it was flair and not fact that made the historian: "For instance," Belloc elaborated, "M. le Directeur has spent the whole morning collecting books and documents in order that I may adequately document my forthcoming work on Robespierre. As we sat down to lunch I suddenly had a flair that there will not be a single fact in all those books and documents. Consequently I do not propose to return to the Archives this afternoon." The shock on the director's pained face, said Fisher, reminiscent of the back-breaking labor expended in gathering these documents, was "an eloquent tribute to Belloc's theories about the true way to write history."[89]

The *modus operandi* of Belloc's historical methodology was more akin to that of Rousseau, a writer with whom he identified because of his ability to expound a fundamental dogma based not on objective facts or the principle of reason but on faith.[90] To H.G. Wells, Belloc wrote that the historian who tried to write from a disinterested, objective viewpoint was condemned to sterility, because history required a flame of conviction comparable to that of religion.[91] Just as conviction made the good historian, so, believed Belloc, the persuasion of personality molded the patterns of history. As opposed to the Marxist school of historiography, which identifies environment as the crucial historical determinant, Belloc seemed to believe in the great man idea. Most of his historical essays concerned personalities (Danton, Napoleon, Robespierre, Richelieu, among others) whose one or two "ideas" or convictions he supposed had shaped the course of history. Perhaps this explains why Belloc searched the bleak political landscape of the 1930s for a great man who could lead Europe out of the impending darkness.

III

"Belloc went into Parliament, smelt it and went out again."
—George Bernard Shaw[92]

The mercurial Hilaire Belloc and G.K. Chesterton first became acquainted through their mutual connections with the *Speaker* group. From the outset, Chesterton was infatuated with Belloc's persona. He was flamboyant, clever, and brazen: "What he brought into our dream was his Roman appetite for reality and for reason in action, and when he came into the door there entered with him the smell of danger."[93]

The two writers' styles conflicted. Chesterton's writings were freewheeling and ironic, and in his polemics he came across as self-effacing and friendly; Belloc wrote in a classical style, and he was vain, bitingly cynical, and cantankerous in debate. Nevertheless they shared much in common. Along with their anarchistic hostility toward the bureaucratic state was their mutual distaste for almost anything described as "progressive" or "modern." One of Belloc's abiding moral objectives, for example, was to find a means for reintegrating people with the tradition of Rome, and this meant rescuing the individual from the rootlessness of modern industrial society. Detached from his Catholic origins, modern man had become a stranger lost in a wilderness of concrete pavements.

In addition to their common aversion to imperialism and modern "progressivism," Chesterton and Belloc had arrived at similar social and moral opinions. Chesterton's feelings about the sanctity of private property and of small rural communities complemented Belloc's idealization of peasant proprietorship. Belloc believed that there were still certain classic features of European culture preserved in the lives of the peasants he had known as a child living in rural Sussex and earlier in the countryside around La Celle Saint Cloud. There he found a respect for tradition and communal cooperation that came from working the land, generating a sense of rootedness, family closeness, and a set of religious mores that gave shape and coherence to the whole social matrix. This was what Belloc called the "Peasant State," a condition of political freedom with an attachment to a specific locality and a love for the produce of the soil. The existence of such an independent rural community, said Belloc, could provide a permanent model of good living to the "unstable, nomadic and creedless creatures who inhabited the floating world of the cities."[94]

Two important experiences provided the practical groundwork for constructing the theory known as Distributism, Chesterton's and Belloc's alternative to the ills of modernity. The first was Belloc's entrance into the House of Commons as a Liberal MP. The second was the cataclysm of labor unrest that nearly brought Britain to open class warfare on the eve of World War I. These experiences served to define the two writers' essential outlooks regarding the necessary programs for change, provided important insights into the workings of the modern political establishment, sharpened the anarchistic, anti-statist dimension of the Distributist alternative to capitalism and socialism, and created both a wider audience and a coterie of activists for the Distributist mission.

Belloc's entrance into the House of Commons as a Liberal MP was a difficult one, though it was a journey for which he had been prepared, he said, since around the age of eighteen, when he became convinced of the need to check the moral corruption of professional politicians. He did not intend Parliament to be a career: "My whole object was to prevent its being a career to anybody."[95] Prior to being elected by slightly more than eight hundred votes in the general election of 1906 to represent South Salford, Belloc had been turned down as a candidate because of his militant Catholicism by five different constituencies.

From the outset, Belloc insisted on pursuing a political career on his own terms. The Liberal caucus was informed that he would not pledge to vote on party lines but only as his constituents or his own conscience dictated. After his election the Liberal Party Central Office tried to discipline Belloc's independence by refusing to help pay his parliamentary expenses, and from this juncture on he was obliged to find such support from certain wealthy friends who believed in his cause.[96] Belloc believed that Parliament rapidly was losing its legislative powers and its control of the executive to a new financial elite who had replaced the old landed gentry. A living symbol of these new forces was the Liberal Party's rising star, David Lloyd George. Lloyd George was a clever politician who knew how to read the mood of the electorate and how to manipulate opinion. Belloc came to detest him as the champion of the new liberalism that betrayed the radical liberal traditions with which he had so closely identified. This new style of mass politics and collectivist-oriented liberalism was especially prone to the manipulation of the financial plutocracy that Belloc saw replacing the old gentry.

Belloc's decision to enter politics was motivated in large part by his belief that there was yet a chance to check such tendencies. Parliament might still serve a useful function as a forum for debate, thereby satisfying the public's need to know. In this sense the House of Commons could provide a crack in the ring of silence engineered by the financial plutocrats who monopolized the press. A member of Parliament at least had the power of criticism, and by asking embarrassing questions in Commons and by raising relevant issues in a few "independent" newspapers the conspirators might be forced into the public spotlight. Here is where Belloc thought he could make a difference.

As the first English politician in modern history to stand for Catholic causes in Parliament, Belloc supported his campaign pledges to oppose the Education Act of 1902 (which withheld public aid to

sectarian schools), resist temperance reform, fight those who opposed Home Rule for Ireland, and work against the importation of
Chinese labor into South Africa. Fighting such battles soon brought
him into conflict with the majority of Liberal MPs.

The first clash was over the Chinese labor issue. Pro-Boers
and labor supporters in the Liberal Party were particularly exercised about the importation of Chinese workers into the Transvaal
gold mines, because they believed it was a ploy by the mine owners
to lower the general wage scales for all miners, thereby maximizing corporate profits. If successful, such tactics might even be tried
in Britain. In December 1925 the leader of the Liberals, Henry
Campbell-Bannerman, pledged his party to work for an end to the
practice. But when a new Liberal government was returned, the
party leadership compromised on their commitment in such a way
as to minimize the losses for those owners who had made large investments in the importation of Chinese workers. Belloc was greatly
disappointed at the Liberals' failure to put an end to all profiteer-
ing in South Africa, but when he was told by the Deputy Speaker
that he would be allowed to address the House only on condition
that he not bring up the Chinese labor question, his indignation
could not be contained. Belloc caused a great stir when he informed
his South Salford constituency of the matter, but the Liberal Party
officially denied the incident.[97] Outraged at the duplicity of his
party, Belloc ignored the order and in his maiden speech demanded
that the government not only stop the practice immediately (it was
the mandate of the 1906 election, he claimed) but commence to
deport the Chinese workers, making the mine owners pay the cost
of doing so.[98]

Belloc concluded that the Liberals had reneged on their electoral promises on the Chinese labor question because a clique of
wealthy capitalists with investments in South Africa had contributed heavily to the party's political funds. He demanded that this
"secret war chest" be audited so the public would know which
people were controlling the political agenda. The proposal was
ignored by the House of Commons, but Belloc claimed he knew
who the guilty ones were: the money came from the pockets of the
"Rand magnates," Jewish financiers who were responsible for the
Boer War.

Other skirmishes concerning Belloc and a variety of foreign and domestic issues ensued after the Chinese labor controversy. Belloc continued to denounce the persistent driving force that controlled events, namely, a group of self-serving plutocrats with foreign financial connections.[99]

The final episode that convinced Belloc to quit Parliament altogether was the Liberal Party's attempt to reform the House of Lords. This effort was prompted by the Lords' failure to support the government's 1909 budget, which called for new revenues from land and income taxes, death duties, and other charges on consumer items to help pay the costs of naval construction (above all, the building of Dreadnoughts to maintain British superiority in the face of the German naval build-up). The House of Lords, the bastion of gentry privilege, rejected the budget, and the Liberals called an election in 1910 as a popular mandate for reforming the upper chamber.

Belloc had been an avid supporter of Prime Minister Asquith's threat to remove the political powers of the House of Lords, hoping that this might help revolutionize the political system by opening it up to more voices of democracy. The Liberal Party's decision to compromise on the issue by calling a constitutional conference with the opposition indicated to Belloc that a conspiracy was in the air. When the conference failed a general election was called for December 1910. However, by this point Belloc had decided not to stand for reelection, for he was convinced that the general election was simply a ploy to postpone the all-important issue. In Belloc's thinking, the general election was all a piece of machine politics, revealing that the so-called opposition was not really working against the government but was in a secret alliance to prevent any significant political change that might weaken the money cliques.[100]

It was clear in Belloc's mind that the leaders of the two political parties, who "controlled rather than were subjected"[101] to the House of Commons, were not responding to popular mandates but rather to the wishes of the financial plutocrats. Given the fact that political reform was not even a central issue for many Tories in the ensuing campaign, Belloc was convinced that his conspiratorial views had been substantiated.

Although Belloc would say that "they" had failed to bribe him heavily enough to stay in Parliament and that he was "relieved to be quit of the dirtiest company it has ever been my misfortune to keep,"[102] his decision to leave Commons was due to other factors as well. He resented being away from his family for extended lengths of time, he wanted to devote more time to his literary career (partly for financial reasons—"Being in Parliament cost me indirectly I suppose about 500 pounds a year"[103]), and he was frankly bored with the work required to be an effective member of Parliament.

The experience left a permanent sour taste in his mouth. In later years, reflecting back on this episode in his career, Belloc confided to his friend Lady Frances Phipps:

> I have never in my life passed years so intolerably tiresome as those during which I was in the House of Commons. I was glad to get in because it raised my income as a writer by advertising me but the surroundings are so tawdry you have to meet such a vast number of scoundrels and equal number of third-rate people daily and the trade as a whole is so impossible that I determined to be out of it as soon as I could. . . . getting out of the House of Commons and associating with decent people again is like getting into the fresh air out of the foulest stuffy room.[104]

Parliamentary politics for Belloc became either the object of cynical jokes[105] or something to be scorned. He attacked its practitioners in the sharpest black and white terms. There was a central purpose to Belloc's vitriolic campaigns against politicians. As he later told Hoffman Nickerson, "my object here is to arouse interest in apathetic people, whose apathy is endangering the State. I should never have succeeded in making the professional politician a byword in England if I acted otherwise."[106]

CHAPTER 5

Against the Servile State

The decade before the outbreak of World War I was a time of social and political turmoil in Britain. George Danger-field in his book *The Strange Death of Liberal England* has argued that the intransigence of the House of Lords, the Irish issue, the excesses of the suffragettes, and the wide-scale industrial unrest had the combined effect of destroying the Liberal Party and, had it not been for those shots at Sarajevo, might well have climaxed in civil war within Britain itself. Historians have taken issue with Dangerfield's thesis, but clearly this spirit of unrest suggested pervasive disenchantment with Britain's traditional political processes. One finds in these years, among both the political left and right, persistent anti-parliamentary sentiments. Of particular concern for the ruling elite was the growing rebelliousness of the working classes, who seemed to be heeding the message of syndicalism, a variety of anarchist thought which arrived in Britain via the United States and France. The syndicalists emphasized the necessity of labor's utilizing so-called "direct action" tactics, outside the halls of Parliament, to win control of their industries. Their ultimate objective was the creation of a new type of society regulated by the workers through their trade unions.

Those responding to the call of syndicalism shared some basic concerns which set them apart from the supporters and practitioners of conventional politics. The workers who identified with revolutionary-style unionism had a deep distrust of their official leadership and the political parties. Middle-class intellectuals welcoming syndicalism were hostile to the political system because they believed it was spawning a new kind of society that would smash the individual for the sake of bureaucratic efficiency. Both these groups shared a common fear of the abuse of state power in the hands of elected officials. The support for syndicalist thinking came chiefly from numerous rank-and-file trade unions, the radical independent labor newspaper, the *Daily Herald*, A. R. Orage's *New Age*, and two journals owned by Hilaire Belloc and Cecil Chesterton, the *Eye-Witness* and the *New Witness*.

Cecil Chesterton, who became an early collaborator with Hilaire Belloc, had been a major figure in the Fabian Society and in Christian Socialist circles. He later converted to Catholicism, though like his brother, Gilbert Keith Chesterton, his path to Rome was a very radical one. Falling under the influence of the Reverend Conrad Noel, a fiery socialist, and Hubert Bland, who was both a Tory and a Marxist, Cecil quickly outgrew the statism of the Fabian crowd, and from 1907 to 1912 he worked closely with A. R. Orage as a major contributor to the *New Age*. From the outset of his journalistic career, Cecil seems to have developed a sour taste for parliamentary politics and, in particular, for the Labour Party, which he believed was an inappropriate vehicle for creating socialism. At the 1909 spring meeting of the Christian Socialist League, for example, Cecil defended the obstructionist political tactics of Victor Grayson, the radical independent Labour Member of Parliament for Colne Valley. He also urged Anglican socialists to keep in touch with "fertile revolutionary activity" and pushed for the acceptance of defiant parliamentary tactics in the face of the collapse of the Labour Party.[1]

Although Cecil initially opposed his brother's and Belloc's antisocialist polemics, it is clear that he shared with Belloc a ferocious dislike of the political parties. As early as February 1908, for example, Cecil applauded Belloc's speech in the House of Commons exposing the venality of the secret party funds.[2] Cecil Chesterton's articles during the next few years in the *New Age* and the *Church Socialist Quarterly* (the journal of the Christian Socialist League) elaborated on the evils of parliamentary politics. These essays, which were published as the book *Party and People* (1910), had a noticeable Bellocian ring to them. *Party and People* asserted that parliamentary government in Britain had ceased to be democratic and representative because the rich administered the front benches through their control of the secret party funds. The Parliamentary Labour Party

was a deliberate attempt to create a political organization independent of these sinister circumstances. Yet it was obvious to Cecil
Chesterton, given the Parliamentary Labour Party's pusillanimous
performance since the 1906 elections, that the Labour Members of
Parliament had become the puppets of their own caucus, which had
as its chief objective the safeguarding of Labour seats through the
continuance of its alliance with the Liberal Party.

Cecil found all of this disconcerting, since the socialist movement, formalized politically through the creation of the Independent Labour Party, had sought to revolutionize British society. Even
the Fabian Society, which Cecil had served with considerable energy,
had as its major objective the creation of a socialist state by collab-
orating with the Liberal Party, though the Fabians intended to "permeate" the Liberals for the sole purpose of dissolving their party.
From the outset, however, Cecil had considered this a dangerous
tactic, since close collaboration with Liberals could lead to co-option
of socialists to the practice of conventional politics. The performance of the Parliamentary Labour Party had borne out Chesterton's
worst fears: in 1906 it refused to protest the Liberals' backsliding
on the Chinese labor question, took no stand for the workingman
in the debate concerning the Licensing Bill, and generally did nothing to force the Liberal government to increase the pace of reform.
Of the forty Labour Members of Parliament returned in the 1910
elections, virtually every one sat at the sufferance of the Liberal
Party. All these Members were more concerned about defending
their own seats than pushing socialist causes, which meant, in effect,
supporting the Liberal government on all issues of importance.

Party and People also pointed out that it was important to keep
the real objectives of socialism in the forefront of public debate,
namely, the upholding of dignity and justice and the abolition of
poverty.[3] Cecil Chesterton showed his concern about the public's
misconception of socialism. It was important, he wrote, to show that
socialism did not entail a growing interference in the lives of individual citizens. Indeed, in anticipation of Belloc's notion of the
"servile state," Cecil voiced his fear of a deadening alternative to
capitalism and true socialism: "chattel slavery" through collectivism
brought on by the "administrative" socialism of the Webbs.[4]

Chesterton's book outlined some sketchy procedures to cure the disease afflicting parliamentary politics. As an antidote to the power of secret party funds, it suggested that the state could pay the salaries of Members of Parliament and underwrite the cost of elections. This procedure might give the public, not the party whips, more control over their representatives. Cecil also made vague suggestions concerning proportional representation and called for the government to publish the names of those who contributed to the party funds. Yet the abject failure of the Labour Party convinced him that there was only one certain path to save Britain from the vast vistas of decay: "We must appeal to Caesar. We must raise the people against the politicians."[5] *Party and People* seemed to suggest the need for a mass movement with sufficient unity and energy to battle the corruption of an enervating parliamentary system.[6]

Despite some differences concerning private property and socialism, Cecil Chesterton and Belloc became fast friends (Cecil eventually accepted Belloc's critique of socialism and by 1911 had become a loyal Distributist). In 1911 they joined together to launch a career in muckraking journalism. The new alliance was signalized by the publication of *The Party System* (1911), which outlined the plutocratic conspiracy that had turned parliamentary government into a sham fight between the two major political parties. The basic theme of the book was that the wealthy contributors to the party funds controlled government without reference to the British electorate. A single coterie of "selected" Members of Parliament directed politics for these monied powers, thus making the old differences between the Tory and Liberal Parties meaningless. The plutocracy continued the party divisions in form only, in order to fool the public into believing that real differences still prevailed. In effect, Parliament was arbitrarily divided into two teams, each of which by mutual consent took turns running the government. This was what the authors called the "party system," a fraudulent game that rendered the House of Commons null and the people of Britain impotent and voiceless in political affairs.[7] The essential function of Parliament, said Belloc, was to manipulate the executive. If that were not possible, then it should control the executive or at least check it. But Parliament had now lost power over even the least of these functions. The purpose of *The Party System*, Belloc insisted, was to plot out this failure and show it to the public "in a time when the press in general had so crystallized upon dead party lines that, save in a book, no wide public could be told the precise truth."[8]

The Party System proposed two specific reforms. The first was a mandatory auditing of the party funds. These secret funds were used for financing the election campaigns of men selected by local party organizations. The existence of this source of money naturally raised questions as to the identity of the contributors and possible rewards that might have been expected of them for services rendered. The second reform proposal was a call to limit the duration of Parliament to a fixed period (four years at the very most), during which the House could not be dissolved. The two authors hoped that this would modify the influence of the party funds, since a vote against the government would not bring the expense of a general election. The book concluded on an optimistic note. There was no need to supplant the present political system:

> All we have to do is make the party system impossible, and that will result when a sufficient number of men are instructed in its hypocrisies and follies and when men begin to ask for an opportunity to express their opinions at the polls. . . . Light on the nasty thing and an exposure of it are all that is necessary.[9]

The second book upon which both the Chestertons and Belloc would construct their attack on parliamentary politics was Belloc's single most important work, *The Servile State*, which appeared in 1912. Here Belloc also first articulated the alternative to socialism and capitalism called Distributism. In *The Servile State* Belloc prophesied that the socialists' attempts at wholesale nationalization would prove too difficult, and that there would be a compromise with capitalism, in which the owners of industry would be allowed to hold the means of production provided they accept the responsibility of keeping their workers in a tolerable living condition. The potentially revolutionary worker would be given security—in short, be bought off by bread and circuses—and thus, for all practical purposes, would become a slave to the capitalists and state bureaucrats.

This would result in a condition where the mass of men would be constrained by law to work for the profit of a minority. As the price of such constraint, the workers would be given the economic protection which capitalism could not provide, but the arrangement would guarantee to the ownership class a monopoly over the devices for producing wealth. The remedy to this system of slavery (the "servile state") which the Chestertons and Belloc demanded was a general redistribution of property into the hands of the widest number of people (in other words, Distributism, an idea derived from *Rerum Novarum*) in place of the present scheme in which a large proportion of property was concentrated in the hands of a few capitalists.

David Lloyd George's National Health Insurance Act (1911) was a major step toward the slave system Belloc warned against. In Belloc's mind, this act created two categories of citizenry: employers and masters, employed and subordinates. Citizens in one group were free but had the legal responsibility of securing the material well-being of their subordinates; citizens in the other were unfree and legally bound to their work but guaranteed a minimum sufficiency. The Insurance Act compelled the workers to register and pay taxes, and the employers to enforce registration and collect the taxes. Belloc believed that the government's continued expansion of unemployment benefits and labor exchanges facilitated the advance of the servile state, for it forced the worker, lacking ownership of the means of production, into a condition of further dependency upon his master.

It is important to realize that the Chestertons' and Belloc's critique of Parliament and their anti-statism were not eccentricities developed outside the mainstream of political and economic thinking. On the contrary, a sizeable element within the trade union movement and those in sympathy with it were moving in similar directions.[10] In this sense, the Chesterton brothers and Hilaire Belloc were part of a larger outburst of anti-establishment opinion. The most visible manifestation of this opposition was a plethora of strikes and various struggles which broke out within the labor movement in Britain prior to World War I. This protest movement not only dovetailed with but also was significantly influenced by the Chestertons' and Belloc's critique of British politics.

I I

A number of theories have been advanced to explain the working-class unrest during these years. Sir George Askwith, the Government's chief industrial advisor, blamed it on the failure of wages to keep up with rising costs of living, while the wealthy increased their conspicuous displays of luxury.[11] Sir Leo Money's *Riches and Poverty* (1905) had a great effect on the public's perception of this. Money used copious and convincing statistics to show the growth of national income and its shockingly unequal distribution. Socialists and Labour Party speakers made ample use of Money's data to bolster their arguments for a redistribution of wealth. Money's figures showed that, despite seven years of progressive reforms and legislation, the average working man was relatively worse off than he had been a decade before. G. D. H. Cole, the labor historian and pioneer of Guild Socialism, recognized the emergence of a new spirit of freedom in this working-class unrest. He called the mood a "new romanticism," though he later concluded that it was primarily a mass reaction against the inability either of trade union leadership or parliamentarianism to improve working-class living standards. Discontent also was fueled by the development of centralized industry-wide collective bargaining agreements, which overlooked particular local variables. On the other hand, many contemporaries believed that the unrest was directly inspired by revolutionary syndicalist ideas.[12]

In recent times, labor historians have tended to minimize the role of syndicalist ideas in these events. This also was the position of the leaders of the Parliamentary Labour Party during the times of unrest, namely, Philip Snowden and James Ramsay MacDonald.[13] The official historian of the South Wales Miners, R. Page Arnot, passes over the syndicalist issue rather hurriedly and considers its influence as transitory at best.[14] The labor historian Henry Pelling argues that syndicalist propaganda received wide publicity, but he believes that contemporary observers attributed to it more responsibility for unrest than it deserves. Active syndicalists were a tiny minority, in his view, and had little influence on union policy after 1912, being completely unsuccessful in their attempts to reorganize the workers along industrial lines. It is certainly true that Labour Party candidates who advocated "direct action" tactics had no success at the polls. Even the Labour Members returned in the radicalized Welsh constituencies in the 1910 election were of the so-called "Lib-Lab" (collaborators with the Liberal Party) persuasion. Pelling also de-emphasizes the anti-parliamentarianism of the trade union movement, maintaining instead that the workers were generally apathetic about politics prior to World War I. Pelling even argues that there is little evidence to substantiate significant working-class despair with the Labour Party during these years. Although there were disagreements about policy, including a revolt of disaffected groups within the Independent Labour Party in 1911, the major labor-affiliated associations, including the British Socialist Party, were not hostile to parliamentary methods.[15]

However, it appears that many labor historians, by focusing on the formal institutional dimensions of organized labor, may have overlooked the informal, local, and provincial levels of working-class sentiment. R. J. Holton, in a lengthy and detailed study of British syndicalism, has demonstrated considerable anarchist influence among the trade union rank and file. Significantly, he shows that there was a large degree of community involvement in the various coal and transportation strikes, which had the effect of forcing the moderate executive leaders to assume more militant policies.[16] Holton also gives evidence of wide-spread disillusionment with conventional parliamentary politics among the rank and file. In 1911, for example, three Devon men, S. Reynolds and Bob and Tom Woolley, published a revealing polemic entitled *Seems So! A Working-Class View of Politics*. The purpose of this essay was to record the views of the "voiceless" historical participants, and the evidence submitted was measurably different from what the institutional labor historians have told us. Its basic message was that working class men, though committed to political party allegiances, were nevertheless highly suspicious of the integrity of labor politicians once they entered Parliament. Much like Victor Grayson, the authors of *Seems So!* complained that Labour Members of Parliament had developed bourgeois mentalities and could no longer be trusted.[17]

Probably the strongest evidence of working-class disillusionment with parliamentary politics was the success of the revolutionary *Daily Herald,* which mounted a ceaseless assault on the Parliamentary Labour Party, and the failure of the *Daily Citizen,* a paper launched by the official labor movement to counteract the influence of the *Herald.*

From labor's inception as a political force, its leaders had been beset by left-wing critics whose purpose was to push the movement into more radical positions and programs. Leftist laborites generally chaffed against the restrictions of the parliamentary system. The founders of the Independent Labour Party (ILP), a national organization representing labor and socialist groups with the aim of building a socialist society, hoped to create a political party giving the working class an independent voice in Parliament. For this purpose, the ILP sought the support of the trade unions, not only to win their votes but also in the hope of using their funds for political purposes. Under the leadership of James Ramsay MacDonald and Philip Snowden, the ILP pursued a gradualist policy of reform through Parliament and urged Labour Members of Parliament to collaborate in this endeavor with the Liberal Party. MacDonald, a man more comfortable in the company of Liberals than of socialists, had a rather woolly idea about the meaning of socialism: in his words, it represented "the growth of society, not the uprising of a class."[18]

In order to secure Labour seats in Parliament, MacDonald and Snowden had a secret agreement with the Liberal Party not to oppose each other in districts where one or the other had a chance to win elections.[19] Both men consistently denied this, and neither their colleagues within the ILP nor the rank and file ever knew about the secret pact. The Parliamentary Labour Party, of which MacDonald became chairman in 1911, had a negligible impact on the House of Commons. The Party was unable to initiate any new legislation in the interest of its labor constituency, and attempts to increase its strength in by-elections ended in complete failure.

One explanation for Labour's unaggressive behavior was the more assertive policy initiated by the Liberals after 1906. In Parliament they assumed the role of social reformers and thereby stole Labour's thunder. After 1910 the Labourites became even more the prisoners of the Liberals. The general election of 1910 returned the two major parties with nearly equal strength, and now the Labour Members of Parliament had to be careful lest they turn the Liberal government out of office. Also, in 1909 the Labour Party was struck a potentially crippling blow by the passage of the Osborne Decision, in which the House of Lords ruled that the trade unions could not use their funds for political purposes. As a result, the Parliamentary Labour Party was bereft of funds necessary to support its Members of Parliament and to fight elections. Because of the Liberal Party's difficulties over Home Rule, it took Labour Members a long while to persuade the government to mitigate the effects of the Osborne Decision. David Lloyd George tried to deal with the problem by instituting state payment of Members of Parliament but did so only after the Parliamentary Labour Party agreed to support his National Insurance scheme.

Meanwhile, the Parliamentary Labour Party came under heavy fire from more radical elements, who felt that not enough was being done to further the cause of socialism. The militants' cause got an important boost in July 1907 when, in a by-election at Colne Valley, Victor Grayson was returned to Parliament as a self-styled "independent socialist." Grayson was a vociferous critic of the Parliamentary Labour Party's gradualist policies and asserted that the amenities of parliamentary life had divorced Labour Members of Parliament from the problems and life-styles of the workers. Although Grayson had the support of his local Independent Labour Party branch, the Labour Party had refused to back him, and, upon entering the House, he refused to sign the Party constitution. Grayson's contumacious conduct in Commons endeared him to labor militants throughout Britain, and he even managed to earn a worldwide reputation for himself. "Parliamentarians," said Grayson in one of his typically colorful but vitriolic perorations, "passed measures for the good of the people only when dragged from their hands by riot and bloodshed."[20]

By October 1908 Grayson's antics had become so outrageous that he was removed forcibly from Parliament. At this point, A. R. Orage convinced Grayson to become political editor of the *New Age*. The position provided Grayson with an excellent platform to vent his anti-parliamentary diatribes, and the *New Age* quickly reached new records in circulation. From the *New Age*, Grayson moved to Robert Blatchford's *Clarion*, where he came to exercise complete control over the paper's policy. Grayson published his views in a book, *The Problem of Parliament: A Criticism and a Remedy* (1909). Urging laborites to "fight" in both Parliament and in the constituencies, Grayson called for a new type of socialist party:

> If the same men are chairmen at the conference, officers of the executive, directors and editors of the official paper and wire-pullers of the political policy all at the same time, why not turn the whole thing into an absolute monarchy or . . . a composite Popedom inside a latter day Vatican.[21]

Grayson's ride to prominence suggested a serious dissatisfaction with the policy of the Labour Party. In 1908 Ben Tillett, leader of the successful 1889 London dock strike, issued an angry pamphlet entitled *Is the Parliamentary Party a Failure?* As part of labor's officialdom, Tillett expressed a minority opinion, though it was representative of the growing frustration of the lower ranks. Developing a line of criticism similar to that used by Cecil Chesterton, Tillett severely denounced MacDonald, Snowden, and others as hypocritical betrayers of their class for serving the interests of what he identified as the temperance-babbling puritans of the Liberal Party. In particular, Tillett condemned the Parliamentary Labour Party's support of such "red-herrings" as the Licensing Bill, which was not in the interests of the workers, and lamented that the more important issues of unemployment and hunger were regularly ignored.

A major event in the history of pre-war labor activity occurred with the return to England in 1910 of Tom Mann, who, along with Tillett, had been a leader of the 1889 London dock strike. Disappointed with the slow progress of social revolution, Mann had emigrated to Australia, where he became active in the labor movement. Mann's experience with state-controlled industry in Australia had undermined his confidence in collectivism, and he came to recognize that nationalization was not the means by which to bring on socialism, for it resulted "in domination by a bureaucracy, entirely in the interest of the capitalist class."[22] In addition, he had discovered that reformist parliamentary politicians and arbitration laws had emasculated the vigor of the Australian trade unions. While abroad, Mann had studied the writings of James Connolly, and, before returning to Britain, he traveled to Paris to learn more about French syndicalism. Mann's major concern was to warn the British workers about the dangers of state socialism and to rouse them against politicians who were taking over the leadership of the labor movement.

Mann's sojourn in Australia and his studies in Paris led him to embrace syndicalism, a doctrine that de-emphasized the efficacy of political reform and turned instead to the use of industrial action by workers to bring meaningful change. Mann became an advocate of industrial unionism, which called for the amalgamation of the multifarious trade associations into one large union that encompassed skilled and unskilled workers across trades and industry. Mann's conversion to syndicalism was extremely important for the British advocates of industrial unionism, because unlike many of the younger, brash, lesser-known rank-and-file syndicalists, Mann's prominent socialist and labor credentials meant that the labor leaders would be obliged to give him both respect and attention. With the assistance of Guy Bowman, Mann published a series of pamphlets that outlined methods for reorganizing the trade union movement along syndicalist lines. In November 1910 a syndicalist conference was held in Manchester, attended by some two hundred delegates representing sixty thousand workers. The conference authorized the creation of the Industrialist Syndicalist Education League (ISEL), which published a monthly journal entitled *The Syndicalist*. The ISEL set no restrictions on membership: it included members of the Independent Labour Party, the British Socialist Party, the Fabian Society, the Church Socialist League, and anarchists of all varieties.[23]

Mann's basic message was that the emancipation of labor could be effected only by the efforts of the working classes themselves, and this could be achieved chiefly by ceaseless struggle in the economic, not the political, arena. Instead of state socialism, which in reality would only ensure control of the government by the capitalists, the proletariat must seek ownership and control of the means of production. In order to accomplish this, *The Syndicalist* insisted that all workers join a union and that all the unions in a given industry unite together to achieve economic freedom. Mann initially did not reject parliamentary politics. His position was nonpolitical rather than antipolitical. Labor should use political tactics, but these were considered of only secondary importance, since, Mann believed, industrial action alone made political maneuvers effective. Essentially, Mann's ideas followed the tack of the industrial unionists, though the ISEL was criticized by some syndicalist groups for its refusal to reject political action altogether.[24] These criticisms ceased by the spring of 1911, since after the general election of 1910 and the growing labor unrest Mann became hostile to parliamentary politics. Instead, he supported what was called "direct action": the policy of workers initiating a fighting policy (by utilizing slowdowns, boycotts, and strikes) to overthrow the capitalist system rather than conciliating the establishment by participating in party politics. By July 1912 Mann could announce that "political action is of no use whatsoever."[25]

Mann's colleague, Guy Bowman, justified this new approach by pointing out that socialism via Parliament would mean bureaucracy, not freedom, a "new tyranny imposed by some six hundred political oracles." Syndicalism sought to liberate the laborer from the clutches of the bureaucrat by teaching him the necessity of self-reliance and individual initiative. The workers, wrote Bowman in the *Daily Herald,* "must think of themselves as something other than articles of merchandise that are bought and sold in the market place." Syndicalism, he explained, was but a means to an end in which the workers would realize their full humanity and need no experts to guide them, or officials to rule them.[26] Henceforth *The Syndicalist* declared that the industrially organized workers should themselves undertake control of both industries and the government. The means to this end was to be prepared as rapidly as possible through a general strike of national proportions.[27]

This outburst of syndicalist sentiment won over several significant elements within the organized labor movement. Echoing Cecil Chesterton, the Socialist Labour Party concluded that Labour's poor showing in the 1910 general election was a direct result of the Independent Labour Party's parliamentary action and its futile "advocacy of reforms": reforms, it argued, led away from socialism.[28] Working-class unrest after 1910 gave credence to this charge. In

November 1910 the Socialist Labour Party's journal, the *Socialist,* announced that the number of issues sold had increased by a thousand during the year and that the Party had a substantial increase in membership. Dissidents within the Independent Labour Party also became more sympathetic to the syndicalist message. Russell Smart, for example, concluded that socialist ideals had been sidelined by "electioneering" and only industrial action would stem the drift toward collectivism controlled by "officials of the class state."[29] Syndicalist ideas were clearly making inroads into the rank and file of labor. The unpopularity of parliamentary tactics reached alarming proportions in the National Boilermakers Union in 1913, when less than six thousand of its sixty-thousand membership voted to engage in political action. A vast majority of the Union members also opposed any kind of affiliation with the Labour Party.[30] Writing in the *Daily Herald* on 8 January 1912, E. W. Sessions claimed that in London and Manchester alone there were fifty thousand avowed syndicalists. Syndicalism also won a wide following in the London building trades,[31] among the railway men (with their own journal, *Syndicalist Railwayman*), and in the mining, engineering, and transport industries. Most importantly, the impact of syndicalist thinking on Jim Larkin and his efforts to organize the Irish transport workers is plain.

The growing dissatisfaction with labor's parliamentary party, the smoldering anger against orthodox trade union leadership, and the appeal of syndicalist thinking coincided with the emergence of Cecil Chesterton's and Hilaire Belloc's critique of party politics and Fabian collectivism. Both Cecil Chesterton and Belloc, along with many within the trade union movement, had recognized serious threats to the liberties of every man in the maturation of plutocratic politics.

III

The most outspoken and consistent supporter of the new spirit of working-class revolt was the unabashedly radical *Daily Herald,* a newspaper that also allowed the Chestertons and Belloc to make bridges into the labor world for the cause of Distributism. This remarkable enterprise was launched in April 1912 as an independent forum for those devoted to revolutionary causes. George Lansbury had controlling interest; it had the backing of Ben Tillett and the financial support of the Countess De La Warr (one of the first aristocratic labor sympathizers),[32] as well as the support of syndicalists and of the leading suffragettes. Lansbury had served as a Labour Member of Parliament, but in 1912, out of disgust with the leadership's refusal to attack the Insurance Bill, its failure to fight the Osborne Decision, and the executive's reluctance to support the vote for women, he resigned from the Party. Lansbury stood as an independent in 1912 but lost the election. He did not return to Westminster for another ten years. Even as Member of Parliament, Lansbury was skeptical of parliamentary politics. Writing in Cecil Chesterton's *Eye-Witness* in 1911, he called for the destruction of the party system through the force of public opinion.[33]

Under Lansbury, the *Daily Herald* was opened to any writer who proclaimed himself a rebel or an enemy of the capitalist system. G. K. Chesterton and Belloc were regular contributors, giving their services for little and sometimes no payment.[34] Although Lansbury worked hard to keep the *Herald* independent, and refused to follow any party line, the major syndicalist spokesmen tended to dominate its columns. Under Charles Lapworth, its editor until 1913, syndicalist propaganda was given preference over all other views. Moreover, leading syndicalists were heavily represented on the paper's management committee, all of which ensured revolutionary-minded opinion in the *Herald's* editorial positions.

Despite the blatant syndicalist proclivities of the *Daily Herald*, under Lansbury the paper made a concerted effort to remain open to all lines of dissident thought. Acting in this capacity, the *Herald* served as an important conduit for the cross-fertilization of Distributist, Christian Socialist, syndicalist, suffragette, and Guild Socialist ideas. Although these movements represented many varying opinions and divisions, they retained a unity of purpose when it came to the larger problems posed by state socialism and the power of capitalism. Belloc and the Chestertons, for example, were vehemently opposed to "votes for ladies" yet at times sympathized with, and even welcomed, suffragette militancy as a tool against the system. The *Herald* noted that the suffragettes were the first to rise against the party system. Not even the labor movement could claim this, wrote its correspondent, "G.R.S.T," for though labor supporters started with a similar political creed, they had been caught up in the parliamentary machine and were mangled in its gears. But the women with their contempt for politicians had taught labor a lesson: they exposed the hypocrisy of a government which claimed to be liberal but allowed half its population to remain political serfs. In this sense the women's movement had infinitely greater influence than simply a demand for the vote: it was part of a larger movement against a sham political system that was creating a servile society, and in rebelling against this system, the suffragettes were really at the side of Hilaire Belloc.[35]

Writers in the *Daily Herald*, despite their different political slants, generally viewed themselves as part of a family of freedom fighters giving battle to what Belloc had called "the servile state." In this sense, these contending schools of thought tended to merge together and complement one another as they assaulted the parliamentary and trade union establishments. Although the socialists who wrote for the *Herald* fundamentally disagreed with the proprietary objectives of the Distributists, there was a steady movement of ideas between the *Herald* and Belloc's and Cecil Chesterton's papers, the *Eye-Witness* and the *New Witness*. These papers had the highest praise for one another. Belloc, for instance, regarded the *Herald* as the only "free" paper available to the working man not controlled by the "official" press (it sold for a halfpenny), while the *New Witness* (selling for sixpence) and the *New Age* were the only two sources of independent news for the middle classes. Though they were different in character, Belloc believed that all three papers shared a common "thirst for freedom."[36]

The *Daily Herald* and the *Eye-Witness* and *New Witness* had similar objectives in throwing their support to the plethora of strikes throughout the period from 1910 to 1914. They attacked the labor proponents of conventional party politics and waged a constant struggle against the National Insurance Act and the Marconi scandal. Belloc's warnings about the impingement of servile legislation led the *Herald* to rebel against every move to increase the powers of the state. In the words of the *Herald's* correspondent, "no one has better claim than Mr. Belloc to claim the honour of being one of the leaders of that revolt."[37] In one of its infrequent and short-lived reformist moods, the *Herald* picked up on the *New Witness's* call for proportional representation as a means for breaking the power of those who pull the wires of Parliament.[38] The *Herald* correspondent hoped for a drastically altered parliamentary structure in which the House of Commons (which the *Herald* dubbed the "House of Pretence") would be replaced by a central assembly similar to the Trades-Union Congress, representing the interests of those who work, rather than "a Parliament along Westminster's lines which only represents those who produce nothing."[39] The syndicalist Leonard Hall, another regular correspondent for the *Herald*, reviewed *The Servile State* in November 1912. Although Hall could not accept its Catholic and Distributist conclusions, he agreed completely with its analysis of the prevailing political trends and declared that no better critique of the capitalist system had ever been written.[40]

In December 1912 Cecil Chesterton wrote a provocative essay in the *Daily Herald* asking the question: "Is socialism dead?" The point of the article was to force socialists to reconsider the old objective of state ownership of the means of production and the notion of using the state as the main tool for the construction of a socialist society. The question triggered a series of responses by prominent dissidents, including Lansbury, Mann, Arthur Lewis, and others, most of whom concurred, in one way or another, with Cecil's anti-collectivism and admitted that they no longer had complete faith in the state as a suitable agency for the achievement of socialism.

A major event for the *Daily Herald* was G. K. Chesterton's decision to join the paper after he broke with the *Daily News* in February 1913. Chesterton informed the *Herald's* readers that he thought it better to resign from the *Daily News* before the next great measure of social reform made it illegal to go out on strike (referring to the government's introduction of labor conciliation boards, to which he was implacably opposed). Chesterton's move to the *Herald* was a front-page story; the importance of the event was revealed in the fact that his weekly column appeared for a time on page 1, something the paper had never done for anyone else.

The *Daily Herald* was clearly the single most important organ of anti-parliamentary opinion in Britain. Its campaign was bolstered considerably by the establishment of the Herald League, which took the paper's message into localities and byways that never could have been reached by newspapers alone. This organization was founded mainly to raise funds at the grass-roots level in order to keep the *Herald* solvent, but it quickly expanded its mission, becoming a vehicle for social, political, and cultural activity. Like the columns of the *Herald* itself, the League was open to all schools of dissident thought, though syndicalists and their fellow travelers seemed to be in the majority. The prominent industrial unionist A. D. Lewis, for example, was national secretary of the League. League members—known as "Heraldites"—addressed one another as "comrades" and "rebels." The ideal "Heraldite" was someone independent in spirit, self-reliant in personal life, and passionately devoted to social reconstruction. G. K. Chesterton wrote a letter to the League saying that he was sorry that he could not attend its inaugural meeting in London, but he applauded its campaign and offered his services to the cause. Belloc also spoke at League meetings. The Herald League generally became involved in the kinds of activities that the Clarion Clubs had undertaken (sponsoring social events and lectures, and doing propaganda work) and, along with the *Eye-Witness's* League for Clean Government, may have provided the inspiration for the New Witness League and the *G.K.'s Weekly*–affiliated Distributist League. Probably the Herald League's most conspicuous contribution to revolutionary activity was its service to the Irish workers during the great Dublin lockout and its subsequent sponsorship of Jim Larkin's British lecture tour.

The *Daily Herald* gave the critics of labor's parliamentary policies, those who opposed the growth of big government, and the foes of conventional trade-union practices a badly-needed forum for airing their unconventional ideas. In doing so, the *Herald* helped to liberate debate from the ideological constraints imposed by the Parliamentary Labour Party and the official trade-union leadership.

IV

The anti-statist campaign of the working-class *Daily Herald* was complemented by an equally radical assault on the politics of the establishment by a few independent journals that represented revolutionary middle-class opinion. One of the most influential of these was A. R. Orage's *New Age*.

Orage and Holbrook Jackson purchased this weekly in the summer of 1907. A major source of support for the venture was the Fabian Arts Group. This group consisted of leading members of the Fabian society who resented the domination of the Webbs and their policies, which they criticized as "collectivist" and prone to an insidious growth in bureaucracy. This splinter group included George Bernard Shaw, H. G. Wells, Lowes Dickinson, and Eric Gill. The *New Age* supporters believed that the Fabian emphasis on state socialism had the potential to stifle individualism; this would result not only in plutocratic political control but would also place a dead hand on art and philosophy. Orage's and Jackson's journal was meant to provide a platform for ideas outside the scope of conventional Fabian discussion, above all for the views of such modern thinkers as Nietzsche, Ibsen, Tolstoy, and Shaw. Many of the writers who contributed to Orage's journal (by the end of 1907 he had sole ownership), though they did not share similar political views, were in revolt against what they discerned to be the decadence of contemporary British social thought. The *New Age's* special mission was laid out in the first issue: the editors declared that "Socialism as a means to the intensification of man is even more necessary than Socialism as a means to the abolition of economic poverty."[41] Orage, for his part, had been very much influenced by Nietzsche and his interpretation of the Dionysian myth. Dionysus was identified with elemental energy, irrational yet democratic, which could be unleashed against institutions that had lost their vitality. It was just such a force that Orage, Shaw, and Wells hoped to attach to socialism as an *élan vital*, a creative power giving men the will to revitalize society. Those who wrote for the *New Age* also called for a hero who would rescue society from the corruption of plutocracy and collectivism. Cecil Chesterton spoke of Caesar; Lowes Dickinson talked of Plato's Guardians; Wells idealized *Bushido*, the chivalric code of the samurai; Gill was passionately devoted to Nietzsche's Zarathustra; and, of course, Shaw championed the Superman. As for Orage, he wrote:

There is no doubt that such ideas as that contained in the Samurai, and again, as that of the Superman, bear a close relationship, if not with actual polices of today, with the near development of the saner political outlook.[42]

In 1908 the *New Age* mounted a long and sustained attack on the Labour Party and the ILP, its chief complaint being that they had failed to uphold revolutionary socialist principles. Grayson's parliamentary harlequinades were hailed as "Dionysian," for they represented the irrational, energized qualities that Nietzsche had extolled. It was during these early years of the *New Age* that Cecil Chesterton began his attacks on the Labour Party, and the paper's editorial policy tended to support his line of argument. Like Belloc and Cecil Chesterton, Orage favored the state payment of members of Parliament because it would free Labour delegates from the clutches of their party caucus. In this sense, Orage denied the legitimacy of the party system. By 1910 Orage had begun to question the relationship between the socialist movement and politics, since he had become convinced that the Labour Party was incapable of absorbing any new socialist ideas. Obviously what was needed, claimed the *New Age*, was a new ". . . personality, intensely individual" and "scornful of the usual bonds of society," a model for true anarchists and revolutionists.[43]

It is not surprising that the *New Age* would welcome the outburst of syndicalist activity, for here was a manifestation of the Dionysian vitalism needed to recharge the socialist movement. The *New Age* editorial of 15 September 1910 concluded that labor's participation in conventional politics was a wasteful expedient, which to date had produced nothing of value. The governing class, the paper contended, was far more afraid of the workingman's strike than his vote. Orage subsequently welcomed the policy of the general strike, not just for its pragmatic value but also because of the moral and spiritual energy it would unleash. The attempts to organize labor politically had failed, though Orage was not surprised; he believed that the workers, being uneducated and untrained, indeed lacking a political tradition altogether, had nothing in their backgrounds to prepare them for such a task. Consequently, the *New Age* considered the Osborne Decision a disguised blessing, since it would force the trade unionists to do what they knew best: combat capitalism through industrial action. Even more importantly, the Osborne ruling might free the trade unions from the leadership of the Parliamentary Labour Party, which was forcing the movement down the road to collectivism. The *New Age* ultimately concluded that the best approach was the dissolution of the Parliamentary Labour Party and the separation of socialists from the trade union movement altogether. The task of tending to theory should be given to middle-class intellectuals, independent of trade unions and political parties, who could further the cause of socialism by drawing on their tradition of learning and engaging in propaganda on a vast scale. The trade unions, being freed from the unfamiliar burdens of political work, could turn their talents to organizing for economic purposes.[44]

Although they fought the same enemies, Belloc had strong disagreements with Orage's elitist views, especially the notion that nothing could help the workingman except the intelligence of the middle class: when Orage is "cut off from religion," said Belloc, "his stupidity is intolerable."[45] Yet the *New Age* had the support of Distributists and syndicalists in its call for industrial action. Tom Mann, for example, wanted trade unionism separated from all political activity and urged the workers to develop their own self-reliance through the industrial union.[46] Belloc and the Chestertons concurred.

Orage, however, could not give his imprimatur to syndicalism per se, for he feared that too much trade union power could lead to a tyranny of its own. A bridge between syndicalism and the *New Age* appeared in the theory of Guild Socialism. As a philosophy, Guild Socialism emerged out of the thinking of A. J. Penty, Hilaire Belloc, Maurice Reckitt, and others, but the variety championed by the *New Age* was a synthesis of these ideas put together by S. G. Hobson. For a time, the Guild Socialism developed in the *New Age* provided hope and sustenance for those middle-class socialists who had lost faith in the Labour Party and the ILP. It also had strong appeal for those in the Fabian Society, where the idea was taken up by G. D. H. Cole and other young people active in the Fabian Labour

Research Department. Guild Socialist thinking made inroads into the Christian Socialist movement as well, being particularly attractive to High Anglicans who were opposed to the state's intrusion into the affairs of the Church.

S. G. Hobson, who articulated the variety of Guild Socialism supported by Orage, had left the Fabian Society in January of 1909, after he failed to convince its leaders to withdraw its affiliation with the Parliamentary Labour Party and to authorize the creation of an avowed Socialist Party. Central to Hobson's criticism of the Labour Party was that it could not free itself from the grip of capitalism unless it became penetrated with the spirit of revolution. By 1911 he concluded that the force for change would come not from political action but only through aggressive industrial fighting. In Hobson's mind the engine-room of social and economic power lay in the workplace:

> Wealth is produced by the workers at the bench, in the factory, in the mine, and (since distribution is an integral part of production) on the railway, in the ship, and in the carrier's van. The power is in the boiler and not in the gauge. Parliament is only the gauge and index; it has no other use.[47]

Hobson believed that the source of working-class servility was the system of wages imposed on labor by those who owned the means of production. Labor's dependency upon the capitalists was ensured by its transformation into a commodity that was subjected to inhumane laws of the market place. Like Belloc, whose anti-collectivism had considerable influence on him, Hobson recognized that political reform and state ownership of the means of production were useless unless the wage system were destroyed. All the legislation supported by the Liberal and Labour parties—the National Insurance Act, the Eight-Hour Day, the Shops Act, and so on—was based on the continuance of the wage system, which perpetuated labor's dependency and guaranteed that economic benefits would continue to accrue to the capitalists. In addition, the expansion of the government into economic matters brought with it larger bureaucracies which increased the state's control over the individual worker. The full emancipation of labor would be possible only after the workers had absorbed every shilling of surplus value, and this necessitated the elimination of rent, profits, and interest.

As a means to this end, Hobson called for the creation of industrial unions that could mobilize a general strike with the specific objective of winning working-class control of the means of production. Under Hobson's scheme, the workers would join national guilds that would have complete control over economic matters. The state, in contrast to the syndicalists' proposals, would not wither away but would simply lose its control over the economy and concentrate exclusively on political administration. Hobson's vision of Guild Socialism was intended to be a solution to the antithetical demands of syndicalism and state socialism; whereas both asked for exclusive management and control over the economy and government, Guild Socialism combined the extremes into a scheme of joint management.[48]

Guild Socialism made converts in the Fabian Society through the work of G. D. H. Cole and William Mellor, two Oxford intellectuals who shared the anti-statism of the syndicalists and Distributists.[49] Both were rebelling against the bureaucratization inherent in collectivism, the reformism of the Labour Party, and the slow advances of the Webbs toward socialism. Cole and his disciples sported red ties and purposely engaged in outlandish revolutionary behavior in order to shock the staid leadership of the Fabian Society. Like most other middle-class intellectuals sympathetic to syndicalist sentiment, Cole was in search of a force that would lead Britain out of the quagmire of Belloc's servile state. Part of the reason he and his colleagues took such an interest in syndicalism (and this was true of Belloc, Gill, Penty, Orage, Hobson, and others as well) was that it provided an approach to the ideals of William Morris: syndicalism offered a form of organization that regarded the workers as "producers" and gave them the freedom to be creative with their labor.

Cole's book, *The World of Labour* (1913), one of the best contemporary discussions of syndicalism, drew heavily on Ruskin, Morris, Belloc, and G. K. Chesterton to make its case for Guild Socialism. Unlike other British aficionados of syndicalism, who were influenced primarily by the American version,[50] Cole had given

French syndicalist theory a close study, and in his discussion of it used turns of phrase that resonated with the rhetoric of Henri Bergson and Georges Sorel. *The World of Labour,* for instance, attacked Fabianism primarily because it was a creed lacking the *élan vital* necessary to rejuvenate society. Thus Cole welcomed the appearance of syndicalism: he saw it as a vitalizing impulse to action, articulating the will of the laboring man.

Cole's position on the trade unions differed sharply from that of his mentors, Beatrice and Sidney Webb. In their plans, the trade unionists were not given a particularly responsible role to play. They were to be excluded from industrial decisions with respect to production and given duties mainly in areas concerning employment. Cole, on the other hand, envisioned unions as the driving force not just for change but also as a means for assuring working-class control over its own affairs once the old system passed away. Like Hobson, Cole called for industrial unions and the abolition of the wage system, both of which would encourage more active citizenship among the laboring class. Cole's proposals differed from the *New Age*'s version of Guild Socialism in a few crucial areas. First, in terms of implementation, he did not believe in the efficacy of the general strike. It was too disruptive and would not draw in new working-class recruits. Second, Cole rejected the syndicalist proposition that industrial action alone would bring on socialism. At least until 1913, he saw the need for some kind of political action, though he had no faith whatever in parliamentarianism. Finally, unlike the *New Age,* Cole was willing to give the state a larger role in the guild system. He was especially concerned that the interests of the consumer be protected. Thus his scheme rejected Hobson's separation of economic and political functions and gave the state co-partnership with the guilds: the state would own the means of production, but the guilds would be responsible for controlling the industrial processes.[51]

The advocates of Guild Socialist theories did not form a unified school of thought. Cole and the *New Age* had their differences, and both were opposed by the Distributist version of Guild Socialism.[52] Belloc, Penty, and the Chestertons, for example, criticized the so-called "National Guildsmen" of the *New Age* because of their acceptance of the factory system, their failure to insist on absolute ownership for the guilds, and their willingness to uphold large-scale organization, which would have the tendency to multiply bureaucracies. Belloc had long predicted the collapse of large-scale capitalist industrialism. Hence, he saw no reason to superimpose an alternative scheme of production on an "abnormal" economic structure, which carried the seeds of its own destruction. Most importantly, the Distributists objected to the large-scale organizational objectives of the *New Age* version of guild socialism. In Penty's view, one insuperable obstacle stood in the path of this approach: all the guild's activities would become choked by the necessity of working through a multiplicity of bureaucracies. Because the average committeeman would get lost in the complexity of details, there would be a natural tendency for power to migrate into the hands of professional bureaucrats. Thus the guild movement could ultimately develop into an inverted form of the bureaucratic monster it initially set out to destroy. To guard against the evil of bureaucracy, Penty insisted upon the utilization of small, self-governing guilds, exercising control on the local level:

> The units of their organization must be as small as is consonant with the function they are required to perform. And if for such purposes as those of finance and the buying of material a larger unit is found desirable, then the larger unit must consist of federated groups. . . .[53]

Like Penty, Belloc also feared that the *New Age* scheme would bind workers to industrial bodies too large for them to control: "You'll have 'leaders' and 'parliamentary committees' and the rest of the rubbish."[54] This would mean that the administration of the guild, though nominally subject to its members, would ultimately fall into the hands of some caucus or machine.

The other two important journals of middle-class opinion that supported revolutionary syndicalism were Cecil Chesterton's and Hilaire Belloc's *Eye-Witness* and its successor, Cecil Chesterton's *New Witness*. The style of these papers and the issues they raised were very similar to those of the *New Age*. Indeed, when the *Eye-Witness* was launched, it drew a number of writers and readers away from Orage's journal, and the *New Age* suffered a serious decline in circulation. The papers of Belloc and Chesterton may have given the *New Age* competition, but it was a friendly philosophical rivalry, and, most importantly, they considered each other as allies in the battle against a common enemy.

Both the *Eye-Witness* and the *New Witness* were chiefly concerned with exposing the secrecy surrounding the political process and laying bare the dangers involved in the encroachment of the state. They focused their energies on two main issues: the National Insurance Act and the corruption involved in the so-called Marconi affair. The *Eye-Witness* interpreted the National Insurance Act as the first major step towards a slave society, in that the entire working force in Britain would be controlled by a state bureaucracy; it also believed that the real motive of the act, like that of the Taff Vale Decision (which ruled that trade unions could be held liable for damages during a strike) and the Osborne Decision, was the destruction of the economic power of the trade unions.[55] The National Insurance Act allowed management to deny coverage to workers discharged for misconduct, and it denied benefits to men on strike. The *Eye-Witness* regarded this as an irrevocable step toward the coercion of labor and as a denial of the employee's freedom. Most significantly, the act stipulated that union unemployment assistance funds could not be used for militant purposes. The Chestertons and Belloc believed that the Labour Party's support of the act was the product of parliamentary chicanery. The plutocrats of Commons had co-opted the Labour Member of Parliament: he had become part of the party system and could no longer represent working-class interests. When the trade union leadership failed to rouse their men against the act, Cecil Chesterton believed that the corruptive disease had permeated the labor movement as a whole. He now recognized the victory of a new kind of trade union official, who, along with Labour Members of Parliament, toured the country, sat in a comfortable London office hundreds of miles away from the nearest workman, and conducted negotiations with capitalists whom he considered charming fellows.[56] The average worker also recognized this, and his disgust with such leadership was responsible for the outbreak of strikes afflicting Britain. The *Eye-Witness* argued that

the time for "political action" would come when the workers organized industrially, realized the treachery of the politician, and set out
not to cooperate with him, but to smash him.

The paper was very clear about what the workers could do about
their predicament. In its lead article of 7 August 1911 it supported
Tom Mann completely and urged the workers to reject their parliamentary leadership (a thoroughly middle-class set of men divorced
from the populace) and to "organize from below." Rejecting the government's scheme for conciliation and arbitration committees as a
means for settling disputes (as contained in the Labour Disputes
Bill), the *Eye-Witness* insisted that the workers must always have the
right to strike rapidly and without notice. Both the *Eye-Witness* and
later the *New Witness* were firm in their support of the strike as a
legitimate weapon of labor and regularly condemned the government's efforts to end strikes through political means. They also lent
their editorial voices to the spread of industrial unionism and were
sanguine about revolutionary changes arising from it. In the words
of Belloc:

> If great masses of labour develop the power to organise from
> below, to insist upon corporate demands, to treat individual
> delegates as their servant, to mistrust labour 'representation' and
> develop a watchdog agency, then there will be great change in
> the industrial towns of England.[57]

Belloc and his associates also took a more active role resisting
those forces that oppressed labor. For example, Belloc was adviser
to the Insurance Tax Resister's Defense Association, which helped
draft pamphlets against the Insurance Act. Upon his advice, this
organization championed what Belloc called the "Voluntary Principle," meaning that workers should not be required to join the
national insurance program. Belloc's alternative to Lloyd George's
plan would have required employers to foot the entire cost of insurance through tax paid directly to the state. Priority for benefits
would be given to subscribers with the lowest family incomes—
whom he estimated to number three million—whereas only the
remaining funds generated by the tax would be distributed to trade

unions and friendly societies. There would be no compulsion in this system. In Belloc's plan the neediest would be helped first, workers would be free to choose their own insurance societies and doctors, and there would be no state official to interfere between them and their freedom. The genius of this scheme was that there would be no opportunity for capitalists to control the workers, while financing of the plan would come from those most able to afford it—"The million of well-to-do who were above the income tax limits."[58]

The Insurance Tax Resister's Defense Association wrote members of the political parties and candidates for public office that it would campaign against anyone who refused to support legislation to make state insurance voluntary. The group urged employers to assist any employee who did not wish to register. In addition to propaganda work against compulsory insurance, the association helped defend many who resisted the National Insurance Act. Their efforts appeared to have had some success in winning converts to the voluntary principle: the *Daily Mail* and the *Globe* took up the idea, and Lord Robert Cecil in speeches at Bethnal Green and Yeovil declared his conviction that compulsion should be abolished.[59]

However, Belloc and his friends also were prepared to entertain extralegal means to reach their ends. The Anti–Insurance Act Committee, for instance, was formed by George Lansbury, Belloc, and others (John Scurr of the dockers' union was president) to head a public campaign to smash the Insurance Act's poll tax by organizing workers to tear up their insurance cards on an agreed-upon date, whereupon they would refuse to permit any further deductions from their paychecks. The Committee reported progress in awakening rank-and-file trade unionists to the dangers of the legislation. It appears that Belloc himself, through various unnamed contacts, even tried to convince a big London labor union to strike against the act. It was important, he insisted, that a move against the Insurance Act be undertaken by those who were oppressed by the legislation, for the politicians themselves would never have the courage to overturn the act, nor would they dare prosecute workers who struck against it.[60]

The most objectionable part of the National Insurance Act was that it created an army of officials who descended on the laboring community, compelling workers to register at labor exchanges where a variety of personal information was recorded. In the words of the Anti–Insurance Act Committee, here the workers were "ticketed and docketed by officials by means of a secret code, which is as follows: looks; clothes; cleanliness; height; strength; sight; speech; hearing."[61] Such data then became part of a worker's private file. Upon receiving a compensation claim, the local labor exchange official consulted a worker's dossier and then sent the applicant's previous employer a form asking for comments. Not only was this an untenable intrusion into the private lives of the citizenry, it also could be a considerable weapon in the hands of employers who might "wish to crush active spirits in the ranks of organized workers."[62]

In a number of articles in various journals and newspapers, Belloc was blunt in his defense of the workers' use of the strike. In the breach of collective bargaining agreements, he claimed, the strike was a morally justified expedient, a legitimate weapon in what had become an issue of class warfare. Since the circumstances surrounding the drafting of such agreements were unequal, the bargains, said Belloc, should have no binding force.[63]

Most importantly, in Belloc's view, the increasing industrial turmoil reflected a shift in the consciousness of the English working class. The workers' hopes and aspirations of earlier times, when thrift and a commitment to labor diligently in the tasks of one's calling had provided access into the ranks of the bourgeoisie, had disappeared. The workers now took the condition of industrial society for granted, and this produced a new moral outlook: "the proletariat now think of themselves as proletariat." As Marx himself would have explained it, the recognition of a class enemy had produced a revolutionary consciousness in the English working class. They despised the system that oppressed them and now were committed to its destruction.[64]

In Belloc's mind the most efficacious method for breaking the chains that bound the laboring classes was the "wildcat" strike, a work stoppage carried out spontaneously and without tangible organization, hitting the owner rapidly with no advance notice. The August 1911 carmen and dockers' strike succeeded, Belloc noted, precisely because it was unanimously supported by the rank and file, was unexpected, and did not involve the bureaucratic leadership of the trade unions. The whole thing, he remarked, had a "military quality about it."[65] Conversely, the railway strike of 1911 failed because the workers relied on their leaders and bureaucratic organizations. Instead of striking unexpectedly "as all men do in a military effort," the railway men gave advance warning, which alerted the government of the necessity to mobilize the armed forces to run the railroads. Although the government kept an even balance between labor and management during the conflict, it sympathized strongly with the capitalists, argued Belloc, and in fact would have sided with the owners if the strike had continued. The men only went back to work because their "so-called leaders" in London lied to them by announcing that the trade union had won a great victory and that the men should return to work. In fact, nothing had been won except the government's commitment to establish a Royal Commission (with no power, and upon which no labor representatives were invited to participate) that would consider working-class grievances. The men were thus duped, said Belloc, and doubly so, since from this time on their interests would be represented by Labour MPs who manipulated trade union officials for their own self-serving purposes. These politicians, in particular, J. Ramsay MacDonald and Philip Snowden, were not even working class in origin, but "theoretically socialists of the regular middle class type" motivated chiefly by private interests and the advancement of their own careers. They had been "captured by the Liberal machine" through the offer of salaries and the actual payment of public money.[66]

Cecil Chesterton and Belloc were disappointed when the strikes were settled without a complete victory for labor. In most cases, they blamed the leadership for bamboozling the rank and file. But in the long run, the *Eye-Witness*, much like the *New Age*, concluded that something spiritual was missing in the labor movement. Conditions were so bad that the workman revolted, but it was a rebellion of the "body" and not of the "soul." The problem with British labor was that the bodily demand was not accompanied by any spiritual force.[67]

The quasi-revolutionary working-class unrest brought a variety of ideas for social and political reform into public discussion. Many socialists and progressives of varying hues, for example, seized upon the introduction of a minimum wage as a fundamental mechanism for improving the condition of labor. This was a remedy supported by many socialists and especially pushed by the Catholic Social Guild. But from the outset the Chestertons and Belloc vehemently opposed the idea as a dangerous subterfuge, an insidious substitute for what labor really needed—ownership of the means of production.[68] Belloc disagreed with the concept because he feared it could become part of a series of legal decisions that might make the minimum wage a national standard wage: "*compelling* the capitalists to pay at least so much for a particular form of labor will *involve* the growth of a corresponding right to see that the labor is performed."[69] If the advocacy of a minimum wage were championed by those desiring to destroy capitalism, then Belloc could support it as a first step toward that end. But since he was convinced it was being forwarded by those hoping to save the present economic system by stanching labor unrest, he would have no part of the package. The minimum wage in the end would produce "compulsory labor," since disputes between workers and management would be turned over to the newly created arbitration courts which, declared Belloc, were managed by the government to support the owners of capital.[70]

Belloc's brief career in Parliament had caused him to despair of reforming England's political traditions from within. Eventually, after the years of labor unrest, he concluded that the parliamentary system itself, as currently constructed, was unsuited to provide governance for Britain. There were several signs of its structural failures. The most obvious was that the basic demands of the wage earners ("the great mass of the English people," as Belloc said) were being expressed not in Parliament but rather out on the streets. Another indicator of parliamentary dysfunction was that the good and talented men who wished to serve the commonwealth no longer believed this could be done by entering the House of Commons (after all, was not Belloc's own parliamentary career proof of this?). And finally, Belloc argued, the man on the street simply had lost interest in what was said and done in Parliament. The "spirit of representative government" had disappeared in the land. Any intelligent MP recognized this and, for this reason, no longer regarded the public political constituency as his master. He now marched to the commands of the real power brokers, the money clique who controlled the party funds.

Prior to 1914 Belloc had hopes that the political system could be reformed through a combination of spotlight journalism, a public auditing of the party funds, payment of members, and proportional representation for the second chamber. This last idea, Belloc believed, would allow minority representation and give voice to a cross-section of opinion heretofore denied political expression. The caucus system potentially might manipulate members of the second chamber just as it did the current party representatives in the House of Commons, but at least it would be more difficult, especially over larger constituencies.[71] Belloc also was prepared to support state payment of MPs. As a matter of principle this would further the democratic process and perhaps even hasten the breakup of the party system by allowing dissidents easier access to Parliament.[72]

Cecil Chesterton, for his part, seemed to think that change could best come through militant parliamentary action.[73] In the summer of 1912, for instance, Cecil Chesterton urged labor to develop tactics similar to those of Charles Stewart Parnell's parliamentary party and the Irish Land League. Parnell's colleagues coordinated obstructionist tactics within Parliament while simultaneously directing the essentially revolutionary action of Irish peasants from without. Parnell won the admiration of the Irish people through his aggressive parliamentary policy; simultaneously, by means of the Land League's militancy, he had made government impossible and encouraged revolution. The *Eye-Witness* suggested that labor needed a similar two-pronged approach: a group in Commons to fight the machine and, simultaneously, an industrial army of labor animated by the same spirit that moved the Land League.[74] Unfortunately, such a bold program required another Parnell, or, as Cecil Chesterton once suggested, a Caesar.

By early 1914 Belloc had come to the conclusion that the reforms he and the *Eye-Witness* and the *New Witness* had earlier supported could only temporarily slow down the decay, at best. An honest auditing of the party funds would be difficult since the caucus would control the procedure; proportional representation might help in the short run, but only if it were coupled by payment of election expenses through public funds.[75] Yet all these proposals were mere mechanical tinkerings with a system beyond the hope of repair. Parliamentary representative governments were now everywhere under attack for the evil consequences of what they produced in each country that accepted the form: "the obedience of parliamentary puppets to financial masters, the welter of petty personal intrigue, the mediocrity of those who achieved power by such intrigue, the unreality of the subjects proposed for debate, and the sham of 'opposition.'"[76] Belloc looked outside England to France, whose revolutionary experiences had popularized the so-called "representative" theory, as the barometer of international political change. When parliamentary government is no longer tolerated in France, said Belloc, the forces of its appeal will be broken everywhere. Moreover, in his view the collapse in France had begun.

By 1914 there was only one other alternative for saving the remnants of a bankrupt parliamentary form of government that Belloc was willing to consider: an addition to Parliament of another type of constituency based not on geographical representation but on vocational groupings along the lines of the medieval guilds. This was a political program that French and Austrian Catholic corporativists had been recommending ever since the closing decades of the nineteenth century. Parliamentary representation from its inception was based on the assumption that the locality was the true unit of the state. But the importance of geographic locality had been superseded by the varying economic interests of the times, in which a man's identity was bound up with his employment. Men sitting for special interests of the vocational kind, representing real-life activities with which they were attached, could revivify English politics: "You would have many speaking at Westminster for the wage earners of the iron, the cotton, the mining, the shipping industries . . . others far less numerous speaking for the interests of capital . . . others for the special interests of the various professions . . . [others for] landowners; others for the peasantry and so forth."[77]

Ultimately, the issue that pushed the journalism of Cecil Chesterton and Belloc to the radical fringes during these interwar years was the infamous Marconi scandal. Cecil took the lead in directing his paper's attacks on the ministers involved, beginning in

August 1912, and his extremist behavior eventually led to his trial and conviction for libel. The Marconi affair, discussed in more detail in chapter 8, indicated that high-ranking government officials were taking kickbacks in the awarding of state contracts. The front benches of both parties clearly soft-pedaled the issue, and those involved not only failed to be reprimanded but were advanced to the highest offices in the land. For the *Eye-Witness* and the *New Witness,* the financial and political dealings in the Marconi case were final proof of the venal and plutocratic character of British government and conclusive evidence of the workings of the wicked party system. The *New Age* and the *Daily Herald,* which covered the episode in great detail, completely supported Chesterton's position throughout the affair and also drew upon the Marconi case as clear proof of the cancerous effects of the party system.

Although Belloc and Cecil Chesterton launched the *Eye-Witness* as a joint partnership, editorial responsibility was mainly Belloc's. In June 1912, Belloc publicly stated that he needed a respite from the rigors of this task and resigned as editor, selling his shares in the paper to Cecil Chesterton. Belloc indeed may have been tiring of the demands of managing a newspaper, but there were other reasons for his formal departure from the *Eye-Witness.* It appears that Belloc found Cecil Chesterton's journalistic style a bit too strong even for his own feisty tastes. The *Eye-Witness* experienced financial difficulties by the autumn of 1912 (the Chestertons and Belloc refused to rely on advertising because it might compromise their independence—thus their papers depended on private backers) and folded by November. However, Cecil was able to put together enough money from his father to reacquire the paper under the title of the *New Witness.* Belloc contributed financially to the enterprise and wrote for the paper on a regular basis, since he shared Cecil's views for the most part. But the *New Witness* under Cecil's editorship became more extremist in its political muckraking, assuming a style much more shrill and monomaniacal than that of the *Eye-Witness.* The paper's campaigns were also marred by a crude anti-Semitism that frequented its pages. Belloc was constantly obliged to defend Cecil's behavior to friends and financial backers. He privately admitted that he did not approve of everything that appeared in the paper and was concerned that the public might think that he was responsible for its contents. As Belloc told E. S. P. Haynes, a close confidant and financial backer of the *New Witness,* Cecil "shares many of my ideas, but not all of them. But that is a very different thing from editorial responsibility."[78]

The early *Eye-Witness* was also scrappy and abrasive in its attempts to expose corruption, but unlike Cecil's paper, it was reasonably well-informed about its subject matter because Belloc had personal contacts who apprised him of the inside business of government. The *New Witness* lacked such inside information, and, because of insufficient money to pay investigators, the alleged facts it publicized were not always properly verified. All of this, in conjunction with Cecil's proclivity for indulging in *ad hominem* attacks, gave Belloc cause for alarm. This kind of policy brought Cecil and his paper national attention when he helped expose the Marconi scandal, but Cecil's reckless allegations led to his conviction for libel.

However, the *New Witness's* exposure of those involved in the Marconi affair proved to be a watershed in the history of Chesterbellocian journalism. The paper's successors, *G.K.'s Weekly* and the *Weekly Review,* cited the scandal as conclusive evidence of the evil machinations of the party system. G. K. Chesterton regarded the event as a turning point in his own career, indeed, a turning point for English politics in general, and it proved to be a factor in the hardening of his political attitudes: "It was during the agitations upon that affair that the ordinary English citizen lost his invincible ignorance; or in ordinary language, his innocence.[79]

Various dissident movements and radical journalists were reacting against the growing power of the British state and its policies prior to World War I. Although the syndicalists, Guild Socialists, and the Distributists had considerable philosophical disagreements, they were nevertheless conscious of being part of a common effort to resist the onslaught of a society engineered by adherents of state socialism. Rather than emphasizing the differences, which are obvious, it is important to keep in mind what these disparate groups had in common. A major concern of the syndicalists and the revolutionary press was to stop the drift toward collectivism and, at the same time, begin building a new, more democratic society that would guarantee freedom to the individual. To accomplish this, the rot in Parliament had to be excised. This required both the elimination of the sham system of party politics and a restructuring of the political order. A means to this end was the construction of a new style of labor organization in the form of industrial unionism. All these movements supported in some fashion the concept of industrial unionism. For most it was a mechanism for unleashing the vital spiritual forces that society needed for its proper rejuvenation. It also was an approach to a more balanced political system that would avoid placing excess power in the hands of the state and, at the same time, would mitigate bureaucratism. Equally important, industrial unionism was recognized as a way of making the individual worker more productive and independent in order that he might reach his full development as a human being. (There was little discussion of female workers among these groups.)

Although the dissidents saw different ways in which to bring about a better social order (socialism, Distributism, and so on), their goals were essentially the same: a social and political organization responsible to the needs of the individual. For example, Guy Bowman's explanation of syndicalism—a means to an end in which the workers would be self-governing and self-reliant, and realize their full humanity without the assistance of experts or officials—would have been recognized by any of G. K. Chesterton's followers as the major plank of the Distributist League. Cecil Chesterton in his socialist phase defined the goals of socialism in essentially the same way as those of Distributism: the maintenance of dignity and justice and the abolition of poverty. The dissidents also agreed about the obstacles that stood in the way of creating this better society: a Parliament controlled by a capitalist plutocracy; a labor leadership that had been compromised by the lure of respectability and money; the "administrative" socialism of the Fabian school; and the use of the state as the organ of socialism. In some ways, the coming together of Cecil Chesterton, the revolutionary socialist, and Hilaire Belloc, the nineteenth-century Radical, was symbolic of the commonality of sentiment that prevailed among all these anti-statists. The partnership also pointed up a looming crisis in the European socialist movement which the question of state sovereignty had raised. The debate over the role of the state caused a serious rift in socialist ranks which, even to this day, has not been resolved.

In many crucial ways, the writings of Cecil Chesterton and Hilaire Belloc served as an arsenal from which the other anti-statists drew their weapons. This can be seen by the large number of anti-parliamentarian critics who made reference to their ideas and freely borrowed the vocabulary of *The Servile State* and *The Party System*. For example, one of the more influential of the syndicalist publications among socialists and radical trade unionists, the organ of the Industrial Democracy League called *Solidarity*, made frequent reference to the servile-state debate raised by the *Eye-Witness* and the *Daily Herald. Solidarity* was an outspoken advocate of union amalgamation, and in its first issue it warned that labor had to fight not only private capitalism but also the extension of the state into the activity of organized labor through such insidious devices as national labor exchanges, compulsory arbitration, and the National Insurance Act. Writing a series of articles in *Solidarity* on the danger of state encroachment into working-class life, Jack Wills, leader of the building-trades amalgamation movement, quoted extensively from Belloc and warned that schemes for labor exchanges were not going to benefit the workers at all but would rather "supply the master class with a regular supply of sober, efficient, and docile wage slaves."[80] This, of course, was exactly the criticism of labor exchanges and conciliation boards that appeared in the *Eye-Witness*.

The views developed in *The Servile State* and *The Party System* formed a paradigm which nearly all anti-collectivist thinkers felt compelled to address. These seminal ideas germinated in the columns of the *New Age*, ensuring that this journal and the journals of Cecil Chesterton and Belloc would always share a certain ideological parentage. But it was in the *Eye-Witness* and the *New Witness* that the anti-statist theories of the Chestertons and Belloc were refined and reached maturity, as these three men tried to explain the ominous forces bringing on what we today recognize as the modern state.

CHAPTER 6

Distributism and British Politics

The Distributist vision of G. K. Chesterton and Hilaire Belloc is difficult to define, in part because it was never spelled out definitively in any single piece of writing. It was more than simply an economic theory: rather, it can best be seen as an approach to life itself, a middle road or "third way" between the inequities of monopoly capitalism and statist collectivism, the most extreme form being communism. A significant dimension to Distributism was the centrality of its moral underpinnings. In fact, this is what separates Distributism from conventional economic theory. Whereas modern economic thinking assumes that the study of economy is an autonomous science, classical economic theory as well as Scholasticism—legacies out of which Distributism emerged—view economics as a subdivision of moral philosophy.[1] Distributism emphasized the importance of widely distributed private proprietorship and a restoration of worker control in commerce, agriculture, and industry along the lines of medieval guilds. The ideal was inspired by *Rerum Novarum*, yet Distributism went beyond what was adumbrated in this encyclical. Ultimately it articulated a system of practical economics and social planning that was far more complete than anything else produced in Catholic circles. As such, it was arguably the single most influential Catholic sociopolitical movement in the English-speaking world, serving both as an inspiration and a model for a large variety of economic and social programs.

The Distributist ideal was a balanced or mixed economy of independent farmers and small industries owned and operated by those who toiled. Political power in the Distributist state was to be decentralized, resembling a New England town hall democracy and offering the maximum opportunity for full participation of each citizen at the local level. At the core of Distributist values were a genuine love and admiration for common, ordinary people. Here was the ultimate creative source of civilization, and, in Chesterton's mind, it was imperative that the "common man" remain free to fulfill his or her religious and social needs in the confined sanctity of family and home. Distributism as it developed in Chesterton's and Belloc's day stood in opposition to the ideas forwarded by George Bernard Shaw and his fellow Fabian imperialists, who had the expansionist's penchant for metaphors of great growing and groping things, like trees. In contrast, as Chesterton put it,

> I believe in the flower and the fruit; and the flower is often small. The fruit is final and in that sense finite; it has a form and therefore a limit. There has been stamped upon it an image, which is the crown and consummation of an aim; and the medieval mystics used the same metaphor and called it Fruition. And as applied to man, it means this; that man has been made more sacred than any superman or supermonkey; that his very limitations have already become holy and like a home; because of that sunken chamber in the rocks, where God became very small.[2]

Distributist ideas reached their maturity in the pages of the successor to the *Eye-Witness* and the *New Witness*, a journal known as *G.K.'s Weekly*. Gilbert Keith Chesterton assumed the responsibility for carrying on Cecil's journalism when his younger brother was killed in World War I. *G.K.'s Weekly* was inaugurated in March 1925, with the avowed aim of continuing Cecil's and Belloc's battle against the prevailing social and political system by championing the principles of Distributism.

Although the journal stood for Catholic ideas, it was not strictly speaking a Catholic paper.[3] *G.K.'s Weekly*, however, wore its Catholic biases with militant pride, and from the outset Chesterton said that his paper would "fight every week for Catholic ethics and economics" in the same manner that the *New Statesman* was fighting for socialist positions.[4] Chesterton's approach to journalism was partly a response to the reluctance of the English Catholic hierarchy to engage in religious and political controversy. Indeed, many Distributists, such as Arnold Lunn and Eric Gill, frequently criticized Catholics for their intellectual timidity and for being out of touch with the problems of industrial society. Gill was perhaps the angriest of the Distributists on this score, since the clergy gave his own famous experiments in Catholic communal work and living at Ditchling little support, and on a number of occasions he lashed out at the hierarchy for lacking the courage to apply the principles of Pope Leo XIII's social encyclicals to the life of their times.

For the most part the Catholic clergy in Britain (and the United States) either ignored or misunderstood papal social teachings. The publication of *Rerum Novarum*, for example, was greeted by a variety of conflicting interpretations. One Catholic writer argued that it indicated Pope Leo's rejection of social democracy, while another viewed it as a justification of Fabian collectivism.[5] But generally, English Catholics paid little attention to the encyclical: it was not even mentioned in the Catholic Truth Society's official short history of the Catholic Church (1895), nor was there any reference to it in Purcell's biography of Manning (1895) or in Snead-Cox's life of Vaughan (1910). Since Catholics knew little or nothing of the content of the papal encyclicals on social issues, they tended to oppose trade unionism as much as they did socialism and communism. This greatly vexed Gill, who explained that when it came to discussing matters of human work and the responsibility of workingmen, ordinary parish priests and laymen were either not interested (owing to their ignorance of the encyclicals) or frankly antagonistic to any reform whatsoever.

In the first years of Chesterton's paper a number of early converts to Distributism played a major role in helping shape the Distributist sociopolitical ideal. Among these was A. J. Penty, the man credited with first introducing guild socialism to England. Penty traced the root of modern economic instability to the growth of big business and the use of machines in the economies of large-scale production. The problem started, said Penty, with the disappearance of the medieval guilds, which under Church direction had regulated prices and restrained the unlimited growth of economic individualism. Penty asserted that the guilds were guarantors of economic stability through their regulation of currency and craft production.[6]

In *The Restoration of the Gild System* (1906),[7] Penty called for a return to the standards of medieval craftsmanship and to the guild traditions of self-regulation and self-government in the various occupations. The book charged that the breakdown of the early guild system had permanently weakened the socioeconomic framework of the state by liberating the rapacious and egocentric side of human behavior. The medieval guilds had succeeded as agencies of social control only by establishing strict discipline over their individual members. As the guilds lost their power, profit became the object of all social action. The inevitable result, argued Penty, was the appearance of a godless, soul-destroying machine age. Penty had a romanticized notion of the healing power of medieval values. He was convinced that alienation of the worker caused by capitalism's bifurcation of the laboring process (the separation of thought from hand work) could be ameliorated by the reestablishment of medieval-type guilds. The result would be a new pride in workmanship and better quality of production; as Penty put it, this would mark an advance toward social reconstruction from the point of view of qualities rather than quantities, of personality and aesthetics rather than external material conditions.

Penty gravitated to Chesterton's Distributism because it proclaimed the paramountcy of religion in economics. Unless the individual were willing to acknowledge and serve some higher principle than that dictated by sensuous appetite, wrote Penty, there could be for him no hope of social or economic salvation.[8]

Another major figure in Distributist circles was Maurice Reckitt, a leader of the Christian Socialist Movement who helped run *G.K.'s Weekly*. Although Reckitt remained an Anglican, he claimed that Chesterton both provided him a sense of social direction and gave him the capacity to relate faith to the realities of everyday living.[9] Reckitt was a key link between Distributism and the Anglo-Catholic wing of the Church of England, a major source of support for Chesterton's and Belloc's social and political ideas.[10]

Perhaps the most colorful and eccentric of the early Distributists, yet also the most influential in many ways, were Father Vincent McNabb and Eric Gill. Gill was an innovative engraver and sculpturer whose radical social and aesthetic views, as well as the craft guild he established at Ditchling Common, helped Distributism gain an international audience. After converting to Catholicism in 1912 (having prepared the way by reading Chesterton's *Orthodoxy*), Gill developed a Thomistic critique of the factory system that emphasized its destructiveness of intellectual creativity and the spiritual and aesthetic qualities of life:

> it makes good mechanics, good machine menders, but men and women who in every other respect are morons, cretins, for whom crossword puzzles, football games, watered beer, sham half-timbered bungalows and shimmering film stars are the highest form of amusement.[11]

Like Chesterton, Belloc, and Penty, Gill proposed that modern men and women return to the higher spiritual values of Christianity, best expressed in the hierarchical guild society of medieval times.[12]

The spiritual force behind Gill's experiment in Distributist communal living at Ditchling Common was Father Vincent McNabb. Father Vincent was one of the best-known Catholic personalities in Britain, an indefatigable campaigner for Distributist causes, and the single most important influence behind the many Catholic back-to-the-land movements of the interwar years. He described himself as "a bit of old England walking about."[13] Father Vincent preferred to don the Dominican white habit and black cappa in public, giving him the appearance of a character out of a Zoe Oldenbourg novel. He was the most unabashedly radical of all the Distributists, always insisting that his close friends Gilbert Keith Chesterton and Hilaire Belloc were too meek in their criticisms of modern society. McNabb believed that only a wholesale return to self-sufficient agriculture could provide the social and economic sustenance for a true Christian life. Like the philosophies of Gill and G. K. Chesterton, McNabb's social philosophy as it emerged out of his experiences at Ditchling had an anarchistic flavor. A cardinal feature of his teaching was a hostility to "the big thing."[14] He was at his most indignant when attacking social and political reformers who championed the nation over the family, the city over the village, and central planning over parental authority. Father Vincent urged his countrymen to turn their backs on industrialism and the sins of the metropolis and return to the land:

There is no hope for England's salvation except on the land. But it must be the land cultivated on a land basis and not on an industrial basis. Nothing but religion will solve the land question. And nothing but a religious order seeking not wealth but God will pioneer the movement from town to land. O that I could make religious men and women see what I see.[15]

G.K.'s Weekly was the vehicle for articulating the Distributist idea, but from the beginning it appears that the enterprise was not well managed. Belloc commented to a friend that the paper is "hardly edited at all" and that things were so chaotic that when he visited the editorial offices he wanted to grab "a strap or whatever else comes handy" to get people into line.[16] The paper might have collapsed in 1926 had not the Distributist League been established with the purpose of keeping the venture alive. The main group of the League was called the Central Branch and met at the Devereux, a tavern near Fleet Street. Other branches soon were set up throughout Britain, eventually spreading to Australia, South Africa, and Canada. *G.K.'s Weekly* served as the unifying element by keeping all the Distributist groups in contact with one another. The League recruited a sizable body of supporters to promote the paper, and with a change in management the weekly became a successful operation, though Chesterton's refusal to depend on advertising revenue meant chronic money problems.[17] After the rescue effort in 1926 Edward Macdonald became the "unnamed acting editor," and he relied heavily on the service of his brother, Gregory Macdonald, who was contributing editor from 1926 to 1928. This arrangement continued until Chesterton's death in 1936.[18]

The fact that Chesterton's prose and commentaries graced the paper meant that *G.K.'s Weekly* would be well known throughout Britain. From the beginning it also was embellished with articles from the old crowd that had written for the Chestertons' and Belloc's earlier papers, men such as George Bernard Shaw, H. G. Wells, Compton Mackenzie, Maurice Reckitt, Walter De la Mare, Maurice Baring, and others. Yet maintaining high circulation was a problem, owing in part, it appears, to resistance in high quarters of the journalistic establishment. Brocard Sewell, a Distributist stalwart who worked for the paper as a young man and was given charge of organizing weekly meetings at the Central Branch of the League, claimed that big news agents like W. H. Smith refused to handle *G.K.'s Weekly* because of its strong stand against big business.[19] The Catholic journalist J. B. Morton said that his employer, Lord Beaverbrook, forbad writers from ever mentioning in print Chesterton's or Belloc's papers. Morton, however, quoted extensively from *G.K.'s Weekly* by using the oblique formula that his information came from "the best paper in Fleet Street."[20]

In the spirit of its predecessors, *G.K.'s Weekly* defended the individual against the encroachment of big government and big business. This threat was posed by socialism and monopoly capitalism, both of which created the conditions for the emergence of a servile state. This struggle for the "small men" (the independently employed shopkeepers, small businessmen, farmers, and the industrial proletariat) took many forms and turns. Each issue of *G.K.'s Weekly*, for example, told of the latest business mergers and the means by which the trusts were buying up and cornering markets, thereby eliminating free competition. The affairs of particular monopoly capitalists, such as Alfred Mond, Lord Ashfield, and the Berry brothers, were regularly featured as illustrations of corruption and political chicanery.

The weekly did more than write about such dealings. One especially colorful episode in the battle against the twin evils of collectivism and monopoly capitalism concerned the Distributist efforts to defeat Lord Ashfield's drive to control the London transportation system. Distributists by the droves came out to defend independent bus owners (most of whom were war veterans who had used government loans to launch themselves in business) as they waged a furious battle for survival against the buses of Ashfield's London General Omnibus Transportation Company. The so-called "London Omnibus War" of spring 1926 was a losing cause, however, for in the end the city's competitive but chaotic transportation business required some kind of central management. However, the problem was settled in the best financial interests of Lord Ashfield, so *G.K.'s Weekly* claimed, for his company, the Bank of England, and the Transport and General Workers' Union pooled their resources to secure a government transportation monopoly for London. This was all done against the wishes of popular opinion, as shown by the fact that more than a million London passengers had signed a petition in favor of keeping the private bus companies in business. Chesterton saw the spunky efforts of the independent busmen (in their distinctively painted vehicles brandishing special names indicating the owner's history and outlook on life, such as the "Vanguard," "Pro Bono Publico," and so forth) as a clear sign that Englishmen desired independent proprietorship versus monopoly. He hoped that the plight of the independents would serve as a catalyst for the public's dormant Distributist instincts: the colorful London traffic "pirates" could be "a beacon for guidance to Distributism."[21] *G.K.'s Weekly* asked its readers to boycott the monopoly's transportation services. Lord Ashfield, who was a business associate of Alfred Mond's in the chemical industry and a partner in the film business with Lord Beaverbrook, the newspaper magnate, was depicted as an "American exploiter of the worst type," a transportation leviathan crushing the freedoms of London's street travelers. *G.K.'s Weekly* was quick to point out that the great monopolists were foreigners: Ashfield hailed from Detroit, Beaverbrook from Canada, and Mond from Palestine.

In matters of domestic politics, Chesterton's weekly followed a moderate course between 1925 and 1928, voicing concern about improving conditions for the working class through trade unionism and reforming economic and social life via Parliament. It seems that while Henry Slesser served as a Labour MP, Chesterton and the Distributists were willing to endorse the Labour Party. Slesser was a highly respected legal mind who embraced Distributism (and later converted to Catholicism) and became a correspondent for *G.K.'s Weekly*. He insisted that his party was the only group in Parliament combating plutocracy and the so-called amelioration of the poor by means that further degraded them. He and Chesterton hoped that the Labourites could be prevailed upon to accept the Distributist guild idea, with its emphasis on private proprietorship. In the issue of 10 October 1926, Chesterton wrote that he could accept Slesser's analysis of the Labour Party (Slesser argued that the Party's resistance to capitalism was rooted in medieval Catholic principles and that it therefore would oppose legislation which impinged upon the dignity of the individual) and that something constructive might be accomplished through parliamentary action. As Chesterton pointed out to his readers, there was no reason why Distributists should surrender Parliament completely to the plutocrats.[22]

While backing Slesser's efforts to move the Labour Party toward Distributist principles, *G.K.'s Weekly* also campaigned hard against what it believed were the government's efforts to undermine the growing political strength of the trade union movement. The test of its commitment came in the spring of 1926 with the outbreak of a general strike.

This unprecedented, seemingly revolutionary trade union response to capitalism was precipitated by years of trouble in Britain's coal industry. Profits dropped steadily after World War I with the recovery of mining in Germany and Poland. These mines were more efficient than Britain's, and with declining profits, British management pushed for longer working hours and a reduction in wages, both of which were bitterly opposed by the miners. Government arbitration failed to resolve the differences, and in April the Trade Unions Congress (TUC) formulated plans for a general strike in support of the miners.

G.K.'s Weekly supported the miners throughout the months of negotiations that preceded the strike. But Chesterton and the Distributists strongly disapproved of a key trade union bargaining demand, namely, its insistence on a minimum or living wage. Focusing on the issue of wages, they argued would only serve to perpetuate the division of property between employer and employee. Wage bargaining rested on the premise that labor was a commodity, and by engaging in such discussions the trade unions simply perpetuated the worker's alienation from the products of his labor and his dependency on a dominating class. Wages were part of the "bread and circuses" of the servile state, designed in large part to diffuse labor's demands for the more important goal of ownership of the means of production. On the other hand, Chesterton saw virtue in the mine owners' offer to gear wages to the prosperity of the mines. This appeared to be an opening for eventual joint business partnership, where remuneration for services would be linked to the industry's profits. The miners were advised to accept the partnership offer along with its logical corollaries: joint cooperation and co-equal power with management in control of the industry and partnership in profits.[23]

In the long run, the workers must go beyond profit-sharing and cooperative production: what they needed, wrote *G.K.'s Weekly's* correspondent B. D. Acland, is part-ownership in the company. A keynote of Distributist industrial policy must be "the utilization of the joint-stock principle of industrial organization for the multiplication of partners." In other words, the present system of capitalism must be smashed so there could be more capitalists.[24]

G.K.'s Weekly offered the workers its unqualified support when the general strike broke out in April 1926. Following the radical traditions of its predecessors, the *Eye-Witness* and *New Witness*, the paper asserted that any workman had a right to strike at any time and for any reason. Withholding such rights represented a denial of liberty.[25]

The paper's strong support for the strike—a special edition of *G.K.'s Weekly* was published during the affair—brought considerable criticism from many lay and clerical Catholics. For weeks the editors received letters from Catholics who considered the strike a revolutionary act.[26] Both the Anglican and Roman Catholic hierarchies condemned the strike in the strongest language. Cardinal Bourne, head of the English Catholic Church, scolded the miners in his Sunday sermon at Westminster and found no moral justification for their behavior: "It is a direct challenge to lawfully constituted authority and inflicts, *without adequate reason,* immense discomfort and injury to millions of our fellow-countrymen. It is, therefore, a sin against the obedience which we owe to God. . . ."[27] Britain's most influential Catholic monthly, the *Tablet,* echoed Bourne's position. It argued that the trade unions were becoming too powerful and that the action was nothing more than a ploy to hold the public ransom for winning "sectional privileges from the People's Government."[28]

In the eyes of many Distributists, the Catholic Church's official reaction to the strike was yet another example of a congenital reluctance to commit itself to political action, a policy driven by the fear of invoking criticism from the governing establishment. Yet there were some associated with *G.K.'s Weekly* who were convinced that the paper's position in support of the strikers had gone too far, and was largely the product of a radical, communist-leaning clique within the editorial offices. Although this political disagreement was masked from the public at the time, in retrospect it appears to mark the beginning of a significant split within the *G.K.'s Weekly* circle that would become more apparent during the controversies surrounding Mussolini and fascism in the 1930s.

In its special strike edition of 15 May 1926, *G.K.'s Weekly* asserted that the industrial combines had goaded the workers into calling for a general strike in order to smash the trade union movement. It also argued that government (thanks to the machinations of Winston Churchill, Lord Birkenhead, and William Joynson-Hicks) with the unofficial support of the British Fascisti had worked to create the impression that the trade unions were under the control of Bolsheviks: "The middle and upper classes have been mobilized in defence of the Combines and the rich, and in defiance of the Trade Unions and the poor. The nominal enemy was Moscow and the Red Flag; the real enemy was the Trade Union." *G.K.'s Weekly* viewed the general strike not as an act of revolution but rather as a "reasonable defence against plutocracy."[29]

Gregory Macdonald, whose brother became the unnamed editor of *G.K.'s Weekly* after the League was formed in 1926 and who has provided valuable "eye-witness" accounts of life behind the scenes at the paper, downplayed the political radicalism of Chesterton's journal.[30] Macdonald emphasized that Chesterton was abroad at the time of the general strike and that the paper's editorial position in support of the workers was shaped by William Titterton (then serving as executive editor), a man, in Macdonald's view, of generous political philosophy but superficial knowledge of social principles. The impressionable Titterton, said Macdonald, was counseled by Cecil Chesterton's widow, an experienced Fleet Street journalist with the paper, who was "an admirer of Soviet Russia."[31] In other words, in Chesterton's absence, a certain unrepresentative element— "troublemakers" in Macdonald's words—pulled *G.K.'s Weekly* to the left in support of the TUC's decision to call a general strike.[32]

Gregory Macdonald was adamantly opposed to this position, and, over the years, he became highly suspicious of certain people in Distributist circles who in his opinion were too sympathetic to the political left.[33] During the general strike *G.K.'s Weekly* under-took some ill-considered, emotional positions, Macdonald believed, which did not represent Chesterton's true feelings about the problem; and when Chesterton returned from his trip abroad, Macdonald insisted, he articulated a more moderate assessment of the situation, which, in the long run, brought the paper into line with the official Church hierarchy.

The record, on the other hand, suggests otherwise. It indicates that Chesterton backed Titterton's position to the hilt. Maurice Reckitt, for example, has written that Chesterton, on returning to London, upheld Titterton's line, endorsing his editor's slogan: "Keep calm, and stand up for the strikers."[34] Evidence in support of Reckitt's recollection can be found in Chesterton's first article published after his trip in May 1926. Here he voiced support for the position his paper assumed during the strike[35] and, furthermore, gave his imprimatur to Titterton's analysis of the causes of the disturbance and its significance in terms of English working-class history. Trade unionism, Chesterton wrote, represents the inevitable reaction of Christian democracy against the abnormal concentration of capitalism.[36]

Chesterton did, however, voice concern about certain troubling tendencies in the trade union movement that threatened to stifle rank-and-file representation. In an earlier article he reiterated support for the trade unions and their right to strike but insisted that "a big trade union" could not in itself be a solution to Britain's industrial troubles. The real issue, wrote Chesterton, is "big organization" in both labor and business. His fear was that the labor movement might be absorbed by the Labour Party and thereby co-opted by the party system:

> And at the end of that process it would be as impossible to introduce a free yeoman or a small guild into the system as it would be to introduce a Green Knight of Chivalry or a Purple Castle of romance into a game of chess played with two colours.[37]

The trade unions, under the control of a single large organization subservient to the Labour Party, could become every bit as powerful as the trusts against which they were supposed to contend. This was Gregory Macdonald's fear and one of the major reasons he opposed the TUC's decision to call a general strike: "I became convinced that if the general strike were successful it would mean the transfer of executive power, or sovereignty, from King and Parliament to a non-elected and untried group of union leaders."[38]

Chesterton, however, had not yet become as pessimistic as Macdonald (though he soon would). His anarcho-syndicalist sympathies fashioned during the pre-war years of labor unrest encouraged him to believe that the workers would be able to reject any attempts by their leaders to establish authoritarian control over the trade union movement. In fact, this hope convinced Chesterton of the necessity of supporting Henry Slesser's efforts to win over the Labour Party to Distributist principles.

For Chesterton, the real significance of the general strike was not the problem of big labor bureaucrats but the courage of the rank and file in challenging those who were determined to destroy trade unionism: "I have been bored . . . by the merely mechanical praises of English moderation and order. I know well that they have often been merely praises of snobbery and apathy. I know well that they have missed many opportunities by which nations at once more logical and more impetuous have done great things."[39] In short, Chesterton's chief concern was not that a successful strike would mean the transfer of power to union leaders but rather that trade unionism ("the pride in England is the pride of the Trade Union") would fail to defend itself in the face of this perilous attack on its existence. Chesterton, therefore, was pleased that the trade unions rose to the challenge, and this is why he could write on his return to London that from the continent England indeed looked like an island but also as a mountain: "And perhaps all the more like a mountain at the moment when it happens to look like a volcano."[40]

Contrary to what Chesterton hoped, but in line with what Macdonald feared, the general strike turned out to be a disaster for the British labor movement. Although the TUC called an end to the strike on 12 May, many disgruntled miners stayed out for another six months. Workers who supported the action in the long run forfeited millions of pounds in lost wages, and thereafter the trade unions experienced a considerable decline in membership. The government throughout the long and arduous months of negotiations had given way to the mine owners, and, consequently, it should have been no surprise that the aftermath would be bitter and vindictive. After the strike was called off, Parliament passed the Trades Disputes and Trade Union Bill. Among other things, this legislation proposed to outlaw sympathetic strikes, forbid civil servants from joining TUC-affiliated organizations, and severely limit the use of trade union political funds.

In the House of Commons, Henry Slesser led the attack on certain legal aspects of the bill for the Labour Party. The bill, in his view, constituted an egregious assault on fundamental principles of individual rights. Along with *G.K.'s Weekly* and the Distributist League, Slesser both in Parliament and in various public debates focused public attention on Labour's claim that the legislation would effectively place workers in a condition of slavery. The bill, they asserted, was a conspiracy of the Federation of British Industries and of conservatives in Parliament to destroy the trade union movement.

The Trades Disputes and Trade Union Bill was passed into law in 1927. From this point on Chesterton and his friends began to lose faith in the possibility of converting the Labour Party and the trade union movement to Distributist ideas. But what ultimately turned Distributists against conventional politics was their conviction that labor had decided to collaborate with industrial capitalism and the governing establishment.

This change in attitude appears to have grown out of the so-called "Mond-Turner" talks. Throughout 1928 and 1929 a group of industrial magnates, inspired by Sir Alfred Mond, chairman of Imperial Chemical Industries (in Chesterton's opinion, the quintessential "monopoly capitalist"), undertook a series of discussions with major trade union officials led by Ben Turner, chairman of the TUC General Council. The purpose of these deliberations was to overcome long-standing differences between management and labor and to arrive at some compromise in the interests of industrial harmony. The discussions were purposely kept secret for fear of raising the wrath of extremists in both camps. In July 1929 the groups published a report which indicated that the employers were willing to make concessions, including recognition of trade unions as the sole bargaining agencies for workers and acceptance of changes in unemployment insurance in favor of labor. Most importantly, the Mond-Turner report recommended the establishment of joint consultative machinery by the Trades Union Congress, the Federation of British Industries, and the National Confederation of Employers' Organizations. These proposals were bitterly attacked by Distributists, for they considered this closer understanding and cooperation between employers and workers as harbingers of the dreaded servile state.

Chesterton, Slesser, and Penty in numerous articles throughout 1928 and 1929 tried to counter the popularity of the Mond-Turner proposals by insisting that the trade unions begin to push for ultimate control and ownership of industrial production. The process should first start, they argued, in the coal industry. As a means to this end they suggested that the government seize control of the mines and lease them to a federation of miners' guilds, which eventually would take over both ownership and management of the industry.[41]

The three men failed to convince either the trade unionists or the government. Disillusionment quickly set in. The TUC's willingness to participate in the Mond-Turner talks represented, for Distributists, an indication that the trade unions had relinquished their struggle for ownership of the means of production. The trade union movement had forsaken the guild idea for the promise of security. From this time on, the Distributists moved further away from conventional politics and sought to gain support for their schemes through a variety of other expedients, including a political alternative proposed by Hilaire Belloc: the restoration of monarchical government.

Was there any validity to Chesterton's and Belloc's political analysis? Was it an exaggeration to assert that by the late 1920s the trade union movement had become absorbed by the party system and that the electorate had no real power to control politicians and bureaucrats? Chesterton's and Belloc's political critique, which assumed the existence of a secret plot to eliminate class and party conflict in the interests of an industrial and financial plutocracy, has frequently been dismissed as the raving of bitter men obsessed with conspiracies.[42]

However, recent scholarship on the structure of British politics that has been able to take advantage of major changes in the Official Secrets Act (reducing the duration of the ban on examining state documents from fifty to thirty years) corroborates certain key tenets of the Chesterton-Belloc political critique. For example, the historian Keith Middlemas has argued that by the early 1920s Britain's nineteenth-century political system had broken down under the weight of industrial conflict, the Irish problems, and World War I.[43] What took its place was a government of "corporate bias," that is, government not by Parliament but by a corporate triangle consisting of the chief representative bodies of business, labor, and, on the government's side, officials of the state. Another contemporary scholar of British politics, Keith Burgess, has corroborated Middlemas's argument, though instead of accepting the latter's triangular model, Burgess identifies a series of "power blocs" which had a similar function. Burgess sheds particular light on the role of bureaucrats who, though supposedly disinterested, had special connections and status-group ties with the various worlds of Oxbridge, industry, and finance. Burgess confirms the emergence of a power bloc by the 1930s that would successfully control British life for the next forty years. This power bloc was dominated by the bureaucrat:

> These were personified by the more 'progressive' sections of big industrial capital, represented by employers in the growing home industries and including huge combinations like ICI with their oligopolistic control of world markets. There was, in addition, the expanding body of salaried employees who phased into a new managerial elite at the highest echelons of administration in commerce, industry, and government.[44]

A major figure in this political transformation was David Lloyd George, the *bête noire* of the Chesteron and Belloc. Lloyd George was one of the first politicians to recognize the necessity of a managerial concept of government to overcome party and class differences. He intended to create a special administrative body, or center group of power brokers, to regulate political and economic life. What particularly frightened Lloyd George and the moguls of industry were the anarcho-syndicalist activities of 1911–1914, in which Chesterton and Belloc had played leading roles. These activities clearly revealed that the official labor leadership was unable to control the extreme fringes of the working-class movement by fusing it with parliamentary democracy. Syndicalist activity had potentially disastrous consequences for industrial production and political order, a situation all the more serious because of worsening diplomatic relations with Germany.

The attempts to formulate a coalition government during the constitutional crisis of 1911, together with David Lloyd George's efforts after the war to form a National Industrial Convention composed of government officials, business, and labor leaders who would discuss industrial problems, were, in Middlemas's thesis, the first attempts to create a formal, triangular power bloc. Supporters of such attempts hoped that a special tripartite national body, through consensus among its leadership, would guide Britain away from class antagonism and political crises and thereby ensure the kind of harmony required for steady economic growth. In the words of W. Milne-Baily of the TUC Research Department, a leading proponent of the new cooperation theory as a means of ending economic conflict, Britain's traditional political institutions were not fit for the task: "A Parliament of the ordinary democratic kind, elected on a territorial basis, is largely ignorant, and is bound to be ignorant of industrial needs and problems, and to that extent is a very unsatisfactory authority for industrial regulation and legislation."[45] What Milne-Baily, Lloyd George, and others had in mind was a managerial concept of government, and this process was capped, according to Middlemas, by the Mond-Turner talks of 1928.

In February 1929 the National Confederation of Employers Organizations, the Federation of British Industries, and the TUC agreed to undertake permanent discussions on fundamental questions of industrial legislation, unemployment, and national economic policy. Due to the fact that the TUC and employers associations had not succeeded in making their institutions fully representative, and because their new alliance with the state was vulnerable to revolt from below, it became official policy from the very beginning to keep this triangular relationship secret. Middlemas argues that by the

1930s the new institutional collaboration had supplemented the parliamentary system and was largely responsible for the relative harmony of the interwar years. During this period the function of the political parties changed, and henceforth, under the tutelage of the triangular bloc, ideological differences and substantive discussions largely disappeared from party warfare. Thus, long before 1945, Parliament had ceased to be the supreme governing body in Britain. It subordinated itself to the managerial powers of the state's bureaucratic apparatus. Parliament's function was to be an electoral source of the majority which provided the party element in government, though, according to Middlemas, the electoral cycle itself had no effect whatever on economic and political decisions.[46] If anything, the old political system was used by the corporate leaders to win popular mandates for decisions they either had already arrived at or would soon make.

Both Middlemas and Burgess describe a process in the consolidation of power away from Parliament and popular democracy that, at the time, was identified with exquisite precision in the political analysis of Chesterton and Belloc. The formation of Middlemas's corporate triangle was called "Mondism" by *G.K.'s Weekly*. The paper frequently remarked on the interlocking interests and relationships between government officers, bankers, industrial magnates, and trade union leaders. Indeed, Mond himself was referred to in *G.K.'s Weekly* as the "Apostle of Rationalization," an appellation that in the Weberian sense accords perfectly with the Middlemas thesis.[47] The studies of Middlemas and Burgess demonstrate the relevance of Chesteron's and Belloc's political analysis. Rather than being an exaggerated or distorted description of political practice, their critique seems to have identified accurately a series of circumstances and events which brought about a substantial shift in power away from the locus of legitimate authority—Parliament—to special interest groups and bureaucrats. The acuity of their political analysis has not yet been recognized by most historians of modern British politics.[48]

As early as September 1928, *G.K.'s Weekly* told its readers that it did not make any difference which party won power at the next general election, because all three parties were pledged to obey the governmental and industrial bureaucracies. As for the Mond-Turner conferences, the paper accurately identified them as marking the accession of the official trade union leadership to the political estab-lishment, thereby completing what Middlemas would later identify as the corporate triangle. The Labour Party politicians, the paper argued, had been converted to "respectability"; they had become a "real party" by entering the full political system with the under-standing that all the rules laid down by parliamentary precedent would be scrupulously observed. Labor had now earned its emblem of respectability; its leaders had graciously become "good parlia-mentarians," in violation of the old socialist revolutionary tradition:

> In the days of William Morris they had talked of destroying the Houses of Parliament by blowing them up or, more pic-turesquely, of shelling them from the river. . . . But now their own aim is to preserve Parliament, to make it permanent, to make it safe.[49]

In February 1930 *G.K.'s Weekly* announced to its readers that it could no longer support parliamentary politics. Henceforth Distributists would work for revolution from without, since any changes would have to be imposed by forces other than legal, parliamentary actions.[50]

Chesterton's comrade-in-arms, Hilaire Belloc, had rejected the parliamentary process long before his Distributist friends and the staff at *G.K.'s Weekly*. In *The House of Commons and Monarchy* (1920), Belloc chronicled the transformation of Parliament as a governing institution from that of a representative body to an oligarchy. In Belloc's opinion no oligarchy could function unless it were aristo-cratic,[51] and the idea of a natural aristocracy had long disappeared in England. Parliament, as the body representing a small money-clique, no longer possessed the moral authority conferred upon it by general respect. The loss of aristocratic spirit was discernable in soci-ety, wrote Belloc, by the decline of principle as the norm of public conduct. When the continuity of such moral tradition is broken, when wealth is divorced from manners and the gesture of the gen-tleman is no longer appreciated as a special thing, the principle dis-appears: "Once broken the thing dies and it cannot be restored."[52]

Belloc argued that the trade unions and other professional cor-porations were rapidly rising to positions of power in the wake of

Parliament's moral collapse. The Mond-Turner deliberations were a clear reflection of this transformation in the network of power. Yet in the long run such varied councils would not be able to exercise sovereign power on their own. These corporate bodies must be arranged and controlled by something external and superior to them in the interests of national unity. Given the disappearance of the aristocratic spirit in Britain, there was only one institution capable of providing this service, and that was monarchy.

The virtues of monarchy, said Belloc, were that it could stand above the political fray, protecting the weak from the strong, preventing the concentration of wealth in the hands of a selfish few, and securing the freedom of the courts of justice and the sources of public opinion from corruption. All this the monarchy could do because it was responsible and would be held accountable for its political behavior. Further, Belloc argued, the lack of overt interference by the British monarchy in public affairs for over a century had brought new respect for the throne. It had now become a symbol, "gathering towards itself the passionate patriotism of the people."[53] On the other hand, a Parliament run by an oligarchy that was not aristocratic could never provide this service, for it was both irresponsible and unpopular. "Each individual in such an amorphous executive does harm with impunity because he can always say that it was not he that did it." In an obvious allusion to that old political warhorse, the Marconi affair, Belloc could assert that "no parliamentarian, since aristocracy failed in England, has gone to prison for a bribe taken or given."[54]

At the end of 1932, in a statement that seemed to mock the League's fantasies of converting the Labour Party to Distributist principles, Belloc wrote that he had given up on Parliament ever since the Marconi scandal:

> I have since that date refused to take any further part in any attempt to cleanse what I think is beyond cleansing. Public life now stinks with the stench of a mortal disease; it can no longer be cured.[55]

Chesterton's own political disillusionment expanded in the wake of Belloc's cynicism. In August 1935 Chesterton could write that as things now stand, he was prepared to examine the offerings of fascism. Parliamentarianism, on the other hand, was not worth looking into at all.[56]

Such were the political dispositions of G. K. Chesterton, Hilaire Belloc, and the Distributist circle at the outset of the 1930s, a decade which, burdened with the economic crisis of capitalism and the rise of the dictators, would make those turbulent pre–World War I years seem like a placid twilight before the storm.

CHAPTER 7

The New Distributists

The English Distributists, armed with an agenda sharply honed by Chesterton's and Belloc's struggles with big business and the governing establishment, entered the decade of world depression with a great deal of self-confidence and strongly committed to radical economic, political, and social reconstruction. The Distributist movement was strengthened at this juncture by the infusion of new and younger recruits, ensuring that the ideas of Chesterton and Belloc would be carried on with energy. Among the more influential of these men were Douglas Jerrold, whom D. B. Wyndham-Lewis called "the brains of the English Right,"[1] Arnold Lunn, Douglas Woodruff, and Christopher Hollis.

Much like the first generation of Distributists, these young lions shared similar views on what they considered the baleful errors of the Renaissance ("the rebirth of pagan pride," said Lunn),[2] the Protestant Reformation, and the Enlightenment. These historical episodes were directly responsible for the three scourges of the twentieth century: liberalism, monopoly capitalism, and collectivist socialism.

Lunn and Hollis, whose conversion to Catholicism was prepared by Chesterton and Belloc, as well as Woodruff and Jerrold, were not mild-mannered religious dilettantes but rather singularly militant Catholics, uncompromising in their political views, and pugnacious propagandists in the fight for Distributism.[3] Arnold Lunn, for instance, in a style appropriate to such spirit, once told a friend, the Duke of Alba, of a "pleasant incident" in which he "flattened out an Oxford don and Eton master, both of whom were wearing the fashionable colour pink," an affectation that apparently offended him.[4] The episode probably involved little more than an exchange of words in heated debate, but the language attests to the

combativeness of Lunn's style—a studied effort on his part to replicate the ways of Hilaire Belloc. He lamented the fact that other
Catholics did not have the courage to carry on as he did. As a Catholic apologist Lunn was notorious for his love of stirring up the mob.[5]

Perhaps the most prominent of the new Distributists was Douglas Woodruff. Woodruff had a distinguished undergraduate career
at Oxford. As a member of the Oxford debating team, along with
his life-long friend, Christopher Hollis, he toured the world with
great success. In 1933 he married the daughter of the Second Lord
Acton. As editor of the London *Tablet* from 1936 through 1967,
Woodruff turned that periodical into a leading voice of English
Catholicism, and, in the opinion of his supporters, one of the most
influential papers in Great Britain and Europe, especially in the area
of international affairs.[6]

The new Distributists learned from Belloc to look beneath the
veneer of political respectability, where they would always find a
sleazy miasma of monied interests, plutocrats, and wire-pullers
manipulating democratic systems for their own selfish ends: thus
their strong distrust of democracy. The political temperament and
public deportment of Lunn and his friends were shaped more by
Belloc than Chesterton. Michael Derrick noted this shift in direction when he observed that Douglas Woodruff, as the years passed,
moved away from the Chestertonian liberalism that marked his
early years. Chesterton, said Derrick, was by instinct a reforming
radical; Woodruff a conserving traditionalist.[7] Like Belloc, the new
Distributists were obsessed with the intrinsic sinfulness of man and
the need to find a fixed and authoritative moral standard to govern
social life. Chesterton's approach to such issues, compared to that of
Belloc and the New Distributists, was far less cynical, more optimistic concerning human nature, and essentially more sympathetic
to the rough edges of the democratic process. Belloc's preoccupation with the folly of human behavior made him less sanguine than
Chesterton about the possibility of realizing democracy in England.
"I still regard democracy as the noblest and least stable of human
forms of government," Belloc wrote Hoffman Nickerson, but
"mechanically impossible in a large state." The habit of calling Par-
liaments democratic, he added, "seems to me like calling petrol a

wine," for all human things are nasty "with the exception of the taste for wine and oysters, first love, good verse, and the victory of one's people in the field. To this catalogue some would add parental affection."[8] It was the politically jaded but bombastic Belloc who set the tone for the vanguard of the new Distributists.

Arnold Lunn wrote to Belloc that as a youth he needed the "blast of dynamite which you effectively provided . . . to shatter my simple boyish faith in the Whig-Don-School of history."[9] After his mentor blasted a breach in those walls of stifling conventionalism, other Catholic writers like Christopher Dawson could receive literary bouquets from the academic establishment that were denied to Belloc, the man who made it all possible. Dawson, wrote Lunn, would later say the same thing as Belloc, but less aggressively and in language sufficiently sanitized to please the English dons. Belloc's breaching the barriers, however, gave such Catholic writers their opportunity.[10]

By the 1930s, after the disappointments of trying to turn the Labour Party in a Distributist direction, the "new Distributists" group began to look on the political right for recruits to their cause. Woodruff, Lunn, Jerrold, and Hollis, for example, believed liberalism was bankrupt in Britain and identified themselves with what they variously called "new," "true," or "radical" conservatism. The "idealistic conservative," wrote Arnold Lunn, by which he meant the old-fashioned country squire who recognized that place brought duties, "has more in common with the idealistic Radical than either has with many of their nominal allies." The virtue of Distributism, he claimed, is that it is more radical and revolutionary than socialism and more conservative than modern conservatism.[11]

The social and political views of Belloc, as well as his interpretation of British and European history, were accepted as gospel by the new Distributists. Belloc's attack on the party system, said Jerrold, was as striking as Luther's denunciation of the sale of indulgences. The *Servile State* could be seen as the equivalent of the "Ninety-five Theses." It was no less then the most "penetrating and prophetic piece of political pamphleteering of the century."[12] In the view of Woodruff, there was no one in the history of English literature who showed such versatility and mastery of his many subjects as Belloc.[13]

In 1931 Belloc, along with Alan Herbert, T. S. Eliot, Roy Campbell, and Wyndham Lewis, by now all stalwarts of the right, convinced Douglas Jerrold to take over editorship of *The English Review,*
an influential and highly-respected literary journal. Between 1931
and 1936 the magazine, under Jerrold's direction, attempted to redefine Tory conservatism along Distributist lines. Jerrold championed what he called a "New Conservatism," which, in contrast to
the party of Stanley Baldwin, opposed big business, low wages,
vested interests, class privilege, and any sympathies with communism. Jerrold and his associates made communism a central focus of
their attacks on contemporary problems; indeed they revealed an
obsession with the expansion of international Marxism.[14] By the
1920s Belloc himself had begun to focus increasingly on the Soviet
Union, which soon displaced the hated Prussia as the principal
enemy in matters relating to international affairs.

Douglas Jerrold at *The English Review* put his own Distributist
twist on the "true meaning" of conservatism: its abiding "axiom," he
insisted, is that the only guarantee of a just social order is "a wide
distribution of private ownership."[15] Unless Parliament under a universal franchise achieved this end, a dictatorship would be not only
inevitable but necessary.[16] However, Jerrold was more optimistic
than his mentor Belloc in that he hoped a revived Tory Party, charged
with the appropriate dose of right-wing principles, might reform
the parliamentary system, obviating the need for a dictatorship.

As of the spring of 1933, however, Jerrold appears to have
despaired of the possibility of finding social justice through a
"reformed" Parliament. In a revealing article in an American journal that claimed to be both Distributist and fascist, he urged the
construction of what he called the "Authoritarian" or "Ethical State"
as a cure for Britain's postwar problems. In a spirit akin to that of
the integral Catholics of the Vogelsang school,[17] Jerrold proposed
an "Anglo-Saxon" version of self-government where decisions and
power would devolve to the various agricultural, craft, and service
professions united through a strong central government (ideally
headed by a monarch) that served the best interests of the nation
as a whole. This was precisely what Belloc had recommended,
namely, a corporate-type system with functional rather than regional
representation held together by a powerful leader above special

interests. Governance in the "Ethical State" would not be "between" but "above" capital and labor, retaining something of the independent tradition of the Tory squirarchy. All this was in the best spirit of Edmund Burke, Chesterton, and Belloc, claimed Jerrold, and would provide the necessary means for reconciling the two most basic wants of the English people: "the passion for Liberty and the passion for Order—the desire for Status and the desire for Freedom."[18]

Douglas Jerrold made repeated efforts to move the Conservative Party toward the right and on many occasions tried to run himself as a Tory MP for the House of Commons. He was never able to secure the backing of the party's selection committee, claimed his friend Douglas Woodruff, because it did not think he "had the right gifts" to be a successful candidate.[19] Finally, Jerrold and some of his right-wing colleagues, notably Sir Charles Petrie, Leo Amery, and Sir Robert Horne, lost patience with the fecklessness of the official party. They organized a splinter group called the "Independent Conservatives" and in preparation for the 1935 general election ran Lord Lloyd on a corporatist platform as a challenger to Stanley Baldwin.

The new Distributists for the most part were not only politically conservative but, like their mentor Belloc, also religiously conservative, with a strong distaste for liberal Catholics. This certainly applies to Woodruff, Jerrold, Lunn, and Hollis. Woodruff was a great admirer of Pius IX's *Syllabus of Errors* for its condemnation of "the dark side of nineteenth-century freedom" (the loss of imagination in thought for Catholic writers was a small price to pay for the preservation of orthodoxy, he claimed), and he established the *Tablet* as the paramount voice of conservative Catholicism in the English-speaking world.[20] Under his direction the paper championed the virtues of traditional Catholicism and the Latin Mass and held forth against liberal efforts to reform the liturgy. (After retirement as editor in 1967 he was greatly saddened by the *Tablet's* new directions embracing liberal causes.)

Woodruff believed that there was a direct correlation between sympathy for a "planned economy" and the prevalence of liberal social and political thinking among Catholics. Not only were such ideas foolish concerning practical matters, they also induced Catholics to soft-pedal on religious dogma. The best example of these tendencies, he claimed, was Dorothy Day's Catholic Worker movement, an influential effort in America, with branches in Britain, to challenge the attraction of communism among the urban laboring classes. Woodruff was scandalized, for instance, when the *Catholic Worker* suggested that the pope consider the canonization of Mahatma Gandhi, whom Woodruff called "the unbaptized, anti-Christian pagan." Day and her followers believed that Gandhi represented the best universal features of the Catholic ideas of brotherhood. But one should not create allies and converts by "watering down the faith to suit the customer," insisted Woodruff. Conversion "means literally a con-version," a turning around of the soul. This "must be crucifying." "Our Faith is and must be to the Jews a stumbling block and to the intelligentsia . . . foolishness."[21]

Arnold Lunn was no less a foe of "modernizing," liberal tendencies. As regards the reforms recommended by the liturgical movement, Lunn wondered in retrospect whether he would have joined a Church that embraced them.[22]

I I

Throughout the 1930s the followers of Chesterton and Belloc worked diligently to inform the public of the virtues of Distributism as an alternative to capitalism and the socialist version of a planned economy. There was no common agreement among Distributists about methods or priorities in their general attack on modern industrialism.[23] One group felt that it was necessary to forsake large-scale industrialism and return to an agricultural village-based economy. Those associated with A. J. Penty and Father Vincent McNabb went further, advocating the abolition of machinery altogether, a position which helped fuel the public impression that Distributists were unrealistic visionaries pining for a return to the Middle Ages. Other Distributists gave priority to monetary reform. Eric Gill, for instance, was persuaded that almost all economic and even moral problems were related to usury and what he called the "trade in money." Gill advocated a new monetary system that would link purchasing power to agricultural and industrial productivity. The currency structure as presently constituted, in his view, served as a tool of bankers and moneylenders in whose interests the power of monarchy had been destroyed. Most Distributists approached money issues along these lines. Belloc, Gregory Macdonald, and others further elaborated on such thinking in various essays exposing what they regarded as an international monetary conspiracy.

As Distributists argued among themselves about the ways to save modern society from the evils of materialism and greed, Chesterton served as a mediator or referee, candidly encouraging their debates in the pages of *G.K.'s Weekly*. Although some critics called the Distributists feckless wind-bags, hopelessly tangled in disagreements with each other, their common agreement about the general ideals upon which the new Christian social order should be built is worth noting. Herbert Shove expressed it best when he said that Distributism was more than a mere redistribution of wealth and private ownership; it was rather a return to "the philosophy of balance," a condition in which both the needs of the heart and the mind would be met. "Intellectual freedom" mattered most, and this could best be satisfied when men held property.[24]

All Distributists were anti-urban; the metropolis removed individuals from "the life-blood of the soil." However, there was never any official position that all people in the new order had to practice farming or handcraftsmanship. Basing his argument on the ideal of liberty emphasized by Herbert Shove, H. E. Humphries, author of the League's first textbook, *Liberty and Property* (1928), pointed out that Distributists were both pragmatic and reasonable:

> The Distributist is not a fanatic. If a man wants to do things by machinery, or work in a factory, he will do so. Some people like hand-made goods, others are indifferent. . . . Those who do not want the responsibility of property and like to rely on a master, will work for a wage on the farm or in the workshop. Our conception of a civilized state is one in which men will want responsibility, and exercise of their own wills in the control of their own business. . . . The essential is liberty, and when there is the variety . . . liberty is as completely established as is possible in economic affairs.[25]

Critics have assailed Distributists for failing to develop a practical, systematic plan for social, economic, and political reform.[26] The charge is somewhat unfair. From the beginning, Chesterton's journal and the League were meant to be organs of propaganda to raise public consciousness about the need for change and to consider alternative methods of production and distribution. They did not fail in this mission: the influence of Distributism has been considerable.[27] Furthermore, over the years Chesterton, Belloc and their followers did develop a Distributist program, though it never appeared in any single piece of writing.

Chesterton's own proposals for a Distributist order appeared in scattered articles throughout the pages of *G.K.'s Weekly* and in a book entitled *The Outline of Sanity* (1926). He recommended a two-pronged assault. The first invited individual citizens to check the drift toward monopoly and the destruction of small ownership by boycotting big shops, chain stores, trusts, and the like. Once the citizenry recognized that they could modify the drift toward the servile state, once the plutocratic pressures were reduced, the appetite for private ownership would return. Government also could take on some responsibilities at this stage of the struggle, both by forbidding plutocratic business practices such as price wars and below-cost selling that undermined small businesses, and by providing legal aid to small property holders.

The second part of Chesterton's reform package called for the construction of a model Distributist community along the lines of Eric Gill's cooperative experiment at Ditchling Common, which Gill hoped would serve as a moral and practical inspiration—a "cell of good living," in the words of Donald Attwater—for building a better society.[28] Again, Chesterton appealed to the government to provide his project a helping hand through a variety of programs, including, among others, differential taxation to discourage the sale of small property to big proprietors, the creation of opportunities for the propertyless to purchase land, the elimination of primogeniture, subsidization of experiments in small property holdings, the sponsorship of educational programs for teaching handicrafts and farming, the construction of a vast network of regional or local market systems to replace the huge marketing centers, such as Covent Garden in London, and so forth. Finally, he urged workers

to organize special guild associations that would exercise cooperative control of all industry, with the ultimate aim of buying out the
capitalists as owners of the means of production. Chesterton's call
for such comprehensive government action had the dreaded odor of
Fabianism, but he was convinced that the legislation could be effective if it were made intelligible to the average citizen. A special Distributist chancellor of the exchequer, not being "a servant of the
F.B.I. or the financiers, or the oil magnates, or any other system of
wire-pulling or back-stair politics . . . could word his act in clear,
simple language, having nothing to conceal, nothing to 'give away,'
and no axe to grind."[29]

Chesterton's appeal for a new Distributist order was clearly
revolutionary, yet he emphasized that participation in it must be
voluntary. it would be counterproductive to coerce people onto the
countryside or into trade guilds because that would undermine the
personal freedom that was the cornerstone of Distributism. Like-
wise, a draconian confiscation of wealth and property would destroy
the love of ownership that Distributists were trying to revive. Unlike
socialism or communism, Distributism was not a thing that could
be "done" to people; it could be realized only through their approval
and active participation. To Chesterton, Distributist reform meant
moral change:

> But it must be done in the spirit of a religion, of a revolution,
> and (I will add) of a renunciation. They must want to do it as
> they want to drive invaders out of a country or to stop the spread
> of a plague.[30]

Besides Chesterton's program of reforms, it is also necessary to
note the work of the various branches of the Distributist League
that formulated numerous practical proposals for social and economic reform. The most significant of these was an unemployment
manifesto called "The Birmingham Scheme," drafted by the League's
Birmingham branch in June 1928. The plan was updated periodi-
cally, and more than seventeen thousand copies had been published
by 1933. The purpose of the Birmingham plan was to eliminate the
economic waste of the dole and relieve industrial unemployment by
reviving Britain's decaying agricultural sector. It called for the gov-

ernment to address the problems of high imported food costs and unemployment by relocating workers on the soil as farmers. The Birmingham Distributists aimed to establish a free peasantry which could sustain itself on the land and yet supply produce to the industrial sector by marketing its surplus. All this could be accomplished, they insisted, by a minimum outlay above the cost of funding the dole. The plan was well received in Catholic circles, some recognizing a striking similarity between the Birmingham plan and President Roosevelt's scheme to encourage economically distressed families in rural areas to become self-sufficient.[31] In April 1930 the Distributist League asked the prime minister to appoint a royal commission to study the feasibility of implementing their proposals. Unfortunately, the government failed to give any serious consideration to the Birmingham scheme.

Belloc's suggestions for the creation of Distributism reached their most complete form in *An Essay on the Distribution of Property* (1936) and *The Crisis of Our Civilization* (1937). Belloc's thinking along these lines was more detailed than Chesterton's yet also more pessimistic, for by 1936 he had almost given up hope of reversing the onslaught of capitalism, socialism, and big government. Any general scheme for the restoration of freedom and property was useless in Belloc's mind because contemporary society had deteriorated beyond the point of repair. Distributism, therefore, could never be created by the state, for what was needed was a change in mood: "It is too late to reinforce it by design . . . our effort must everywhere be particular, local, and in its origins, small."[32] This explains why there is a deliberate vagueness in Belloc's writings about the specific economic and political steps needed to bring about Distributism. The conditions for its success demanded a popular recognition of the evil effects of capitalism and collectivism, which would then be followed by a revolution in values and ideas; political change would come after this requisite moral transformation. But Belloc was not sanguine about the matter: "To restore private property, however, must be a very long business, and has no chance of success unless people desire it, which I think in this country they no longer do."[33] Still, in *An Essay on the Restoration of Property* Belloc labored to develop a fairly detailed plan for the reestablishment of a small independent peasantry and classes of craftsmen and merchants, the three socioeconomic groupings he regarded necessary for the creation of a free society. Since the pervasiveness of monopoly capitalism had almost completely destroyed the possibility of a wide division of property in Britain, Belloc felt it necessary to invoke the power of the state to aid the small man in regaining his freedom. In even more detail than Chesterton, he outlined a series of suggestions for differential taxation schemes, state-protected cooperative credit institutions, progressive taxes against the sale of property, and, most importantly, the creation of self-governing, legally charted guilds modeled along medieval lines to serve as protective agencies for the private ownership of property. Belloc underscored the necessity of the interventionist state because a well-balanced system of property holding could never naturally emerge in the face of monopolistic economic tendencies. The new order would have to be artificially induced and, once restored, constantly sustained lest it lapse back into capitalism. Just as unchecked parliamentary politics turned to plutocracy, so private property tended to capitalism in a free enter-prise economy and thereby threatened to choke the middle classes, the "fly-wheel" of society, as Belloc called them. By 1937 Belloc was suggesting that it may well require dictatorial powers to save what he called "the middle class standard" from the powers of plutoc-racy and high finance.[34]

Yet any talk of merely political and economic reform was so much persiflage, for in Belloc's thinking essential change required first and foremost a recovery of the general spirit of Catholicism. Institutions, he insisted, were shaped by the moral spirit of the cul-ture, and they were sustained only so long as people adhered to the spiritual impulse from which the institutions arose. Convinced that economic freedom historically had grown out of the Catholic faith, Belloc maintained that Distributism could not remedy social fail-ures until the world were converted to Catholicism. "We cannot build up a society synthetically," wrote Belloc, "for it is an organic thing; we must see to it first that the vital principle is there from which the characters of the organism will develop."[35]

As in all matters, Belloc was more cynical than Chesterton and less tolerant of the untidiness of the democratic process; thus there was little chance, in his mind, that effective reform would come

through the system as presently constituted. "In every respect, wherever I turn," he wrote Nickerson, "the same conclusion is borne in
upon me, that our social and political condition in this country is
incurable."[36] England would need a dictatorship, one that could
wield effective power over the autonomous guild networks that
would be part of the Distributist state. Since monarchy had been a
traditional component of England's governing practices, Belloc was
convinced that a monarch, aided by what he called the "Councils
of Real Interests" (representatives of the various guilds), could most
effectively provide the responsible authoritarian leadership necessary for the large modern state. However, unlike his inspiration,
Charles Maurras and the *Action Française*, Belloc was never enamored of the idea of royalty per se; he rather saw it as the most practical mechanism for meeting the authoritarian role that degenerate
society so desperately needed. What Belloc really desired was a
dynasty of heroic strong men who could force society out of the
narrow paths of petty hedonism: "I have no doubt that monarchy
is what is needed now in every European nation . . . but . . . an existing dynasty like that of Philip of Orleans would be of the least
effect. . . . What will save our society when it comes will be some
new line of dynasties sprung from energetic individual men who
shall seize power."[37]

CHAPTER 8

The Appeal of Fascism

The anti-parliamentarian sentiments of Chesterton and Belloc, combined with Belloc's quest for a Napoleonic hero, made them and the new Distributists favorably disposed to the exploits of Mussolini and his mission to create a "New Roman Empire" in the robes of Catholicism. For this reason, the careers and political ideas of Chesterton and Belloc have been linked to the extreme Right that came into full bloom in the interwar years. For example, a leading historian of the British Right, J. R. Jones, suggests that Distributism reached its fullest articulation in the programs of Sir Oswald Mosley, leader of the British Union of Fascists. In some circles, both Chesterton and Belloc earned the reputations of having been fascist fellow travelers or, at the least, enemies of democracy.[1]

Mussolini deliberately appealed to Catholic sympathies by linking his Fascist regime to traditional Catholic corporatist ideas. Italy's corrupt legislative assembly with its bickering politicians was to be replaced by a corporative chamber consisting of professional and trade associations. The nation, achieving integration through the corporations, was declared an "organic whole." Labor of all kinds was now a social duty. The various corporations were to be democratically controlled by their membership, private property was safeguarded, excessive competition curbed, and disputes between management and labor were to be settled collectively with the aid of arbitration courts. The Fascists claimed to use the idea of corporatism as an instrument to suppress excessive individualism, special interest groups, and big business and finance for the national good of the organic state.

In what ways did G. K. Chesterton share the Fascist worldview? The syndicalist, anti-statist ideas that Fascism had appropriated to its cause would have found a natural resonance in the political concerns of Chesterton and Belloc. Those English laborers who had marched to the drums of syndicalism in the turbulent years before World War I had a deep distrust of the trade union officials and party politicians, who, they believed, had sold out to the moguls of capitalism. As we have seen, the men involved in this revolutionary-style unionism were influenced by Chesterton and Belloc, and the two writers offered the movement strong journalistic support. They viewed syndicalist activity as a healthy reaction to the advancement of the servile state, and they welcomed the kind of participatory democracy and desire for ownership that this revolutionary unionism encouraged.

Chesterton must be understood during these pre-war years as an integral part of a larger intellectual movement in protest against the state.[2] This protest appeared on the political level in the guild socialist movement; it was manifested philosophically in what was called pluralism.

The intellectuals who were associated with pluralism drew their inspiration from a variety of sources, but chiefly from Lord Acton, a Catholic thinker who was keenly aware of the corruption of state power, and who also was sympathetic to the Whig notion that freedom is best preserved when power is dispersed.[3] Above all, pluralism was a revolt against the Hegelian idealistic theory of state, which taken to its logical end would destroy the liberty of the individual. Belloc played a central role here, for his concept of the servile state was not only a protest against German idealism but a prognostication of the form which a future Hegelian society would assume.[4] What united the pluralists was their rejection of the state as morally sovereign and their opposition to using its agencies as tools for social reform.[5] It must be remembered that the Liberal Party's decision to expand the social role of government had helped drive Chesterton and Belloc from its ranks. The Fabians carried these statist tendencies even further. George Bernard Shaw, for example, championed a paternalistic government: "the State may be trusted with the rent of the country . . . with the land, the capital, and the organization of national industry—with all the sources of production, in short, which are now abandoned to the cupidity of irresponsible private individuals."[6]

The leading pre–World War I English pluralist was John Neville Figgis. Figgis worked out his ideas with the help of the legal theorist F. W. Maitland, and by drawing on the writings of Otto von Gierke, a German historian who believed that the medieval corporate ideal underlay the whole of Western historical development. Accepting the anarchist assumption that large-scale organizations necessitate oligarchy and dehumanizing bureaucracies, Figgis asserted that individuals should be allowed to pursue their own self-development within the framework of voluntary associations with a minimum of interference from governmental authorities. Like Chesterton, his theory of associations, according to which the group would have rights over the state, recognized that the best social structure was one that provided for the greatest development of individual personality.[7]

Figgis's pluralist arguments were carried out chiefly in terms of the Anglican Church, which in his view possessed a corporate personality that had evolved independently of any government. Thus he insisted that the state had no natural right to wield unrestricted power over it. Although he focused on the Anglican Church, Figgis contended that his theory of corporate freedom had a wider context and could be applied to all groups that had functions of primary socialization: the family, trade unions, universities, and various professional organizations. The state did not create any of these groups: they arose out of the "natural associative instincts of mankind" and should be treated as individuals.[8]

The pluralist state envisioned by Figgis was reflected in both guild socialism and Distributism. As noted previously, these movements had important links to Anglican intellectuals and both advocated voluntary, self-governing corporations with claims over the state. Figgis himself praised guild socialism and Distributism as illustrations of pluralism in practice; guild socialists and Distributists of many stripes acknowledged their debt to pluralist writers.[9]

Concern for the independence of groups within the state led many guild socialists and Distributists to welcome the appearance of corporatist governments following World War I. The first to win their praise was Gabrielle D'Annunzio's short-lived "Regency of Carnaro," established in Fiume in 1919. D'Annunzio vowed to turn Fiume into a model city amidst a Europe gone mad with capitalism. His constitution called for the creation of corporations for workers and employers, universal suffrage, a governing body based on functional representation, and dictatorial power for the leader in times of crises.

Similarly, Mussolini's experiment in corporatism initially received wide support from guild socialists and Distributists. A. J. Penty, for instance, held that the Italian Fascists were putting into practice the principles of *Rerum Novarum*. Like many pluralists, Penty took Mussolini's corporatist constitution at face value and believed it similar to his own vision of Distributism. On paper at least, Italian industry was to be controlled by self-governing corporations (which Penty saw as just another name for the regulative guild), large-scale industries were closely regulated by a central authority functioning in the public interest, wages were fixed, profits limited, and the state's governing body—Mussolini's Chamber of Deputies—operated on functional, not territorial, principles. Penty also complimented the Fascists for their efforts to foster a prosperous peasantry and their emphasis on national economic self-sufficiency, two ideas close to the hearts of all Distributists. In short, "Fascism . . . exists to defend tradition and human values while it seeks a wider distribution of property; it is Distributist rather than Collectivist."[10]

The corporate aspect of Fascism won Penty's approval, but there was a side to Mussolini that greatly troubled him, and that was Mussolini's self-professed totalitarianism. Penty ultimately concluded that these two faces of Fascism could not be reconciled. The state's claim to total sovereignty implied the centralization of authority and, as such, was opposed in principle to the true corporatist state, which reposed on the pluralistic postulate of federalism.

Chesterton's analysis of Fascism had much in common with Penty's assessment of the matter. Like Penty, Chesterton initially welcomed the emergence of Italian Fascism, in his case because it did away with what was most loathsome about parliamentary politics: the corruption of polity through the hidden power of money. In this respect, Mussolini's attack on parliamentarianism was a healthy response to the treason of Liberalism. The true Liberal was supposed to stand against the spirit of oligarchy, against the big estates that undermined small proprietors and the big employers who oppressed the workers. Republican government in the tradition of Jefferson and of the leaders of the French Revolution was open and honest. But then, lamented Chesterton, entered the secret society, the creation of finance and selfish interest groups. While the true Liberals thought they were building a brotherhood of all men, power secretly passed to the conspirators who used money for private, not public interests. Chesterton believed that Mussolini was rebelling against this perversion of republican principles: "He had reverted to the original ideal that public life should be public; and emphasized it in the most dramatic manner by stamping on the Secret Societies as on a tangle of vipers."[11] This was merely the acceptance of what Robespierre had called the civic necessity of virtue. Chesterton believed that Thomas Jefferson and the early Republicans would have understood Mussolini perfectly.

Chesterton frequently could defend Italian Fascism for the above reasons, and, of course, his deep affection for Catholic culture, which he thought Mussolini was reviving, also strongly influenced his views on the matter. Yet, Chesterton never gave his imprimatur to Fascism, either as practiced in Italy or as championed in Britain. Although he could point out the positive dimensions of Mussolini's rebellion against a rotten Liberalism, he was never taken in by the Fascist corporate state. Indeed, Chesterton condemned the totalitarian, statist tendencies in Fascism from the moment they appeared. In his mind, Fascism's rebellion against secrecy led to a problem as sinister as the evil it replaced, and that was the one-party state. A similar proclivity in British politics had spawned the "party system" and Chesterton's own disaffection from Parliament. His objection to Parliament was not that it was the domain of a two-party system, consisting of brawling Tories and Liberals with concrete disagreements, but that it only pretended to be so. The party system was a facade designed to hide the fact that power was already centralized: "It occupied a central position between the Prime Minister and the

Leader of the Opposition; not infrequently in the form of an unknown financier who was advising them both."[12] Mussolini's destruction of the secret societies and of the power of finance simply cleared the decks for a new kind of undemocratic, centralized power, only this one was more lethal in that it lacked what Chesterton called a "fixed moral principle" and was totalitarian. His position on Fascism could be summed up quite succinctly: "The whole of the real case for Fascism can be put in two words never printed in our newspapers: secret societies. The whole case against Fascism can be put in one word now never used and almost forgotten: legitimacy."[13] In short, Fascism was justified in smashing a corrupted Parliament, but it was never a satisfactory political solution because it rested not on authority but only on power.

Thus, to label Chesterton a fascist fellow traveler and an anti-democrat is a misreading of his career and the pluralist principles upon which it was built.[14] The irony here is that Chesterton criticized Italian Fascism precisely because it was not democratic. Nor is there adequate appreciation for the fact that Chesterton was a persistent foe of British fascism. The British Union of Fascists assiduously tried to convert Distributists to its cause. Many of the movement's programs were close to the hearts of Chestertonians (the establishment of peasant proprietorship, the destruction of chain stores and monopolies, the elimination of what it called the "party game," functional representation, and so forth). Yet, while Chesterton was alive, the Mosleyites were unable to convince Distributists to accept their version of the corporatist state. Chesterton demonstrated quite clearly that fascist government, with its insistence on the unquestioned sovereignty of the state, could never be accepted by either Distributists or Catholics, because it ultimately denied the dignity and liberty of the common man.[15]

The tendency to associate Chesterton with fascism is largely the product of his relationship with Belloc and the fact that, after his death in 1936, his journal and various Distributists became increasingly enamored of fascism, both in Italy and in Britain. Belloc was never able to bring himself to denounce Mussolini's totalitarianism, and by the late 1930s he was writing fulsomely of fascism in Italy and Spain. As late as 1939, for example, Belloc could argue that

Mussolini's Fascists had saved Italy and the heart of Western civilization from communism and that Mussolini, in the process, had created "for the first time within living memory a guild system."[16]

Chesterton's opposition to fascism rested firmly on pluralist grounds: he regarded its version of corporatism as bogus because the principle upon which it reposed was illegitimate, statist, and totalitarian. In the face of fashionable Fascism and the "toppling simplifications of the Totalitarian State," wrote Chesterton, there was much to appreciate in liberalism and its language of liberty:

> The Totalitarian State is now making a clean sweep of all our old notions of liberty, even more than the French Revolution made a clean sweep of *all* the old ideas of loyalty. It is the Church that excommunicates; but, in the very word, implies that a communion stands open for a restored communicant. It is the State that *exterminates;* it is the State that abolishes absolutely and altogether; whether it is the American State abolishing beer, or the Fascist State abolishing parties, or the Hitlerite State abolishing everything but itself.[17]

The British, Mosleyite version of the Fascist creed would never have appealed to Chesterton because it was, in large part, a reincarnation of the pre-1914 Right. This tradition was diametrically opposed to the anarcho-syndicalist, pluralistic pre-War legacy out of which Chesterton emerged. Like the Tory imperialists and the "Coefficients" (a "brain trust" to create an efficiently organized British empire) who gathered around the Webbs, Lord Milner, Leo Amery, and others who were the true predecessors of British fascism, Oswald Mosley was motivated primarily by the desire for strong government and was obsessed with the idea of using experts who could streamline the administration of the state. Indeed, Mosley's main criticism of Parliament was that it was simply inefficient. The historian Henry A. Turner has called Mosley an "authoritarian modernizer" in a society which had "resolved unwittingly to stand on the ancient ways."[18] Nothing could be further removed from the philosophy of Chesterton, who was a warrior against modernity seeking solutions to its evils precisely by returning to the spirit of "ancient ways."

Belloc's relationship with the Latin varieties of fascism was more complicated and sympathetic than that of G. K. Chesterton. This can best be appreciated in the context of his ideas about Jews and communism. From the beginning of his journalistic career, Belloc had established himself as a critic of Jewish influence in British political and financial affairs.

Both Gilbert Chesterton and Belloc believed that Jews, a "people apart" who had withstood assimilation into European national communities, had been given an opportunity to maximize their quest for economic gain in the individualist environment fostered by the Protestant revolt. They were solvents of medieval culture and the driving force behind the rise of capitalism. The Jews were always for Chesterton and Belloc a symbol of the financial power ("usury," as they called it) that destroyed medieval (Catholic) civilization. Belloc, however, later began to see certain connections between Jews— who, he claimed, worked in secret behind the scenes and were in the habit of changing their names—and a host of evils: corruption of parliamentary politics, international finance (imperialism), Freemasonry, and communism.

Scholars recently have noted an important linkage between the conspiracy theories of British fascists and the anti-Semitism of Belloc and the group of writers associated with his early journalistic endeavors.[19] The defining issue for Belloc's and Cecil Chesterton's *Eye-Witness* and the later *New Witness* was the war against corruption in public life, and from the outset both claimed that Jews were a key source of this problem. Their journals highlighted the increasing involvement of Jews in important economic and political sectors of British life. Belloc's literary stature gave considerable weight to this campaign, and the publicity associated with what the Witness group called the "Jewish factor" created a rich imagery and a legend, indeed a subculture, that future British fascist groups could draw upon.[20] The language and programs of the British Union of Fascists, in particular, struck a familiar chord in Distributist ears. Its message fell on intellectual soil fertilized by Belloc's conspiratorial theories, and there was significant cross-over between the two movements by the late 1930s.

In addition, some have argued that the more blatant anti-Semites and fascists in the 1930s who warned of an international

Jewish-communist-Freemason plot to take over the world (an updating of that notorious forgery, *The Protocols of the Elders of Zion*) were elaborating on a set of positions already established in some detail by Belloc.[21] Indeed, many of these extremists, like Belloc, were Catholics.

Most disconcerting were the fascist tirades of the influential radio priest of Royal Oak, Michigan, Father Charles Coughlin. Father Coughlin shared Chesterton's and Belloc's populism and antipathy to modernity. He voiced the frustrations of a rural American mentality that could not reconcile itself with the growth of big government and monopoly capitalism. Coughlin's campaign against the New Deal, Jews, communism, and Freemasons had the imprimatur of his superior and protector, Bishop Michael J. Gallagher of Detroit. Gallagher as a young seminarian had studied in Innsbruck, where he fell under the influence of the Austrian/Vogelsang version of social Catholicism with its authoritarian, corporatist, and ideological anti-Semitic underpinnings. Coughlin's journal was the widely circulated *Social Justice Review*, which provided a forum for his anti-Semitic, conspiratorial rantings. Belloc contributed a good many articles to this paper, further cementing his name to the cause of British and American fascism. Coughlin deeply appreciated Belloc's work.[22] Father Coughlin's commentaries articulated three themes which previously had been elaborated upon by Hilaire Belloc: the Jews, he asserted, were responsible for the abuses of international banking and the rise of materialistic communism; Nazism was a defensive reaction to protect Germany from an alliance between Jews and communists; and the democracies, being weak and decadent, were themselves responsible for the problems of world depression.

A number of influential Catholics in both Britain and America felt compelled to speak out against the association of their faith with fascism and anti-Semitism (for example, George Shuster, Father H. A. Reinhold, Donald Attwater, Father James Gillis, Dorothy Day, and Wilfrid Parsons, S.J.), and in many instances they addressed Belloc's influence in the matter. The Catholic Association for International Peace, for instance, in its pamphlet "The Church and the Jews," condemned what it called the "moderate anti-Semitism" of men like Belloc. Father Lawrason Riggs of Yale

University's More House in his attack on a scurrilous anti-Semitic article by Father Stanislaus Hogan, O.P., given wide circulation in America, also remarked on the Belloc connection.[23] Father Riggs told his readers that although Belloc was a great defender of the faith, he was "primarily an artist," whose political and economic views frequently needed correction and in many cases had caused considerable harm to the Church.[24]

One of the most sweeping condemnations of Father Coughlin and Catholic anti-Semitism, accompanied by a detailed scholarly analysis of the sources of such thinking (in this case Alfred Rosenberg's *The Myth of the 20th Century*), was written by George Shuster.[25] He was especially concerned about the work of the Coughlin-affiliated Christian Front. This organization had close ties to the Nazi-funded German-American Bund. The New York branch of the Front was headed by Marcel Honore and Walter Ogden. At one of their meetings, Shuster noted, members praised Hitler's accomplishments and recommended a wholesale massacre of Jews.[26] Shuster's attack on Father Coughlin seems to have been prompted by the desires of a committee of influential New York Catholics to disassociate the Church from Coughlin's anti-Semitic propaganda.[27] This was no easy task, as much of Father Coughlin's prestige came from his priestly office and from his habit of lacing his remarks with references from Catholic social teaching. Adding to his apparent authority was a group of Coughlinite priests who banded together under the name "Clerical Reservists of Christ the King." Some Holy Name societies, Knights of Columbus Councils, and Catholic War Vets in the New York City area also espoused his doctrines with great enthusiasm.

Belloc first established a high public profile on the issue of the Jewish problem in the *Eye-Witness* and the *New Witness*. Yet long before this journalistic crusade, Belloc as a Liberal MP had suggested that the plutocratic wire-pullers behind the scenes were Jews. In fact, Belloc's opposition to the Boer War was based, in large part, on this assumption. He believed that the Liberal Party's political fund was in the hands of certain rich men with financial stakes in South Africa, the "Rand Magnates" like Barney Barnato, who, Belloc asserted, initiated the Boer War to protect their investments.

Belloc also saw the hand of Jews behind the Congo Reform Association, an organization formed by E. D. Morel in 1904 to force the Belgians to treat Congo natives more humanely. In a series of articles in the *New Age* Belloc implied that the real powers behind Morel's campaign were Jewish financiers who hoped to destroy the Belgian government's monopoly in order to make a fortune for themselves in the Congo rubber trade.[28]

The specter of a Jewish conspiracy also was a feature of Belloc's pre–World War I novels. Throughout *Emmanuel Burden* (1904), *Mr. Clutterbuck's Election* (1909), *A Change in the Cabinet* (1909), and *Pongo and the Bull* (1910) there lurk wealthy Jews who continually change their names, speak with heavy foreign accents, and have unsavory physical appearances (greasy curly hair, swarthy complexions, hooked noses, and so forth). These men own important newspapers and devise exploitative development schemes in India and Africa, working behind the scenes while using respectable, hardworking English businessmen as fronts. They control the party system through the power of bribery. In the end, Belloc's stories show how the old elites—honest, good folks with deep roots to the English soil but naive about the power of hidden money—pass from the scene. It is the men of cosmopolitan wealth who inherit the new world.

The conspiracy of finance was soon linked in Belloc's mind with that traditional enemy of Roman Catholicism, international Freemasonry. Belloc began to make connections between Masonry, Jewish associations, and anti-Catholicism in a series of articles on the infamous Ferrer affair.

Francisco Ferrer Guardia was a Spanish apostate Catholic with a deep hatred of the Church who became well known as a freethinking education reformer. His goal was to liberate Spanish education from the control of Catholicism and, through a curriculum of rational, scientific studies, prepare what he called "a better humanity."[29] Such ideas were considered a serious threat to Spain's traditional culture, one in which Church and state were intimately linked. Ferrer's educational philosophy made him sympathetic to anarchism (he called himself an *acrata*, a philosophical anarchist), but he denied that he was ever a complete convert to the creed. He had personal affiliations with individual anarchists but apparently was not associated with them in any organizational fashion. Ferrer had also consistently condemned anarchist acts of violence. However, when the librarian of Ferrer's libertarian school in Barcelona, the so-called *Escuela Moderna,* threw a bomb at the Spanish king and queen in May 1906, Ferrer was arrested and charged with complicity. He was soon released due to lack of evidence. But an oppressive environment in Spain (the government closed the *Escuela Moderna*) forced Ferrer to emigrate to Paris and London, where he had contacts with the anarchist Prince Peter Kropotkin.

Ferrer returned to Barcelona in the summer of 1909, just as a prolonged political crisis produced outbursts of social protest. Anarchists and members of the Radical Republican Party exhorted their followers to turn this anger against the Church, a convenient symbol of political and economic tyranny. Matters became worse in July when the government called up reservists in Catalonia for service in an unpopular war in Morocco. In what came to be called the "Tragic Week" (*Semana Tragica*)," Barcelona was seized by the passion of a general strike which soon erupted into a spontaneous social rebellion. Anarchists quickly claimed responsibility for the affair. The enraged lower-class rioters singled out religious property rather than the persons of clergy, government, army, the upper classes, or the economic system itself. Church property was targeted as a protest against the failings of the clergy to fulfill their religious and social responsibilities.[30]

The government's response was extreme, and in the aftermath it undertook a witch hunt for anarchists whom it blamed for the destruction. Ferrer's educational ideas, his strong anticlericalism, and the government's frustration over his previous acquittal made him a prime target of the crackdown. Although the police had no clear evidence against him (indeed, Ferrer had opposed plans for a general strike and established himself as an outspoken critic of anarchist violence), a court martial found him guilty of having "decisively influenced" the Radical party to rebellion. He was executed in October 1909. By all accounts, this was a grave miscarriage of justice, and an international outcry condemning the reactionary behavior of the Spanish government soon followed.[31]

Belloc's response to these events adumbrated his reaction to the outbreak of the Spanish Civil War some twenty seven-years later. The violence against the Church was the defining issue here, and, as in 1936, he was quick to smell conspiracy. Belloc recognized that the *Semana Tragica* was a carefully planned attack on Church property, but he failed to appreciate the reasons behind the action. Although the rebellion had started as an antiwar protest, no military establishment was attacked; nor, for that matter, were banks, factories, or the homes of wealthy capitalists so hated by the laboring masses. The Radicals who directed the violence once it erupted saw the destruction of Church property as an end in itself. The issue, however, was not essentially religious but rather political and economic. Because of its special relationship with the established elites, the Spanish Church had become the symbol of privilege and oppression and the reviled instrument of state authority. The Spanish Catholic hierarchy was perceived as having sacrificed its spiritual obligations to the cause of conservative politics. Anticlericalism was not confined to the laboring classes. Army officers, for example, were notably passive during the attacks and Catholic bourgeois laymen failed to defend clerical property.[32]

Belloc, on the other hand, had a far simpler explanation for the Barcelona uprising: the city had been ripe for a violent explosion because it was full of Jewish usurers despised by the poor. Yet in this bastion of capitalism, not a single piece of capitalist property was touched by rioters, Belloc noted, suggesting that the conspirators had diverted the destitute to a false target.

Working-class alienation from the Spanish Church and the long history of anticlericalism in that country were important factors in the "Tragic Week," as they would be in the later, even more tragic events of civil war. Belloc, rather than examining the social roots of these factors, a task he undertook eagerly in analyzing institutional Catholicism at the time of the French Revolution, simply charged that the *Semana Tragica* resulted from a tripartite conspiracy against the faith engineered by communists, Jews, and Freemasons.[33] These events, he claimed, were part of a "synchronized" action by the press and those who hated religion. As for Ferrer, Belloc had no doubt as to his guilt: "his views upon human morals in general . . .

were such as would not be tolerated . . . in any strictly governed country, not the least of all in England."[34] Belloc pointed out that Ferrer had been a high-ranking official of Grand Orient Free-masonry. When Ferrer fled Spain for Paris in 1906 he made friends with the "Jew Nacquet," whose political business was to introduce divorce into the French Code of Law. In England Ferrer took up with his Bloomsbury friends, most of whom were "Dissenters of one kind or another" interested in undermining Catholicism in Spain.[35] The Freemasons rushed to Ferrer's defense, Belloc noted, and when this failed, they engineered riots all over Europe.[36]

Belloc gave a warning in his analysis of the Ferrer case, one that would be elaborated more fully in the *Eye-Witness* and *New Witness* and in his book *The Jews*. The violent events in Spain in 1909 were a presage of worse to come, he claimed. The masses of Europe were utterly discontented. Their condition in crowded cities was becom-ing increasingly wretched and inhumane, and they could not be expected to tolerate much longer an economic and spiritual sickness repellent to all European instinct and tradition. The Church lost its hold on these urban masses at the onset of the industrial revolution, and throughout the nineteenth century it had struggled to win them back from the grip of secret societies and men of wealth, who used the workers' hunger and thirst for social justice in the service of their own ends. Such would be the source of the inevitable outbursts of violence that would plague European society in the years ahead.

Belloc possibly was correct in regarding the *Semana Tragica* as a turning point of sorts in Europe's political history; but it was so for reasons far different from those he recognized. The vigorous repression that followed, and the mistaken impression that the re-bellion was primarily fueled by separatist aspirations, seriously crip-pled the reformist efforts of Catalan politicians, who represented the vanguard of change for Spanish politics. After the crisis ended, Spanish politicians ceased to use the legislature as a tool for effect-ing much-needed reform. Furthermore, the failure of the workers to achieve any semblance of representative government in Catalonia, the most industrialized section of the nation, was a major setback for the cause of Spanish democracy and would have a direct bear-ing on the origins of civil war in 1936. Henceforth, Spanish workers turned exclusively to labor movements, not political parties, for social and economic salvation, and these functioned outside the political structure.[37]

Belloc's analysis of the Ferrer affair, informed chiefly by a religious polemical agenda, revealed his inadequacies as a commentator on Latin politics. As early as 1909 his writings show that he failed completely to appreciate the way in which the Spanish Church had become identified in the popular mind with defense of a hated feudal social order, thereby fueling the intense anticlericalism of the *Semana Tragica*. Contrary to Belloc's arguments, the Barcelona uprising had no significant international connections.[38] The issues that inspired it were largely social and religious, and its chief objective was to destroy the property and wealth of the clergy.[39] The reactionary Spanish hierarchy refused even moderate political reform lest it open the door for separation of Church and state. Pope Leo XIII's encyclical *Rerum Novarum* was largely ignored in Spain, its precepts seldom even discussed in high Church circles. Not surprisingly, the clergy were frequent targets of working-class violence, since they symbolized the source of social and economic unhappiness.

Hilaire Belloc's obsession with the intrigues of international Masonry and Jewish financiers increasingly blinded him to the more complex issues of class warfare that were behind the social upheavals in Spain and later in Italy. Those in his intellectual orbit manifested the same myopia. Nowhere was this better illustrated than in a major financial scandal that soon unfolded in Britain in 1912.

There was a dramatic shift in the *Eye-Witness's* suspicions of Jews as well as parliamentary political corruption with the disclosure of the so-called Marconi affair, discussed briefly in chapter 5. Following this incident the editors were convinced that the "Jewish connection" was proven beyond all doubt. In the words of Cecil Chesterton, who coined the term "Marconi scandal" and who played a major role in exposing those involved, the event was the fulfillment of a prophecy and thus the justification of a hypothesis.[40]

The details of the Marconi affair were complex and need only be briefly touched on here. The British Admiralty proposed to construct a chain of wireless radio stations throughout the Empire in order to attain instant communications with its war vessels. Negotiations for building the project were undertaken in March 1910 with Godfrey Isaacs, the managing director of the London Marconi Wireless and Telegraph Company. Godfrey was a brother of the attorney general, Sir Rufus Isaacs. In March 1912 the postmaster-general, Herbert Samuel, provisionally accepted the contract. But before this decision was made public, Godfrey Isaacs travelled to the United States where he bought up the assets of a competing company and reissued the new shares for the American Marconi subsidiary at a higher cost. In April 1912 he offered shares of the American company at a reduced cost to his brother Harry Isaacs. The announcement of the British government's contract with the London Marconi company naturally would have increased the value of these stocks. Harry quickly sold his shares to his brother Rufus, who in turn offered some to the chancellor of the Exchequer, David Lloyd George. All this took place before Parliament made public its decision to give the London Marconi company the contract.

Rumors and questions about ministers making money at public expense forced the government to investigate matters. In the autumn of 1912 a parliamentary select committee was charged with conducting an inquiry. Its report split on party lines, and the men involved essentially were cleared of any corruption charges.

Cecil Chesterton in his *New Witness* along with Leo Maxse's *National Review* (a journal of the right that criticized the Conservative Party for its failure to entertain direct action political tactics) led the charge on what they declared was a sell-out to plutocratic interests. The *New Witness* saw a clear connection between the party system and Jewish influence. The journal claimed that the peerage was a Jewish monopoly, its "alien gold" having bought the soul of the Liberal Party. The *New Witness* group's attacks on those implicated in the scandal were nothing short of savage. Rufus Isaacs, wrote Cecil Chesterton, was a Jew who could not be expected to understand the subtle workings of a Christian conscience: "He is an alien, a nomad, an Asiatic, the heir of a religious and racial tradition wholly alien from ours. He is amongst us: he is not of us."[41] The *New Witness* alleged that the Marconi affair involved others outside the country and that it was part of a wider conspiracy in international finance. An important secret role, the journal asserted, was played by Amsterdam Jews who had created the boom in Marconi shares in the first place.[42] Cecil Chesterton spearheaded the *New Witness's* assault on the Marconi men, making crude references to what he called "the chosen" and "alien money-lenders." Considerable space in the paper was given over to Frank Hugh O'Donnell, an intemperate former Irish Nationalist MP whose anti-Jewish diatribes seemed to be lifted straight from the pages of the *Protocols*. O'Donnell appears to have been speaking for a number of anti-Semites who were beginning to establish close links to the paper and its campaign against corruption. O'Donnell's opinions were featured in a weekly column entitled "Twenty Years Later." His commentaries on the behavior of Jews in France closely resembled the articles by the French monarchist Charles Maurras in *Action Française*, a proto-fascist journal which he regularly singled out for the highest praise.

O'Donnell was certainly mirroring Belloc's opinions on the subject, for he too was an avid reader of *Action Française* and expressed admiration for its social, political, and economic positions. In a letter to E. S. P. Haynes, for example, Belloc wrote that Maurras was "perhaps the most intelligent man of our generation."[43] Belloc's enthusiasm for such people increased during the interwar years. Belloc urged his good friend Maurice Baring to become acquainted with Robert Brasillach, the French literary fascist ("we have long since seen Fascism as a poem, the very poetry of the twentieth century")[44] who, along with Pierre Gaxotte, a right-wing historian known for his anti-Freemasonry vitriol, were the backbone of *Je suis partout*. This was a sophisticated anti-Semitic weekly review dominated by young *Action Française* epigoni who eulogized Italian Fascism and worked toward a better understanding between France and the Nazis. Along with its attacks on communism, Belloc found the paper's campaign against Judeo-Marxists and Freemasons appealing. *Je suis partout*, he wrote Baring, was intelligent and well written, and he urged that Baring take up reading it "unless you are put off by the violence of its opinions."[45]

O'Donnell's strident columns in the *New Witness* assailed the poison of hidden conspirators in a style that even Belloc thought excessive. O'Donnell ceaselessly excoriated the Third Republic for its Marconi-type scandals, the first of which was triggered by Dreyfus, who, in the *New Witness* group's view, symbolized the international evil of the Marconi men. The "constant element" in the development of French Republicanism was a "Jewish Directory," "traitorous, corrupt and decadent."[46] England and France were but a small part of the picture, insisted O'Donnell. Hundreds and thousands of people in several modern countries were being "registered, marked down, tabooed, reduced to helplessness and poverty, solely through the vast organization controlled by the Jew."[47] Everywhere, in the United States, England, in India and South Africa, enormous confederations of "Judean promoters and directors" were engineering a complex cosmopolitan plan to exploit all the world's wealth. Its victory would reveal "Le Juif Roi de L'Epoque."[48]

Such crude anti-Semitic diatribes were too much even for Belloc. In a number of letters to Maurice Baring, Belloc expressed dismay at the paper's careless attacks on Jews, fearing that it could destroy the *New Witness's* credibility.[49] Belloc also received many letters critical of Cecil Chesterton's rudeness and poor editorial responsibility from his close friend and confident, E. S. P. Haynes, who himself was a source of financial support for the *New Witness*. Belloc responded apologetically, essentially agreeing with Haynes and fearing that the public would hold him responsible for what was said in the paper. Yet it was style, not substance, with which Belloc took issue, for the *New Witness*, he insisted, "only goes forward by the power that truth has inherent in itself."[50]

Cecil Chesterton eventually was convicted of libel for his scurrilous assaults on Godfrey Isaacs in the Marconi scandal, an attack which had served to launch the *New Witness's* wider campaign against international Jewry. Isaacs' civil suit greatly discredited Cecil Chesterton and his friends for their nefarious role in the Marconi affair. But in a perverse sort of way the Chesterton people saw this as a moral victory, mainly because they had caught the attention of the nation and were given a platform for their scandalmongering. Unfortunately, the damage done to the Jewish families wrongfully implicated by the *New Witness* group was deep and long-lasting. The whole affair contributed to the further deterioration of political decency and dialogue in Britain, exacerbating the negative climate of discourse brought on by labor unrest and the women's suffrage movement.[51]

The libel conviction by no means throttled the anti-Semitism of the *Eye-witness* and the *New Witness*. Soon thereafter the campaign against Jews was carried over into organized group activity with the formation of the National League for Clean Government. After 1918 the movement was resurrected under the name of the "*New Witness* League." From the outset the League's two key figures were Cecil Chesterton and F. Hugh O'Donnell. Chesterton was its central publicist; O'Donnell was one of the League's main speakers and chairman of the Organizing Committee.

The *raison d'être* of this organization was the Marconi scandal, which for the *New Witness* circle represented Britain's Dreyfus affair. Although the League's main objective was to fight corruption in Parliament, it was always assumed that this problem was part and parcel of a Jewish plot to subvert political life. As O'Donnell pointed out, the issue of clean government was interlinked with all other problems, and the constant element is the "reign of the Judean." The Jew, he wrote, "finds everywhere material for his activity and willing flunkies for his tips and his ground floor prices. No larva can thrive and multiply except in the soil or the sediment which is its suitable environment."[52]

Many who joined the League were not hostile to Jews and came from all over the political spectrum—for example, the right-wing Conservative Leo Maxse supported it, as did Fred Jowett, Labour MP for Bradford West, Thomas Burt, Lib-Lab MP for Morpeth, and various radical trade union activists with syndicalist proclivities. However, there was an active core of anti-Semites from literary, political, and journalistic circles who, along with the editor of the *New Witness*, managed to shape the propaganda to fit their particular vision. The cartoonist David Low attended one of the League's first meetings called to expose the sale of honors and corruption in the House of Lords. There was much to be said about such matters, Low noted, but he quickly became uneasy and irritated by the vague anti-Semitism that filled the air.[53]

Two leading figures of the League were Rowland Hunt, an anti-Semitic Conservative MP, and Vivian Carter, editor of the *Bystander*. Carter voiced an ethnocentric hostility to Jews, much like that of the Chestertons and Belloc, which asserted that their cosmopolitan loyalties were incompatible with British patriotism. Carter insisted that Jews be prevented from changing their oriental-sounding names so they could be easily identified. She also recommended that Jews be given special sectors of the cities in which to reside, thereby preventing an unhealthy mixing of the populations.[54]

The League had some successes in promoting the candidacy of independent MPs in by-elections and campaigning against what it called "place men." It raised public awareness about laws abusive of human rights, exposed food scandals, probably was partly responsible for defeating the sterility provisions of the so-called Mental Deficiency Bill, and worked diligently against the eugenicists' campaign for birth control. Yet even these battles were colored by tones of anti-Semitism. The *New Witness,* for example, asserted that the eugenicists were part of a Jewish-German conspiracy designed to decrease the British population and undermine the foundation of common morality by destroying the home.[55]

The League for Clean Government and the later *New Witness* League incorporated three dimensions of anti-Semitism that were reenacted in the British fascist movements of the interwar years: the articulation of an ethnocentric "Britain-for-the-British" idea; the specter of a politico-economic conspiracy; and the creation of a refuge for racists like O'Donnell, serving in this sense as a respectable front legitimated by the more august names of others attached to the movement.[56] For these reasons, contemporary scholars of British politics and racism, in particular Kenneth Lunn and others, consider the *New Witness* group and the League precursors of the fascist movements of the 1930s. Indeed, Lunn has gone so far as to argue that the Distributist League of the interwar years was an extension of the League for Clean Government, since G. K. Chesterton's association claimed a common heritage and promised to continue the approach of its predecessor.[57] However, there was a marked difference in tone in the Distributist movement while G. K. Chesterton was involved in its activities, and nothing was ever written in *G.K.'s Weekly* that resembled the vituperative anti-Semitic diatribes of his brother's papers. During Chesterton's years at the helm the Distributist League did not perpetuate the Jewish conspiracy thesis, nor would it accept any affiliation with British fascist organizations.

However, Kenneth Lunn makes it clear that one of the main avenues to the 1930s fascist subculture of anti-Semitism was Belloc's final updating of the conspiracy thesis in his book *The Jews* (1922). This book was nothing more than a reiteration of what Belloc already had written during the *Eye-Witness* and *New Witness* days (suggesting a certain continuity in thought between these formative years and the postwar period), differing only in that it incorporated the Bolshevik Revolution of 1917 in the broader context of the Jewish problem.

Belloc went to great lengths in insisting that his book was not inspired by a dislike of Jews as a people. Indeed, he dedicated the work to his Jewish secretary, Miss Ruby Goldsmith. His objective in writing the book was to alert both Jews and Gentiles to a serious problem and to make suggestions for avoiding a tragedy that racial anti-Semitism could produce. It was necessary to accept the fact, wrote Belloc, that the Jews were an "alien body" producing great friction within the organism in which it resided. To acquaint his readers with the "Jewish problem," Belloc outlined their rise to prominence in politics and finance. Jews had gained a monopoly in the international news media, garnered enormous power through an alliance with Freemasonry, and by the end of the century had strong representation within the governing institutions of Western Europe "fifty or one hundred fold" more than was their due in proportion to their numbers. All this, along with Jewish imperialist conspiracies via their domination of international finance, and the exposure of their involvement in political corruption (Dreyfus and Marconi), triggered the outbreak of late-nineteenth-century anti-Semitism.

The unfortunate culmination of these cosmopolitan tendencies, insisted Belloc, was Jewish control of Bolshevism. Expanding on the fact that Marx, Trotsky, and several of the prominent Bolsheviks were Jewish, Belloc asserted that Jews engineered the Russian Revolution of 1917 and that their secret international networks were the glue holding the communist movement together throughout the world. The Russian Jews, he admitted, were possessed of a positive political ideal in communism: it was a force that could destroy the excesses and evils of capitalism. Jews were well suited to this task, wrote Belloc, because communism as a creed ran against the natural strivings of European nationalism. The Bolsheviks sought to destroy private property, and the Jews could direct this endeavor because they were not compromised by the sympathy of civic instinct. The Jew could destroy capitalism, the spawn of unfettered greed, because he had "neither the political instinct for the sanctity of property in his national tradition nor a religious doctrine supporting and expressing such an interest."[58] Jewish consciousness transcended national boundaries, since Jews did not possess the European sense of patriotism. A Jew's patriotism was of a different complexion, for he lacked traditions rooted in a common soil.

Belloc hoped this problem could be resolved amicably. However, the solution required that Jews be recognized as a wholly separate nationality and treated legally as such, replete with certain rights and privileges. What worked against this, he said, was the Jew's power to conform externally to his "temporary surroundings."

Throughout his career, Belloc insisted that he was not an anti-Semite, a prejudice he equated with racism. The true anti-Semite, he argued, disliked or hated Jews as a people. It is important to remember that Belloc was an early critic of the Nazis, condemning their abominable and immoral persecution of Jews. He claimed that such behavior was exactly what he had warned against in his book *The Jews.*[59] What distinguished the Nazis from Belloc was that he opposed Jews for religious and nationalistic reasons (their cosmopolitan culture mitigated sentiments of patriotism), not because of their race. Belloc was legitimately horrified at the Nazis' war against the Jews. He viewed the Nazis as irrational extremists: it was not possible to appeal to a group's intelligence when their passions were moved by the far greater emotion of hatred for people as a race.[60] Just because communism was under Jewish direction and is essentially a Jewish movement, wrote Belloc, "it is not necessary to turn savagely on the whole Jewish people as the Nazis did."[61] Belloc also showed scorn for English racists. For example, he called Nesta Webster's scurrilously anti-Semitic *The Cause of the World Unrest* a "lunatic book" and soundly denounced its obsessions.[62]

II

Belloc was an avid supporter of Mussolini from the beginning of the dictator's experiments in Fascism, primarily because he believed that

Il Duce was resurrecting an empire of Roman proportions grounded upon Catholic principles and traditions. Mussolini's mission appeared to complement Belloc's singular idea of Catholicism as culture. Only on rare occasions, and then only privately, would Belloc offer a critical evaluation of Mussolini's behavior.[63]

As a young man, however, Belloc believed that the inspiration and power for resurrecting a Catholic Latin civilization would come from France. Writing to his wife from Sienna in 1901 while preparing *The Path to Rome*, Belloc lamented that "Italy *has been* dead and I have no great passion for dead and putrefying things." Yet if the French were wise and carefully avoided war, "they will lead Europe and all the Latin race will grow up in their shadow." At this early date, Belloc prophetically observed that, despite the dreary influence of effete Italian priests, the salvation of the Mediterranean would come from popular rule:

> The test of Italy's renovation will be the hatred of England. When you find the English running down Italy then you may be sure she is all right. I am waiting for that day.[64]

In the meantime, unlike his friend Hoffman Nickerson, who believed the troubles of the postwar years lay with democracy and the concept of egalitarianism (Nickerson thought President Roosevelt embodied many of the negative attributes of both), Belloc identified the problem as far deeper. On the most fundamental level it was rooted in the loss of religion. The real battle today, Belloc wrote Nickerson, is between the Church and those trying to destroy it. The issue "will depend largely upon the arrival or non-arrival of a man or groups of men who are prepared to make heavy sacrifices in the attempt to revive religion."[65] The heroes were soon to arrive: for Belloc they were Mussolini, Salazar, Dollfus, and Franco.

Belloc was convinced that there was a diplomatic conspiracy against the faith which commenced with the Versailles Peace Treaty. Belloc's analysis of the settlement sheds additional light on the reasons for his support of Mussolini's imperialist claims.[66] In Belloc's view, Italy had been unjustly deprived of the spoils of victory after World War I by the international bankers in Paris, London, and

New York. Not a single colony, not a mile of the Eastern Adriatic coast was granted to Italy as payment for her considerable sacrifices. Working in tandem with the financial conspirators was the Masonically organized, anticlerical political machinery of Europe. These forces made sure that Catholic Bavaria was separated from Austria, and they worked against the creation of a Catholic Danubian state and a Catholic Renish nation, assuring, instead, that the anti-Catholic Prussia would be reinstated on the Rhine. Of the new nation states erected after the Armistice, only Czechoslovakia, claimed Belloc, was given favorable treatment, and this was because Prague was violently and cruelly anti-Catholic. On the other hand, Poland had every imaginable obstacle put in its path to nationhood, and this was due, insisted Belloc, to the fact that Poland was the bastion of Catholic culture in Eastern Europe.[67] Italy's postwar international objectives, Belloc believed, were shaped by the need to overcome this anti-Catholic political and financial alliance. The first step toward this end was the creation of a strong state, and this Mussolini had accomplished by smashing a corrupted parliamentary government (putting an end to the nefarious "party system," similar in nature to that which plagued and perverted English politics), shutting down the conspiratorial Masonic lodges, and throttling a so-called "free press." Thereby Mussolini had laid the groundwork for a restoration of Caesarism, or, as Belloc preferred to call it, a "return to monarchy."

By the late 1930s Belloc could inform his readers that Fascist Italy and Nazi Germany were two major examples of the popular return of monarchy (a force which back in 1901 he believed would be the salvation of the Mediterranean). In his analysis, Britain's disagreements with Germany and Italy were simply the clash between monarchy and "money power" for the soul of Europe. The new Reich and Italy had risen up to do battle on a double front, establishing a new corporativism against the strength of monopoly capitalism and its "twin brother," international communism. However, Belloc emphasized that there were vital differences between these neo-monarchies. The Italian variety was conducted by a man of genius who had inherited all the political talent of a special race. Mussolini lived in the "real memory" of Rome, while the German monarchy paraded about on an opera stage immersed in the darkness of Teutonic barbarism:

> The new Italian monarchy evokes the classics; the new German monarchy evokes Wagnerian actors, elderly and bawling in tow coloured wigs. . . . But the major and permanent difference between the two is in their contrasting attitude towards the religion that made Europe.[68]

Belloc's enthusiasm for the mission of Mussolini appeared to know no bounds. Belloc and his circle could not even bring themselves to criticize publicly the Italian Fascist's anti-Jewish policies (though they had no trouble denouncing Hitler's pogroms). The *Weekly Review,* successor to *G.K.'s Weekly* after Chesterton's death, insisted in the face of the obvious that the Italian pogroms should not be seen as a mere copy of German policy. Although the paper admitted that Mussolini's campaign was a cruel one, it refused to condemn him: the fact remains "that it [the Jews] is a people apart, with ideals and habits often violently opposed to the nature of its surroundings." "Jewish energy has been responsible for a great number of anti-national activities—the Communist Revolution being the most notorious—and thus a country with strong national ambitions cannot afford to harbor a Jewish population."[69]

Belloc's ultimate public endorsement of Italian Fascism came in June 1939. Mussolini's dictatorship, he claimed, saved the state and the heart of civilization from breaking under the vile hand of Moscow. In the process of saving Western culture, the Italian Fascist created for the first time within living memory a guild system: "*This,* rather than the excess of highly centralized control, is what we ought to associate with the name of Mussolini."[70] In short, dictatorship was an acceptable means for the greater purpose of preserving Catholic culture if it were carried out in the spirit of Belloc's version of Distributism.[71] In any case, by 1939 Belloc seems to have concluded that the enemies of the faith were so formidable that Mussolini's solution was the only option. Nevertheless, he did not believe that the Fascist dictatorship was intended to be permanent: "Italy is the most civilized of the European nations and civilization and despotism do

not go well together."[72] Authoritarian government was a dangerous expedient and must be short-lived. As Belloc put it to Maurice
Baring, "Despotism is excellent as a sharp momentary remedy, but
it is no more a permanent food than raw brandy."[73]

In contrast to the fawning Belloc, Chesterton tended to see
Mussolini as a rather comic figure and frequently poked fun at him.
It was a case of extreme "self-dramatization which causes the Fas-
cist to see himself as the heir of Imperial Rome," Chesterton wrote
regarding the invasion of Abyssinia; possessing another nation's ter-
ritory was an assertion of the doctrine of force in its ugliest form.[74]
Chesterton also was not especially enamored of the men on the
French Right who had cast such spells over his friend Belloc. Chester-
ton, for example, privately deplored the defense of Maurras in *G.K.'s
Weekly*.[75]

G. K. Chesterton's most personal and difficult struggle with Italian Fascism occurred with Mussolini's invasion of Abyssinia in 1935.
As opposed to his friend Belloc, Chesterton was far less certain
about what the invasion represented, and he was deeply troubled by
the imperialist implications of Mussolini's action and the suffering
and injustice inflicted on the Abyssinians. The episode became a
watershed in the history of Distributism, for it permanently divided
the followers of the Chesterton and Belloc. Chesterton died before
the controversy was resolved within Distributist circles, and thereafter the movement split apart. One group, represented by the more
liberal-minded of Chesterton's followers, drifted away from *G.K.'s
Weekly*. Another faction sympathetic to Belloc's increasingly extremist thinking endorsed a radically right-wing approach to politics and
economic issues. Many became fascists and fellow travelers. This
latter group, with Belloc's support, took control of *G.K.'s Weekly* in
August 1937 and renamed it the *Weekly Review* in March 1938.

Belloc had no doubt about the meaning of Mussolini's Abyssinian adventure. He wrote to Chesterton that the American-led move
against Italy represented "the conspiracy" in action:

It is an error to exaggerate the importance of the Masonic organization. It is a much bigger error to be as ignorant of it as our
people are. There are more Masons in America than in all the

rest of the world. The Lodges all over resent their suppression by Mussolini and hate the growth of a new and strong Catholic power.[76]

Belloc publicly stated his analysis of the Abyssinian invasion in *G.K.'s Weekly* in December 1935. A strong Catholic power in the Mediterranean was a clear military threat to Britain, he argued, and this could explain the Foreign Office's opposition to the Italians. But this was only one part of an anti-Catholic alliance poised against Mussolini, claimed Belloc, the most highly organized element being the communist movement led by intelligent and active Jews who work from Moscow. The third component, of course, was international Freemasonry, whose natural antipathy was increased by the emergence of a new powerful Catholic nation: "Wherever the Catholic Church is powerful masonry becomes the organization or caucus directing the political forces which aim at a destruction of a Catholic society."[77]

The invasion of Abyssinia, for Belloc, was simply Mussolini's revenge for the slights of the Versailles peace settlement: "What the Italians want is a country in which to invest and to exploit such as France and England have; they were cheated out of it after the War and have been angry since."[78] The outrage expressed by the so-called democratic countries was sheer hypocrisy, said Belloc, an "odious Puritan itch for mixing up ordinary policy with morals,"[79] since the Italians merely were doing what Britain, France, and others had done in the previous century. In this case, however, the Italians were motivated by more than the cash nexus of economic imperialism. Mussolini was carrying forward his Catholic cultural mission, namely, converting the barbarian to Christianity. Talk of an Abyssinian "nation" was nothing more than political propaganda preceding from the Jews of London and New York. The people of Abyssinia, Belloc wrote his son, "are a mass of more or less barbaric tribes, slave-owning and slave raiding." They certainly do not understand or feel patriotism; it is rather "a feeling that they do not want work and worry and organization."[80] These comments were in stark contrast to what Chesterton and Belloc had said about the natives of South Africa who had suffered the blows of British imperial aggression during the Boer War. Was Belloc applying a double standard in his analysis of European imperialism? Was Mussolini's imperialist adventure different because it was allegedly driven by Catholic ideals?

Those who supported Belloc's position on Abyssinia got the upper hand in the editorial room of *G.K.'s Weekly*. Chesterton himself noted that he did not agree with these people, but in the spirit of openness that governed his paper, he had always permitted them to express their differences.[81]

The faction that shaped the journal's posture on the Abyssinian affair—an element that closely corresponded to what Donald Attwater appropriately labeled the "Latinophiles"[82]—asserted that Mussolini had been coerced into invading Africa by the machinations of international capitalism. Gregory Macdonald, for instance, maintained that Mussolini was in a desperate race against a consortium of New York-London-Paris financiers who were trying to gain control over the mineral riches of Abyssinia before he did.[83] Essentially, the Latinophiles placed the Abyssinian campaign in the context of a conspiracy of international moneylenders to undermine Italian financial independence by forcing the country off the gold standard. An important step in the "Money Power's" goal of monopolizing international wealth was to make the major European economies dependent upon American finance. At times this could be done by issuing special loans calculated to draw the recipient closer into the clutches of Wall Street. Such had been the case with Britain when she had been extended credit in the sterling crisis of 1931 and forced off the gold standard due to pressures from American moneylenders (of course the Latinophiles always assumed that these people were Jews). Now an assault was underway against those states that had maintained their financial independence.

In a series of articles in *G.K.'s Weekly* concerning the workings of the "international credit system," Gregory Macdonald and C. Featherstone Hammond argued that the Abyssinian invasion was the result of Mussolini's efforts to break through this financial blockade by obtaining raw materials outside the sterling market and the capitalist oil monopoly. These journalists criticized the imposition of sanctions on Italy. They were convinced that it represented a political extension of the "Money Power's" assault on the gold bloc nations. Macdonald reasoned that the various proposals for an international boycott of Italian products were simply a ploy to make Italy lose gold reserves by forcing it to pay in gold for imports. Instead, he and Mr. Hammond proposed a wider solution to the Abyssinian problem which was designed to counterattack the conspiracy of international financiers. Rather than supporting sanctions against Italy, which only favored Wall Street's money conspiracy, they called for an international conference to settle the outstanding European debt, currency, and trade problems. Macdonald hoped that such a conference would promulgate plans for the free distribution of raw materials, since it was Italy's need for resources that prompted the Abyssinian crisis in the first place.[84] Such journalistic wishful thinking, uncomfortably close to Mussolini's own justification for the campaign, was thought sufficient to preclude Italian imperialist claims in Africa.

Another facet of the Latinophile thesis was that Mussolini was on a mission for higher civilization; the invasion was prompted by the duty to bring a more wholesome Christian way of life to benighted Africans.[85] This was an argument given prominence by the Catholic writer Evelyn Waugh. Although few contemporaries took Waugh's analysis of the Abyssinian conflict seriously (a recent scholar considered his account of the war so "provably inaccurate" and "openly biased in favour of Italy that his testimony could not be taken as any more factual than his very entertaining novels"),[86] it was given a highly positive profile in Douglas Woodruff's *The Tablet* and the *Catholic Herald*. Waugh wrote that Abyssinia was so depraved and worthless that Italy had a Christian mission to conquer the land, thereby bringing a higher culture to its barbarous people.[87]

A number of Distributists vehemently denounced Mussolini's imperialist behavior as a case of unprovoked aggression akin to Britain's deplorable action in the Boer War. Chesterton took a middle path on the issue, condemning Mussolini's behavior as a throwback to the discredited ways of the nineteenth century.[88] Il Duce, he wrote, was a reactionary in so far as he "thinks that whatever Palmerston thought good for England, or Bismarck thought good for Germany, will naturally be good for Italy . . . he thinks patriotism involves imperialism." Chesterton's position turned on what he called "the whole matter of the relapse." "The instant immediate effect, at this moment, of Italy resuming the old attack on niggers, is England and America resuming an old attack on dagoes. All this amounts to a shrinking back into nationalism in the narrowest sense."[89] Yet, wrote Chesterton, one should not single out the Italian campaign as blind barbarism, for it must be seen as atavistic, part and parcel of an imperialism practiced by all the major powers at the end of the previous century.

The more moderate, liberal Distributists expressed shock at the Latinophile thesis (which appeared sufficiently pro-fascist to win praise from Ezra Pound) and demanded an adamant denunciation of Mussolini. Even Chesterton's criticism was not strong enough medicine for this group, since it lacked the hard, satirical edge of his earlier pro-Boer campaign. Maurice Reckitt was so upset with the editorial positions of *G.K.'s Weekly* that he privately wrote Chesterton to say that he was prepared to resign from the paper's board of directors. Chesterton responded by explaining that he had been out of town when the crisis broke and urged Reckitt to hold off until he had time to issue a complete statement on the affair. Between the two of us, wrote Chesterton, "I do think myself that there ought to have been a more definitive condemnation of the attack on Abyssinia."[90]

A major figure in the Distributist movement, Archie Currie, along with Conrad Bonacina, deputy chairman of the Distributist League, publicly attacked the *Weekly's* editorial line and lamented the fact that Chesterton's response lacked the fury of the Boer War days. What was the "black and special sin," asked Currie, "that these wretched people have committed alone of all the nations in all history, that the last champion of liberty should yawn politely at the spectacle of their enslavement?"[91]

Currie's comments were a blow to Chesterton, which he felt personally. Chesterton pointed out that he sympathized with his critics, and in *G.K.'s Weekly* he denounced what he called "the return of conquest," whether it be in the form of an armed Italian or an English capitalist acting for an American company that was secretly buying up Abyssinia. Although the latter was more insidious and dangerous than the soldier, both were contemptible and deserved condemnation.[92] We hold the aggression of Italy, wrote Chesterton, "every bit as abominable and indefensible as all aggression *in Africa.*" But it was important to keep the regrettable Abyssinian escapade in the proper perspective, namely, that of the evils of international finance in which Britain herself had a large share.[93]

None of this was enough to mollify the liberal Distributists. As Bonacina put it, they agreed with what Chesterton said but were unsatisfied with what was not said. In the case of Abyssinia the soldier himself was tainted by the banker, for he was behaving as the financier's best friend. Mussolini was motivated by the claims of glory and finance: nothing will convince me, said Bonacina, "that Prussianism suddenly loses its savour of iniquity, just because it finds a Latin practitioner."[94]

The Abyssinian crisis and Chesterton's uninspired criticism of Italian imperialism created a deep fissure in Distributist ranks.[95] this fissure was only deepened following Chesterton's untimely death in June 1936.

Gregory Macdonald has spoken and written about the power struggles behind the scenes of *G.K.'s Weekly* and the League. The public criticism by the Currie faction, he revealed, greatly troubled Chesterton, caused an explosion of anger within *G.K.'s Weekly*, and destroyed a healthy equilibrium between diverse groups of opinions.[96] Macdonald was convinced that the liberal Distributists were being manipulated by communists, and that the refusal of the *G.K.'s Weekly* to go along with the Left on an anti-fascist campaign (he says that the paper recognized Marxism and Nazism as two aspects of the Hegelian exaltation of the state) led to the false accusation that the paper was fascist.[97] For Macdonald and the right-wing Distributists, the League of Nation's criticism of Mussolini and especially the British and American denunciations of the Abyssinian invasion were an integral part of the Left's efforts to remake the cultural landscape of Europe.

After Chesterton's death the Distributist movement broke apart along liberal and reactionary lines. The Latinophiles gained control of the newspaper, and from this point on there was a steady drift into the world of fascists and fellow-travelers.[98] The *Weekly Review*, successor to *G.K.'s Weekly*, upheld what could be called a philo-fascist line in matters relating to international affairs, and a num-

ber of its leading writers had associations with British fascist organizations.[99] The paper provided its readers with an obsessive screed
of anti-communist, anti-Jewish commentaries that disgraced the
legacy of G. K. Chesterton's journalism. The association of Chesterton's name with the *Weekly Review* has had the unfortunate effect
of linking his career with the extreme right and fascist fellow-
travelers. One of Britain's better-known fascists, A. K. Chesterton,
wrote regular columns in the *Weekly Review* urging a return to a
guild society; but unlike his cousin, G. K. Chesterton, he called for
a dictator to establish the corporate state. Maurice Reckitt captured
the tragedy of these events best when he wrote that with the death
of the author of *Outline of Sanity*, Distributism, now also bereft of
sanity, died too: "When England's greatest modern democrat laid
down the flaming torch he held aloft through so long a night, the
movement grouped round him spluttered out as a damp squib mid
the showy and mechanical fire works of Fascism."[100]

 After Chesterton's death, Belloc tried to fill in as editor of *G.K.'s
Weekly* and the *Weekly Review*, but he soon left these journals to join
forces with a number of other right-wing English writers who embraced fascism so as a suitable ally against the danger of international communism. Belloc had an important influence on such
people. His ideas on the Jewish problem, Latin fascism, and the
unholy alliance between Jews, communism, and Freemasonry
stretched well beyond immediate Distributist circles. What could
be called the "Bellocian line" on such issues seemed to be echoed
in a variety of publications of the right, such as Lady Houston's
Saturday Review, the *London Mercury* under the editorship of John
Squire, Jerrold's *English Review*, Seward Collins' *The American
Review*, and the two Catholic journals, the *Tablet* under Woodruff
and the *Catholic Herald*. The group of writers associated with the
January Club, discussed at more length in chapter 12, also expressed
an anti-Semitic, pro-fascist sociopolitical vision that was inspired
by Belloc's writings.

CHAPTER 9

Early Catholic Critics
of Fascism

The Latinophiles' response to Mussolini stands in sharp contrast to that of a small number of liberal Catholics, especially Italians and Germans who felt the boot of fascist terrorism firsthand. They gave Mussolini's corporativism a close critical analysis, and their conclusions were very different indeed from those of Belloc's circle. As early as 1926, for instance, A. Grandi wrote a harsh critique of the Italian version of corporatism in the Catholic weekly *Cronaca sociale d'Italia*. Grandi noted that *Rerum Novarum* and every Catholic political philosopher from Ketteler to La Tour du Pin had insisted that Catholic corporatism must repose on the fundamental principles of freedom for individuals, free elections, and guild autonomy from the state. Not a single one of these principles was upheld by Fascist corporativism.[1]

Drawing extensively from *Quadragesimo Anno,* an updating of *Rerum Novarum* by Pope Pius XI drafted in 1931 and largely ignored by Belloc and his circle, the liberal Catholics examined how Italian Fascism compared in theory and practice to the corporatism outlined in the labor encyclicals. Their ultimate criticism of Mussolini's Fascism was essentially the same as G. K. Chesterton's: its excessive bureaucratism designed to centralize total power in the state was in defiance of natural law. Referring to the Fascist political program, Pope Pius XI warned:

> The new syndical and corporative organization tends to have an excessively bureaucratic and political character . . . and it ends in serving particular political aims rather than contributing to the initiation and promotion of a better social order.[2]

A central argument of *Quadragesimo Anno* was that the true purpose of social activity was to help individual members of the corporate body, never to destroy or absorb them. Barbara Ward, translator of the writings of the Italian politician and sociologist Father Don Luigi Sturzo, echoed Grandi's critique of Fascism when she claimed in 1939 that Mussolini's state-forged, state-imposed, and state-controlled corporatism "bears as much resemblance to the Catholic ideal of an organic society as does a lath-and-canvas pantomime oak to a living tree."[3] An essential tenet of the Catholic notion of a just society, Ward emphasized, was the sanctity of the human personality. Both state and society must exist for the sake of the individual (a central point in Chesterton's attack on collectivism). Yet to be truly human the individual requires freedom, and the basic safeguard of such liberty is the right to possess private property: Fascism claimed rights of state over individual rights.

The highly influential American Benedictine educator Father Virgil Michel, an advocate of Distributism, editor of *Orate Fratres*, and founder of the American liturgical movement, also condemned Italian corporativism on fundamentally Chestertonian principles. In the totalitarian states, he wrote, autonomy and the power of self-determination are taken away from individuals and small groups and centered more and more in larger units, ultimately in the one all-embracing society of the state. In a true corporative order, on the other hand, power would devolve to smaller units, the larger group merely safeguarding the autonomy of the small.[4] In any case, wrote Michel, reiterating what both Chesterton and Belloc had always stressed, the essential prerequisite for regenerating the social order is not the establishment of any specific political or economic structure, but rather a "change of heart," a return to the Christian spirit of the Gospels. Ultimately, it is the spirit behind the institutions that will give shape to the social order. This was absent in Mussolini's Italy.

Ironically, perhaps the most incisive critique of Italian corporativism along the lines of Catholic social principles came from the German economist Wilhelm Röpke, himself not a Catholic.[5] Röpke was startled at the general lack of analysis—Catholic or otherwise—of the Italian corporate state. Outside Marxist circles, virtually no one had undertaken a serious study of the documents of Italian corporativism. At the London International Studies Conference in 1933, for example, at which Italian economic theory and practice were discussed with representatives of Mussolini's government, not a single person questioned whether such a thing as the *corporozione* actually existed. In fact, noted Röpke, fascist economics escapes scientific analysis altogether because free discussion and inquiry are not allowed in the nations that embrace it.[6] Thus, he asserted, there "is perhaps no other sort of literature containing so high a percentage of worthless trash."[7] However, since Italian Fascism was monopolistic, interventionist, and totalitarian, its version of the corporate state was fundamentally incompatible with the Catholic teachings on the virtues of the medieval corporative order. In Fascism, claimed Röpke, it is not the state that is "corporativo" but the corporation that is "statale." As such, the state strangles spontaneity and individual creativity. Yet the Fascist state is more than window dressing. It is rather a mechanism for achieving three purposes: it serves a political function by organizing the national economy so it can be penetrated by Fascist control; it restricts free enterprise so as to facilitate the growth of a command economy; and, thirdly, it regiments society so it can be manipulated more rationally by a totalitarian dictator. The only way to fully appreciate the profound incompatibilities between Fascism and the economics of modern Catholicism, emphasized Röpke, was to consult Pope Pius XI's *Quadragesimo Anno*.[8]

Indeed, there was hardly a single Italian Fascist institution that did not seek to absorb the individual into the clutches of state bureaucracy. In this sense, Fascist corporativism was the very reverse of Catholic corporate thinking: Mussolini intended the corporations to be instruments for maximizing the control of his state. To Leo XIII their main value was the opposite, namely, to serve as a brake on the two chief threats to Christian freedom: unrestricted capitalism and excessive interference by the state.[9] This also was a distinction emphasized by Pope Pius in *Quadragesimo Anno*.

The eminent Catholic historian D. A. Binchy, who wrote a seminal study in 1941 of church-state relations in Mussolini's Italy, noted the singular failure of many Catholic publications to analyze critically the programs of Mussolini's Fascists. For instance, the

London *Tablet's* assertion that the Italian corporate state was "recovering the system traditional to Catholic Europe" and its claim that there were parallels between Fascist corporations and the self-governing professions in Britain revealed, suggested Binchy, that the writer simply knew nothing about the Italian system, or, even worse, was advancing some political agenda.[10]

The most knowledgeable Catholic source of information about Mussolini's corporatism was a priest who personally experienced its violent birth and suffered dearly from its excesses. This was the scholar-politician Father Don Luigi Sturzo. Founder of the Popular Party (Partito Popolare), out of which emerged the Italian Christian Democrats, Sturzo was Fascism's fiercest critic. In May 1924 Mussolini personally forced Sturzo to resign as General Secretary of the Popular Party, and after persistent harassment by the secret police he was eventually driven into exile.[11] After Sturzo's departure from politics, the democratic Popular Party, which had resisted Mussolini steadfastly in Parliament, split into factions, and the Fascists began a program of systematic violence against Catholic clergy, institutions, and lay organizations throughout the country.

Don Luigi Sturzo initially took refuge in England, where he received a cool welcome from right-wing Catholics. Broken in health, Sturzo had the good fortune of being rescued from the German bombing of London in 1941; a poor Sicilian worker from America brought him to Brooklyn, where he took up residence in a back room among the poor. A committee of prominent Catholics led by Father H. A. Reinhold, a refugee from Nazi Germany who, like Sturzo, had also been victimized by Catholic conservatives, convinced the Bishop of St. Augustine to take in the Italian priest.[12] Sturzo wrote regularly for French Catholic journals and the *Commonweal*, the *Dublin Review*, *Blackfriars*, and Dorothy Day's *Catholic Worker*. Sturzo quickly established an international reputation as a historical sociologist. But he was given little space and attention in the conservative American and English Catholic media. Hilaire Belloc, who by the 1930s was recognized as the best-known and most influential Catholic writer in the English language,[13] chose to ignore Sturzo for the most part, and what little attention he did give the Italian priest was mostly negative. Francesco Saverio Nitti, for example, a pioneering scholar of modern Catholic social philosophy who served as prime minister of Italy from 1919 to 1920 and, like Sturzo, was forced to flee the country, wrote Don Luigi from Zurich in March 1925: "Who is this journalist Belloc who has written so many stupidities about you, about freedom and about fascism. He must be an ignorant swindler or at the very least a person of repugnant cynicism."[14]

Belloc's response to Sturzo might initially seem puzzling, since the Popular Party pursued essentially a Distributist program. But, as earlier chapters make clear, Belloc by the 1930s was consumed with the fear of international Marxism and what he perceived to be the insidious plans of Jews and Freemasons. To his way of thinking, Mussolini provided the only hope for rolling back this tripartite threat to Christian civilization. Sturzo's commentaries only served to weaken "Rome's mission" to resurrect a Christian civilization in the Mediterranean. From Catholics who shared Belloc's thinking on the matter, Sturzo suffered the same fate as his refugee friend and fellow liturgist, H. A. Reinhold. Both were targeted by conservative British and American Catholics as dangerous leftists and denounced for disloyalty to the tribe.[15] Dorothy Day, for instance, claimed that even mentioning Sturzo's name in some Catholic circles during the 1930s was sufficient to bring down upon one the charge of being a communist.[16]

In the spirit of the Leonine encyclicals, Don Luigi Sturzo's lifelong political mission was to harmonize Christian teachings with democracy. As opposed to most Catholic intellectuals and clergymen, Sturzo, who for fifteen years was the mayor of Caltagirone in Sicily, had a long and distinguished career as a social and political activist. His political experiences were brutal to the extreme. The obstacles to carrying the torch of democracy in Fascist Italy were a far cry from the frustrations of political reformers in countries with a long tradition of freedom and political pluralism. Unlike Belloc, however, Sturzo never gave up on the system of democracy.

Sturzo's positive approach to political problems owed much to his teacher Giuseppe Toniolo, an apostle of Christian democracy, an eminent professor of political economy at the University of Pisa, and a major collaborator in the preparation of *Rerum Novarum*.

Under Toniolo's inspiration, Sturzo did extensive research on Marxism, and his voluminous writings on the sociology of knowledge reveal a kinship with the thinking of Marx, Emile Durkheim, Max Weber, and Karl Manheim. Ultimately Sturzo came to believe that the historical process was fueled by a dialectic between conservative and progressive forces—an ongoing struggle in which, despite setbacks, the rational and the good would endure.[17] The sociologist Nicholas Timasheff, who knew Sturzo well during his stay at Fordham University, has described his sociology as essentially "synthetic" with an inclination toward personalism. This is reflected in Sturzo's refusal to recognize society as legitimate outside or above the individual personality: society is a sum total of its individual parts, yet a person cannot act without membership in some organization which he himself must form and control.[18]

Sturzo's political objective was twofold. In the spirit of the papal labor encyclicals he called for an improvement of social conditions and, closely linked to this, the participation of the masses in the life of the nation. This required an awakening of popular consciousness that went beyond merely social and political levels. Like those involved in the British-American liturgical movement, Sturzo recognized that real social reform had to spring from a religious insight that accepted the individual personality as the transcendent core of all social action.

This insight informed Sturzo's vision as a historical sociologist, which was uniquely Catholic and at variance with mainstream sociological thinking. It asserted that the spiritual quest was every bit as intrinsic to human needs as were economic drives. Sturzo's position dovetailed with the sociological thinking of the liturgists in the sense that he believed that civilization could achieve a happy equilibrium only by integrating the natural, humanistic world with the force of grace. This demanded a "re-enchantment" of the universe, a transmutation of values with Christ the divine being brought back into the process of history.

Sturzo's sociology also was shaped by his personal involvement in the rough-and-tumble of Italian provincial politics. While a young Sicilian priest and advocate of radical agrarian reforms, he led a three-month strike of eighty thousand peasants until they reached a satisfactory settlement with landlords. Sturzo was an advocate of what he defined as "Popularism," a call for radical reconstruction of the capitalist system in which property would be widely distributed and property-owners would commit themselves to use it in a socially responsible manner.[19] He also was a firm believer in a co-partnership between capital and labor, and these notions became important platforms in the political movement that centered on the Italian Popular Party.

Sturzo's radical agrarian ideas, especially his advocacy of the expropriation of land for destitute peasants, brought accusations that he was a socialist. This was a fate he shared with his radical predecessors Bishop Ketteler and Cardinal Manning. Of course, like Ketteler and Manning, Sturzo was no socialist, for he believed in the sanctity of private property. The goal of his Popular Party was to encourage the Distributist ideal of a politically decentralized nation of small proprietors. The party demanded government compensation for landlords whose excess property would be redistributed to the needy.[20] Furthermore, like the Distributists, Sturzo believed in the efficacy of free enterprise. His reform plan called for a "vocational corporatism," a fraternal and equal collaboration between capital and labor. The function of the state was to oversee this enterprise, protecting the rights and interests of each partner but never interfering in their internal governance.[21]

Sturzo's career as a young priest in Sicily and as mayor of Caltagirone had convinced him that the social evils he hoped to overcome on the local level had their roots in the activity of the Italian national state. Therefore, he concluded, it became a pragmatic and moral imperative to use the state as the instrument for change, since Christian teaching emphasized that maintaining the public order was a first objective, indeed the *raison d'être*, of government. To accomplish this in Italy, however, would mean overcoming the alienation of Church and state that had developed out of the Risorgimento and the occupation of Rome by the national army. Italian unification was carried out from above—not from within the context of an idealized confederation of states—through the power of the kingdom of Piedmont. The system imposed on Italy's varied regions and cultures was a unitary one, grafted from British and French experiences and forged on wholly political fixtures without well-defined social and economic underpinnings.

Following the unification of Italy the Italian Church went into political isolation. It ultimately forbad Catholics to become involved in the political process. This policy was known as the *non-expedite* (political participation "is not expedient"), and as a result, Catholic action in Italy permeated social and cultural life independent of politics. Sturzo played a major role in convincing the Vatican to lift the prohibition against lay political abstentionism, for he believed that the political process was the only means of integrating the state with the diverse social, cultural, and economic traditions of regional Italy. Only then, after establishing a rapport with the citizenry, could the government formulate realistic reform programs for rectifying the social and economic ills of the nation. Within a month after the revocation of the *non-expedite*, Sturzo founded the Popular Party (January 1919).

The driving purpose of the Popular Party was to overcome the alienation and bureaucratic distance between state and people, thereby bringing to completion the Risorgimento along the principles of a healthy pluralism. In order to protect Italy's rich regional traditions and to expand the democratic process, Sturzo's party called for parliamentary reform through proportional representation, votes for women, and various legislative, judicial, and labor reforms designed to encourage the expression of diverse national interests. It also hoped to improve the conditions of the working class and to promote the popular ownership of private property.

Many Americans who studied Sturzo have believed that his ideas complemented the political vision of Jeffersonian democracy. Like Jefferson, Sturzo appreciated the vitalism that sprang from a decentralized political order. The manifesto of his Popular Party, published in January 1919, not only reflected the sentiments of Thomas Jefferson but equally could have been drafted by the English pluralists, a tradition that molded the political liberalism of G. K. Chesterton:

For a centralizing state, seeking to restrict all organizing powers and all civic and individual activities, we would substitute, on

constitutional grounds, a state . . . respectful of the natural centers and organisms—the family, occupational groups, townships,
communes—giving way before the rights of human personality
and encouraging its initiatives.[22]

Unlike Hilaire Belloc, who veered from liberalism to authoritarian integral Catholicism, Don Luigi Sturzo stands firmly in a tradition that embraces the political principles of Ozanam, Ketteler,
Manning, Pope Leo XIII, and finally Chesterton. Like them, he saw
no reason why Catholic theology was incompatible with liberal
democracy. The Church, Sturzo emphasized, is indifferent to political form so long as the imperatives of morality and religion are
respected. Sturzo knew from personal experience that Mussolini's
Fascist regime did not pass this basic test. But democracy—the
Anglo-Saxon liberal/pluralistic variety—had revealed a capacity to
govern justly by protecting the moral and religious spheres of the
community.

It was upon the principles of liberal democracy that Sturzo
spoke out against Mussolini's Fascism. From the outset, Sturzo
pointed out to his constituents that the "Law of 1926" (also known
as the "Rocco Law," since it was drafted by Mussolini's minister of
justice, Alfredo Rocco), which abolished the right to strike and
established compulsory procedures for settling labor disputes, was a
tool of totalitarian rule since it only recognized the legality of Fascist trade unions. (It is interesting to recall that Belloc condemned
similar ideas of compulsory labor arbitration in Britain during the
pre–World War I labor disputes.) The secretaries of each union, who
were given the power to settle labor disputes, were not elected by
union members but were rather official appointees of the state.

The so-called corporations in Mussolini's Italy were constructed
upon Fascist syndicates. The syndicates represented employers,
workers, and state officials and met regularly under the supervision
of Mussolini. All delegates to the syndicates, however, were hand-
picked by the government, and the entire setup was ultimately under
the control of Il Duce himself. In short, the syndicates were monopolies of the state, a fact to which Pius XI referred in *Quadragesimo
Anno*. This was far removed from the corporatism discussed in *Rerum*

Novarum, which stressed the principle of autonomy for the guilds. Catholic corporate thinkers insisted that each syndicate enjoy freedom and freely elect representatives to a national corporative council.

Sturzo's "hands-on" views of the real character of Fascist corporatism were corroborated by various disinterested journalistic and academic sources to which any well-read, non-Italian Catholic had access. For example, an independent scholarly analysis of the Italian political system was undertaken by Carl T. Schmidt, a lecturer in economics at Columbia University. Having written an impressive book on Italian agricultural programs, Schmidt was awarded a Social Science Research Council Fellowship in 1935 in order to study corporative policy in Italy. His *The Corporative State in Action: Italy under Fascism* (1939) laid bare the hollowness of Mussolini's claims to have established a society along lines set forth by the papal labor encyclicals and the programs of the Distributist movement.

Schmidt showed that the Fascists, contrary to their claims of making Italy safe from anarchy and Bolshevism, were really waging war on liberalism and democracy. In this respect they were "carrying on the old battle of privileged groups against the masses of their countrymen."[23] To accomplish their objectives, the Fascists had to destroy institutions that served the common man, in particular, the Italian labor movement. With the creation of the Fascist syndicates in 1926, ushered in by strike-breaking Blackshirt squadrists who crushed both socialist and Catholic unions, Mussolini had achieved this goal. As Sturzo had pointed out as early as 1926, Schmidt noted that the twenty-two "corporations" that emerged from such syndicates were composed of employers and party officials selected by the Fascist Party. These were tools for binding the Italian workers firmly to their employers, and beyond that, to the political chiefs of the state. In a phrase that could have been penned by the author of *The Servile State*, Schmidt asserted that Mussolini's corporations were "the ball and chain that reduces wage-earners to helplessness, making them into passive raw materials for the 'higher' purposes of the nation."[24]

Schmidt's research also exposed the fraudulence of Fascist agrarian reform. Mussolini's highly publicized land reclamation schemes, largely underwritten by public funds, had provided next to nothing for the rural masses they were touted to benefit. Despite the claims by Fascist politicians that landless peasants would be given a greater share in ownership, the real beneficiaries were large landowners. Schmidt's studies showed that after 1926, during the very years when the regime was supposedly strengthening small proprietors, there was a systematic elimination of independent farmers, the number of "operating owners" having fallen by nearly 750,000 from 1921 through 1936. Yet, at the same time, the number of cash-and-share-tenants and sharecroppers increased by 1.2 million.[25] Schmidt concluded that when stripped of its "spiritual" and anti-Marxist rhetoric, the real purpose of the Fascist corporations was to make Italy safe for the traditional ruling elites.[26]

These assessments flew in the face of pronouncements by conservative, right-wing Catholics such as Minister of Justice Rocco and the clerico-fascists who persistently drew parallels between Catholic corporatism and Mussolini's programs. The Fascist press naturally dismissed the pope's criticism of their corporatism. Mussolini's brother, Arnaldo, declared that the regime did not need Pius's imprimatur anyway. On the other hand, too many Italian Catholics overlooked the pope's criticisms and even tried to show that *Quadragesimo Anno* supported the basic tenants of Fascist corporativism in that it, as well as Mussolini, weighed in against Marxism, laissez-faire economics, and liberalism.[27] Much like Belloc and his circle, the Italian Catholic publicists simply assumed that the Fascist order was grounded on ethical principles and thereafter ignored the large body of Catholic social doctrine against which Mussolini's behavior should have been judged.

Mussolini himself was a far cry from the defender of religion that his Catholic admirers made him out to be. In fact, it was always difficult for Il Duce to contain his lifelong animus toward the Church,[28] and after the Lateran treaties, which forged his opportunistic alliance with the Vatican, he would occasionally, in public forums, lapse into vitriolic anti-Catholic diatribes. The philo-fascist Catholics never seemed to notice. Only three months after signing the 1929 concordat, for example, Mussoline announced in the Chamber of Deputies that in Fascist Italy the Church was neither sovereign nor free. Christianity would have found its grave ages ago, "leaving no trace" of its existence, had it remained in Palestine. It was Rome, said Mussolini, that made the Church Catholic. As for the recently concluded Lateran agreements, they had not "resurrected the temporal power of the popes," but merely left the papacy "enough territory to bury its corpse."[29] Mussolini for the most part was able to conceal this hatred for the Church from public view, though his anticlericalism was always made clear to high-ranking Fascist functionaries, whom he allowed to attack the Church with impunity.[30]

Sturzo's analysis of Mussolini and Fascism seems to have been shared by only a minority of British and American Catholic publications. Journals and associations that were particularly concerned about industrial and social problems and were well-informed about the message of the social encyclicals tended to be highly critical of Italian Fascism. Those Catholics supportive of Mussolini, on the other hand, generally paid little attention to the labor encyclicals or were woefully ignorant of them.[31] Catholics concerned with social justice had a better understanding of Marxism than the philo-fascist Catholics; they realized that its appeal to the laboring population had much to do with the Church's failure to pursue its mission of social deaconry. Consequently, their energies focused on what should be done to mitigate the conditions that made revolutionary socialism attractive to workers in the first place. These Catholics certainly were critical of communism, for the same reasons that moved conservative Catholics, but their approach to the problem was more balanced, firmly grounded sociologically, and thus more analytical; it was not driven by the impulse of a crusade.[32] What separated them politically from their co-religionists on the right was their recognition that Fascism was every bit as evil as Marxism.[33]

Perhaps the most outspoken and ground-breaking American critic of Mussolini was Father James M. Gillis, editor of the Paulist Fathers' *Catholic World,* a journal intended for Catholic intellectuals. Father Gillis's journal criticized Mussolini and Fascism on conservative grounds, founded in large part on Gillis's nineteenth-century belief in individualism. In many respects, Gillis would have found comfort in the company of Chesterton and the English pluralists, for he voiced a strong objection to big government, an evil

he called "statism." Father Gillis's editorial columns supported
Catholic moral theology and the integrity of the family, defended
the Church against persecution, and expressed a firm belief in the
fundamental compatibility between American democratic principles and Catholicism. In the view of his most recent biographer,
Father Gillis saw himself as a conservative guardian of the nation
against those who ignored President Lincoln's dictum "government
by the people."[34] Yet for years Gillis remained a lonely voice of
Catholic outrage against Italian Fascism.[35]

Father Gillis's unvarnished criticism of Mussolini was a response
to the dictator's attacks on the Church and his use of the state as
an instrument to undermine the freedoms of the Italian people.
Mussolini was a Nietzchean, not a Catholic, Gillis insisted, and his
wild diatribes and threats of violence would bring ruin to Italy and
possibly bring on another European war. In short, wrote Gillis,
"Mussolini is mad."[36] Although Il Duce and his boosters claimed
that he saved Europe from Bolshevism, Father Gillis observed that
he certainly did not choose to save it for democracy. Mussolini's
contempt for Parliament showed that he was not a democrat but a
demagogue.[37]

Father Gillis, much like Virgil Michel at *Orate Fratres,* recognized that the Fascist concept of an omnipotent state ran contrary
to the claims of Catholic teachings, for it refused to accept the fundamental premise that the spiritual and sacred were the domain of
the Church. In America Catholics had long been yoked with the
charge of a "divided allegiance," that is, a split loyalty concerning
matters of religion and politics. But Gillis asked if there might also
be another, more important "divided allegiance," namely, the evil
of an exaggerated nationalism which pitted loyalty to state against
one's conscience.[38]

What Mussolini was really reviving, argued Gillis, was not a
Catholic Rome but rather a pagan Rome, a state absolutism redolent of the tyrannical caesar where those who refused divine honor
were crucified, decapitated, burned alive, or offered to the lions. The
central issue in Italy, said Gillis, was that the state was transgressing
the boundaries of the Church. Mussolini's ploy was to isolate the
Church, to keep it in the cloister without any ties to the social and

political world. Yet in practice Church and state had a thousand points of contact. Rather than being mutually repellent, the nature of these institutions was to coalesce in such a fashion as to promote the common good. In this respect the true destiny of religion and government was mutual cooperation. However, Fascist doctrine denied this possibility, for it asserted that the citizen belonged to the state, not the state to the citizen.[39]

Not only did Father Gillis eviscerate Mussolini's Fascism, but most notably he went after other Catholics who failed to appreciate its evil. Those who defended Mussolini, asserted Gillis, were so pre-occupied with communism that they failed to see the true nature of Fascism, and this was largely because they were not really concerned with tyranny unless it was anti-Catholic. The London *Tablet* was singled out here, as was the post-Chesterton *G.K.'s Weekly* and the English Catholic journalist Douglas Jerrold. In fact there were very few Catholics who showed such a warm heart for Fascism as did Belloc's friend Douglas Jerrold. In *The Future of Freedom* (1938), for example, Jerrold went so far as to say that there was no perse-cution of religion in Hitler's Germany, an assertion that the pope himself contradicted in the 1937 encyclical *Mit brennender Sorge*. As for Italy, Jerrold made the outlandish argument that any Christian in Italy was better off than in England insofar as the practice of his religion was concerned. In response to Jerrold, Gillis asked what the practice of religion actually meant: did it involve social injustice? Were Catholics supposed to rise from their knees after Mass and venture forth into the light of day to apply what the Church taught? Could men of Catholic action in Italy go into the streets, factories, shops, and stores to preach social justice? Was there freedom of speech and press in Italy so that citizens might address papal teach-ings on racism or the state's rights over family and Church?[40] In fact, in the encyclical *Non abbiamo Bisogno* (1931), which America's Mon-signor Francis Spellman smuggled out of the Vatican to be pub-lished in Paris (such was the environment of oppression in Italy), Pius XI criticized the Fascists for not allowing Catholics to pursue Christian social action. Fascists, said the pope, had "committed acts of oppression" and "terrorism" against the Church. *Non abbiamo Bisogno* concluded with a warning against "pagan worship of the

State." After reading the encyclical, Mussolini flatly declared that Fascism and Catholicism were incompatible. Jerrold, of course, conveniently overlooked all such issues in his panegyrics on Mussolini. He made no reference whatever to *Non abbiamo Bisogno* in *The Future of Freedom*.

Finally, Father Gillis raised the moral question of a just war after Mussolini's invasion of Abyssinia, an issue that would take on even greater significance when Franco rebelled against the Republican government in Madrid one year later. Augustine and Thomas Aquinas, noted Gillis, established that a "just war" can occur only when all efforts to avoid it have failed. Since Italy had defied all attempts at arbitration by the League of Nations, its invasion of Abyssinia, on strictly Catholic grounds, was unjust and thus unethical.[41] The Fribourg Congress of 1931 set out the Catholic ethics of war in a document signed by seven of the best-known moralists of the day. It concluded that "a war declared by a State on its own authority without previous recourse to the international institutions which exist cannot be a lawful social process."

Father Gillis's position on the injustice of the Abyssinian war was also echoed in the writings of Don Luigi Sturzo and was similar to that adopted by other Catholic journals, such as *Les Etudes*, *La Vie Intellectuelle*, *Blackfriars*, and *Commonweal*.[42] Gillis was especially critical of English Catholic publications such as *G.K.'s Weekly*, the London *Tablet*, and the *Month*, which downplayed the evil of Mussolini's behavior by equating it with nineteenth-century British and American imperialism. These commentaries, claimed Gillis, ignored the primary ethical issue, which must always take precedence over the imperatives of politics. Gillis called Chesterton's stance equating Mussolini's Abyssinian invasion with the "soiled hands" of English colonialism as "journalistic tripe . . . more sickening than any bad logic or false ethics that has appeared in the American papers."[43]

The *Catholic World* was particularly incensed with the Italian hierarchy's support of the African campaign. One of the most influential Italian churchman, Cardinal Schuster of Milan, asserted that the war in Abyssinia was justified because it would end slavery and bring the blessing of the faith to Africa. Gillis, however, pointed out that a war otherwise unjust can not be made morally correct because of the good results that might accrue. In this sense the end does not justify the means, for a basic maxim of Catholic theology is that an evil may not be perpetrated in order to bring good.[44]

Father Gillis was buried in a deluge of vituperative condemnation from Catholics for his editorial stance, in particular for what some called blatant anti-Italian prejudice. This was the first significant expression of editorial criticism in the nearly fourteen years since Gillis had taken over the *Catholic World*.[45] Gillis responded that a basic tenet of Catholic journalism that fundamentally set it apart from all other journalism was the necessity of being universal, of speaking "urbi et orbi" (to the City and the World), as the popes frequently asserted in making their opinions and judgments. Good Catholic writers had to be both supra-national as well as supra-racial. To be truly Catholic, insisted Gillis, "a paper must be consistently, invariably, impartially universally opposed to tyranny and injustice."[46]

The *Catholic World* under the editorship of Father James Gillis and a small number of liberal Catholic publications in Britain and the United States lived up to such standards. Far too many others, however, lost their perspective and balance in an anticommunist crusade that took on religious proportions. The zeal of holy war blinded conservative Catholics to the faults of what turned out to be false friends on the political right.

CHAPTER 10

Social Catholicism and the Career of H. A. Reinhold

His was one of the classical cases of the pioneer unnoticed, the inventor whose rightful rewards are reaped by others, the humble hero who goes through life unknown, unhonored and unsung and whose place is left to history.
—Msgr. George W. Casey on Father H. A. Reinhold,
The Pilot, 17 February 1968

Father James Gillis, discussed in chapter 9, was one of America's most respected and powerful Catholic journalists; his editorship of the *Catholic World* was a badge of respectability and a shield of sorts against the criticisms of conservative Catholics (Gillis was ranked third among American Catholic writers in *America's* national poll of the greatest living Catholic authors). It was far more difficult for those on the fringe, such as supporters of Dorothy Day's and Peter Maurin's Catholic Worker movement and liberal Catholics involved with the fledgling liturgical movement. Members of the latter group were frequently held in suspicion by the Church hierarchy and regarded as "revolutionary" and "dangerous" communists, or as "fools who do not like Benediction," as one official called them.[1]

Perhaps no Catholic suffered more for the courage of his convictions on such issues than the German refugee priest, Hans Anscar Reinhold (H.A.R., as he liked to refer to himself). Father Reinhold, along with Father Virgil Michel, O.S.B., the founder of *Orate Fratres* (later *Worship*), was a mainspring of the American liturgical movement. In fact, besides Father Michel (who died before the results of his pioneering work were realized), H. A. Reinhold, his successor as writer of *Orate Fratres's* "Timely Tracts," was probably America's single most influential proponent of liturgical renewal.

Reinhold was a "planter of ideas," as one member of the clergy described him, whose liturgical work helped fertilize the soil from which sprang the reforms of Vatican Council II.[2]

H. A. Reinhold's own spiritual rejuvenation began during the revolutionary upheaval that followed Germany's defeat in World War I. Personally disillusioned by the breakup of Germany after having risked his life at the front (he was decorated with the Iron Cross, the *Hanseatenkreuz*, and the *Schwartz Verwundetenabzeichen*), Reinhold seemed to have lost his intellectual and spiritual bearings. Everything changed with his discovery of Romano Guardini's *The Spirit of the Liturgy*.[3] Reinhold read the book twice at one sitting. Too excited to sleep that night, his mind was filled with a new vision of the Catholic Church. Like many German Catholics of his day, Reinhold had been brought up on an authoritarian, didactic religion that was devoid of intellectual substance and wanting in spirituality. His religious teachers, he recalled, could never even explain the meaning of the Mass. They could only describe its form and ritualistic appearances. Guardini's book showed him that the Mass itself was a distillation of a new way of life: "The legalistic body of restrictions and commandments which I used to have in mind and which I used to defend in fierce and dull despair, had vanished before the vision of Christ's Mystical Body and the incredible beauty of His Mystical life among us through His sacraments and mysteries."[4]

Following his encounter with Guardini's liturgical insights, Reinhold entered the University of Freiburg as a student of philosophy. After graduation he attended a Jesuit seminary at Innsbruck and spent a year with the Benedictines at the Abbey of Maria Laach, the birthplace of European liturgical renewal. Reinhold was eventually ordained as a secular priest. From the outset he devoted himself passionately to the ideas he had absorbed at Maria Laach. He immediately introduced the dialogue Mass in his first priestly assignment in 1925, only to have it forbidden by his superiors. He also devoted himself to one of the central objectives of liturgical reform: Catholic social action.

In 1930 Reinhold helped found the International Council of the Apostleship of the Sea. As secretary-general of this association he organized a German branch of the Apostolate, which soon became an early center of resistance to Nazi seamen's unions. A central objective of the Apostleship of the Sea was to help seamen develop spiritual independence and to train them as apostles for religious and social causes. Father Reinhold wrote a monthly magazine for the sailors and a bimonthly newsletter for officers. In these articles the outspoken and independent-minded priest stressed the spiritual and political dangers of communism, but unlike so many other German Catholics at the time, he avoided seeking help in this struggle from the political right. In fact, he excoriated the followers of Hitler in the same tones as the Marxists. Reinhold soon concluded that the Nazis were the more serious threat to German democracy and the Christian religion. He informed his charges of this fact openly in writing and in lectures, attacking the Nazis as perverters of religion and an immediate threat to world peace.

Father Reinhold's considerable influence among seamen prompted the Nazis to infiltrate his organization with spies. They eventually gained access to his personal secretary, who informed the Gestapo of Reinhold's various political activities, including his secret meetings with former prime minister Heinrich Bruening and with the French Consul, and his reports to Catholics in England.[5]

One of Father Reinhold's early contacts outside of Germany was E. J. Oldmeadow, editor of the London *Tablet*. From the outset Reinhold was apprehensive about writing in the foreign media for fear of Nazi reprisals against himself and his family. His correspondence with Oldmeadow and others, however, reveals a perspicacious and prescient understanding of the true nature of Hitler and Nazism. Writing to Oldmeadow in 1935, Reinhold chastised him for thinking that Hitler would vanish as quickly as he arrived and for believing, along with many others, that Hitler was a puppet of conservative special interests. Reinhold warned that Hitler was really his own man and would "stand to his last aims" as declared in the first edition of *Mein Kampf*, as soon as the European and world situation allowed him the opportunity. (Very few of Hitler's critics in 1935 took what he said in *Mein Kampf* seriously). There was only one solution to the Nazi problem, insisted Reinhold, and that was a second world alliance against Germany, whose dictator was intent on world war. Reinhold's fear of Nazi spies was such that he asked Oldmeadow to take his letter to the nearest fireplace and burn it.[6]

The central purpose of Father Reinhold's activities immediately after Hitler became chancellor was to alert the outside world that the Nazis were targeting for persecution not only Jews but also Christians, Catholic and Protestant alike, as well as dissident politicians, writers, and artists. In spite of Nazi propaganda stressing the importance of Christianity and family values, claimed Reinhold, Nazism represented "the German form of Bolshevism." Hitler aimed to create "a German shinto religion" by deifying the state, the so-called Aryan race, and his own person. Germany was rapidly becoming totalitarian, and in this respect there was little difference between Berlin and Moscow.[7]

Reinhold's warnings were largely dismissed by the Catholic hierarchy in Germany, whose general consensus was that a deal could be made with Hitler in common defense of the old verities of religion against communism. What made matters especially troublesome for Father Reinhold, however, was the misfortune of being under the jurisdiction of Wilhelm Berning, bishop of Osnabrück. Berning was an ardent defender of Cardinal Adolf Bertram of Breslau, chairman of the Fulda Bishops' Conference, the official body representing the Catholic Church in Germany. The cardinal was himself no devotee of democracy; nor, would it seem, were a great many German Catholics in general.[8] Although Bertram found National Socialism repugnant and a deadly threat to Catholicism (the real danger of the Nazis, Bertram said, was the fanatical fashion in which they sought their goals),[9] he appreciated their anti-Bolshevik and anti-liberal positions. These were sentiments shared with his close friend, the reputedly pro-Nazi papal nuncio to Germany, Cesare Orsenigo.[10]

Although Cardinal Bertram was not as optimistic as his fellow bishops that the much-discussed 1933 Concordat with Berlin would resolve church-state conflicts with the Hitler regime,[11] he was convinced, once the agreement was concluded, that the Catholic Church must adhere to its provisions and seek accommodation with the Nazis. In his mind, open opposition, as exemplified by Father Reinhold, brought the risk of Nazi persecution and incalculable harm to Catholics. Most significantly, Bertram feared the return of another *Kulturkampf*. He and most other bishops of the

Fulda Conference felt it better to find agreement with Hitler than to resist the Nazi regime.[12]

Since Bishop Berning was an outspoken and trusted supporter of Bertram's policies of conciliation, the cardinal appointed him to serve as the Church's chief negotiator with Hitler's government. Berning also had the advantage of being held in high regard by the National Socialists. Much to the surprise of many Catholics, in July 1933 he was appointed by Hermann Goering to be a member of the reorganized Prussian Council of State. The bishop of Osnabrück took great pride in his official rank as Prussian *Staatsrat,* although the Vatican appears to have had some doubts about the wisdom of assuming such a position.[13] At times Berning gave the appearance of being a zealot in his service to the regime. For instance, at his inauguration as member of the Council of State he declared that German bishops not only accepted and recognized Hitler's Reich but would serve it "with ardent love and with all our energies."[14] The important thing in Berning's mind was for Catholics to demonstrate their loyalty as German patriots. It was in such a spirit that the bishop reminded the inmates at the concentration camp Aschendorfer Moor that they had an obligation to be obedient and show fidelity toward the state, as this was demanded of them by their faith; and he praised the camp guards for the patriotic work they were doing for the Nazi regime.[15] Like many other Catholic ecclesiastics in Germany, Berning regarded Hitler as a force of rejuvenation; his movement was a great popular wave on whose crest the Church must ride, lest, once again, it miss the chance to join the cause of the masses as had happened during the time of Martin Luther.

Father Reinhold believed that Bishop Berning was well-meaning but naive about political matters and thus was duped by Hitler. For his part, Berning deflated Reinhold's numerous and very detailed reports of Nazi atrocities as merely "regrettable excesses in the first flush of revolution."[16] In any case, joked the callow Berning, Reinhold was nothing but an "old Bolshevik."[17] The benighted bishop may have been making light of the matter, but the charge stuck, and Reinhold, via Nazi propaganda filtered through conservative Catholics, suffered the curse of bearing the Marxist label throughout his years in exile.

Matters became increasingly difficult for Father Reinhold after the signing of the Concordat between Berlin and the Holy See in July 1933. Bishop Berning, along with Archbishop Konrad Gröber of Freiburg (who believed that Catholicism and National Socialism were in principle reconcilable), played an important role in paving the way for the negotiations. A fatal mistake, however, was Gröber's and Berning's failure to persuade Berlin to accept a list of Catholic organizations that would be protected from state interference. The papal secretary of state, Cardinal Eugenio Pacelli, thought it wise to hold up the agreement until a list was accepted, but the bishops, eager to limit Nazi actions by legal agreements, urged the Vatican to ratify the document. This proved to be a costly mistake, for in the absence of a list of protected associations the Nazis could attack Catholic groups with legal impunity. Despite this tactical error, Bishop Berning was so satisfied with the final agreement that he ordered a *Te Deum* of thanksgiving to be rung in all the churches in his diocese of Osnabrück.

Father Reinhold blamed Franz von Papen, the Catholic vice-chancellor of the Third Reich, for maneuvering the Holy See into signing the ill-fated Concordat. Von Papen had been a zealous promoter of rapprochement between the Church and National Socialism. He believed that Nazism could fulfill so many of Germany's national ambitions that the Church was obliged to make compromises with Hitler. This was made more palatable to many Catholics, it seems, after von Papen discovered a myriad of affinities between Catholicism and the teachings of Hitler: both were conservative, supported corporative ideals, emphasized the importance of authoritarian guidance, attacked liberalism and Bolshevism, and preached the importance of family values and religion. This was precisely the line of argument put forth by Catholic philo-fascists when they explained why the Church had a friend in Mussolini.

The Concordat was signed on 20 July 1933. It was an unmitigated disaster in Reinhold's view. Among other things, the legal agreement undermined the possibility of a united Catholic political front against Hitler, since it prohibited Catholic clergy from all political activity. The majority of the German hierarchy and those who controlled the *Centrum* (the Catholic political party) had made a tragic blunder, wrote Reinhold. Their actions revealed a complete misunderstanding of Hitler. Such Catholics were blinded by wishful thinking. They hoped to tame Hitler by the same devices with which they had boasted of controlling Bismarck.[18] Reinhold was deeply disillusioned with the bishops: "The German Church looked like a strong, heroic and courageous army without leaders." The episcopate was incapable of recognizing that Hitler was behind the outrages against Christians and Jews (many thought such deeds were perpetrated by Nazi functionaries without the Führer's explicit knowledge).[19] The German bishops, said Reinhold, "were keeping up a policy of feeding the tiger to keep him quiet."[20] He dedicated himself to exposing the folly of the agreement.[21]

H. A. Reinhold was first arrested by the Gestapo in July 1934 on the charge of "hostility to the state and the party" but was soon released due to insufficient evidence. Friends and family advised him at this point to leave Germany, but he refused so long as he still had a chance to expose Nazi policy. Meanwhile, as member of the executive board of the International Seamen's Apostolate, he traveled throughout Europe in the capacity of attaché priest, where he spread the word of Nazi brutalities and secretly helped German anti-Nazis who had fled into exile.

Reinhold's continued outspoken criticism of the regime was a source of great embarrassment to Bishop Berning, who, along with Cardinal Bertram, still worked diligently to placate Hitler. Moreover, according to article V of the Concordat, which required clergy to protect the state in the same fashion as public officials, Reinhold's behavior was clearly illegal. By 1934 any criticism of National Socialism on the part of priests laid them open to arrest.

In December 1934 the Nazis enforced a law forbidding "malicious slander of State and Property," which led to the arrest of numerous Catholic clergy. The Gestapo had now compiled a large dossier on Reinhold's anti-Nazi activities abroad and implicated him as a communist. Bishop Berning had little sympathy with Reinhold's circumstances, insisting that the priest had fathered his own problems with inveterate "pacifism" and an unnecessary polemical attitude toward the Nazis.

Although Berning made some halfhearted efforts to intervene on Reinhold's behalf, the Nazis completely ignored him; the local

Gestapo chief even refused to return his phone calls. On 30 April 1935 Reinhold was expelled from the states of Hamburg, Bremen, and Schleswig-Holstein. Yet Berning insisted that his priest stay with him in Osnabrück and ignore an impending order to report to Gestapo headquarters in Frankfurt for questioning.

Bishop Berning, meanwhile, left his diocesan residence in Osnabrück for Bremen in order to have dinner with Hitler. Reinhold would have been left alone at the bishop's residence when the Gestapo called. He fled to Muenster, where two Jesuit priests, Fathers Maring and Wahle, helped him cross the German border. From there Father Reinhold traveled to England, where he was promised asylum by the British secretary general of the Seamen's Apostolate.

From this point on Father Reinhold labored under the burden of Nazi and German Catholic propaganda, for Berning sent out word that his priest "was not a bona fide refugee" fleeing political persecution, but rather someone with left-wing sympathies who "simply lost his nerve" and ran away from his clerical responsibilities. In short, Reinhold was "on leave" without permission.[22] These charges followed Reinhold wherever he went. For example, a German priest, whom Reinhold identified as Father Groesser, came to America in 1936 with a letter and documents approved by the Gestapo from Bishop Berning for the Chancellery of New York, spreading the rumor "that nobody knew why" Reinhold left and that he was "a restless person who never staid [sic] anywhere more than a year." Father Groesser's documents and claims appeared to have been accepted completely by the chancellor of the archdiocese of New York, James Francis McIntyre. There was no persecution of the Church in Germany, argued Groesser, and in fact the German Catholics, in many ways, were better off than their American counterparts, since Hitler paid for their schools and salaries.[23] Added to this were the encouraging reports about the virtues of the new regime from such German religious luminaries as Karl Adam and Joseph Lortz.[24]

With such references, and as a secular priest without the benefit of support from an international order, Father Reinhold was unable to find parish work in England, where he was obliged to live on charity.[25] One of Father Reinhold's benefactors, A. Hudal, wrote that in the spring of 1935 the priest was "entirely destitute of all means." Mr. Hudal sent Father Reinhold a small sum to help him through this period of difficulty and wrote a number of letters to other Catholics in America and Europe calling attention to his precarious situation.[26] After two months in Britain, not a single bishop gave Reinhold even a brief audience, with the exception of Archbishop MacDonald of Edinburgh. He was generally handled, Reinhold said, by "petty secretaries," although the lower clergy and lay officials of the Seamen's Apostolate were kind and supportive.[27]

Father Reinhold moved to Switzerland, where he found temporary work as a curate in a parish in Interlaken. He also managed to travel extensively, briefing many high-ranking European Catholic officials about conditions in Germany and warning them that the apparent cooperation between the German Church and Hitler was no more than a Nazi diplomatic ruse. Reinhold gained conferences with the papal secretary of state, Cardinal Eugenio Pacelli, Cardinal Theodor Innitzer of Vienna, Bishop Edward Myers of London, Archbishop Emmanuel Anatole Chaptal of Paris, and Archbishop Johannes de Jong of Utrecht. All I received, wrote Reinhold, was a "doubtful reputation as an 'excited' emigrant. . . . Who was I, when in Germany everything—a few minor incidents subtracted—was in peace."[28]

As a refugee priest, Father Reinhold was driven to tell the world of Hitler's persecution of Christians and to warn of his plans for war. The first objective was difficult in the face of Goebbels' propaganda, for common opinion was that only Jews and communists were targets of Nazi persecution. Reinhold was deeply upset over the lack of civic courage exhibited by German Catholics in their failure to speak out against the Nazis: "Men, leaders at that, who privately admitted that Hitler was a murderer and knave, stood in the market places and invited the Catholic German youth to be loyal to their beloved 'Fuehrer.'"[29]

Perhaps the most ironic of Reinhold's many meetings with Catholic hierarchs was that with Cardinal Innitzer of Vienna. The Cardinal listened quietly for an hour or more without interrupting as Reinhold held nothing back concerning the Nazis. Then Innitzer

offered his own point of view. First, he told Reinhold that his opinions were obviously jaundiced by the wrongs he had suffered and
thereby dismissed his warnings. Hitler, he asserted, would never
seize Austria. The Führer had said that he had all he needed, and
with unemployment in decline Germany would soon be normal
again. Even if he should be tempted, commented the cardinal,
Hitler was like himself and like Austria: "we are both Sudetan Germans. Austria has always lived through subtlety and outfoxing her
adversaries. We are very different from your clumsy north German
bishops. Hitler would never get anywhere in Austria. We have a tradition of cleverness and astuteness."[30] When Austria was invaded
in March 1938, Cardinal Innitzer called it "providential" and tried to
deal with Hitler as a fellow Sudetanlander. In an open and fawning letter to Hitler, Cardinal Innitzer pledged that the Catholic
hierarchy and the people of Austria would cooperate fully with the
Nazis. He concluded his offer with the signature "Heil Hitler." The
Cardinal was quickly summoned to the Vatican for a fiery scolding
from Pius XI, after which he feasted on crow: Innitzer published
his errors in a long apology to the Pope and the world at large in
L'Osservatore Romano.[31]

   "I have no other intention," wrote Reinhold under the assumed
name Adolf Schuckelgruber in *The Catholic World,* after a detailed
exposé of Nazis methods of obtaining German Christian support,
"than to demonstrate to the American public that the Catholic
Church in Germany lives under the same threat as the Russian
orthodox community" under the dictatorship of Stalin.[32] It was
always Reinhold's contention that Nazism was designed to serve as
a surrogate religion, a modern secular replacement of that one great
Christian idea that had united Europe in the Middle Ages. In order
to broaden its appeal, Nazism utilized existing beliefs and emotions
as far as possible—the outrage over the Versailles peace settlement,
the growing public distrust of Weimar economic and social organizations, and especially the authoritarian Christian religious sentiments and cultural tendencies of the German people—to serve its
totalitarian creed. In this respect, the Nazis learned from Russia's
mistakes. Rather than destroy a positive religious force, Hitler chose
to graft it to Nazi ideology in order to solidify the party's outreach

to the German masses.[33] Thus, insisted Reinhold, totalitarianism must be recognized as a religion, one that is absolute and knows no compromises, a form of life that pervades the whole of a people. Christians can live under such regimes only if they understand their true character, but they can never be active Bolsheviks, Fascists, or Nazis in the full sense of such creeds. The life of a Christian must serve as a living protest against a system that claims their whole personality for worldly purposes. Liberal and democratic principles had shielded Europeans from such horrible possibilities in the past. But as the "Prince of this World arises in the Place of God and His Saviour we can only reply with the old warfare of Christians: resistance unto martyrdom against the old enemy, be he clad in red, or brown or black robe."[34]

It is important to stress the fact that Father Reinhold condemned his German co-religionists not only for their silence on Hitler's attacks on Christians but also for their silence on atrocities against Jews. As long as the Nazis shot communists and Jews, noted Reinhold, German Catholics did not see it as their affair. Catholics seemed to think that "to protest against these outrages . . . and to investigate their case or to cry injustice was only prejudicing their own cause." German Catholics simply had not learned the truth about totalitarianism, nor did they understand the indivisibility of justice.[35] Reinhold had a keen historical and sociological understanding of anti-Semitism, was sensitive to Jewish issues, and had a deep aversion to Catholic manifestations of anti-Semitism.[36] As a refugee in America, for example, he worked closely with Catholic groups fighting anti-Semitism and was especially supportive of "Opus Sancti Pauli," organized by Father Johannes Oesterreicher to counteract anti-Semitism in Catholic ranks. The fight against anti-Semitism, the Pope told Oesterreicher, "is a most important apostolate of our times." Reinhold appreciated the imperative of Pius's charge: the campaign against Jews could be "the death blow to our catholicity and universality." Those who attack Hebrews, he noted, do not have any liking for Catholics either. Once they finish with Jews the guns would be turned on Catholics. Not only do Catholics share the Old Testament in common with Jews, "but we also support a universalism, an anti-rationalism, and a moral and ritual law, all of which are equally annoying to anti-Semites."[37] Yet despite such appeals, Reinhold's own writings in America on the evils of anti-Semitism brought charges from some Catholics that he himself must be Jewish.[38]

Father Reinhold showed very little tolerance for his fellow German Catholics in positions of spiritual leadership who could not see what he saw or, even worse, preferred to keep their eyes and mouths closed for the sake of peace. These were the pusillanimous "irenic clergy," as Reinhold scornfully referred to them, "the worst pack of people on God's earth" whose tactics could at times be terroristic.[39] As Nazi violence increased, many German bishops blamed the excesses on overzealous followers of the Führer. They failed to appreciate, claimed Reinhold, that it was really Hitler who was behind the outrages perpetrated by his henchmen. The bishops "were keeping up a policy of feeding the tiger to keep him quiet," an unfortunate stratagem to which the German hierarchy had grown accustomed ever since the passing of Bishop Ketteler. If the Church survives in Germany, lamented Father Reinhold, it will only be through the "stubbornness, patience, and sound instinct of the faithful and the rank-and-file parish clergy."[40]

In addition to waging a propaganda campaign against Hitler, Reinhold's other major activity as a refugee both in Europe and later in the United States was to raise aid for Christian refugees from Germany. World opinion held that only Jews were being persecuted by the Nazis. This was due, in part, to the fact that Hitler's government refused to recognize any refugees other than Jews. The Nazis did not want Jews to remain in Germany, but non-Jews—so-called Aryans—who left the country were regarded as traitors and political enemies. This placed severe constraints on the German bishops, for to acknowledge the existence of Catholic refugees would have made them guilty of aiding the enemy in the eyes of the Nazi government.

There were a sizeable number of non-Jewish exiles from Germany in the 1930s in Europe, and in fact by 1936 they vastly exceeded Jewish refugees. Among these were former politicians of the Catholic Center Party, numerous editors of Christian papers, and various types of professional people who found Nazism repugnant. In all these totalled some fourteen thousand, of whom roughly one-sixth were Catholic.[41] The countries bordering Germany had been flooded with refugees and were unable to absorb them into their economies. Living conditions were wretched, many refugees of middle-class background being completely unable to support themselves. Furthermore, as Father Reinhold told one wealthy American whom he solicited for refugee financial aid, police restrictions regarding working permits in Europe were so heavy that most turned to beggary. Their socialization in a bourgeois/intelligentsia world proved insufficient for finding their living on the streets.[42]

A turning point in Father Reinhold's life was his decision to travel to the United States. The journey was prompted by Dorothy Day, who wrote him in Switzerland in 1936 explaining that nothing was being done by the American Church to help Catholic refugees from Hitler's regime.[43] Nazi propaganda, however, had so poisoned the air that non-Jewish refugees in America were generally regarded as "contaminated." In Father Reinhold's case, the suspicion endured. His friend, Father Thomas Carroll, remembered that Reinhold's stories were scoffed at by all too many people: "I can recall, before knowing him, hearing verbally of a German priest in this country who was telling very exaggerated stories about the danger of Hitler and Nazism. He was a prophet here too, but even he could not know the full horror which was to be."[44]

Despite impressive letters of introduction by reputable Catholics, including the best reference possible from Monsignor Kreutz, for many years president of the German Caritas-Verband, Father Reinhold found no hospitality from the New York Catholic Chancery and therefore contacted a group of Protestants who were concerned about the refugee problem. Many of these people were willing to listen to him and provide shelter.[45] The American Catholic Church at this juncture did not recognize the necessity of refugee work. Father Reinhold, however, found a handful of American Catholics, including Professor Carlton J. Hayes of Columbia University, Michael Williams, founder of *Commonweal,* and George Shuster, who, along with his new Protestant acquaintances, were willing to join forces across religious boundaries to address the refugee problem. This resulted in the formation of an interdenominational organization of clergy and laymen called the American Committee for Christian

Refugees. Father Reinhold was a member of the group's executive committee representing Europe. He hoped to use this association as a catalyst for the establishment of an official Catholic effort, thereby aiding many of his fellow German Catholics who had fled Hitler's regime.

In October 1936 the American Committee for Christian Refugees held a conference at Riverside Church in New York City. Acknowledging that the Nazis were targeting not only Jews but Christians as well, the committee passed a resolution calling on Christian churches throughout the United States to extend relief and disseminate as widely as possible information regarding the deplorable plight of these people so that "funds may be raised to save them from extinction and to provide for their permanent establishment in countries where they can become self-supporting."[46]

Those working for German Catholic refugees decided they needed the support of the American bishops to help organize a committee of their own. Toward this end Father Reinhold and others appealed to several influential bishops, including Cardinal Patrick Hayes of New York, for permission to provide information on the situation in Germany to American Catholics (strictly unpolitical, they emphasized) for purposes of raising funds. Progress here was very slow and terribly frustrating. Reinhold complained to the executive director of the American Committee for Christian Refugees that by October 1936 he had written over a hundred letters to important American Catholics about setting up a Catholic branch of the interdenominational committee, but yet he had no success.[47] Persistence, however, paid off: Father Reinhold and his friends were eventually successful in their endeavors, and in fact, Reinhold's reports concerning the condition of Catholics who had fled Germany were decisive in founding the American Bishops' Committee on Catholic Refugees. After this point, however, Father Reinhold was shut out of the process. The one man who knew more than anyone else about the plight of German émigré Catholics and whose knowledge was seasoned by years of clandestine experience helping refugees, a tireless worker with numerous international contacts, was excluded by the American hierarchy from all participation in refugee work. The decision to isolate Reinhold was made by Cardinal

Hayes, who, with information from Bishop Berning and other high-ranking Catholic Nazi collaborators, was convinced that he was a pro-communist agitator.[48]

Efforts to aid German Catholic refugees were seriously handicapped at this juncture by opposition from Father Charles Coughlin's followers. Coughlin's influential journal *Social Justice,* which found few fascist-type movements it did not like, never offered so much as a single line of sympathy for Catholic exiles. His supporters in New York City claimed that these people were not "Catholics of good standing" (meaning that they had leanings to the political left) and on several occasions openly heckled speakers from the American Bishops' Committee on Catholic Refugees.[49]

Father Reinhold's situation in the United States was made even more difficult by the head of the New York Chancery, Monsignor James Francis McIntyre. His contacts with German Catholics sympathetic to Nazism had encouraged him to keep Reinhold away from American Catholics because of his "unreliable" and "revolutionary" political ideas.[50] It appears that McIntyre distrusted Reinhold from the moment they met; he found it impossible to believe that there could be any legitimate refugee priests from Nazi Germany, such was the quality of religious life under Hitler.[51] Consequently, McIntyre was unwilling to provide Father Reinhold with any parish work and even restricted his right to say Mass by stipulating that he not give public addresses on the German situation or speak about his own experiences in Germany. In fact, Father Reinhold was forbidden by the New York Chancery from preaching, writing, saying anything about Germany in public, and even performing weddings.[52] McIntyre's obduracy was further stiffened by the Spanish Civil War, since Father Reinhold failed to view Franco's uprising against the Republic as a religious crusade, a great battle between the forces of good and evil. This only added to his reputation as an unstable radical; McIntyre increased his pressure, even admonishing Reinhold for casual discussions with old friends from the Hamburg seamen's mission who visited the Catholic Worker's offices in New York City.[53]

Father's Reinhold's sojourn in New York would have been unbearable, save for the kindness of Dorothy Day, Paul Tillich, and George Shuster, editor of *Commonweal.* The latter helped him locate a congenial place to stay in the diocese of Brooklyn, though it took nearly three years to find a diocese that would accept him as its pastor. So desperate was Father Reinhold's desire for ministerial work that in 1936 he considered going to Argentina, the one place where he was offered meaningful employment working again with the Seamen's Apostolate. His removal to Argentina was exactly what the New York Chancery hoped for. Yet there remained the persistent problem of Nazism. All German seamen were forbidden contact with Father Reinhold, and the port of Buenos Aires was honeycombed with Nazi agents. In addition, Italian and Spanish ships were now off limits to him. Argentina was governed by pro-fascists, and Buenos Aires' large community of Germans was highly sympathetic to Hitler's regime. For an outspoken critic of Nazism, Argentina presented many dangers. When his sponsor, Father William Cushing, and the bishop of Buenos Aires were unable to provide sufficient assurances for his safety, Father Reinhold sadly declined the offer.[54]

Father Reinhold's sense of abandonment and rejection was increased by relations with his family. His brother, a Nazi collaborator, had called Reinhold a publicity-hungry, self-centered prima donna who was sacrificing his family on the altar of vanity. If he had been Hitler, wrote Reinhold of his brother, "he would have shot me and my ilk the moment he came to power." The brother charged that Reinhold's activities abroad were bringing financial ruin to the family business, thereby condemning his mother to starvation. Father Reinhold begged his brother to disown him, to throw him out of the family, and to call him a criminal and a traitor, if this could save them from Nazi molestation, and, finally, to send on his mother whom Reinhold would gladly support in exile.[55]

Despite frequent bouts with depression and a growing sense of abandonment, Father Reinhold continued to labor on behalf of fellow refugees. He worked unofficially behind the scenes to liberate them from concentration camps, raise private money to pay medical bills, find teaching and writing positions, help them evade the clutches of Nazi agents, and generally provide the encouragement and sympathetic ear that eased the loneliness and alienation that so many of them felt living in strange lands.[56] All this he did without any help from the American Bishops' Committee for Catholic

Refugees. The best-known recipients of Reinhold's largess were Don Luigi Sturzo and Waldemar Gurian.

Dr. Gurian was a preeminent scholar in European circles and was known as one of the most brilliant and best informed Catholic writers on German and Russian affairs. Born in St. Petersburg, Gurian emigrated to Germany with his Jewish family where, while still a young boy, his mother brought him into the Catholic Church. He authored several important books on a wide range of topics, including studies of the political and social ideas of French Catholicism and of the theory and practice of Bolshevism, Nazism, and nationalism, and was a regular contributor to the best German academic journals.[57] Like Father Reinhold, Dr. Gurian had been an outspoken critic of the Nazis in Germany. Forced into exile, he fled to Buchrain, near Lucerne, Switzerland. Within a short time bitterness set in, for he felt that the German Catholic exile community had largely forgotten him. Gurian was especially stung by conservative Catholics, who interpreted his anti-fascist positions as inspired by a crypto-socialism; some claimed that he was an agent in the pay of the Third International. This of course was a canard, prompted in part, it appears, by Gurian's detailed critique of the political behavior of Heinrich Bruening, the Catholic chancellor of Germany, which angered many Catholics. Gurian, in fact, was a severe critic of Bolshevism and held that it was contradictory to the spirit of Europe and a direct threat to Western civilization.[58]

In many respects, Dr. Gurian suffered the same fate as his friend Father Reinhold: both were attacked by right-wing Catholics antagonized by their criticism of those who were willing to make common cause with fascism against the Bolsheviks. Several important Catholic journals, of course, persisted in claiming throughout the 1930s, in the face of mounting violence against German Jews and Christians, that Soviet Russia was the enemy of Christian civilization, whereas Nazi Germany was a bulwark state, guilty of certain excesses perhaps, but essentially Christian and committed to defending Europe against the wave of atheistic communism. Gurian made it very clear in his private letters and published essays that the extreme right was every bit as dangerous as Bolshevism, his life in Hitler's Germany having schooled him in that reality.

Although Gurian regarded Bolshevism as the greater long-term threat, he believed that Nazism was the immediate danger. Nazi anti-Bolshevism should not be taken seriously, wrote Gurian, for it was simply a propaganda tool to attract various religious, economic, and social groups to Hitler's cause. In fact, the National Socialists and Bolsheviks were nothing more than competitors for power, "children of the same spirit" wielding the same methods for similar goals: total domination of the state and its citizens.[59]

In order to alert German and European Catholics to the real meaning of Nazism, Gurian and another German émigré, Otto M. Knab, a former editor-in-chief of the Starnberg Catholic daily *Land und Seebote*, launched *Die Deutschen Briefe* out of Lucerne, Switzerland, on 5 October 1934. The editors, having precious little money, ran the enterprise on a shoestring budget (it was mimeographed on type-script once a week and Gurian himself wrote over 75 percent of the articles). The paper never reached a circulation beyond two hundred, but it offered incisive analyses of Nazism and had considerable influence well beyond its limited circulation. *Le Temps* and *L'Osservatore Romano* used its material. The Gestapo made several attempts to arrest those within Germany who provided the paper with information, and various German bishops, worried about *Die Deutschen Briefe*'s criticisms of their collaboration with Hitler, sent emissaries to Gurian in an attempt to explain why they felt compelled to cooperate with the Nazis.[60]

The Roman Church would fail in its earthly mission of social justice, wrote Gurian to Reinhold, if the current thinking that pervaded many Catholic circles, namely, that whoever is against communism is immediately a friend of the Church, were carried to its logical end.[61] The fascist's open appeal to authority, the call for a new morality to replace the current culture of unfettered individualism, and the suppression of anticlerical and Marxist organizations had the effect on Catholics of a narcotic. Their ability to recognize the many defects of fascism was numbed, and in the process, said Gurian, they were seduced into believing that such programs would restore power to the Church. This was a serious miscalculation, a misjudgment of the totalitarian ethos that marked the political experiments of the new century.

The utopian civilization promised by Bolshevism, which envisioned man as an automaton governed by utilitarian, mechanistic impulses, was replaced in fascism by the appeal to heroism and national power, which, in itself, became a totalitarian secular religion fundamentally at odds with Christianity. In both Bolshevism and fascism the machinery of the state rejected rights of truth and rights of humanity. What Catholics overlooked (hence the necessity of exposing the true nature of the new Reich), wrote Gurian, was that the fascist anti-Bolshevik would tolerate the Church only so long as it served to increase the power of the state and conformed to the wishes of the party.[62] The fascists, in short, simply "mediate God." That is, they employ Him as a means for legitimizing their power, then use this power to stimulate nationalist activity as an ultimate end blessed by the Almighty.

It was a gross oversimplification to judge the Left according to the measure of "enlightened-Marxist or secularized-Puritan 'mysticism,'" wrote Gurian, just as it was folly to condemn the Right en bloc as antiprogressive and antisocial. The extremes at either end of the political typology should never be used to define the social good. What Catholics needed to remember after the fires of anger against the Left had subsided was that the Church historically had gained enormously by the legal rights wrought from liberal-democratic traditions. These had provided it protection under the rule of law side by side with other bodies within the state. Alsatian Catholics, Gurian noted, were able to fight openly and with uncompromising vigor for their denominational schools against the claims of the leftist Blum government in France. The German bishops, on the other hand, were not permitted to publish their pastoral letters in defense of threatened Catholic schools.[63]

Gurian was in dire straights by 1936. Exile had cut him off from his former means of financial support. Sales of *Die Deutsche Briefe* provided some income, but this was never sufficient. Though his work was highly regarded, Gurian complained of being mired in abject poverty, without access to the scholarly sources he required to continue research. Gurian's despairing letters to Father Reinhold bristled with bitterness toward those German Catholics whom he felt should have been doing more to help him. Reinhold, for his part, assumed responsibility for Gurian and worked tirelessly to find

journals in Britain and the United States that would accept his articles. He also made contacts with publishers for Gurian's books,
assisted with editing and translations, and encouraged him to continue studying English in order to find employment in America.
Throughout these difficult times Reinhold tried to counter Gurian's
bleak views and bolster his fading self-confidence by explaining the
special circumstances that made it difficult for the exile community
to respond to his needs. He offered positive perspectives on those
whom Gurian, in his despondency, believed were abandoning him.[64]
Most significantly, Father Reinhold informed the British and
American public about the plight of Gurian, and through his contacts with such important Catholics as George Shuster, Father
James Gillis, Wilfrid Parsons, S.J., Bernard Wall, and various academicians at American Catholic colleges and universities, he mus-
tered support for a professional appointment and a home for his
friend. Waldemar Gurian's subsequent impressive career as an American academic—as professor at the University of Notre Dame and
founder of the *Review of Politics*—owed much to the efforts of
Father Reinhold.

Father Reinhold's relationship with Don Luigi Sturzo grew out
of their shared plight as exiles from fascism and their active involvement with their respective refugee communities. The two priests
also were strongly committed to the cause of social deaconry. Their
liberal political, economic, and religious views would eventually find
a natural home in Virgil Michel's liturgical movement.

Like Reinhold, Father Sturzo had been frustrated with the
Church's failure to help anti-fascist refugees. After his flight from
Italy, Sturzo continued his contacts with other exiles from the political organization he founded, the Popular Party, and with their assistance helped set up Catholic unions for Italian foreign workers.
However, the anti-fascist Italians who worked in France and other
European countries found little help from the Church hierarchy, and
this disappointment, along with frustration over the pro-fascist pronouncements of several bishops, convinced many to join socialist
and even communist trade unions.[65]

In these years before the world appreciated the true political
ambitions of Hitler, Sturzo had become a forgotten man, a lonely
but strong voice against totalitarianism who worked in the obscurity

of a dark little room in the West End of London. Reinhold and a few of Sturzo's more stalwart friends maintained contact with him; they labored to inform British and American Catholics of Sturzo's stature as a religious and political leader, and they tried to sensitize them to the difficult conditions under which the once famous priest had to live. In addition, Father Reinhold seems to have served as a literary agent of sorts for Sturzo. He sought safe storage for Sturzo's manuscripts, eventually placing them in his own bank box. Thanks to Reinhold's connections with such journals as *Commonweal* and the *Christian Front,* Sturzo was able to publish his first articles for an American audience.[66] Reinhold sought out various companies to publish Sturzo's books, and tried to find a teaching position for him at Fordham, St. John's University in Minnesota, and Harvard. Sturzo eventually succeeded in his efforts—with a good deal of help from his friends—to come to America in 1941. A special committee of prominent Catholics, among whom were Reinhold, Carlton Hayes, George Shuster, Monsignor John A. Ryan, and others, was established to raise money and care for Sturzo while he lived in American exile. It was this committee that found a home for Father Sturzo with Bishop Joseph Patrick Hurley of St. Augustine, Florida.

I I

Father Reinhold's greatest and most notable work was in liturgical renewal and social reform. In these areas he represented the best traditions of the papal labor encyclicals and Distributism. As a Catholic social and political commentator he can be placed in the pioneering liberal democratic path chartered by Ozanam, Ketteler, and Manning.

H. A. Reinhold eventually found his American spiritual home at St. John's University in Collegeville, Minnesota, the birthplace of the American liturgical movement. After so many encounters with unsympathetic conservative American Catholics, it was a refreshingly agreeable surprise, wrote Reinhold, to find that so many of the Benedictine monks at St. John's shared his liberal social and political views.[67]

The dean of the College of Arts and Sciences at St. John's University was Father Virgil Michel, O.S.B., already introduced (in chapter 9) as a staunch critic of fascism and as founder of *Orate Fratres* (later *Worship*), the voice of the American liturgical movement. Dom Virgil Michel was one of America's most inspirational Catholic leaders. His friendship and collaboration with French Catholics such as Emmanuel Mounier, editor of *Esprit*, and Jacques Maritain facilitated the infusion of a cosmopolitan, liberal-minded Catholicism into American religious life. Among Virgil Michel's prominent protégés were Dorothy Day, founder of the Catholic Worker movement, and Norman McKenna of the *Christian Front*. Father Michel's vision of the social mission of the Church, called in America the "New Social Catholicism," meant, in the words of Rev. Paul H. Furfey, "a return, with a new loyalty, to the traditional social doctrines and methods of the Catholic Church"[68] and had its roots in the nineteenth-century European liturgical revival centered in the German Rhineland at the Abbey of Maria Laach.[69]

Virgil Michel, along with fellow-Minnesotan Monsignor John A. Ryan, offered some of the clearest and most trenchant explications of *Rerum Novarum* and its successor, *Quadragesimo Anno*, to American audiences. Michel's own success had much to do with the breadth of his education: like Sturzo he had studied carefully the writings of St. Thomas and Karl Marx and had a deep understanding of both philosophers. Michel admitted that he had learned much from Marx's critique of capitalism and of the ways that capitalism objectified and dehumanized the laboring process. He claimed that many of his conservative Catholic critics failed to see the ultimate social bearing of their own basic Christian principles because they had not allowed their minds to be opened to the reality of contemporary social problems by reading Marx.[70]

Virgil Michel developed his socioeconomic ideas in the mid-1920s while studying in Europe, where he fell under the influence of Dom Lambert Beauduin of Mont-César, professor of theology at Benedictine College in Rome. Father Beauduin began his career as a secular priest working with industrial laborers in the Belgian diocese of Liège. As a young priest he was deeply influenced by *Rerum Novarum*, and in his capacity as "Chaplain of Workmen"

Beauduin associated directly with the laborers, encouraging them to organize into trade unions for achieving a living wage and an improvement in working conditions. However, in 1906, after eight years of struggle and little success to show for his efforts, Father Beauduin became disillusioned; in a state of frustration he retreated into the Benedictine monastery at Mont-César. It was there that he found an answer to his own spiritual dissolution as well as to the problems of industrial society. He joined the Benedictine Order. For Beauduin, the rootlessness and anomie that so marked modern society, the real source of the industrial problem, could be overcome by applying Benedictine monastic ideals to the secular world. The Benedictines insisted on replicating the communitarian character of the early church, most powerfully expressed in the sacrament of the Holy Eucharist. The Rule of the Benedictines emphasized the importance of following the example of Christ as set forth in the Gospels: St. Benedict's monastic ideal was to permeate secular living with Scripture so that God would be truly "all in all."[71] Beauduin concluded that if lay Catholics could actively participate in the Eucharistic liturgy and, in the process of acting out its rituals, think of themselves as part of a *Gemeinschaftlichkeit* of believers, they could begin to address the true nature of the social problem, which in an industrial society was rooted in the alienation of the individual from his work and community. Beauduin insisted that the Catholic Church must not remain aloof from factories, trade unions, and strikes but rather must reach out and become part of that world, filthy belching smokestacks and all.

An exposure to the teachings of Dom Lambert Beauduin led to Virgil Michel's own spiritual renewal. He returned from Europe in 1925 determined to transport Beauduin's vision to America. St. John's Abbey would serve as the working center of a liturgical revival for the United States. Within the next five years ten monks from St. John's were sent to Europe to undertake liturgical study. The vehicles for carrying the Benedictine social message to the public were the magazine *Orate Fratres* (meaning "Pray, Brethren"), which by 1930 reached three thousand subscribers and appeared in twenty-six countries, and the establishment of the Liturgical Press at St. John's University. Michel's journal was designed to reach clergy, seminarians, and the educated laity, essentially those who could lead and teach other Catholics the true meaning of liturgical reform.[72]

The goal of the liturgical movement was the direct involvement of Catholics in their religion by a return to traditional, more intimate medieval forms of worship. Yet its concerns went far beyond mere prayer and ritual: more than anything else the liturgists aimed to reintegrate Christians with the Mystical Body of Christ. In this endeavor they emphasized the Mass as a means of extending Christianity into the broader life of the community. Much like Chesterton and Belloc, Virgil Michel and the liturgists believed that the ills of extreme individualism, manifested in the creed of capitalism, and its opposite, collectivism, could be overcome only by restructuring the thought processes, values, and social personalities of those who lived in modern society. In short, social reconstruction had to be preceded by a renewal of the Christian spirit.

The best source of such regeneration, insisted Michel, was the liturgy of the Catholic Church. At the core of Church liturgy was the doctrine of the Mystical Body of Christ, a concept that served as the primary inspiration in the life of the early Christians. This doctrine was always embroidered into the preachings of the church fathers, but in the modern era of agnostic individualism it had become peripheral, largely unappreciated by laity and clergy alike. St. Paul had captured the meaning of the Mystical Body of Christ most succinctly with the image of the human body composed of a head and various appendages. Christians enter the faith through the liturgical ritual of baptism, thus becoming united with Christ as members of the Mystical Body of which He is the Head. This is what constituted the "Christian paternalistic ethic,"[73] the ethos of medieval European civilization, which envisioned society as a corporation headed by God the father and a family of Christian children, brothers and sisters intimately united in Christ: "In this holy fellowship," said Michel, "we find a harmonious combination of the two complementary factors of humankind, that is, organic fellowship coupled with full respect for human personality and individual responsibility."[74]

According to the liturgical reformers, the principle of "supernatural living solidarity" symbolized by the offertory procession in

Holy Communion could not be confined simply to prayer or ab-
straction but rather required enactment as idea in praxis. This was
fully understood by the early Christians who actively participated
in the liturgy of the Mass. The common offering "made by them to
God became at the same time a common act of love and charity to
the poor and needy, so that in one and the same collective but unitary action they worshipped God directly and served Him indirectly
in their countrymen."[75] In this respect the Mystical Body of Christ
serves as the link between liturgy and sociology that "cannot fail to
revive and foster a determination to carry Christ-life into the social
and economic sphere."[76]

The desire to make Catholics more active participants in the
liturgy eventually convinced Michel to advocate the use of the vernacular in the Mass. This was a tall order, for there was considerable
ignorance of and opposition to liturgical reform in America. Indeed,
Father Michel established his own press mainly because no commercial house would take a chance publishing liturgical material.[77]
Many Catholics thought that liturgical reform was a sterile exercise
in rubrics and aestheticism and, on the whole, a submission to the
secularism of modern culture.[78] The issue was also complicated by
ethnic and regional rivalries. Many Catholics on the East and West
coasts, especially Irish bishops, seemed to regard the liturgical movement as part of a search for German identity. In addition, Irish
ecclesiastics generally were more conservative than German Catholics and may have been discomfited by the egalitarian communal-
ism of the liturgists.[79]

The Irish clergy, on many accounts, were resistant to liturgical
reform in Britain. English parishes were "very stony ground" for the
wheat of the liturgy, wrote Father Clifford Howell, S.J., to his friend
H. A. Reinhold. As of the 1930s, the great majority of English
Catholic clergy were Irish born and trained. The English liturgists
constantly complained that the Irish were somehow "allergic" to the
liturgy. In Irish seminaries there was very little study of *Rerum
Novarum* or *Quadragesimo Anno*, the consequences being a priesthood largely unprepared to teach Catholic ideas on social reconstruction. Indeed, Father Howell complained that the main obstacle
to the progress of liturgical reform in Britain was the "prevalence

and persistence of a completely individualist, sentimental, unintelligent type of piety based on personal emotion." This, he claimed, was indigenous to the training of Irish clergy and laity alike and perpetuated by the continued importation of Irish priests. This was by the decision of Irish bishops, who deemed it cheaper than training English boys for the priesthood.[80]

In the United States there was, no doubt, a tendency for some Catholics to dismiss the liturgical movement as part of a populist sentimentality that issued from the Farm Belt. As Sister Antonia McHugh, president of the College of St. Catherine in St. Paul, Minnesota, put it: "The thought of connecting the psalms with socially activated prayers is too irritating to be considered. The whole commotion is doubtless of German origin."[81]

Yet another stumbling block for the American liturgists was the generally poor religious instruction provided in Catholic parochial schools at all levels. With its uninformed, simplistic catechetical texts and its emphasis on rote memorization of dogma, such education failed to produce graduates capable of understanding, let alone appreciating, the positions set forth in the papal social encyclicals.[82] Catholic education did not create an intellectual or spiritual environment conducive to social action. Stanley Vishnewski, an associate of Dorothy Day, claimed that American lay Catholic activity in the 1930s "was confined to the five Bs: Bingo, Bridge, Bowling, Bazaars, Beers."[83] As a young man Vishnewski discovered that, outside the religious orders, there was little opportunity for Catholics who wanted to follow the social message of the Gospels within the framework of Catholic organizations. Yet, said Vishnewski, had "I written a letter to the Communists or to the Jehovah Witnesses or some Bible sect I would have soon found myself distributing literature and preparing myself for an apostolic ministry."[84]

The American leaders of the "New Social Catholicism" were determined to change all this.[85] The group had a strong sense of corporate identity: they were all committed to liturgical renewal, championed a more rigorous intellectual attack on communism, and, almost to a person, were highly vocal in their criticism of fascism as a friend or ally of Christianity. As Norman McKenna put it to Father Furfey in reference to the possible topics and invitees for a conference on New Catholicism: "As for pussyfooting on the Ethiopian business, we aren't having any, as the English say. We will state our reasons for opposing Fascism in an early issue, and anyone who wants to defend Fascism will have to tilt a lance with *Non Abbiamo Bisogno*, the *Syllabus of Errors*, *De Regimine Principum* and other authoritative documents."[86] Most significantly, the New Social Catholics were determined to attack the abuses of wealth and privilege. Father Michel warned that Catholics had been far too negligent about denouncing such evils; some, he lamented, had even "falsely hidden" their own social injustices "beneath the cloak of the Church."[87] Virgil Michel's commitment to consciousness-raising as a prerequisite for transforming the social and economic order assured that there would be a steady cross-fertilization of ideas between the liturgists and the English Distributists throughout the 1920s and 1930s.[88]

A key figure linking the American liturgical revival with Distributism was the English Catholic convert Donald Attwater. As an associate editor of *Orate Fratres*, he was one of the most influential lay members of that journal's board of directors.[89] Virgil Michel said that Attwater was his "ideal of an alert and apostolic Catholic layman."[90] Attwater arrived at Distributism through his association with Eric Gill, for whom he served as personal secretary. Attwater introduced Gill to Michel's liturgical ideas, and Gill became an avid supporter of the movement's magazine. (Gill even designed the cover page for the first number of *Orate Fratres*.)

Eric Gill also had important connections with the Catholic Worker movement. Dorothy Day's colleague, Peter Maurin, was a keen student of Gill, and his ideas concerning the virtues of handcraft production and the worker's claims to ownership of the means of production were major influences on Maurin's writings.[91] Dorothy Day claimed that Maurin was the primary source for her own constructive notions about social reform. He brought to the Catholic Worker movement, she wrote, the ideas of Guardini, Karl Adam, Luigi Sturzo, Maritain, Eric Gill, Belloc, and Chesterton.[92] Arthur Sheehan, Maurin's biographer, noted his subject's careful study of Chesterton and Belloc and believed him to be the purest American voice of Distributism.[93] But Gill was the most widely quoted writer in Maurin's "Easy Essays," and in this respect one could argue that Gill was the main conduit of Distributist thinking to the Catholic Worker movement.

Virgil Michel also had a close working relationship with Dorothy Day and Peter Maurin. The Catholic Worker movement and the organizations affiliated with it were shelters for intellectuals bitter about what they believed to be the reactionary policies of the Catholic hierarchy.[94] This was undoubtedly part of the reason that the movement was so frequently attacked by right-wing, philo-fascist Catholics, such as Patrick Scanlan, editor of the *Brooklyn Tablet*. Virgil Michel sent the *Catholic Worker* all publications of the Liturgical Press free of charge. The generosity was returned in thanks and action. Dorothy Day wrote that those who were attracted to the Catholic Worker movement because of its emphasis on social justice had also, from the beginning, an equal interest in liturgical renewal. Almost always, she said, the long discussions at Catholic Worker offices came around to the doctrine of the Mystical Body of Christ.[95] The zesty intellectual atmospheres of the *Catholic Worker* offices was legendary. Jacques Maritain, a frequent visiter whenever he was in New York, said that the place had the feel of Charles Pèguy's workshop in the Rue de La Sorbonne, and "so much good will, so much courage, and so much generosity. It is thus, with meager means, but with much love, that we prepare the future, with great hope."[96] The *Catholic Worker* regularly featured articles on liturgical reform.

In addition to his friendship with Dorothy Day and Peter Maurin, Virgil Michel collaborated extensively with Norman McKenna, who, along with Richard Deverall, broke away from the *Catholic Worker* and published the *Christian Front* (not to be confused with another paper of the same name published by those associated with Father Charles Coughlin). McKenna and his group wanted a more aggressive and intellectual approach to America's social and economic problems. Their journal drew on the labor encyclicals and Distributism, and was outspoken in its condemnation of communism, fascism, and anti-Semitism.[97] Virgil Michel wrote many articles for the *Christian Front* and served as chief advisor to McKenna and Deverall.

The liturgist-Distributist linkages also extended into the German Catholic Central Verein of America. The latter was America's oldest national Catholic social organization and the first to take a serious interest in the issuance of *Rerum Novarum*. Under the aegis of Frederick P. Kenkel, a student of the teachings of Ozanam and Ketteler, the Central Verein published a bilingual magazine, *Central-Blatt and Social Justice*, which was the first journal to explore the ways in which Catholic ideas of social justice could be applied to America.

Kenkel believed that a true Christian society depended on the existence of a sturdy middle class. Yet his concept of a bourgeoisie could not be understood in Marxist terms, for Kenkel's ideal was a vigorous *Mittelstand*, a broad grouping of small property owners, tradesmen, shopkeepers, and farmers that closely corresponded to what Chesterton and Belloc defined as the core elements of a Distributist society. In an effort to strengthen this *Mittelstand*, Kenkel and the Central Verein were supporters of labor and professional cooperatives along the lines suggested by Bishop Ketteler. To promote better understanding of contemporary social and economic matters, the Central Verein established libraries, study circles, summer schools, and scholarships. The association also had a long tradition of working closely with the Benedictines of St. John's Abbey.[98]

Finally, the influence of the liturgical-Distributist revival is shown in the fact that Virgil Michel and *Orate Fratres* expanded their spiritual alliance outside narrow Catholic circles. Father Michel, for example, had a long working relationship with Maurice Reckitt and the Christendom group, the Anglican advocates of Distributism, and he was an avid reader of their publications.[99] In April 1936 *Orate Fratres* welcomed *Christendom*, the High Anglican quarterly, into the ranks of the liturgical revival. Its vigorous efforts at spreading the doctrine of the Mystical Body of Christ as the operative path for social reconstruction, said Michel, meant that this Anglican group was seeking the same ends through the same means as the Roman Catholic liturgists.

As founder of both *Orate Fratres* and the Liturgical Press, Virgil Michel championed a good many liberal and even radical causes and programs. These included, among others, trade unionism, Distributism, personalism (a Belgian Catholic philosophical movement

that stressed the rights of the human personality against capitalis-
tic individualism), and, most emphatically, a recommendation to
study what was called "cooperativism." This last effort, promoted by
the International Consumers Cooperative Movement, was gaining
popularity throughout Britain, Scandinavia, and the Catholic countries of Europe in the 1930s. It was chiefly concerned with achieving a more economically egalitarian society along lines outlined in
the papal labor encyclicals and supported by the Distributists. "Production for use and not for profit," the battle cry of the cooperatives,
resonated nicely with the concerns of such English Distributists
as Father Vincent McNabb and A. J. Penty. Important tenets of its
program were democratic government, voluntarism, and the organization of economic activity not according to the mechanisms of
profit, which ignored the main purpose of economics, but according to consumption needs. A major purpose of the Consumers
Cooperative Movement was to enable members to purchase goods
more cheaply by eliminating the unnecessary profits of the middle-
man, thus reducing costs of distribution. The movement was held
together by international alliances. In Sweden, for instance, the
Consumers Cooperative Societies accounted for over 20 percent of
the nation's retail and wholesale trade and 10 percent of all manufacturing. In 1935, forty countries were represented by the International Cooperative Alliance with three hundred thousand societies
and a total membership of a hundred million consumers.[100]

Cooperative economic ideas were among many subjects of study
undertaken by the Institute of Social Study at St. John's University.
The Institute was founded by Virgil Michel, with the collaboration
of the Minnesota branch of the Central Verein, while he was at St.
John's University. Its purpose was to train lay leaders in Catholic
social philosophy so they might play a direct and active role in the
community by establishing credit unions and cooperative self-help
programs. Michel and his associates viewed their enterprise as a
positive response to the pope's calls for the promotion of social study.
But most importantly, and in a very idealistic fashion, they called for
their students to gradually reform social and economic institutions
by participating as a living community in the spirit of the liturgy,
thereby regenerating not just Christian life but eventually all of
America.

The Institute's seminars and its educational enterprises undertaken in the spirit of freedom of inquiry, the *raison d'être* of institutions of higher learning, brought a torrent of criticism from
conservative elements in the Catholic community. These difficulties
were exacerbated by Peter Maurin's arrival at the Institute. Maurin's
anarchistic opinions had made him unwelcome at many Catholic
college campuses. Michel, whose understanding of the papal social
encyclicals as well as his training as an educator made him sympathetic to Maurin's predicament, defended Maurin's presence at St.
John's. Peter Maurin was an original, Michel claimed, a fountainhead of good ideas and worthwhile projects.[101]

Opposition to the Institute of Social Study came from two main
sources, both of which symbolized the kind of resistance that generally surfaced against the liberal thinking that undergirded the
labor encyclicals: conservative businessmen who claimed its seminars were preaching communism, and the bishop of St. Cloud, the
Most Reverend Joseph Busch, who felt the need to control what
went on at the Institute in order to prevent the infusion of "dangerous" socialistic ideas. The bishop objected to what he described
as a "laissez-faire" approach to education that was insufficiently
didactic concerning church teachings, thereby permitting too much
room for "incorrect" thinking.[102]

The persons critical of Michel's program were convinced that
ideas about consumers' cooperatives discussed at the Institute of
Social Study represented communism, pure and simple. As one correspondent explained it, those nations that "went radical like Mexico, Spain, and Russia" all started down the path to communism by
first experimenting with consumers cooperatives. Critics such as
these threatened boycotts against the university unless the "Red propaganda" ceased.[103] Father Michel and his associates did their best
to counter these criticisms with patience and reason, pointing out
that the great orthodox theologian Tanquerey had himself advocated
cooperatives and that it was an approach to economics deeply rooted
in church teachings, most particularly in the tradition of the Benedictines. In any case, Father Michel offered his critics the opportunity to send speakers to the Institute who could present the case
against cooperatives. The challenge, however, was never accepted.

The Benedictines were largely successful in staving off attacks from such uninformed, authoritarian elements, but the opposition was emblematic of the unfavorable environment with which Catholic reformers with advanced social and economic ideas were obliged to contend.[104]

In the last few years of his life, Virgil Michel set forth a practical program for industrial reconstruction, one which, in the final analysis, was highly Distributist in its goals. His program called for worker involvement in the management, ownership, and profits of the productive process; the promotion of private proprietorship; a new credit system to serve the public good; and regulation or abolition of irresponsible absentee ownership of factories. In order to achieve these objectives, Father Michel recommended the creation of a corporative system in which workers' councils would have a direct role in running factories and where all individuals would have the choice of joining autonomous, freely organized socioeconomic associations that corresponded to their employment. He also advocated a general "down-sizing" in the living and production structures of society (a move away from large, impersonal bureaucratic associations) in order to create a more humane environment for all.[105]

Following the death of Father Michel in November 1938, the new editor of *Orate Fratres,* Father Godfrey Diekmann, O.S.B., needed someone who could carry on the important column "Timely Tracts." The loss of Virgil Michel left a huge void for the paper, not to mention the American liturgical movement, and Father Godfrey searched desperately to find a writer armed with the requisite knowledge of European liturgical thought and a zesty pen, who could continue the paper's tradition of provocative essays. Father Reinhold had visited St. John's campus in the previous year and since then had maintained a correspondence with Father Emeric Lawrence, O.S.B., an influential figure in the liturgical revival at the college. Reinhold and Father Emeric had become friends while both were doing research at Harvard's Widner Library. Father Emeric had been impressed with Reinhold's broad knowledge of the liturgical tradition and especially with his appreciation of the linkages between Benedictine monastic ideals and social issues, as well as his familiarity with architecture and liturgical art. Although Father

Reinhold had only been in America for a few years, he had managed to master the English language and was already challenging
conventional Catholic thinking in provocative articles in *Commonweal*. For all these reasons Father Emeric recommended him to the
editor of *Orate Fratres*, and Father Reinhold was taken aboard.

Reinhold's freely-roaming mind and his personal contacts with
important, avant-garde continental Catholic thinkers provided the
continuity that Godfrey Diekmann sought for *Orate Fratres*.[106] Not
only did Reinhold fully endorse Virgil Michel's mission, he had the
sharpness of wit, breadth of knowledge (the product of an excellent European education), and the tenacity of spirit to bring great
power to the column. "What characterized him more than anything
else," Father Emeric recalled, "was his keenness in getting at the
base of things, seeing things and issues as they are and should be.
He never wasted time on anything that was not fundamental." In
H. A. Reinhold *Orate Fratres* inherited, in the words of one reader,
a "firebrand, a whirlwind, a cyclone," whose unflinching criticism of
what was wrong with American and worldwide Catholicism was
always anchored in a solid understanding of Christian history.[107]

As the author of "Timely Tracts," Reinhold continued in the
same vein as his predecessor (maintaining, as he put it, a "close interconnection of four apostolates: the social, liturgical, educational and
biblical"),[108] though there was a sharper edge to his essays. Reinhold
was less the diplomat than Virgil Michel, less gentle with those who
failed to heed the message of the Gospels, and bolder in what he
believed Catholics should do to change things.[109] Like Michel,
he regularly criticized the Catholic Church for its failure to take the
lead in fighting social and economic injustice and for its tendency,
in too many countries, to side with the wealthy and powerful. He
was especially harsh on what he called the "irenic clergy," churchmen who were afraid of disturbing the delicate balance between the
institutional church and those who had the advantage of possessing
power and wealth.[110] In fact, Reinhold went so far as to suggest that
the appeal of socialism and Marxism to workers was a direct result
of the clergy's reluctance to understand or take seriously the warnings of the earlier popes.

Virgil Michel's social research corroborated Reinhold's assessment of the Church's failure in such matters. Michel had studied the

Antigonish cooperative movement in Nova Scotia,[111] and one of his contacts, a former member of the United Mine Workers' board of governors, told him that prior to their knowledge of the papal labor encyclicals, almost all Catholic miners voted communist.[112] In 1920, he said, United Mine Workers' representatives passed resolutions which were "communistic from A to Z," even advocating the use of force. Indeed, the most devout Catholic miners voted for communist candidates "because the communists were the only ones that wanted to help the poor people to better their lot." Catholics at this point did not yet know that the Church offered any way out; they knew only that it condemned communism.[113] Catholic laborers in Nova Scotia had become lukewarm, almost reluctant followers of the Church. Catholic leaders always talked about what was wrong with both communism and the condition of the workers, but they never spoke of a cure. However, once the miners learned about the message of the papal social encyclicals they turned away from Marxism. In fact, Michel discovered that some of Nova Scotia's most stalwart communist union officials were now among its leading Catholics.[114]

Father Reinhold's bold assaults on what he found objectionable in contemporary Catholicism were inspired by the social and aesthetic criticisms of Eric Gill. Gill was at the forefront of a handful of Catholic writers who were arguing that the diffusion of "bourgeois-commercial" values was transforming modern culture into a vast wasteland of vulgarity. Its markings were a plethora of bad taste exhibited in all forms of art, literature, politics, education, and even in leisure activities. The "new bourgeois," a term employed by several contemporary Christian philosophers (Maritain, Etienne Gilson, Christopher Dawson, Karl Adam, and Romano Guardini, among others), added to Marx's materialist, class definition of "bourgeois" a Weberian notion of the acquisitive mind-set, fathered by Puritan values, that led to capitalism. The crass materialist values of the bourgeois vulgarian were singled out for special condemnation in Reinhold's column.

In addition to dominating secular culture, the acquisitive spirit of the bourgeois had also made significant inroads into the Church itself, most notably in the "irenic clergy" that Reinhold so despised. A bourgeois, wrote Reinhold, is a "surface man" more concerned about the conventions of polite life than with truth, honesty, and genuineness. Above all, he seeks "safety" in every respect, financial, political, social, and moral. His greatest delights are found in mediocrity, efficiency, and respectability. For three centuries the Church had resisted the onslaught of the bourgeois, but by the nineteenth century its spirit had breached the barriers. What better documentation of this, noted Reinhold, than modern drab and uncreative Church architecture, the timid and sterile progeny of masters of imitation and make-believe. Reinhold recommended that Catholics look to Gill as someone who knew how to break the siege of the vulgarians: he administered the shock treatment that Catholics needed to "snap out" of their Puritan stuffiness in art, sexual matters, human relations, economics, and politics. Gill was opening the gate toward a road that would allow all to find themselves again as Christian, Catholic, and human.[115]

Finally, in the Distributist tradition that was so important to the founder of *Orate Fratres* and the American liturgical movement, Father Reinhold in his "Timely Tracts" columns continued to call his readers' attention to the proper understanding of property and ownership in a Christian society. Most Catholic moralists had properly excoriated the evils of collectivism, but in too many cases this had become an obsession; they overlooked the equally pernicious danger of unlimited and depersonalized proprietorship associated with the ethos of capitalism. Far too many Catholics were afraid of alienating their benefactors and loath to disturb the political quiescence encouraged by the ruling elites. They had remained silent about the Christian responsibilities that went with the ownership of wealth. Rights to the ownership of property, Reinhold emphasized, drawing on the writings of Maurice Reckitt and the Anglican Distributists, cannot be something absolute; they must meet certain functional criteria, namely, to improve the quality of living for the commonweal as a whole.[116] Reinhold concurred with Gill that it is just that a man should possess that portion of the field, shop, or factory upon which he can leave the "impress of his personality" for the purpose of perfecting his nature and for the benefit of others. But men must share without hesitation when others were in need. Does such sacred personal property in the Christian liturgical sense sanction the workings of the American capitalist system, asked Reinhold, in which a single individual, such as J. P. Morgan, controls directly or indirectly 70 percent of forty-two railroad companies and 55 percent of fifty-two other utility companies?[117]

Father H. A. Reinhold was a worthy successor to the pioneer of American liturgical renewal, Dom Virgil Michel. His labor with *Orate Fratres* and later with *Worship*, the corpus of his writing for liturgical reform, and his service to his parish and the Seamen's Apostolate in the United States were distinguished by a rare courage and a willingness to bring Catholicism into the secular world. Even when gravely ill (he suffered from Parkinson's disease and episodes of severe depression), he found time to bridge the religious and secular worlds as writer and social activist by assisting his friends at the *Catholic Worker*. Like his predecessor, Reinhold was a sophisticated scholar with an extraordinary sensitivity to the plight of the poor, underprivileged, and oppressed. For Reinhold, religious belief was always related to action and to the problems of communism, fascism, democracy, war, peace, poverty, and wealth.

CHAPTER 11

American Catholics Move to the Right

The rise of fascism and the growing strength of communism exacerbated political divisions in the British and American Catholic community. By the mid-1930s the Vatican had established a much clearer position on Marxism, as was manifested in the encyclical *Divini Redemptoris* of March 1937, a root-and-branch condemnation of communism. On the other hand, the concordats with Hitler and Mussolini, Catholic support for reactionary authoritarian governments that came to power in Portugal and Austria, and the philo-fascist writings of those associated with the highly influential Hilaire Belloc and other reactionary Catholic intellectuals, gave the appearance that Catholicism was prepared to ally itself with dictators to offset the Red menace. This was not necessarily the case, as the encyclical *Mit Brennender Sorge,* also of March 1937 and sharply critical of Nazi religious policies, suggests. But the Church's ambiguity toward fascism certainly gave the impression of general and even official Catholic support and sympathy. In any event, Rome's clearly articulated opposition to Marxism had the general effect of making British and American Catholics especially vigilant in their efforts to battle the infusion of communist influence in all spheres of life.

Although many Catholic leaders emphasized that the best way to check communism was to combat the social injustice that spawned the creed in the first place, far too many of their co-religionists became obsessed with Red subversion and in the process turned a blind eye to social and economic oppression and fascism.

A major force giving shape to American Catholic opinion in the 1930s was Francis X. Talbot, S.J., editor of the Jesuit magazine *America*.[1] Father Talbot succeeded Wilfrid Parsons, S.J., as editor of *America,* and under his direction the tone of the journal shifted noticeably to the political right. In contrast to Father Talbot, whose interests and training were primarily in the area of literary criticism, his predecessor, Father Parsons, had been schooled in the disciplines of history and sociology and, partly for this reason, showed a greater interest in and more sophisticated appreciation of the social and economic issues that confronted American Catholicism.[2] This was revealed in the character and orientation of *America* while Parsons was editor. Prior to 1936, when Father Talbot took charge of the paper, *America* devoted far more space to papal labor thought, and Parsons himself maintained a busy lecturing schedule, visiting all kinds of associations and groups where he expounded on the applications of the social encyclicals to American life. In one radio talk, for instance, Parsons emphasized that *America* operated from a central idea, namely, that religion had a lot about it which could "occupy the brain" and that above all, he insisted, Catholicism was "a *social* thing."[3] In this spirit Parsons regarded it as necessary for his paper to support the American labor movement's collective bargaining efforts, its claim of the right to strike, and demands for a living wage, all of which were threatened by "yellow dog" contracts, the dangerous proliferation of company unions, and court injunctions in labor disputes. In fighting these evils Parsons was quick to point out that Pius XI's 1931 encyclical, *Quadragesimo Anno,* must be seen not so much as mere protest against injustice and inhumanity but as a call for the adoption of a new social order founded on a "fair distribution" of wealth. He also claimed that if the Great Depression were in itself insufficient to undermine the current capitalist system, then the state "must see to it that this is done, by taxing the wealthy, if necessary, to make them do what they will not do of their own free will."[4] Parsons certainly had his concerns about the expansion of Marxism and its appeal to American workers, but this problem, he argued, could be avoided if the government allowed labor its natural right to organize and provided it some protection from capitalist exploitation.

America under the editorship of Wilfrid Parsons was an uncompromising critic of the Hoover administration. The administration's laissez-faire approach to the nation's economic troubles betrayed a bias that smacked of what Parsons called the "old liberalism," giving liberty to the men of industry, finance, and commerce independent of legislative curbing or any standards of social morality. Mr. Hoover, he wrote, "stood for every principle, economic and social, that is condemned by the Popes in their encyclicals," and it is our duty, he added, to refute the ethical fallacies upon which his administration functioned.[5]

Parsons' writings in *America* and his lectures and correspondence showed a sophisticated understanding of the central issues of the 1930s: economic depression, the idea of corporatism, management/labor disputes, fascism, communism, and Nazism.[6] Father Parsons was an early supporter of Franklin Delano Roosevelt's presidency, for he sympathized with the administration's attempts to introduce legislation for social reform and the regulation of industrial activity in favor of labor. There was something new and quite special with Roosevelt, wrote Parsons, for he was attempting to establish, for the first time in American history, a system founded on the recognition of basic working rights through which labor might achieve its fair economic rewards. In a culture steeped in the ethos of rugged individualism, the president was encouraging the principle that the ownership of property carried with it social responsibilities, that there was an important moral dimension to economics. FDR's administration seemed to be willing to assume the burden of achieving true social justice.[7] Parsons later concluded that the National Recovery Administration, though a good idea and launched with the best intentions, was put into the hands of the wrong people, who opposed its goals of finding a proper balance between the rights of property and labor and the reconciliation of social justice with individual justice. In too many cases, Parsons concluded, the "oldstyle individualists" were put in full control of enforcing NRA codes. The New Deal, in other words, was administered by old methods: "It was a Democratic idea, and it was run by Republicans."[8]

Father Parsons was a strong supporter of the American labor movement, but he became increasingly doubtful that the major union representing craft workers, the American Federation of Labor

(AFL), offered much promise for solving the social problem along lines favorable to most American workers. The elitist AFL ignored the majority of unskilled workers, and its conservative social philosophy and refusal to entertain militant methods gave little hope to Catholics who saw the need to redistribute wealth and power as called for in the papal labor encyclicals. Consequently, Parsons and several other Catholic leaders, notably Monsignor John A. Ryan and his colleagues in the Social Action Department of the National Catholic Welfare Conference, looked to the federal government as an agent for reform.[9] In the meantime they urged workers to join a union and use the strike as a weapon to achieve economic justice.

The persistent refusal of the AFL to open its doors to unskilled workers led to the formation of a rival association in 1935. In that year those who favored industrial unionism in the factories of mass production formed the Committee for Industrial Organization (CIO). Although many Catholics had urged the unionization of unskilled workers and were disappointed in the AFL's limited social vision, they deplored a split in the American labor movement. The militancy of the CIO, the presence of communists in its ranks, and the rash of strikes that broke out in 1937 caused grave concern for many Catholics. The more conservative condemned this militancy and became convinced that communists were behind the unrest. The liberal Catholics associated with the liturgical movement and *Catholic Worker* circles were more sympathetic, recognizing that such tactics as the sit-down strike were the only weapons that labor could employ to prevent further erosion of its power. Father Virgil Michel, for example, argued that the worker's job was itself a form of property carrying with it prerogatives comparable to other property rights. Since strikes were a legitimate means to protect labor's interests, the sit-down could also be seen as a morally legitimate weapon.[10]

Such sentiment clashed with the views of conservative Catholics. Reverend Charles Coughlin and the influential Bishop John F. Noll of Fort Wayne, Indiana, editor of *Our Sunday Visitor,* for instance, went so far as to charge that the CIO was itself a front organization for communists. Given the Church's condemnation of Marxism, Coughlin said, Catholics should be forbidden to join CIO unions. Bishop Noll claimed he had plenty of evidence that a great many well-meaning Catholic ecclesiastics were being "terribly fooled" and becoming the "unwitting tools" of the communists.[11] Noll criticized the *Catholic Worker* in this context: the paper was too radical, its tactics perilously close to those of the communists.[12]

Catholic supporters of the American labor movement, however, came to the CIO's defense. Voices of approval were heard from several socially progressive bishops (George Mundelein of Chicago, Edward Mooney of Detroit, and Robert Lucey of San Antonio, among others). Archbishop Lucey, for example, asserted that the pope endorsed industrial unionism and that the CIO should go further in its demands against capital by claiming the right to manage industry. Labeling the CIO communist, he said, was palpably untrue and a slander of America's laboring classes.

Outside the official hierarchy, support for the CIO came from Father Wilfrid Parsons, Father John Ryan, the liturgists, the Catholic Worker movement, and, perhaps most uncompromisingly, from those associated with the *Christian Front*. Founded by Norman McKenna, a close friend of Virgil Michel, and Richard Deverall, the *Christian Front* supported a socially conscious unionism as the means for bringing about a corporate system based on vocational groups as recommended in *Quadragesimo Anno*. Rather than moralize about the evils of communist infiltration of the labor movement, McKenna and Deverall insisted that Catholics should demonstrate to the American worker that the Church was more concerned, more selfless, and more dedicated than communists in efforts to solve the social problem. Only by doing so would labor ever recognize that there was something called Catholic social teaching. Instead of simply dismissing the CIO as a communist front organization, Catholics needed to burrow within it, support its legitimate claims for power, counter communist influence, and push the movement toward accepting corporatist principles.

McKenna and his colleagues were helped in this endeavor by the creation of the Association of Catholic Trade Unionists (ACTU) in 1937. Its purpose was to encourage Catholic workers to become union activists and to introduce them to the programs of the social encyclicals. The ACTU did not aim to seize control of the American trade union movement for its own sectarian ends but rather sought to show that Catholics could move beyond tribalism and cooperate with others for the attainment of common objectives beneficial to labor as a whole. Conservative Catholics were highly suspicious of ACTU policy, however, since its cooperative ethic opened the door to communist contamination, while the insistence that labor actually share ownership of the means of production (which was central to Distributist labor programs) was perceived as radically dangerous to the American system.[13]

America under the editorship of Father Parsons gave considerable support to Catholic plans to revitalize the trade union movement and assumed a pro-New Deal profile because Roosevelt was believed to be a true friend of the working class. Father Parsons also had been prepared to take on the enemies of FDR's reformist objectives. Along with Rev. John A. Ryan, for example, he was one of the first well-known Catholics to point out the mistaken notions of Father Charles Coughlin, who by 1935 had become one of Roosevelt's most vociferous critics.[14] Although an initial supporter of Roosevelt, after 1934 Coughlin became increasingly critical of the New Deal because it failed to address what he believed to be the main cause of the depression: a financial conspiracy by international bankers. Father Parsons recognized an authoritarian dimension to Coughlin's ideas that did not square with the papal social encyclicals. The "Radio Priest," as Coughlin was called (his program out of Royal Oak, Michigan, was one of the most popular in America), recommended that strikes be abolished in favor of federally-mandated arbitration boards. Parsons objected essentially for the same reason as had Chesterton and Belloc in their support of the British labor movement: this would place labor under the tutelage of government and thus liable to be easily manipulated by big business.

Father Coughlin's views on corporative reform also were called into question by Parsons. Coughlin's program, Parsons pointed out, called only for the worker to enter vocational groups. *Quadragesimo Anno*, on the other hand, emphasized the necessity of both labor and management forming vocational associations so that each could bargain more equally. Coughlin's plan placed the workers at a disadvantage, since it perpetuated the division between a unionized working class and the powers of management.

In addition, Parsons saw problems with Coughlin's campaign for credit reform. It continued the dangerous tendency toward increasing the power of the state, since Coughlin recommended the creation of a national bank to replace the Federal Reserve system, which he regarded as a privately owned tool of the financial plutocracy; he would place the actual ownership and control of credit in the government's hands.

Finally, Parsons noted, Coughlin's social credit theories were murky, untried, overly simplistic, and obfuscatory. They had the effect of diverting attention from demand side economics, according to which the real sources of the depression were maladjustments between production, distribution, and consumption. On this issue Parsons supported Monsignor Ryan, who pointed out that "what business needs is not more credit but more sales, and this is an industrial not a monetary problem."[15] The real danger concerning Father Coughlin, warned Parsons, was that by dragging his own mistaken views on social justice into presidential politics, which ultimately would fail, he might undermine Catholic confidence in papal social thought. America, wrote Parsons, would be saved by no mechanical, automatic plan but only through a change of mind and soul: "It seems a shame that Father Coughlin, with his power over the popular mind, has not restricted himself to the reformation of his mind, but has risked all on doubtful economic legislation."[16]

Parsons' articles in *America* on Coughlin's economic ideas, which revealed, he claimed, a misunderstanding of the papal social encyclicals, brought a deluge of letters to the paper denouncing the editor. Indeed, in reaction to the series Coughlin personally attacked Father Parsons in a speech at Madison Square Garden.[17] Parsons, however, had no regrets for his actions. Even before publishing the series on Coughlin, he had written Rev. Hugh Francis Harte that the radio priest's economic ideas appeared completely unfounded in fact, and he expressed his fear that they could lead the Church into a regrettable adventure.[18]

America's initial enthusiasm for the Roosevelt administration waned rapidly after Father Francis Talbot became its editor. Rather than concentrating on the papal labor encyclicals, the magazine became increasingly sympathetic to business interests and obsessed with the threat of communism. First, Talbot and his staff became convinced that New Deal reforms and the Roosevelt administration's attacks on the Supreme Court would strengthen the powers of the federal government at the expense of the states and thereby upset the balance of powers guaranteed by the Constitution. Parsons also had some concerns about federal powers undercutting individual liberties (as did a good many Catholic intellectuals), but he believed an antidote to this was to go beyond the New Deal to a cooperative system that would devolve power to vocational groups.[19] The second development that turned *America* against Roosevelt was the administration's recognition of the Soviet Union in 1933, followed by its refusal to denounce religious persecution in Mexico. Adding to these vexations was the rise to prominence within the administration of a number of liberal advisors believed to be sympathetic to communism.

This shift against the New Deal was even more pronounced in two other influential Catholic publications that enjoyed support from Talbot's magazine, namely, Patrick Scanlan's *Brooklyn Tablet* and Father Charles Coughlin's *Social Justice*. Both Scanlan and Coughlin were moved to action by fears of communism and over-centralization of power in the federal government. These papers, along with Bishop Noll's *Our Sunday Visitor,* mounted a coordinated attack on America's largest industrial union, the newly founded (1935) Congress of Industrial Organizations (CIO), arguing that its ranks were falling under communist control.

Patrick Scanlan and Father Coughlin had also orchestrated a vitriolic campaign against the liberalism of Father John Ryan, an enthusiastic and highly influential supporter of Roosevelt's New Deal legislation. Ryan was not one to hold his tongue on issues close to his heart, and he had openly questioned Father Coughlin's understanding of the labor encyclicals. He had also defended the CIO against charges of being communist controlled. Moreover, there was a scandalous lack of understanding among Catholics of both papal social teachings and the doctrines of communism, a problem compounded, in Ryan's view, by what Church leaders had to say about such matters. Ryan, for example, had told Bishop John O'Hara that, in his opinion, Bishop Noll's assessment of communist doctrines and challenges, widely circulated in *Our Sunday Visitor* and in a pamphlet entitled "It Is Happening Here," were the most superficial and unreliable collection of writings ever published by an American bishop. His analysis of communism, claimed Ryan, had "about as much substance as the diatribes of the Hearst papers."[20]

Father Ryan's critics bit back with vengeance. Father Coughlin, for instance, charged that Ryan was a paid agent of the communists and that he had collaborated in writing a book which denied the divinity of Christ. Ryan preferred to fight with Coughlin behind the scenes, recognizing that public battles would only serve to divide the Catholic community. Yet he was acutely aware of Coughlin's capacity for damage. Ryan told his fellow Catholic journalists that Coughlin "is the worst enemy to Catholic causes that exists in the United States today."[21] In general, however, Ryan refused to respond to Coughlin's lies because the great majority of his followers were abusive and so set in their ways that nothing he could say would move them.[22] In any case, Ryan never felt that Coughlin should be silenced. The principle guaranteeing freedom of speech was more important than Father Coughlin's demagogic preaching, and it certainly could serve as a better corrective than enforced silence.[23] Ryan was also circumspect in replying to Patrick Scanlan's attacks in the *Brooklyn Tablet* for the same reasons. One of Scanlan's tactics, for example, was to publish anonymous abusive, untruthful, and misleading letters concerning Ryan without providing him opportunities to respond in a timely or fair-minded fashion. Privately Ryan considered Scanlan to be not merely an "unfair controversialist" and "reactionary nuisance" but "downright crooked."[24] Scanlan at one time had been friendly with Ryan; but after the latter spoke out in favor of FDR Scanlan angrily turned against him. This is also a reason Scanlan became an ardent supporter of Charles Coughlin: their friendship was forged by mutual hatred of Roosevelt.[25]

Besides Roosevelt and the New Deal, the other matter of dispute between liberal Catholics and Talbot's allies was how to address the challenge of communism. Whereas Wilfrid Parsons as editor of *America* had been preoccupied with the exploitation of labor by the wealthy and powerful, Talbot's *America* focused its energies on fighting communism. Parsons, for his part, had feared a reaction to communism which, in a frenzied effort to protect property and class interests, could be so strong as to destroy American democracy itself. In Father Talbot's thinking, the greatest danger confronting both

America as well as the Catholic Church was the Popular Front, a coalition against fascism which he believed was inspired and controlled by the Bolsheviks as a means of bringing communism to the West.[26] It was Comintern (Communist International) policy after 1935 to encourage alliances with bourgeois governments in Western Europe. Stalin by this time recognized the importance of securing Russia from German invasion and therefore was determined to encourage a united front against all forms of fascism. However, the labor movement in Europe had already been working for a united front, well before Stalin joined the cause. Numerous working-class parties and associations throughout Europe and America supported the idea of a united front against fascism. It was clearly Stalin's intention for the Comintern to control these efforts, yet with the exception of Spain, the Bolsheviks failed to completely dominate or control the various united front efforts; they had stiff competition from independent socialists, anarchists, liberals, and radical groups, many of whom did not accept the objectives of the Russian Revolution. The majority of these elements were moderates who wanted change to occur gradually and only through parliamentary means. Certainly the communists were able to exert a good deal of influence within the front's anti-fascist drive because of their organizational expertise, but it is an exaggeration to say that all Popular Front activity was controlled by Moscow.

Talbot contended that Marxism, abetted by American liberals, was swiftly infiltrating all areas of American life. Communists, he insisted, instigated labor unrest, directed the impetus for labor reform, had taken control of the liberal media, and were making great strides in the arts and theater.[27] One of Father Talbot's major interests was the work of communists in Hollywood. In its "Comment" column of 19 March 1938, for example, *America* played up an anonymous advertisement published in the Hollywood *Daily Reporter* that was meant to be a gag about communists and their influence in the film industry. *America* inferred from the advertisement that Hollywood was indeed in "the closed fist of Communists." The editor of the *Daily Reporter,* W. R. Wilkerson, who was himself a Catholic, wrote to Talbot informing him of the satirical nature of the advertisement and expressing his concern that *America's* response might give the mistaken impression that the motion picture business was run by Marxists. The editor also approached Archbishop Cantwell of Los Angeles to express his concerns about the potential danger of the inferences made by *America*. Archbishop Cantwell concurred with Wilkerson that Hollywood communists were few in number and possessed negligible influence.

Father Talbot wrote a revealing response to Mr. Wilkerson, setting the stage for the crusade he was orchestrating against communism in America. Talbot said he published the advertisement because it was a confirmation of other evidence he had "on very good authority" of subversive activity in the film industry. Although the author of the bogus advertisement had himself written Talbot (in a style that continued the joke), and despite Wilkerson's clarifications, Talbot concluded that even though the advertisement may have been somewhat exaggerated, "is there not a great deal of truth" in what was said? "Has not there been a very definite attachment on the part of Hollywood, its producers, and its stars, to the Loyalist communist government of Spain?"[28]

Talbot cultivated connections with the extreme right in his campaign against communism. One of his allies was George S. Viereck, a notorious Nazi sympathizer who wrote articles in a magazine called *Liberty* under the name of Donald Furthman Wickets. Viereck was indicted in 1941 as a German agent and spent four years in prison. In carrying out his work as a Hitler apologist, Viereck published information from someone he called "Comrade XYZ," a one-time party member, concerning communist activity that the House Committee on Un-American Activities had overlooked. According to Viereck, the communists had not only burrowed into the American government at the state and federal levels but had actually secured a foothold in President Roosevelt's cabinet. Communists had planted key agents in the railroad and shipping industries and in the utilities, and when Moscow gave the order they would tie up communications and shut off power and light throughout America. Viereck claimed to have knowledge that laborers in the Works Progress Administration, which he called a communist-controlled front organization, were mixing explosives with their cement to blow up dams and roads "whenever the hour in Moscow strikes." In

fact, Washington, wrote Viereck, was honeycombed with under-
ground secret passages, one leading straight from the headquarters
of John L. Lewis (leader of the United Mine Workers' Union) to
the White House, and Roosevelt himself had already "passed word"
to the Comintern to assassinate his political enemies. These frightening pictures of subversion painted in lurid detail by Viereck reached
levels of the phantasmagoric, but in the view of *America's* editor,
Viereck was performing a valuable journalistic service to the nation.
Father Talbot congratulated Viereck on his "splendid" articles: "I am
glad that *Liberty* shows such courage and would recommend its
example to the other major publications of the U.S. who [*sic*] are
pussyfooting on the real issues."[29]

In contrast to Father Talbot, Wilfrid Parsons' approach to the
Popular Front issue was more measured and dispassionately analytical. Most significantly, he feared that an unbalanced, extreme
reaction to its challenge would be dangerous to Catholics. Parsons
pointed out that the appeal to join communism in the fight against
fascism took on different forms according to the varying ways that
countries had evolved historically. The challenge, in short, was different in Spain, France, and England. In America the debate was
being framed by the Popular Front as a simple alternative between
democracy and fascism, with the corollary assertion that opposing
communism makes one a fascist and antidemocratic. This was the
problem facing Catholics, who knew communism was a threat to
their religion and, contrary to Popular Front propaganda, not a force
for democracy. The Popular Front debate presented a false dilemma,
for opposing communism did not mean forsaking democracy or liberal ideas. The problem for Catholics, Parsons emphasized, was losing a sense of proportion between the relative evils of communism
and fascism, thereby blinding themselves to political reality.

The dangers posed by the political right and left were different
in character. Communism, Parsons insisted, was the greater threat
to civilization because it was not simply a socioeconomic-political
system but also a philosophy of life (diametrically opposed to Christianity) designed for export to other countries. Fascism was also an
institution contrary to Christianity and democratic government, but
it was primarily an extreme reaction to communism and had not

been packaged for resale in other countries. Consequently, Catholics should oppose fascism on political and economic grounds in the name of democracy. Communism, on the other hand, should be rejected for political, economic, and religious reasons. Therefore, concluded Parsons, Catholics must be united in convincing Americans that the alternatives are not fascism and democracy, but "democracy and all forms of totalitarianism, whether direct, as Communism, or Fascism, as the indirect result of Communism." Meanwhile, the Church should not abate its demands for social justice, especially in the industrial field, which, because of the political ambitions of communists, threatens to be abandoned by Catholics.[30] Parsons' analysis was similar to Father H. A. Reinhold's assessment of Marxism as the "legitimate offspring" of capitalism, and of fascism as the progeny of communism, and the two men shared remarkably similar views of what the Church must do to fight the evils of all three.[31]

For Father Parsons, Catholics must oppose communism and fascism by adhering to American liberal democratic traditions. This imperative was not always paramount in his successor's policies and opinions. Talbot's *America* had a proclivity for linking liberalism with communism, and this shaped its attitude toward the New Deal. Indeed, Talbot's distaste for Roosevelt became so great that he saw fit to embrace the ideas of Father Charles Coughlin.

Soon after Francis Talbot was appointed editor in 1936, *America* began finding positive things to say about Father Coughlin. In a private letter to Rev. Patrick Dowd, O.P., Talbot admitted that under his direction the paper had expressed approbation of the work that Coughlin had undertaken: we do not agree with all the facts as he alleges them, wrote Talbot, but "we heartily agree with his principles."[32] Coughlin's views by 1936 had become far more extreme than they were in 1935, when Father Parsons had criticized Coughlin. By 1938 Coughlin had become a peddler of hate, a raging anti-Semite, and an apologist for both Hitler and Mussolini.[33] His movement had now become a focal point for American fascists. Like Hilaire Belloc, who became a regular contributor to the radio priest's *Social Justice,* Coughlin had discovered a connection between Jews, plutocracy, and communism.[34] This certainly explains why Father Coughlin took such a keen interest in Hilaire Belloc. The disproportionate numbers of Jews in the financial oligarchy and the many Jews who were Bolsheviks suggested an international conspiracy. As evidence of this conspiracy, Coughlin published the *Protocols of the Elders of Zion,* a notorious forgery by Russian anti-Semites that outlined a Jewish plan to take over the world.[35] Jews, Coughlin claimed in a fashion that echoed Hilaire Belloc, were persecuted in Europe because of their affiliation with communism and their lack of patriotism. American Jews would suffer a similar fate, he warned, if their monopoly of the media continued to support the communist cause in Spain.

Several of *America's* more conservative readers were quick to appreciate the shift in political orientation. Father Joseph A. Luther, S.J., of the University of Detroit, wrote Talbot about his fears concerning intrigues by Archbishop Mundelein of Chicago and President Roosevelt together to persuade the Vatican to muzzle Coughlin by replacing his superior and protector, Bishop Michael Gallagher of Detroit.[36] Talbot remarked that he too was disturbed by this possible turn of events. Father Luther was delighted with the breath of fresh air coming from the "new" *America.* Now it was time, said he, to convince people that the paper was permanently freed from the "reactionary mossbacked barnacled-studded days of Wilfrid Parsons."[37]

By 1937 it was clearly evident that the magazine was allied with ultra-conservatism. Gerard J. Murphy, S.J., who wrote for the journal during the summer months of 1937 and fit in so well that he became *America's* literary editor for a time, made a strong plea for linking *America* with the cause of reaction. The "true conservatism" with which Catholicism must ally itself, he argued, was best articulated in Douglas Jerrold's *English Review* and Seward Collins' *American Review.* The former publication expressed a strong fondness for Mussolini's corporatism and his adventures in Abyssinia; Collins had the distinction of having openly declared his magazine "Fascist."[38]

A common theme that emerged in *America* was that communism and liberalism were fellow materialistic philosophies, essentially "blood brothers tarred with the same atheistic smudge."[39] Apparently ignoring the Anglo-Saxon liberal traditions upon which the

U.S. Constitution was constructed, *America* under Francis Talbot presented the issues of the 1930s in the framework of a Manichean struggle between Lucifer and Christ.[40]

Several prominent clergy strongly objected to *America's* move to the political right and its abandonment of labor causes.[41] For instance, Rev. Laurence K. Patterson, S.J., criticized Talbot for betraying the magazine's earlier commitment to liberal social reform. Talbot, in response, attacked Patterson for building up a hostile campaign to unseat him as editor. A well-known labor activist, Father Owen Rice of the Pittsburgh Catholic Radical Alliance (a group of clergy and laymen committed to applying the social encyclicals to the American trade union movement), also objected to the general tenor of *America's* articles on trade unions. Father Rice wished to be allowed to write an essay in *America* stating the case for the CIO.[42]

In his early years Father Rice had developed a reputation as a tough-talking radical "labor priest" who was willing to take on all comers in the cause of furthering the interests of Catholic workers. He even crossed swords with Monsignor Fulton J. Sheen and Cardinal William O'Connell, the archbishop of Boston. O'Connell retaliated by barring Rice from speaking in the archdiocese. Initially Father Rice provided balanced critiques of capitalism and communism as he struggled to find the "third way," an alternative to both as outlined in the papal social encyclicals and championed by the Distributist movement. The Catholic Radical Alliance, said Rice, was "going to the roots" of the capitalist society by reintroducing the guild idea: "We are dissatisfied with the present Social and Economic set up: we want it drastically changed."[43] The Pittsburgh chapter of the ACTU, which Father Rice and his fellow "labor priest," Father Carl Hensler, had founded, worked closely with the CIO and the Catholic Worker movement and consulted with H. A. Reinhold (who was also instrumental in convincing Rice to forsake his commitment to pacifism) during its efforts to organize laborers in the steel and textile industries.[44] Rice insisted that workers had a duty to join unions, which were their only hope against the pernicious designs of employers. Fathers Rice and Hensler were proud of the fact that their organization was at the forefront in fighting for labor. As to why they took the name "radical," Hensler said it was

only appropriate because "we advocate a program that is more radical than any other program of social reform."[45]

Another radical Catholic trade union group at odds with
America's political orientation was associated with H. K. Kendall's
Seattle-based magazine *Social Action*. Kendall's journal made bold
attacks on the Catholic hierarchy's flirtation with fascist causes, in
particular calling attention to the suppression of pertinent anti-Nazi
news that was supposed to come through the National Catholic
Welfare Conference News Service. Along with the *Pittsburgh Catholic*, an outspoken supporter of Catholic trade unionism, *Social Action*
published anti-fascist stories that the official Catholic news association refused to release. For this and other reasons the paper was
criticized by Catholic conservatives.

Kendall's paper would have made G. K. Chesterton proud, for
there were precious few publications in America that paralleled
more closely the policies and vision of *G.K.'s Weekly*. Following the
lead of Chesterton's journals and the Distributist movement, *Social
Action* mounted furious attacks on "monopolistic capitalism,"
though like its British counterpart, the journal announced that it
was only prepared to undermine the creed within the constitutional
framework of the nation's legal system. As Kendall put it in a personal letter to his friend and mentor, Father Reinhold:

> We are in earnest about eliminating the present capitalist system—
> just as much so as are the Communists. Only instead of estab-
> lishing a Marxist collectivist socio-economic structure in the place
> of modern finance capitalism, we would set up a Co-operative,
> Distributist form of economic democracy that would guarantee
> the dignity of the human person, the sanctity of the family, per-
> sonal responsibility through the restoration of property to the
> people, etc.—all so that men might the more easily gain eter-
> nal salvation.[46]

Kendall's writings suggest that he was not only steeped in British
Distributist ideas but also well acquainted with the French Personalist philosophy of Eduard Mournier, which had considerable
influence on Peter Maurin, the liturgists at St. John's University, and

the writings of Paul Hanley Furfey. *Social Action's* objective, claimed Kendall, was to work through the trade union movement, serving as a "a spark plug" for FDR's New Deal policies, making certain that they would be implemented with as many "Christian Distributist elements as possible." It might be more effective if we employed the sophisticated "*New Yorker*" style, claimed Kendall, but *Social Action* lacked such talented writers and, in any case, could not afford the subtlety. For Catholics primarily and Christians generally, *Social Action* "in a miniature way" was to serve the same function as did the *Daily Worker* and the *People's World* for the misguided cause of communism.[47]

While *America* and other conservative Catholic publications and clergy were mounting an energetic campaign against the CIO for its alleged communist tendencies, Fathers Rice and Hensler and progressives in the ACTU along with *Social Action* were emphasizing what they considered to be a far more important issue, namely, the social injustice of employers. With respect to charges that the CIO was communist, Rice retorted that the notion was "ill-advised and asinine, especially when they come from Catholics." These were claims, said Rice, that issued from smug, bourgeois Catholics who were afraid of the workers gaining control of the means of production.[48]

However, by the early 1940s even Father Rice was swept up in the anticommunist hysteria of the Catholic establishment. He became increasingly conservative and for the most part subordinated his earlier commitment to Catholic social teachings to a war against Marxism. It was Rice who spearheaded the effort to purge communists from the CIO.[49] Father Talbot ultimately found an ally in Father Charles Owen Rice.

The career of Father Charles Owen Rice is illustrative of a shift in American Catholicism from radical social reform to defense of the status quo. When Rice broadened his forum to become a radio priest in 1939 he brought into his program the ideas of Peter Maurin, Dorothy Day, John Paul Furfey, John A. Ryan, and the liturgical views of H. A. Reinhold. These ideas faded when Rice joined the all-consuming struggle against communism.[50] Dorothy Day spoke out against the frenzied CIO purges inspired by Rice (his broadsides were sweeping and disquieting, since Rice believed communists should be denied civil rights) but to no avail.[51]

In the view of Douglas P. Seaton, a historian of the Catholic trade union movement, the effect of the anticommunist crusade of Rice and others was not merely to remove communists from the CIO but to destroy the spirit of independent militancy the union greatly needed to make meaningful gains from the powerful capitalist establishment. Henceforth the fight for social justice would take a back seat to the struggle against communism.[52] In the long run, Catholic influence, argues Seaton, was a major reason why American industrial unionism became a force for conservatism.[53]

One influential journal that failed to follow in the conservative trajectory of the Catholic mainstream was *Commonweal*. Talbot's political repositioning of *America* led to heated and bitter disagreements with the editors of *Commonweal*. However, Talbot did everything he could to keep the feuds out of public view.[54] What particularly provoked Talbot was *Commonweal's* falling under the control of Philip Skillin and his associates, who continued to support George Shuster's position that Catholics should maintain a position of neutrality on the Spanish Civil War. Talbot was convinced that these dangerous liberal tendencies served to remove *Commonweal* from the Catholic fold: "Their training and present attitudes are not 100 percent Catholic in our sense of the term."[55] Despite Talbot's efforts at concealment, the squabbles between *America* and the *Commonweal* circle became more pronounced, spilling into the public domain because of the two journals' opposing interpretations of the Spanish Civil War. Writing privately to *Commonweal's* founder and former editor Michael Williams, who lost out to Shuster's group in the struggles over the journal's Spanish policy, Talbot suggested that *Commonweal* as well as the *Catholic Worker* (which also refused to endorse the Spanish Civil War as a crusade for Christ) should be investigated by the Catholic Press Association. These are times, said he, that members of that assembly must either express themselves in a Catholic way (as defined by Father Talbot) or cease to call themselves Catholic.[56]

Father Talbot's anticommunist campaign also targeted H. A. Reinhold indirectly. Reinhold's sympathies and close association

with progressive and radical elements in the American labor movement and his connections with liberal Catholics, including his friends
at *Commonweal*, made him a person of questionable character in the
eyes of Catholics like Father Francis Talbot.[57] By the late 1930s
Reinhold's liturgical ideas, as well as his refusal to embrace Franco,
opened him to public attack by Patrick Scanlan's *Brooklyn Tablet*.
Scanlan was always on the hunt for communist agents. Unlike most
Catholic social activists, Scanlan refused to accept the idea that
communism as a political force was encouraged by social and economic oppression. For him, the spread of Marxism was the result of
alien intrusion: it was directly brought to America through Russian agents. If the government could suppress communist propaganda and deport aliens, the "red peril" would largely disappear.[58]

The attacks on Father Reinhold continued unabated, eventually
convincing him of the wisdom of disassociating from groups labeled
by conservative Catholics as "untrustworthy" or with "socialist tendencies." In the end, fearing such right-wing assaults would compromise his application for American citizenship, Reinhold painfully
severed his affiliations with Catholic trade union activists and other
such reformers who relied on his advice and inspiration.[59] The
attacks on Reinhold had a chilling effect on his frankness about
speaking out against social and political evils. In the future, if an
organization to which he belonged or person with whom he had a
professional relationship was placed under the suspicion of having
connections with communist groups, Reinhold severed his affiliation. These tactics, of course, served to silence what the right-wing
Catholics called the "liberal party" functioning illicitly within the
Church, liberal in this case being a code word for "Red." Such was
the case with Reinhold's association with the Committee of Catholics for Human Rights (CCHR), an organization formed in 1939
to fight anti-Semitism. Its board of directors included Senator
James E. Murray, Bishop Joseph M. Gilmore of Helena, Montana,
Bishop Francis H. Haas of Grand Rapids, Michigan, Bishop
Bernard J. Sheil of Chicago, and John Brophy, director of the CIO
Industrial Councils, among other Catholic luminaries.

The CCHR published a monthly called the *Voice*, which stood
as a forum for rational discussion and toleration among the pro-

fascist and oblique anti-Semitic ramblings found in a good many Catholic papers at the time, in particular Scanlan's *Brooklyn Tablet*, Coughlin's *Social Justice*, and Bishop Noll's *Our Sunday Visitor*, which claimed to have the largest circulation of any Catholic diocesan paper in America. The *Voice's* executive board included Monsignor John A. Ryan and Reverend Paul Hanley Furfey. The paper had a large circulation that ranged from 60,000 to 120,000, reaching some 110 cities throughout America. The founder and chairman of the Committee of Catholics for Human Rights was Professor Emmanuel Chapman of Hunter College. Chapman was attacked by the *New Leader* in October 1946 for being a communist. The assault continued in Gerald L. K. Smith's *The Cross and the Flag* and in the *Brooklyn Tablet*, where Joseph Corriden accused the CCHR of being a communist front organization and its honorary chairman, Senator James E. Murray, of being soft on Reds.

Within a month of these attacks, Father Reinhold wrote Chapman to say that he was obliged, out of self-protection, to abrogate his ties with the CCHR. Long before the appearance of Senator Joseph McCarthy and the witch hunts of the 1950s, Father Reinhold had detected the emergence of a sinister tendency in American politics, a phenomenon uncomfortably close to the experience he had had in another land: "Something is shaping up in this country," wrote Reinhold, "either planned or just by accident which looks to me rather familiar in spite of its definitely American outward symptoms."[60]

CHAPTER 12

The Religious Crusade in Spain

In fact, to the writer it seems that the whole world is suffering
from some kind of psychosis of excess nationalism and deficiency
of calm thought, and to him this explains at least in part the
cocksureness with which statements are made pro and con
on so many questions by both Catholic and non-Catholics.
St. Augustine said long ago: "I hold that one never errs more
surely than when he errs as the result of an excessive love of
truth or an excessive fear of falling into error."

—Virgil Michel[1]

The outbreak of the Spanish Civil War in July 1936 created a deep moral crisis for European and American Catholics, both in terms of its effect on political consensus within intellectual ranks and in terms of the negative public image it created for the Church.[2] The strident American Catholic campaign for Franco and its related attacks on liberalism, for example, earned the Church the dubious distinction of winning second place (ahead of the Ku Klux Klan and Nazi agencies) in the 1937 American Civil Liberties Union's poll of institutions that most threatened individual freedoms. Beginning in the same year, several notable American and British Protestant theologians and publications became openly critical of the Catholic Church for what appeared to be its international alliance with the forces of Fascism. The journalist Herbert Matthews held that the Spanish Civil War had divided America along religious and political lines for the first and only time in U.S. history.[3] Pro-Franco Catholic opinion may have played a decisive role in the Roosevelt administration's decision to maintain an arms embargo on Spain, thus helping to assure a Nationalist victory.[4]

After a large anti-monarchist vote in the Spanish municipal election in April 1931, King Alfonso XIII relinquished the throne and transferred power to a provisional government which introduced a republic. The first government of the Second Spanish Republic was made up of a coalition of diverse republican parties and socialists. The regime seems to have had the support of the majority of politically conscious Spaniards.[5] In city plazas and on parade grounds, cries of *vivas* for the Republic and strains of the "Marseillaise" were heard throughout the land. This popular enthusiasm for democracy was encouraging, given Europe's current drift toward authoritarianism. Those in support of the change in government closely identified it with the legacy of 1789, though, in contrast, Spanish republicans could claim that their king had left peacefully and that the revolutionaries had agreed beforehand to an equitable distribution of power. In actuality, the transition was fraught with tensions and bitter emotions stemming from intense regional aspirations, from industrial and agrarian struggles, and, very significantly, from anger against the Catholic Church, which in the popular mind was associated with the privileges and oppression of the old order. Spain had been dominated by a landed aristocracy and a small cadre of industrialists who assiduously resisted economic and political reform. The fact that the Republic was supported by considerable numbers of peasants and factory workers imbued the ensuing conflict with the tones of class war.

The ownership of land in Spain was in the hands of a small group of aristocrats and wealthy bourgeoisie (who were given the opportunity to purchase confiscated Church properties under nineteenth-century Liberal governments) The landless peasants were brutally exploited.[6] Adding to this volatile brew was the rapid industrialization of a few key areas of Spain (Catalonia and the Basque Provinces).[7] The inability of the growing numbers of working poor to protect their interests against the extortionate claims of capitalist financiers and industrialists made them receptive to a wide range of radical, revolutionary social ideas. Much of the peasant/proletarian unrest that grew out of this situation took on distinctly anti-clerical tones, owing to the Church's close association with the economic elites and its own reluctance to encourage economic and social reforms.

The Spanish Church offers striking parallels with the French Church at the time of the French Revolution. However, as an institution and in terms of its economic role in society, the Spanish Church was far different from its eighteenth-century Gallican counterpart. Following the confiscation of Church property known as the *desamortización*, begun under the Liberal government of Prime Minister Alfredo Mendizábal in 1835, the Church ceased to be the country's largest landowner. In compensation, and in order to be able to liquidate its holdings in the face of possible future hostile action, the Church including various religious orders, in particular the Jesuits, began investing in other forms of wealth.[8] By the 1930s they had accumulated enormous amounts of mobile property in the form of capital investments. Many believed that the Spanish Church had become the country's single richest shareholder.[9]

The *desamortización* had profound consequences. Although the move was engineered by Liberals hoping to break up the power and entrenched privileges of the Church, only those of considerable wealth could afford to purchase the confiscated property. Thus the transactions had the effect of increasing the wealth and power of Spain's elites and further retarding the emergence of a rural middle class. The *desamortización* also tended to make those wealthy Liberals who purchased religious property increasingly dependent on maintaining the new order, hence becoming in the long run wedded to the status quo. It is important to point out, moreover, that the *desamortización* affected not only Church property but also public-owned common land. The mass dispossession of poor peasants from municipal land led to the emergence of a surplus population, soon to be transformed into a new proletariat. Along with the rural masses, the industrial laborers represented a formidable revolutionary bloc against the Spanish industrial and agricultural oligarchy.

The loss of the Church's landed revenues meant that it was obliged to become heavily dependent on the ruling class for economic support. In return, the clergy assumed a more partisan, elitist position on social and economic issues, alienating themselves further from the masses. Consequently, as the hierarchy jockeyed to garner other forms of capital wealth and preserve its privileges, the Church became increasingly committed to perpetuating the arrangements of oligarchy.[10] Even the conservative Catholic writer José María Gironella, in his epic novel *The Cypresses Believe in God*, dramatized this fact. The hero, a fictional projection of Gironella by the name of Ignacio Olvear, in an exchange with the priest Mosén Alberto, who could not understand why people would use violence against the Church, tells Alberto that the clergy's lives have been too completely disconnected from the lowly, too unaware of the working class and the needy: "it was friendship that was needed."[11]

Politically, the Spanish Church served as the ideological bulwark of monarchy and was intimately connected to it. Prior to 1931, canonical law and civil law existed side by side. Religious indifference was a civil offense, bishops were nominated by the monarch (generally only those with unquestioned loyalty to the ruling elites were appointed), and all ecclesiastics were paid by the state.[12]

What little affection the common people may have felt for an institution so closely allied to an oppressive ruling establishment quickly dissipated when the leaders of the Spanish Church attacked the idea of the Republic and urged the masses to vote against it.[13] This call for resistance, however, was the product of class bias. The episcopate, being closely allied with the oligarchy, was largely opposed to the Republic. However, as noted by William F. Montovan of the National Catholic Welfare Conference (NCWC), a close observer of the Spanish situation, the majority of the clergy below the rank of bishop supported the new experiment in democracy.[14]

As director of the legal department of the NCWC, Montovan was sent to Spain in 1931 to observe the formation of the new government. Montovan concluded at the time that the Republicans had wide popular support and were committed to constitutional reform.[15] His confidential report to the Vatican on the Spanish situation was unusual for its dispassionate objectivity. Montovan noted the seriousness of the Church's failure to support long overdue social and political reforms, and he was especially critical of the decision of Catholics to withdraw from the constituent Cortes after the approval of anticlerical articles. The refusal of Catholic politicians to push for change within this legally-established political institution and thereby to protect Church interests, wrote Montovan, was an "act of cowardice . . . by men who were amateurs in statesmanship; it was an unpatriotic betrayal of a responsibility to the nation solemnly accepted with election."[16] Montovan's report to the Vatican pointed out that Catholic opinion was divided regarding social, economic, and political reforms. Therefore it was incumbent upon Catholic leaders, wrote Montovan, to formulate a program that could forge consensus. A major problem in this regard was the failure of the Spanish bishops to encourage Catholic action along lines set forth in the papal social encyclicals. In what must be seen as a damning indictment of the Spanish hierarchy, Montovan averred that reform had begun "at the wrong end." The Cardinal Primate had written a constitution for Catholic action. The archbishops gave it their imprimatur and sent copies to the suffragan bishops. There the effort died.[17] Montovan concluded that the organization for Catholic social action must begin where it would receive popular support: at the individual parish level.[18] Perhaps Montovan's most significant recommendation to the Vatican was that Spanish Catholics must take the responsibility of working for reforms through the elected bodies of the Republic. Of critical importance, he suggested, was the presence of an intelligent Catholic opposition (staking out a moderate ground that could appeal to voters) in the public sectors of Spanish life.[19]

William Montovan's report should not have been a great surprise, for the institutional malaise of Spanish Catholicism was frequently commented upon by visitors to that country. Sir Peter Chalmers Mitchell, who lived in Málaga before and during the Civil War, wrote that "it was odd, to English eyes, to find that the parish priesthood was simply a privileged bourgeois profession, doing nothing for parishioners except exacting fees for ceremonies or rites deemed necessary." In no country, noted Mitchell, had he ever seen such a vast contrast between the poverty of the poor and the luxury of the rich, the latter of whom were carefully tended by the Church.[20]

Virgil Michel traveled through Spain in 1924–25 and made it a point to talk extensively with people from all walks of life. He read the local newspapers and studied Spanish culture with consummate care. His diary during this period highlights the yawning gap between ordinary people and the Church hierarchy. The higher Spanish clergy, he observed, lived in lavish luxury in close alliance with the ruling classes and large landowners. They were wholly ignorant of both the condition of the laboring masses and the papal social teachings. His entry for 20 June 1925 reads:

> Priests in Spain do not go after stray sheep. Religious education of people is wanting. Thus fewer real vocations, and others enter the priesthood because a living is assured from the government. Priests do not know who belongs or should belong to the parish. Bishops confirm when they please; go about with retinue, sometimes do not get to certain places for 10–15 years.[21]

On the other hand, Father Michel was highly impressed by the religiosity and social activism he observed among the Basque clergy. The priests in this part of Spain were well schooled in the labor encyclicals and their religious houses overflowed with vocations.[22] Yet social and economic conditions in the rest of Spain were so abysmal that Michel claimed it almost shocked him into embracing the visceral message of radical socialism.[23] Indeed, so powerful were these experiences that Virgil Michel's biographer believes they may have been a seminal factor in the development of his positions on Catholic social action and liturgical renewal.[24] The religious and economic situation in Spain was a topic upon which Virgil Michel spoke frequently after his return to the United States. For him, the outbreak of civil war in 1936 was not unexpected.[25]

Although Spain was known as "the most Catholic of all the nations," vast numbers of the population failed to practice their religion.[26] Much of this was a direct consequence of the Church's failure to provide confessional and educational leadership. Even in the most Catholic provinces of Navarre and Catalonia many villages lacked schools. In Andalusia, for example, 45 percent of the people were illiterate. One well-placed and influential student of Catholic culture observed that there were few Spaniards who knew anything at all about Catholicism.[27] The leadership ranks of the Spanish Church were top-heavy and constituted a considerable drain on the limited economic resources of the state, whereas parish clergy were abysmally remunerated. The Catholic journalist Lawrence Farnsworth wrote that he frequently encountered sixteen to twenty high-ranking ecclesiastics at modest funerals, each collecting a sizeable fee: "And how many times have I walked into some cathedral to find a solemn or a pontifical mass being celebrated in all liturgical pomp with the assistance of the entire cathedral chapter and in the presence of only 3 or 4 of the faithful."[28]

A devout Spanish Catholic academic, Enrique Moreno, concluded that his countrymen had become indifferent to Catholic culture. As a frequenter of ancient cathedrals, Moreno noted that High Mass was often celebrated before no more than two or three parishioners.[29] He also commented on the failure of the educational mission of the Jesuits, who controlled the curricula of 50 percent of Spanish universities.[30] According to José María de Semprún Guerra—a lecturer in the philosophy of law at the University of Madrid, a leading member of the Conservative Party, and founder and long-time contributor to the Spanish Catholic review *Cruz y Raya*—at least 80 percent of Spanish middle-class youth had been educated in Catholic colleges yet knew nothing of the theological traditions of their religion.[31] Semprún Guerra had been educated at a religious college and left after six years of uninterrupted attendance without acquiring more than a vague idea of Pascal's *Pensées*, without having read more than a few extracts of Saint Teresa, scarcely knowing the significance of the writings of the Church fathers, and without having read the Gospels in their entirety.[32]

Clearly, the clergy's association with the landholding classes served as a formidable obstacle to economic reform. It has been estimated that at the beginning of the nineteenth century the Church owned roughly one-third of Spanish national territory; the hierarchy was naturally embittered by the efforts at land redistribution enforced by liberal politicians. Churchmen came to identify opposition to these liberal efforts with defense of the Catholic social order represented in their *latifundios*. As a consequence of this linkage of religion with property, the Spanish public suspected that there were always economic motives at the base of Church attitudes. The public associated the clergy with the defense of an unjust social order and hence included them as the enemies of their liberties. For its part, the Spanish Church associated liberal reforms and all things modern with foreign influences. This linkage stemmed in large part from what the Spanish Church viewed as the Rousseauistic evils of the French Revolution: evil foreign influences designed to destroy national culture.[33] The Spanish Church's attitude toward liberalism was aptly summed up by Reverend Genadius Diez, O.S.B. The "French influence," Rev. Diez claimed, invaded not only the throne and aristocracy but also the class of men who posed as "intellectuals." Only the Church and lower classes, he argued, remained mentally and spiritually loyal to the "Spain of the Reconquest," i.e., to that of Ferdinand and Isabella. The word "liberal," wrote Diez, meant in Spain far more than "progressive views"; it was rather a revolutionary attempt to undermine moral ethics and theology and to bring about the absolute domination of the Church by the state. Today, insisted Rev. Diez, liberalism means the same as anarchism, communism, and socialism.[34]

The reactionary bent of the Spanish Church had engendered a long tradition of anticlericalism that was frequently accompanied by mass violence. Contrary to the assumptions of many conservative American and British Catholics, unbridled anger against the Church and its association with the organs of oppression certainly was not something sparked by the anti-God revolution in Moscow and nor was it unique to the twentieth century. As the Spanish writer Ramos Oliveira observed:

> The people began withdrawing their support from an institution which could reform nothing because it stood in need itself of a sweeping reform. In 1834, there occurred the first murder of friars in Madrid, and the following year saw a repetition of the disorders. Already convents were burning in Barcelona, Saragossa, Reus and Murcia.[35]

II

The Second Spanish Republic was politically unstable from the moment of its inception. Both the aristocracy and wealthy bourgeoisie as well as the major groups representing lower-class interests were dissatisfied with it. The Republic's main source of support came from moderate republicans with democratic and liberal leanings. From the outset the new government made a serious mistake in failing to address land reform as the first order of business, focusing instead on legislation to secularize the state. This approach served to exacerbate ill feelings among nearly all parties. In June 1933 President Niceto Alcalá Zamora (a practicing Catholic), following the wishes of the Cortes, signed the Law of Religious Denominations and Congregations, a sweeping effort to prohibit Catholic educational, industrial, and commercial activities and to nationalize Church property. Many Spanish Catholics were outraged, and even Pope Pius XI felt it his duty to denounce the legislation, calling upon Spaniards to unite and remove the dangers that threatened their spiritual and civil welfare.

Those on the Left were also dissatisfied with the performance of the new government. A timid agrarian reform law angered peasants, and failure to address working-class needs fanned urban unrest. Insurrections in the countryside and urban violence forced the government to call on the military to restore order. By the summer of 1933 it had become clear that the moderate republican cabinet, having alienated Catholics and the laboring masses, could no longer govern. New elections were called for November 1933.

The forces of the Right prevailed in the 1933 national elections. In terms of satisfying the nation's social and political needs, however, the triumph of conservatism brought no more success than had the pro-republican elements in 1931. The pro-Church politician José María Gil Robles, who hoped to put together a coalition of rightist groups in the new government—based on an umbrella party called CEDA (Confederación Española des Derechas Autónomas)—was unable to effect any constructive change, in part because his partners were committed to maintaining the status quo. The limited reforms of the previous government were quickly reversed.

CEDA, the most influential grouping on the Right, was a party of moderate Catholic opinion, and many of its members were prepared to support the Republic. Essentially, CEDA pursued a policy called "accidentalism": to CEDA, the forms of government were immaterial provided they protected Catholic interests. The organization called for a restoration of "the religious rights" of the Church and the inauguration of a social program along the lines set forth by *Rerum Novarum* and *Quadragesimo Anno*. Following through on the papal labor encyclicals, however, would have required a redistribution of landed wealth and industrial reform favoring workers. Since CEDA's bankers were chiefly the landed oligarchy, the redistribution of land and other pertinent social reforms that the party called for never went beyond rhetorical flourish and served mainly as a verbal tactic to win proletarian and peasant support. Although CEDA's republicanism was ambiguous and at best faint-hearted, the party was very clear about its Catholic agenda: the restoration of the Church to its former position of dominance.

Another problem was Gil Robles himself. He was a political opportunist who was never completely trusted by republicans on his left, nor, because he thought in terms of a movement willing to accommodate disparate groups of moderate liberal and conservative opinion, could he manage to win the complete confidence of the Right. Although Robles claimed he was supportive of the Republic and for the most part was a man of reasonable and tempered views, his rhetoric, carefully crafted to appease his right-wing constituents, frightened republicans of every stripe. "For us," declared Robles, "democracy is a means, not an end. . . . When the time arrives, [the Cortes] will submit to us or we will do away with it."[36] On many occasions Robles used language that suggested he favored fascism.

In October 1934 Asturias and Catalonia erupted in a fiery leftist-led rebellion against what was called the "fascist" government of CEDA. The rebels were in no sense united except in anger.[37] Although the so-called "Red" October Revolution was defeated, the violence that marked the affair had the effect of making all parties on the Left, especially the socialists who heretofore had been moderate and even legalistic in their tactics, more uncompromising and sanguine about the efficacy of armed revolt. The most serious upheaval, in the words of Franz Borkenau, "more heroic than any working-class rising since the days of the Paris commune,"[38] occurred in Asturias. Socialists with the help of anarchists took the lead. They set up a Soviet-style regime and began a massive

campaign of terror against their enemies. The government was able
to subdue this working-class uprising only by calling in the elite Foreign Legionaries and Moorish troops. The repression appears to
have been even more gruesomely cruel than the uprising itself. In
the words of a conservative republican and avid foe of the Left: "The
accused were tortured in jails; prisoners were executed without trial
in the courtyards of the barracks, and eyes were closed to the persecutions and atrocities committed by the police during these sixteen months."[39]

The heroic resistance of the rebels and the vicious counteraction
by the rightist government created martyrs, new leaders (Dolores
Ibarruri, the famous "La Passionaria," began her meteoric rise to
fame during the uprising in Asturias), and a legacy of revolution that
would serve as a catalyst for future action. Indeed, most historians
of the Spanish Civil War trace the dissolution of the Second Republic, the beginning of its grisly unraveling, to the October Revolution
of 1934. In effect, the Left had revolted against a legally elected government.[40] The Right would replicate this behavior in 1936.

The armed combat served to draw together the multiplicity of
factions on the Left in defense of the 1934 revolution: the republicans now saw the necessity of allying in electoral battle with socialists. This led to the emergence of the "Popular Front," a coalition of
republicans, socialists, and, with Moscow's approval, the Spanish
communists. Communist participation was made possible by the
Comintern's *volte-face* in mid-1935, when it decided to support alliances with liberal-bourgeois parties advancing revolution in the
developing world.[41] Even the anarchists realized that their best
hopes lay with the electoral success of the Left; they too decided to
support the Popular Front.[42] The decision of a sizeable bloc of anarchists to reverse their previous policy of electoral abstention was vital
for the Popular Front: it won the election of February 1936. Yet as in
1931, the new government of the Left, in the hands of liberal and
moderate republicans led by Premier Manuel Azaña (the socialists
and anarchists gave the government their votes but refused to participate in it), failed to find common agreement on land reform. The
liberal republican proposals for change were stymied by the more
radical ideas of socialist and anarchist elements. In frustration, the

peasant masses soon took things into their own hands and, in rebellion against the old regime, began seizing land. Workers throughout Spain engaged in a series of crippling strikes and attacks on property. Azaña condemned the acts of violence in the Cortes, but his government was powerless to temper the revolutionary rage of the workers and peasants.[43]

Meanwhile, a rejuvenated Right prepared to challenge the new order. The government's inability to throttle anarchy—anarchosyndicalists released from prison, for example, had immediately resorted to violence against their enemies—convinced many that brute force was the only solution to Spain's problems. The most influential leader on the Right, Gil Robles of CEDA, found it impossible to staunch the radicalization of conservative opinion. Indeed, once Gil Robles reiterated his opposition to violence and commitment to work through the established political structures of the Republic, the CEDA began to disintegrate. There was a massive defection of Robles' followers to the Renovación Española (a party of monarchist and Catholic integralists) and, even more ominously, to the Falange, the Spanish fascist party led by José Antonio Primo de Rivera that drew heavily on the programs of Mussolini and Hitler. In the minds of those who trembled from the volcanic eruption of assassinations, illegal seizures of land, and violence against property and persons, only one path offered security: the dictatorship of fascism. In the words of Augustín Calvet, director of *La Vanguardia:* "almost without realizing it, the people 'feel' themselves fascist. Of the inconvenience of a dictatorship they know nothing. . . . Of these they will learn later. . . . But meanwhile they see in that form of strong government nothing more than an infallible means of shaking off the insufferable vexations of the existing lawlessness."[44]

The spreading anarchic violence against established order convinced influential, high-ranking officers in the army that they must move quickly or be overcome by a massive popular uprising. On the 17th of July 1936 the Spanish military declared war against the government. The coup d'état (*pronunciamiento*) had the immediate effect of unifying the Left in support of the Republic. The masses—poor peasants, the urban working classes, and the "little" people—rose in ferocious anger against the Right. Such popular insurrection could not be controlled by the government. In both Madrid and Barcelona armed workers overcame the military and, through the establishment of their own defense committees, became the real source of power. The generals' revolt against the Republic, which they called the *Movimiento Nacional* or *Alzamiento,* achieved what had eluded the socialists and anarchists since 1931: it brought to power in half of Spain and in almost all its larger cities a revolutionary proletariat.[45]

In many regions sympathetic to the Republic a sweeping social revolution followed that was even more far-reaching than what the Bolsheviks had accomplished in 1917. It was not a result desired by the Popular Front, and indeed was actively resisted by many Popular Front members in positions of influence. The commitment of radicals on the Left to bring a Marxist revolution to Spain by any means necessary now openly confronted the ultra-Right's equally zealous commitment to fascist-style dictatorship.[46] Little space was left for moderates in the Popular Front government who wished to save the constitution of the Republic. In a last-ditch effort to encourage army officers to negotiate, and thereby defuse the socialist-communist-anarchist endeavors to organize their own militias and arm the citizenry, Azaña, recently made President of the Republic, asked Diego Martínez Barrio, leader of the most moderate elements in the Popular Front, to form a new, more conservative government. The Republic's efforts to negotiate with the rebels failed: General Emilio Mola, the man who initiated the *pronunciamiento,* claimed that his men would overthrow his own leadership if he entertained compromise. The hour was too late. "Neither of us," said Mola to Prime Minister Martínez Barrio, "can now control the masses."[47]

The government of the Republic that rose to defend Spain against the generals was indeed powerless to throttle the social revolution. It should come as no surprise, given the popular anger at the Church's alliance with the legions of reaction and the absence of government defense forces, that terrible violence was unleashed against organized religion. At no time in European history or even, perhaps, in that of the world, noted the historian Hugh Thomas, had such hatred been shown toward religion and all its works.[48]

III

A seminal figure providing inspiration and ideological focus for British and American Catholic intellectuals of the Right who gave their services to the Insurgents (or Nationalists, as they were called by supporters) in the Spanish Civil War was Hilaire Belloc.[49] However, the man who had such considerable influence on subsequent Catholic opinion on Spain appeared to be confused initially by the issues. From the outset Belloc was at least superficially appreciative of the deep-seated class struggle at the core of the conflict. Writing to his son in the summer of 1936, Belloc identified as the basic problem in Spain the fact that peasants did not possess their own land (a consequence of the elites' resistance to reform) and that a revolutionary industrial proletariat were denied their just rewards by greedy capitalists.[50] In various articles in British political journals Belloc had argued that the revolt against industrial capitalism was the spiritual inspiration behind the Republic, which represented an economic and social system wholly unsuited, in his opinion, to the traditions of Spain. Moreover, as he had recognized in the case of the French Revolution, the Church was attacked because it had lost its vitality and was associated with the the interests of the rich.[51]

Yet, as Belloc put it, this was only "half of the truth." He was convinced that the spiritual force behind the Republic was not indigenous, for he did not believe that the revolt had proceeded from the victims of industrialism themselves. It was rather managed as a "crusade" from without, its chief point of attack being the Catholic Church.[52] For Belloc, the catalyst was the Communist Party, an organization which everywhere claimed to represent the will of the national proletariat but which, in fact, was completely at the orders of Moscow. In the final analysis, Soviet involvement in the Spanish Civil War and what he deemed the Soviet intentions for world revolution brought Belloc down firmly on the side of the Nationalists. The Republic's inspiration was an anti-capitalism controlled by Moscow; the general who quickly emerged to lead the Nationalists, Francisco Franco, possessed a spiritual energy driven by a special Spanish patriotism and by an allegiance to Catholic tradition which, Belloc believed, was triggered by foreign intervention.

Belloc was convinced that the Spanish Civil War was the king-pin of a "new revolution" engineered by Moscow and its secret allies that was engulfing Europe and threatening the core of Christian culture. Its first objective was the uprooting of Catholicism, a pre-liminary to the substitution of communism for private proprietor-ship and the elimination of the family. The Bolsheviks had conducted a rampage of terror against the Russian clergy designed to eliminate Christianity altogether, since it constituted an island of separateness not allowed in a totalitarian regime, and now the process was under-way in Spain.[53] Belloc noted similar attempts in Italy, Germany, Hungary, and Poland, though these were checked by the "counter-offensive," by which he meant fascism.[54]

In Belloc's assessment the Bolsheviks were assisted in their efforts to destroy Spain by two other forces: international Jewry and Freemasonry. Belloc, of course, had long believed in a direct con-spiratorial linkage between Jews, Masons, and Spanish sociopoliti-cal problems,[55] and he had warned as early as 1910 of impending civil war.[56] The conspiracy was broadened, in his mind, when Jews engi-neered the Bolshevik Revolution of 1917. Belloc asserted that the Jews were especially well suited for destabilizing nationalist gov-ernments (for instance, the Spanish revolution was being directed, he argued, by Moses Rosenberg, nominally the Soviet ambassador, and France was under the leadership of another Jew, Léon Blum), since they had a natural capacity for such matters: Jews were detached both from the patriotic sentiment of the various European ethnic groups and from the traditions of Christendom, and thus were indifferent to the destruction of each. Spain was vital in this re-gard, for it represented the last in a series of Bolshevik efforts to destroy Christianity as a necessary step toward absorbing the whole of Europe.[57]

The Freemasons contributed to this tripartite revolutionary con-spiracy, claimed Belloc, by directing their highly-placed agents in the Republican government to secretly incite mob action against Church property. As Belloc wrote during the 1909 Barcelona upris-ing, "Not a single case of violence was directed against the house of a capitalist or upon any great capitalist work or bank."[58] Contrary to what gullible English newspapers had reported, there was nothing spontaneous about such acts of disdain for religion. It was, Belloc asserted, simply a ruse by the authorities to produce popular hatred against religion. A major factor that conditioned Belloc's analysis of the Spanish situation was the Comintern's advocacy, noted earlier, of a united front to oppose the forces of fascism. Recognizing the threat posed by Hitler, the Seventh Congress of the Comintern (Communist International), which gathered in August 1935, determined that it was necessary to collaborate with bourgeois parties. The goal was to infiltrate such organizations in order to transform them into tools for communist revolution. The idea was developed by Stalin and publicly introduced by the Bulgarian General-Secretary of the Comintern, Georgi Dimitrov:

> Cannot we endeavor to unite the Communist, Social Democratic, Catholic and other workers? Comrades, you will remember the ancient tale of the capture of Troy. The attacking army was unable to achieve victory until, with the aid of the Trojan Horse, it penetrated to the very heart of the enemy camp. We, revolutionary workers, should not be shy of using the same tactics.[59]

The Trojan Horse idea convinced Belloc that Moscow's aid to the Republic, the rapid growth in Spanish Communist Party membership,[60] and its collaboration with Popular Front parties were part and parcel of the blueprint for world revolution.[61] The Comintern's new program was enormously successful in Spain. Their carefully calculated "moderate policies" (designed to look respectable to the middle classes), an insistence on stopping anarchist revolution in the countryside, and the fact that their allies, the Soviets, had the guns needed by the Republic, were all sufficient reasons to attract a myriad of elements into the communist fold, most of whom had never read a word of Marx. In fact, many Spaniards joined the Communist Party as a means of stopping the Republic's social revolution.[62] "Representative government," a polity Moscow had decided to cultivate and which Belloc, from his own experiences in England, had long denounced for its corruptive tendencies, seemed the ideal spawning ground for the Comintern's Trojan Horse program.

Just as the French Revolution had its heroes in Danton, Robespierre, and Napoleon, so the Spanish Republic, for Belloc, had a hero who symbolized in his person the Christian crusade in Spain.

This hero was General Francisco Franco, who had assumed control of the rebellion against Spain's democratically elected Republic. Here was a leader, in Belloc's mind, who had the qualities of both
a Charlemagne and a Napoleon. Central to Belloc's lionization of
Franco was his belief that the general had the popular and moral
support of the Spanish people. Belloc also insisted that the masses
were behind the Church.[63] In short, Belloc regarded Franco, like
Napoleon, as the repository of the general will, a force incapable of
manifesting itself through the diseased parliamentary government
of the Republic. Franco would save Western civilization, just as his
predecessors rescued Christendom from the yoke of Islam.

After having made a personal visit to the Nationalist front line
in 1939 where he had a private interview with his hero, Belloc was
moved to write the following panegyric:

> When I entered Franco's presence I entered the presence of one
> who had fought that same battle wherein Roland of legend died
> fighting, and Godfrey in sober history had won, when his bat-
> tered remnant, a mere surviving tenth of the first crusaders,
> entered Jerusalem. They came in on foot, refusing to ride where
> God and man had offered up the Sacrifice of Golgotha.[64]

In Belloc's public commentaries on the Spanish Civil War there
was nary a hint of any parallels with the French Revolution and the
related issue of class struggle. The probing economic and sociopolitical analyses that undergirded his earlier books on Robespierre,
Danton, Napoleon, and the French Revolution itself, are notably
missing in his writings on Spain.

One of Belloc's admirers, Arnold Lunn, who was studying the
older man's writings on the French Revolution, could not help but
notice striking parallels between what Belloc said about France's history and what was presently occurring in Spain. Lunn had started
with a strong bias against the French Revolution and was perplexed
at Belloc's enthusiasm for it. Lunn wrote Belloc and asked if he
had changed his mind about that pivotal historical event.[65] Belloc
responded by asserting that the French and Spanish events were
separated by a profound spiritual difference:

The French Revolution was founded on patriotism and property, the Spanish is founded on Jewish Communism which specially attacks those two fundamental ideas of our Western civilisation. What the two movements have in common is hostility to the Catholic Church, but in the French case that hostility came in from the side, it was incidental. It took root because religion had been lost in the directing mind of the French people. The civil constitution of the clergy was the consequence and started the whole quarrel; but the Communist attack on the Church is a *main* activity: indeed, the two great forces now facing each other in the Western world are Communism and Catholicism. That is why it was good strategy on the part of the Moscow Jews to attack Spain. I think they would have succeeded if it had not been for Franco forestalling them. It was a close thing.[66]

Once Belloc had found what he believed to be the "key" to the Spanish imbroglio, he appears to have felt no need to analyze the affair any further: like Procustes with his bed, everything would be made to fit the thesis. Belloc's vision was Manichean. In his mind Spain was on the verge of an Armageddon-like struggle between good and evil. In this sense his assessment of the situation was identical to the propaganda of the radical counter-revolutionaries in Spain. They, like Belloc, also saw their enemies as the anti-Christ, composed of three parts: Jews, Freemasons, and Marxists.[67] From this point on, Belloc's objective was to get the message out, to undertake a massive campaign of propaganda to show the world that Franco was wrestling the anti-Christ in a noble but insufficiently appreciated struggle to save Western civilization. As he told a Queen's Hall meeting of the Friends of Nationalist Spain in March 1939:

> . . . in spite of the contradictions and cross purposes of the moment, one major fact still stands out. The Spanish struggle has been a crusade: a struggle between forces organized for the destruction of religion and forces organized in the defense of religion. . . . It was to restore the Spanish nation and the religion with which that nation is identified that Franco rose and that he and his followers have fought. . . ."[68]

There was a lacuna of critical analysis in Belloc's visions of Spain, as was the case with most others on both the Left and Right who chose sides in 1936. Objective, analytical evaluations were not necessary—a strong emotional response was sufficient. Nowhere is this more apparent than in Belloc's failure to study carefully the case of the Spanish anarchists. If he had looked more closely, Belloc might have recognized some striking parallels between the motives of workers and peasants in Catalonia and his own involvement with the virtually revolutionary upheavals in British labor circles prior to World War I. This broader perspective might have made him, and those who followed his lead, more sensitive to the complex social dynamics that drove the conflict in Spain. However, this is probably a moot point, since Belloc's circle had no interest in such matters as regards the civil war: the anticlerical fury at the beginning of the conflict defined the issues in a purely religious, emotive perspective. Yet in terms of Belloc's perceptive critique of industrial capitalism there was a sharp rupture with respect to what he analyzed in Britain and what he chose to see in Spain.

Belloc does not appear to have noted any affinities whatever between the working-class revolution directed by the Spanish anarchists and syndicalist activity in pre-war Britain. As we have seen in *The Party System, The Servile State,* and in numerous articles in the *Daily Herald,* the *New Age,* and other such avant-garde papers, Belloc, along with Cecil Chesterton, had condemned conventional English political processes as irrelevant for satisfying working-class interests. The two chastised trade union leaders for "selling out" to the oligarchy of capitalists and urged the workers to take things into their own hands and smash the bureaucracies that oppressed them. Belloc and both the Chesterton brothers (Gilbert and Cecil) urged the British laboring classes to reject wage slavery and demand control and ownership of the means of production.

The Catalan anarcho-syndicalist trade union, the Confederation Nacional de Trabajo or C.N.T., was probably the most radical element in the mélange of revolutionary groups in Spain. Their members were bitter foes of the Spanish communists. The C.N.T. was founded in 1910–11 to accomplish the same objectives as the syndicalist and industrial unionist groups (formed at the same time) that Belloc and his friends had supported in the pre–World War I years. Like their British counterparts, the Spanish anarchists opposed "bourgeois" politics and urged their members to use "direct action" tactics against their employers with the objective of bringing control and ownership of the productive system into the hands of the workers. Rather than prolong collective bargaining, the Spanish anarchists, much like the British syndicalists who were appreciative of and seemingly influenced by Belloc's views on the subject, fully distrusted management and preferred the swiftness of the strike to reach their goals. The C.N.T. was essentially libertarian. It had no permanent officials. The association's literature celebrated the independence of the worker and opposed all forms of bureaucratic and elitist structures because they stifled the individual's creative capacities. They were uncompromising in their resistance to the wage slavery of modern capitalism. Not unlike Distributists, the Spanish anarchists were communitarians who championed a return to life on a small scale.

As opposed to their communist and socialist rivals, whose "nationalization" programs hinged on control by the party standing "above" workingmen with a tight leash on the rank and file, the C.N.T. spoke of what it called "collectivized" policies, meaning control from "below," essentially from the factory floor.[69] The urban workers in the C.N.T. were syndicalists, meaning that they favored a "vertical" social restructuring along lines familiar to Britain's guild socialists: workers would be organized into self-governing guilds or syndicates interacting in democratic fashion with other related vocational units. These arrangements were supposed to restore the freedom and dignity workers lost in the soulless tyranny of the modern factory system.

Peasants associated with the C.N.T. advocated a rural social order based on the *pueblo* or "small town" whose inhabitants would form democratic, cooperative, self-sufficient mini-communities free from outside interference.[70] The rural visions of G. K. Chesterton and Belloc had been colored by the idyllic *Rural Rides* of William Cobbett of a century ago; the Spanish anarchists were inspired by their ideas of the primitive communes that existed in the medieval, supposedly halcyon days of sixteenth- and seventeenth-century Spain.

The writer Gerald Brenan, who experienced the civil war first-hand and subsequently came to appreciate the vitality of Spanish Catholicism, has called the anarchists uniquely Spanish. His description of their ideals, however, would seem to apply equally to Distributism, which G. K. Chesterton and Belloc thought uniquely English. The Spanish anarchists, Brenan wrote, managed to "canalize" feelings that were deeply seated in the Spanish soul:

> One may describe this as a hatred of political shams, a craving for a richer and deeper social life, an acceptance of a low material standard of living and a belief that the ideal of human dignity and brotherhood can never be obtained by political means alone, but must be sought in a moral reformation (compulsory, it is needless to say) of society. That is what one might call the characteristic Spanish attitude. Contrary to the Liberal doctrine which separated Church from State and society from government, it aims at an integration of political and social life. But it is not totalitarian. Far from asserting the moral supremacy of the State, it holds the Christian view that every human being, whatever his capacity or intelligence, is an end in himself, and that the State exists solely to advance these ends. And it goes further. The long and bitter experience which Spaniards have had of the workings of bureaucracy has led them to stress the superiority of society to government, of custom to law, of the judgement of neighbours to legal forms of justice and to insist on the need for an inner faith or ideology, since this alone will enable men to act as they should, in mutual harmony, without the need for compulsion.[71]

As was clearly the case with Distributists, Brenan viewed Spanish anarchists as similarly driven by a strongly idealistic, moral-religious vision reflecting a nostalgia for an earlier *Gemeinschaft* order where individuals had dignity and the security of place.[72]

The anarchists were primarily responsible for the violence unleashed against the Spanish Catholic Church. But this was a rage fueled by an intense anticlericalism and the Church's solidarity with the traditional institutions of tyranny; it was a collection of hatreds not unlike those that spawned terror against the Church during the French Revolution. Yet this terrifying fury, as Brenan correctly observes, was not strictly anti-religious. It was rather a violence fed by the fires of the social Gospels. At the core of New Testament teaching is the damnation of the rich and the blessedness of the poor. The Christian notion of the social good is tied to the functioning of a corporate ethos in which the rich have a paternalistic responsibility to serve the poor. There was always a persistent danger, Brenan pointed out, that any weakening of the Church, any large-scale failure of the priesthood to fulfill its mission of social deaconry, could lead to more emphasis by its critics on the social principles of equality and brotherly love; for those failing to heed such injunctions, it could lead to the pain of the sword.[73]

There were both obvious and significant differences between Spanish anarchism and the industrial unionist elements supported by Belloc and company. The anarchists opposed all forms of private property as oppressive (yet this was also the case with some of the guild socialists with whom the G. K. Chesterton and Belloc allied themselves), and, like the French revolutionists, they were violently anticlerical. All this was behind anarchist-directed, not communist, violence against the Church. Belloc's outrage at the anticlerical fury clearly outweighed any visceral sympathy he may have had for the Spanish revolutionaries. Yet it is clear that he did not bother to examine their social situation and programs very closely, which suggests that Belloc's understanding of the Spanish situation was limited, reductionist, and ultimately subordinated to his larger thesis that Europe was the faith, and the faith was Europe. In this perspective, Spain, the most Catholic of nations, represented the unbroken tradition of Catholic culture (that is to say, the faith in its purest form). Since Europe's culture was determined by Greco-Roman traditions preserved in the mother Church, Spain's struggle against communism was, in effect, a battle to preserve Western civilization.[74] In the final analysis, Belloc's purpose was not to analyze the Spanish tragedy with any scholarly objectivity. His mission was to wage a propaganda campaign to save civilization from the rabble. One of Belloc's more ardent disciples, Arnold Lunn, said it best: "it is infinitely more important to write propaganda for the Faith than to write anything else. For Catholicism is not only a culture it is culture."[75]

Many Catholics who rushed to the defense of Franco interpreted the issues along lines that had been set down by their mentor, Belloc.[76] The most articulate and persuasive of the English were Belloc's protégés Arnold Lunn, Christopher Hollis, Gregory Macdonald, Douglas Jerrold, and Douglas Woodruff. The Spanish Civil War for them was a religious "White Crusade" against communism, a struggle to save the West from the perdition of atheism.[77] The complex web of social, economic, and political factors that contributed to the wrenching conflict in Spain were given short schrift by these writers, for they were seen as secondary issues in a struggle that was inherently religious.[78]

The extraordinary violence against the Church and its representatives in territory under control of Republican loyalists when the revolution first broke out was the immediate catalyst in bringing many Catholic intellectuals to play an active role on Franco's behalf and as the war dragged on this remained the defining issue for most Catholics. Arnold Lunn was typical of this mind-set when he wrote that "the persecution of the Church by the Spanish Reds would have been decisive for me even if I had not numbered among my friends a single Spaniard."[79] The Catholic publisher Frank Sheed later admitted that his friends knew very little about conditions in Spain, "but as between people who murdered priests and nuns and people who didn't, we preferred those who didn't. It was practically a reflex reaction."[80]

The response of Belloc and his associates to the Spanish situation, with some exceptions, essentially mirrored general English Catholic thinking on the Republican experiment in Spain. When the Republic of 1931 first took shape, most English Catholics were hopeful that the Spanish Church would reform itself and make an effort to work constructively with the new government.[81] As the *Catholic Herald* put it, the cause of freedom and religion were linked and only in a "free, instructed, religious and moral" democracy could the Church find a true ally.[82] Even after the wave of anticlerical violence in May 1931 the conservative Jesuit magazine *The Month* felt that the popular anger with Catholicism was due to the Church's close ties to a corrupt and exploitative state, and it criticized Spain's Catholic leaders for failing to serve the poor.[83]

The general view in England was that the Spanish Church ought to support social change along lines outlined in the papal labor encyclicals (the matter was all the more urgent as *Quadragesimo Anno* had just been published) and that the current situation offered an ideal opportunity to make common cause with the Republic to initiate such reforms. There was considerable hope that the Catholic Action group under Gil Robles (which stressed the replacement of class warfare by the social Gospels and the establishment of a Christian corporative state) could come to terms with the new government. Increasingly, especially after the Asturias revolt, English Catholics saw Gil Robles as the only barrier to a Marxist takeover in Spain. However, as reports of mounting extremism and violence grew more ominous in the spring and summer of 1936, English and American Catholics became convinced that the central issue in Spain was less the failure of the Church to promote social reform than revolutionary Marxism, a sentiment given further credence in the following year with the publication of Pius XI's encyclical *Divini Redemptoris* condemning atheistic communism. Once the generals revolted, all Catholic aspirations for the creation of a new Christian order in Spain disappeared, and the defining issue now became the battle against Bolshevism.[84]

The fury unleashed against the clergy after the *pronunciamiento* solidified the issue. For most Catholics the matter was now purely one of religious freedom. As the Jesuit journal *The Month* was quick to point out, if the Nationalists were defending the faith, all else was of no consequence.[85] Thus from the very outset of the conflict there was little interest in examining the social and political context of the Spanish Civil War; Hilaire Belloc and his fellow propagandists had a frightened, ready-made audience for their message.

One of the most zealous proponents of Belloc's "White Crusade" idea was Reginald Dingle, the translator of an unabashedly propagandistic panegyric of General Franco (George Rotvand's *Franco Means Business*, with an introduction by Gregory Macdonald) and a regular contributor to most of the influential Catholic periodicals in England. Rotvand's main thesis was that Franco was a hero of epic proportions: he was a military genius, a charismatic intellectual with almost perfect qualities in every sense. In fact, claimed

Rotvand, he is a man with "no weakness."[86] Dingle was merciless with Catholic writers who failed to see Franco the way Rotvand described him. Such Catholics, he insisted, lacked the faith.[87] Dingle was singularly incapable of recognizing the resentment of many working-class Catholics against the Spanish Church's relationship with wealth and privilege. Throughout the conflict he insisted that attacks on the Church were unequivocally the product of a diabolical hatred of the supernatural.[88]

The writings of Belloc's young disciple, Gregory Macdonald, revealed a common feature of nearly all right-wing Catholic views on the Spanish conflict, namely, a deep-seated animus for liberalism. In fact, a central feature of the crusade idea was not an attack on the conditions that spawned communism (and this is what so annoyed liberals like H. A. Reinhold, Luigi Sturzo, and Virgil Michel) but an assault on movements and individuals with liberal political views. In this effort, many prominent British and American Catholics were willing to accept "anti-democratic disreputables" as allies.[89] Macdonald put Franco in the company of the great defenders of Christendom (Roland, Alfred the Great, Godfrey deBuillon, Don John of Austria, and others) because Franco was holding forth against the combined forces of the nineteenth-century liberal tradition, which Macdonald labeled the "Left Wing." In this category he lumped together such seemingly disparate groups as Manchester liberals, democrats, internationalists, humanitarians, philanthropists, and communists. Like Belloc, Macdonald regarded all these categories as cloaks for a series of sinister conspiracies. Liberalism, for instance, was considered a gospel of rights and freedoms for the wealthy to exploit the poor. Democrats were people who hoped to control the commonweal through secret committees; humanitarianism was a ruse for the denial of a belief in God. And finally, the communists, representing the apogee of the left-wing conspiracy utilizing the false doctrines of Genevan international law (the League of Nations was presumably vitiated from its origins by Protestant and Jewish connections), were operating through the guise of the United Front to destroy Christian Europe. For all these reasons, Macdonald and his fellow right-wing Catholics saw the Spanish Civil War as a turning point in history.

A most revealing assessment of the Christian crusade idea was put forward by the English Catholic convert and writer Stanley B. James in *The Month* of September 1937. Rather than recognizing the call to arms in Spain as an unfortunate human tragedy, James deemed the struggle largely positive, offering hope for a new type of "Catholic Action." James saw a clear parallel between the civil war and the crusades of the eleventh century. Although the latter failed, the spiritual energies they unleashed transferred the militant crusading ideal to a higher plane and, as it reappeared in the religious revivals of the Middle Ages, not only saved Europe from falling to the prey of commercialism but sparked a Christian cultural renaissance. In James's view, Europe of the 1930s was in need of a similar revitalization. The spiritual and economic collapse that followed World War I produced a moral vacuum, a fertile breeding ground for "amoral liberalism" and the atheistic propaganda of Marxists. Given the low morale of Western Europe, the war in Spain offered Catholicism a golden opportunity. General Franco's vigorous offensive against what Gregory Macdonald called the "Left Wing" would give new heart to Catholic Action, which had wallowed too long in a defensive siege mentality. In tones reminiscent of Georges Sorel's myth of the general strike and the mystical musings of José Antonio Primo de Rivera's fascist dreams, James welcomed Franco and the Spanish bloodletting as a means of breathing life into a Catholic renaissance:

> Has it to be confessed that the forms of Catholic Action proposed to us, admirable as they are, have as yet failed to create widespread enthusiasm? If so, that is because there is no Peter the Hermit among us, nor anything like a Crusade to which he could summon us. Need this be so? For the creation of a popular movement, now as in the time of the Crusades, something spectacular and physical is required.[90]

James's wishes were fulfilled in the eyes of the eminent American Jesuit publicist and scholar, Joseph Thorning, S.J. After having returned from Spain in the autumn of 1937 Thorning waxed rhapsodic in praise of Franco's soldiers: "War has few attractive features but it must be acknowledged that the war-time tempo occasionally lifts a nation from lethargy and *dolce far niento* into the zone of time-tables and the systematic dispatch of business."[91] There were a good number of Belloc's disciples who accepted Stanley James's challenge to revitalize the faith through Nietzschean combat. Indeed, a special feature of the Catholic Right's crusade for Franco was its love of a good fight. Once again, Arnold Lunn provides a model of the style. Lunn was stimulated when he could intimidate large crowds, in particular, said he, when they shouted with anger: "I like to make these enemies of everything which I love." Lunn claimed that he believed it would be infinitely easy to enjoy "burning a mob of Reds." He feared that American Catholics were insufficiently militant. One of Lunn's major objectives as Visiting Professor of Apologetics at the University of Notre Dame was to raise the level of militancy in his students. "Unless they get stirred up," said Lunn, Americans will "get it in the neck."[92] Lunn went so far as to urge his audiences to kill for their religion. Father Virgil Michel, with redolent disgust, reported that when Lunn spoke at St. John's University he not only called Franco's campaign a holy war of the Catholic religion but told the students: "You must be ready to die for your faith; yes sometimes you must be ready to kill for your faith."[93]

Arnold Lunn's ally in militant religious polemics, Douglas Jerrold, saw something both ennobling and biologically imperative in combat. His words had an uncomfortably fascist ring to them:

> An idea for which a man is not prepared to die is not an idea sufficiently dynamic to stimulate the instinct to serve, and it is on the stimulation of this instinct, on its predominance over all else that, as a matter of mere biological necessity, the health of the race depends. For it is only in serving that the male can attain moral dignity, without which the race must deteriorate and ultimately decay.[94]

Arnold Lunn was a great admirer and close friend of the Spanish grandee and ardent monarchist, Captain Gonzalo de Aguilera, Count de Alba y Yeltes, Nationalist Spain's diplomatic agent in London. After Britain recognized Franco's government in 1939, Alba was appointed Ambassador to the Court of St. James, where he stayed until 1945.[95] Lunn was fond of dropping the Count's name and that of other notables as a way of impressing people with his close connections with the Spanish aristocracy.

Despite his pedigree (he was a descendant of James II, which endeared him to English Catholic notables), educational training (Beaumont and Madrid University), and government experience (he was appointed Spanish Minister of Education in 1930 and subsequently Foreign Minister in the Berenguer Government), the Count de Alba was a brute in nobleman's clothing. He seems to have been much more popular in Britain than in his native country, and London, where he spent most of his time, afforded him the congenial company of other well-placed aristocrats. The Count owned almost 222,000 acres of property in Spain but seems to have been the quintessential absentee landlord. [96] Aguilera served the Nationalist cause in many different capacities, but he turned out to be somewhat of an embarrassment as Franco's press liaison officer in the north of Spain. For example, on the day the civil war broke out, which he helped plan, the Count proudly informed an English visitor that he promptly lined up the laborers on his estate, selected six from the group, and shot them in front of the others—*"pour encourager les autres,* you understand."[97] The troubles in Spain, Aguilera announced to the American journalist John T. Whitaker, were due to the introduction of public sanitation. Before city drainage the *canaille* had been killed off by diseases:

> Had we no sewers in Madrid, Barcelona, and Bilbao, all these Red leaders would have died in their infancy instead of exciting the rabble and causing good Spanish blood to flow. When the war is over, we should destroy the sewers. . . . Sewers are a luxury to be reserved for those who deserve them, the leaders of Spain, not the slave stock.

Whitaker claimed Aguilera told him that

> We have got to kill and kill and kill, you understand. . . . It's our program . . . to exterminate one third of the male population of Spain. That will purge the country and we will be rid of the proletariat.[98]

Whitaker was disgusted by the Count's talk, yet he wrote that it was typical of what he heard expressed by hundreds of others on Franco's side.[99]

Arnold Lunn, on the other hand, found Aguilera "not only a good soldier but a scholar" whose general philosophy was positively enlightening.[100] Lunn told the Count that he wished he himself had been born a Spaniard, for there were only two types of Christian he found appealing: "Saints like St. Theresa and St. Peter Claver, and real tough conquistadors such as my good friend Aguilera." Lunn took considerable pride in his own tough guy image, which he carefully cultivated as a militant Catholic figuratively bashing heads for Franco. Lunn reassured his friend Aguilera that he was every bit as tough as the Count: "Hair shirts or beautiful guns looted at Bilbao. I've not much more use for anything in between."[101] The Count responded in kind. When Lunn boasted of having a debate in which he "flattened out" an Oxford don and an Eton master who were wearing the fashionable color of pink, Aguilera wrote that he himself would have enjoyed immensely "to have been present and have helped to jab at these pinky products of protestantism."[102]

Perhaps the best example of the merging of civil war machismo and religious zealotry can be seen in the career of a South African Catholic poet, Roy Campbell. Campbell can rightly be called the "Hemingway of the Right." Like Campbell, Hemingway was also a convert to the faith but one who served the other side. Campbell's persona was that of a rough man of the bush, though in fact he came from a wealthy South African family. Yet Campbell seems more the genuine article than Hemingway, for he actually supported himself in Provençe as bullfighter and fisherman. His male chauvinism may also have exceeded Hemingway's: Campbell boasted of shaking up the illusions of his new wife that she was going to wear the pants in the family by hanging her out of a fourth-floor window. This, he wrote, earned her respect.[103]

Roy Campbell welcomed the struggle promised by civil war:

> I was disgusted at what I took to be the tame, cringing fatalism of the Nationalists who, after all, formed the majority. They had turned both cheeks so many times that it began to look cowardly

rather than Christian. . . . Little did I know what a feast of hero-ism was in store![104]

The conflict did more than simply inspire Campbell to flex his lit-erary muscles: it also convinced him and his wife to forsake their amorphous Anglo-Catholicism for the real thing. In a secret nigh-time ceremony in June 1936 they were received into the Roman faith by Isidro Gomá y Tomás, cardinal-archbishop of Toledo and pri-mate of Spain. With this, Campbell claimed, he could at least step into the front ranks of the Regular Army of Christ.

Campbell hoped to serve in the ranks of the Carlist militia, the *Requetés,* but Marqués de Pablo Merry del Val, chief of the Nation-alist Press Service, persuaded the poet that Franco needed "pens not swords." Nevertheless, in his autobiography Campell writes of having killed Bolsheviks in self-defense as he fought his way out of Toledo, and in the poem "We/Who Are in the Legion" describes taking part in a cavalry charge.[105] Campbell deliberately created an image of himself as a zealous soldier taking up arms for Franco. He was indeed zealous, points out his biographer, Peter Alexander, but as a writer not a soldier. In fact, Campbell's single battlefield experi-ence consisted of a one-day motor tour of the front on 1 July 1937 as a correspondent of the London *Tablet.*[106] The South African poet David Wright, who came to know Campbell very well after the war, wrote that Roy was almost the exact reverse of the truculent persona he projected in his writings. All this was part of Campbell's theater to the world: it was a "put on," part of the mask of vainglory brag-gadocio behind which hid a modest man.[107]

Campbell's writings on Spain, which one critic has called pre-posterous distortions of fact,[108] had the hard edge of combat about them. The celebration of slaughtering one's enemies was so graphic in his epic philo-fascist poem of the civil war, *Flowering Rifle,* that Stephen Spender claimed to have become physically ill reading pas-sages from it.[109] Hilaire Belloc and his circle, on the other hand, found the book, in Belloc's words, "a really good thing," a work of art against which all of Campbell's other work would pale.[110]

As might be expected, Campbell was not one to sit back and accept Spender's criticism lightly. He struck back by calling Spender

and his leftist friends "cowards." The following lines were aimed at
Spender and his party:

> . . . these three hundred Red-Necks thrilled and caught,
> By Prophecy, on the live wires of thought,
> Brought here to learn why communists 'feel small'
> And we so perpendicular and tall
> (Like a Catholic over Comrades' Hall)[111]

Campbell did more than attack Spender in print. One evening he
mounted the stage where Spender was giving a lecture and punched
him.[112]

Campbell's style and sentiments were mirrored in a coterie of
reactionary English writers associated with the January Club. Founded
on New Year's Day 1934, this was an informal association of like-
minded thinkers, many of whom expressed great admiration for the
works of Hilaire Belloc. The group gathered at luncheons and din-
ners to discuss the virtues of fascism.[113] Although they did not agree
on all matters, the members were convinced that the democratic
political system in Britain had to be scrapped. A companion and
protégé of Hilaire Belloc, Sir John Squire, editor of the *London Mercury*, became the first chairman of the January Club. Many who
joined this group wrote for Jerrold's *English Review* and Lady Houston's *Saturday Review*, a journal that championed Mussolini and
all forms of fascist dictatorship. Among the January Club's more
prominent members were Francis Yeats-Brown, Sir Charles Petrie,
Muriel Currey, and Major-General J. F. C. Fuller, all of whom were
unabashedly philo-fascist.[114] The January Club articulated various
positions on Fascist Italy that were essentially the same as Belloc's,
and, not surprisingly, its members became some of the most vocal
and influential sources of pro-Franco propaganda in Britain.

Sir Charles Petrie, an Irish baronet and, in the words of Douglas Jerrold, a "genius" on foreign affairs whom he alone had the good
fortune to have discovered, was one of England's more ardent monarchists. Petrie's ideas on the subject appear to owe much to Belloc.
Indeed, even his language and literary imagery resembled Belloc's.[115]
Petrie praised Belloc's exceptionally insightful attacks on England's

parliamentary system and deeply respected what he called his anti-democratic authoritarianism.[116] Like Belloc, Petrie was a close reader of *Action française* and regarded the Catholic writers Paul Déroulède, Maurice Barrès, and Charles Maurras, among other French reactionaries, as the true intellectual sources of the fascist ideology he so admired.[117] Although he praised fascist dictatorship, Petrie realized that this political form was highly personal and lacked adequate mechanisms for transferring authority. In the end he believed it must give way to a feudal-style monarchy, which to Petrie's mind was inherently more stable than aristocracy or democracy.[118]

Along with James Strachey Barnes, the fascist triumphalist and El Duce sycophant whose views on Italian politics he completely accepted, Charles Petrie was one of Britain's foremost champions of Mussolini. The Italian dictator was the best representative of "a revival of monarchy"; his invasion of Abyssinia gave Italians pride and confidence once again as the true heirs of imperial Rome. For this deed, claimed Petrie, Mussolini "deserves to rank among the greatest leaders in history."[119] To Petrie, Mussolini was a benevolent and patriotic despot. As for his purging of the liberal democratic priest Don Luigi Sturzo, it was a necessary consequence of the politics of the Popular Party, which the Fascist government could ill afford to tolerate. Indeed, wrote Petrie, the Vatican's troubles with the Fascists were directly caused by the intrigues of Sturzo's party.[120]

Sir Charles Petrie's position on the Spanish Civil War mirrored his interpretation of Italian Fascism. The followers of Franco were the progenitors of the true Spanish monarchical tradition. Like the reactionary Carlists, they had no time for the "imported" social and political customs of the French Revolution but rather were trying to restore to Spain the praxis of throne and altar found in Catholic corporativism.

Many of the writers associated with the *English Review* circle and the January Club were members of the "Friends of Nationalist Spain," the most important pro-Franco organization in Britain. This group was founded by the Count of Alba and Luis Bidwell Bolín, who before the war was a journalist for Spain's chief Catholic and pro-monarchist paper, the Madrid daily *ABC*. Bolín served Franco in many capacities, eventually acting as press attaché at the

Spanish embassy in London. The idea behind the Friends of Nationalist Spain, wrote Bolín, was to make "the truth better known" about what was happening in that country.[121] Bolín himself, however, was notorious for ensuring that only his version of the truth about Spain was made known. As Nationalist Chief of Press in the south of Spain, Bolín had been instructed by his boss, General José Millán Astray y Terreros, to intimidate foreign journalists into following the Nationalist line.[122] Bolín pursued his orders with zeal, especially in the case involving Arthur Koestler, whom he had imprisoned. It appears that Bolín was prepared to hang Koestler on the spot after arresting him in Málaga (Bolín disapproved of Koestler's journalism) but was persuaded from doing so by the intervention of Sir Peter Chalmers Mitchell, a well-connected English nobleman.[123]

There were five "original" founding members of the Friends of Nationalist Spain: Bolín, the Count of Alba, Charles Petrie, Victor Raikes, MP, and Douglas Jerrold. Jerrold and Bolín claimed that they "lit the fuse" for the civil war by conspiring to smuggle Franco out of the Canary Islands on a secret flight in order to take charge of the military uprising in Morroco.[124] The Friends quickly attracted supporters, and Bolín could boast that the group had a considerable amount of political clout in appropriate circles. Such pressures served to influence banks and the government in favor of Nationalist interests.[125] Arnold Lunn related that Neville Chamberlain had told Sir Martin Melvin, owner of the Catholic weekly *The Universe*, that if it had not been for the forceful action of Catholics he would have been obliged to take action extremely embarrassing to Franco's cause.[126]

An important member of the "Friends" who served as an active propagandist carefully working behind the scenes was the Marquis del Moral, Frederick Ramón Bertodano y Wilson. Moral was born in Australia, served in the British army in the Boer War and World War I, and later acquired a Spanish title and citizenship. Along with Jerrold and Bolín he published an anti-Republican book called *The Spanish Republic* in 1933.[127] The purpose of the book was to expose the Republic's corruption, human rights abuses, and general drift toward anarchy. Christopher Hollis gave *The Spanish Republic* a very favorable review in the *Catholic Herald* (29 July 1933), and it was well received among English Catholic readers.[128] Douglas Jerrold claimed that Moral was the spark plug behind the Friends, a "remarkable and buoyant personality" whose "overflowing hospitality kept our small group in being and in remarkable amity over a number of years."[129] Moral had personal access both to Franco and to a number of conservative MPs, over whom he had considerable influence.[130] In August 1936 Moral submitted to the British Foreign Office photocopies of "certain secret reports and orders of the Socialist-Communist Headquarters in Spain," supposedly obtained for him with considerable difficulty, calling for an uprising between early May and late June 1936. This was part of the evidence used by the Catholic Right to prove that the *pronunciamiento* was prompted by the necessity of averting a communist takeover in Spain. These documents, which the British Foreign Office found to be forgeries, were later published in Arthur Loveday's books *World War in Spain* (London, 1939) and *Spain, 1923–1948; Civil War and World War* (London, 1949). Loveday was pro-Insurgent and a former president of the British Chamber of Commerce in Barcelona, and his books were vehicles of propaganda for Franco's cause. Close analysis of the documents and the circumstances in which Loveday procured them suggest that they were concocted before the civil war by some pro-fascist group to convince the Spanish people that the Reds were planning a revolution. Variations of this so-called "secret evidence" were published in 1937 by the Nazi-controlled anti-Komintern in Berlin and reprinted in a number of other publications in France, the United States, and elsewhere.[131] These documents served as "indisputable evidence" for the British and American supporters of Franco's cause that the *Movimiento Nacional* was the only thing that prevented a communist takeover in Spain. Typical of this attitude was Owen B. McGuire, a regular commentator on the Spanish Civil War for *The Sign*, the national Catholic magazine of the American Passionist Fathers. Reference was seldom made, wrote McGuire, to plans for a Red revolution in the spring of 1936, which only failed because of the army uprising.[132]

Another key activist for the Friends was the Tory MP, Brigadier-General Sir Henry Page Croft. Like his friend Hilaire Belloc, Croft proclaimed that Franco was a gallant and heroic Christian figure and worked indefatigably for his cause both inside and outside Parliament.[133]

Hilaire Belloc also did his part for the Friends of Nationalist Spain. He wrote the chairman of the Friends Committee, Lord R. F. Phillimore, a seminal figure in the Franco propaganda campaign and unofficial envoy to Nationalist Spain for Prime Minister Chamberlain, that he supported their cause "from the bottom of my heart." Phillimore recruited Belloc as a keynote speaker for a major public meeting of the Friends to discuss the importance of Spain for Christian civilization. The gathering was held at Queen's Hall on 29 March 1939; its main purpose was to "scant" the idea of Italian and German domination in Spain.[134]

Belloc also worked actively in a confidential, behind-the-scenes fashion for the supporters of Nationalist Spain. He served as a recruiter of wealthy and influential conservatives willing to tour Nationalist territory and thus provide support for Franco's crusade. Among a host of potential recruits on Belloc's "strictly private and confidential" list were Duff and Lady Diana Cooper, Mrs. Raymond Asquith, Lady Helen Asquith, J. M. Morton, and Desmond McCarthy.[135]

Douglas Woodruff's London *Tablet,* which was the most prominent organ of Catholic opinion in Britain,[136] Jerrold's *English Review,* the Chesterton-Belloc alliance's *G.K.'s Weekly* and the *Weekly Review,* and the Jesuit paper *The Month* were all English journals of some influence among Catholic intellectuals that took up the propaganda campaign for Franco. Another was the *Colosseum.* This feisty, impolite quarterly was founded and edited by the young Bernard Wall (he was twenty-five years old when the first issue appeared). Inspired by Chesterton's and Belloc's papers, though with a decidedly more highbrow touch, the *Colosseum* provided a forum for Catholic-minded thinkers who sought to recover spiritual balance and Christian moral integration in a world consumed by the blind power of science and machines. Echoing Chesterton, the energetic Wall pointed out in one of the journal's early issues that "Modern life is on the average no more than a meaningless circle, unsanctified by any ideal, ordered towards no end, a frightful hash and chaos of old survivals and new fads."[137]

The youthful Bernard Wall had drunk deeply from Bellocian wells while a student at the Jesuit school, Stonyhurst. "Where triumphalism touched the nerve of my schooldays closest," he wrote, "was in the influence of Hilaire Belloc."[138] Having been taught history in his last two years at Stonyhurst by Christopher Hollis, Wall entered Oxford with a physical *joie de vivre* fueled exclusively by Belloc's polemical works. His deep convictions about the truths of Belloc's book *The Servile State* led Wall to seek out the fledgling Distributist League at Oxford. He soon took charge of the movement, and, thanks to his prodigious energies, the League grew enormously in numbers.

The appearance of the *Colosseum* in March 1934 was Wall's debut as a publicist. The operation was comparatively successful. It quickly built up a subscription list in England and the United States with a circulation that exceeded that of T. S. Eliot's *Criterion*. *Colosseum* published a number of distinguished continental writers, including Jacques Maritain, the Russian Christian philosopher Nicholas Berdyaev, Gonzague de Reynold, an eminent nobleman and professor at the University of Fribourg, and the Belgian writer Marc de Munnynk. British writers who appeared regularly in the journal were J. M. Turnell, Eric Gill, Christopher Dawson, and E. J. Oliver, Wall's Oxford friend who frequently helped him edit the paper.

The young and impressionable Bernard Wall, following the lead of his intellectual mentors Arnold Lunn and Christopher Hollis, argued in his writings that the Renaissance was a chief source of the twentieth-century malaise.[139] In the same vein as several reactionary intellectuals who had been influenced by the brilliant T. E. Hulme and Ramiro de Maeztu[140] (notably, Wyndham Lewis, Ezra Pound, and William Butler Yeats), he contrasted the roving, restless romantic of the day unfavorably with the "classical type" of Christian eras.[141] Not surprisingly, the youthful Wall continued to walk the paths suggested by de Maeztu and, much to the chagrin of his more liberal-minded Catholic friends and advisors (including Eric Gill, Father Victor White, Don Luigi Sturzo, and Jacques Maritain), became infatuated with fascism as a movement in tune with the moral integration of classical times. As Wall's assistant E. J. Oliver observed, the reactionary impulse all over Europe against the French revolutionary tradition represented a return to morality. The object of the Royalists in France and the critics of democratic, Republican government was moral as political: ". . . it is the characteristic of these modern movements that they reunite politics with morality."[142]

The *Colosseum* threw its undivided and engergetic support to the Nationalist crusade because, taking up a line of argument so eloquently expressed by the *éminence gris* Hilaire Belloc, Franco was saving Spanish Christian culture from Bolshevism. But Wall went further than Belloc and most other conservative Catholics who supported the rebels: he was willing to accept the fascist label for Franco. To the editor of *Colosseum*, the rightist totalitarian alternative to Marxism had many qualities, both positive and negative. Fascism, like democracy, might occasionally bring accidental evils and dangers. But it was capable of being a good political form the Church could accept and with which it could collaborate.[143] Most significantly, wrote Wall, fascism was the best weapon against Bolshevism:

> Fascism has saved Italy from the fate of Spain, and it may also save Spain from the fate of Russia. Italy has a youthful healthiness which is badly needed in the world, and the fact that Fascism has made Italy a great power is a good thing primarily because the whole mode of life, the way of civilisation that Italy represents so superbly, has been resurrected at a time when the basic culture of Europe may have disappeared entirely.[144]

Bernard Wall's eventual embrace of fascism was rooted in his strong distaste for liberal democracy. Like many other conservative Catholics, he regarded communism as its natural outgrowth. His main criticism of liberalism was its antipathy for tradition. Wall admitted that conservatives and the elites of the old orders had provided good cause for such hostility, for they had lost touch with the masses and their ideas and programs had favored the rich. Since the defeat of conservatism in World War I, however, liberal politicians through their control of the League of Nations had mounted a root-and-branch attack on all vestiges of tradition in European culture as retrograde and evil. In their laudable quest for social justice, the forces of the left were aiming to create a new world order in which religion, patriotism, and family values would become outmoded historical curiosities. Liberalism, "the philosophy of Geneva," was grounded in a deracinated view of humanity: it denied the legitimacy of national historical traditions as integrative forces in the cultures of Europe. What liberals failed to appreciate, claimed Wall, was that tradition was as essential to civilized life as social justice, that the one could not be achieved without the other. In a phrase derivative of Belloc, Wall noted that the movements of the left were strongest amongst "those classes which do not share the heritage of European culture."[145]

Bernard Wall came to believe that the fascist movements in Italy and Germany were positive reactions to the excesses of deracinated, cosmopolitan liberalism. Fascism represented a "revival of traditionalism," not entirely like the old conservatism it replaced, but rather evincing a willingness to embrace scientific development constructively while at the same time preserving the basic cultural life of people by subordinating technical and commercial development to traditional beliefs. Fascism in Wall's view was a herald of the "new Middle Ages":

> The strictness of its discipline is suggestive of feudalism, and this discipline may be a necessary means for giving mankind today a corporative social conscience.... The very exaggerations of the claims of the Fascist State over the individual and its use of military discipline for knitting the atoms of society into a corporative whole suggest a comparison with the achievement of feudalism in building up our civilisation.[146]

In its October 1938 issue *Colosseum* published for its readers the complete text of José Antonio Primo de Rivera's official doctrine of the Phalanx (or Falange Espanola, the party of Spanish fascism). It was a full-fledged attack on democracy and liberalism that called for the construction of what de Rivera named the "totalitarian State." *Colosseum* announced that de Rivera's fascism represented the true spirit of the Nationalist revolution in Spain.[147]

Wall's quarterly also distinguished itself from other British and American Catholic publications on the issue of Nazi Germany. Its editor occasionally had good things to say about Hitler. In January 1939, for example, Wall wrote a long article discussing the merits of Nazi racist policies, noting how they compared favorably with Catholicism as a force for creating national solidarity. Racism, argued Wall, "gives the people unity and hope."[148] *Colosseum* supported a rapprochement between Germany and Britain. Wall asserted that it was important for the British to appreciate the fact that Germany needed *Lebensraum*. Like Great Britain and the United States, Germany, with the most "technologically developed" and "educated" people on earth, had the right to expand.[149]

In some ways Bernard Wall's views were the apotheosis of the continental integralist ideas that infused the English-speaking world through the pens of such persuasive writers as Hilaire Belloc and his Latinophile coterie. Given the authoritarian and anti-Semitic proclivities of integralist thinking, it was only natural that those who were seduced by its creed would feel sympathy for the reactionary posturings of fascists and fellow-travelers who defended Franco's rebellion as a crusade for Christian culture.

CHAPTER 13

Against the Tide: The Catholic Critics of Franco

We are certain ... that those who must refute at a later time the perverse historians diligently calumniating Catholicism for its contacts with the powers of evil, will not be angry to find, when they search the archives, some Catholics who raised their voices against the destruction of Guernica.

—Jacques Maritain[1]

The Catholic Right's reductionist depiction of the Spanish Civil War as an Armageddon between atheistic communism and Christianity was resisted by less ideologically-driven Catholic intellectuals. A major voice of reason in opposition to the inquisitional attacks of the Right, one whose critique had a seminal impact on liberal British and American Catholics, was the French philosopher Jacques Maritain.

Maritain and several Catholics of the *cercle Thomiste* (which included François Mauriac, Gabriel Marcel, Hélène Iswolsky, and Emmanuel Mounier, among others) made their first public statement on the proper role of the Christian in politics in the wake of the so-called Stavisky riots of February 1934, an ugly event that raised the specter of a fascist takeover in France. Their response took the form of a manifesto, *Pour le Bien Commun,* drawn up by Maritain and signed by some fifty-one prominent Catholic writers, artists, and scientists. This was a key document in the emergence of Maritain's political philosophy. It publicly announced the basic principles upon which he believed the conscientious Catholic should face the secular challenges of the twentieth century.

332 CATHOLIC INTELLECTUALS AND THE CHALLENGE OF DEMOCRACY

The manifesto had two main purposes. First, it emphasized the obligation of Catholic philosophers to move from the spiritual realm of theological speculation and ivory-tower academics into the turmoil of the political marketplace. The increasing public struggles between fascist and Marxist extremists called for peacemakers, voices of Christian sanity in a society whose discourse had sunk to the level of political vitriol.

The second purpose of the manifesto was to caution the Catholic intellectual against becoming part of the marketplace in the sense of actually identifying with a single political party. Becoming a partisan of a particular political movement could only compromise the independence of the true Christian. The signatories emphasized that the Christian must be "*in* the world" but "not *of* the world."[2] Maritain and his colleagues fundamentally opposed the idea of a Catholic political party, nor did they feel it legitimate for any other group in the marketplace to assume the posture of a Catholic party.[3] This position stemmed from the signatories' acceptance of the papal condemnation of Charles Maurras' *Action Française,* a movement which sought to use Catholicism as an instrument for reactionary political objectives. Maritain's group sought the construction of a Christian society but not through the agencies of a theocracy. A Christian social order along the lines put forth in the papal encyclicals had to be forged through the ideals of Catholic justice and charity, by Christian principles infusing the consciousness of the secular city.

In addressing the specific dangers arising out of the Stavisky riots, *Pour le Bien Commun* pointed out two evils that would seduce European and American intellectuals for the rest of the decade. As Maritain's friend Hélène Iswolsky noted, the February upheavals had divided France into two camps:

> . . . one of them, being specially conscious of present-day political corruption, aspires confusedly to a revolution and an 'order,' which might in the long run assume a dictatorial form.

The other

> . . . is especially aware of present-day social injustice; it aspires more or less to a 'revolution' and an order, but by means of a collectivist regime oppressive to the human person.[4]

The danger was that Christians would see the obligation to chose between fascism and communism as solutions to the turmoil of the marketplace. For Maritain this was a false choice, since both "solutions" would destroy individual freedom. Rather than remain silently passive, the Catholic should exercise his or her Christian responsibility and oppose any doctrine which, in order to stanch fascism or communism, demanded the sacrifice of human liberty or dignity.

Pour le Bien Commun drew attention to one other principle upon which the Christian should guide political conduct, and that was the obligation to heed Pope Leo XIII's warnings against the capitalists' exploitation of the working classes. *Quadragesimo Anno,* an updating of Leo XIII's *Rerum Novarum,* had asserted that Catholic failure to take up the cause of labor had directly contributed to the drift of the working classes away from the Church and into the arms of Marxism. Most significantly, *Pour le Bien Commun* urged Catholics to measure political programs on the basis of their promotion of individual freedom and moral responsibility. Only what Maritain called a "pluralist" political order, one "assembling in its organic unity a diversity of groups and of social structures incarnating positive liberties, deserved Catholic support."[5] In subsequent manifestoes, lectures, books, and articles, many of which responded to specific political issues (the Abyssinian invasion, the suppression of the working classes in Austria, racism, and so forth), Maritain reemphasized and further refined the fundamental principles set down in *Pour le Bien Commun.*

Maritain and the *cercle Thomiste* were also active during the 1930s writing for *Sept* and *Esprit,* two highly respected Catholic periodicals which advocated social reform along lines similar to those of the English Distributists who followed Chesterton's way of thinking. Maritain had helped establish the two journals. *Sept* was launched with Dominican affiliation on the promptings of the Vatican in order to articulate the Church's new emphasis on social reform and pluralistic forms of political organization in the aftermath of the *Action Française's* condemnation. The journal was guided by the shibboleth "above party politics." Its intent was not to avoid political action but to preserve an independent voice. *Sept* hoped to find a common meeting ground for reasoned debate above the squabble of parties: ". . . we remain above the *mêlée.*" "Neither of the Right nor of the Left, independent of all politics, the better to serve the city."[6]

The moving force behind *Esprit* was Maritain's friend Emmanuel Mounier. A deeply religious man, Mounier championed the necessity of a personal spiritual revolution as the foundation of a new Christian social order. Mounier's philosophy of "personalism," directly inspired by Maritain's pluralistic teachings and the writings of Charles Péguy, was an appeal for the reawakening of the human personality through direct participation in community affairs.[7] Like G. K. Chesterton, Mounier had been influenced by anarchist thinking and revolutionary syndicalism. His journal, *Esprit*, condemned the dehumanization wrought by industrial society and the capitalist ethic, yet it also recognized the evils of their socialist antidote, which sacrificed individual personalities to the bureaucratic necessities of collectivism. Much like the core ideas of Distributism and the social principles that inspired the liturgical movement, Mounier's call for a spiritual renaissance aimed to integrate the individual fully into the community. The personalist revolution sought to liberate man from his social chains, but this transformation could not be accomplished through violence. It must be realized through spiritual means, for, as Péguy had insisted, "revolution must be moral, or it is not a revolution."[8] Politically, Mounier and his colleagues supported a corporatist state, one which offered a maximum of individual participation through professional and labor unit representation.

Maritain, Mounier, and their associates assessed the Spanish conflict in the context of the cultural imperatives that informed *Pour le Bien Commun, Esprit,* and *Sept.* After carefully examining the issues, they concluded that the Civil War was the result of complex social and economic problems which had undermined a political system unable to adjust to the demands of modernization. The violent outburst of anticlericalism that marked the onslaught of the Civil War was the logical outcome of a tragedy already identified by Popes Leo XIII and Pius XI, namely, the failure of the Church to satisfy the needs of the laboring classes. Given the social and economic roots of the Spanish Civil War, Maritain and his friends could not in good conscience support the Insurgents simply because they claimed the banner of Catholicism.

In fact, religion itself had never been a central motivating factor in the military revolt that triggered the Civil War in the first place. The officer coup was a rightist reaction against what the Insurgents considered revolutionary policies of the Republican government. Early pronouncements by the Insurgents made no reference to religion, in part because the conspirators desired broad middle-class support and did not want to antagonize moderate anticlerical opinion. The leading figures behind the *pronunciamiento* were not religious themselves. Only four of the ten members of the rebel Junta de Defensa Nacional had shown sympathy for political Catholicism, and senior general Miguel Cabanellas was not only a liberal but a Freemason.[9] The marriage of reaction and religion came later, after some of the Insurgents recognized the political advantage of using Catholicism to consolidate Nationalist support among groups that were already predisposed to the military's counterrevolutionary goals. As the fury against religion intensified, Church leaders threw their support to Franco.

Although he had shown no particular religious faith as an officer in Morocco, General Francisco Franco soon discovered the advantage of playing up Spain's long cultural and political association with the Catholic Church. He was the moving force behind the "Collective Letter" of the Spanish bishops supporting the Nationalists' cause. Franco's strategy was to link the Catholic faith with the creation of a Nationalist-authoritarian state which he openly called "totalitarian" in the tradition of the monarchism and culture of the ancient Spanish kings. In April 1937 Franco made the fascist Falange the official state party—renamed the National Movement—and essentially adopted its programs as the core of his new regime. By 1938 all Catholic secular associations (excepting its agrarian organization) were absorbed into state-controlled syndicates.

This linkage of tradition with totalitarianism did not seem to disturb Cardinal Isidro Gomá y Tomás, the primate of Spain, and the other leading Spanish hierarchs, nor did they at any time voice public criticism of the brutality of Franco's policies, which were responsible for the political executions of tens of thousands of Spaniards.

The American historian Stanley G. Payne, who is certainly not an unsympathetic observer of the Insurgent cause, has argued that

Franco's National Movement inaugurated the most reactionary cultural policy of any Western state in the twentieth century, an enterprise, in his words, "virtually without parallel."[10] Yet Cardinal Gomá remained convinced that the Nationalist crusade would lead to a spiritual awakening in Spain. No compromise was possible, he insisted. The Left must be totally defeated. At the close of the Civil War, Cardinal Gomá's pastoral "Catolicisimo y Patria" read, "Let us give thanks to God that he [Franco] has willed to make of Spain a Christian people from the heights of [state] power."[11]

Jacques Maritain recognized that General Franco's authoritarian political program contradicted the standards that guided *Pour le Bien Commun*. Maritain and his friends felt compelled to alert the international Catholic community to the dangers of identifying with a reactionary regime that was cynically using religion for political purposes.[12] In this endeavor the Maritain circle discussed Franco's regime in the context of Pope Pius XI's encyclical *Mit brennender Sorge* (March 1937), which the Nationalists refused to publish. The encyclical criticized Nazi doctrine as inherently totalitarian and godless. The Vatican's warning to the Germans was grounded on principles akin to those that undergirded its earlier condemnation of Charles Maurras' movement, which had employed Catholicism for tendentious political purposes.[13] On the other hand, it seemed anomalous, to say the least, that the Nationalist government saw fit to translate and give wide circulation to the anti-Christian writings of Alfred Rosenberg and Julius Streicher.

An exceedingly awkward situation occurred for the Catholic Right when the deeply religious Basque country threw its support to the Republican cause. This required a quick-witted Nationalist response, demanding the very best in Jesuitical casuistry. The British Catholic press rose to the challenge by suggesting that the Basques were under the sway of communists. Arnold Lunn, Douglas Jerrold, and others argued that only a minority of those in the Basque land fighting Franco were Catholic, and Lunn claimed that even among these a mere handful were what could be called "genuine Catholic." Once again, an a priori assumption was that anyone who opposed Franco was weak in the faith. The driving force behind the "schismatic" Basques was provided by the extreme Leftists, said

Lunn, and the few devout Catholics in their ranks had subordinated their religious principles to the narrow interests of nationalism.[14]

Lunn's assessments could not have been further off the mark. The Basques found themselves on the same side as the communists, but this was out of necessity. They were fighting for survival, and support of the military coup would have led to wholesale slaughter by radical leftists in Basque industrial centers.[15] Contrary to the claims of Nationalist propaganda, Marxism had no influence on Basque nationalism. The major influence on the radical economic thinking of the Basque Nationalist Party (PNV), which essentially determined the direction of Basque politics, was papal social philosophy. This was by no means a working-class party. Its political base was non-revolutionary, pro-Catholic, and essentially bourgeois, consisting mainly of small landowners, owners of small to mid-size businesses, and members of the professional classes. Those in the PNV were recognized by the Basque hierarchy as representing the "best" of Basque Catholicism in spirit and in works.[16] In no way was their commitment to nationalism, that is, to Basque autonomy against the dominance of Castile, considered incompatible with the faith. Even the most ardent followers of Franco admitted that the Basques "were the most Christian people in Spain."[17]

Unlike the hierarchy elsewhere in Spain, the leaders of the Basque Church developed close ties to the community, putting into flesh Leo XIII's encyclical *Rerum Novarum*, which called for the implementation of social and economic democracy. The Basque clergy had spearheaded educational, religious, and agrarian reforms and gave its full support to the provinces' aspirations for political and cultural autonomy against Castilian hegemonic pressures. Indeed, the Basque Church was so successful in social welfare work and in its encouragement of Christian trade unionism that socialism, anarchism, and communism found no appreciable audience in its industrial centers. Heeding the corporative suggestions of *Rerum Novarum*, the Basques had created Christian syndicates of industrial workers, day laborers, fishermen, and farmers, and set up professional associations for doctors, lawyers, and journalists, among others. Alongside these stood a large number of producer and consumer cooperatives as well as syndical savings institutions.[18]

Not only were the Basque provinces of Guipúzca and Vizcaya considered the most Catholic areas of Spain; they were also the most European in orientation and culture. Early commercial and industrial growth had led to strong links with Western Europe. Nearly half the peasants owned their own homes and farmlands, their population was the most highly literate in Spain, the economy was more fully developed and balanced than in other provinces, their people had a proud tradition of self-government, and the Church, as opposed to that institution in Castile and Catalonia, had been transformed by the winds of modernity. The Basque clergy lived close to the people, and priests played a central role in social and labor reform. Anticlericalism, a social virus that plagued the rest of Spain for nearly a hundred years, was virtually nonexistent. Moreover, unusually large numbers of the Basque population joined holy orders.[19] For all these reasons, the Basque country experienced no social revolution in 1936.

It follows that Basque Catholics in general were far less isolated theologically than their co-religionists in the rest of Spain. It was only in the Basque country, for example, that translations of the papal encyclicals were regularly published for all to read. The very limited number of encyclicals translated in regions that supported the Nationalists were frequently altered to fit the ideological needs of the propertied classes.[20] As implied earlier, *Mit brennender Sorge,* the encyclical that condemned Nazi practices, was actually suppressed by Franco and Cardinal Gomá.[21] At this time the German Condor Legion was playing a crucial role in the Nationalists' struggle with Basque autonomism, and Franco had no desire to give offense to Hitler by publicizing the text.

Prior to the *pronunciamiento* the Basques had been both courted and buffeted by the Spanish Left and Right. Their progressive social philosophy was welcomed by the Left, but Leftists were not at all pleased by the Basque's assiduous opposition to the laical orientation of the Republican constitution. The Right had lobbied for the Basque vote prior to 1933 by promising to support their Statute of Statehood in the Cortes. This statute would have given the Basque provinces certain local powers as an autonomous region within the Spanish state. But once the threat of a communist takeover receded, the Rightists lost interest in granting the Basques devolutionary rights. They were especially angry with the Basque bishop of Vitoria for voting in favor of the statute and for his support of Christian syndicalism. After assuming power in 1933, the Right pursued an anti-autonomistic course, at times violently persecuting the Basques. In the February 1936 elections the Basque Nationalist Party denounced the anti-Christian programs of the Leftists as well as the statist policies of the Right, supporting instead what it called the "eternal program": Christian civilization, social justice, and Basque liberties.

The Rightists invited the Basques to join the rebellion against the Azaña government. Senior José Antonio Aguirre, the Jesuit-educated Catholic activist leader of the PNV and later president of the Basque country under a statute of autonomy given by the Republic during the civil war, spurned the offer, replying that "sedition and rebellion are not Christian weapons."[22] The Basques supported the Republicans as soon as the military revolt occurred and never swayed in their loyalty throughout the course of the civil war.

Basque Catholics justified their alliance with the Republic on several grounds. A Collective Letter of the Spanish Episcopate published on 20 December 1931 had urged Catholics to obey the legal government of Spain; another issued in 1933 asked Catholics to work against unjust laws but within the confines of the constitution and without recourse to violence. These instructions were still in force by the *pronunciamiento* of 18 July 1936.[23] Equally compelling was the necessity of assuring Basque cultural survival in the face of coercive, even terrorist policies of the followers of Franco. The Nationalist government intended to suppress the Basque language and press and close down their schools. There were even plans to exile the Basque clergy to other provinces in Spain. We fight, said an official declaration of the Basque Nationalist Youth, for "God and the ancient Laws," so as to assure a peaceful society "based on justice, fraternity, and the dignity of the human person, help for the workers, veneration of the family, and respect for authority."[24] Finally, the declaration expressed a profound appreciation of the democratic conception of life, and this also was a reason why Basques felt compelled to support the Spanish Republic.

In the final analysis, the Basques remained loyal to the Republic because their survival depended on it. The Republic was the legally established government, one which had expressed belief in the democratic process and offered them assurances of political and cultural autonomy. The steadfastness of Basque support for the Spanish Republic belied the Nationalist notion of a holy war.

A major source of trouble for the Catholic Right's religious crusade was the Nationalist government's campaign of violence against civilians, the most notorious being the attack on the town of Guernica and the murders of Basque priests and civilians.[25] Basque resistance to Nationalist troops proved so resolute and unexpected that Franco decided to employ systematic terror to break the morale of the civilian population. Writing to Roberto Cantalupo, the Italian Ambassador to Nationalist Spain, Franco emphasized that he was not interested in territory but in the minds of its inhabitants. "The reconquest of the territory is the means, the redemption of the inhabitants the end."[26] Franco's experiences in Africa had taught him that good government was assured by the endless intimidation of the ruled.[27]

In their "pacification" of the northern Basque country the Nationalists rounded up some three thousand Basques and nineteen labor missionary priests, all of whom were shot without trial. More than five hundred Basque priests were persecuted, imprisoned, or forced into exile.[28] It may be the case that more Basque priests were executed by the Insurgent military in their campaign in the northern provinces than the number of clergy killed in the earlier civil conflict in Mexico, a grisly event which deeply shocked and angered the American Catholic community, especially since the government of the United States did nothing about the carnage. The Mexican civil war made Catholics in America extremely sensitive to the violence against the Spanish Church.[29] However, in contrast to the Mexican tragedy, the Vatican was essentially silent on the assassination of Basque priests.[30]

The Nationalists' *modus operandi* was far different from that of the Basques. The latter practiced political democracy, continued to champion social and economic reforms in agriculture and industry, abjured negative commentaries on Jews and Freemasons, and scrupulously followed international rules governing treatment of prisoners and noncombatants. The Basques would not have continued their support of the Republican government if such policies had been overruled. Their reactionary co-religionists on the other side, the Carlists and Castilians with the Nationalists, praised dictatorship, denigrated democracy, denounced international conventions concerning prisoner exchange, and shot their opponents, including those who wore the collar. It was for these reasons that the Basques, in defeat, hoped to surrender to the Italians, who were appalled by the cruelty of the Spanish Catholic Rightists.[31]

General Franco's image outside Spain was seriously compromised by the behavior of Nationalist troops in the Basque country. In its defense, the Burgos government claimed that the executed priests were agents of the Basque Nationalist Party. The Republican government vigorously denied that this was the case, stating that not a single Basque priest even belonged to the PNV.[32] Equally troublesome was the fact that very little was written about the executions in official Church publications. None of the media close to the Vatican, not even *Osservatore Romano,* published anything on the deaths of the Basque priests. According to canon law, Catholics who perpetrate such crimes against clergymen are automatically excommunicated. Cardinal Gomá, Spain's highest-ranking Church official, did not condemn the executions as such, though he did urge the rebels not to repeat such behavior.[33]

The single greatest public relations problem for the Nationalists centered on the fate of the small Basque town of Guernica. On the afternoon of 26 April 1937 aviators of the German Condor Legion in Junker and Heinkel aircraft conducted a massive raid on Guernica. The assault was chosen to coincide with market day, when the town would be filled with the maximum number of people. Guernica was on the Nationalist army's line of march to Bilbao, the important industrial center of the Basque country. It was without defenses or military significance, but it was important as the ancient center of Basque culture.

The bombardment lasted approximately three hours and a quarter, during which aircraft unceasingly dropped an assortment of state-of-the-art German bombs, a good number of which were aluminum incendiary devices. In the midst of this firestorm from above, Heinkel fighters dropped from the skies and machine-gunned terrified civilians who ran through the streets and fields for shelter.

"The whole town of 7000 inhabitants, plus 3000 refugees, was slowly and systematically pounded to pieces. Over a radius of five miles round a detail of the raiders' technique was to bomb separate *caseríos,* or farmhouses. In the night these burned like little candles in the hills."

The above was part of the report of that day's events cabled by George Lowther Steer to the *Times* of London. The paper's correspondent had arrived in Guernica from Bilbao on the night of 26 April. The story was reproduced in the *New York Times* on April 28. Steer was known as a superbly accurate and responsible observer, whose account of the tragedy remains a classic of reporting.[34] Steer described a town that was nearly completely engulfed in flames, the reflections of which could be seen in clouds some ten miles away.[35]

The assault on Guernica represented something entirely new in military history: the terror bombing by air of civilians. It appears to have been deliberately engineered to break the morale of the Basque population so that Nationalist forces could take Bilbao more easily. The symbolic significance of the event was captured by Don Luigi Sturzo, who presciently observed a short while later that

> ... in the past such bombardments were tolerated because they were not prominently in view. From now on, the history of future wars, in speaking of aerial bombings, will refer to Guernica as now one refers to the Lusitania, in speaking of torpedoing by submarines.[36]

George Steer's report on the events in Guernica was corroborated by two other British reporters and a Belgian journalist present in the town on the night of 26 April, who sent similar descriptions to their respective papers. It is noteworthy that Steer's report originally appeared in the *Times,* a conservative newspaper sympathetic to the Nationalist cause and one whose owner had been lobbying for a better understanding between Britain and Germany. There also were more than a hundred survivors who told essentially the same story. Among these eyewitnesses were the mayor of the town and some nine Basque priests, including Canon Alberto Onaindia of Valladolid, a man of "unchallengeable veracity,"[37] who sent their accounts to the pope. These stories were further confirmed by field research undertaken in Guernica by the historian Hugh Thomas in 1959.[38]

The news from Guernica quickly became a public relations disaster for the Nationalists, since the truth of the affair would give the lie to their claim that Franco's cause was a sacred one, a holy war to save Catholic Spain and Western civilization from Marxism. The task of holding back the rising tide of world outrage fell to Luis Bolín, whose office in Salamanca controlled information in the Nationalist zone. Bolín had always been overzealous as Chief of the Press Services of Nationalist Headquarters, a title and position which seems to have become his, at least in part, as a reward for having arranged Franco's flight from the Canaries to Morocco.[39] As we have seen, Bolín's methods of censorship had made him widely loathed by foreign journalists. His style was to bully newsmen, making it known that he would have them shot for "transgressions" in reporting. For example, the Count of Alba, who took orders from Bolín, told the American journalist John T. Whitaker that he was not to venture anywhere around Nationalist lines without permission from headquarters: "The next time you're unescorted to the front, we'll shoot you. We'll say that you were a casualty to enemy action. Do you understand?"[40]

In matters concerning the press, Bolín and his associates were guided by at least three imperatives: the conflict must be seen as a holy crusade; it must be portrayed as strictly a Spanish affair; and no mention could be made of the existence of foreign troops, especially German and Italian. For a time their strong-armed methods brought results: few newsmen working in the Nationalist zone dared write of massacres, or, for a good while at least, of the presence of Germans and Italians.[41] Even after leaving Spain they did not speak out for fear that those reporters who remained would pay the price of their indiscretions.[42]

Bolín crafted the initial denial of Nationalist responsibility for the Guernica bombing,[43] and the explanation stuck. On 27 April *Radio Nacional* at Salamanca issued a sharp response entitled "*Mentiras, mentiras y mentiras*" ("Lies, Lies, Lies"). Franco's government claimed that there were no German or foreign aviators working for the Nationalists, and that Nationalist planes could not have bombed Guernica because the weather that day was too inclement for flight.[44] Guernica, claimed *Radio Nacional,* was burned not by bombs from the air but by arsonists on the ground, who, in fleeing, did not want to leave anything of value for the advancing Nationalist army. Salamanca offered no evidence for such charges. There certainly were no Nationalist officials who could have investigated the matter: the so-called "official" statement was given a day after the bombing of Guernica and two days before the Nationalist army entered the city. Not long after this, however, the Nationalists began to contradict themselves, admitting that bombs may have been dropped (the craters left behind could not be ignored—the thousand-pound bombs made holes twenty-five feet deep) but claiming that Guernica, in any case, was of considerable military significance because of its strategic railway connections and armament factories.

The explosive public outrage in Britain over the fire bombing of Guernica panicked the Friends of Nationalist Spain and galvanized them to action. Bolín, dismayed at the way the foreign press was making hay with Guernica, paid a personal visit to Franco. Through his efforts the Duke of Alba was appointed Franco's special agent in London. Alba, said Bolín, was as much at home in England as Spain. He had weight and influence, knew the right people, had entrée everywhere, and was well "qualified to speak for us in the right quarters."[45] Douglas Jerrold quickly emerged as the general spokesman of authority on the Guernica affair for the Nationalists. Jerrold served as the "visible commander" of the Guernica myth-makers, but behind him stood the furtive but steady hand of the Marquis del Moral.[46] Others who joined the fray as leading propagandists were Arnold Lunn and Sir Henry Page Croft. The ensuing counterattack—according to one who received its harshest blows, the newsman who broke the story for the *Times,* George Lowther Steer—represented "some of the most horrible and inconsistent lying heard by Christian ears since Ananias."[47]

After visiting Nationalist Spain in March 1937, Jerrold, General J. F. C. Fuller, and Major Francis Yeats-Brown dedicated themselves to legitimizing Franco's endeavors. Their chief objective was to discredit the Republican position on Guernica. Jerrold admitted that

Guernica was bombed "intermittently" by the Germans (he claimed that there were military imperatives for doing so), but that the damage was minimal. Jerrold essentially provided a reiteration of Bolín's thesis. The massive destruction was the result of the Basques burning their own town. Why?

> The 'incident' would stiffen the resistance of the Catholic Basques. It would influence neutral opinion; strengthen the attitude of the British government in regard to the blockade of Bilbao and possibly even lead to its abandonment.[48]

In order to substantiate his arguments that Guernica was fire-bombed by the retreating Basques, Jerrold appears to have distorted the words of correspondents who observed the bombing in Guernica and made false accusations about Steer's testimony.[49]

In the end, Bolín's and Jerrold's account became the Catholic Right's official version of the Guernica affair. Variations on this theme (complete with contradictions) were repeated regularly by such writers as Arnold Lunn, Arthur Bryant, Major Yeats-Brown, and Sir Henry Page Croft in England, and by a variety of influential American Catholics, including, among others, Father Joseph F. Thorning, Wilfrid Parsons, S.J., and Father Joseph B. Code.[50] Reflecting back on these tortured, casuistic arguments, Herbert Rutledge Southworth, author of the definitive work on Guernica, remarked that "it seems incredible that they were proposed by rational persons."[51]

The tragic events in Spain and the unmitigated violence against civilians and clergy on both sides were the apotheosis of Jacques Maritain's political prognostications. The cause of justice and humanity was overridden because both adversaries had succumbed to the ideology of dictatorial complexes, neither of which was compatible with Christian values. The Nationalists' program of terror against civilians and the totalitarian aspirations of their political order convinced Maritain and several other French Catholic intellectuals to actively campaign against the idea of Franco's "holy war."

It is important, however, to appreciate the fact that Maritain's campaign against the Spanish Civil War was also driven by his analysis of a fundamental weakness in modern industrial social structure of which capitalism was the central framework. According to Maritain's humanistic vision, the good society provided for the basic needs of the masses, assuring them of the right to work and fundamental spiritual satisfaction. The social significance of this humanism, wrote Maritain, was that it "should assume the task of radically transforming the temporal order, a task which would tend to substitute for bourgeois civilization, and for an economic system based on the fecundity of money, not a collectivist economy, but a 'personalistic' civilization and a 'personalistic' economy, through which would stream a temporal refraction of the truths of the Gospel."[52] Maritain's condemnation of capitalism as an amoral economic system and, by extension, a source of trouble for Spain became yet another reason for the thunderous criticism brought down on him by conservative Catholics who had embraced the economic and political establishment.[53] In Maritain's mind, the Spanish Civil War was emblematic of conditions preventing the emergence of a Christian social order. In Spain, the Church itself had seemed increasingly aligned with the capitalist status quo.

The events which had the most decisive impact on Maritain and his associates were the bombing of Guernica and the testimony of Canon Onaindia, who personally witnessed the catastrophe. On 8 May 1937 two Catholic dailies in Paris published a manifesto signed by numerous eminent Catholic intellectuals protesting the bombing and requesting an immediate end to the killing of non-combatants.[54] Soon after this Maritain and his friends formed the Committee for Civil and Religious Peace in Spain, an organization of people who pledged to work for an end to the Civil War. The effort was encouraged and sponsored by Cardinal Jean Verdier, the archbishop of Paris. The group had several objectives: it sought to help Catholics on the Loyalist side restore public worship; to mitigate the suffering brought on by the war; to protect the civilian population from harsh reprisals once one side found victory; and to influence international public opinion and governments toward finding a peaceful solution to the conflict in such a way as to allow the Spanish people the opportunity to live in freedom and dignity. The Committee made contacts with Catholic members of the Loyalist government and Basque leaders in order to help them obtain relief from anti-religious measures.

Jacques Maritain made it a special point to speak out against those who depicted the events in Spain as a holy crusade for Christianity. He asserted that the very concept of a holy war only had meaning in a sacral civilization where the entire focus of life was religious. Such an ethos had disappeared with the waning of the Middle Ages. Modern man's orientation was now secular, not sacred, and his entire energies were concentrated on independence, freedom, and other such concerns of the temporal realm. In short, the direction of modern living was not "Godward" but pragmatic. It was contemporary man's independence from, rather than dependence upon, God that motivated his behavior.[55] Any attempt to carry the principle of holy war into secular, political squabbles could only result in making religion subservient to Mammon. Therefore, the notion of a Christian crusade could have no meaning whatsoever in a civilization that had become profane.[56]

Maritain and his supporters believed that the emotive language of those who spoke of a holy crusade and who called down fire and brimstone on the Reds had the effect of both sowing hatred and inflaming the kind of passions that encouraged extremist behavior. This helped escalate the fratricidal violence and closed the door to any solutions requiring dispassionate, diplomatic compromise. Luigi Sturzo, for instance, argued that it was the "first duty" of responsible officials in the Church to eliminate the religious factor from the war motives in Spain, for not only was such a claim un-Christian (it was, said he, "entirely Mohammedan"), but it would arouse "in the name of religion the worst instincts of slaughter and extermination."[57]

The fiery propaganda of holy war certainly contributed to the terror of Nationalist repression. For its part the Republican government tried to throttle unauthorized violence against the Church and clergy carried out by anarchists and others. Although such violence had largely stopped by the end of 1936, sporadic violence against the clergy did continue throughout the Civil War in the Republican zone. Both sides were guilty of pursuing a policy of physically liquidating their enemies. Yet on the Nationalist side the tempo of killing and terror was more systematic, and it actually increased as time went on, accelerating even further when the war was over. The Spanish clergy, caught up in the maelstrom of a crusade mentality, at no point questioned the necessity of this systematic purge.[58] Why would they have done otherwise, when Cardinal Gomá, in his first public pronouncement on the war while celebrating the relief of the Alcázar, claimed that the day had arrived "on which Jews and Masons . . . threaten the national soul with absurd doctrines, with Tartar and Mongol ideas" and with a political and social system "manipulated by the Semitic International."[59]

Maritain's views on the Spanish conflict found corroboration from an unlikely quarter: the outspoken Catholic royalist, Georges Bernanos.[60] Bernanos and Maritain had fallen out with one another over the former's anti-Semitism and disagreements concerning the Church's condemnation of *Action Française*. Bernanos intrinsically reviled democracy and was the *bête noir* of liberal Catholics. It would be hard to find a more militant or reactionary Catholic than Bernanos.[61] In 1934 he moved his family to Spanish Majorca, partly to escape the deadening hand of bourgeois liberalism which he saw overtaking French urban life. Bernanos had a profound attraction to the medieval, mystical quality of Spanish Catholicism, which, for him, seemed to hold firm against a world rapidly falling under the sway of capitalism and communism. Before the generals' coup, Bernanos did not hide his fascist sympathies and violent feelings about what should be done to those responsible for the disorders of Spain. His former friend Francisco Ferrari Billoch pointed out that Bernanos advocated a root-and-branch change for Spain. Bernanos, wrote Billoch, "was not in favour of a *coup d'état* which would confine itself to removing the *Frente Popular* from power; but, on the contrary, he favored a complete revolution which would last long enough for all the whole Communist class to be shot—yes, shot."[62] At the beginning of the Nationalist revolt, Bernanos's son had become a lieutenant with the Falangist forces, fighting, in his father's view, a just war against the materialism and hypocrisy of the antichrist.

As a resident of Majorca Bernanos soon became an eye-witness to one of the many savage sideshows of the Civil War. Majorca was occupied by Nationalist and Italian forces without any resistance. The reprisals that began after their arrival deeply shocked and repelled Bernanos. The population of Majorca, Bernanos had earlier observed, was generally indifferent to politics. There were no factories, hence the absence of a significant working-class movement; even the head of the Majorcan Falange admitted that one could not find a hundred communists on the whole island.[63] The ensuing campaign of terror against countless civilians who were falsely labeled "Reds" laid bare the hypocrisy of a crusade that was supposed to be both nationalist and Christian. The horrible carnal reality of the vicious purgation overturned Bernanos's political views.[64]

Bernanos witnessed Italian units on Majorca, with the aid of local Falangists, "cleaning up" the island by carrying off truckloads of farmers to be shot. His descriptions of these horrors bristled with rage. The peasants had just returned from the fields. Their clothes were still wet from the day's work. Left behind were the evening's soup on the table and a wife who arrived too late at the garden gate. Bernanos noted one ecclesiastical document sanctimoniously reporting that "only ten percent of those dear children refused the last sacraments before being dispatched by our good officers."[65]

It was not simply the killing that so incensed Bernanos. More disturbing was the behavior of the Church authorities in Majorca, who not only failed to speak out against these atrocities but openly and willingly gave their support to them. When the archbishop of Palma, José Miralles y Sbert, was questioned about the Church's position on the use of terror, he replied, wrote Bernanos, that exceptional measures were justified when during the previous year only 14 percent of the population performed their Easter duties.[66] This reign of terror would have long burned itself out, insisted Bernanos, but for the endorsement of priests and churchgoers who gave it religious sanction.

Bernanos's explosive book, *Les Grands Cimetières Sous La Lune* (published in English as *The Diary of My Times*), was more than an exposé of the assassinations in Majorca, which certainly had revolted his conscience and altered his political thinking. Above all, it was an angry protest against the clergy for aiding and abetting the fascist terror against innocent civilians. The Spanish Church, Bernanos announced, failed in its mission as father to the people, as a conciliator and healer. Bernanos described a clergy who, for the sake of expedience, came down swiftly and unequivocally on the side of a dictatorship every bit as evil as communism. He believed this would prove suicidal for the Church, since the alliance with Franco could only lead to a permanent estrangement of the masses from Christianity.

Bernanos's account of events in Majorca was written largely for his right-wing associates in France, who, like himself, had pined for a fascist-type revolution to sweep out the "trash" of liberal democracy. As Thomas Molnar has noted, Bernanos knew the number and names of people on both the Left and Right who were waiting to play the same roles in France. When the war first broke out, Bernanos wrote in his diary that he was grateful to the Lord for having given him the opportunity to witness "a kind of general rehearsal of the universal revolution." But three months later, following the occupation of Majorca, the tone shifted: "Now the hyenas appear on the scene. What follows is not for people like you and me.... A counter-revolution is not at all what the idiots think it is, back in France." By the beginning of 1937 Bernanos wrote that he was in the midst of a nightmare: "I am witnessing a revolution made by the military and the clericalists. It is a disgusting spectacle and it would be hard to imagine so paradoxical a mixture of cynicism and hypocrisy."[67]

Like Maritain and others who had recognized the hypocrisy of "holy war" from afar, Bernanos, having personally experienced the fires of civil war, discovered that his beloved medieval and mystical Spanish Church had forsaken the common man and tied its cause to that of the privileged classes and their brutal right-wing protectors. Whereas Hilaire Belloc and his circle had viewed the Spanish Civil War as a struggle for the survival of European Christianity—after all, claimed Belloc, "Europe is the faith, and the faith is Europe"—Bernanos saw something else: "Christianity has been the making of Europe. Christianity is dead. And therefore Europe must die too."[68]

Conservative Catholics and those associated with the political right launched a vigorous assault against the critics of Franco's crusade.[69] One of the early casualties of this campaign was the liberal journal *Sept*, which had dedicated itself to the promotion of social reform and democratic, pluralistic forms of social organization.

From its inception in March 1934 *Sept* had applied Maritain's political principles to the Spanish Civil War and had urged Catholics to take a position of neutrality on the conflict. The magazine was forced to close down under orders of the Holy Office in Rome because its Dominican editor, Reverend Bernadot, refused to support the pro-Franco position advocated by the anticommunist papal secretary of state, Cardinal Pacelli.[70] The rise of Pacelli, the future Pope Pius XII, meant the increasing domination of conservative clerics in the Vatican. In August 1937 the Holy Office formally recognized Franco as head of the legitimate government of Spain, and a papal nuncio was sent to his capital. One of Pacelli's first acts when elevated to the papacy was the lifting of his predecessor's ban on *Action Française*.

Jacques Maritain became the chief target of the Right's attack. He was identified as the ringleader of muddleheaded and disloyal Catholics ("chrétiens rouges," as the French right-wing press called them) who strayed from what the Right regarded as a Vatican party line. Such voices of criticism had contacts with reactionary elements in the Vatican, and the general effect of their denunciation was to engender a hostile climate of suspicion against independent thinking in the conservative Catholic press throughout Europe and the Americas. Some of these sources gave the impression that Maritain's anti-Francoism was the product of insidious Jewish influence.[71]

In Britain the attack on Maritain and recusant Catholic attitudes on Spain was spearheaded by Reginald Dingle, who was given a prominent forum in the Jesuit journal, *The Month*. A distinctive feature of the Catholic Right's attack on their co-religionists was a resolute refusal to assess the allegation of Nationalist terror against civilians. Dingle in his articles, for example, made vague passing references to the "lurid accounts of Guernica" but insisted that the "comfortable theory" concerning atrocities committed by both sides could not stand up to serious analysis.[72] Dingle never bothered to examine the facts himself, instead preferring to fall back on the so-called "unimpeachable testimony" of the Spanish bishops' joint letter to the "Bishops of the World."

This letter was published in July 1937 at the request of the Nationalist government in Burgos to convince international Catholic opinion that Franco's rebellion was justified on religious grounds.

Cardinal Gomá was given the task of writing the document, an undertaking he willingly accepted given his strong anticommunist sentiments. The signatories explained that since 1931 the Republic, with Bolshevik aid, had engineered a legislative revolution to eradicate the traditional framework of Spanish culture. The Comintern ultimately assumed a more direct role in this effort when it armed "a revolutionary militia to seize power." The bishops claimed to have "irrefutable" documentary evidence of a communist coup in Spain (documents the British Foreign Office determined were forgeries). Thus Franco's military revolt was a justified response to a conspiracy to destroy religion in Spain. It was a "civic-military" venture by the best-qualified civilians and military leaders carried out primarily to preserve the Church and the basic national traditions of Spain.[73]

Contrary to Nationalist propaganda, the joint letter did not express the unanimous opinions of the Spanish bishops. Two episcopal signatures were notably missing, those of the cardinal-archbishop of Tarragona, Francesc Vidal i Barraquer, and Mateo Múgica, the bishop of Vitoria in the Basque country. Both were in exile because of persecution by communists but refused to sign the letter. The Bishop of Vitoria had defended the Basque priests against Franco's purges and had made the awkward accusation that there was no religious freedom in Nationalist Spain. A number of Catholics abroad were also distressed by the Spanish bishops' allegation that the Basque leaders were blinded by narrow sectarian political interests, and that they had taken the side of communism against Catholicism. This assessment, as Luigi Sturzo pointed out, had failed to take into account the fact that the Nationalists and various parties of the Spanish Right had refused to recognize the historic rights of the Basques.[74]

The credibility of the bishops' letter was further compromised by the political associations of the moving force behind the document, Cardinal Gomá. Long before the military revolt the Cardinal had waxed ebullient on his affections for Mussolini and Hitler. In a 1934 speech in Buenos Aires, for example, he had urged his audience to cast its eyes reverently to the old world, for "over the sea which has interred the democracies, stand forth the summits of the dictatorships."[75] Gomá's subsequent writings and radio broadcasts revealed a fixation with leftist conspiracies: Freemasons, Jews, and communists, he claimed, were out to destroy Spain.

The Catholic Right validated its interpretation of the Spanish Civil War by drawing on the "irrefutable truth" of the collective letter to the "Bishops of the World," which in itself was a highly partisan and polemical political document, written primarily to link the Church with Spanish nationalism as defined by Franco. By casting this letter in the rubric of episcopal approval and in the context of the universality of Catholic principles, the supporters of Franco could argue that there was no need to give the causes of the Civil War further analysis. In short, the bishops' letter precluded the necessity of examining the issues for oneself.[76] Reginald Dingle criticized Maritain for an ivory-tower approach to politics, far removed from the everyday realities that informed the Spanish bishops:

> . . . all that he has written on the Spanish issue confirms the impression that a long sojourn in the realm of pure ideas may lead to an imperfect appreciation of facts and to a failure to give them their due importance in contingent matters, with which politics is mainly concerned.[77]

Yet, in the same essay in which he charged that Maritain was insufficiently engaged, Dingle made the curious assertion that although the conduct of Franco could be evaluated only in light of all the facts, it was not a Catholic's responsibility to pass judgment on such matters. Instead, in Dingle's line of thinking, Catholics had a religious responsibility to support the Nationalist cause. It would appear that the stalwart crusader should suspend moral judgment concerning complex social and political issues, for the die already had been cast; the overriding religious dimension was fixed, once the proper authorities determined that Russia via the Popular Front had decided to extirpate Catholicism from Spain. This was at the core of Dingle's attacks on Maritain, and was repeated in similar form by all other such critics. The "philosopher mystic," as Dingle called him, failed to "see the facts for the general principles"; the "principle" in this case was Maritain's refusal to become a partisan in a struggle which Dingle's "facts" had established as purely religious.[78]

Since the war in Spain was a crusade, there could be no room for dissent. The point was clarified for the confused by Douglas Woodruff's *The Tablet,* which printed a theological defence of Franco by Salamanca University Dominicans: "resistance to the Popular Front is not only right and lawful but also obligatory—a holy war."[79] Joseph Keating, S.J., editor of *The Month,* could write of his surprise at the liberty the Church permitted French Catholics who opposed the idea of a Nationalist crusade, since to challenge it and even to attack fascism could be seen as an assault on the Church itself.[80] The Nationalists, wrote Keating, were courageously fighting off "an unholy alliance of Jews, Freemasons and atheists, but we Catholics can give them the support of our sympathy and prayers."[81] Reginald Dingle, for his part, did not mince words when he described the folly of the recusants: all notable French Catholics who opposed the White Crusade were unbalanced and aberrant, hovering on the "dangerous edge" of heresy.[82] Even Christopher Dawson, a supporter of Franco, came under fire as editor of the *Dublin Review* for not sufficiently echoing the Catholic Right's united front on Franco as the "last Crusader." Dawson's boss, Douglas Jerrold, was greatly annoyed at Dawson's decision to publish articles on Maritain and Bernanos. Jerrold eventually ousted his former mentor from the editorial chair in a maneuver that was anything but pretty.[83]

This crusading mind-set meant that Georges Bernanos's *Les Grands Cimetiéres Sous La Lune* would be greeted with the venom of vipers. Adding to this poisonous mix was the bitterness of right-wing Catholics who had already become suspicious of Bernanos's "orthodoxy" when he had turned against *Action Française* in the mid-1930s. Maurras' paper launched the campaign against "the traitor Bernanos" when it published a letter condemning his book, written by the archbishop of Parma, whom Bernanos had singled out as the quintessential evil Churchman for having aided and abetted the Nationalist atrocities in Majorca. It is important to point out that few, if any, rightist responses to Bernanos's book bothered to analyze the serious charges he brought against the Church's complicity in the terror. In fact, in the United States there was some hesitation in the Catholic press to even mention the book.[84] *The Month* labeled *Les Grands Cimetiéres Sous La Lune* "shallow in its Catholicity, violent and ill-balanced," but the magazine had nothing to say about the issues it raised.[85] *The Tablet,* without a single word about the book's central arguments, simply said that there was nothing in the conduct of the Nationalists to justify its author's abusive comparisons of the "hypothetical massacres of the 'poor' as Marxists with the all too real massacres of priests."[86]

The Month was one of the few Catholic publications in Britain to give Bernanos's book the lengthy review it deserved. However, the reviewer, James Broderick, unleashed a polemical diatribe against Bernanos, discussing virtually nothing of the book's thesis. As to the three thousand or so civilians Bernanos claimed were murdered by Nationalists and Italians, Broderick could only say that more evidence was needed, especially since Bernanos himself was like a chameleon (he turned his back first on *Action Française* and then on Franco), changing his color from one page to the next. The thrust of Broderick's review was that Bernanos represented a twentieth-century version of the Roman Tertullian, a soul-destroying, puritanical fanatic whose self-righteous Christian bullying pushed him into the heresy of Montanism. Like Tertullian, Bernanos's call for honesty, fairmindedness, and compassion presumably was demanding too much of Christians. Broderick rejected Bernanos's charges (without articulating what they were for his readers) and called the book a nightmarish fantasy. Without mustering a single shred of evidence to substantiate his argument, and rejecting out of hand Bernanos's eyewitness testimony, Broderick could write that it was an open question whether the Nationalist authorities were excessively draconian in their administration of justice on Majorca.[87]

I I

In Britain and America the Christian crusaders for Franco were challenged by a small but intellectually significant minority of Catholic journals and newspapers. The two best known in Britain were the quarterly *Dublin Review* (which opened its pages to the views of Don Luigi Sturzo) and *Blackfriars,* the English Dominican monthly.[88] In the United States the only major Catholic journal to resist the crusaders was *Commonweal*, and its decision to do so produced a serious internal conflict and a precipitous decline in readership.[89]

Blackfriars attempted to replicate in England the work of the French Dominicans, who assiduously opposed European fascism on Thomistic grounds from its very inception. As regards Spain, its Dominican editors recognized that the problems were too complex to be caused by communism alone and pointed out that if the Spanish Church had taken seriously the messages of papal labor encyclicals, there might well have been no civil war.[90] What especially concerned *Blackfriars* was an issue largely ignored by its British Catholic counterparts (*The Tablet*, *The Month*, the *Universe*, the *Catholic Times*, *G.K.'s Weekly*, and the *Weekly Review*): the political turpitude of those states that came to the aid of Franco. Might not this make the remedy of fascism to save Christianity worse than the disease? *Blackfriars* noted that with the exception of the first outburst of anti-religious terror against the clergy, which was largely beyond the control of the Azaña government, Hitler's persecution of the Church and its servants was every bit as evil as the policies of anticlerical groups who supported the Republic. *Blackfriars* urged Catholics not to confuse two distinctly different kinds of anticommunism: that of the pagan, hate-inspired Nazis, whose policies were scarcely less poisonous than Bolshevism itself, and that of Christianity.[91]

Blackfriars's anti-fascism did not go unchallenged by Catholics on the right. Bernard Wall in the *Colosseum*, for example, who was a good friend of Father Victor White, O.S.B., the paper's editor, considered *Blackfriars*'s condemnation of fascism too sweeping and extreme. Essentially, argued Wall, democracy and liberalism were at least as dangerous and anti-Catholic as Mussolini's brand of politics.[92] Donald Attwater, in support of *Blackfriars*'s position, wrote that Christian anti-Bolshevism fights its enemy by understanding and removing the social and economic factors that cause people to embrace communism in the first place. The causes of communism, emphasized Attwater, cannot be fought with the politics of the Right. They can only be fought with true religion: "One of the gravest dangers is that religious people allow themselves to be thrown by communist violence and success into the arms of opposite parties in which Christians should not be found."[93] On the other hand, Douglas Woodruff's *The Tablet* disagreed: the Church certainly does have sympathy and good will for Fascism, it confidently asserted, just as she does for democracy.[94]

Blackfriars's approach to the issues of Spain and fascism was supported by an association of English Catholics and other like-minded Christians who, under the direction of Virginia Crawford (a pupil of Cardinal Manning and admirer of Frédéric Ozanam),[95] formed in 1936 the "People and Freedom Group" and launched a paper, *People and Freedom*. Crawford's association sought to educate youth in the principles of Christian democracy. Its mottoes were *Magna est Veritas et Praevalebit* against the lying propaganda of fascists, and *Fiat Justitia* in opposition to Britain's appeasement policy toward the dictators. The People and Freedom Group immediately declared its opposition to the Spanish Civil War and, in alliance with the Maritain circle, formed an English branch of the Paris-based Committee for Civil and Religious Peace in Spain. Its purpose was to work for conciliation between both sides in the Civil War and to prevent a fascist-style dictatorship from coming into power.[96]

One of the most prudent and objective English commentators on the issue of Spain was Father Gerald Vann, O.P., founder of the Union of Prayer for Peace and a professor at the Dominican Blackfriar's School. A neo-Thomist in the tradition of Maritain, Father Vann, like Don Luigi Sturzo, recognized the impossibility of disentangling religion from the social, political, and economic factors behind the Spanish Civil War. Vann cautioned Catholics about reducing the struggle to issues of mere religion. "To simplify is to falsify," wrote Vann, for the conflict also involved issues of class, regional autonomy, and political philosophies, the complexities of which made it impossible to sort the warring sides into neat categories of good and evil. Catholics who refused to recognize such facts, claimed Vann, had falsified the issue and, in doing so, caused the Church to be identified with a position contrary to the teachings of Christ. Although it seemed natural to support the side that identified with the faith, not many considered what sort of Catholic Spain might emerge from the conflict. What were the implications for the new order when the Right had savaged the Catholic Basques and refused to accept the teaching of the social encyclicals? Pro-Franco Catholics in a tempest of rage had forsaken critical reasoning for a "one-track" religious crusade: *la colère des imbèciles remplit le monde.*" Not content with this, the Catholic Right, lamented Vann, had gone on to denounce all those who refused to share such simple-mindedness and *colère* as traitors to the faith. In so doing the Catholic defenders of Franco had fallen into the same mind-set as that of the Left, which identified everything emanating from the Nationalists as reactionary and fascist. It is not possible for Catholics, claimed Vann, to sell the truth to political expediency without paying for the treason of allying with the enemies of Christ.[97]

Gerald Vann's jeremiads dovetailed with the assessment of Catholicism's most experienced critic of fascism, Don Luigi Sturzo. Writing in the *Dublin Review* (January 1937), Sturzo likened the Christian crusade in Spain to the folly of the nineteenth-century Holy Alliance, which had been opposed by Pope Pius VII for essentially the same reasons that the Vatican remained aloof from the Spanish affair. Sturzo recognized that the Church's aims might run parallel at times with the policies of particular rulers and political movements, but these aims should never be identified completely with secular affairs; in order to give its full weight to spiritual problems the Church must be freed from political entanglements that would have the effect of subordinating religious issues to secular ends.

It would be especially unwise, said Sturzo, for the Church to identify herself with totalitarian regimes simply because they were directed by Catholic rulers. This would require accepting responsibility for the state's oppression of dissenting populations and, equally immoral, associating a sacred institution with the profane myths (of race, class, empire, nationality, and so forth) which are the *raison d'être* of such regimes. The Church, insisted Sturzo, must pursue the same policy followed in the previous century when she maintained her autonomy above the political forms of liberalism, democracy, and socialism.[98]

Sturzo had been diligent in his efforts to expose the hypocrisy of Hitler's and Mussolini's version of the Christian crusade against communism. As he demonstrated in numerous articles over the years, their own anti-Soviet policies were adapted to ends that had nothing to do with religion. Hitler's anticommunist campaign was clearly bogus, since the Nazis had several friendly agreements with Russia prior to 1935, shifting gears only after a treaty had been drawn up between Russia and France. Even more duplicitous was Mussolini's anticommunism. Fascist Italy had a long record of friendly relations with Moscow, distinguishing itself as the first Western state to recognize Lenin's government. Sturzo also noted that Moscow was the first nation to support the withdrawal of sanctions after Italy's invasion of Abyssinia. In short, modern states established their policies on the basis of national interests, and to support dictatorships because of their publicly-stated religious policies was both foolish and dangerous. Contemporary dictators simply used religion to legitimize political and cultural objectives that were inherently un-Christian.[99]

Sturzo fully accepted Jacques Maritain's analysis of the troubles in Spain as well as his solution to the problems of Church-state relations as outlined in *Integral Humanism* (1936). Like Maritain, Sturzo in his writings criticized the notion that the conflict in Spain was essentially religious. Religion, as Sturzo labored to point out, was originally a subsidiary issue, although it became a central part of the Right's justification for overthrowing the Republican government. In fact, the Insurgents' *pronunciamiento* made no mention of religion, and even General Emilio Mola, one of the leading conspirators, was slow in adopting the jargon of the "cruzada." Apparently, he did so only after the Spanish Church encouraged the idea.[100] The generals' main justification for rebellion was the necessity of challenging the basic tenets of the French Revolution, which the conservative officers believed were being replicated by the Republican government. The religious motive certainly served to sustain the Nationalist cause, but the matters that substantially divided the two sides were political and social. The case of the Basques proved the point. In general, wrote Sturzo, the lines of demarcation were not absolute. Many Spaniards had to work through the issues on the bases of conscience, class, and geographical interests. In any case, the depiction of the Spanish conflict as a "holy war," claimed Sturzo, was blasphemous and contrary to Christian doctrine. The concept was Islamic: the "Jihad" meant an armed conquest for the faith of Mohammed in which the kingdom of God would be established through the physical destruction of every other religion.[101]

Finally, Sturzo, along with Maritain and his friends, challenged the Catholic Right's defense of the *pronunciamiento* on the grounds of a "just war." In their attempts to establish an interdenominational coalition against communism in Spain, the United Christian Front Committee in Great Britain, for example, had cited St. Thomas's writings on civil disobedience as a justification of Franco's war against the Republic.[102]

Much of the groundwork on this question had been done in France. In 1925 Charles Maurras was prosecuted for threatening to assassinate the minister of the interior. His organization, *Action Française,* had also advocated the forcible overthrow of the anti-clerical Republican government. Out of this developed a public discussion regarding the right to resist unjust laws and tyrannical government. The Jesuit review *Etudes* gathered a number of opinions from jurists, philosophers, and theologians on the matter, and Père Michel Riquet published them under the title *Enquête sur les Droits du Droit et Sa Majesté la Loi.* Père Riquet concluded that from Déguit to St. Thomas, from Locke to Bellarmine, there had been common agreement that one may use violence to oppose the execution of unjust law. But action of this kind must be measured by the demands of the common good. This position had already been underlined by Pope Leo XIII in his letter to the French bishops in February 1892 concerning Catholics and the French Republic. Acceptance of the new government, he asserted, "is not only permitted, but demanded . . . by the necessity of the social weal which has made them and maintains them." This duty would persist, he added, "so long as the exigencies of the common good demanded it, since in society this good is, after God, the first and last law."[103]

The central question regarding justified rebellion concerned cases in which the "exigencies of the common good" might no longer demand public support. This problem was examined carefully in the encyclical *Nos es muy,* issued by Pius XI in September 1932, addressing the religious problem in Mexico. Here, for the first time, a modern pope drew a distinction between an unjust and just rebellion against civil authority. In this encyclical Pius XI asserted that the citizenry had the right to defend their freedoms through "lawful and appropriate" means (that is to say, by means not intrinsically bad), but such actions should be proportionate to the end and employed in such a manner as to save the community from greater evils than those they sought to remedy.[104]

In Sturzo's view, the conditions established in *Nos es muy* regarding means and ends were not sufficient to justify the *pronunciamiento*. In Spain, Sturzo asserted, there was no fundamental Christian moral standoff between citizens and tyrant but rather a conflict between two sections of one people each determined to destroy the other. The affair was inherently secular and therefore did not fit the Christian moral imperatives governing legitimacy of rebellion.[105] Religion was certainly a factor in the Spanish Civil War, but Sturzo believed it was blown entirely out of proportion in the "impassioned atmosphere" of the "frenzied religious persecutions" of the early stages of the rebellion, thereby obscuring the more central social, economic, and political issues.[106] A certain religious criticism is not unfounded, he insisted, "but it is too general."[107]

Sturzo's position was echoed in many other Catholic quarters as well. Maritain, for example, noted that rather than improving the status quo—one of the imperatives of the "just war"—the *pronunciamiento* had led to the intervention of foreign forces and the murders of thousands of innocent people on both sides. The psychological and political damage would not heal for generations:

> Think of the priests slain, the nuns outraged. . . . Think of the women and children slaughtered by aerial bombardments. . . . Think of the cities of Spain—among the noblest of cities—which have become proving grounds for international air forces. Picture the exhaustion of the country, the immense damage, physical and moral . . . the accumulation of hatred and bitterness amassed on both sides, the despair of so many souls. And tell me what good one can expect from such a civil war and its pitiless prolongation.[108]

Pope Pius XI on 14 September 1936 in his address to Spanish exiles warned of the danger of allowing party interests to cloud the morality of their actions. In subsequent statements regarding the conflict in Spain the Vatican offered nothing to suggest a crusade or holy war. In fact, there is sufficient evidence to suggest that Pope Pius XI wished Catholics to follow a policy of neutrality on the civil war in Spain.[109] Several influential Catholic organs in France, Germany, Belgium, and Switzerland also rejected the *pronunciamiento* as a justified response to civil tyranny.[110] It is worthy of note that in more recent times Pope John Paul II has publicly denounced the idea of religious war. In his welcoming address to the assembly of the World Conference on Religion and Peace in the Vatican City on 3 November 1994, John Paul II said that killing or waging war in the name of religion was a blatant contradiction: "No one can consider himself faithful to the great and merciful God who in the name of the same God dares to kill his brother."[111]

Sturzo gave the lie to the accolades offered Franco in his role as a latter-day El Cid, an image carefully cultivated by the dictator and willingly devoured by his sycophantic rightist Catholic supporters. Nor did he regard Franco as the pure fascist that the Left made him out to be. In reality, Franco was never loyal to either the creed of fascism or the creed of Catholicism; he only used their nomenclature, enthusiasms, and some of their programs to solidify his own personal power. Sturzo concluded that in the final analysis it all made little difference, for

> if we call it Fascism or Communism, though each be placed at the opposite ends of the arch of a pendulum, they have the same impulses, the same fundamental concepts, namely: the spirit of violence and the use of force as a means to acquire and maintain power, the subordination of the legal rights and moral values of the human personality to the interests of the State, the loss, be it gradual or violent, of Liberty![112]

III

The outbreak of civil war in July 1936 prompted Francis X. Talbot, S.J., editor of the influential Jesuit magazine *America*, to call a meeting of New York's Catholic editors to discuss whether a common position should be taken on the Spanish conflict. At this meeting, to which Talbot had invited an agent of Franco's government, the managing editor of *Commonweal,* George Shuster, suggested that it would be prudent to gather additional information; he proposed inviting Gil Robles, the leader of the Catholic Party who was presently in exile and soon to arrive in New York, to address the group regarding what should or should not be done by the Catholic Press. Shuster believed that his recommendation was accepted, but it soon became clear that Talbot felt confident enough concerning the issues to launch his own campaign for Franco. Although Shuster thought that Talbot had been "pressured" into making propaganda for the Insurgents,[113] the Jesuit's monarchist inclinations and close contacts with certain individuals of the Spanish Right would have swung *America* into the battle on Franco's side in any case. Father Talbot seems to have been a bit of a romantic concerning Spain, and, according to Shuster, he was more suited by training and disposition to write poetry than to discuss political affairs.[114]

America's initial response to the crisis in Spain was considerably searching. Its editorials cited the social failures of the old regime as a major source of the troubles. Problems spawned by land monopolies and absentee landlords, together with the poverty and ignorance of peasants and workers, were all analyzed as the results of the apathy and greed of an entrenched Spanish ruling class. The only way to ameliorate the communist menace that these conditions encouraged, claimed the editor of *America,* was to eliminate the social misery on which it fed. This could be accomplished only in a society organized along Christian lines.[115] However, soon after the *pronunciamiento,* following directly on the heels of the meeting of Catholic editors summoned by Father Talbot, *America* came out solidly in favor of Franco and the Insurgents. Irrespective of what kind of regime the Right might create, claimed Talbot, it could never be as evil as that promised by the Red government currently in power. Those who viewed Franco as reactionary, asserted *America,* were simply "lovers of communism and Sovietism."[116]

George Shuster was surprised by Talbot's rush to judgment and decided to respond in *Commonweal* by warning Catholics of the danger of a fascist victory in Spain. Franco's admiration of Hitler and Mussolini, he feared, might well mean the application of total-itarianism to that country. Fascism, as practiced in Italy and Germany, wrote Shuster, was the antithesis of the social reforms needed in Spain. Although the dictators gave rhetorical service to religion, there was no possibility that fascism would serve Christianity. Thus Catholics should not applaud the rebels: "The lessons of history are too plain for that."[117]

Commonweal was deluged with irate letters charging the editor with giving aid and comfort to the enemies of the Church. Yet these were trifling compared to the outburst of anger resulting from *Commonweal's* publication of an article by Barbara Barclay Carter, an English Catholic journalist and translator of Don Luigi Sturzo, outlining how European Catholics viewed the Spanish conflict. Carter's essay gave credence to Shuster's warnings, pointing out that many influential European Catholics had condemned the idea of a "holy war" in Spain (she noted that the Basques and many supporters of the Popular Front were in fact Catholic) and were deeply fearful of a fascist take-over.[118]

George Shuster's views on the Spanish situation were strongly influenced by his knowledge of what was happening to the Catholic Church in Germany. Shuster had been a careful observer of German affairs, having undertaken two lengthy tours of study in that country, the second of which (1933–34) coincided with the rise of Hitler to power.[119] He was the first American journalist to expose the Nazi war on religion.[120] Disturbed by Hitler's failure to uphold agreements established by the Concordat with the Church, in particular the Nazi ban on Catholic athletic organizations and the regime's anti-Semitic policies, Shuster in 1935 tried to enlist support for a boycott of the 1936 Olympic Games scheduled in Berlin.[121] These efforts were resisted by the archdiocese of New York, however, and without this important institutional support Shuster's plans collapsed.

Shuster was associated with a small group of Catholics in New York who met frequently to discuss the Church's struggles with European fascism. Among these were Heinrich Bruening, the exiled former chancellor of Germany, who was in seclusion under an assumed name at the Immaculate Conception Seminary in Huntington, Long Island,[122] Carleton J. H. Hayes, professor of history at Columbia University, and the anti-Nazi refugee priest, H. A. Reinhold. Shuster found Reinhold especially helpful regarding the current situation of Catholics in Germany.[123] The group was also in close contact with Luigi Sturzo and the eminent German Jesuit, Friedrich Muckermann, publisher of the anti-Nazi *Der deutsche Weg* and an ally of H. A. Reinhold's, who was then in Rome and able to keep his friends informed about Vatican affairs.[124] Shuster received much valuable information from these contacts about events in Germany. Nazi violence against the clergy and their perfidious evasion of Concordat agreements made Shuster particularly sensitive about the possible impact of fascist ideology and programs on religious life in Spain.

Shuster answered *Commonweal's* critics in a lengthy article entitled "Some Reflections on Spain," which appeared on 12 April 1937. It was prefaced by a statement from the editor and founder of *Commonweal*, Michael Williams, who expressed his disagreement with Shuster's analysis. Williams was convinced that communism and anarchism were far more responsible for the troubles in Spain than Shuster suggested.

There were at least three key points to Shuster's arguments on the Spanish Civil War. First, he asserted that Catholic supporters of Franco as well as those on the Left were simplifying the issues. Reliable, authoritative information on Spain was difficult to obtain, owing to great passion and violence perpetrated by both sides. In any case, Shuster had never found conservative Catholics in Britain (the source of most pro-Franco sentiment) particularly open-minded or committed to Christian notions of truth and justice. In 1933 Shuster had visited London to enlist the major Catholic journals in a campaign opposing Nazi laws against non-Aryan Christians. "To my amazement," he claimed, "these gentlemen looked upon every adverse reference to Hitler as 'French Propaganda.'" Ever since then, lamented Shuster, "I have found it difficult to believe that the palm for objective visualization of major Catholic problems was to be hung on certain quasi-official door-posts in London."[125] Shuster pointed out, however, that there were many well-informed, reliable European Catholic narrators on continental politics who did not accept the assertion that communism was the sole cause of the Spanish Civil War. Their reports made it abundantly clear that Franco was not a white knight selflessly battling Satan for Christ. The methods employed by Franco against his opponents—especially the Basques—were proof enough of this mistaken notion. How could such a regime represent Catholic interests or protect the faith? Moreover, Shuster pointed out to his readers that the source of propaganda for Franco as savior of the Catholic religion and culture was none other than that "eminent defender of the faith, Dr. Goebbels."[126]

The above problem raised a second issue for Shuster. Pro-Franco Catholics, he warned, were ignoring the "shadows which fall upon the scene from without." Shuster and his associates knew far more about what was happening in Europe than did the Talbot group (their intelligence, for example, indicated that there was a good chance that the French armies in North Africa could invade the homeland, overthrow the Popular Front government, and make common cause with fascism).[127] What kind of arrangements had Franco made with Mussolini and Hitler? What was the extent of Italian and German involvement in Spain? Why was it, asked Shuster, that a dictator who put Alfred Rosenberg in the saddle to destroy the Catholic Church in Germany felt it his duty to save Catholicism in Spain?

Finally, Shuster focused attention on Spanish Catholicism itself as a major source of the problem. Making reference to Father Ludwig Veit's definitive study of the nineteenth-century Spanish Church, Shuster pointed out that the Spanish hierarchy was forced to depend on a state hostile to even the most elementary demands of social justice. Veit himself had warned that unless working-class and peasant problems were addressed, the blows struck against religion in Spain would replicate the violence brought down upon the Church in revolutionary France. It was the despair of the Catholic proletariat, argued Shuster, that brought success to Marxism and anarchism in Spain.

Catholic reaction to Shuster's "Reflections" on the Spanish situation was quick and vexatious. Within the week he received volumes of hate mail, including threats to his life. The New York Chancery, seemingly the command headquarters for Franco's cause, phoned

Shuster's parish priest in Connecticut inquiring whether he attended Sunday Mass regularly. The most mean-spirited assaults came from the Coughlinite *Brooklyn Tablet*, which depicted Franco as "the George Washington of Spain." Shuster could only conclude from all this that Catholic New York had envisioned the world outside America as engaged in a Manichean struggle between the followers of Mussolini and Hitler and the devotees of Karl Marx, and it had therefore come down on the side of fascism.[128]

Perhaps the greatest disappointment to Shuster was Father Talbot's attack, which appeared in a lengthy editorial in *America*. Both men had nourished a long personal relationship and respected each other's convictions. As opposed to Shuster, Talbot asserted that "Moscowism" was the greater danger in Spain. Franco, he claimed, was no fascist and could be relied on to bring a Catholic social order to Spain. Talbot accused Shuster's anti-Francoism of "splitting the influence of corporate Catholicism" and thus giving succor to the Church's enemies. Shuster's writings, claimed Talbot, amounted to an arsenal of "ammunition for all the Communistically controlled organizations in this country."[129]

Shuster quickly responded to Talbot's charges, though it marked the last time he would do so as editor of *Commonweal*. Hoping to disabuse Talbot of his sympathy for communism, Shuster defined himself as a "Borah Republican and, I hope, a Catholic," who wished to see the establishment of a sound conservative social order in Spain.[130] He wanted neither a dictatorship of the left nor a dictatorship of the right in Spain.

Especially troubling to Shuster was the impression conveyed by certain influential Catholics that fascism could be tamed by the Church and that its inherent sins were far less evil than communism. Both were evil, and the two shared similar methods and objectives. As regards Germany, Shuster made this prescient observation: "a system is coming into being which differs so little from 'Moscowism' that the eventual alliance between the two states is no longer the fear of just a few dreamy mortals."[131]

One of Shuster's greatest fears was the negative repercussion on the working class as well as on general public opinion brought about by Catholics who linked their religion with the aims of Franco and his reactionary and fascist supporters. The "patriotic tradition" to which Franco appealed was a shibboleth; behind it lay a policy crafted to freeze the old social order in the interests of the wealthy and privileged. The condition of labor in Spain was worse than anywhere else in Europe, owing largely to the Spanish Church's failure to promote social justice. It was the despair of the Catholic proletariat, argued Shuster, that fueled the success of communism and anarchism in Spain. A true conservative Christian social order could never be constructed through an alliance with Franco's variant of fascism, since, like its Moscow-based totalitarian twin, it rested on the concept of a purely autarkic economy which subordinated both labor and capital to a martial state. In Shuster's view, a sound social order required two things: the rights of labor had to become a central concern of the state and such rights needed to be freely and creatively exercised. For Shuster, the chief practical problem with the Christian crusade for Franco was that by backing the cause of fascism it created international working-class antipathy to the Church, thus widening the gulf between Catholicism and the masses.

George Shuster's response to *America* was his swan song with *Commonweal*. Michael Williams objected strongly to Shuster's views, as did the Catholic establishment in New York. Subscriptions to the *Commonweal* had fallen dramatically, and the fund drive currently underway to relieve the magazine's financial crisis could ill afford controversy. Shuster gave all these reasons for his decision to step down from the magazine's editorship, but those who were close to him claim he left because of a desire to dissociate himself from Williams's position on Spain.[132] Father Talbot had the final word. Shuster's "further reflections" were certainly good news to editors and orators infected with Marxism, he wrote in the next issue of *America*. It was impossible for a Catholic to be neither left nor right on Spain. The only choice must be for a "White Spain," claimed Talbot, because unlike communism, the Catholic Church could indeed collaborate with fascism.[133]

Shuster's departure allowed Michael Williams to position *Commonweal* solidly in the pro-Franco camp. Not content with journalistic support for the Nationalists, Williams helped organize what was called the American Committee for Spanish Relief, of which he was secretary-general. In cooperation with the American Association against Communism, whose president was Father Edward Lodge Curran, a man of extremist political views and a close ally of Reverend Charles Coughlin, Williams and his organization planned a mass rally at Madison Square Garden for purposes of raising money for victims of the Spanish war. From the outset plans for the rally swirled in controversy because many feared that the relief funds might be used solely to help the Insurgents.[134] At the last minute the Committee announced that it would aid both sides.

Michael Williams had become emotionally distraught by the Spanish situation, and the strain of the Madison Square rally took a toll on his health.[135] The numbers who turned out for the event were disappointing, and the triumphalist, circus-like atmosphere of the affair was considerably embarrassing to more sober-minded Catholics. Williams, for example, composed a hymn for the occasion to be sung by a choir "of a thousand voices." Mrs. S. Stanwood Menken donned a costume with peacock-like headdress studded with glittering stones to portray the "Spirit of Spain," prompting Heywood Broun's comment that the stunning lady was "pleased to proffer their radiance to the starving children of Bilbao who cry loud for bread."[136] Although the rally was supposed to call attention to the suffering of all Spaniards on "a non-partisan and non-sectarian basis," practically all the speakers glorified the cause of the Insurgents and minimized the tragedy of Guernica. One of the featured guests, Father Rev. Dr. Bernard Grimley, editor of the *Catholic Times* of London, got straight to the point, thereby establishing the real purpose of the rally. The situation in Spain, he declared, could be clarified only by religion: "the issue is God or anti-God." With thundering applause from the audience he denounced the secular press for ignoring the murders of thousands of priests and other religious. "Are not these sufferings as worthy to be reported," asked Father Grimley, as the deaths of women and children "who seem always to get in the way of the bombs and shells of the other side?"[137]

Soon after the rally several prominent members of *Commonweal's* board of directors, the Calvert Associates, the most influential being Carleton Hayes, arranged for Williams's retirement. In a private letter to Williams, Hayes pointed out his personal objections to associating *Commonweal* with the campaign for Franco but claimed that the Madison Square rally was "only one of a series of regrettable incidents" suggesting a need for change in the magazine's editorship.[138]

Williams had been strident and uncompromising in his campaign for Franco, calling those who opposed his views a miscellaneous set of radical fanatics, congenial ignoramuses, and badly educated riffraff. Such sentiments clashed sharply with the ideas of several on *Commonweal's* editorial staff. These younger, more liberal-minded individuals had been studying the Spanish situation in biweekly meetings with a number of lay faculty in the Department of Philosophy at Fordham University. Some of these meetings included Jacques Maritain. Three members of this group—Harry Binesse, Philip Burnham, and Edward Skillin—had been protégés of Shuster and Maritain, with whom they had discussed their objections to Williams's policies. Having become so disturbed with *Commonweal's* stand on Spain, the men thought about issuing a manifesto of dissension.

As opposed to the founding generation of *Commonweal* leaders who represented the assimilated British and American interests of the Church, the young Binesse, Burnham, and Skillin were more in touch with the grass-roots Catholicism of the immigrant community; and wanting to broaden their religion's outreach, they felt that Catholics should be actively engaged in debating issues of political importance for the American nation as a whole. They were especially sensitive to the ravaging effects of economic depression and recognized that the social and political teachings of the Church must address such issues. American Catholic leaders in their view were largely ignoring the messages of the papal labor encyclicals. This lapse in social deaconry, compounded by an embarrassing ignorance of the myriad economic and political factors behind the Spanish Civil War, was serving to marginalize the Church among the laboring classes.

After lengthy negotiations with the Calvert Associates, in which they received the important support of Carleton Hayes, Skillin and Burnham were able to put together the requisite financing to purchase *The Commonweal*. The "new" *Commonweal* announced that it would fight totalitarianism in all its guises. But the magazine did not take up the Spanish issue until some two months after the transfer of ownership. On 24 June 1938 the three young editors set out their position on the Spanish Civil War, and the response, in the words of one commentator, "brought the heavens down." Although the facts regarding Spain remained unclear given the thick haze of propaganda, there were a number of troubling matters, claimed the editors, that made it difficult if not impossible to single out either side for praise, let alone support. Loyalists had instigated or at least permitted violence against nuns, priests, and lay people. They pursued their objectives with ruthlessness and showed a degree of allegiance to Soviet communism. The Insurgents, on the other hand, gave rhetorical support to the Church, yet, against the protests of the Holy Father, indiscriminately murdered innocent civilians through aerial bombing and were intimately associated with totalitarian dictators of the Right.

The new editors of *Commonweal* were mainly concerned, however, with the impact of the Spanish conflict on America. The bitter divisions it had created within the Catholic community made it difficult for the Church to address the social and political problems created by the Great Depression. What could America learn from Spain in its efforts to create a more just society? One path was that already taken by the Spanish themselves, one which involved uncompromising partisanship. This, it seems, was an approach assumed by most American Catholic organs of opinion. An alternative was to avoid the passion that both blinds and simplifies and seek instead what the editors called "a positive impartiality" in search of what is right, good, and just. Embracing wholeheartedly one side or the other would mean accepting the bad, not only because the facts were obscure but also because both sides advocated ideas that ran against American political tradition. The Spanish situation offered a false choice, since both fascism and communism were anti-Christian and secularist. *Commonweal* urged its readers to maintain "positive impartiality" and "sanity of judgement" on Spain, and warned against being uncritical partisans of either side.[139]

The young editors of *Commonweal* had been strongly influenced by the ideas of Jacques Maritain and Emmanuel Mounier. They concluded that the real choice for Catholics lay between the Hegelian secular state in its current Marxist and fascist variants and the "personalist" state, which exists for the protection of its citizens, allowing each the free pursuit of mental, social, and spiritual life without the dictation of an exterior force.

There was a powerful negative reaction to the new *Commonweal's* stand. Archbishop John T. McNicholas of Cincinnati banned the sale of the magazine in his diocese. Almost all of the major American Catholic publications strongly opposed "positive impartiality," and the fact that the liberal *Christian Century*, Reinhold Niebuhr, and the *Nation*, among others, welcomed the approach only created more problems. *America* found the controversy conclusive proof that failure to embrace the Nationalists only served to give comfort to "Loyalists, Leftists, and Liberals," since Franco and everything he stood for was "a positive good."[140] *The Sign* counterattacked *Commonweal's* position by criticizing "Liberal Catholics" (they "pooh-pooh the dangers of Communism in spite of Popes, bishops and priests") in its June 1938 issue; *Ave Maria*, the voice of the Holy Cross fathers at the University of Notre Dame, saw the hand of Maritain in *Commonweal's* policy and attacked the French philosopher and *Commonweal* for their "dangerous" liberal proclivities.

The Sign's Owen B. McGuire held a position typical of most of the American Catholic establishment on "positive impartiality." *Commonweal* claimed that outsiders simply did not have enough "facts" to judge the Spanish situation. McGuire, on the other hand, claimed that there were at least twelve "absolutely certain" facts regarding the Spanish conflict, including the fact that it was a planned revolution directed by Moscow to set up "an Atheistic Communist Union of Soviets in the whole Peninsula." Any good Catholic, McGuire argued, had no need to know anything else about the situation: "It should be sufficient for him to read the joint letter of the Spanish Bishops."[141]

Since the bishops had spoken, Catholics were expected to rally to their side. Those who questioned were traitors to the faith. Edward Skillin received the most violent hate mail of his life, most of which appears to have come from Coughlinites and the profascist constituency of Patrick Scanlan's *Brooklyn Tablet*. Within the year *Commonweal* lost nearly a quarter of its subscribers.[142]

Only two members of the American Catholic hierarchy supported *Commonweal*'s position, namely, George Cardinal Mundelein of Chicago ("positive impartiality" was welcomed in his paper, *The New World*) and Archbishop Edmund V. O'Hara of Kansas City, who privately praised the magazine.[143] Dorothy Day's *Catholic Worker* enthusiastically endorsed neutrality, as did Virgil Michel, editor of *Orate Fratres*. Day's followers, the *Commonweal* circle, and Virgil Michel had long been allies in the struggle for liturgical renewal, which they saw as a means of energizing Catholics for social action.

Prior to Skillin's and Burnham's stand on the Spanish Civil War, Virgil Michel had created a stir in the pages of *Commonweal* by attacking an article in the *Catholic World* which had depicted Christ as "the first preacher of capitalism." This was blasphemy, claimed Michel, for capitalism had sacrificed the social ends of economic endeavor for material gain. He urged Christians to be on their guard and not allow "iniquitous capitalism to lead to its logical conclusion in either communistic collectivism or the equally totalitarian fascism."[144]

Virgil Michel wrote a personal letter to Edward Skillin for publication in which he supported *Commonweal*'s neutrality. A true Christian social order, Michel emphasized, did not entail setting up a theocracy; the Church should never be identified with the fortunes of any particular political arrangement.[145] In explaining his own position on the Spanish situation, Michel drew on the advice of the well-known poet and journalist José Bergamín, editor of the Spanish Catholic review *Cruz y Raya*. Bergamín had been permitted to travel through Insurgent territory under Franco's auspices. He was not convinced of the righteousness of the Loyalist cause, however, and urged his fellow Catholics to remain neutral on the civil war. Virgil Michel believed the situation too complex to be understood at a distance. The struggle, he insisted, was not simply between democracy versus autocracy, or religion versus atheism, but was rather rooted in Spain's complex cultural and historical experiences.[146]

The *Catholic Worker* had voiced its opposition to the Spanish Civil War long before *Commonweal* did so and was the first American publication to recommend the policy of neutrality. In September 1936, soon after the fighting erupted, the paper argued that the issues were not sufficiently clear to be judged fairly and that there certainly was much right and much wrong on both sides. "Forget your anger," urged the editors. "Let your indignation die. Remember only that the Body is being rent asunder, and the only solution is Love."[147]

In December 1936 the *Catholic Worker* published the full text of a long letter written to Emmanuel Mounier's *Esprit* by the Spanish writer and educator Alfredo Mendizábal.[148] The author had experienced firsthand the partisan hatred unleashed by the war, which, he observed, was threatening to submerge all that was human in man. The only sensible Christian response to such brutal stupidities was non-partisanship:

> To take sides under these circumstances would be for me to renounce in some manner this independence which is the mark of the Christian in his power over the world. It would also permit me to be led by people who have unpardonably lost their reason in the ocean of their passions.[149]

No one anathematized the combatants more forcibly than Mendizábal. Catholics in Spain had compromised their Church by binding it to a reactionary political cause, and in revenge furious hordes pillaged, burned, and killed all that in their eyes represented religion. But Mendizábal was especially scandalized by the vulgar and murderous uses being made of religion by the Insurgents to justify a criminal action, namely, fomenting a civil war, the most wholly immoral of means to achieve a political objective. Although both sides aligned themselves with anti-God philosophies, the sins of the Right, claimed Mendizábal, were worse:

> . . . justice compels us to a severity in judgment, all the greater if we perceive a like hatred among those who claim for themselves the name of Catholics. For we owe to the Truth of Christ, to the Love that Christ had for all men, the homage of the conquest of souls, not the insult of the massacre of bodies in a hatred which prevents the conversion of souls.[150]

The *Catholic Worker* also raised warnings about the fascist connection in the Spanish Civil War. Father H. A. Reinhold had become the paper's Hamburg correspondent in 1934 and passed on important information to Day's group about Nazi campaigns against German Catholic and Protestant churches as well as the Jewish religion. In the summer of 1935 the *Catholic Worker* began publishing a series of articles on the dangers of fascism, and a number of Day's inner circle (Norman Mckenna, Dorothy Weston, A. H. Coddington, and William Callahan) as well as Day herself picketed the German consulate, inciting demonstrations against Nazi persecution of Catholics and Jews.[151] Several of the articles on fascism provided detailed information about the Nazi oppression of religion in Germany and warned that the same could be expected from a fascist victory in Spain.[152]

The Catholic Worker group's street activities frequently brought criticism from various Catholic quarters, but this was trifling compared to the protest sparked by the letter from *Esprit*. Many readers withdrew their support from the paper, claiming its position on Spain was playing directly into the hands of the communists. Yet the *Catholic Worker* was also attacked by readers on the left, who regarded neutrality abetting fascism.[153] As a result of the *Catholic Worker's* stand on the Spanish Civil War, circulation dropped from a high of 175,000 a month to a low of 100,000, as both readers on the left and right canceled their subscriptions.[154]

Commonweal under the editorial triumvirate of Binesse, Skillin, and Burnham, along with Dorothy Day's Catholic Worker movement, represented a politically progressive, social-activist Catholicism linking together the British and American liturgical revival with the Maritain circle in France. The so-called "Commonweal Catholics"—an initially derogatory term suggesting disloyalty to the religious establishment's party line—for whom the new editors spoke were unyielding in their commitment to social reform in the spirit of the papal labor encyclicals. They championed a liberal political agenda, essentially a pluralistic form of "Christian Democracy" consistent with the thinking of Luigi Sturzo, Emmanuel Mounier, and Jacques Maritain.[155] *The Commonweal's* relationship with Maritain was crucial in this endeavor and was solidified in their common struggle against the holy war in Spain.

In the face of withering attacks from right-wing Catholics in Europe and America, Maritain and his associates on the Committee for

Civil and Religious Peace in Spain steadfastly continued their endorsement of *Commonweal's* "positive impartiality." As they saw it, this was the only prudent approach for Catholics regarding the struggle in Spain.[156]

Maritain himself was encouraged by developments in American Catholicism during these difficult years. In particular, he was pleased with its efforts to assimilate religious beliefs with the democratic, pluralistic traditions of American political practice. In this regard he singled out for praise the philosophers at Fordham University, the liturgical work of Virgil Michel, and the social deaconry of Dorothy Day, as well as the work of a diverse group of American non-Catholics, who, in the language of Father Gerald Vann, were practicing a policy of "integration," that is, attempting to merge spiritual life with the cultural, social, and political affairs of the nation.[157]

These efforts and activities resonated with Maritain's hopes for a revived Christian culture that could provide the necessary social healing after the traumas wrought by communism and the varieties of fascism. Maritain's allies in the fight to bring a reflective and balanced approach to the conflict in Spain shared with him a deep commitment to the democratic and pluralistic principles of the Western tradition, a set of principles which, as the pioneering encyclicals of Pope Leo XIII had shown, were consistent with the historically evolving teachings of the Church. Maritain's own political philosophy had been inspired by the Leonine encyclicals. It envisioned a pluralistic body politic bringing together in organic unity a diversity of social groupings and structures each claiming the right to exercise basic freedoms independent of the larger, superimposing political organizations so characteristic of both communist collectivism and fascism. Citing *Quadragesimo Anno*, which spoke of the injustice of higher political institutions arrogating to themselves functions performed more efficiently by smaller bodies, Maritain insisted that a "new Christendom" (his term for a future temporal regime whose structures in varying degrees reflect the imprint of a Christian conception of life) would allow maximum autonomy for individual persons and the social groups that give direction and meaning to their lives.[158] The groundwork for this new Christian order was to be found not in Nationalist Spain, whose political and social models were authoritarian and paternalistic, and certainly not in the integral Catholicism that saturated the thinking of reactionary Catholics of the Vogelsang school, but in the democratic and liberal institutions that had evolved in Britain, France, and the United States.

CHAPTER 14

Completing the Circle

I think it is wrong to look upon the Catholic religion as by its very nature hostile to democracy. Of all the various interpretations of Christianity, Catholicism strikes me as by far the one most favourable to the equality of [social and political] conditions. In Catholicism, the religious community is made up of two elements only: priest and people. Only the priest is raised above the rest of the faithful: all below him are equal. In Catholicism, so far as dogma is concerned, men of every degree of intelligence are placed on the same level. The wise man and the ignoramus, the man of genius and the man in the street, all are subject to the same creed in all its details.

. . . It strikes no bargain with any child of earth, and, weighing each man by the same standard, it brings every class of society without distinction to the foot of the same altar, just as such distinctions are confounded in the sight of God.

—Alexis de Tocqueville[1]

The conditions that led to the Spanish Civil War of 1936, framed as they were by a retrograde social and political climate untouched by the Reformation and Enlightenment experiences that had altered the culture of the rest of Western Europe, were markedly similar to those that produced the French Revolution. The men who started the Civil War certainly believed this to be the case: the officers of the *Movimiento Nacional* justified their declaration of war on the grounds of preventing a French-style revolution from destroying traditional Spain.[2]

The excesses of the French and industrial revolutions, followed by what the historian Carleton J. H. Hayes has called the "Generation of Materialism," had been anticipated by the pioneering Catholic social thinkers, including Ketteler, Ozanam, and others. Their critique of modern society and programs for reform, a middle road between capitalism and socialist collectivism, informed the great labor encyclical *Rerum Novarum*. Although this document's immediate objective was somewhat limited (establishing the right of workers to organize into mutual benefit societies), it reposed on a set of moral principles that allowed for a continued expansion of social doctrine into other spheres of life that enabled Catholics to keep their faith relevant in a world of constant political and economic change.[3] Leo XIII's approach to social problems was purposely broad and intended to remain outside party rivalries and changing political fashions (partly as the result of a plurality of voices giving advice to the papacy). The intellectual architecture of *Rerum Novarum*, however, strengthened the conviction that Catholics must take the initiative for promoting economic and political reforms by working through the various agencies of secular society.

Rerum Novarum provided a trenchant critique of industrial society and set out the general principles for constructing a Christian social order, but there was no consensus within Catholic intellectual circles concerning the practical methods for doing so. Fundamentally, Catholic political thought and action during the nineteenth century were largely riven by two opposing approaches to modernity: the Christian democracy of Ozanam and Ketteler and the reactionary politics of the integralist tradition associated with Vogelsang, de Maistre, and others.[4] The former was progressive and prepared to find common ground with modern pluralistic political practices. The integralists, on the other hand, rued the loss of medieval culture, admired authoritarian political forms, and essentially rejected modern culture.[5] For example, the influential American historian Ross J. S. Hoffman, one of Hilaire Belloc's admirers, took seriously the possibility of retrieving the cultural verities lost in modern society by returning to the ethos of the twelfth and thirteenth centuries, a historical era that for him represented a "fresh world" of "vigor . . . health . . . passion, heroism and hard thinking."[6] The political consequences of Hoffman's religious thought found little resonance in American culture, and his advocacy of a Bellocian "monarchical" concept of state brought him uncomfortably close to fascism. The Catholic mind, wrote Hoffman, never took easily to the liberal system of parliamentary oligarchies, behind which the real powers of government lay hidden. Thus Catholics, he pointed out, "can look with considerable favor . . . upon the Fascist State in Italy because Mussolini's state does appear to be solicitous equally for the well-being of all classes. . . ."[7] The extreme Romantic Austrian Catholic writer Anton Orel, regarded as Karl von Vogelsang's successor, also sounded very much like Hilaire Belloc when it came to liberal politics. Democracy, he wrote, was nothing more than the governance of a moneyed oligarchy greased by unscrupulous demagogues. The cancer of such politics must be excised:

> We desperately need an authority whose ultimate source of power is God. All the democratic instruments like universal suffrage have turned out to be frauds. . . . There is not a trace of true democracy anywhere, instead we have been saddled with an oligarchy of demagogues in cahoots with the plutocracy.[8]

In many respects the careers of Hilaire Belloc and H. A. Reinhold symbolize these two divergent political tendencies as they were played out in British and American Catholicism. Belloc and his epigones were highly critical of Western parliamentary democracy, and a good number championed Mussolini-style authoritarianism as a solution to the ills of the interwar years. Douglas Woodruff, for instance, could write as late as 1938 that the Church "plainly" has "sympathy and good will" for Fascism. For Woodruff there simply was no choice for Catholics between democracy and the virtues of Fascism.[9]

Woodruff's views were outside the liberal/progressive Catholic stream discussed in this study, one that had adjusted successfully to the meaning of the French Revolution and sought accommodation with a secular world order. Yet these liberal Catholics—Reinhold and many others discussed here—were a distinct, almost overlooked minority by the 1930s, and it took an individual of strong, independent constitution to withstand the force of conservative Catholic political opinion. There was a striking lack of support in the public forum for the few voices of progressive Catholic ideas. One notes, for instance, a conspicuous absence of strong democratic conviction in the vast majority of British and American Catholic organs of opinion during these years. Even the highly influential English

Catholic historian, Christopher Dawson (whose political views would later earn him the editorship of the *Dublin Review*), reflected this tendency when he asserted that liberal individualism, which found its political expression in parliamentary democracy, was entirely inconsistent with Catholic principles. There certainly was no necessary connection between Christianity on the one hand and liberal democratic forms of government on the other, claimed Dawson. Thus there was little reason why the passing of democratic forms of government should be opposed by Catholic sentiment: "It is at least theoretically possible that the limitation of political and economic freedom by the extension of social control should be actually favorable to the cause of spiritual freedom."[10] Indeed, Dawson went so far as to say that liberalism with its various democratic political forms was the most dangerous enemy and rival that the Catholic Church had to meet in modern times.[11] Dawson at this juncture was convinced that the social ideals articulated in *Rerum Novarum* and *Quadragesimo Anno* were more in line with Fascism than with either liberalism or socialism.

Hilaire Belloc and H. A. Reinhold, symbols of two conflicting Catholic paths to modernity, paid a high price for the courage of their convictions. Although Belloc was far better known than Father Reinhold, indeed he was perhaps the most prominent Catholic figure of the age, his career as an academic was painfully compromised by a contentious personality and religious triumphalism.[12] A giant as a man of letters in Edwardian England, Belloc's politically extremist views make him an intellectual pariah today. His reactionary and anti-Semitic opinions are a source of considerable discomfort to contemporary Catholics. Belloc, for many such Catholics, is someone to be hidden away in the family closet and not talked about. This is an unfortunate and distorting legacy, since, as this study has labored to point out, it has tended to obscure the considerable influence (not altogether negative) and significance of the man for the era in which he lived. No single individual was more responsible for breaking down the siege mentality of English Catholics than Hilaire Belloc, and his perspicacious social and political ideas were fertile soil for the growth of new and imaginative approaches to the problems of industrial society.

H. A. Reinhold became well known in American and European liturgical circles, but he never achieved the high public profile and international influence of Hilaire Belloc. His selfless struggle for social justice in the tradition of liberal, progressive Catholicism led to exile and persecution. The pain and loneliness brought by separation from family and country, along with the persistent attacks from right-wing Catholics, took a heavy toll. As he wrote Father William Cushing,

> To be a refugee is in itself a curse. No one who has not been in this terrible position will ever understand what it means to be an outsider and a suspected man all life long. If I had known this before, I might have preferred to face the concentration camp and the hardships of one of the famous staged trials for high-treason in Germany.[13]

The fact that the reactionary, integralist tradition has been allowed to define the Catholic response to the political and social challenges of the modern age is a distortion of the historical record. This is partly the consequence of the behavior of the Church hierarchy in Germany, Italy, and Spain, as well as the weighty influence of many British and American conservative Catholics who were inclined toward authoritarian ways.[14] Consider again the opinion of Christopher Dawson (who in some ways seems to have inherited the exalted position once claimed by Hilaire Belloc) that the Church is naturally more comfortable with fascist forms of governance than with democratic parliamentary ones.[15] In their attempt to overcome the "mechanical element as represented by the party machine," the fascists cultivated a direct relation of personal loyalty between leader and the man in the street. Their success, wrote Dawson, owed much to the fact that they resembled religious orders rather than the political party of the old type. Fascist movements, he claimed, "were organized in an hierarchical fashion, based on authority, discipline and subordination." As such, they tended to foster the same strong *esprit de corps* as Catholic religious orders.[16]

Dawson's assessment of the natural cultural affinity between Catholicism and authoritarianism was vigorously rejected at the time by such liberal Catholics as Don Luigi Sturzo and the historian

D. A. Binchy.[17] Sturzo argued that the political forms that best met
Catholic values were not fixed but shifted with historical circumstances. Monarchy, so highly esteemed by Belloc, Ross Hoffman,
Charles Petrie, and others, may well have fit the needs of a premodern culture that reached integration through a communitarian
ethos—the accent here being placed on rights of single communities represented by the head: *Cuius regio illius et religio*. But democracy satisfies a society that has become pluralistic. In the twentieth
century, asserted Sturzo, democratic political forms best complemented the *Civiltà Cattolica*'s (1864) definition of the ethical and
religious principles of Christianity.[18]

Nevertheless, many historians have accepted Dawson's assessment, regarding the Catholic Church's collaboration with dictators,
as well as its failure to provide progressive leadership for social change,
as an inevitable consequence of antidemocratic institutional bias.[19]
For example, the successful campaign to purge communism from
the American labor movement led by Fathers Francis X. Talbot, S.J.,
Owen Rice of the American Catholic Trade Union, and others—
an obsessive struggle that forced Catholic social teachings to the
sidelines and ultimately weakened trade unionism in America—
has convinced the labor historian Douglas Seaton that Catholicism
itself is inherently incapable of supporting progressive or radical
labor programs.[20] However, a broader analysis of the issue suggests
that Seaton's judgment is too historically confined. The important
role played by Hilaire Belloc and the Chesterton brothers during
the era of labor unrest in pre–World War I Britain shows very
clearly that Catholic social thought could be employed to support
not only progressive but outright revolutionary labor objectives. One
must also appreciate the aggressive role played by the American
labor-priests in helping workers organize against the large monopolies in the coal, steel, and oil industries in the decades before World
War I. One of the most colorful and influential was Father Peter C.
Yorke of San Francisco. Father Yorke used *Rerum Novarum* as his
labor bible, and as a charismatic educator, orator, and trade union
organizer he established a legacy of progressive Catholicism in the
tradition of the social gospels. When he died in 1925 a labor newspaper eulogized him as the "Father of the organized labor movement of San Francisco."[21] One historian recently has equated Father

Yorke's role in the history of American labor with Martin Luther King Jr.'s leadership of the civil rights movement.[22]

Several contemporary students of Catholic social teaching have identified important connections between the Church's traditional grass-roots commitment to supporting the poor in their struggle against economic injustice and various radical streams of socioeconomic theory. Radical theory is generally understood as having its roots in Marx's classical critique of capitalism. It recognizes the interlocking structural relationships of political, social, and economic institutions and emphasizes human labor as the source of all value.[23] There is a certain symmetry between radical theory and Catholic social and economic thinking, especially as manifested in Distributism. Both recognized the interconnectiveness of economics with all aspects of social behavior. Catholic economic philosophy from Ozanam to Chesterton and Belloc accepted the labor theory of value, and their ultimate vision of social justice—as is the case with radical notions of democratic socialism—required the empowerment of marginalized people; popular control of the productive and political processes (thus a rejection of corporate capitalism, since this meant sharing power between management and labor); decentralization of economic structures; and the creation of a new ethos of social solidarity.[24]

The Catholic Church's relationship with right-wing dictators in the 1930s has raised a number of troubling questions concerning its commitment to traditional Christian principles of equality, justice, and the social gospels. Guenter Lewy's ground-breaking study of the Church and Nazism emphasized, among other things, the German hierarchy's limited understanding of Hitler's revolution.[25] However, the German bishops' continued failure to penetrate the Nazi myth, Lewy insisted, suggests something deeper and more politically disturbing: a lack of concern over the abrogation of civil rights except as they impacted on the special freedoms of the Church.[26] The Brown Shirts tortured and murdered, but the bishops, motivated by short-sighted and parochial humanitarian interests mixed with institutional pragmatism, saw no reason to denounce such behavior as contrary to Catholic teachings. In addition, there was a certain attraction for aspects of Nazi ideology (in particular, its appeal to tradition and resistance to the "red tide" of communism), claimed Lewy, that prevented the episcopate from understanding "the true inhumanity of Nazism."[27] In the final analysis, Lewy has argued, the German hierarchy's limited opposition to Hitler was calibrated to meet institutional interests rather than any higher standards of liberty and justice.[28] For well over a hundred years the main enemy of the Church was communism, and almost any social and political principle could be sacrificed to meet this challenge, even its own moral teachings.[29]

Lewy's analysis stands in sharp contrast to the views of conservative Catholics. The highly influential Bishop John F. Noll of Fort Wayne, Indiana, editor of America's largest circulation Catholic paper, *Our Sunday Visitor* (reaching more than five hundred thousand homes, making it the widest circulating Catholic weekly in the world), praised the German bishops for their courageous opposition to Hitler.

> In Germany itself no one denounced National Socialism so frequently and in such a nation-wide manner as did the Bishops of Germany who, as often as three or four times a year met jointly to issue Pastorals to be read from the pulpits of the Catholic Churches, or to be distributed clandestinely among the Catholic people.[30]

Yet Bishop Noll's own assessment of fascism seems to corroborate Lewy's thesis. Noll, for instance, appreciated certain aspects of Hitler's mission, in particular his anti-Bolshevism. In 1938 Noll went so far as to write to Adolf Hitler explaining how he, as bishop and editor of a high-profile Catholic paper, felt "compelled to defend Nazism from communist attacks, as well as from attacks in the secular press of this country." Bishop Noll invited Hitler to write an article for *Our Sunday Visitor*, as one who could speak officially for the Nazi program: "The article might contain about 2000 words, and should declare the philosophy of Nazism, its main objectives and its need in your particular country." Following the article's publication in *Our Sunday Visitor*, Noll wrote, he would like permission to use it in a book, which would have wide circulation.[31] Noll also tried to set up a symposium on problems of current economic and social justice; Mussolini and Hitler, along with Catholic spokesmen for liberal causes (including Fathers John A. Ryan, R. A. McGowan, and Peter Dietz), would be invited to attend. Father Ryan, much to his good sense, thought the proposal completely inappropriate and refused to participate.

Many influential Catholic leaders passionately defended authoritarian forms of governance. The Vatican's official response to modern democratic governance was dilatory and was not clarified until Pope John XXIII's 1963 encyclical *Pacem in Terris*. Yet the arguments it made for the acceptance of constitutional democracy had already been set down by the liberal Catholics of the Sturzo-Maritain persuasion.[32] All this suggests that the Church as an institution guided by the requisites of bureaucratic self-preservation is not as flexible philosophically in responding to social change as are individual Catholics. (Nor, it should be added, has the Vatican always shown wisdom and a sense of Christian justice in its behavior and pronouncements.) All too often institutional imperatives have encouraged the Vatican to follow rather than lead the faithful within a modern secular society.[33]

There are of course good historical reasons for the authoritarian ethos of the papacy. Authority in the Church generally has followed secular political patterns. Yet, since the Church is of necessity inherently a conservative institution, keeping alive unique events that occurred over two thousand years ago, a time lag has developed between secular affairs and institutional vision. As the theologian Robert Nowell has observed, in the Church "attitudes towards authority which the secular world has long since outgrown are apt to be found fossilised within it like flies in amber." Nowell argued that the Reformation and the defensive and conservative reaction to it by the Church enormously increased this time lag, and it was only with the Second Vatican Council that Rome started to emerge from the age of absolutism, which in the secular world began to decay with the American and French revolutions.[34]

One is compelled to ask what it was that made so many leading British and American Catholics political reactionaries and apologists for fascist-type regimes, while only a minority drew on Catholic social teachings to justify an accommodation with liberal politics. Why did the Catholic Church in general show greater leniency toward the Right? Part of the answer is that many Catholics were intuitively uncomfortable with democracy, temperamentally more at home with the certitudes of hierarchy and authority, and generally willing to follow the directions of their conservative clerical leaders. This was certainly the case with Hilaire Belloc and his circle. Although he voiced a philosophical belief in democracy, Belloc never thought it could function properly because the unsophisticated masses were susceptible to manipulation by corrupt politicians. One of Belloc's critics, the English liturgical reformer Father S. J. Gosling, called attention to this disposition when he claimed that Belloc began by fighting for the underdog, but when the underdog turned to other leaders Belloc bit him.[35] The parliamentary system in England, Belloc had argued, owed its past success to the aristocratic character of the nation's social and political tradition. But with the rise of the "money cliques" the nobleman lost his influence. As Christopher Dawson noted, democratic institutions when left to themselves were apt to become tools of sordid and selfish interests.[36] Belloc gravitated to *Action Française* because he idealized the medieval function of aristocratic leadership and monarchical political forms. G. K. Chesterton, on the other hand, exhibited opposite tendencies, namely, a suspicion of privilege and an abiding respect for the common man.[37]

It also has been noted that a good number of British and American Catholic apologists for fascism were converts from Protestantism. Many of these converts commented on the influence of Chesterton and Belloc concerning their decisions, and the militant Latino-centric views of the latter might account for their appreciation of Mussolini and Franco. As the Catholic historian D. A. Binchy observed, the converts tended to identify the Italian nation as the citadel of Catholicism, its spiritual fatherland, whereas cradle Catholics were more apt to separate the Italian government from the Vatican, possessing an "instinctive, or perhaps inherited, grasp of the realities of the Church's relation to Italy."[38] The prominence of the convert Catholic men of letters, along with their close working relationships with respectable journals of intellectual opinion, conveyed the mistaken impression that their views were official.[39]

The dichotomy between liberal and conservative Catholics was strikingly evident in an ongoing private debate between Father S. J. Gosling and Douglas Woodruff. Gosling was one of the most vocal

critics of Belloc's identification of Catholicism with European culture. He particularly objected to Belloc's support of Latin fascist dictators simply because they claimed to be Catholic.[40] Gosling had
the opportunity to vent his views on the subject over a period of
time with Woodruff, who, in Gosling's mind, had absorbed most of
Belloc's religious and political ideas.[41] Gosling complained that
Woodruff and his influential friends in the Catholic hierarchy were
curiously silent about "wage slavery," seldom if ever making reference to the major purpose of the papal social encyclicals.[42] Woodruff, in response, claimed to have a more extensive knowledge of the
encyclicals than his interlocutor. Gosling admitted that it might
be so, but there was a danger of not being able to see the wood for
the trees. The object of two great social encyclicals was to raise the
material condition of the working classes, and Woodruff and friends
said very little about this.[43]

Such squabbling over social encyclicals, however, was only a
symptom of the main problem, for what fundamentally divided
Gosling and Woodruff were questions concerning freedom and
authority. Like Belloc, Woodruff had a deep affection for the institution of medieval monarchy and thought the world considerably
less civilized since its demise, a death he attributed in part to the rise
of liberalism and participatory politics. This process, in his mind,
was abetted by "the Court Chaplains of Demos"[44] who curried favor
with the mob. The crux of the whole business between us, wrote
Gosling to Woodruff, is that "you would convert the world from the
top downwards. I would begin with the bottom upwards. The first
looks speedier, easier, and more attractive. The second is surer and
more lasting."[45] A suspicion of popular political participation, based
on a fundamental bias in favor of authoritarian leadership buttressed
by religion, marked the thinking of all Catholics of the Right.[46] This
also explains why the social reforms of the British and American
liturgists found no support among such Catholics. The liturgical
reformers urged the Church to reach out and involve the faithful
more directly in the liturgy of the Mass. Conservatives thought the
granting of such freedom a dangerous tendency.[47] This antidemocratic bias certainly conditioned the Catholic Right's approach to
the Spanish Civil War. Franco deserved support chiefly because he

claimed to save a traditional, clerico-authoritarian order from the consequences of liberalism.

A wide gulf naturally separated Gosling and Woodruff regarding international affairs. Bellocian Latino-centric Catholicism and Woodruff's own distaste for democracy conditioned the *Tablet's* support of Mussolini, Franco, and Portugal's Salazar. But Gosling noted a double standard here. Woodruff and Belloc had frequently condemned the corruption of British politics but complacently accepted the turpitude of the Latin dictators: "Demos, as you have reminded me, has his court chaplains; but there is no sting in that remark so long as you do not hold that *all* court chaplains are suspect."[48]

Why was Woodruff always pointing out the evils of communism, asked Father Gosling, which was only dangerous when totalitarian in practice? Totalitarianism in any form—including the fascist variety—was fundamentally opposed to Catholic philosophy. But for Woodruff a Catholic Fascist bishop was allowed to steal a horse, whereas the Protestant Socialist bishop may not look over the hedge. This equation, wrote Gosling, needed balancing somewhere.[49]

What troubled Father Gosling had not gone unnoticed by one of the age's great moral voices, the writer George Orwell. Few have analyzed more incisively the modern authoritarian mind than George Orwell. It is noteworthy that he detected a philosophical linkage between reactionary Catholicism and the totalitarian twins of Marxism-Fascism. All three, he claimed, contradicted the moral values of the Western intellectual tradition. A close reading of Orwell's critique of right-wing Catholicism reveals a remarkable affinity with the political positions articulated by H. A. Reinhold, Jacques Maritain, Don Luigi Sturzo, and other liberal Catholics represented in this study.

Orwell was a special breed of socialist whose self-declared mission was to battle dogma, especially the communist, fascist, and Catholic varieties.[50] Orwell went straight to the moral failing that so weakened the cause of the Catholic Latinophiles. As Orwell made clear in an article for the *Partisan Review*, one of his major tasks was to fight the intellectual tendencies of three literary cliques: the "Stalinist gang, the Fascist gang, and the Catholic gang."[51] All three had in common a reliance on a religious priesthood separated from the ordinary citizen and an adherence to dogma. All three distrusted and limited the individual's ability to judge matters independently. Any writer embracing these orthodoxies did so by suppressing his sensibilities and intellectual integrity.

The "orthodoxy-sniffers," as Orwell labeled those intellectuals who sold their careers to the cause of a particular dogma, were guilty of what he called "the drunkenness of nationalism." This was different from the passion of patriotism, by which he meant devotion to a particular place and way of life without the jingoistic desire to force it upon other people. Nationalism, on the other hand, was by nature aggressive and exclusive. It was generally a blind and irrational attachment to a country, but it also had the quality of being "transferred" to a system of beliefs. The "nationalist" placed the object of his attachment above everything else, beyond good and evil, recognizing no other duty than to advance its interests. A popular form of such sentiment among intellectuals of the 1930s was that of communism: "a Communist, for my purpose here," explained Orwell, "is one who looks upon the USSR as his Fatherland and feels it his duty to justify Russian policy and advance Russian interests at all costs."[52]

Orwell also identified other contending forms of "nationalism," and although they were opposing currents of thought, they were bound together by a common principle. For him, the variety most closely corresponding to communism was political Catholicism. By this Orwell meant the kind of militant Catholicism exhibited in the *Tablet* and through the writings of Douglas Jerrold, Arnold Lunn, and others in Belloc's circle. Unfortunately, he identified Chesterton rather than Belloc as its main source and most notable exponent. Not seeing the complete Chesterton, Orwell could say: "Every book that he wrote, every paragraph, every sentence, every incident in every story, every scrap of dialogue, had to demonstrate beyond possibility of mistake the superiority of the Catholic over the Protestant or the pagan."[53] This superiority was not simply spiritual or intellectual but was translated into national culture entailing what Orwell called an "ignorant idealisation of the Latin countries," particularly France and Italy. Orwell never forgave Chesterton for his failure to denounce Mussolini's imperialism with the same vitriol that he had applied to British expansionism. Orwell praised Chesterton for being a "patriot" in affairs concerning Britain, and he greatly admired Chesterton's "Little Englander" politics. But when he turned to international affairs, said Orwell, orthodoxy induced Chesterton to forsake his principles without being aware of it. A major characteristic of "transferred nationalism" was an indifference to reality, an inability to see congruity between a similar set of facts. Chesterton, chided Orwell, had little to say against imperialism and the conquest of colored races when it was practiced by Italians and Frenchmen. "His hold on reality, his literary taste, and even to some extent his moral sense, were dislocated as soon as his nationalistic loyalties were involved."[54] As pointed out earlier in this study, Chesterton did not succumb to the Latinophile vision of Hilaire Belloc. He ultimately condemned fascism because it lacked a fixed moral principle and was totalitarian. The irony that eluded Orwell was that Chesterton had criticized fascism precisely because it was not democratic: fascist government, with its insistence on the unquestioned sovereignty of the state, could never be accepted by Catholics because it ultimately denied the dignity and liberty of the common man.[55]

On the other hand, Orwell's objections to Chesterton were brilliantly accurate when applied to Hilaire Belloc. Unlike his friend, Belloc had indeed gone over to orthodoxy in precisely the fashion that so irritated Orwell. Orwell was an intellectual who understood the necessity of staying out of the marketplace of advocacy politics. Orwell could never sell his services to a party, as did Belloc, because it meant giving up one's freedom to an ideology. Becoming part of a party also meant committing oneself to the propagation of doctrine: "the mere sound of words ending in—ism," wrote Orwell, "seems to bring with it the smell of propaganda."[56] In this respect Orwell was in step with Jacques Maritain (whose Catholicism was a creed that transcended nationalism). Both played the role of the so-called "Julien Benda intellectual."[57] This is a writer who takes on the responsibility of being a truth-telling moralizer, an intellectual who strives to remain above the passions of politics and refuses to descend into the agora where he is obliged to compromise the ideal of abstract justice for a partisan cause.[58] For Orwell, this did not mean that the intellectual had to avoid the political fray. It meant only that when he did soil his hands in the mud of advocacy (distributing leaflets, lecturing in dingy halls, even fighting in civil wars), he should do so as a citizen, as a human being, but not as a writer. "But whatever else he does in the service of his party, he should never write for it. He should make clear that his writing is a thing apart," something that must be done as an individual, an outsider, an unwelcome guerrilla on the flank of an army.[59] Belloc and his circle, from Orwell's perspective, were too much the "true believers," too much the insiders in their commitment to the orthodoxy of Rome.

Orwell's analysis of the sins of the Catholic Right applied equally to his colleagues on the Left who became partisan communists. In Orwell's view, the writers of the 1930s—Stephen Spender, W. H. Auden, Edward Upward, and others—had moved away from the despairing "twilight of the gods" mind-set of their 1920s predecessors into a Boy Scout atmosphere of "bareknees and community singing." Unlike the Pounds and the Eliots, this new generation was more conscious of itself as a group, being the product of public school–university–Bloomsbury conditioning. Although some forsook organized Christianity, their loss of faith in nationalism and religion made it necessary for them to find something else to believe in, and this was Marxism. To Orwell, this "Communism" of the English intellectual was nothing more than the patriotism of the deracinated.[60] Nor were intellectuals of the 1930s egalitarians. Like their "mystagogic" mentors, the temperament was decidedly elitist, sanitized of working-class life and values. As is the case with all elites, these writers were prepared to impose their vision of socialism on the rest of society.

A distinctive feature of those on the communist Left was their style of thinking, which was essentially the same as the style of those on the Catholic Right who had either moved into the fascist camp or served as fellow travelers. Neither side would brook a heretic. In other words, as was so graphically revealed with the Catholic Right during the Spanish Civil War, criticism and independent thinking were not allowed. Orwell discovered this for himself when Victor Gollancz of the Left Book Club refused to publish *Homage to Catalonia* and *Animal Farm* and when the left-wing *New Statesman* turned down his articles on Spain, in both instances because he made inconvenient, unorthodox political observations. The Right responded in kind. T. S. Eliot at Faber and Faber declined to publish *Animal Farm* because "we have no conviction . . . that this is the right point of view from which to criticize the political situation at the present time."[61] At this point the term "totalitarian" had not yet become a household word, but Orwell was one of the first to recognize that the similarities between communism and fascism were more significant than their differences: "the sin of nearly all left-wingers from 1933 onwards is that they have wanted to be anti-Fascist without being anti-totalitarian."[62] The same substantive criticism, of course, was made by Father Gosling in his debates with Woodruff.

George Orwell understood the mind-set of the conservative Catholics as well as any. He also knew that their line of thinking found generous institutional support. From the outset of the Church's struggle with modernity it found natural allies among political reactionaries. The first and most loyal defenders of the ancien regime, with which the Church was intimately entwined, were inevitably aristocrats and monarchists who were defending their social and economic privileges. This coalition for the maintenance of the status quo expanded in the later nineteenth century to include the upper middle classes who had succeeded in enlarging their property through industry and finance. These same elements in the twentieth century could be depended upon to support the Church's struggle against atheistic communism.[63]

Adding to the strength of conservatives who rallied to the defense of the Church was an institutional anti-liberal tradition that accompanied the Vatican's struggle with Enlightenment rationalism. Reactionary sentiment within Church officialdom reached its zenith in 1832 when Pope Gregory XVI condemned Félicité de Lamennais (*Mirai vos*), dealing a near fatal blow not only to liberal philosophy but also to "liberal Catholicism" as a political movement. Karl von Vogelsang and the Vienna School, along with de Maistre and Frederic Le Play in France, went further along this trajectory by articulating a romantic alternative to the capitalist order that called for an authoritarian guild society designed to restore a pre-revolutionary, pre-liberal form of living.

While part of its political vision remained unrealistically medieval, the Church's very institutional survival in most European countries demanded a secular incorporation with the propertied classes. Thus by the end of the nineteenth century the Catholic Church had developed a stake in the maintenance of the status quo and was therefore reluctant to support alterations in power arrangements. This served to alienate the laboring masses. The history of the Spanish Civil War is a vivid illustration of this dynamic. Liberal Catholic social activists such as George Shuster and Luigi Sturzo warned of the dangers of this power relationship, citing Spain as a living example of its consequences, but for the most part they failed to generate institutional support for their views. Caught up in the maelstrom of anticommunism, their fellow Catholics, both lay and clerical, remained unmoved by the programs of Christian renewal set forth in the social encyclicals. By this juncture their fear was godless Marxism, a very real threat to the faith, and all the Church's energies were devoted to the struggle against communism.

On the other hand, those aspects of the Catholic political consciousness that had been conditioned by nostalgia for an "organic" medieval order unsoiled by the modern diseases of capitalism and communism (for the integralists, both were the offspring of liberal philosophy) fit closely with the rhetoric of fascist and Nazi theoreticians. By appropriating the vocabulary of organic thought the totalitarians of the Right were able to garner wide support among bourgeois Catholics threatened by the breakdown of the capitalist world order and the expansion of communism.[64]

The fascist propaganda campaign was abetted by right-wing Catholic intellectuals, who, in blindingly uncritical fashion, sought allies from any quarter to fight the atheistic, materialist threat of Marxism. As Kevin L. Morris has pointed out, why should Catholics in general have been suspicious of Fascism when so many of the Church's charismatic literati closed the door to any close examination of the creed and its continental practitioners? It is disappointing, wrote Morris, "that their grasp of what was good in republicanism, parliamentarianism, and Christian democracy was so frail while, in a most un-Catholic manner, to different degrees they acquired faith in a novelty, a modern secular panacea."[65]

The points of light represented by the liberal thinkers given prominence in this book represent the other face of Catholicism: historically, they can be seen as the spiritual forerunners of today's Catholics who identify with and celebrate the progressive, democratic legacy of their faith.[66] Such thinkers affirm the central thesis of this study, namely, that the Catholic tradition has been flexible enough to adjust to the architecture of modern secular culture and, at the same time, offer new and imaginative solutions to the problems that have grown out of it. The great social thinkers of the nineteenth century had long warned of the collapse of capitalism (to which fascism was in part a response) and the dehumanizing potential of Marxism. The liberal Catholics provided a rational solution to the ills of industrial society through the infusion of Christian values into a purely materialistic economic system.[67] They accomplished this by drawing on the legacy of Catholic social teaching, proving that there was nothing inherently reactionary in a religious tradition which, through the voluminous contributions of the Church fathers, had evolved symbiotically with the Western secular historical experience.[68] In the final analysis, it was not Catholicism that failed; rather, individual Catholics failed their historical heritage. The point was insightfully made by Barbara Ward in her analysis of the Church and fascism. If Catholics, wrote Ward, "had known *Rerum Novarum* as communists knew Marx, if their activities in the spiritual sphere had been as revolutionary as those of the Fascists in the material order, the masses in Europe would not have been brought to the impasse where, every rational order having failed, they grasped at the solution of unreason."[69]

Notes

Introduction

1. For a highly critical assessment of the outcome of *aggiornamento* see James Hitchcock, *The Decline and Fall of Radical Catholicism* (New York, 1971), and Benedict M. Ashley, O.P., "The Loss of Theological Unity: Pluralism, Thomism, and Catholic Morality," in Mary Jo Weaver and R. Scott Appleby, eds., *Being Right: Conservative Catholics in America* (Bloomington, Ind., 1995). Anti-modernist, anti–Vatican II positions are also a regular feature of the magazine *The Wanderer*. More orthodox views can also be found in the *Catholic Social Science Review*.

2. Langdon Gilkey, *Catholicism Confronts Modernity* (New York, 1975), pp. 34–35, as discussed and quoted in Jay P. Dolan, *The American Catholic Experience: A History from Colonial Times to the Present* (Garden City, N.Y., 1987), p. 428.

The Catholic historian of Christian democracy Hans Maier makes the same argument: "The Protestant churches were spared the harsh cut of secularization, not least because a lengthy process of secularization had already achieved what Catholicism was forced to achieve in one short period. Many of the ideas which surfaced during the French and the American revolutions were already domesticated in Protestantism" (*Revolution and Church: The Early History of Christian Democracy, 1789–1901* [Notre Dame, Ind., 1965], p. 25).

3. A myriad of historians and political commentators who have dealt with the issues and experiences of social change in Europe and America have noted how Catholicism served socially regressive and politically reactionary causes. The following list is by no means complete but illustrates the point. For Germany, see the works of Guenter Lewy, Gordon Zahn, Waldemar Gurian, Richard Rolfs, and Walter Adolph. For France, see Eugen Weber, Robert O. Paxton, J. S. McClelland, and Richard Griffiths.

For Britain, see J. R. Jones, Alastair Hamilton, Colin Cross, John R. Harrison, and Margaret George. For America, see John Patrick Diggins, Alan Brinkley, James P. Shenton, and George Seldes.

4. This argument has been made elsewhere as well. See the discussion that followed the presentation of Paul E. Sigmund's paper "The Catholic Tradition and Modern Democracy" at a conference at the University of Notre Dame sponsored by the *Review of Politics* and the Office of Policy Studies, February 1986, in Leslie Griffin, ed., *Religion and Politics in the American Milieu* (Notre Dame, Ind., 1986).

5. There are some recent exceptions. See Thomas Bokenkotter, *Church and Revolution: Catholics in the Struggle for Democracy and Social Justice* (New York, 1998).

Of course, others have seen problems with liberal trends in the post–Vatican II era. Msgr. George A. Kelly, for example, believes that American Catholics have made a major mistake attempting to arrive at a peaceful coexistence with forces of the French Enlightenment and philosophies that underpin the *modus operandi* of modernity. If the renewal promised by John XXIII has failed, he argues, it is because blocs of bishops were more willing to follow "the thinking of Rudolf Bultmann, Martin Heidegger, Max Weber, or Carl Rogers than the wisdom contained in Matthew, Mark, Luke, and John, along with a variety of Pauls and Piuses down through the centuries" (*Battle for the American Church (Revisited)* [San Francisco, 1995], p. 139). See also Joseph A. Varacalli, *Toward the Establishment of Liberal Catholicism in America* (Washington, D.C., 1983).

6. This tradition can be seen as part of the continuing effort to reify Vatican I and the idea of a papal monarchy. In the view of Rosemary Radford Ruether and Eugene C. Bianchi, and the contributors to their book on Catholic Church governance, such endeavors are essentially unhistorical. They are grounded on the notion that the Church is an unchanging hierarchy of being and social order firmly placed in a sacral cosmos outside and impervious to human experience. Bianchi, for his part, fundamentally disagrees with the commonly accepted notion that "the church is not a democracy" and offers compelling historical evidence that pluralistic ideas and administrative structures have been deeply rooted in the Catholic tradition from its earliest sources. (See his "A Democratic Church: Task for the Twenty-First Century," pp. 34–51, in Eugene C. Bianchi and Rosemary Radford Ruether, eds., *A Democratic Catholic Church: The Reconstruction of Roman Catholicism* [New York, 1992]. For a critical assessment of this approach see the works of George Weigel, especially his *Freedom and Its Discontents: Catholicism Confronts Modernity* [Washington, D.C., 1991].)

7. American Catholic leaders from the outset interpreted *Rerum Nova-rum* in a narrow and restrictive fashion, emphasizing its anti-socialism at the expense of the encyclical's equally strong warnings about the excesses of capitalism and its pro-labor and social reformist messages. However, thanks to the pioneering work of Fathers John Ryan, Peter Dietz, William Kerky, and others, the American Church after World War I officially committed itself to progressive reform. The culmination of John Ryan's efforts to merge Catholic social thought with American progressivism came in February 1919 with the promulgation of the "Bishops' Program of Social Reconstruction," a proposal to link Leonine social teachings to the conditions and needs of the times. This represented the most advanced, forward-looking social document ever to come from an official agency of American Catholicism (Francis L. Broderick, *Right Reverend New Dealer John A. Ryan* [New York, 1963], p. 105). Its appearance was given formidable fanfare by the Catholic press, and the daring and imaginative proposals of the program (including a minimum wage and working age, public housing, and old age and health insurance) had the effect of shifting the popular impression that Catholicism was socially and politically conservative. Implementing the social gospel now became part of the Catholic mission. In the words of historian Jay P. Dolan, "Catholics were now known not just for what they opposed—socialism—but also for what they advocated: social reform" (Dolan, *The American Catholic Experience*, p. 345). Within a decade, however, this social and political progressivism was drowned out by the Catholic crusade against socialism.

8. In some ways this anti-liberal tradition prepared the ground for the emergence of the "new conservatism" of Catholic traditionalists whose influence has been considerable in America since the era of Ronald Reagan. For a discussion of such Catholics see Patrick Allitt, *Catholic Intellectuals and Conservative Politics in America, 1950–1985* (Ithaca, N.Y., 1993).

9. See Guenter Lewy, *The Catholic Church and Nazi Germany* (New York, 1964) and *Religion and Revolution* (New York, 1974).

10. This is the judgment of John Patrick Diggins. See his "American Catholics and Italian Fascism," *Journal of Contemporary History* 2, no. 4 (1967): 68.

11. Walter Lippmann, "Autocracy Versus Catholicism," *Commonweal*, 13 April 1927, p. 627. Reinhold was a close friend of Luigi Sturzo and played a key role in helping him emigrate to the United States. See Reinhold's letters to Sturzo, "Correspondence: S File," Reinhold Papers, Burns Library, Boston College.

Yet another non-Catholic, the eminent German economist Theodore Röpke, also pointed out that Catholics should be led to condemn fascism on moral grounds because it fundamentally contradicted Church teachings. See his "Fascist Economics," *Economica* 20, no. 5 (1935): 35–100.

Not surprisingly, Hilaire Belloc had no liking for Lippmann's liberalism. Writing to Hoffman Nickerson, Belloc said that he had "met the Jew Lippmann once or twice. . . . He has to the full the Jewish quality of understanding the superficial and obvious thing in any European affair . . . but never getting anything beyond that, and making a complete muddle of half the motives of the European" (Belloc to Nickerson, 6 September 1938, Belloc/Nickerson Correspondence, Hoffman Nickerson Collection, Burns Library).

12. Michael P. Fogarty, for instance, argues that liberalism along with socialism provided for Christians excellent examples of improved community management which they should have been able to see for themselves from the principles of Catholic social doctrine. Christians returned the favor: their resistance to statism and the tyranny of majority rule at the expense of different spiritual communities forced liberals and socialists "to face up to the true meaning of their own principle of tolerance in a plural society" (*Christian Democracy in Western Europe, 1820–1950* [Notre Dame, Ind., 1957], p. 152).

13. For a broad historical overview of how these issues played out in American Catholic experience see David J. O'Brien, *Public Catholicism* (Maryknoll, N.Y., 1996); Margaret Mary Reher, *Catholic Intellectual Life in America: A Historical Profile of Persons and Movements* (New York, 1989); George Weigel, *Freedom and Its Discontents: Catholicism Confronts Modernity* (Washington, D.C., 1991) and *Catholicism and the Renewal of American Democracy* (New York, 1989); and Michael Novak, *Freedom with Justice: Catholic Social Thought and Liberal Institutions* (New York, 1984).

Chapter 1.   European Catholics Confront Revolution

1. Quoted in Raymond Corrigan, S.J., *The Church and the Nineteenth Century* (Milwaukee, Wis., 1938), p. 4.

2. A discussion of *Sozialreform* and its opposite, a willingness to seek reforms through the existing social framework (*Sozialpolitik*), can be found in Heinz Herber, *Eine wirtschaftssoziologische Ideengeschichte der neueren Katholischen Soziallehren in Deutschland* (doctoral diss., University of Bern, 1933).

3. The term "liberal" Catholic has a special meaning in this study. It refers to those Catholics who were accommodationists, that is, willing

to engage and grapple with the issues of modern industrial society through the prism of democratic ideas that evolved out of the English and American revolutionary experiences. In the words of Mary Jo Weaver, "liberalism" is "an embracing term for those who welcome modernity and adopt many of its cultural markers" (*What's Left? Liberal American Catholics* [Bloomington, Ind., 1999], p. xi). In this respect "liberal" Catholics fall within the tradition of *Sozialpolitik* and, in later years, were active in the school of social reform known as "Christian democracy." See Michael P. Fogarty, *Christian Democracy in Western Europe, 1820–1950* (Notre Dame, Ind., 1957).

For a further discussion and definition of the meaning of "liberal" Catholicism and its relationship with Christian democracy see Hans Maier, *Revolution and Church: The Early History of Christian Democracy,* trans. Emily M. Schossberger (Notre Dame, Ind., 1965), pp. 1–28 and Appendix, pp. 290–297. Maier argues that Christian democracy recognized democracy as the surest guarantee of Catholic security and thus obligated the Church theologically toward democratic solutions (p. 22). A discussion of these ideas as applied to the American experience is found in the writings of John Courtney Murray, S.J. See his "Contemporary Orientations of Catholic Thought on Church and State in the Light of History," *Theological Studies* 10 (1949): 177–234.

My use of the term "liberal" Catholic should not be associated with what Kenneth L. Grasso and others have identified as "liberalism." Grasso has described liberalism as a particular theory of politics which rejects teleology and is driven by an inner logic that subordinates everything to the promotion of individualism. None of the liberal Catholics discussed in my study would have accepted such a model for the advancement of their cause. (See his "Beyond Liberalism: Human Dignity, the Free Society, and the Second Vatican Council," in Kenneth L. Grasso, Gerard V. Bradley, and Robert P. Hunt, eds., *Catholicism, Liberalism, and Communitarianism: The Catholic Intellectual Tradition and the Moral Foundations of Democracy* [Lanham, Md., 1995].)

4. The idea of "social deaconry" is developed fully by Edgar Alexander, "Church and Society in Germany," in Joseph N. Moody, ed., *Church and Society* (New York, 1953).

5. Quoted in Robert Cross, *The Emergence of Liberal Catholicism* (Cambridge, Mass., 1967), p. 9.

6. For an examination of Ozanam's career and contributions to social Catholicism see James Patrick Derum, *Apostle in a Top Hat: the Life of Frederic Ozanam* (New York, 1960); Kathleen O'Meara, *Frederic Ozanam*

(New York, 1883), preface by Cardinal Manning; Henry Louis Hughes, *Frederick Ozanam* (London, 1933); L. Celier, *Ozanam* (Paris, 1956); E. Galopin, *Essai de bibliographie chronologique sur Antoine-Frédéric Ozanam* (Paris, 1933); G. Goyau, *Ozanam* (Paris, 1925); and Albert Paul Schimberg, *Frederick Ozanam* (Milwaukee, Wis., 1966). Ozanam's career and influence on the development of social Catholicism are also discussed in Thomas Bokenkotter's *Church and Revolution: Catholics in the Struggle for Democracy and Social Justice* (New York, 1998).

7. From Lillian Parker Wallace, *Leo XIII and the Rise of Socialism* (Durham, N.C., 1966), p. 186.

8. Cross, *Emergence of Liberal Catholicism*, p. 11.

9. H. L. Hughes, *Frederick Ozanam* (London, 1933), p. 56.

10. Ibid., p. 53.

11. Ozanam had in fact begun to study the social question some twelve years earlier than Marx. His own views on social problems and the role of religion were informed by the writings of Louis Veuillot, Jean Baptiste Henri Dominique Lacordaire, Vicomte Armand de Melun, Villeneuve-Bargemont, and others.

12. French revolutionists had outlawed labor unions in July 1791 on the grounds that they were a danger to individual freedom. The text of the law read: "No longer will there be corporations in the state; there remains only the interest of each individual person" (from I. Voshchynin, *Solidarism and Economics* [n.d.], unpublished translation by Joseph Curran, p. 2).

13. John A. Ryan and Joseph Husslein, *The Church and Labor* (New York, 1920), p. 18.

14. Kathleen O'Meara (Grace Ramsay), *Frederic Ozanam: His Life and Work* (New York, 1883), p. 225.

15. *Extraits de l'Ere Nouvelle*, vol. 7, p. 272, from O'Meara, *Frederic Ozanam*, p. 238.

16. James Patrick Derum, *Apostle in a Top Hat: the Story of Frederic Ozanam* (St. Clair, Mich., 1962), p. 177.

17. O'Meara, *Frederic Ozanam*, p. 236.

18. The best study of Ketteler is Fritz Vigener, *Kettler. Ein deutsches Bischofsleben aus dem 19. Jahrhundert* (Munich, 1924). See also William E. Hogan, *The Development of William Emmanuel von Ketteler's Interpretation of the Social Problem* (Washington, D.C., 1946).

19. George Metlake (pen-name for J. J. Laux), *Christian Social Reform: Program Outlined by Its Pioneer, W. E. Baron von Ketteler, Bishop of Mainz* (Philadelphia, 1923), p. 224.

20. Kettler defined it as "self-seeking gone wild on the part of those who hold the reins of state power" (Bishop Wilhelm Emmanuel von Ket-

teler, "Freedom, Authority, and the Church," trans. Rupert J. Ederer, *Social Justice Review*, March 1976, p. 359).

21. Ketteler, "Freedom, Authority, and the Church," trans. Rupert J. Ederer, *Social Justice Review*, April 1976, p. 7.

22. Wallace, *Leo XIII*, p. 184.

23. From Metlake, *Christian Social Reform*, pp. 231–232.

24. Ketteler, "The Relationship of the Labor Movement to Religion and Morality," trans. Rupert J. Ederer, *Social Justice Review*, May 1976, p. 37.

25. Metlake, *Christian Social Reform*, p. 230.

26. From Ryan and Husslein, *Church and Labor*, p. 42.

27. Metlake, *Christian Social Reform*, p. 160.

28. Ibid., p. 127.

29. From "On the Care of the Church for Factory Workpeople, Journeymen, Apprentices and Servant Girls," paper delivered at the Conference of Fulda, 5 September 1869, quoted in Metlake, *Christian Social Reform*, pp. 181–182.

30. Quoted in Metlake, ibid., p. 48: "not poverty, but corruption of the heart, is the source of our social misery."

31. Henry Somerville, *The Catholic Social Movement* (London, 1933), p. 41.

32. Ryan and Husslein, *Church and Labor*, p. 44.

33. Metlake, *Christian Social Reform*, p. 206.

34. Ketteler, "The Relationship of the Labor Movement to Religion and Morality," trans. Rupert J. Ederer, *Social Justice Review*, May 1975, p. 36.

35. Metlake, *Christian Social Reform*, p. 215.

36. See Alexander in Moody, ed., *Church and Society*, p. 430. This author considers Hitze to be the best living example of the Catholic social deacon, "beyond suspicion of clerical narrow-mindedness or clerical pressure politics," fully committed "to the social interests of the nation as a whole."

37. A more complete coverage of Vogelsang's career can be found in Johann Allmayer-Beck, *Vogelsang: Vom feudalismus zur Volksbewegung* (Vienna, 1952).

38. Alfred Diamant, *Austrian Catholics and the First Republic: Democracy, Capitalism, and the Social Order, 1918–1934* (Princeton, N.J., 1960), p. 42.

39. Anti-Semitism was pervasive throughout aristocratic and bourgeois classes in nineteenth-century Europe and it was especially strong in central-European Catholic circles. These sentiments even spilled over into the judgments of liberal-minded scholars. For example, Francesco S. Nitti, an esteemed professor of political economy at the University of

Naples and an authority on Catholic social philosophy, who claimed his methodology was "positive" in the Comtian tradition and his treatment of subjects "strictly objective," could write the following in trying to explain why the Austrian Christian Social Movement was anti-Semitic (from *Catholic Socialism*, London, 1895): "We must not lose sight of the fact that, especially in Austria and Hungary, the Jews enjoy an almost exclusive monopoly of industrial revenue, nor should we forget that the press, the banks, and the stock-exchange are all in the hands of Jews. . . . In a country [Austria] where the aristocracy of capital is almost entirely Jewish, where the old feudal nobility, as well as the small landed proprietors, are threatened with being absorbed by the Jews, it is easy to understand the welcome and success which met the theories of the Catholic Socialists, and that they found a soil disposed to receive them and to render them fruitful" (pp. 200 and 202).

Even the English liberal Catholic, Henry Somerville, a harsh critic of Hitler and Mussolini, explained in 1933 that the "marked anti-capitalism" of the Hapsburg countries could be attributed to the fact that "their capitalist class was [to] an amazing degree Jewish, and its yoke more hateful because it was alien" (*The Catholic Social Movement*, p. 75).

40. Andrew Whiteside, "Austria," in Hans Rogger and Eugen Weber, eds., *The European Right: a Historical Profile* (Berkeley, Calif., 1966), p. 322.

41. Alexander in Moody, ed., *Church and Society*, p. 421.

42. For a fuller discussion of this see Diamant, *Austrian Catholics and the First Republic*, pp. 54–63.

43. Alexander in Moody, ed., *Church and Society*, p. 425.

44. See Parker Moon, *The Social Catholic Movement* (New York, 1921), p. 61.

45. Parker Moon argues that de Mun and La Tour du Pin were inspired to become involved in Catholic social action after having heard about Ketteler's work during their imprisonment in Germany (Moon, *Social Catholic Movement*, p. 138).

46. Moon, *Social Catholic Movement*, p. 85. The clubs failed to attract large numbers of industrial workers owing partly, it appears, to their reluctance to join organizations controlled by paternalistic aristocrats and a basic inability to understand why the upper classes would be involved in labor movements.

47. Ibid., p. 86.

48. See Paul Misner, *Social Catholicism in Europe: From the Onset of Industrialization to the First World War* (New York, 1991), chapter 9. Mis-

ner also shows linkages between Vogelsang, La Tour du Pin, and Charles Maurras (p. 181).

49. Moon, *Social Catholic Movement*, p. 104.

50. Ibid., pp. 143–144.

Chapter 2. The Development of Catholic Social
Action in Nineteenth-Century England

1. Robert Cross claims that Newman was the "the greatest liberal Catholic spokesman to modern culture." (See his *The Emergence of Liberal Catholicism* [Cambridge, Mass., 1967], p. 13.) For more on Newman consult Ian Ker, *John Henry Newman: a Biography* (Oxford, 1988). Ker regards Newman as a figure of monumental genius, whose ideas ranged from conservative to radical. See also Sheridan Gilley, *Newman and His Age* (London, 1990).

2. In Raymond J. Corrigan, S.J., *The Church and the Nineteenth Century* (Milwaukee, Wis., 1938), p. 155.

3. See Alva S. Ryan, "The Development of Newman's Political Thought," *Review of Politics* 7 (1945): 210–240. Ryan believes that Newman charted a course later taken by Jacques Maritain, Luigi Sturzo, and Christopher Dawson.

4. Alec Vilder, "The Tractarian Movement, Church Revival and Reform," in Harmon Grisewood et al., eds., *Ideas and Beliefs of the Victorians* (New York, 1966), p. 118.

5. Newman wrote to W. B. Ullathorne, Bishop of Birmingham, in August 1887: "I have been indoors all my life, whilest you have battled for the Church in the World" (from Vincent Alan McClelland, *Cardinal Manning: His Public Life and Influence, 1865–1892* [London, 1962], p. 22).

6. Vilder, "The Tractarian Movement," p. 118.

7. Ronald Knox, "Newman and Roman Catholicism," in Grisewood, *Ideas and Beliefs of the Victorians*, p. 129.

8. Robert Gray, *Cardinal Manning: a Biography* (London, 1985), p. 304.

9. From Henry E. Manning, "A Charge Delivered at the Ordinary Visitation of the Archdeaconry of Chichester," London, 1842, p. 35, in McClelland, *Cardinal Manning*, p. 11.

10. Shane Leslie, *Cardinal Manning: His Life and Labours* (New York, 1921), p. 348.

11. Hilaire Belloc, *The Cruise of the Nona* (London, 1925), p. 48.

12. Ibid., p. 48.

13. Dermot Quinn, *Patronage and Piety: the Politics of English Roman Catholicism, 1850–1900* (Stanford, Calif., 1993), p. 184.

14. Quoted in Gray, *Cardinal Manning*, p. 147.

15. The census in 1851 recorded that 519,959 living in England had been born in Ireland, 75 percent of whom were estimated to be Roman Catholic. The total Catholic population of England was calculated at 679,067. (See G. Kitson Clark, *The Making of Victorian England* [New York, 1969], p. 165, n. 2.)

16. From Gray, *Cardinal Manning*, p. 272.

17. From McClelland, *Cardinal Manning*, p. 21.

18. Henry E. Manning, "On the Subjects Proper to Academia," Session 1866–7, from his *Miscellanies* [London, 1877], vol. 3, p. 95.

19. A good discussion of Manning's friendship with Sir Charles Dilke, along with a brief discussion of his activities with Dilke on the Royal Commission on the Housing of the Working Classes, can be found in Francis Bywater, "Cardinal Manning and the Dilke Divorce Case," *The Chesterton Review*, vol. 18, no. 4 (November 1992): 539–553.

20. Henry Slesser, "Forword," in abridged version of Shane Leslie's *Cardinal Manning: His Life and Labours* (New York, 1958), p. xx.

21. Gray, *Cardinal Manning*, p. 301.

22. Leslie, *Cardinal Manning*, pp. 348–349.

23. Ibid., p. 349.

24. McClelland, *Cardinal Manning*, p. 23.

25. Leslie, *Cardinal Manning*, p. 350.

26. McClelland, *Cardinal Manning*, p. 135. For a fuller discussion of how and why labor should be regarded as property see Henry E. Manning, *The Dignity and Rights of Labour* (London, 1934). As Manning saw it, "whatever rights capital possesses, labor possesses" (p. 18). A short but succinct description of Manning's Christian social vision can be found in V. A. McClelland, "Manning's Work for Social Justice," *The Chesterton Review*, vol. 18, no. 4 (November 1992): 525–537. See also Thomas Bokenkotter, *Church and Revolution: Catholics in the Struggle for Democracy and Social Justice* (New York, 1998), chapter 6: "A Bishop Who Heard What Marx Was Saying: Henry Edward Manning (1808–1892)."

27. Leslie, *Cardinal Manning*, p. 367.

28. Manning, *The Times*, November 1886.

29. Leslie, *Cardinal Manning*, p. 368.

30. Bokenkotter, *Church and Revolution*, p. 194.

31. Gray, *Cardinal Manning*, p, 302.

32. Ibid., p. 304.

33. For Manning's role in settling the dock strike see Terry McCarthy, *The Great Dock Strike of 1889: The Story of the Labour Movement's First Great Victory* (London, 1988), and Tom Mann, *Memoirs* (London, 1923).

34. Leslie, *Cardinal Manning*, p. 376.

35. Manning, *Dublin Review*, July 1891, p. 163.

36. Leslie, *Cardinal Manning*, p. 362.

37. Manning, *Dublin Review*, April 1917.

38. Corrigan, *The Church and the Nineteenth Century*, p. 162.

39. The *Gazette de Liege*, 8 September 1890, from Francesco S. Nitti, *Catholic Socialism* (London, 1895), pp. 319–320.

40. Ibid., pp. 319–320.

41. Bokenkotter notes that Manning's labors for the cause of social justice were so emphatic that they became a permanent legacy of the English Church in spite of its generally conservative character (Bokenkotter, *Church and Revolution*, p. 204).

42. Slesser, in Leslie, *Cardinal Manning*, p. xx.

Chapter 3. Leo XIII and the Principles of *Rerum Novarum*

1. Michael P. Fogarty, *Christian Democracy in Western Europe, 1820–1953* (Notre Dame, Ind., 1957), p. 7.

2. Pope Leo XIII, *The Church and Civilization* (New York, 1878), pp. 10–11. Quoted in Raymond H. Schmandt, "The Life and Work of Leo XIII," p. 20, in Edward T. Gargan, ed., *Leo XIII and the Modern World* (New York, 1961).

3. A papal encyclical is a pastoral letter similar to those delivered by bishops to the Catholics of their diocese. But since the pope is Bishop of Rome and the successor of St. Peter, as head of the Christian community his letter (encyclical) is addressed to all Catholics and, in many cases, to all people irrespective of race, nation, or creed. Unlike an ecumenical council, an encyclical does not define doctrine but is rather designed to interpret the teaching of the Church concerning problems that arise in everyday affairs. In this respect, the encyclical is the paramount pedagogical tool of the Church, the vehicle by which the pope teaches the Christian community. Since the pope imparts his knowledge with the higher guidance of the Holy Spirit, and on matters of faith is infallible, going against the teaching of an encyclical can place the Catholic in danger of serious error.

4. See Schmandt, "Life and Work of Leo XIII," p. 34.

5. It should be pointed out, however, that it was never Pope Leo XIII's intention to open the Church to the secular forces of the day, in effect "modernizing" the Vatican. As Thomas Bokenkotter has observed, Leo was a political realist who recognized that the Church's past efforts at linking throne and altar were doomed. He rather saw the practical necessity of reorienting the Church to the people as a safer path for restoring Christendom and his own temporal power: in this sense democracy was a better means than monarchy for achieving traditional ends. See Thomas Bokenkotter, *Church and Revolution: Catholics in the Struggle for Democracy and Social Justice* (New York, 1998), p. 242.

6. John McManners, *Church and State in France, 1870–1914* (London, 1972), p. 46.

7. Ibid., p. 48.

8. Joseph N. Moody, "The Church and the New Forces in Western Europe and Italy," in Joseph N. Moody, ed., *Church and Society: Catholic Social and Political Thought and Movements, 1789–1950* (New York, 1953), p. 69.

9. From *Immortale Dei*, article 18, in Joseph Husslein, S.J., *Social Wellsprings: Fourteen Epochal Documents by Pope Leo XIII* (Milwaukee, Wis., 1940), p. 83.

10. There has been much confusion about liberalism among Catholics. Liberal Catholics have always asserted that continental liberalism represented a perversion of true liberalism. A leading Catholic authority on this subject, John Courtney Murray, S.J., has argued that continental liberalism and French revolutionary ideology have nothing in common with liberalism as it is known in Britain and the United States, representing instead a "deformation of the liberal tradition," simply another form of "absolutist state-monism, to which the liberal tradition stands in opposition" ("The Problem of State Religion," *Theological Studies* 12 [1951]: 162).

Those conservative Catholics who assailed liberalism in the interwar years failed to note the difference between these two different forms of political philosophy. The reasons for this failure are complex, but certainly a good number of the anti-liberal Catholics made no effort at distinction because they themselves were inherently hostile to democracy. Yet, as Murray pointed out, even to this day European students of canon law are unaware of the difference between Jacobin and Anglo-Saxon liberal-democratic thinking. Murray believed that the battle with continental liberalism was so great that it drowned out the voices of American liberalism, so in European Catholic academic circles they were never given a fair hearing. (See ibid., p. 164.)

For more on the life and ideas of John Courtney Murray, see Donald E. Pelotte, *John Courtney Murrary: Theologian in Conflict* (New York, 1976).

11. From *The Declaration of the Rights of Man and of the Citizen,* in *Introduction to Contemporary Civilization in the West,* prepared by Columbia College, vol. 2 (New York, 1961), p. 34.

12. Quoted in "The Decline and Fall of the French Revolution," *New York Review of Books,* 15 February 1990, p. 49.

13. Ibid., p. 50.

14. Joseph Emmanuel Sieyès, "What is the Third Estate?", in *Introduction to Contemporary Civilization,* vol. 2, p. 31.

15. From Marcel Gauchet, "Rights of Man," in Francois Furet and Mona Ozouf, eds., *A Critical Dictionary of the French Revolution* (Cambridge, Mass., 1989), p. 821.

16. "In truth, that the source of human power is God the books of the Old Testament in very many places clearly establish. 'By me kings reign . . . by me princes rule, and the mighty decree justice.'" *Diuturnum,* Article 9, as cited in Etienne Gilson, ed., *The Church Speaks to the Modern World: The Social Teachings of Leo XIII* (Garden City, N.Y., 1954), p. 144.

17. *Diuturnum,* Article 11, Gilson, p. 151.

18. The encyclical *Diuturnum* was drafted in the wake of Tsar Alexander II's assassination; the incident most certainly had an impact on the pope's thoughts on civil obedience.

19. *Diuturnum,* Article 11, Gilson, p. 145.

20. This would become a burning and divisive issue for Catholics during the 1930s in Spain, when many Catholics supported Franco's resort to force against the Spanish Republic. The issue is examined in chapters 12 and 13 of this book.

21. Joseph N. Moody, "Leo XIII and the Social Crisis," in Edward T. Gargan, ed., *Leo XIII and the Modern World* (New York, 1961), p. 73.

22. *Rerum Novarum,* Article 3, Gilson, pp. 206–207.

23. *Rerum Novarum,* Article 19, Gilson, p. 214.

24. John A. Ryan and Joseph Husslein, *The Church and Labor* (New York, 1920), p. xii.

25. *Rerum Novarum,* Article 5, Gilson, p. 207.

26. *Rerum Novarum,* Article 20, Gilson, pp. 215–216.

27. *Rerum Novarum,* Article 47, Gilson, p. 231.

28. *Rerum Novarum,* Article 62, Gilson, pp. 238–239.

29. *Rerum Novarum,* Article 14, Gilson, pp. 212.

30. *Rerum Novarum,* Article 32, Gilson, pp. 222.

31. *Rerum Novarum,* Article 36, Gilson, pp. 225.

32. Pope Leo XIII quoting from *Ecclesiastes*, 4:9–10, *Rerum Novarum*, Article 50, Gilson, p. 232.

33. *Rerum Novarum*, Article 55, Gilson, p. 235.

34. *Rerum Novarum*, Article 45, Gilson, pp. 230.

35. *Rerum Novarum*, Article 56, Gilson, pp. 235–236.

36. Wallace, *Leo XIII*, p. 273. *Rerum Novarum's* insistence that workers act independently of the state and that they should organize according to their own nature (apart from the employer) stands in sharp contrast to the fascist corporatist theories that prevailed in the 1930s. This issue is examined in some detail in chapters 7 and 8.

37. The Austrian and French corporativists, for example, did not want owners to share power with labor and in general showed no appreciation of the European working class's increasing self-confidence. (See Moody, "Leo XIII and the Social Crisis," in Gargan, p. 79.)

38. *Rerum Novarum*, Article 58, Gilson, pp. 237.

Chapter 4. The Appearance of the "Chesterbelloc"

1. Christopher Hollis, "Social Evolution in Modern English Catholicism," p. 823, in Joseph N. Moody, ed., *Church and Society: Catholic Social and Political Thought and Movements, 1789–1950* (New York, 1953).

2. Leslie Toke, "Some Methods of Social Study," *Downside Review*, March 1907, p. 3. Reprinted by the London Catholic Truth Society, 1908.

3. J. G. Snead-Cox, *The Life of Cardinal Vaughan* (London, 1910), vol. 1, p. 2.

4. Quoted in Mary Vivian Brand, *The Social Catholic Movement in England* (New York, 1963), p. 7.

5. Quoted from E. R. Norman, *The English Catholic Church in the 19th Century* (Oxford, 1964), p. 352.

6. F. Rogers, *Labour, Life and Literature: Some Memories of Sixty Years* (London, 1913), p. 246.

7. Quoted in Georgiana Putnam McEntee, *The Social Catholic Movement in Great Britain* (New York, 1927), p. 152.

8. Snead-Cox, *Life of Cardinal Vaughan*, vol. 1, p. 457.

9. Sheridan Gilley, "Manning and Chesterton," *The Chesterton Review*, vol. 18, no. 4 (November 1992): 492.

10. Denis Rolleston Gwynn, *A Hundred Years of Catholic Emancipation (1829–1929)* (London, 1929), p. 227.

11. See Snead-Cox, *Life of Cardinal Vaughan*, vol. 1, pp. 457 and 476.

12. McEntee, *Social Catholic Movement*, p. 155.

13. Snead-Cox, *Life of Cardinal Vaughan,* vol. 1, p. 197.

14. All this was the result of "a quaint instance of unfamiliarity with ordinary social terminology," wrote Leslie Toke. See Leslie Toke, *Some Methods of Social Study* (London, 1908), p. 2.

15. Ibid., p. 4.

16. See Toke, *Some Methods of Social Study.*

17. McEntee, *Social Catholic Movement,* p. 189.

18. Henry Browne, S.J., *The Catholic Evidence Movement* (London, 1921), p. 60.

19. Distributism is fully discussed in chapter 6.

20. "Aspects of Distributism," *The Newman,* vol. 4, no. 1 (January 1969): 4. From the Patrick Cahill Collection, Burns Library, Boston College.

21. Ibid., p. 4.

22. Quoted in Peter d'A. Jones, *The Christian Socialist Revival, 1877–1914* (Princeton, N.J., 1968), p. 12.

23. See Barbara P. Petri, *The Historical Thought of J.-J.-B. Buchez* (Washington, D.C., 1958).

24. K. S. Inglis, *Churches and the Working Classes in Victorian England* (London, 1963), p. 21. In other words, as Peter d'A. Jones put it, "alienation was a two-way relationship" (Jones, *Christian Socialist Revival,* p. 79).

25. Maurice Reckitt, *Maurice to Temple* (London, 1947), p. 151.

26. Jones, *Christian Socialist Revival,* p. 45.

27. See Conrad Noel, *Autobiography* (London, 1945), p. 57.

28. See J. A. Hobson, *Imperialism* (London, 1902).

29. Quoted in André Maurois, *Prophets and Poets* (New York, 1935), p. 193.

30. G. K. Chesterton, *What Is Wrong with the World* (New York, 1910), p. 105.

31. Maurice Evans, *Chesterton* (Cambridge, England, 1939), p. 49.

32. Conrad Noel, *Socialism in Church History* (London, 1910), p. 257.

33. G. K. Chesterton, *The Autobiography of G. K. Chesterton* (New York, 1936), pp. 167–169.

34. *Church Socialist* 1, no. 2 (February 1912): 4. See also Noel, *Socialism in Church History,* p. 272.

35. See Noel, *Autobiography,* pp. 28–29.

36. See P. E. T. Widdrington, "The History of the Church Socialist League II," *Commonwealth,* no. 7, July 1927.

37. No single intellectual or political circle could claim Chesterton as exclusively its own, yet he seemed to share the platform with a variety of Christian Socialist Leaguers more regularly than with people from other organizations during the pre–World War I years.

38. G. K. Chesterton, *Heretics* (London, 1905), p. 36.

39. G. K. Chesterton, *Orthodoxy* (London, 1908), p. 12.

40. Ibid., p. 10.

41. Ibid., p. 45. Chesterton here touched on one of the most salient features of Catholic social theory adumbrated in the teachings of Pope Leo XIII and more formally set down in Pope Pius XI's *Quadragesimo Anno* and Pope John XXIII's *Mater et Magistra* and *Pacem in Terris* as well as Vatican II's *Gaudium et Spes*. This is the principle of subsidiarity. In addition to recognizing that the individual and the family precede the state, subsidiarity affirms that governments and larger organizations should never undertake activities that are better suited to either individuals or smaller social associations.

42. From *The Speaker*, 1900, as quoted in D. J. Dooley, "Chesterton in Debate with Blatchford: The Development of a Controversialist," paper delivered at Seattle Pacific University, June 1987.

43. Margaret Canovan, *G. K. Chesterton* (New York, 1977), p. 29.

44. G. K. Chesterton, *The Everlasting Man* (New York, 1925), p. 269.

45. This comes from a notebook of Chesterton's to which Leo Hetzler made reference in his "Chesterton's Political Views, 1892–1914," *The Chesterton Review*, vol. 8, no. 2 (Spring 1981): 122–123.

46. Ibid., pp. 123 and 137.

47. G. K. Chesterton, "The Apology of the Partisan," *Daily News*, 21 October 1905.

48. Sidney Webb, *Fabian Essays* (London, 1889), p. 58.

49. From Sidney Webb, *A Stratified Democracy*, p. 5, in Anthony W. Wright, "Fabianism and Guild Socialism: Two Views of Democracy," *International Review of Social History*, vol. 23 (1978), part 2, p. 230. The Webbs' social ideal became the Soviet Union. In 1935, after a visit to Russia where they saw Stalinism in action, the Webbs published two exuberant volumes on the Soviet system hailing it as the dawn of a new civilization.

50. This is an observation made by George Orwell in *The Road to Wigan Pier* (London, 1937), p. 180. It is interesting to note that Orwell's criticism of socialism and the faith that he placed in the common man were remarkably similar to those of Chesterton. Indeed, Orwell and Chesterton were fellow spirits in many crucial respects. For more on Orwell and Chesterton see the concluding chapter of this book.

51. From Shaw, *Fabian Essays in Socialism*, p. 119, as quoted in Alex Zwerdling, *Orwell and the Left* (New Haven, Conn., 1974), p. 34.

52. From Wells, *New Worlds for Old*, p. 261, as quoted in Zwerdling, *Orwell and the Left*, p. 35.

53. As quoted in F. A. Hayek, *The Road to Serfdom* (Chicago, 1944), p. 143.

54. G. K. Chesterton, "A Gap in English Education," *The Speaker,* 4 May 1901.

55. Hilaire Belloc, *The Cruise of the Nona* (London, 1925), p. 48.

56. Belloc to Lady Frances Phipps, 24 October 1936, Box 363, Personal Letters "P," Belloc Papers, Burns Library, Boston College.

57. "Position of English Catholicism Contrasted with 50 Years Ago," written for the Jubilee number of the *Catholic Herald,* n.d., Box 9 MSS, Belloc Papers, Burns Library.

58. Belloc to Lady Phipps, 28 April 1936, Personal Letters, 1935–36, 581–B, Belloc Papers, Burns Library.

59. E. S. Purcell, *The Life of Cardinal Manning* (London, 1896), vol. 2, p. 630, as cited in A. N. Wilson, *Hilaire Belloc: A Biography* (New York, 1984), p. 24.

60. Belloc said that he became interested in national politics "from the moment I could think on public affairs at all—say from 12 to 14 years old. As to why I so began it was because it was a tradition in my English family. . . . for three hundred years, they having been . . . Nonconformist yeomen from the 17th century." Belloc's response to an inquiry by J. C. Wedgewood, Personal Letters "V," "W," and "Z" 1936, Box 363, Belloc Papers, Burns Library.

61. Manning was about the only person whom Belloc admitted had influenced his politics. Certainly, he said, there were no books that did. My political views, wrote Belloc, "are due to the natural action of the human conscience in the presence of any morally repulsive thing, such as the corruption of our professional politicians" (ibid.).

62. Belloc, *Cruise of the Nona,* p. 170.

63. Ibid., p. 172.

64. Hilaire Belloc, "The Liberal Tradition," in *Essays in Liberalism,* Hilaire Belloc et al. (London, 1897), p. 7.

65. See Robert Speaight, "The European Mind: Hilaire Belloc's Thought and Writings," *Times Literary Supplement,* 21 May 1954, p. 322.

66. Marie Belloc Lowndes, *Where Love and Friendship Dwelt* (New York, 1943), p. 59.

67. Belloc to Goodwin, 4 May 1932, Box 331, Correspondence "G," Belloc Papers, Burns Library.

68. Ibid.

69. Belloc to Hoffman Nickerson, 15 January 1931, "Belloc/Nickerson Correspondence," Hoffman Nickerson Papers, Burns Library.

70. For an elaboration on these connections see John P. McCarthy, "Hilaire Belloc: Jacobite and Jacobin," *The Chesterton Review*, May 1986, pp. 165–173.

71. See John P. McCarthy, *Hilaire Belloc: Edwardian Radical* (Indianapolis, Ind., 1978).

72. Belloc to Nickerson, 3 November 1931, "Belloc/Nickerson Correspondence," Hoffman Nickerson Papers, Burns Library.

73. See Belloc's *A Shorter History of England* (London, 1934).

74. Douglas Woodruff, "Hilaire Belloc: His Life and Work, An Outline of Activities and Achievements," *The Tablet*, 25 July 1953, p. 79.

75. Hilaire Belloc, *The French Revolution* (London, 1911), p. 133.

76. Hilaire Belloc, *Danton* (London, 1899), p. 10.

77. In the 1927 introduction to *Robespierre,* after he had become disillusioned with Parliament, Belloc apologized for his failure to point out more clearly the problems with representative government in the book's first edition.

78. Hilaire Belloc, *Napoleon* (London, 1932), p. 16.

79. Belloc to Van den Hout, 17 September 1936, Personal Letters, "V," "W," and "Z" 1936, Box 363, Belloc Papers, Burns Library.

80. Douglas Woodruff, Broadcast on Belloc for the BBC, 27 March 1949, Woodruff Papers, Box 17, Folder 13, Special Collections, Georgetown University.

81. Upon completing his book on Napoleon, Belloc wrote Hoffman Nickerson that he really had no love for it: this "was hack work done to order because Lippincotts . . . offered me my year's income for it." Belloc to Nickerson, 14 December 1932, "Belloc/Nickerson Correspondence," Hoffman Nickerson Papers, Burns Library. Belloc confessed to Nickerson that he wrote more than he should and did so too quickly. See Belloc to Nickerson, 26 March 1931, "Belloc/Nickerson Correspondence," Hoffman Nickerson Papers, Burns Library.

82. Belloc to Nickerson, 20 December 1932, "Belloc/Nickerson Correspondence," Hoffman Nickerson Papers, Burns Library.

83. Belloc was boycotted by the Harmsworth publishing empire. See A. J. P. Taylor, *Beaverbrook* (New York, 1972), p. 229.

84. Belloc to Nickerson, 6 February 1932, "Belloc/Nickerson Correspondence," Hoffman Nickerson Papers, Burns Library.

85. See Belloc to Lady Phipps, 17 September 1936, Box 363, Personal Letters, "P" 1936, Belloc Papers, Burns Library.

86. A claim made by Arnold Lunn, *And Yet So New* (New York, 1958), p. 65. For an opposing view see Rev. Philip Hughes, "Mr. Belloc's Reviewer

Replies," *Clergy Review*, April 1935, pp. 317–322. Lunn asserts that Belloc was a careful researcher who simply refused to flaunt his scholarship by copious footnotes. This was part of his errant contempt for academic convention—after all, it had rejected him.

87. When asked by Father Philip Hughes why he refused to give references, Belloc replied: "I am not a historian. I am a publicist." From Lunn, *Yet So New*, p. 79.

For a Catholic assessment of Belloc as historian see Patrick McGrath, "Catholic Historians and the Reformation—II," *Blackfriars*, vol. 14 (April 1963): 156–163.

88. Belloc to Gordon Smith, 8 July 1936, Box 363, Personal Letter "S," Belloc Papers, Burns Library.

89. Typed notes on a talk with historian Harold Fisher, n.d., Arnold Lunn Papers, Box 2, Folder 14, Special Collections, Georgetown University.

90. Belloc, *Danton*, p. 37.

91. Hilaire Belloc, *A Companion to Mr. Wells' 'Outline of History'* (San Francisco, 1927), p. 4.

92. Quoted by Hilaire Belloc to J. C. Wedgewood, n.d., p. 3, Personal Letters "V," "W," "Z" Box 363, 1936, Belloc Papers, Burns Library.

93. C. Creighton Mandell and Edward Shanks, *Hilaire Belloc: The Man and His Work* (London, 1916), introduction.

94. Hilaire Belloc, *The Place of Peasantry in Modern Civilization* (Manchester, England, 1910), pp. 279–280.

95. Belloc to J. C. Wedgewood, n.d., p. 1, Personal Letters "V," "W," "Z" 1936, Box 363, Belloc Papers, Burns Library. This was Belloc's reply to a questionnaire sent by J. C. Wedgewood, head of the Committee on House of Commons Records, on 7 July 1936, asking him to respond to a series of inquiries concerning his political views and experiences in Parliament. In his usual fashion, Belloc's replies had a sharp edge of sarcasm to them, and he prefaced his letter to Wedgewood by stating that they would not be of much use "save as a comic turn." Yet Belloc's candor revealed some interesting insights into what he remembered about his parliamentary career.

96. Ibid., p. 2.

97. Hilaire Belloc, "The Eye Witness," *Weekly Review*, 29 October 1939.

98. Parliamentary Debates (Commons), 4th series, 152 (22 February 1906): 614, from John McCarthy, *Hilaire Belloc: Edwardian Radical*, p. 103.

99. For example, see the series of articles Belloc wrote for the *New Age* concerning E. D. Moral and the Congo Reform Association: 7 and 21 December 1907; 6 August 1908. The events described in these articles seem

to have provided the material for the novel *Emmanuel Burden*, one of Belloc's many stories that focused on the corruption of party politics by secret monied interests. The symbol of these new forces was "Peabody Yid," the Jewish political kingmaker who pulled wires behind the scenes in several of Belloc's novels.

100. In the final analysis Belloc failed to appreciate the fact that after the 1910 election Asquith's government had a substantially reduced majority, that at this point only a small number of radical Liberals desired to destroy the upper chamber, and that the new monarch was deeply opposed to Asquith's plan for flooding the House of Lords with five hundred new peers.

101. McCarthy, *Hilaire Belloc: Edwardian Radical*, p. 152.

102. Wilson, *Hilaire Belloc*, p. 171.

103. Belloc to Wedgewood, n.d., p. 2, Personal Letters "V," "W," "Z" 1936, Box 363, Belloc Papers, Burns Library.

104. Belloc to Lady Phipps, 1 April 1938, Box 359, Personal Letters from Hilaire Belloc "1938," Belloc Papers, Burns Library. In this same letter Belloc told Lady Phipps that he only sat for a second term in Commons in order to rebuff a certain rich political leader, a swindler with a purchased peerage, who threatened Belloc because of his defense of the poor. "I went through another election in order to teach him manners. He was so frightened that he bolted at once to the House of Lords. He was in the soap business and had plantations in the tropics."

105. "Talking of bad sherry, you know where the Devil would go if he lost his tail? He would go to the bar of the House of Commons, where bad spirits are re-tailed." Belloc to Oriana Haynes, 20 May 1931, Personal Letters, Belloc Papers, Burns Library.

106. Belloc to Nickerson, 21 June 1922, "Belloc/Nickerson Correspondence," Hoffman Nickerson Papers, Burns Library.

Chapter 5. Against the Servile State

1. Stanley Pierson, *British Socialists: the Journey from Fantasy to Politics* (Cambridge, Mass., 1979), p. 186.

2. "Notes of the Week," *New Age*, 29 February 1908.

3. Chesterton's sense of the true objectives of socialism were markedly similar to those articulated by George Orwell in his book *The Road to Wigan Pier* (London, 1937), p. 214.

4. Cecil Chesterton, *Party and People* (London, 1910), pp. 171–172.

5. Ibid., p. xx. Cecil had called for a "popular Caesarism" as early as 1905 in *Gladstonian Ghosts* (London, 1905), p. 230.

6. Cecil praised the Marxist Social Democratic Party, for example, because, though sectarian, its members were good "fighters" and had a solid doctrinal foundation necessary for battle (*Party and People*, p. 182). He also appreciated Victor Grayson, for Grayson had the power to move and inspire great masses of men (*Party and People*, p. 185).

7. Cecil Chesterton and Hilaire Belloc, *The Party System* (London, 1911), pp. 33–34.

8. Belloc, "The Party System," n.d., Box 9 MSS, Belloc Papers, Burns Library, Boston College.

9. Ibid., p. 158.

10. Although this chapter focuses on trade union sentiment, a variety of other people were voicing similar criticisms. Libertarians, such as George Howell, the working-class member of Parliament, had long argued that state regulation was against the true interests of the laboring man (see F. M. Leventhal, *Respectable Radical: George Howell and Victorian Working Class Politics* [Cambridge, Mass., 1971]). A pluralist critique of statism was developed by F. W. Maitland and J. N. Figgis. The pluralists emphasized the importance of protecting the freedom of smaller groups within the state and vehemently opposed the centralization tendencies of socialism (see David Nichols, *The Pluralist State* [New York, 1973]). On the political right, certain conservatives also objected to the growth of state power. This was best expressed by Hugh Cecil and the anti-socialist writer W. M. Mallock. Conservative anti-parliamentary sentiment was also represented by the followers of Lord Milner and the so-called "Round Table" group, which included several "protectionist" elements from within the Tory Party. These people developed some rather elitist notions of government that were highly critical of the dilatoriness of parliamentary processes and the party system.

11. See G. R. Askwith, *Industrial Problems and Disputes* (London, 1920). Belloc made a similar argument, though he thought it possible that the rapid influx of South African gold onto the world market at the end of the Boer War—an increase of more than 30 percent by 1910—was largely responsible for the increase in prices. This rapid increase in supply was greater than the world's commercial systems could absorb. As gold accumulated, prices went up and the real value of wages fell (see Hilaire Belloc, "The Unrest of This Year," sent to the *Manchester Daily Dispatch*, 17 October 1910, MSS, Box 9, Belloc Papers, Burns Library).

12. See, for example, the *Daily Mail*, May 1912; Sir Arthur Clay, *Syndicalism and Labour* (London, 1912); and Margaret Cole, "Labour Research," in Margaret Cole, ed., *The Webbs and Their Work* (New York, 1974).

13. See, for example, James Ramsay MacDonald, *The Social Unrest: Its Causes and Solution* (London, 1913), and Philip Snowden, *Socialism and Syndicalism* (London, 1913).

14. See R. P. Arnot, *The Miners: Years of Struggle* (London, 1948). A similar position is taken by K. O. Morgan, "The New Liberalism and the Challenge of Labour: the Welsh Experience, 1885–1929," in Kenneth D. Brown, ed., *Essays in Anti-Labour History* (London, 1974).

15. See Henry Pelling, ed., *Popular Politics and Society in Late Victorian England* (London, 1968), pp. 155–162.

16. R. J. Holton, "Syndicalism and Its Impact in Britain with Particular Reference to Merseyside, 1910–1914," D. Phil. thesis, Sussex University, 1973, pp. 212–214. Holton's work was published as a book entitled *British Syndicalism, 1900–1914: Myths and Realities* (London, 1976).

17. Ibid., pp. 222–223.

18. Ralph Miliband, *Parliamentary Socialism: A Study in the Politics of Labour* (London, 1961), p. 2.

19. Ibid., p. 2.

20. Roger Moore, *The Emergence of the Labour Party 1800–1924* (London, 1978), p. 114.

21. Walter Kendall, *The Revolutionary Movement in Britain 1900–1921* (London, 1969), p. 37.

22. R. J. Holton, "Syndicalism," p. 124.

23. See "The Smart Philosophy," *Daily Herald,* 9 January 1923.

24. For Mann's syndicalist views see *Tom Mann's Memoirs* (London, 1923) and the July 1911 edition of *The Syndicalist.*

25. Speech at Holborn Hall. Reported in the *Daily Herald,* 18 July 1912.

26. Guy Bowman, "Syndicalist Realities," *Daily Herald,* 4 November 1912.

27. See *The Syndicalist,* March 1911 and January 1912.

28. Pierson, *British Socialists,* p. 266.

29. Ibid., p. 269.

30. Robert Williams, "The Greater Unionism II," *Daily Herald,* 19 March 1913.

31. See R. W. Postgate, *The Builders' History* (London, 1923).

32. Arthur Marwick, *Clifford Allen, the Open Conspirator* (Edinburgh, 1964), p. 16.

33. John P. McCarthy, *Hilaire Belloc: Edwardian Radical* (Indianapolis, Ind., 1978), p. 254.

34. R. W. Postgate, *The Life of George Lansbury* (London, 1951), p. 138.

35. G.R.S.T., "Reflections," *Daily Herald,* 29 June 1912.

36. Hilaire Belloc, "The Point of the Herald," *Daily Herald,* 15 April 1913. For additional insight into the cross-fertilization of ideas among those who wrote for the *Herald,* see R. J. Holton, "*Daily Herald* vs. *Daily Citizen,* 1912–1915," *International Review of Social History* (1974). Holton is one of the few labor historians who has written on the importance of Distributist thinking for the labor Left.

37. G.R.S.T., "Reflections," *Daily Herald,* 29 June 1912.

38. G.R.S.T., "Reflections," *Daily Herald,* 27 August 1912.

39. G.R.S.T., "Reflections," *Daily Herald,* 4 September 1912.

40. Leonard Hall, "The Servile State," *Daily Herald,* 8 November 1912.

41. S. T. Glass, *The Responsible Society: The Ideas of the English Guild Socialists* (London, 1966), p. 26.

42. Quoted in Donald Thatcher, *Nietzsche in England 1890–1914: The Growth of a Republican* (Toronto, 1970), p. 229.

43. *New Age,* 26 May 1910.

44. See "Notes of the Week," *New Age,* 25 August 1910.

45. Belloc to ESP Haynes, 29 December 1913, Belloc Papers, Burns Library.

46. Tom Mann, "Why I Am a Rebel," *Daily Herald,* 15 April 1913.

47. S. G. Hobson, *Pilgrim to the Left: Memoirs of a Modern Revolutionist* (London, 1938), p. 149.

48. For more details see A. R. Orage, ed., *The National Guilds* (London, 1919), and the *New Age* articles on Guild Socialism commencing in April 1912.

49. Orage had recommended Cole to Belloc, who was chagrined to discover that the young Turk was a "peace crank." It seems that in Belloc's mind his allies generally had flaws: "The instruments to one's hand always turn out to be lunatics or thieves and in general people who have nothing to lose or no sense of proportion" (Belloc to H. A. L. Fisher, 2 November 1915, Belloc Papers, Burns Library).

50. The first type of syndicalism to make its appearance in Britain, via the Scottish dissidents in the Social Democratic Federation known as the "impossibilists," was that associated with an American Marxist with anarchist tendencies, Daniel DeLeon. DeLeon championed industrial action by the workers along the lines of relentless class warfare, de-emphasizing political reform.

51. For a good discussion of the similarities and differences between Cole's version of Guild Socialism and that articulated by Hobson, see A. W. Wright, *G. D. H. Cole and Socialist Democracy* (Oxford, 1979), pp. 40–43; L. P. Carpender, *G. D. H. Cole: An Intellectual Biography*

(Cambridge, England, 1973), pp. 24–26; Stanley Pierson, *British Socialists: The Journey from Fantasy to Politics* (Cambridge, Mass., 1979), pp. 212–213; C. Bechofer and Maurice Reckitt, *The Meaning of the National Guilds* (London, 1918); A. R. Orage, ed., *The National Guilds* (London, 1919); and G. D. H. Cole, *The World of Labour* (London, 1913).

52. For a discussion of the differences between the *New Age* and Distributist ideas, see Jay P. Corrin, "The Formation of the Distributist Circle," *The Chesterton Review*, vol. 1, no. 2 (Spring-Summer 1975), and *G. K. Chesterton and Hilaire Belloc: The Battle against Modernity* (Athens, Ohio, 1981), pp. 84–88.

53. A. J. Penty, *Post-Industrialism* (London, 1922), pp. 98–99.

54. Hilaire Belloc, "An Examination of the National Guild System," VIII, *New Age*, 4 December 1913.

55. See "Will the Bill Do?" *Eye-Witness*, 22 June 1911.

56. Junius, "Open Letter to a Trade-Union Official," *Eye-Witness*, 6 June 1912.

57. "Two Strikes: 1889–1911," *Eye-Witness*, 17 August 1911.

58. Belloc, "Honest and Dishonest Insurance," *Eye-Witness*, 6 June 1911. See also "The Fraud of the Poll Tax," *Daily Herald*, 24 November 1913.

59. See Box L, 1,2,3,4, Belloc Papers, Burns Library.

60. See letters from Belloc to Watson, 12 October 1914, and Watson to Belloc, 16 October 1913, Box L, nos. 1,2,3,4, Belloc Papers, Burns Library.

61. "Anti-Insurance Act Committee," Box 6, nos. 1,2,3,4, Belloc Papers, Burns Library.

62. Ibid.

63. For example, see "The Present Industrial Dispute," sent to the *Daily Dispatch*, 15 September 1910, MSS Box 9, Belloc Papers, Burns Library. The editor in this case had asked Belloc's opinion on the London Boilermakers' Lockout.

64. See Belloc, "The Unrest of this Year," Manchester *Daily Dispatch*, sent on 17 October 1910, MSS Box 9, Belloc Papers, Burns Library.

65. Belloc, "The English Railway Strike," sent to Movement Social de November, n.d., MSS Box 9, Belloc Papers, Burns Library.

66. Ibid.

67. "Crisis in Trade Unionism," *Eye-Witness*, 8 February 1912.

68. This issue was one of many reasons why the CSG under the leadership of Henry Somerville refused to support the programs of Belloc, G. K. Chesterton, and the Distributists.

69. Hilaire Belloc, "On the Minimum Wage and the Servile State," sent to the *Catholic Times*, 27 December 1913, MSS Box 7, Belloc Papers, Burns Library.

70. Ibid.

71. See Belloc, "Proportional Representation," sent to *Academy*, 3 April 1911, and "The Best Proposal (?) or a Real Reform (?) or True Representation (?)," sent to the *Daily Dispatch*, 1 March 1911, MSS Box 9, Belloc Papers, Burns Library. See also Belloc, article sent to *The Sunday Chronicle*, 12 January 1914, MSS Box 7, Belloc Papers, Burns Library.

72. Hilaire Belloc, "On Payment of Members," sent to the *New Age* on 20 October 1910, MSS Box 9, Belloc Papers, Burns Library.

73. Belloc, however, seems to have given up on Parliament altogether by this juncture. In December 1912, Belloc in the *New Witness* asked Lansbury why he even bothered to run for Parliament, since in his mind nothing of merit could be accomplished there. Lansbury answered Belloc in the *Daily Herald*, arguing that Parliament might eventually respond to the control of the people through the creation of mechanisms for popular initiative, referendum, and the recall. (See Lansbury, "Parliament's Uses," *Daily Herald*, 20 December 1912.)

74. "The Strike and the Vote," *Eye-Witness*, 27 June 1912.

75. See Belloc article sent to the *Sunday Chronicle*, 12 January 1914, MSS Box 7, Belloc Papers, Burns Library.

76. Belloc, "The Present Situation in France," sent to *The New Weekly*, 18 April 1914, MSS Box 7, Belloc Papers, Burns Library.

77. See article sent to the *Sunday Chronicle*, 12 January 1914, and "The Osborne Judgement," n.d., MSS Box 9, Belloc Papers, Burns Library.

78. Belloc to Haynes, 26 October 1912. Haynes complained about Cecil's rudeness and inept management and regretted ever having promised any money to the *New Witness*. See his letter to Belloc, 19 December 1912. For Belloc's criticisms of Cecil's journalism see letters to E. S. P. Haynes, 12 October 1912; 2 May 1913; and 3 December 1913, Belloc Papers, Burns Library.

79. See G. K. Chesterton's *Autobiography* (New York, 1936), pp. 205–206.

80. R. J. Holton, "Syndicalism and Its Impact in Britain," pp. 566–567.

Chapter 6. Distributism and British Politics

1. For a full discussion of how Distributist economic theory contrasts with contemporary economic thinking, see Gerald Alonzo Smith, "Distributism and Conventional Economic Theory," *The Chesterton Review*, vol. 5, no. 2 (Spring 1979).

2. G. K. Chesterton, *The Autobiography of G. K. Chesterton* (New York, 1936), p. 232.

3. It had no official connections with the Church, and non-Catholics wrote for the paper and were members of the Distributist League. In fact, Charles Dokin, a prominent man in the League's Central Branch, and Archie Currie, a regular contributor to the weekly who signed his material "Agag," were atheists. (See Lyle Dorest interview with Brocard Sewell, pp. 23 and 34, Wheaton College, Special Collections.)

4. Dudley Barker, *G. K. Chesterton* (London, 1973), p. 26.

5. See K. S. Inglis, *Churches and the Working Classes in Victorian England* (London, 1963), p. 26.

6. See A. J. Penty, *Old Worlds For New* (London, 1917).

7. Ever true to his love of the old, Penty preferred the medieval spelling of guild.

8. A. J. Penty, *Towards a Christian Sociology* (London, 1923), p. 45. For a clearer understanding of how Penty merged his thinking with the ideas of Chesterton see his *Distributism: A Manifesto* (London, 1937).

9. Maurice Reckitt, *G. K. Chesterton: A Christian Prophet for England Today* (London, 1950), p. 9.

10. For example, P. E. T. Widdrington, leader of the Church Socialist League, helped fashion a program against party politics and examined new ways to bring a Christian sociology to industrial society that paralleled work on the subject being done by the Chester-Belloc papers. (See the League's journals during these years: *The Commonwealth* and the *Church Socialist Quarterly*.) In fact, it can be argued that Reckitt and his Anglican friends represented the purest form of Distributist social thinking in the interwar years. As editor of the Anglican *Christendom*, Reckitt managed to attract important German Catholic liturgical reformers to write for his magazine, such as Father H. A. Reinhold and Waldemar Gurian. The Catholic writer Bernard Wall, editor of the influential journal *Colosseum*, admitted that the Christendom group was "exceedingly good—on many social questions perhaps more to the mind of the Church than most Catholic reviews" (Box "Correspondence, W-File," letter from Bernard Wall to H. A. Reinhold, n.d., H. A. Reinhold Papers, Burns Library, Boston College).

11. Eric Gill, *Money and Morals* (London, 1934), pp. 21–22.

12. Gill and other Distributists gained the reputation of being unrealistic medievalists and machine breakers. (See Donald Attwater, *A Cell of Good Living: The Life and Opinions of Eric Gill* [London, 1969], pp. 145–146. See also Gill's *It All Goes Together* [London, 1944], a compilation of his ideas on industrial society and how to improve it; *Eric Gill: Autobiography* [New York, 1971]; and Robert Speaight, *The Life of Eric Gill* [New York, 1966].)

13. Brocard Sewell, "Father Vincent McNabb," *The Aylesford Review,* Summer 1988, p. 9. For more on Father McNabb see *The Chesterton Review,* February and May 1996, a special commemorative issue.

14. See Ferdinand Valentine, *Father Vincent McNabb, O.P.* (Westminster, Md., 1955), p. 172.

15. From a letter written on a turnleaf of a discarded exercise book, Attwater, *Cell of Good Living,* p. 59.

16. See Belloc's letters to Hoffman Nickerson, 29 November 1925 and 3 May 1926, "Belloc/Nickerson Correspondence," Hoffman Nickerson Collection, Burns Library, Boston College.

17. Much of the work on the paper was done gratis, though Chesterton himself put substantial sums of his own money into the project—as much as five thousand pounds—to keep the operation going. (See Dudley Barker, *G. K. Chesterton,* p. 266.) Gregory Macdonald recalled that the total weekly payroll of *G.K.'s Weekly* was about eight pounds, and of this his brother, Edward, received about four pounds weekly for his efforts as editor (Gregory Macdonald, "Forty Years After: A Note by Gregory Macdonald," unpublished memoirs, 1974, Gregory Macdonald Papers, Wade Collection, Wheaton College, Wheaton, Illinois).

18. See Lyle Dorsett interview with Gregory Macdonald, 19 July 1985, p. 5, Wade Collection, Wheaton College. Gregory Macdonald claimed that his brother kept in touch with Chesterton on a regular basis by telephone and that it was by such means that the paper was brought out on a weekly basis. Throughout these years the Macdonald brothers seem to have had an intimate working relationship with Chesterton. Gregory, for example, claimed that he and his brother were the only ones who knew that Chesterton was dying in 1936, and that they were told just before Mrs. Chesterton wrote to Gilbert's confessor, Father John O'Connor (Gregory Macdonald, "Forty Years After," pp. 1 and 9, Wade Collection, Wheaton College).

19. Lyle Dorsett interview with Brocard Sewell, 25 April 1985, p. 5, Wade Collection, Wheaton College.

20. Gregory Macdonald, "Forty Years After," p. 6, Gregory Macdonald Papers, Wade Collection, Wheaton College.

21. G. K. Chesterton, "Straws in the Wind: The Mystery of Mussolini," *G.K.'s Weekly,* 24 April 1926.

22. G. K. Chesterton, "Straws in the Wind: Representative Government," *G.K.'s Weekly,* 17 April 1926.

23. G. K. Chesterton, "Straws in the Wind: Wages and Profits," *G.K.'s Weekly,* 24 April 1926.

24. See B. D. Acland, "Distributism in Industry," *G.K.'s Weekly*, 27 February 1926.

25. "The Great Lockout," *G.K.'s Weekly*, 8 May 1926.

26. See "Notes," *G.K.'s Weekly*, 5 June 1926.

27. *The Tablet*, 15 March 1926, p. 639.

28. Ibid., pp. 638–639.

29. "The League Against the Poor," *G.K.'s Weekly*, 15 May 1926.

30. For Macdonald's strong disagreements with my own assessment of the politics of Chesterton's paper, see "And Now the Pink Legend: A Response to Jay P. Corrin," *The Chesterton Review*, Fall-Winter 1976–77.

31. Ibid., p. 7.

32. See Dorsett interview with Macdonald, p. 3, Wade Collection, Wheaton College.

33. See his "Forty Years After," Wade Collection, Wheaton College.

34. Maurice Reckitt, *The World and the Faith* (London, 1954), p. 58.

35. In fact Chesterton claimed personal responsibility for all unsigned copy in his journal. (See *G.K.'s Weekly*, August 1925, p. 476, and A. Herbold, "Chesterton and *G.K.'s Weekly*," Ph.D. diss., Department of English, University of Michigan, 1963, p. 39.)

36. See G. K. Chesterton, "The Pride of England," *G.K.'s Weekly*, 22 May 1926.

37. G. K. Chesterton, "Straws in the Wind: Our Critics: Trusts and Trades Unions," *G.K.'s Weekly*, 10 April 1926.

38. Gregory Macdonald, "Pink Legend," *The Chesterton Review*, Fall-Winter 1976–77, p. 9.

39. G. K. Chesterton, "The Pride of England," *G.K.'s Weekly*, 22 May 1926.

40. Ibid.

41. See "Distributism and the Mines," Parts I and II, *G.K.'s Weekly*, 7 April and 14 April 1928.

42. For example, see Patrick Braybrooke, *Some Thoughts on Hilaire Belloc* (London, 1923); the writings of Henry Somerville, leader of the Catholic Social Guild and editor of the *Christian Democrat* during the 1920s; Wilfrid Sheed, *The Morning After: Essays and Reviews* (New York, 1972); and Michael Mason, "Chesterbelloc," in *G. K. Chesterton: A Half Century of Views*, ed. D. J. Conlon (New York, 1987). Two of Chesterton's biographers, Maisie Ward and Dudley Barker, also have been critical of Chesterton's political obsessions.

43. It should be pointed out that Belloc had emphasized that the Irish problem was a key factor in destroying the House of Commons. Along with increased suffrage, the advent of the secret ballot, and "the genius" of

Irish political organization in the appearance of a united Irish party, the party system, which up until the mid-nineteenth century had an aristocratic spirit and a certain elasticity to it, became "infected with a mechanical discipline" imposed by the new oligarchs. This is what undermined the independence of individual MPs. Irish obstructionism (singled out for praise by Cecil Chesterton), employed as a political tool for winning national independence, forced the oligarchs to defend themselves, and they did so by enforcing a new discipline on parliamentary debates and individual voting, making the whole process nothing more than a sham, mere window dressing to preserve the impression that what an MP said and did really mattered. This, of course, is why Belloc was muzzled once he entered Parliament. (See Hilaire Belloc, *A Shorter History of England* [London, 1934], pp. 585–587.)

44. Keith Burgess, *The Challenge of Labour: Shaping British Society, 1850–1930* (New York, 1980), p. 248.

45. Quoted in Keith Middlemas, *Politics in Industrial Society: The Experience of the British System since 1911* (London, 1979), p. 213.

46. Ibid., p. 22.

47. For example, see the 3 January 1931 issue of *G.K.'s Weekly*.

48. A similar tendency was identified in American politics after World War II. See C. Wright Mills, *The Power Elite* (New York, 1956).

49. G. K. Chesterton, "The Respectable Radicals," *G.K.'s Weekly*, 22 February 1930.

50. Ibid. Ironically, the Chesterton-Belloc analysis of the Mond-Turner talks dovetailed with that of the leading English Marxist of the day, Mr. R. Palme Dutt. In the *Labour Monthly* Dutt pointed out that if the trade unionists accepted the Mond-Turner proposals it would mark their conversion "from organs of class struggle into organs of co-operation in the capitalist organisation of industry" (as cited in "Notes of the Month," *The Commonwealth*, September 1928).

51. An aristocracy he defined as a governing class accepted by the community as a natural organ of control (Hilaire Belloc, "The Crown and the Breakdown of Parliament," submitted to the *English Review*, January 1934, MSS Box 7, Belloc Papers, Burns Library, Boston College).

52. Hilaire Belloc, *The House of Commons and Monarchy* (London, 1920), p. 95.

53. Hilaire Belloc, *A Shorter History of England* (London, 1934), p. 619.

54. Belloc, *House of Commons and Monarchy*, p. 184.

55. Hilaire Belloc, "Were We Wrong?" II, *G.K.'s Weekly*, 5 November 1932.

56. G. K. Chesterton, "The First Reply to Fascism," *G.K.'s Weekly*, 29 August 1935.

Chapter 7. The New Distributists

1. As noted by Robert Speaight. "It is no disparagement of Jerrold's considerable abilities," wrote Speaight, "to suggest that here he had not much competition." Speaight believed that Belloc and Christopher Dawson had decisive influences on Jerrold's ideas. But Jerrold took too much from Belloc, a more brilliant yet less erudite and balanced guide than Dawson. Speaight thought it an exaggeration to label Jerrold a fascist, although he was so obsessed with the problems of industrial capitalism and the corruption of parliamentary democracy that he became indulgent to fascism wherever it reared its head (*The Property Basket: Recollections of a Divided Life* [London, 1970], p. 155).

2. Arnold Lunn, *Now I See* (London, 1956), p. 55.

3. Before converting to Catholicism, Arnold Lunn in June 1929 began a lengthy correspondence with Belloc concerning religion that ran on for many years. These letters chronicle Lunn's reasons for eventually embracing the faith, especially the role Belloc's apologetics played in the matter: "You and Chesterton have been the two biggest influences in my life since, as a undergraduate, I read your *Path To Rome* and *Orthodoxy*. To you and to him I owe, under God, my faith" (Arnold Lunn to Hilaire Belloc, 26 June 1936, Box 2, Folder 14, Arnold Lunn Papers, Special Collections, Georgetown University).

Lunn's family, especially his father, Henry Lunn, had strong reservations about this conversion and disapproved of his son's subsequent, single-minded devotion to militant apologetics. (See Henry Lunn to Arnold Lunn, 18 November 1937, Box 5, Folder 10, Douglas Woodruff Papers, Special Collections, Georgetown University.) Arnold Lunn's brother, Hugh Kingmill, shared their father's concerns. He hoped that Arnold would not spend the rest of his life in controversy, especially since he was not following the best of paths to wisdom: "Chesterton is not the man he was"—i.e., since converting to Catholicism—"and no one can escape the warping effects of always arguing" (Kingmill to Lunn, 6 December 1933, Box 3, Folder 15, Arnold Lunn Papers, Special Collections, Georgetown University).

4. See Duke of Alba to Arnold Lunn, 21 September 1937, Box 2, Folder 13, Arnold Lunn Papers, Georgetown University.

5. During a visit to America Lunn apparently engineered a riot in the winter of 1938 while addressing a crowd on the Spanish Civil War, where, as he put it, "Jewish faces predominated" (the new Distributists also tended to absorb Belloc's unfortunate anti-Semitic proclivities). "What I

helped to provoke was a flavour of the kind of mob fury which has burnt the churches and murdered the priests in Red Spain," but the real purpose of this behavior was to develop a fighting *esprit de corps* among the young Catholics. The press reported the rage Lunn unleashed as "sad and shameful," but Lunn commented that the episode was mild compared to any meeting in Glasgow (Arnold Lunn to unidentified recipient, 5 December 1938, Box 3, Folder 20, Arnold Lunn Papers, Georgetown University).

6. See "The Douglas Woodruff Papers: A Register," prepared by Anna T. Zakarija, Douglas Woodruff Papers, Georgetown University, and an essay by Auberon Waugh on Woodruff for the *Dictionary of National Biography* which appears in the Woodruff Papers, Box 7, Folder 25. Belloc was also appreciative of Woodruff's important contributions to Catholic journalism: "The *Tablet* gets better every week and I rejoice in it! It is the only Review which has a knowledge of foreign affairs and I read it avidly" (Belloc to Woodruff, 30 May 1940, Box 1, Folder 14, Woodruff Papers, Georgetown University). Michael Derrick believed that Woodruff made the *Tablet* as influential and respectable as the *Spectator,* the *Economist,* and the *New Statesman* ("An Editorial Jubilee: Profile of Douglas Woodruff," 23 May 1961, Box 16, Folder 19, p. 2, Woodruff Papers, Georgetown University). In his later years Woodruff received many honors as a guiding light of English Catholicism, the most notable being the Grand Cross of the Order of St. Gregory the Great (1968). He was a close friend of Pope Paul VI before his election as pontiff and was acquainted with many high-ranking Vatican ecclesiastics.

7. Derrick, "An Editorial Jubilee: Profile of Douglas Woodruff," 23 May 1961, p. 6, Box 16, Folder 19, Douglas Woodruff Papers, Special Collections, Georgetown University.

8. Belloc to Hoffman Nickerson, 30 December 1933, "Belloc/Nickerson Correspondence," Hoffman Nickerson Papers, Burns Library, Boston College.

9. See Lunn to Belloc, 13 December 1933, Box 2, Folder 14, Arnold Lunn Papers, Georgetown University.

10. Ibid.

11. Arnold Lunn, *Come What May* (London, 1940), p. 75.

12. Douglas Jerrold, "Hilaire Belloc and the Counter-Revolution," in Douglas Woodruff, ed., *For Hilaire Belloc: Essays in Honor of His 71st Birthday* (New York, 1942), p. 5.

13. "Half a dozen sufficient reputations could be shared out and thankfully received if the authorship of his works could be transferred to writers less generously endowed. But this profusion of talent was offset by the extremely uncongenial environment in which he had to display his

428   Notes to Pages 179–183

gifts" (Broadcast on Belloc for the BBC, 27 March 1949, Box 17, Folder 13, Douglas Woodruff Papers, Georgetown University).

14. For example, when Lunn was engaged by Father John F. O'Hara, president of the University of Notre Dame, as an assistant professor of apologetics, a title he did not much like because of its modern defensive tone, he said that the subject he most desired to teach, indeed the only thing that really mattered, was "the threat of communism." Lunn hoped to trace the whole movement historically beginning with the French Revolution through a century of liberalism to Russia and Spain, the last of which, he claimed, Catholics know too little about (Arnold Lunn to Father O'Hara, 9 April 1937, Arnold Lunn Correspondence, 1935–37, UP, OH, Box 69, File 27, Archives, University of Notre Dame).

15. Douglas Jerrold, "Comments," *The English Review*, January 1933.

16. Douglas Jerrold, "Comments," *English Review*, December 1933.

17. For Vogelsang, see chapter 1.

18. Douglas Jerrold, "English Political Thought and the Post-War Crisis," *American Review*, May 1933, p. 178.

19. These included, it seems, less the problem of ideas than a fetching physical appearance. See Douglas Woodruff's unpublished memoirs, p. 42, Part II, Box 14, Folder 1, Douglas Woodruff Papers, Georgetown University.

20. For Woodruff's views on the *Syllabus of Errors*, see "Pope and Church," n.d., Box 15, Folder 9, Douglas Woodruff Papers, Georgetown University.

21. Douglas Woodruff, "Manuscripts, Notes," pp. 10, 11, 12, undated, Box 14, Folder 9, Douglas Woodruff Papers, Georgetown University.

22. Arnold Lunn to Douglas Woodruff, n.d., "Confidential," Box 5, Folder 10, Douglas Woodruff Papers, Georgetown University.

23. For a detailed analysis of this topic see Jay P. Corrin, *G. K. Chesterton and Hilaire Belloc: The Battle against Modernity* (Athens, Ohio, 1981), pp. 125–136.

24. "The Distributist League," *G.K.'s Weekly*, 13 December 1930.

25. H. E. Humphries, *Liberty and Property: An Introduction to Distributism* (London, 1928), pp. 12–13.

26. Chesterton's first major biographer, Maisie Ward, wrote to Douglas Woodruff that Father Ignatius Rice and James Walsh, who served Chesterton's cause as members of the Distributist League, told her that Chesterton did not want Distributists to do anything practical and that it was largely his doing that the Central Branch made so little effort to carry their principles into practice. What he asked of them was to be amus-

ing and convivial (Maisie Ward to Douglas Woodruff, 29 December 1949, Box 6, Folder 34, Douglas Woodruff Papers, Georgetown University).

27. For example, see Jay P. Corrin, *G. K. Chesterton and Hilaire Belloc*, chapter 8, "The Influence of the Distributist Idea," and Dermot Quinn, "Distributism as Movement and Ideal," *The Chesterton Review*, vol. 19, no. 2 (May 1993).

28. Gill set up a highly-regarded craft guild where workers lived with their families in a self-sufficient, loosely knit commune guided by the religious principles of St. Thomas and the philosophy of Distributism.

29. G. K. Chesterton, "How Are You Going to Do It?" *G.K.'s Weekly*, 1 October 1927.

30. G. K. Chesterton, *The Outline of Sanity* (New York, 1927), p. 246.

31. Michael Derrick, "Distributism and Primitivism," *Blackfriars*, April 1934. For more on the activities of the Distributist League and its various branches during these years see Michael Thorn, "Filling a Gap in the Distributist Record: 1930–1936," *The Chesterton Review*, vol. 24, no. 3 (August 1998).

32. Hilaire Belloc, *An Essay on the Restoration of Property* (London, 1936), p. 11.

33. Belloc to J. Stafford Johnson, 22 October 1932, Box 374–F, File 1932 "C," Belloc Papers, Burns Library.

34. Hilaire Belloc, *The Crisis of Our Civilization* (New York, 1937), p. 214.

35. Ibid., p. 235. Belloc did not insist that reform demanded conversion of everyone to the Catholic Church; rather, it depended on the existence of "Catholic culture," a condition in which the governing, economic, and social institutions were motivated by the Catholic spirit.

36. Belloc to Nickerson, 22 June 1936, Box 54, Letters 1935–36, "M,N,O," Belloc Papers, Burns Library.

37. Letter to Mrs. Reginald Balfour, 28 June 1922, in Robert Speaight, ed., *Letters from Hilaire Belloc* (London, 1958), p. 122.

Chapter 8. The Appeal of Fascism

1. See J. R. Jones, "England," in Hans Rogger and Eugen Weber, eds., *The European Right: A Historical Profile* (Berkeley, Calif., 1966); Alastair Hamilton, *The Appeal of Fascism* (New York, 1971); John P. Diggens, "American Catholics and Italian Fascism," *Journal of Contemporary History*, vol. 2 (1967), and his *Mussolini and Fascism: The View from America* (Princeton, N.J., 1972).

2. See E. Barker, *Political Thought in England* (London, 1915), p. 223.

3. See David Nicholls, *Three Varieties of Pluralism* (New York, 1974), p. 6.

4. This is noted by Anthony W. Wright, "Guild Socialism Revisited," *Journal of Contemporary History*, vol. 9 (1974), p. 167.

5. One could include in these ranks John Neville Figgis, G. D. H. Cole, Mandell Creighton, F. W. Maitland, Harold Laski, Chesterton, Belloc, and others.

6. From David Nicholls, *The Pluralist State* (New York, 1975), p. 3.

7. This position, of course, is similar to that taken by the Catholic personalist philosophers.

8. John Neville Figgis, *Churches in the Modern State* (London, 1913), p. 47.

9. Nicholls, *Three Varieties of Pluralism*, p. 54.

10. A. J. Penty, "Communism and Fascism," Part II, *American Review*, October 1936, p. 495.

11. G. K. Chesterton, *The Resurrection of Rome* (London, 1930), p. 263.

12. G. K. Chesterton, "On the One-Party System," in *Avowals and Denials* (London, 1934), p. 149.

13. G. K. Chesterton, *The Well and the Shallows* (New York, 1935), pp. 60–61.

14. The tendency to paint Chesterton with the brush of philo-fascism continues. Even those who admire the man have given credence to this mistaken legacy. For example, Michael Thorne, writing an appreciation of the Distributist League in the 1930s, associates Chesterton with Belloc and Gregory Macdonald, a major contributor to *G.K.'s Weekly*, as the "most prominent and persistent" advocates of the Fascist cause ("Filling a Gap in the Distributist Record: 1930–1936," *The Chesterton Review*, vol. 24, no. 3 [August 1998]: 313–314).

Kevin L. Morris, who has written one of the most insightful analyses of Catholics and Fascism to date, also overlooks Chesterton's condemnation of Fascism on pluralistic grounds. Morris writes that Chesterton appears to have followed Belloc in matters concerning Fascism but with slightly less enthusiasm. On balance, avers Morris, "Chesterton seems to have said more in favour of Fascism than against it." At best, he claims, Chesterton's attitude was ambivalent, and he failed to pursue its denunciation ("Fascism and British Catholic Writers, 1924–1939," *The Chesterton Review*, vol. 25, nos. 1 and 2 [February/May 1999]: 6).

15. See "A Socratic Symposium—III," *G.K.'s Weekly*, 25 July 1935.

16. Hilaire Belloc, "Mussolini and the Guild," *Weekly Review*, 15 June 1939.

17. "The Return of Caesar," *G.K.'s Weekly*, 27 July 1933, as reprinted in *The Chesterton Review*, vol. 25, nos. 1 and 2 (February/May 1999): 18–19.

18. From Robert Skidelsky, *Oswald Mosley* (New York, 1975), p. 17. This is the interpretation of Henry A. Turner as developed in his "Fascism and Modernization," *World Politics*, June 1972. Richard Thurlow, in *Fascism in Britain: A History, 1918–1985* (London, 1987), also emphasizes the continuity between the pre-1914 political right (notably Milner, Chamberlain, and the Unionist "Die-hards" who voted against the Parliament Act in the House of Lords in 1911 and who were strongly opposed to militant trade unionism) and British fascism. Thurlow, however, fails to note the significance of the Chesterton-Belloc group's leftist, syndicalist sympathies during these years and mistakenly links them with the Right. It is important to appreciate that it was not simply the Right that believed in political and economic conspiracies.

Barbara S. Farr's *The Development and Impact of Right-Wing Politics in Britain, 1903–1932* (New York, 1987) argues that a main source of British fascism was the right-wing political inspiration surrounding the new imperialism that came out of the Boer War. The major post–World War I events that stimulated right-wing and fascist organizations were the general strike threats of 1920 and 1921.

19. For example, see Colin Holmes, *Anti-Semitism in British Society, 1876–1939* (New York, 1979); Thurlow, *Fascism in Britain* and Kenneth Lunn, "Political Anti-Semitism before 1914: Fascism's Heritage?" in K. Lunn and R. Thurlow, eds. *British Fascism* (London, 1980). Richard Griffiths in his *Fellow Travellers of the Right* (London, 1983) considers the Chesterton-Belloc group to have been one of the main sources of British anti-Semitism. He argues that their positions owed much to the French Right, especially the theories of Le Play. Griffith's *The Reactionary Right* (London, 1966) provides a good discussion of the ideas of the French Right which can be compared to the programs and thinking of the Distributists.

20. K. Lunn, "Political Anti-Semitism," p. 28.

21. See Norman Cohn, *Warrant for Genocide* (Chico, Calif., 1981), for an examination of the impact of the *Protocols* on England, pp. 151–156.

22. See letters from Father Coughlin to Belloc, beginning in January 1938, Box I, Belloc Papers, Burns Library, Boston College. Belloc contracted to write fifty-two articles—not less than a thousand words each, for the total sum of one thousand pounds—for the *Social Justice Review* on the world's social and economic problems. The first appeared on 31 January 1938. This contract ended after the twenty-sixth article, when Coughlin claimed that the American depression cut deeply into his operating budget and the paper could no longer afford such expense.

23. Father Hogan charged that the real purpose of communism was to destroy Christianity, and that the effort was engineered by a clique of Jews who worked through a satanic organization called "Illuminized Freemasonry." See *Catholic Worker,* January 1939.

24. See "Priest Lashes Anti-Semitic Article," *Catholic Worker,* January 1939.

25. See "Father Coughlin," Parts I and II, n.d., Box 8; Folder 1, Shuster Archives, University of Notre Dame. At this time Coughlin was also taken on by *Commonweal.*

26. Ibid., Part II, p. 2. For important information on the Coughlin movement's activities beyond New York see Philip Jenkins, *Hoods and Shirts: The Extreme Right in Pennsylvania, 1925–1950* (Chapel Hill, N.C., 1997), and Kenneth J. Heineman, "A Catholic New Deal: Religion and Labor in 1930s Pittsburgh," *Pennsylvania Magazine of History and Biography* 118 (1994): 363–394.

27. See Norman Thomas to George Shuster, 25 July 1939, Box 5; File 17, 1939, Shuster Archives, University of Notre Dame.

28. See *New Age,* 7 December and 21 December 1907; 8 August 1908.

29. James Joll, *The Anarchists* (New York, 1964), p. 234.

30. See Stanley G. Payne, *Spanish Catholicism: an Historical Overview* (Madison, Wis., 1984), p. 133. Payne believes that the rioters were primarily inspired by the anticlericalism of the Radical Republican party led by Alejandro Lerroux rather than by anarchists, who at this point had little influence on Barcelona's working classes.

31. An examination of the events surrounding the *Semana Tragica* can be found in Joan Connelly Ullman, *The Tragic Week: A Study of Anticlericalism in Spain 1875–1912* (Cambridge, Mass., 1968). Irrespective of the question of Ferrer's culpability (the evidence Ullman provides shows that Ferrer was innocent of the charges), the sheer magnitude of the popular explosion against the establishment could never be explained by the work of one man (p. 298).

32. There were a number of possible explanations for the Radicals' decision to exclusively target Church property, most of which relate to the party's endeavors to create alliances with military elements within the government and to undermine Catalan separatist efforts. In fact, a compelling theory for the action is that the Radicals used anticlerical violence as a safety valve to diffuse tensions that had built up in Spanish society and that they could no longer control effectively. For more on this see Ullman, *Tragic Week,* chapter 15.

33. This analysis (replicated in Belloc's later assessment of the Spanish Civil War) overlooks the resentments that had led to similar anti-

clerical outbursts in 1835, 1868, and 1873. Another more astute and objective English historian of Spain correctly identified the problem. In his book on the Spanish Civil War, Hugh Thomas noted that the Spanish workers had a long and deep resentment of the clergy. They attacked churchmen, he wrote, "because they thought them hypocrites and because they seemed to give a false spiritual front to middle-class or upper-class tyranny" (Hugh Thomas, *The Spanish Civil War* [New York, 1963], p. 175). As Guenter Lewy has observed, the thesis that the violence against the Spanish Church was caused primarily by anticlericalism rather than hatred of religion can be seen from the fact that Protestant chapels in Madrid, Valencia, and other cities were not touched during the outbreak of the Spanish Civil War in 1936. Indeed, one mob in Barcelona that had set fire to a Protestant church quickly extinguished the blaze once the rioters realized their error (Guenter Lewy, *Religion and Revolution* [New York, 1974], citing John David Hughey, Jr., *Religious Freedom in Spain: Its Ebb and Flow* [London, 1955], p. 133).

34. "The International: V: The Motive Force," submitted to the *Dublin Review*, April 1910, Belloc Papers, Burns Library.

35. "The International: I: The Ferrer Case," submitted to the *Dublin Review*, January 1910, Belloc Papers, Burns Library.

36. It is interesting to note that the many international demonstrations for Ferrer also convinced the young Francisco Franco and his cadet classmates that the *Semana Tragica*, with its tones of anti-militarism, anti-clericalism, and Catalan separatism, was the product of an international conspiracy of Freemasons. Such events, claims a recent Franco biographer, must have been deeply resented by the impressionable young cadet and probably were "burnt deep into his consciousness." (See Paul Preston, *Franco: A Biography* [New York, 1994], p. 12.)

37. Ullman, *Tragic Week*, p. 315.

38. Despite Barcelona's importance as a seaport and the fact that many Frenchmen and Italians labored in her textile factories, almost all those arrested were of Spanish origin.

39. The workers identified the religious orders as close allies with capitalists and raged against what one of their leaders called the "existence of the plutocratic-clerical trusts" which "sucks up the blood of the workers and absorbs all wealth produced by labor" (Ullman, *Tragic Week*, p. 328. See also pp. 284–287).

40. Cecil Chesterton, "The Wrath of Mr. Wells," *New Witness*, 27 July 1916. For more on the Marconi affair see Frances Donaldson, *The Marconi Scandal* (London, 1962).

41. Cecil Chesterton, "For the Defense," *Eye-Witness*, 4 July 1912.

42. See *New Witness*, January 1913.

43. Belloc to Haynes, 26 August 1913, Box 1, Belloc Papers, Burns Library.

44. Hans Rogger and Eugen Weber, eds., quoting Brasillach in *The European Right*, p. 108.

45. Belloc to Baring, 25 March 1939, Letters to and/or from Belloc, 1939, Correspondence "B," Box 374–F, Belloc Papers, Burns Library.

46. F. H. O'Donnell, *New Witness*, 12 February 1914.

47. F. H. O'Donnell, *Eye-Witness*, 28 March 1912.

48. F. H. O'Donnell, *New Witness*, 2 July 1914. "Le Juif de L'Epoque" was the title of a French anti-Semitic book.

49. Belloc to Maurice Baring, 31 August 1916, in Robert Speaight ed., *Letters from Hilaire Belloc*, p. 73.

50. Belloc to E. S. P. Haynes, 13 December 1913, Box 1, Belloc Papers, Burns Library.

51. See Bernard Wasserstein, *Herbert Samuel: A Political Life* (Oxford, 1992), pp. 134–146.

52. F. H. O'Connell, *New Witness*, 9 October 1913.

53. From David Low, *Autobiography of David Low* (London, 1956), p. 133, as quoted in Holmes, p. 102.

54. Carter contributed to a series in the *New Witness* entitled "What shall we do with the Jews?" See *New Witness*, 25 September 1913. Her position on separating Jews from everyone else was the policy eventually advocated by the *New Witness*.

55. *New Witness*, 4 October 1918.

56. Kenneth Lunn, "Political Anti-Semitism before 1914: Fascism's Heritage?" p. 31, in Lunn and Thurlow, eds., *British Fascism*.

57. See Ibid., p. 34.

58. Hilaire Belloc, *The Jews* (Boston, 1922), p. 174.

59. The "worst peril of all," Belloc wrote Hoffman Nickerson, was that no Jew, however intelligent, "has any conception of either the imminence of the peril, or of the causes of it." The Jews, he predicted, were destined for terrible suffering (Belloc to Nickerson, 21 June 1922, "Belloc/Nickerson Correspondence," Hoffman Nickerson Papers, Burns Library).

60. See interview with Belloc in the *American Hebrew and Jewish Tribune*, 20 December 1935, MSS Box 7, 2 of 2, Belloc Papers, Burns Library.

61. Hilaire Belloc, "Portugal," p. 328, 22 July 1937, "Papers of G. K. Chesterton," Hoffman Nickerson Papers, Burns Library.

62. The commentary got Belloc entangled in legal troubles, for Nesta Webster threatened prosecution for libel. See Belloc's biographer's mem-

oirs, Robert Speaight, *The Property Basket: Recollections of a Divided Life* (London, 1970), p. 373.

63. Mussolini appreciated the support. In a personal audience with some American Catholics in the summer of 1935, Il Duce singled out both Belloc and Chesterton for their supreme reputation as Catholic writers. In his efforts to gain Italian-American backing for the Fascist regime, Mussolini had made assurances that he worked for the good and peace of Italians everywhere. The first principle for any political action, he insisted, had to be religious, and that was why Belloc and Chesterton achieved greatness:

> Ci dice a gl'Italiani di rimanere tranquilli perche io lavoror per il bene e per la pace di tutta l'Italia in qualunque cost.

> Ci dice agli uomini di essere uomini di buona religione, perche l'uomo senza religione non puo mai andare avanti. Considerate Belloc e Chesterton, i due gran scrittori Inglesi. Loro non potovavno mai arrivare alla grandezza della loro gloria se primo non avevano visto la luce della vera fede. (Letter from Father William Rowan to Hilaire Belloc, 10 September 1935, 581–B, Correspondence "R" 1935–36, Belloc Papers, Burns Library)

Father William H. Rowan wrote Belloc to inform him of Mussolini's statement, which was given to two of Rowan's friends who visited Il Duce in Rome. Belloc responded by saying that he was indeed most honored and delighted to hear praise from such an important governing quarter, the transcript of which he would keep as a most precious memorial (Belloc to Father William H. Rowan, 23 September 1935, 581-B, Correspondence "R" 1935–36, Belloc Papers, Burns Library).

64. Postcards and letters from Belloc to his wife while doing research for *The Path to Rome,* 24 June 1901, Box 2, Folder 14, Lunn Papers, Special Collections, Georgetown University.

65. Belloc to Nickerson, 7 May 1932, "Belloc/Nickerson Correspondence," Hoffman Nickerson Papers, Burns Library.

66. Unlike Belloc, G. K. Chesterton was far more critical of Mussolini's foreign policy. For example, see "Notes of the Week," *G.K.'s Weekly,* 9 November 1929, a critical commentary on Mussolini's belligerence toward Belgrade and his aspirations of turning the Adriatic into an Italian lake: as a European Mussolini "is not entitled to preach a policy of national aggrandizement unless the safety of Italy is endangered."

67. See Hilaire Belloc, "The Truce," *G.K.'s Weekly*, 9 November 1929.

68. Hilaire Belloc, "The Two Monarchies," *Weekly Review*, 25 August 1938.

69. "Notes," *Weekly Review*, 8 September 1938.

70. Hilaire Belloc, "Mussolini and the Guild," *Weekly Review*, 15 June 1939.

71. This essay appears to mark a shift in Belloc's thinking about Mussolini's heavy-handed methods. A year earlier, for example, he had written to his daughter Elizabeth that Mussolini had done wonders by re-organizing the guild system, but that there was no necessity for such despotism. A guild system "could arise quite naturally in a free society." This letter underscores the difficulty Belloc had criticizing Mussolini in the public forum. It was important, at all costs, to keep a tribal united front against the enemies of the faith. (See Belloc to Elizabeth, 21 April 1938, Box 1, Belloc Papers, Burns Library.)

72. Belloc to W. W. Blair-Fish, 27 October 1939, Box L16, Correspondence 1938–39, Belloc Papers, Burns Library. Belloc had mixed feelings about what he said concerning Mussolini in print. For instance, the personal sufferings of his friend, Max Beerbohm, gave him pause in his seemingly uncritical endorsement of Il Duce. Official anti-Semitism had forced Beerbohm as an old man to leave his family estate at Rapallo. This, wrote Belloc to Baring, was yet another example of the "injustice and folly" of the anti-Jewish policy in Italy. At least the Germans had an excuse for what they had done. (See Belloc to Baring, 25 March 1939, Box 374–F, Letters to and/or from Hilaire Belloc, 1939 Correspondence "B," Belloc Papers, Burns Library.)

73. Belloc to Baring, 21 March 1939, Box 374–F, Letters to and/or from Hilaire Belloc, 1939 Correspondence "B," Belloc Papers, Burns Library.

74. G. K. Chesterton, "Abyssinia," *G.K.'s Weekly*, 18 January 1935.

75. This was said by Geoffrey Davies, who claimed Chesterton would not have approved of the Distributist drift into the fascist camp. (See "At the Devereux," *G.K.'s Weekly*, 11 February 1937.)

76. Belloc to Chesterton, 29 November 1935, G. K. Chesterton Correspondence/Belloc, 1931–40, Wade Collection, Wheaton College, Wheaton, Illinois.

77. Hilaire Belloc, "Masonry and Italy," *G.K.'s Weekly*, 26 December 1935.

78. Belloc to his son, 5 August 1935, Box 1, Belloc Papers, Burns Library.

79. Belloc to Father Holland, 1 May 1936, 581–B, Letters 1935–36, "H," Belloc Papers, Burns Library.

80. Belloc to his son, 5 August 1935, Box 1, Belloc Papers, Burns Library.

81. *G.K.'s Weekly,* 11 June 1936. Chesterton wrote here that he hoped to write further on this subject in the next issue, but by that time he was dead.

82. See Donald Attwater, "English Catholic Fascists?" *Commonweal,* 10 January 1941, pp. 296–302. Attwater informed his friend Father H. A. Reinhold that this article got him into serious trouble with several leading conservative English Catholics (Attwater to H. A. Reinhold, 5 March 1946, Correspondence "Austin-Attwater-Auden," Number 8, H. A. Reinhold Papers, Burns Library, Boston College).

In this essay Attwater had described a "Latinophile" attitude, produced largely by Hilaire Belloc, which created the impression that Italy and France could do no wrong because they were rooted in Catholic culture. Attwater was commenting on a group of writers who had fallen under the sway of such attitudes and who had thereby created a fascist image for English Catholics in the American press. Generally, he wrote, the Latinophiles pushed for closer political cooperation between Britain and Mussolini and excused Italy's imperialism on the grounds that she was anti-communist and was forced into Abyssinia by the "folly of sanctions." The group also had a preoccupation with communist conspiracies (they blamed the fall of France on the "Reds," i.e., the Popular Front, and regarded Franco as a defender of Christianity against communism), and believed that Europe was dominated by a combination of bankers, secret societies (Freemasons), and Jews.

For a vigorous criticism of my own analysis of this group and the role of *G.K.'s Weekly* in the Abyssinian affair, see Gregory Macdonald, "And Now the Pink Legend: A Response to Jay P. Corrin," *The Chesterton Review,* vol. 3, no. 1 (Fall-Winter 1976–77); Lewis Filewood, "'Fascism' and the *Weekly Review*: a Response to Gregory Macdonald and Jay P. Corrin, *The Chesterton Review,* vol. 3, no. 1 (Fall-Winter 1976–77); and Gregory Macdonald, "Forty Years After: A Note by Gregory Macdonald," unpublished memoirs, 1974, Wade Collection, Wheaton College.

83. Gregory Macdonald, "Memoirs," p. 8, Wade Collection, Wheaton College.

84. See C. F. Hammond, "Financial Armageddon, Second Phase," *G.K.'s Weekly,* 24 October 1935, and G. Macdonald, "Looking On," *G.K.'s Weekly,* 17 October 1935.

85. This was put forward by Douglas Jerrold in *The Necessity of Freedom* (London, 1938), pp. 249–250. It was also Oswald Mosley's position. See Colin Cross, *The Fascists in Britain* (London, 1961). Perhaps the most

strident proponent of Mussolini and Fascism along lines similar to Belloc's came from the English Catholic writer James Strachey Barnes, who became a member (*honoris causa*) of the Italian National Fascist Party. Barnes claimed to have played the role of chronicler and prophet for the Fascist Revolution. See the autobiographical account of his work for Mussolini, *Half a Life Left* (New York, 1937), and his *Fascism* (London, 1934).

86. Thomas M. Coffey, *Lion by the Tail* (London, 1974), p. 307, as cited in Morris, "Fascism and British Catholic Writers, 1924–1929," p. 42.

87. For more see Evelyn Waugh, *Waugh in Abyssinia* (London, 1936).

88. Brocard Sewell said that there was a right and left faction in the Distributist movement at the time (he considered himself a man of the right) and that both Chesterton and Belloc represented the center. However, Belloc's private correspondence and what he wrote in the public domain bely this notion. Belloc not only sympathized with the right-wing Distributists, he was, as Donald Attwater correctly surmised, the very fountainhead of the Latinophile mentality. On the other hand, Sewell's memory serves him well in that Belloc, as opposed to Sewell himself, Herbert Shove, and a number of other Distributists, did not directly embrace the ideas of Mosley and the British Union of Fascists. (See Lyle W. Dorsett's interview with Brocard Sewell, 25 April 1985, Wade Collection, Wheaton College.)

89. G. K. Chesterton, "The Relapse," *G.K.'s Weekly*, 4 June 1936.

90. Chesterton to Reckitt, 19 September 1935, in Maisie Ward, *G. K. Chesterton* (New York, 1943), p. 548.

91. Archie Currie, "Cockpit," *G.K.'s Weekly*, 12 September 1935.

92. See G. K. Chesterton, "Which Is the Herring," *G.K.'s Weekly*, 19 September 1935.

93. G. K. Chesterton, "The Disaster," *G.K.'s Weekly*, 10 October 1935.

94. Conrad Bonacina, "Cockpit," *G.K.'s Weekly*, 26 September 1935.

95. Many of Chesterton's friends believed his lack of fire over Abyssinia was influenced by an intense commitment to Catholicism, which, as was always the case with Belloc, would have clouded his judgment. (See Mrs. Cecil Chesterton, *The Chestertons* (London, 1941), p. 298; Frank A. Lea, *The White Knight of Battersea: G. K. Chesterton* (London, 1946), p. 74; Jay P. Corrin, *G. K. Chesterton and Hilaire Belloc: The Battle against Modernity* (Athens, Ohio, 1981), pp. 210–211; and Morris, "Fascism and British Catholic Writers, 1924–1939.")

96. Lyle Dorsett interview with Gregory Macdonald, pp. 6–7, Wade Collection, Wheaton College.

97. Macdonald, "Memoirs," p. 7 ff., Wade Collection, Wheaton College.

98. See Corrin, *G. K. Chesterton and Hilaire Belloc.*

99. These included Jorian Jenks, A. K. Chesterton—the intellectual spark-plug of Mosley's British Union of Fascists and editor of its two chief propaganda organs, *Blackshirt* and *Action*—and J. L. Benvenisti.

100. Maurice Reckitt, *As It Happened* (London, 1941), p. 185.

Chapter 9. Early Catholic Critics of Fascism

1. See Carlo Francesco Weiss, "Corporatism and the Italian Catholic Movement," pp. 123–126, Ph.D. diss., Yale University, 1955.

2. *Quadragesimo Anno,* Article 95, in Oswald Von Nell-Breunning, S.J., *The Reorganization of Social Economy: The Social Encyclical Developed and Explained* (New York, 1936), pp. 426–427.

3. Barbara Ward, "Planned Economy in Catholic Social Thought," *Dublin Review,* January 1939, p. 88.

4. Virgil Michel, *Christian Social Reconstruction* (Milwaukee, Wis., 1937), pp. 98–99.

5. Röpke is one of the best examples of post-World War II efforts to amalgamate neoliberalism with Distributism. Röpke is considered the father of Germany's postwar economic recovery and had a major influence on similar programs undertaken in France and Italy. (See Jay P. Corrin, "The Neo-Distributism of Friedrich A. Hayek and Wilhelm Röpke," *Thought,* December 1988.)

6. Another impediment to interpretative analysis of Fascist corporatist ideas was the absence of patterned ideas to buttress its institutional structures. As Carlo Weiss has noted, Fascism was not an idea that had found some bayonets; it was not the embodiment of a creative principle, and it certainly was not, as Mussolini proclaimed, the "social content of the revolution." Fascism was rather "a de facto situation institutionalized." Its vital impulse was expressed through the actions of its charismatic leader, not through laws or institutions. That is why the only significant piece of writing on Fascism was Mussolini's own article in the *Encyclopedia Italiana,* which, of course, he actually did not write himself (Weiss, "Corporatism and the Italian Catholic Movement," p. 176).

7. Wilhelm Röpke, "Fascist Economics," *Economica,* vol. 2, no. 5 (February 1935): 87.

8. Ibid., p. 99.

9. See D. A. Binchy, *Church and State in Fascist Italy* (London, 1941), p. 338.

10. Ibid., p. 340.

11. For details, see George Seldes, *Sawdust Caesar* (New York, 1935), p. 99. Thomas Bokenkotter also has a chapter on Sturzo and Fascism in *Church and Revolution: Catholics and the Struggle for Democracy and Social Justice* (New York, 1998). See chapter 9, "Don Sturzo (1871–1959) vs. Mussolini's Revolution."

12. See H. A. Reinhold, "Don Luigi Sturzo," 16 May 1943, intended for *Orate Fratres*'s "Timely Tracts," Box 1, "Manuscripts," Reinhold Papers, Burns Library, Boston College.

Reinhold had a long relationship with Sturzo and his private papers contain many letters discussing the difficulties they both had trying to find support for their anti-fascist crusade among Catholics in America.

13. In 1935 the Jesuit magazine *America* conducted a national plebiscite for the purpose of deciding who were the greatest forty living Catholic authors. Those selected would be inducted into an Academy of the Gallery of Living Catholic Authors established at Webster College, Missouri. Twenty-five places were allotted to foreign writers, and fifteen to those of the United States. Father Francis X. Talbot, S.J., editor of *America*, announced the results in October 1936. G. K. Chesterton ranked the highest, but since he had just died and was also deemed the greatest Catholic writer of the generation, a special status was created for him. At the top of the list of the most important living Catholic writers was Hilaire Belloc, surpassing the likes of Jacques Maritain and Paul Claudel (see *America*, 10 October 1936).

14. Quoted in John N. Molony, *The Emergence of Political Catholicism in Italy* (London, 1977), p. 13.

Belloc may not have had much liking for Father Reinhold either. In a letter to a friend in September 1935, for instance, he made disparaging and facetious remarks about "a disquieting fellow named Reinhardt [*sic*]" who became dreadfully frightened when the Nazi party came to power and feared they would come over the Austrian border and kidnap him. "I am told that he has crawled back again." (File 581–B, Letters 1935–36 "H," Belloc Papers, Burns Library, Boston College).

15. See chapters 10 and 11 on H. A. Reinhold's work and travails.

16. Interview with Dorothy Day by Dean Brackley and Dennis Dillon, New York City, 28 January 1972, "Dorothy Day/Catholic Worker—Barry" Papers, W-9 Box 1, Special Collections, Marquette University.

17. Sturzo's sociological views are most fully detailed in *The Inner Laws of Society: A New Sociology* (New York, 1943; first published in Italian, 1935).

18. Nicholas S. Timasheff, *The Sociology of Luigi Sturzo* (Baltimore, 1962), pp. 67–68.

19. Luigi Sturzo, *Church and State* (New York, 1939), p. 479.

20. Luigi Sturzo, "Corporatism: Christian-Social, and Fascist," *Catholic World,* July 1937, pp. 398–399.

21. For a discussion of Sturzo's ideas on agrarian reform see Malcolm Moos, "Don Luigi Sturzo—Christian Democrat," *American Political Science Review* 39 (April 1945): 269–292. Sturzo's views were very similar to the English Distributists with whom he corresponded.

22. Luigi Sturzo, *Italy and Fascism* (New York, 1945), p. 97.

23. Carl T. Schmidt, *The Corporative State in Action: Italy under Fascism* (London, 1939), p. 44.

24. Ibid., p. 96.

25. Ibid., p. 112.

26. Other American Catholics also gave witness against Mussolini. Father James Cox, for example, had studied Italian Fascism firsthand in 1932. Upon returning to the United States he denounced the complete denigration of religious and political freedom under Mussolini. See "Father Cox Has a Closeup View of Mussolini," *Christian Century* 49 (27 July 1932), pp. 925–926, and John Hearley, *Pope or Mussolini* (New York, 1929), which also exposed for American Catholics the antidemocratic nature of Mussolini's regime.

27. See Weiss, "Corporatism and the Italian Catholic Movement," pp. 170–171.

28. Mussolini's hatred for religion was a product of primary socialization. His father had named him after Benito Juarez, the Mexican archenemy of Church privilege. From his earliest youth, Mussolini had been steeped in an environment of intense anticlericalism.

29. John P. McKnight, "The Papacy and Fascism," from his *The Papacy: a New Appraisal* (London, 1952), as quoted in Charles F. Delzell, ed., *The Papacy and Totalitarianism between the Wars* (New York, 1974), p. 23.

30. This is made clear in Count Caleazzo Ciano, *The Ciano Diaries* (Garden City, N.Y., 1946). Although Il Duce generally kept his contempt for the Church close to the vest for political purposes, any well-informed Catholic would have come across the well-documented occasions when he expressed hatred for that institution and everything it held sacred.

31. For instance, the archbishop of Boston, Cardinal William O'Connell, who openly expressed admiration for Il Duce and was highly suspicious of the Catholic Worker movement because he feared it might be crypto-communist, resisted efforts to involve his clergy in social action. After having spoken with the cardinal at length in Boston, Norman McKenna, editor of *The Christian Front,* told his friend Father Paul Furfey that O'Connell did not grasp the situation confronting the American

working class, had very few substantive questions to ask concerning the activities of the *Catholic Worker* group, and "simply does not understand the purport of the latest encyclicals." (See McKenna to Furfey, 20 December 1935, "McKenna-Furfey Correspondence," Z-26, Virgil Michel Papers, St. John's University.)

32. For example, the most informed and perceptive analyses of the various fascist movements were written by Catholic liberals: Sturzo, Waldamer Gurian, H. A. Reinhold, and George Shuster, one-time editor of *Commonweal*. Their studies of Nazism and Italian Fascism have withstood the test of time and are supported by current scholarship on the subject.

33. Catholic publications and associations critical of Fascism from the outset included those of the American and British Dominicans, especially the latter's magazine *Blackfriars*, Harold Robbins' *The Cross and the Plough* (a back-to-the-land English Distributist publication), the English Catholic Social Guild and its publication, *Christian Democracy*, the *Dublin Review* when it was under the editorship of Christopher Dawson, and *PAX*, a journal of the British liturgists edited by Donald Attwater. In America, Dorothy Day's *Catholic Worker* was a leading opponent of Fascism, as was a related publication, Norman McKenna's *The Christian Front*. The Paulist monthly *Catholic World*, *Commonweal*, and *Orate Fratres*, the mouthpiece of the American liturgical movement started by the Distributist Benedictine educator Virgil Michel, also assumed a highly critical stance concerning Fascism.

34. See Richard Gribble, C.S.C., *Guardian of America: The Life of James Martin Gillis, C.S.P.* (New York, 1998). An earlier biography is James F. Finley's *James Gillis, Paulist* (Garden City, N.Y., 1958). The latter is a popular, straightforward and rather uncritical account of Gillis's life. Gribble's treatment is more scholarly, disinterested, and analytical.

35. When the Jesuit journal *America* finally published an anonymous article critical of Mussolini in March 1939—the fact that the author chose not to reveal his name suggests the chilling environment for Catholics critical of Fascism—Gillis remarked that for the first time he did not feel so isolated concerning his analysis of Mussolini. (See "Editorial Comments," *Catholic World*, April 1939.)

36. "Editorial Comments," *Catholic World*, March 1926.

37. "Editorial Comments," *Catholic World*, December 1924.

38. See "Editorial Comments," *Catholic World*, February and December 1930. Father Gillis's concerns about such matters were shared by America's best-known Catholic social activist, the influential Father John A. Ryan. Note Ryan's criticism of Fascist statism in *Declining Lib-*

erty (New York, 1927). Indeed, like many liberal Catholics, Ryan believed that the great danger to America came not from communism but from some source of fascism. (See letter to H. A. Reinhold, 14 January 1943, "R" Number 8, Reinhold Papers, Burns Library, Boston College.) Ryan appreciated the danger of Father Charles Coughlin's movement in such light, and he, along with Gillis, became one of the radio priest's most outspoken critics. (For the details surrounding Ryan's battles with Coughlin and his right-wing supporters with the *Brooklyn Tablet*, see John A. Ryan Papers, Boxes "Coughlin" and "Ryan Writing, 1935–40," Special Collections, Catholic University of America.)

39. "Editorial Comments," *Catholic World*, August 1931.

40. "Editorial Comments," *Catholic World*, April 1939.

41. See "Editorial Comments," *Catholic World*, November 1935 and August 1936.

42. See *Church and State*, pp. 502–505. The Parisian Jesuit publication *Les Etudes, La Vie Intelectuelle* of the French Dominicans, *Blackfriars*, the *Commonweal*, and the *Catholic Worker* also supported this position.

43. "Editorial Comments," *Catholic World*, November 1935.

44. "Editorial Comments," *Catholic Review*, December 1935.

45. Richard Gribble, *Guardian of America*, p. 147. Gribble reveals that Frank Hall of the National Catholic Welfare Conference News Service received so many letters critical of Gillis's columns that he asked him to "shift to something less controversial." Gillis's harsh criticisms of Mussolini were unpopular both in Italy and with the Vatican. The Paulist Superior General John Harney was informed that the Italian consulate in New York had placed the Paulist Fathers "and particularly Gillis" under observation. Moreover, the Secretary of the Sacred Congregation of Extraordinary Ecclesiastical Affairs had also contacted the Paulists in Rome to complain about a Gillis *Catholic World* editorial and radio talk which had attacked Mussolini. (See Richard Gribble, *Guardian of America*, pp. 148 and 291.)

46. "Editorial Comments," *Catholic World*, July 1936.

Chapter 10. Social Catholicism and the Career of H. A. Reinhold

1. From an interview with Father William Leonard, S.J., of Boston College, an early participant in the American liturgical movement, Chestnut Hill, Mass., 21 October 1990. Father Leonard was founder of Boston College's Liturgical Library Collection, "Liturgy and Life."

2. John S. Kennedy, "Variations in Accomplishment," *Hartford Transcript*, 26 January 1968.

3. For more on the life and work of Romano Guardini (1885–1968) see Robert A. Krieg, C.S.C., ed., *Romano Guardini: Proclaiming the Sacred in a Modern World* (Chicago, 1995).

4. Quoted in Warren G. Bovee, "H.A.R., Front Line Fighter," *Today*, December 1954, p. 4.

5. The Nazis closed down the Catholic seamen's clubs in 1939.

6. H.A.R. to Oldmeadow, 18 September 1935, Box "Correspondence: T File," H. A. Reinhold Papers, Burns Library, Boston College.

Reinhold always was cautious when writing about conditions in Germany, such was his fear of the Gestapo. He frequently wrote articles under different names and refused to grant interviews, lest the Nazis hurt his family. For example, see H.A.R. to Frederic Kenkel, 27 August 1936, Box "Correspondence: Immigration and Naturalization File," Reinhold Papers, Burns Library.

7. H.A.R. to Father ?, 30 November 1935, Box "Correspondence: W File," Reinhold Papers, Burns Library. Reinhold's analysis of Nazism appears to have been influenced by his contacts with the German Catholic publicist Waldemar Gurian. As early as 1932 Gurian had equated Nazism and Bolshevism as secular religions. (See *Um des Reiches Zukunft* [Freiburg, 1932]. Gurian wrote this book under the name of Walter Gerhart.)

8. When the German bishops withdrew their prohibitions against the Nazi regime in the spring of 1933, many Catholics responded with great enthusiasm. Bertram pushed for lifting the ban on Nazism, fearing that failure to do so would lead to massive Catholic defections to the Protestant Church. (See Richard Rolfs, "The Role of Adolf Cardinal Bertram . . . in the Church's Struggle in the Third Reich," Ph.D. diss., University of California, Santa Barbara, 1976, p. 30.)

9. Ludwig Volk, S.J., *Catholische Kirche und Nationalsozialismus* (Mainz, 1987), p. 258.

10. See Guenter Lewy, *The Catholic Church and Nazi Germany* (New York, 1964), p. 316; Walter Adolph, *Sie sind nicht Vergessen* (Berlin, 1972), pp. 23–24; and Richard Rolfs, "The Role of Adolf Cardinal Bertram." Rolfs conducted numerous personal interviews with Father Adolph, a confidant of the bishop of Berlin, Konrad von Preysing. This bishop was a consistent opponent of the German episcopate's dealings with the Hitler regime, and Rolfs's interviews shed valuable light on the Church's relationship with the Nazis. See also Walter Adolph, *Geheime Auszeichnungen aus dem Nationalsozialistischen KirchenKampf 1935–1945* (Mainz, 1979).

It is interesting to note that when Cesare Orsenigo was under fire by several German bishops in 1937, especially by Bishop Preysing, for being too sympathetic with the Nazis, Cardinal Bertram wrote a letter to the Vatican extolling the work of the papal nuncio and requesting that he be allowed to remain in Berlin (Adolph, *Geheime Auszeichnungen aus dem Nationalsozialistischen KirchenKampf,* p. 40).

11. See Volk, *Katholische Kirche und Nationalsozialismus,* pp. 257–258.

12. For background on the Concordat see Stewart A. Stehlin, *Weimar and the Vatican 1919–1933: German-Vatican Diplomatic Relations in the Interwar Years* (Princeton, N.J., 1983), and John Zeender, "The Genesis of the German Concordat of 1933," in Nelson H. Minnich, Robert B. Eno, S.J., and Robert F. Trisco, eds., *Studies in Catholic History in Honor of John Tracy Ellis* (Wilmington, Del., 1985), pp. 617–665.

13. See Adolph, *Geheime Auszeichnungen aus dem Nationalsozialistischen KirchenKampf,* pp. 39–40.

14. Ernst-Wolfgang Böckenförde, "German Catholicism in 1933," trans. Raymond Schmandt, *Cross Currents,* vol. 2, no. 3 (Summer 1961): 289.

15. Lewy, *The Catholic Church and Nazi Germany,* pp. 172–173.

16. H. A. Reinhold, *The Autobiography of Father Reinhold* (New York, 1968), p. 81.

17. Appendix to letter of H.A.R. to Bishop W. Berning, S.T.D., of Osnabrück, Germany, Box "Correspondence: File B," Burns Library. Reinhold sent this letter to Berning on 15 April 1947, after the bishop had invited him to return to Germany.

18. Adolf Schuckelgruber (pen name of H.A.R.), "The Church in Germany," n.d., p. 294, Box 1, "Manuscripts," Burns Library.

19. Even Cardinal Michael von Faulhaber, Archbishop of Munich, and one of the most ardent critics of the Nazis and Cardinal Bertram's conciliatory policies toward the regime, could never be convinced that Hitler himself was the source of all the trouble. He was blinded from recognizing this evil, writes the historian Ludwig Volk, S.J., by Hitler's charisma and "statesmanlike aura" (Ludwig Volk, S.J., "Lebensbild," in Andreas Kraus, ed., *Acten Kardinal Michael von Faulhabers,* vol. 1: *1917–1945* [Mainz, 1978], p. lxxiv).

20. Scrutator (pen name of H.A.R.), "The Catholic Church in Germany and Nazi Persecution," n.d., p. 7, Box 1, "Manuscripts," Burns Library.

21. The Church's response to National Socialism has been a subject of considerable controversy. Immediately after the war Johann Neuhäusler published a two-volume, richly documented book, *Kreuz und Hakenkreuz* (Munich, 1946), showing that the German bishops had vigorously but unsuccessfully resisted Nazi rule. Neuhäusler's view, buttressed by other

books authored by Johanna Maria Lenz, *Christus in Dachau* (Vienna, 1956), Konrad Hoffman, *Zeugnis und Kampf des deutschen Episkopats* (Freiburg im Breisgau, 1946), Gerhard Ritter, *The German Resistance: Carl Goerdeler's Struggle against Tyranny* (London, 1958), and Hans Rothfels, *The German Opposition to Hitler: An Assessment* (London, 1961), along with a spate of biographies on Catholic anti-Nazis, held sway through the early 1960s. For an American view along such lines, see Mary Alice Gallin's *German Resistance to Hitler: Ethical and Religious Factors* (Washington, D.C., 1961). In the view of Gallin, "Catholic bishops offered straightforward and courageous opposition to the ideology and tactics of the Nazis" (p. 229). H. A. Reinhold, Walter Gurian, and a few émigré intellectuals took strong objection to the "Neuhäusler thesis," though they constituted a distinct minority.

Eventually a number of younger German revisionist historians and dissident journalists began to cast a more critical eye on the episcopal relationship with the Hitler regime. One of the first influential critiques of the Church's record was Ernst Böckenförde's article "Der Deutsche Katholizismus im Jahre 1933," which appeared in the liberal Catholic journal *Hochland* in 1960/61. (The significance of this study was such that Raymond Schmandt translated it for *Cross Currents* in the summer of 1961.) Böckenförde's argument essentially corroborated Reinhold's position, namely, that the German bishops had not been solidly opposed to the National Socialists and that the signing of the Concordat in 1933 was a disaster for the Church in that it made it impossible for the episcopate to lead Catholics in opposition to Hitler. Reinhold's prescient arguments were given further support by a number of other scholars, including Hans Müler, "Zur Behandlung des Kirchen Kampfes im der Nachkriegsliteratur," *Politische Studien* 12 (July 1961), and *Katholische Kirche und Nationalsozialismus* (Munich, 1965). For a good overview of this controversy see Richard Rolfs, "Adolf Cardinal Bertram," pp. 2–6.

American scholars soon joined the fray. Gordon Zahn, for example, concluded that the average German Catholic had no desire to oppose the Nazis and that his religious leaders actually called upon him to support Hitler's wars. After rigorous investigation, Zahn learned of no more than seven Catholics who openly refused Nazi military service. (See his *German Catholics and Hitler's Wars* [New York, 1962], p. 54.) Zahn's arguments appear to have caused vexation in certain high Church circles. Zahn wrote H. A. Reinhold that the German hierarchy formally protested his research report. The president of Loyola University in Chicago was told that some "top-ranking prelate" in Rome was monitoring Zahn's work and might demand "redress." It appears that neither Zahn nor the president of Loyola were intimidated by such pressures (Zahn to Reinhold, 1 March 1960, Box "Correspondence: File Z, Burns Library).

Perhaps the most searing critique of the German Catholic hierarchy and the Nazis has come from Guenter Lewy. Drawing on copious unpublished German sources, Lewy showed that the bishops were largely supportive of dictatorship, that by 1935 they were diligently trying to find common ground with Nazism, but that in the end they totally misunderstood the nature of Hitler and his movement: "One must conclude," writes Lewy, "that the [Catholic] view of the Nazi regime as merely another conventional political system was based on unsophisticated political perspective" (*The Catholic Church in Nazi Germany*, p. 169). Finally, note the recent assessment of Klemens von Klemperer. In *The German Resistance against Hitler* (Oxford, 1992), Klemperer writes that on balance, the churches in Germany took no part in the *Widerstand* against Hitler (p. 37). The German Catholics, for their part, were consumed with the need to demonstrate their "national" reliability. This patriotic imperative, combined with a fear of communist dictatorship, made it far more politically expedient to equivocate on the issue of National Socialism (p. 38).

22. See letter from H.A.R. to friends, 19 June 1935, "Hapsburg File, 1936–1938," Reinhold Papers, Burns Library.

23. See appendix to letter of Rev. H. A. Reinhold to Bishop W. Berning, S.T.D., of Osnabrück, Germany, Reinhold Papers, Burns Library.

24. Joseph Lortz, the distinguished Reformation historian, argued that Catholicism and National Socialism occupied the same ground in opposing the destructive forces within the Weimar Republic, namely, liberalism, immorality, relativism, atheism, and Bolshevism (Robert Anthony Krieg, C.S.C., *Karl Adam: Catholicism in German Culture* [Notre Dame, 1992], p. 115).

25. In a letter to Father Ostermann in March 1936 Reinhold wrote that he subsisted on handouts for about three months in 1935, mostly from American benefactors: "You hardly imagine what an emigrant's life is! One month I spent about 15 (fifteen) Dollars for postage writing letters to all parts of the world to find out a position!" Box "Correspondences, File O," Reinhold Papers, Burns Library.

26. A. Hudal from Rome to "My Lord," 27 May 1935, Box 2: "Correspondences, 1935–36," Reinhold Papers, Burns Library.

27. Letter from H.A.R. to friends, 19 June 1935, "Hapsburg File, 1936–38," Reinhold Papers, Burns Library.

28. H.A.R., appendix of letter to Berning, Reinhold Papers, Burns Library.

29. Ibid.

30. Box 3, "The Cardinal of Vienna," p. 7, n.d. or source where published, Reinhold Papers, Burns Library.

31. Pope Pius XI made it clear that he himself had no responsibility for Innitzer's statements about Hitler. Pius insisted that the cardinal publicly modify his position on the Nazis. (See Gordon Zahn, "The Unpublished Encyclical—an Opportunity Missed," *National Catholic Reporter* 9, no. 8 [15 December 1972], p. 9.)

32. "The Church in Germany: Kulturkampf or Persecution?" written for *The Catholic World,* n.d., Box 1, "Manuscripts," Burns Library. Recent scholarship shows that Reinhold's analyses were very accurate. His writings, along with those of Konrad Heiden and Waldemar Gurian, were some of the very best contemporary analytical accounts of the activities of Hitler. For example, see "Princeps Huius Saeculii: the Church and Totalitarian Systems," by Johann Hiedler (a.k.a. H.A.R.), and "The Catholic Church in Germany after Four Years of Hitler's Dictatorship," by E. H. R. Lich-Keith (a.k.a. H.A.R.), Box 1, "Manuscripts," Reinhold Papers, Burns Library. Reinhold was the source of much information on German affairs for those who wrote for *Commonweal,* in particular for George Shuster.

33. A good example of this can be seen in Leni Riefenstahl's "Triumph of the Will," a Nazi film documentary on the great Nuremberg rallies. These gigantic gatherings graphically reveal the extent to which the Nazis went to link their message with ancient Catholic rituals.

34. "Princeps Huius Saeculii," p. 7.

35. "What About Christians in Germany," n.d., Box 1, "Manuscripts," Reinhold Papers, Burns Library.

36. Reinhold's private papers contain numerous personal letters to his friends Don Luigi Sturzo and Waldemar Gurian, for example, where the priest comments extensively on the shocking rise of anti-Semitism even among Catholics and offers his own personal feelings about the matter. (See "Gurian, Waldemar" File, Reinhold Papers, Burns Library. Gurian concurred with Reinhold's sentiments and observations on the issue.)

37. "Let us Fight Anti-Semitism in Our Own Ranks," pp. 6–7, n.d., Box 1 "Manuscripts," Reinhold Papers, Burns Library. Reinhold also helped Oesterreicher expand his work into England through his contacts with Donald Attwater, who introduced Oesterreicher and his mission to Father Victor White, John Epstein, and Eric Gill. (See H.A.R. to Attwater, 25 July 1938, "Correspondences, File O," Reinhold Papers, Burns Library.)

38. Reverend Joseph Stang of Colfax, Washington, wrote Reinhold a nasty letter in 1943, suggesting that his liberal ideas were the result of Jewish blood. Reinhold responded to Stang pointing out that he was not

Jewish—though wished it were so, thus sharing the same blood with Christ. Reinhold said that he came to America, in part, to escape the scourge of anti-Semitism, which he had mistakenly thought infected mostly Nazis. He quickly discovered, he informed Rev. Stang, that a hatred of Jews was rife in the U.S., even among the Catholic clergy. (See H.A.R. to Rev. Joseph Stang, 11 January 1943, Box "Correspondence: Moenius, Stang, et al. File," Reinhold Papers, Burns Library.)

Kathleen Hughes in her book on Godfrey Diekmann also makes the mistake of identifying Reinhold as Jewish (*The Monk's Tale: A Biography of Godfrey Diekmann, O.S.B.* [Collegeville, Minn., 1991], p. 113). Reinhold noted in his autobiography that even as a youngster he had been thought to be a Jew, though this was not the case.

39. Letter from H. A. R. to Waldemar Gurian, 12 September 1936, Box "Correspondence: Gurian File," Reinhold Papers, Burns Library.

40. "The Catholic Church in Germany and Nazi Persecution," by Scrutator (a.k.a. H. A. R.), Box 1, "Manuscripts," Reinhold Papers, Burns Library.

Reinhold's assessment was shared by a friend, the Jesuit anti-Nazi Friedrich Muckermann. Muckermann wrote in 1946 that the German Catholic laymen saw much more clearly the dangers of Nazism than did the bishops or academicians (Friedrich Muckermann, S.J., *Der deutsche Weg* [Zurich, 1946], p. 25).

41. E. Forelicher to Cardinal Hayes, n.d., Box "Correspondence: File F," Reinhold Papers, Burns Library.

42. H.A.R. to Mrs. N. Brady, 13 June 1936, Box "Correspondence: File B," Reinhold Papers, Burns Library.

43. "The Cardinal of Vienna," n.d. or source where published, Box 3, Reinhold Papers, Burns Library.

44. Father Carroll to Sister Adele and Sister Rosemary, St. Francis General Hospital, Pittsburgh, 18 February 1967, Box 6, "Reinhold Estate," Reinhold Papers, Burns Library.

45. There were few Catholic charities at this time in either the United States or Europe where people could turn for sympathy and understanding, the exception being Holland, where political exiles were given shelter by Catholic Church authorities.

46. "Summary of Conference on Christian German Refugees," 6 October 1936, "Correspondence: File A," Reinhold Papers, Burns Library.

47. H.A.R. to Frank Ritchie, 6 October 1936, "Correspondence: File A," Reinhold Papers, Burns Library.

48. See appendix of Reinhold letter to Berning.

49. See George Shuster, "Father Coughlin," n.d., Part I, Box 8, Folder 1, Shuster Archives, University of Notre Dame.

50. The archdiocese of New York at this time required that any visiting priest who said more than three Masses in any parish or religious house within its jurisdiction report to the chancery office to have his credentials approved (See Reinhold, *Autobiography*, p. 105).

51. See letters of H.A.R. to McIntyre, Box "Correspondence: Chancery-New York City," Reinhold Papers, Burns Library.

52. H.A.R. to Waldemar Gurian, 12 September 1936, Box "Correspondence: Gurian, Waldemar," Reinhold Papers, Burns Library.

53. See H.A.R. letter to McIntyre, 13 January 1937, Box "Correspondence: Chancery–New York City," Reinhold Papers, Burns Library.

54. H.A.R. to Cushing, 11 January 1937, Box 6: "Cushing, September 29, 1936–January 14, 1937," Reinhold Papers, Burns Library.

55. Appendix of letter to Berning, p. 3, and H.A.R. to Friends, 19 June 1935, Box "Correspondence: Hapsburg, 1936–1938," Reinhold Papers, Burns Library.

Reinhold's brother tried to convince him to return to Germany in order to settle family business matters. Reinhold decided against it only after Henrich Bruening, the former chancellor of Germany, warned that the Gestapo was waiting to arrest him. See Box 5, "Miscellaneous, My Colorful Uncle," Reinhold Papers, Burns Library.

56. For example, see H.A.R. to Rev. Joseph Ostermann, 12 January 1940; H.A.R. to John J. O'Connor, Catholic News Editor, National Conference of Jews and Christians, 24 January 1937, Box "Correspondence, File O," and letter of 11 December 1939, "Correspondence, File P and Q," Reinhold Papers, Burns Library.

Reinhold frequently kept a low profile in his work for refugees. For example, he contacted Father John LaFarge, S.J., in 1938 to see what could be done through the State Department to save the former chancellor of Austria Kurt von Schuschnigg (the State Department had rescued Bruening from Germany in 1933). Reinhold in this particular instance worked quietly, since, as he told La Farge, he did not want American Church authorities to regard him as an activist (LaFarge to W. Parsons, 23 March 1938, Parsons Papers, Box 6/*America* 1938 D-6, Special Collections, Georgetown University).

57. His scholarship was highly regarded. Hannah Arendt, for instance, praised Gurian's brief essay on German anti-Semitism in Koppel Pinson, ed., *Essays on Antisemitism* (New York, 1946) as "outstanding" and "extraordinary," fully reflective of the profundity of thinking that Gurian brought to everything that interested him (Hannah Arendt, "The Per-

sonality of Waldemar Gurian," *Review of Politics*, January 1955, p. 34). In fact, Gurian's analyses of Nazism, Bolshevism, and anti-Semitism were similar to that of Arendt as outlined in her monumental study, *The Origins of Totalitarianism*, 1951. The January 1955 edition of *Review of Politics* is devoted to the career of Waldemar Gurian.

58. See his *Bolshevism as a World Danger* (New York, 1935), and Gurian to H.A.R., 19 July 1936, Box "Correspondence: Gurian, Waldemar," Reinhold Papers, Burns Library.

59. *Deutschen Briefe*, 31 May 1936, quoted in M. A. Fitzsimmons, "Die Deutschen Briefe: Gurian and the German Crisis," *Review of Politics*, January 1955, p. 62.

60. See M. A. Fitzsimmons' article on *Deutschen Briefe* in the *Review of Politics* for more on Gurian's work in exile.

61. Waldemar Gurian to H.A.R., 24 May 1937, Box "Correspondence: Gurian, Waldemar," Reinhold Papers, Burns Library.

62. See Waldemar Gurian, "Bolshevism and Anti-Bolshevism," *Colosseum*, June 1937.

63. See "Correspondence," *Colosseum*, September 1937. Gurian was undoubtedly pleased that Bernard Wall, editor of *Colosseum*, had allowed him to publish in his journal, for the article under review was a criticism of Wall's own philo-fascism. Wall, like Belloc and his circle, had regarded Mussolini as an acceptable partner in the fight for Christianity against the perils of Marxism. It was Wall's contention, for example, that the "Right" was less dangerous than the Left for Christians, since religion and social justice could be achieved under its rule, but never under communism. The fact that Wall permitted contrary views to be published in his journal convinced Gurian that Wall was not yet a fascist (Gurian to H.A.R., 10 March 1937, Box "Correspondence: Gurian, Waldemar," Reinhold Papers, Burns Library). Despite Gurian's liberal positions, Wall collaborated with Father Reinhold in helping him find employment in America.

64. In Gurian's mind, these included George Shuster, whom Gurian believed had taken Bruening's side in their quarrels, Frank Sheed, and Godfried Briefs, among others. (See H.A.R. to Gurian, 1 June 1937; Gurian to H.A.R., 10 March 1937, 19 March 1937, and 29 March 1937, Box "Correspondence: Gurian, Waldemar," Reinhold Papers, Burns Library.) In frustration, Gurian even lashed out at Father Reinhold at times. (See H.A.R. to Gurian, 18 July 1937.)

65. See Sturzo to P. Meegan, 7 April 1937, Box "Correspondence, S File," Reinhold Papers, Burns Library.

66. H.A.R. to Sturzo, 26 August 1940, Box "Correspondence, S File," Reinhold Papers, Burns Library.

67. Reinhold, *Autobiography,* p. 125.

68. Paul Furfey to Norman McKenna, 30 October 1936, "McKenna-Furfey Correspondence," Z-26, Michel Papers, St. John's University.

69. Father Reinhold had studied at Maria Laach. His experiences with the Benedictines had a profound impact on his spiritual growth and were undoubtedly a strong source of Reinhold's liberal social ideas.

70. Mortimer Adler, "A Christian Educator," *Orate Fratres,* 22 January 1939.

71. R. W. Franklin and Robert L. Spaeth, *Virgil Michel: American Catholic* (Collegeville, Minn., 1988), p. 39.

72. A large number of subscribers were laity, who from the outset, it appears, showed more interest in promoting the liturgy than did the clergy. (See Paul Marx, *The Life and Works of Virgil Michel* [Washington, D.C., 1957], p. 126.) According to John Cogley, after Reinhold took over Virgil Michel's column "Timely Tracts," many of the clergy regarded the journal as "downright subversive" for its open-mindedness concerning the use of the vernacular in the Mass. Cogley also wrote that even during the era of John XXIII the liberal magazine *Commonweal* had to be passed around surreptitiously in many religious houses and seminaries (John Cogley, *A Canterbury Tale, Experiences and Reflections: 1916–1976* [New York, 1976], p. 72).

73. This is a term coined by E. K. Hunt to describe the moral code that governed the Middle Ages. See his *Property and Prophets: The Evolution of Economic Institutions and Ideologies,* 5th ed. (New York, 1986).

74. Virgil Michel, "The Liturgy: The Basis of Social Regeneration," an address given at the thirty-seventh annual convention of the Minnesota branch of the Central-Verein, Mankato, Minn., September 22–24, 1935, reprinted in *Orate Fratres,* 2 November 1935, p. 541.

75. Ibid., p. 543.

76. Virgil Michel quoting Christopher Dawson, ibid., p. 545.

77. Marx, *Life and Works of Virgil Michel,* p. 92.

78. This sentiment continues to be a source of contention among American Catholics. See Peter Steinfels, "Latin Mass at St. Patrick's Brings Conservative Discontents to the Fore," *New York Times,* 12 May 1996.

79. H. A. Reinhold, for instance, wrote his English friend Arthur Gannon that he had a "bitter experience with the American Irish clergy" because of his liberal views (H.A.R. to Gannon, 8 May 1936, File "Correspondence: Arthur Gannon," Reinhold Papers, Burns Library).

80. Clifford Howell to H.A.R., 5 June 1948, Box "Correspondence: Howell, Clifford, S.J.," Reinhold Papers, Burns Library.

81. Helen Angela Hurley, *On Good Ground* (Minneapolis, Minn., 1951), p. 261, quoted in Franklin and Spaeth, *Virgil Michel,* p. 62.

82. Father Michel, for example, waged an ardent campaign against the distortions of Catholic social teachings produced by some of the more popular Catholic catechisms on communism. (See his letter to *Catholic Worker*, n.d., "Virgil Michel" file, W-2.2, Box 2, Dorothy Day/Catholic Worker Papers, Marquette University.)

83. Stanley Vishnewski, "Days of Action," p. 3, unpublished MSS, W-12.3, Box 1, Dorothy Day/Catholic Worker Papers, Marquette University.

84. Ibid., p. 5.

85. Early leaders of what was called "New Social Catholicism" included Virgil Michel, Dorothy Day, Richard Deverall, John LaFarge, S.J., Norman McKenna, Father James Gillis, and Rev. Paul Hanley Furfey, among others.

86. Norman McKenna to Paul Furfey, 12 November 1936, "McKenna-Furfey Correspondences," Z-26, Virgil Michel Papers, St. John's University.

87. Virgil Michel, "The Fight against Communism," *Orate Fratres*, 24 January 1937.

88. For Michel's embrace of Distributism and what he regarded as the virtues of its programs see his "Timely Tracts: On Social Environment," *Orate Fratres*, 15 May 1938; "Timely Tracts: City or Farm," 12 June 1938; and his *Christian Social Reconstruction* (Milwaukee, 1937), p. 121.

89. Attwater was lay editor of Caldey Abbey's *Pax*, an English Benedictine publication, and its *Notes of the Month*. He also was well known for his translations of the principal works of the Russian philosopher Nicholas Berdyaev.

90. Marx, *Life and Works of Virgil Michel*, p. 118.

91. Eric Gill, claimed Ed Turner, the author of an unpublished biography of Peter Maurin, was the best exemplar of Maurin's economic ideals. Gill was the man Maurin most liked to paraphrase. In making a collection of Maurin's condensations and paraphrases from other writers' works (Maurin's "Easy Essays," printed over the years in the *Catholic Worker*), Turner found that of fifty-one of these essays some thirteen were based on works by Eric Gill, and these ran to over seventy-seven pages. Maurin had eight notebooks of material on the work of Eric Gill ("Typescript of Unpublished Book on Peter Maurin" by Ed Turner, n.d., pp. 16–19, Box 4, W-10, Dorothy Day/Catholic Worker Papers, Marquette University).

92. Dorothy Day to Brendan O'Grady, n.d., probably June or July 1954, "General Correspondence—Outgoing," Box 1, W-2, Dorothy Day/Catholic Worker Papers, Marquette University.

93. Arthur Sheehan, *Gay Believer* (Garden City, N.Y., 1959), p. 12.

94. Stanley Vishnewski, "Intended Article on the Catholic Worker Movement," p. 12, Box 4, W-123, Dorothy Day/Catholic Worker Papers, Marquette University.

95. Marx, *Life and Works of Virgil Michel,* p. 374.

96. Maritain to Peter Maurin, 17 November 1934, W-10, Box 1, "Peter Maurin Correspondence," Dorothy Day/Catholic Worker Papers, Marquette University.

97. In launching the *Christian Front,* McKenna said that the venture "won't be any intellectual stuffed shirt affair which has to be read with a dictionary in one hand. Our writers are men of action, as well as men of ideas, and it is to a similar type of reader that we appeal for support" (Norman McKenna to John Fortier, 22 November 1935, "McKenna-Furfey Correspondence," Box Z-26, Virgil Michel Papers, St. John's University). McKenna's group initiated their project in part to combat the philo-fascism of Coughlin's followers.

98. An excellent study of Kenkel and his ideas can be found in Philip Gleason, *The Conservative Reformers: German-American Catholics and the Social Order* (Notre Dame, Ind., 1968).

99. Michel's personal papers at St. John's University contain numerous correspondences with Reckitt and the Christendom Anglicans.

100. See the Association Contract, 15 October 1936, p. 1, *The Service Bulletin for the Members of the Minnesota and South Dakota Retail Hardware Associations.*

101. Maurin's visit to St. John's was a great success. Peter wrote Dorothy Day that he found a very receptive audience for his radical ideas (Peter Maurin to Dorothy Day, 19 January 1936, Box 1, W-10, "Peter Maurin Correspondence," Dorothy Day/Catholic Worker Papers, Marquette University).

102. Bishop Joseph Busch to Virgil Michel, 15 February 1935, Box Z-27, Virgil Michel Papers, St. John's University. Bishop Busch wrote to the prior of St. John's Abbey that before any lectures were delivered at the Institute an outline should be forwarded to him first for prior approval.

103. See letters to Virgil Michel from Henry J. Blenker, 26 October 1936 and 11 December 1936, Box Z-32, Virgil Michel Papers, St. John's University.

104. Michel wrote to his friend Dorothy Day, who regularly weathered the assaults of reactionary Catholics, that he was also under attack for his radical pamphlets, but that he could console himself with the "good company" he was in, and "in that I include the *Catholic Worker,* and above all our common Head Christ" (Virgil Michel to *Catholic Worker,* 5 Octo-

ber 1935, Box 2, W-2.2, Dorothy Day/Catholic Worker Papers, Marquette University).

105. Franklin and Spaeth, *Virgil Michel,* pp. 92–93.

106. Besides his relationships with Heinrich Bruening, Gurian, and Sturzo, Reinhold also was personal friends with Jacques and Raissa Maritain and Hélène Iswolsky.

107. Warren G. Bovee, "H. A. R., Front Line Fighter," *Today,* December 1954, pp. 4–5.

108. "Dom Virgil Michel's Columns," *Orate Fratres,* 19 March 1939, p. 224.

109. For instance, he went much further than Father Michel in calling for changes in the Eucharistic feast and the introduction of vernacular in ritual, and in recommending Saturday evening Mass for those who had difficulty attending Sunday services. He also made unabashed criticisms of the horrible state of religious art and architecture. Father Emeric Lawrence, for example, wrote that Reinhold could become violent whenever cheapness and artificiality offended good taste, and it was the brashness of his opinions that usually angered his opponents (including many bishops) rather than the criticisms themselves, for nearly everyone realized that he was probably right, being one of the most scholarly authorities on such matters (Emeric Lawrence, "H. A. R.—Death of a Friend," *Commonweal,* 8 March 1968).

110. Virgil Michel was far less combative than Reinhold, and in fact was noted for doing anything possible to avoid controversy.

111. This experiment turned out to be highly successful. It was an example of what Donald Attwater called a Distributist "cell of good living," where arts and crafts and self-sufficient agriculture were encouraged as counterforces to industrial capitalism.

112. The comments of Michael F. McNeil, who was himself a former communist.

113. From Virgil Michel's unpublished diary, entry for 13 April 1938, p. 13, Virgil Michel Papers, St. John's University.

114. Ibid., pp. 15–16.

115. See H.A.R., "Inroads of the Bourgeois Spirit," intended for *Commonweal,* 1941, Box 3, Reinhold Papers, Burns Library.

116. Reckitt and the Anglican social activists were also great supporters of the Roman Catholic liturgical movement. See Maurice Reckitt, "Anglo-Catholic Aspects," *Colosseum,* December 1937.

117. H. A. Reinhold, "Timely Tract: Nature Mirrors Supernature," *Worship,* 28 December 1941.

Chapter 11. American Catholics Move to the Right

1. Francis X. Talbot, S.J., played a seminal role in the American Catholic literary revival in the 1930s and 1940s. He was one of the founders of *America*, where he served as literary editor from 1923 to 1936 and then editor-in-chief from 1936 to 1944. He also was editor of the *Catholic Mind* from 1936 to 1944, one of the founders of *Thought*, the Catholic journal of ideas, and editor of *Thought* between 1936 and 1940. In 1928 Talbot founded the Catholic Book Club and in 1930 the Catholic Poetry Society, and he was president of Loyola College, Baltimore, from 1947 to 1950. His career with *America* and his important contributions to Catholic literary culture are covered well in Arnold Sparr, *To Promote, Defend, and Redeem: The Catholic Literary Revival and the Cultural Transformation of American Catholicism, 1920–1960* (New York, 1990).

Father Talbot was hypersensitive to communism. He especially objected to the use of art as propaganda, which seemed to be the trend by the 1930s as various writers pursued radical social agendas through literary channels.

Talbot had particularly strong views on Catholic culture and literature, and he did much to break down Catholic provincialism in *America* through the creation of the "Gallery of Living Catholic Authors." Talbot, however, was very thin-skinned when Catholics criticized the Church for any reason. It was because of this that he first crossed swords with Reinhold's friend George N. Shuster. In *The Catholic Spirit in Modern English Literature* (New York, 1922), Shuster pronounced the bulk of American Catholic fiction inferior as literature because of its pious and sentimental bent. Talbot responded strongly in an unprecedented long review entitled "'The Catholic Spirit' in Literature," *America* 27 (15 July 1922): 304–305. He argued that Shuster had slighted Catholic literary accomplishments just when American Catholics needed a better sense of their cultural successes. This literary disagreement was the first step in a long struggle, culminating in an open break over the Spanish Civil War. For an excellent treatment of Shuster's career see Thomas E. Blantz, C.S.C., *George N. Shuster: On the Side of Truth* (Notre Dame, Ind., 1993). An informative and far-reaching discussion of the Jesuits in the United States and their magazine *America* can be found in Peter McDonough, *Men Astutely Trained: A History of the Jesuits in the American Century* (New York, 1992).

2. Having earned a Ph.D. from the College of St. Jean Berchmans in Louvain in 1910, Parsons went on to help found the journal *Thought* and then served as editor-in-chief of that publication as well as *America*

from 1925 to 1936. After leaving *America* he was appointed a professor at Georgetown University and became dean of the Graduate School in 1938. He was an important figure in the American Political Science Association and a prolific writer on American social and political issues as well as international relations. Parsons had the distinction of being appointed the first Jesuit to serve on the regular faculty at the Catholic University of America.

3. Radio Talk, n.d., Box 1, A-34, *America*/Parsons Papers, Special Collections, Georgetown University.

4. "The Rights of the Worker according to the Encyclical 'Quadragesimo Anno'," a lecture given at the Negro Industrial Political Conference, 3 September 1932, Box 1, A-34, *America*/Parsons Papers, Georgetown University.

5. Parsons to Rev. Joseph J. Donovan, S.J., 11 April 1933, Box 1, 1933 D, *America*/Parsons Papers, Georgetown University.

6. Of special interest in this context is Parsons' correspondence with Seward Collins, editor of the *American Review,* who believed that Distributism had the best chance of coming to America through fascist-style corporatism (i.e., through dictatorship). Parsons, of course, took objection and tried to convince Collins to look at the issue from a more democratic perspective.

See also Wilfrid Parsons, S.J., *Which Way Democracy?* (New York, 1939). The purpose of this book was to show the common linkages between democracy and Christianity. Along with a number of other Catholics of the 1930s (for example, W. F. Obering, S.J., *The Philosophy of Law of James Wilson* [Catholic University of America, 1938]), Parsons attempted to demonstrate that the founding fathers were guided by a political view that was inherently grounded in religion, not dissimilar from the Thomistic tradition expounded by Bellarmine and Suarez.

Parsons asserted that communism and fascism were essentially totalitarian siblings and thereby deadly threats to democracy and all religions. However, in his mind fascism was a more serious problem, owing to its *faux* corporatism which duped Catholics, its virulent anti-Semitism, and the authoritarian and militaristic fashion in which it claimed to have "solved" the labor problem (*Which Way Democracy?*, pp. 182–183).

7. See Parsons' "Social Legislation in America," submitted as an article to Jean M. Hanssens, S.J., Pontificia Universitas Gregoriana, Rome, 11 October 1935, Box 1, "Parsons—Writings," File A-16, *America*/Parsons Papers, Georgetown University.

For a good survey of Catholic social teaching and the Roosevelt administration see Francis L. Broderick, *Right Reverend New Dealer: John A. Ryan* (New York, 1963). Father Ryan was one of America's most prominent social reformers and devoted his life to the application of *Rerum Novarum* to the problems of labor. Ryan was an avid supporter of the New Deal. In the long run his ability to show the unity between Catholic natural law teachings and American democratic culture helped bridge the gap between secular misunderstandings of Catholicism and Catholic self-confidence about living up to the ideals of American citizenship. Ryan's importance in this context is discussed in Joseph M. McShane, S.J., *"Sufficiently Radical": Catholicism, Progressivism, and the Bishops' Program of 1919* (Washington, D.C., 1986).

8. Wilfrid Parsons, "On Relations of NRA with Papal Encyclicals," p. 3, n.d., Box 1, A-35, *America*/Parsons Papers, Georgetown University.

9. The influence of Rev. John A. Ryan was crucial within this circle of Catholic social activists. Ryan was adamant in his insistence that the Church had a responsibility to insert itself into the business of capital and labor. Industrial relations, he emphasized, were not merely economic but above all human and thus subject to moral law: "Inasmuch as the Church is the accredited interpreter and teacher of moral law, her authority and function in the field of industrial relations are quite as certain and normal as in domestic relations, or in any other department of human life" ("The Teaching of the Catholic Church," *The Annals of the American Academy of Political and Social Science,* September 1922, from the John A. Ryan Papers, Department of Archives and Manuscripts, Catholic University of America). In this respect the remaking of the social order had to be seen as an integral piece of the Church's primary mission, which was the saving of souls.

10. David O'Brien, *American Catholics and Social Reform* (New York, 1968), p. 109.

11. Noll to Joseph Husslein, S.J., 22 August 1938, *"Our Sunday Visitor,* Noll Correspondence File," 1935–1938, Box 1, John F. Noll Papers, University of Notre Dame.

12. See Noll to Edward Squitieri, Association of Catholic Trade Unionists, 7 August 1939, *"Our Sunday Visitor,* Noll Correspondence File," 1939–46, CNOL 1, Box 1, John F. Noll Papers, University of Notre Dame.

13. A thorough treatment of Catholicism and the American trade union movement can be found in Douglas P. Seaton, *Catholics and Radicals* (East Brunswick, N.J., 1981), and Patrick J. McGeever, *Reverend Charles Owen Rice: Apostle of Contradiction* (Pittsburgh, 1989).

14. Informative sources on Father Coughlin's career are Alan Brinkley, *Voices of Protest: Huey Long, Father Coughlin, and the Great Depression* (New York, 1982); James Terence Fisher, *The Catholic Counterculture in*

America, 1933–1962 (Chapel Hill, N.C., 1989); and Charles J. Tull, *Father Coughlin and the New Deal* (Syracuse, N.Y., 1965).

15. *Catholic Charities Review,* April 1935, p. 105. Ryan's analysis was reaffirmed by Pope Pius XI's *Quadragesimo Anno.*

Parsons had seen fit to consult Monsignor Ryan before drafting his own analysis of Coughlin's economic ideas. Ryan offered minor emendations and thought Parsons' critique "about as well done as it could possibly be done within the space that you have set for yourself" (Ryan to Parsons, 17 May 1935, Box "Ryan Correspondence 1934–35, 'P'," Department of Archives and Manuscripts, Catholic University of America).

16. Wilfrid Parsons, "Father Coughlin and Social Justice," *America,* 18 May 1935. See also Parsons, "Father Coughlin and the Banks," *America,* 25 May 1935, and "Father Coughlin's Ideas on Money," *America,* 1 June 1935.

17. *America* devoted a special section to letters on Parsons' articles concerning Coughlin in two of its subsequent editions: "Letters on Father Coughlin" (8 June 1935 and 22 June 1935). Eighty-seven letters were received: sixty-two opposed Parsons' point of view; twenty-five favored it; yet only sixteen of those opposed had actually read the articles (from "Father Coughlin: the Aftermath," *America,* 29 July 1935).

18. Parsons to Harte, 23 April 1935, Box 2, 1935 H, *America*/Parsons Papers, Georgetown University.

19. See Wilfrid Parsons, "Philosophy of a New Deal," *America,* 19 May 1934.

20. John Ryan to Alice S. Duffy, 26 April 1937, Pamphlet Box, Ryan Correspondence, 1936–37, Bio-G/File C, John A. Ryan Papers, Department of Archives and Manuscripts, Catholic University of America.

21. John Ryan to Daniel A. Lord, S.J., editor of *The Queen's Work,* 20 February 1939, Box "Ryan Writing, 1934–40," Folder re: Coughlin, John A. Ryan Papers, Department of Manuscripts and Archives, Catholic University of America.

22. By the fall of 1936 Ryan had already received over twelve hundred letters from Coughlin's supporters, the majority of which seem to have come from poor and uneducated persons badly hurt by economic recession.

23. John Ryan to B. K. Jones, 16 February 1935, ibid. For more concerning Ryan's views on Father Coughlin see the many letters, essays, and unpublished materials in the John A. Ryan Papers, Catholic University of America.

24. John Ryan to Michael Williams, 1 June 1937, Box "Ryan Correspondences, 1936–37," Michael Williams Folder, and John Ryan to Nan

Moynahan, 12 November 1936, Folder M H-Q, John Ryan Papers, Catholic University of America.

25. See John Ryan to John D. Moore, National Labor Relations Board, 10 March 1937, and Moore to Ryan, 12 March 1937, Box "Ryan Correspondences, 1936–37," Folder M H-Q, John Ryan Papers, Catholic University of America.

26. There were two Popular Front governments in Europe at this time: Leon Blum's coalition in France and the democratically elected government of Spain of January 1936 against which General Francisco Franco led the rebellion in July of that year. Blum himself was not a communist. His government was brought to power by a combination of peasants, workers, small tradesmen, schoolteachers, and intellectuals who demanded social justice. Blum himself was a socialist who mistrusted the French Marxists, recognizing behind them the iron fist of Stalin.

The Popular Front government that came to power in Spain was not controlled by Marxists, though once the Soviet Union came to the aid of the Republic it eventually was able to use that government for its own purposes. See Burnett Bolloten, *The Spanish Civil War: Revolution and Counterrevolution* (Chapel Hill, N.C., 1991).

27. Talbot to Rev. F. Woodlock, S.J., 18 November 1936, Box 17, 1936, V-Z, *America*/Talbot Papers, Special Collections, Georgetown University.

28. See letter to Talbot from "An American," 14 April 1938; W. R. Wilkerson to Talbot, 15 April 1938; and Talbot to Wilkerson, 20 April 1938, Box 17, 1938, W-Y, *America*/Talbot Papers, Special Collections, Georgetown University.

29. Talbot to Viereck, 10 January 1939, Box 17, 1939, V, *America*/Talbot Papers, Special Collections, Georgetown University. *America* welcomed *Liberty's* exposure of the communist menace. See "Comment," *America*, 5 August 1939. For *America's* views on related issues see Farrell Schnering, "Communists Burrow Way into Key Positions in CIO," 12 August 1939, and "The Wisconsin C.I.O. and the In-Borers," 26 August 1939.

30. See Wilfrid Parsons, "Popular Front and Catholicism," n.d., Box 1, "Parsons-Writings," A-18, *America*/Parsons Papers, Special Collections, Georgetown University. However, by 1939 Parsons had come to believe that fascism was a greater threat than communism to American Catholics. (See *Which Way Democracy?*, p. 183.)

31. See Reinhold's Newman Club lecture to students at the University of British Columbia, Vancouver, B.C., 26 October 1950, Box 1, "Manuscripts," Reinhold Papers, Burns Library, Boston College.

32. Talbot to Dowd, 11 January 1939, Box 4, 1937, *America*/Talbot Papers, Special Collections, Georgetown University.

33. By 1938 Father Coughlin had started writing to Mussolini. Coughlin asserted that he supported the Italian dictator's policies to the fullest and proposed that some type of formal agreement be drawn up between them to promote common causes. Mussolini was advised to decline the offer, since a formal pact might alienate American public opinion. (See Philip V. Cannistraro and Theodore P. Kovaleff, "Father Coughlin and Mussolini: Impossible Allies," *Journal of Church and State* 13 [1971]: 427–443).

34. *America* under Talbot found a similar connection: "The Alliance of International Jewry and International Communism and International Masonry is a Natural." See "Comment" section, 3 April 1938.

35. The *Protocols* began appearing in *Social Justice* in July 1938. Although the document was known to be a forgery, various people continued to argue for its authenticity. Rev. Francis A. Brien, for example, sent Father Talbot a pamphlet purporting to keep up the claim and to prove that the *Protocols* were not faked. (See Rev. Francis A. Brien to Talbot, 9 June 1939, and Talbot to Brien, 12 June 1939, Box 4, June-December 1939, *America*/Talbot Papers, Georgetown University.)

36. For Coughlin's relationship with Bishop Gallagher see Earl Boyea, "The Reverend Charles Coughlin and the Church: The Gallagher Years, 1930–1937, *Catholic Historical Review*, vol. 71, no. 2 (April 1995): 211–225.

37. Luther to Talbot, 8 July 1936, Box 6, L, 1936, *America*/Talbot Papers, Special Collections, Georgetown University.

38. Gerard J. Murphy, S.J., "Plea for Conservatives," *America*, 31 July 1937.

39. Raymond Corrigan, "Materialist Communism and Liberalism Are Blood Brothers: Why a Capitalist Press Favors Both," *America*, 9 October 1937.

40. Father Parsons, on the other hand, was more appreciative of the Anglo-Saxon liberal traditions out of which America's practice of democracy had developed. He recognized the difference between continental liberalism, that associated with the Manchester school of laissez-faire economics and Rousseauist thinking, and the form of liberalism which had inspired the founding fathers of the American constitution. (See his talk at the Brooklyn Knights of Columbus Forum, 13 March [no year given] and a series of addresses on the Catholic Hour Program of NBC [probably 1929], Box 1, "Addresses, Lectures," A-33 *America*/Parsons Papers, Georgetown University. Parsons' ideas on the subject can be seen in more mature form in *Which Way Democracy?*)

41. Although the Jesuit Provincial approved of Talbot's editorial line, there were some voices of criticism at the spring 1939 provincial meeting

in New Orleans. Some thought that *America* had been a bit hard on the FDR administration (Talbot to Paul Blakely, 5 May 1939, Box 5 1939, January-May, *America*/Talbot Papers, Georgetown University).

42. There were others who also objected to the unbalanced treatment of labor. See letters between Parsons and Patterson, Box 7, PC, 1935–37; Parsons and John J. Morrisson, S.J., of Woodstock College, Maryland, 23 March and 24 March 1937, Box 6, M, 1937, *America*/Parsons Papers; and Rev. Charles Owen Rice to Talbot, 11 August 1938, Box 17, Re-Ri 1938, *America*/Talbot Papers, Special Collections, Georgetown University.

43. Quoted in Patrick J. McGeever, *Rev. Charles Owen Rice*, p. 52.

44. Ibid., p. 63. Reinhold's stories of Nazi persecution of Christians and Jews and his having "exploded" at Rice's anti-interventionism convinced the labor priest of the folly of pacifism.

45. Quoted by Richard Deverall, "Catholic Radical Alliance," *Catholic Digest* 2 (November 1937): 93.

46. Kendall to Reinhold, p. 3, 25 September 1942, "Naturalization File," Box 9, Reinhold Papers, Burns Library.

47. Ibid., p. 3.

48. Ibid., p. 94.

49. Rice had always harbored a strong dislike of communists. What seems to have pushed him over the edge on the subject was the American Communist Party's turning a blind eye to Stalin's crimes and its willingness to toe Moscow's line without question. The story of how the ACTU succumbed to anticommunism is told in Seaton, *Catholics and Radicals*.

In the long run, claims the labor historian Steve Rosswurm, the obsession with communism (so typified by Talbot and his circle) was dangerous for the Church, even more so than communism itself. In Rosswurm's view the furious anticommunist crusade of the Catholic trade unionists led by Father Rice had the unintended effect of making Catholic social teaching largely irrelevant for the American working class. (See Steve Rosswurm, ed., *The CIO's Left-Led Unions* [New Brunswick, N.J., 1992], p. 137.)

50. Patrick J. McGeever, *Rev. Charles Owen Rice*, p. 94. The attacks on ACTU progressives were led by William J. Smith, S.J., Director of the Crown Heights Labor School in Brooklyn and a regular correspondent for *America*. Father Smith disagreed with the progressive position that the primary enemy was management's failure to fulfill the needs of labor. In his view the fight for social and economic reform had to be subordinated to the more pressing struggle against communism (Seaton, *Catholics and Radicals*, p. 82).

51. Rice's systematic purge of the CIO was spearheaded in Bishop John F. Noll's *Our Sunday Visitor*. Rice had previously refused to write for the paper because of its extreme conservatism. But in 1947 he made a deal with its editors to do a series of articles attacking communist influences in the union movement. This led to the publication of a highly influential and widely distributed pamphlet entitled "How to Decontrol Your Union of Communists," of which some thirty to forty thousand were printed. Thirty-five years later when ABC television prepared a documentary on McCarthyism the network found copies of the pamphlet all over the nation (McGeever, *Rev. Charles Owen Rice*, p. 102).

52. Seaton, *Catholics and Radicals*, p. 82.

53. Ibid., p. 235.

54. See Talbot to Rev. Francis P. Connelly, S.J., 7 June 1937, Box 4, "Correspondence 1937," D File, *America*/Talbot Papers, Special Collections, Georgetown University.

55. Talbot to Rev. Edw. Duff, S.J., n.d., Box 5, 1938, *America*/Talbot Papers, Georgetown University.

56. Talbot to Williams, 14 June 1939, Box 17, 1938, W, *America*/Talbot Papers, Georgetown University.

57. For example, Reinhold believed that Father Talbot had been responsible for spreading a story that he was in the pay of communists. This incident involved the accusations of a Mr. Dudley P. Gilbert, an influential member of St. Mary's Parish in Newport, Rhode Island, where Reinhold had been residing. Gilbert informed a priest at St Mary's that Reinhold might be a Freemason and a communist under the employment of the Loyalist government in Spain. It seems that Gilbert found it incredible that a priest of the Church could not favor Franco or could fail to see that the conflict in Spain was a religious war. Reinhold's unorthodox position on such matters, Gilbert concluded, may be explained by his friendship with the Dorothy Day–ACTU crowd. Talbot, for his part, denied having anything to do with these accusations. (See Gilbert to Talbot, 25 May 1938, Box 17, Re-Ri, 1938, *America*/Talbot Papers, Georgetown University.)

58. The *Brooklyn Tablet*, 26 July 1930.

59. See, for example, Reinhold's correspondence with H. K. Kendall, the Seattle-based Distributist who launched the magazine *Social Action*. When conservative Catholics accused Kendall's efforts of being "communistic," thus implicating Reinhold, their advisor, as a communist, Reinhold decided to break his relationship with the Catholic trade union group. (See Kendall to Reinhold, 25 September 1942, and Reinhold to Kendall, 26 September 1942, "Naturalization File," Box 9; Reinhold to Kendall,

2 September 1942, Box 2, "1935–1936," Box 9; Reinhold to Kendall, 2 September 1942, Box 2, "1935–1936," Reinhold Papers, Burns Library, Boston College.

60. Reinhold to Emmanuel Chapman, 13 December 1946, "Committee of Catholics for Human Rights File," Reinhold Papers, Burns Library, Boston College.)

Chapter 12. The Religious Crusade in Spain

1. "Catholics and the Catholic Spirit," p. 14, unpublished manuscript, 1938, Box Z-32, Virgil Michel Papers, St. John's University, Collegeville, Minnesota.

2. The Spanish Civil War remains an emotive issue. The truth about the affair may never be fully told because of the difficulty of overcoming the prejudice of those who wrote about it. (Such is the view of Antony Beevor, *The Spanish Civil War* [London, 1982], p. 8.) The London *Tablet* on 28 July 1951 noted that even fifteen years after the war events concerning Spain were still so mired in propaganda that it was nearly impossible to fully grasp the roots of the tragedy. Joseph N. Moody, editor of the voluminous *Church and Society: Catholic Social and Political Thought and Movements, 1789–1950* (New York, 1953), felt obliged to offer only an abbreviated treatment of Spanish Catholicism because a non-partisan analysis of the complex social and religious situation was so difficult to achieve (p. 723).

An insightful though somewhat partial contemporary treatment of the Spanish Civil War is Gerald Brenan's *The Spanish Labyrinth: An Account of the Social and Political Background of the Spanish Civil War* (Cambridge, England, 1943). Brenan was an active supporter of the Republic and had a firsthand view of events while living near Málaga during the early stages of the Civil War (he left for England in 1937). A later and more objective, comprehensive study that drew on almost all relevant primary and secondary sources available at the time is Hugh Thomas's *The Spanish Civil War* (New York, 1961; revised and enlarged edition, 1977). See also Burnett Bolloten, *The Spanish Revolution* (Chapel Hill, N.C., 1979) and his last, most detailed study, *The Spanish Civil War: Revolution and Counterrevolution* (Chapel Hill, N.C., 1991); Raymond Carr, *The Spanish Tragedy* (London, 1977); and Gabriel Jackson, *The Spanish Republic and the Civil War, 1931–1939* (Princeton, N.J., 1965).

American and English Catholic sources on the Spanish Civil War, for the most part, were unreliable, reductionist, and largely committed to propaganda. See the judgment on this by John David Valaik, "American

Catholics and the Spanish Civil War, 1931," Ph.D. diss., University of Rochester, 1964, and his "American Catholic Dissenters and the Spanish Civil War," *Catholic Historical Review*, January 1968. In the view of Allen Guttmann, Douglas Jerrold's articles on Spain were some of "the least accurate accounts of the war" (*The Wound in the Heart* [New York, 1962], p. 23). Jerrold was a key figure in the creation of the myth concerning Guernica, which, contrary to the distortions of pro-Insurgent propaganda, was in fact destroyed by German air bombardment. Herbert Rutledge Southworth, who wrote the definitive study on the subject—*Guernica! Guernica! A Study of Journalism, Diplomacy, Propaganda, and History* (Berkeley, Calif., 1977)—concludes that Jerrold's tendentious but highly influential work on the Spanish Civil War was not only unreliable but the product of deliberate lies. A very good balanced treatment of the conflict from a contemporary Catholic historian's perspective can be found in José M. Sánchez's study, *The Spanish Civil War as a Religious Tragedy* (Notre Dame, Ind., 1987).

The American Catholic press was not far behind the sensationalist Hearst papers in its embellishment on the atrocity stories coming out of Spain. (See Robert Morton Darrow, "Catholic Political Power: A Study of the Activities of the American Catholic Church on Behalf of Franco during the Spanish Civil War, 1936–1939," Ph.D. diss., Columbia University, 1953.) After Franco's victory, Rev. Timothy Rowan, editor of the Catholic Chicago *New World*, assessed the American Catholic press's coverage of the Spanish Civil War. He concluded that many Catholic writers and their press "had lied" about conditions in Spain, and that the secular media, against which Catholic journalists loyal to Franco inveighed for its bias, was far more reliable in its analysis and coverage (*New World*, 30 June 1939, as cited in Darrow, "Catholic Political Power," p. 192).

The study of the Civil War from the Spanish Church's perspective has greatly benefited from two recent publications: Cardinal Francesco Vidal i Barraquer's papers (a monumental twenty-year project) and a detailed history of the Spanish Church during the 1930s by Gonzalo Redondo. For more on these and other Spanish Catholic sources see José M. Sánchez, "The Spanish Church and the Second Republic and Civil War, 1931–1939," *Catholic Historical Review*, vol. 82, no. 4 (October, 1996): 661–668. This is a survey of some of the important documentary literature and secondary works on the history of the Spanish Church during the Civil War. At the time of Professor Sánchez's writing, few, if any, of these works had been reviewed in English-language publications.

3. Herbert Matthews, *Half of Spain Died: A Reappraisal of the Spanish Civil War* (New York, 1973), p. 182.

4. Secretary of the Interior Harold Ickes wrote in his diary that in 1938, when there was a good chance to lift the embargo, Roosevelt said frankly it "would mean the loss of every Catholic vote next fall and the Democratic members of Congress were jittery about it and didn't want it done" (ibid., p. 181). There was a mistaken notion in American politics that Catholics politically moved in lockstep with the views of their clergy and would therefore vote as a bloc against those who ignored the wishes of the hierarchy. For a different interpretation see George Q. Flynn, *Roosevelt and Romanism: Catholicism and American Diplomacy, 1937–1945* (Westport, Conn., 1978). Flynn argues that despite Catholic opinion Roosevelt had determined to maintain the embargo because of pressure from England, France, and the Low Countries. These nations, as well as FDR himself, were convinced that a policy of nonintervention would contain the fighting, preventing it from spreading to the rest of Europe (p. 51).

5. Stanley G. Payne, *Spanish Catholicism: An Historical Overview* (Madison, Wis., 1984), p. 152.

6. Serious peasant rebellions had broken out in 1840, 1892, and 1919. According to Don Enrique Moreno, in the year 1931 estates of more than 250 hectares covered 36 percent of Estremadura, 39 percent of La Mancha, and 45 percent of Andalusia. In Seville, 5 percent of the landowners held 72 percent of the total land value (Don Enrique Moreno, *Catholics and the Spanish State* [London, 1937], p. 21). This situation is also discussed in Jackson, *The Spanish Republic and the Civil War,* pp. 7–11.

The monarchist politician José Calvo Sotelo, whose assassination by *Asaltos* (the police force loyal to the Republic) was the immediate cause of the military uprising in July 1936, admitted to an American correspondent that 30 percent of the upper classes in Spain consumed 60 to 70 percent of the national revenue—"only about one third goes to the 70 per cent who live on the land" (Frederick Birchall, *New York Times,* 28 June 1936). Even some influential foreign conservatives who later were sympathetic to Franco's cause admitted that such conditions, along with the social irresponsibility of the Spanish aristocracy, made civil war inevitable and nasty. A distinguished British diplomat, Sir George Rendel, K.D., M.G., who was himself a right-wing Catholic, described the fashionable parties he attended in Madrid during 1917 as occasions for lavish displays of jewellery and furs. Such spectacles, "Los Lunes de Moda" as they were called, attracted the poor and destitute who gathered at the curbside to watch the "smarter set" arrive. Rendel observed that "after some of the intensely cold nights of the Castilian winter the papers would announce without comment that such-and-such a number of beggars had been picked up frozen to death." The extremes of wealth and poverty in Spain corresponded to conditions in the England of Charles Dickens. Rendel found the social irresponsibility of the Spanish aristocracy to be "quite extraordinary" (*The Sword and the Olive* [London, 1957], pp. 40–41). The historian José M. Sánchez has called the Spanish "possessing classes" the most materialist group in modern history (*Spanish Civil War as a Religious Tragedy*, p. 4).

7. Between 1915 and 1930 there occurred the most rapid proportionate expansion of urban population and industrial labor growth in Spanish history. During the years 1910 through 1930 factory employment almost doubled, from 15.8 percent of the labor force to 26.5 percent. This was a greater increase than during the boom years of the 1960s. See Stanley G. Payne, *Spain's First Democracy: The Second Republic, 1931–1936* (Madison, Wis., 1993), pp. 23–24, 148–155.

8. The German sociologist Franz Borkenau claimed that by the twentieth century the Spanish Church and Jesuits were no longer the country's largest landowners but rather the heaviest investors in *mobile* property, thus the richest capitalists. (Franz Borkenau, *The Spanish Cockpit: An Eye-Witness Account of the Political and Social Conflicts of the Spanish* [Ann Arbor, Mich., 1937; reprint 1963], p. 9).

9. The Catholic journalist Lawrence A. Farnsworth, who served as a correspondent in Spain for the London *Times* and the *New York Times*, wrote that it was estimated in the 1931 Cortes that the Jesuits alone owned a third of the country's wealth. (From *Fortune*, April 1937, article reproduced in "Catholics Speak for Spain," p. 10, North American Committee to Aid Spanish Democracy, Abraham Lincoln Brigade Archives, Special Collections, Brandeis University. It should be noted that the pamphlet "Catholics Speak for Spain" was issued by a communist publisher.) Once the government began to confiscate Jesuit wealth, this estimate was shown to be greatly exaggerated (see José M. Sánchez, *Reform and Reaction: The Politico-Religious Background of the Spanish Civil War* [Chapel Hill, N.C., 1962], pp. 49–50). In any case, it was difficult to assess the true value of Jesuit wealth because much of the order's mercantile and commercial property was registered in the names of laymen.

10. A Church more closely linked to the soil, observed Franz Borkenau, would never have become so distant from the masses (*Spanish Cockpit*, p. 9). As the Church struggled to protect its traditional interests, the clergy steadily forsook their pastoral responsibilities.

11. José María Gironella, *The Cypresses Believe in God*, trans. Harriet de Onis (New York, 1955), vol. 1, p. 258.

12. In fact, some bishops were partisans of the working classes and did not walk in lockstep with the ruling elites. But for the most part clerical salaries were so low that the clergy were obliged to collaborate with the political establishment as a way of getting contributions to augment their inadequate incomes.

13. The Church's ambiguous stand on the campaign for a republic seemed to be clarified in a pastoral letter issued in April 1931 by the bishop of Vitoria, Monsignor Mateo Múgica. His excellency pronounced that in the approaching elections Catholics could not vote for any republican candidates. The letter had the effect of seriously compromising the efforts of moderate republicans to win over Catholic support, for Múgica suggested that those who did not vote monarchist would fall into mortal sin. The letter served to fan the flames of extremism on both the left and right. (See Sánchez, *Reform and Reaction,* chapter 6, and his "The Spanish Church and the Revolutionary Republican Movement, 1930–1931," *Church History* 31 [December 1962], p. 437.)

14. Montovan letter to the *New York Times,* 18 November 1931.

15. "The Truth About Spain," *The Catholic Mirror,* October 1931, p. 6.

16. "The Position of the Church in Spain," p. 1, Confidential Memorandum prepared at the request of Msgr. Pizzardo for the Vatican, Box 3, William Montovan Papers, Special Collections, Catholic University of America.

17. Montovan wrote that he could not find a copy of the primate's pamphlet on Catholic action anywhere in the city of Madrid and that only in the offices of the nuncio and the newspaper *El Debate* did he locate men who had even heard of the document.

18. "The Position of the Church in Spain," Part II, p. 2.

19. "The Position of the Church in Spain," p. 1.

20. Sir Peter Chalmers Mitchell, *My House in Málaga* (London, 1940), pp. 21 and 140.

21. "Diary on Trip to Spain," 20 June 1925, Box Z-22, Virgil Michel Papers, St. John's University.

22. From Paul Marx, *The Life and Work of Virgil Michel* (Washington, D.C., 1957), pp. 30–31. The Basque country had the highest rate of practicing Catholics, as much as 100 percent in rural areas and over 50 percent in urban centers. By contrast, in southern Spain the level of practicing Catholics was as low as 15 percent (Sánchez, *Spanish War as Religious Tragedy,* p. 72). In neighboring Navarre, the clergy also had kept close to the people and worked diligently to protect their interests. As in the Basque country, the commoners of Navarre had great affection for the

Church and were known for their deep devotion to Catholicism. For an intimate, sympathetic depiction of Basque culture and religion from the perspective of an English wartime journalist, see G. L. Steer, *The Tree of Gernika* (London, 1938).

23. *Der Wanderer,* 14 April 1927.

24. Marx, *Life and Work of Virgil Michel,* p. 32.

25. Nor, it appears, was it a surprise for Pope Pius XI. The pope was deeply worried about Spain and convinced that the Spanish hierarchy was too complacent and wealthy to carry out needed social reform. He believed a revolution there was imminent (William Teeling, *The Pope in Politics* [London, 1937], pp. 138–139).

26. The Catholic paper *Correo Espanol* estimated the population of "active" Catholics at 1.5 million men and 3.5 million women (Farnsworth, *Fortune,* April 1937, p. 10). A more accurate and complete assessment can be found in Thomas, *The Spanish Civil War,* pp. 31–37. He notes, for instance, that moderate Catholics estimated that two-thirds of the Spaniards in the 1930s were not practicing Catholics (p. 31).

27. Teeling, *The Pope in Politics,* p. 138.

28. From *Foreign Affairs,* October 1936. In "Catholics Speak for Spain," Abraham Lincoln Brigade Archives, Brandeis University.

29. Moreno, *Catholics and the Spanish State,* p. 15.

30. Many well-known Spanish intellectuals and artists, including José Ortega y Gasset and Juan Miro, had become atheists despite their Jesuit educations. As José Sánchez has noted, not a single one of modern Spain's literary, scientific, and artistic luminaries defended the Spanish Catholic cultural ethic, even though they were products of Church schools (*Spanish Civil War as Religious Tragedy,* p. 7).

31. "A Catholic Looks at Spain," p. 23. Reprint from an essay published in *Esprit,* November 1936, Abraham Lincoln Brigade Archives, Brandeis University.

32. Ibid., p. 25.

33. An informative contemporary discussion of this can be found in Moreno, *Catholics and the Spanish State,* pp. 5–13.

34. Pamphlet by Rev. Genadius Diez, n.d., Abraham Lincoln Brigade Archives, Brandeis University. The Catechism of the Spanish Church published in 1927 labeled liberalism "a most grievous sin against the faith." It went on to ask, "What sin is committed by him who votes for a Liberal candidate?" "Generally a mortal sin" (Brenan, *The Spanish Labyrinth,* pp. 51–52).

35. A. Ramos Oliveira, *Politics, Economics and Men of Modern Spain, 1808–1946* (London, 1946), p. 36.

36. Quoted in Sánchez, *Reform and Reaction*, p. 169. Gil Robles admitted years later in his memoirs that in theory he had always been a monarchist (Payne, *Spain's First Democracy*, p. 168).

37. The labor movement, for example, was seriously divided between anarchists and socialists who warred against each other. Marxists at this point were not yet a factor.

38. Borkenau, *Spanish Cockpit*, p. 56.

39. Quoted in Bolloten, *Spanish Civil War*, p. 9.

40. This is a point often overlooked by defenders of the Republic. The Asturias rebels acted against a legally-elected rightist government, yet no liberals in the democratic countries raised a voice of protest. This fact did not go unnoticed by those who supported Franco's cause. A leading historian of the day, Professor E. Allison Peers (a Protestant), could argue that the "Moscow-instigated" rebellion set up the first Soviet Republic in Spain a full two years before a single Italian or German landed in that country (Arnold Lunn, *Spain and the Christian Front: Ubi Cux Ibi Patria* [New York, 1937], pp. 4–5).

The Spanish journalist and diplomat Luis A. Bolín also made note of the liberal double standard regarding Spain: the *New Statesman*, he wrote, enthusiastically supported the armed revolt in Asturias against the conservative Spanish government in 1934 but denounced Franco for doing the same thing against the leftist-dominated Republic (Luis Bolín, *Spain: The Vital Years* [New York, 1967], p. 4).

41. The Spanish communists at this juncture were few in number and negligible in influence. Contrary to their own propaganda and that of Catholic conservatives, they were not the creators of the Spanish *Frente Popular* (it was rather the product of a revival of the 1931 Republican-Socialist coalition), nor did they play an important part in the Left's subsequent electoral victory.

42. The anarchists did not join the Popular Front, but since the coalition promised a general amnesty for political prisoners—most of whom were anarchists—they decided to vote for Front candidates. The prospect of violently anticlerical anarcho-syndicalists being freed from jail was very frightening to the Church. The episcopate issued pastoral letters urging rejection of Popular Front candidates. The Left denounced the hierarchy for blatant political meddling.

43. Azaña himself may have lacked the stomach for such a battle and also probably doubted the reliability of the military to put down the uprising in the name of the Republic (Stanley Payne, *Politics and the Military in Modern Spain* [Stanford, Calif., 1967], p. 318).

44. Quoted in Bolloten, *Spanish Civil War,* p. 20.

45. Borkenau, *Spanish Cockpit,* p. 63.

46. Violence played a decisive role in destabilizing the Second Republic and seems to have been more proportionately severe than that which accompanied the breakdown of democratic order in Italy, Germany, and Austria. However, as opposed to these three countries, the main source of systematic violence in pre-war Spain came from the Left. The Republican government certainly did not encourage terror, but the leaders could not restrain those who practiced it nor successfully prosecute its perpetrators. See Payne, *Spain's First Democracy,* pp. 361–364.

47. Quoted in Bolloten, *Spanish Civil War,* p. 40.

48. Thomas, *The Spanish Civil War,* p. 175.

49. Belloc's influence on the Right and the Spanish Civil War has not been fully appreciated. For example, Katharine Bail Hoskins in *Today the Struggle: Literature and Politics in England during the Spanish Civil War* (Austin, Tex., 1969) includes a chapter on the Right, but surprisingly makes no mention of Belloc. Nor are Belloc's contributions discussed in Rowland Smith's article on the subject, "The Spanish Civil War and the British Literary Right," *Dalhousie Review,* vol. 51 (Spring 1971): 60–76, which focuses on R. J. Campbell and Wyndham Lewis. On the other hand, it is noteworthy that Sir Robert Hodgson, who served as Britain's *chargé d'affaires* to Nationalist Spain, mentions that Belloc, along with Douglas Jerrold, Douglas Woodruff, and a few other stalwart English-Irish Catholics, was a major player in the propaganda campaign for "The Cause," a term Franco's supporters called the "Crusade against Asiatic Barbarism" (Robert Hodgson, *Spain Resurgent* [London, 1953], p. 91). Stanley Weintraub's *The Last Great Cause: The Intellectuals and the Spanish Civil War* (New York, 1968) has a chapter which deals briefly with Belloc and more extensively with Douglas Jerrold, Roy Campbell, and Arnold Lunn.

Although there are several good studies of American rightists and Catholic support for Franco (see the contributions of Allen Guttman, John David Valaik, and Robert Morton Darrow), there is very little on the pro-Nationalists in England. Scholars have largely ignored the literary right because the collective quality of their writings on the Spanish affair was not high. Britain's most talented men of letters were committed to the Republic, and this involvement had a profound impact on their literary and intellectual lives. However, the literary right certainly had considerable influence on British attitudes toward the Spanish civil war. See Southworth, *Guernica!*

It is difficult to document a causal connection between Belloc's views on Spain and the position taken by American Catholic publications. However, given the fact that Belloc during the 1930s was the best-known and perhaps most influential Catholic writer in the English-speaking world and that numerous writers made reference to him when they wrote about Spain, one can reasonably conclude that his influence was seminal. His disciples, Douglas Jerrold and Arnold Lunn, had enormous influence on American Catholic opinion (notably on the ideas of Father Joseph Thorning, Wilfrid Parsons, S.J., and Father Joseph B. Code). Several observers, for example, complained that American Catholics, despite their Anglophobia, were too willing to follow the intellectual lead of English Catholics on international affairs. (See Robert Morton Darrow's interview with Edward Skillin, editor of *Commonweal*, 24 August 1950, p. 72, "Catholic Political Power: A Study of the Activities of the American Catholic Church on Behalf of Franco during the Spanish Civil War, 1936–1939," Ph.D. diss., Columbia University, 1953.)

50. Letters of 10 August and 29 August 1936, Hilaire Belloc Papers, Burns Library, Boston College.

51. Hilaire Belloc, "Commentary on the Spanish Victory," *Tablet*, 15 July 1939.

52. Miscellaneous Manuscripts, Hilaire Belloc Papers, Burns Library. As early as May 1931 Belloc detected a conspiracy by outsiders in the affairs of the Spanish Republic. Among the active politicians in the government, he claimed, were strongly anti-Catholic Freemasons who were arranging to undermine religion. (See "The Press and Spain," *G.K.'s Weekly*, 23 May 1931.)

53. The major violence perpetrated against the Catholic Church in Spain came from anarchists, not communists. Belloc, of course, made no distinction between the two. (Belloc was not alone; even a highly respected expert like Professor Allison Peers was unable to differentiate accurately between the various parties of the left. See Antony Beevor, *The Spanish Civil War* [London, 1982], p. 176.) In the words of Gerald Brenan, who greatly admired the anarchists: "Without going far wrong one may say that all the churches recently burned in Spain were burned by Anarchists and that most of priests killed were killed by them" (*The Spanish Labyrinth*, p. 189). The same assessment can be found in the works of José M. Sánchez, Burnett Bolloten, and others.

54. See Hilaire Belloc, "Moscow," *G.K.'s Weekly*, 13 August 1936.

55. See Belloc's response to the Ferrer affair, chapter 7.

56. See Hilaire Belloc, "The International: I: The Ferrer Case," submitted to the *Dublin Review*, January 1910, and "The International V: The

Motive Force," submitted to the *Dublin Review*, April 1910, Hilaire Belloc Papers, Burns Library.

57. See Hilaire Belloc, "Notes," *G.K.'s Weekly*, 7 January 1937; "Moscow and Berlin," *G.K.'s Weekly*, 11 January 1937; "Correspondence," *G.K.'s Weekly*, 4 February 1937; and "Portugal," *G.K.'s Weekly*, 22 July 1937.

The notion that communists and Jews were manipulating events in Spain became a common feature of rightist Catholic propaganda. For example, in Douglas Woodruff's paper, the London *Tablet* (whose object in the editor's words was "to keep English Catholics informed about the grim realities of Spain"), Marcel Chaminade could claim, without any evidence whatever, that the anarcho-syndicalists in Barcelona were controlled by a small group of Moscow agents directed by the "great Russian Jew publicist, Ilya Ehrenburg," who was operating out of Paris ("Soviet Influence in Spain, 1919–1936," *The Tablet*, 8 October 1938. See also Douglas Woodruff to Frank Sheed, 8 April 1975, Box 6, Folder 34, Douglas Woodruff Papers, Georgetown University Special Collections).

58. "The Press and Spain," *G.K.'s Weekly*, 23 May 1931.

59. Minutes of the seventh meeting of the Comintern, published by the Communist Party of Great Britain, as cited in Thomas, *Spanish Civil War*, p. 90.

60. When the war broke out, the Communists were the smallest of the revolutionary parties (having sixteen Members out of a total of 475 in the Cortes). Party membership numbered around twenty thousand. By mid-1937 their ranks had swelled to one hundred thousand (Jackson, *The Spanish Republic and the Civil War*, p. 360).

61. Belloc's analysis of events in Spain was essentially the same as that outlined by the influential *Entente Internationale contre la Troisième Internationale*, a Swiss-based organization whose journal was devoted to studying the activities of the Communist International. The Entente's *Bulletin* was violently anti-Bolshevik, anti-Semitic, and supportive of fascism and military dictatorships as effective counterweights to communism. It depicted the Spanish Republic as a "Trojan Horse" for communists and Freemasons designed to destroy Spain's Christian culture. The *Bulletin* was read carefully by the highest-ranking officers of the Spanish army and played a significant role in transforming Francisco Franco's political ideas. Franco came to see communism as the force behind every manifestation of ideas and activities that challenged the status quo in Spain. The General had the highest regard for the Entente: along with the birth of his daughter, he claimed that the organization had been the single most important influence on his life. (See Paul Preston, *Franco: A Biography* [New York, 1994], p. 61.)

There was a certain irony here in that the Left also interpreted Gil Robles' "accidentalism" as a "Trojan horse" policy. Since the Right was too weak to overthrow the Republic, Robles' critics believed that his willingness to work legally through the government's institutions was simply a ploy, a tactic that would allow CEDA to infiltrate the Republic and thereby destroy it from within. (See Carr, *The Spanish Tragedy*, p. 44.)

62. Hugh Thomas in Philip Toynbee, ed., *The Distant Drum: Reflections on the Spanish Civil War* (London, 1976), p. 40.

63. Most reliable accounts of the origins of the Spanish Civil War indicate otherwise, namely, that Franco and the Catholic Church had limited popular appeal mainly because they were exponents of the interests of oligarchy and the upper classes. See Jackson, *The Spanish Republic and the Civil War*; Thomas, *The Spanish Civil War*; Borkenau, *The Spanish Cockpit*; Brenan, *The Spanish Labyrinth;* and Stanley G. Payne, *Falange: A History of Spanish Fascism* (Stanford, 1961).

64. "The Salvation of Spain," *The Tablet*, 25 February 1939.

65. Lunn to Belloc, 21 May 1938, Box 2, Folder 14, Arnold Lunn Papers, Georgetown University Special Collections.

66. Belloc to Lunn, 27 May 1938, Box 2, Folder 14, Arnold Lunn Papers, Georgetown University Special Collections.

67. The Left was no different. It too saw the world in Manichean terms, namely as a great struggle between the evil of fascism and the pure goodness of democracy, of which communism was supposed to be the most representative. Stephen Spender's Oxford tutor, the idealist philosopher E. F. Carritt, described the Spanish Civil War as the only conflict to occur in his lifetime in which clearly and indisputably the forces of good—the Republicans—were arrayed against the forces of evil—the Fascists (Stephen Spender, *The Thirties and After: Poetry, Politics, People, 1933–1970* [New York, 1978], p. 7). This sentiment has not eroded with the passage of time. For example, the eminent British historian E. J. Hobsbawm in his recent book *The Age of Extremes* (New York, 1994) writes that the Spanish Civil War and the alliances and allegiances it helped shape remain "the only political cause which, even in retrospect, appears as pure and appealing as it did in 1936" (p. 160). This comment, wrote Tony Judt in reviewing Hobsbawm's book, illustrates the inability of the author to provide his readers with a serious analysis of Bolshevism except on its own restricted terms ("Downhill All the Way," *New York Review of Books*, 25 May 1995, p. 22).

68. Letter from Belloc to Lord R. F. Phillimore, Chairman of the "Friends of Nationalist Spain," 22 March 1939, read to Queen's Hall meeting, 29 March 1939, Box 374–F, Hilaire Belloc Papers, Burns Library.

69. See Raymond Carr, *The Spanish Tragedy: The Civil War in Perspective* (London, 1977), pp. 96–103.

70. See Thomas, *Spanish Civil War*, pp. 40–44.

71. Brenan, *Spanish Labyrinth*, preface, pp. xvii–xviii. The author pointed out that this description of anarchist ideals could apply equally to their political antagonists, the deeply conservative Carlist movement.

72. Franz Borkenau also argued that the Spanish anarchists were essentially religious because they were motivated by a traditional Christian moral vision rooted in the Gospels. "Anarchism *is* a religious movement," believing "in the creation of a new world out of the moral resurrection of those classes which have not yet been contaminated by the spirit of mammon and greed" (*The Spanish Cockpit*, p. 22).

73. Brenan, *The Spanish Labyrinth*, pp. 192–193.

74. This understanding of the Spanish Civil War became the mainstay of most Catholic pro-Loyalist writing. For instance, see Owen McGuire, "Spanish Democracy Linked with Regionalism," *America*, 24 April 1937. The distinctive Bellocian view on the Spanish situation is most striking here. McGuire wrote that every Spaniard who does not want to break with and repudiate the past is a traditionalist and sees his life inseparably bound up with Catholicism (p. 54). Belloc's spin on the civil war can be observed in some of the most influential British and American journals of the day: *The Month*, the *Colosseum*, the London *Tablet*, and the *Brooklyn Tablet*. And, of course, it was at the core of Douglas Jerrold's and Arnold Lunn's propaganda on the Spanish Civil War.

75. Arnold Lunn to Etta Bonacossa, 4 November 1938, Box 2, Folder 20, Arnold Lunn Papers, Georgetown University Special Collections.

76. This is graphically illustrated in Arnold Lunn's *Spanish Rehearsal* (New York, 1937). "I regard communism," wrote Lunn in the introduction, "as the final form of the servile state." On Belloc's influence on Douglas Woodruff and even Evelyn Waugh, see Bernard Wall, *Headlong into Change: An Autobiography and Memoir of Ideas since the Thirties* (London, 1969), p. 24.

77. It is unclear who first claimed that the rebels were engaged in a Christian crusade for civilization. The bishop of Salamanca, Dr. Enrique Plá y Daniel, who had long been a supporter of the rebels, first used the word "crusade" to describe the civil war in a pastoral letter entitled "The Two Cities" issued on 30 September 1936. The text was submitted to Franco before publication. The General not only gave it his imprimatur but readjusted the wording in such a way as to maximize his political gains. (Preston, *Franco*, pp. 184–185). The Dominican priest Father P. J. Mendendez-Reigada, in an article in *Ciencia Tomista* of Salamanca, wrote: "The

Spanish National war is a holy war, the most holy war registered by history." His essay was later published as a pamphlet, *La guerra racional española ante la moral al derecho* (Salamanca, 1937) (as cited in Don Luigi Sturzo, *Church and State* [New York, 1939], p. 511).

One of the first outsiders to apply the label "Religious War" to the Spanish conflict was the French monarchist Charles Maurras, editor of *Action française*. (See Eugen Weber, *Action Française: Royalism and Reaction in Twentieth-Century France* [Stanford, Calif., 1962], p. 380.) This judgment was issued within three days of the *Pronunciamento* of 17 July 1936. Belloc was an avid reader of Maurras' journal and thought highly of both its editor and the movement's (*Action Française*) ideas. Belloc was not given to citing sources, but his thoughts on the Spanish situation, as well as his views on European politics in general, were strikingly similar to what one finds in Maurras' journal, *Action française*. The "Holy War" idea was most widely propagated in the writings of Belloc's followers, Douglas Jerrold and Arnold Lunn. The sentiment also appeared in *Osservatore Romano* on 8 January 1937: "*To a militant conception of life struggle for a doctrine is a holy war,* something which, for spiritual reasons, is inevitable...." (quoted in K. W. Watkins, *Britain Divided: The Effect of the Spanish Civil War on British Political Opinion* [London, 1963], p. 2).

George Shuster claimed it was Dr. Goebbels, that "eminent defender of faith," who initiated the propaganda campaign depicting Franco as the savior of religion. (See "Some Reflections on Spain," *Commonweal,* 2 April 1937.) In any case, the archbishop of Valencia and the bishops of Segovia and Pamplona were soon making public statements describing Franco's cause as a holy crusade: in the Bishop of Segovia's view, it was a hundred times more important than the *Reconquista*. Nationalist troops dispatched to battle were issued leaflets with photo-montages of Christ at the side of Generals Franco and Mola (Beevor, *The Spanish Civil War,* p. 174). Major support for the "Cruzada" idea also came from reactionary elements in the Roman Curia, one of the most influential being Msgr. Ildebrando Antoniutti, papal nuncio to Spain. (See Norman B. Cooper, *Catholicism and the Franco Regime* [London, 1975], p. 11.)

Father Slyvester Pancho, O.P, rector of the University of Santo Tomas, Manila, who spent much of 1936 in Avila, near Madrid, went on a speaking tour in the United States, the purpose of which was to demonstrate the resurgence of the Catholic spirit in Nationalist Spain. Under Franco, he claimed, throngs fill the churches, Nationalist volunteers go to the front wearing scapulars singing hymns, and Franco, with wife and child at his side along with members of his staff, recites the Rosary every evening before retiring (NCWC News Service Report, *America* Material," Box 5, 1938, Georgetown University Special Collections). If this were not sufficient, other right-wing Catholics were prepared to go so far as to recognize parallels between the Spanish situation and America's civil war. Father Edward Lodge Curran, an influential but politically extremist Brooklyn priest, identified Franco as a latter-day Abraham Lincoln (*Franco: Who is He? What Does He Fight For?* [International Truth Society, New York, 1937]).

78. In England this line of argument was also taken up by many non-Catholic Christians and political conservatives. For more on this see Richard Griffiths, *Fellow Travellers of the Right: British Enthusiasts for Nazi Germany, 1933–39* (London, 1980), pp. 260–264, and Simon Haxey, *England's Money Lords; Tory M.P.* (New York, 1939).

79. Arnold Lunn, *Memory to Memory* (London, 1956), p. 122. A similar sentiment was expressed in the English Jesuit journal, *The Month*. Its editors claimed that the issues in the Spanish Civil War were secondary compared to the fact that religion was being attacked by the Reds. "What conclusion can be drawn from these facts other than that Catholics as Catholics are bound in conscience to sympathize with the defenders of the Faith and withhold support from its enemies? All else is beside the point" (Editorial Comments, December 1936).

80. Frank Sheed, *The Church and I* (New York, 1974), p. 199.

81. Belloc was the exception here. From the outset he was suspicious of the Republican government and never felt it wise for the Church to collaborate with its leaders. The editors of *G.K.'s Weekly* seemed to support Belloc's line from time to time. In August 1932, for instance, the paper referred to the current government in Spain as an "alien junta" that had seized power. It did not represent the spirit of Spain ("Notes of the Week," 20 August 1932).

82. *Catholic Herald,* 11 July 1931, as cited in Thomas R. Greene, "The English Catholic Press and the Spanish Republic, 1931–1936," *Church History* 45 (March 1976): 73.

83. *The Month,* October 1931.

84. The initial Catholic support for the 1931 Republic and its ultimate disillusionment by 1936 is the subject of Thomas Greene's "The English Catholic Press and the Spanish Republic."

85. *The Month,* September 1936, p. 193.

86. George Rotvand, *Franco Means Business* (New York, n.d.), p. 26.

87. Arnold Lunn went even further than Dingle on such matters. For instance, he had particular contempt for Waldemar Gurian, a refugee from

Nazi Germany who was teaching at Notre Dame during Lunn's sojourn at the university. Gurian was a convert to Catholicism from Judaism. Writing to Etta Bonacossa, Lunn described a lecture he attended given by Gurian, who spoke English with a heavy German accent. Gurian, noted Lunn, had very "semitic features" and great "difficulty with the Aryan paragraph." Could one ever trust a Jew? "It is a curious thing," continued Lunn, that any Catholic who has Jewish blood or Jewish affiliations is "invariably bitterly anti-Franco and bitterly anti-Chamberlain. Maritain is a case in point. He married a Jewess" (Lunn to Etta Bonacossa, 4 November 1938, p. 2, Box 3, Folder 20, Arnold Lunn Papers, Georgetown University Special Collections).

This line of reasoning was typical of Belloc's circle. Christopher Hollis, who also had a strong dislike for Gurian (Hollis's visiting professorship at Notre Dame overlapped with Lunn's), complained to Douglas Woodruff that America was unfair to Hitler, grotesquely overstating the case against him, and that such hostile sentiment toward the dictators was partly due to Jewish power in the American press: "the *New York Times* is entirely Jewish and most other papers take their cue from that" (Hollis to Woodruff from Notre Dame, undated, Box 4, Folder 4, Douglas Woodruff Papers, Georgetown University Special Collections). Hollis does not seem to have dated most of his correspondence, of which little remains. He destroyed his own copies (as reported by his daughter to Nicholas Scheets, Archivist, Georgetown University Special Collections). In general, this linkage of liberalism and anti-Fascist sentiment with Jewish influence was a common feature in Catholic journals (see Darrow, "Catholic Political Power," p. 70).

88. For an example of Dingle's style and views see his review of Luis Carreras' *The Glory of Martyred Spain* in the *Dublin Review*, October 1939. Also see his frequent articles in *The Month* and his own book on the Spanish tragedy, *Democracy in Spain* (London, 1937).

89. See Darrow, "Catholic Political Power," p. 213. Francis Talbot, S.J., editor of *America*, for example, was happy to work with Rev. Charles Coughlin, Patrick Scanlan, the pro-fascist, anti-Semitic editor of the *Brooklyn Tablet*, the Nazi sympathizer George Viereck, and Merwin K. Hart, a leading organizer of American fascist support for Franco. (On Hart, see letters of 9 November and 14 November 1939, *America*/Talbot Papers, Box 5, 1939 H, Georgetown University Special Collections.) Talbot, however, did draw the line on publishing James Strachy Barnes, the English Catholic fascist journalist who idealized Mussolini. Barnes wanted to be a regular contributor to Talbot's *America*, whose political line

he obviously admired, but Talbot, though initially interested in having Barnes write on the Fascist constitution in Italy, ultimately declined the offer. At this point it seems that Barnes's notorious fascist triumphalism was too strong a brew even for *America*. (See letters between Talbot and Barnes, 19 October and 21 November 1938, *America*/Talbot Papers, Box 5, 1938, Georgetown University Special Collections.)

90. "Jerusalem and Madrid," *The Month,* September 1937. Such sentiments concerning the civil war as a catalyst for religious reawakening became increasingly common in Catholic pro-Franco propaganda. Even *Osservatore Romano* made this observation, and several writers, again following Belloc's lead, saw the "last crusade" and its many martyrs as a harbinger of the revival of Catholic civilization. (For example, see Aodh de Blacam, "For God and Spain: The Truth about the Spanish Civil War," Office of the *Irish Messenger,* Dublin, 1936, Abraham Lincoln Brigade Archives, Special Collections, Brandeis University.)

91. Quoted in Darrow, "Catholic Political Power," p. 34.

92. Correspondence from Arnold Lunn to an unknown recipient, 5 December 1938, Box 3, Folder 20, Arnold Lunn Papers, Georgetown University Special Collections.

93. Virgil Michel, "Catholics and the Catholic Spirit," p. 23, unpublished manuscript, Virgil Michel Papers, Box Z-32, St. John's University.

94. Douglas Jerrold, introduction to René Quinton, *A Soldier's Testament* (London, 1930), quoted by Herbert Read in *Poetry and Anarchism* (London, 1939), p. 67.

95. The British government recognized the Republic, but Aguilera (also known as the Duke of Alba) served as Franco's special agent in London. Even before the Nationalist victory in 1939 when the British government gave *de jure* recognition to Franco's regime, Alba was accorded essentially diplomatic status by a good number of people in the Ministry of Foreign Affairs. Aguilera, along with the Duke of San Lucar la Mayor (later chargé d'affaires in London) and Pablo Merry del Val, drew on a network of old-boy relationships with high-ranking British diplomats that went back to their Catholic public school days in England. The Beaumont, Downside, Ampleforth, and Stonyhurst connection, wrote Sir Robert Hodgson, "created an Anglophile nucleus among Spain's aristocratic elite that made it easy for us to get on with them." (See Sir Robert Hodgson, *Spain Resurgent* [London, 1953], p. 89).

96. Frederick Birchall, *New York Times,* 28 June 1936. A different view of Alba is provided by Peter Kemp, an Englishman who fought with the Requetés and later, with the help of Pablo Merry del Val, served as an

officer in Franco's elitist Spanish Foreign Legion. In his autobiography Kemp provides a colorful but somewhat unflattering picture of the Count. Because of his command of vituperation, Alba had earned the nickname *El Capitán Veneno* (Captain Poison). Yet, Kemp claims that Alba was not an absentee landlord and spent the greater part of his time looking after his estates near Salamanca (Peter Kemp, *Mine Were of Trouble* [London, 1957], p. 50).

97. Kemp, *Mine Were of Trouble*, p. 50. It was also known that Aguilera personally had shot his chauffeur after he had made the mistake of turning too sharply and running the Count's car off the road. "He was a red all the time," explained Aguilera (John T. Whitaker, *We Cannot Escape History* [New York, 1943], p. 115).

98. Whitaker, *We Cannot Escape History*, p. 108.

99. Ibid., p. 110.

100. Arnold Lunn, *Spanish Rehearsal* (London, 1937), pp. 42 and 108.

101. Lunn to Aguilera, Count de Alba y Yeltes, 26 July 1937, Box 2, Folder 13, Arnold Lunn Papers, Georgetown University Special Collections.

102. Alba to Lunn, 21 September 1937, Box 2, Folder 13, Arnold Lunn Papers, Georgetown University Special Collections.

103. Roy Campbell, *Light on a Dark Horse* (Chicago, 1952), p. 224.

104. Ibid., p. 311.

105. Cited in Katharine Bail Hoskins, *Today the Struggle*, p. 44.

106. Peter Alexander, *Roy Campbell: A Critical Biography* (Oxford, 1982), p. 173.

107. David Wright, *Roy Campbell* (London, 1961), p. 39.

108. Weintraub, *The Last Great Cause*, p. 164.

109. *The New Statesman and Nation*, 1 March 1939, p. 370. Spender also was appalled by the poem's unsavory diatribes against Jews. The virulent anti-Semitic remarks in *Flowering Rifle* were comparable to what appeared in the columns of Julius Streicher's Nazi paper, *Der Stürmer* (Hoskins, *Today the Struggle*, p. 48). Like Belloc, Campbell here lays out for his readers the Masonic, Jewish, and communist conspiracy to take over Spain as part of a long-range plan to destroy Christianity.

110. Campbell was delighted with Belloc's judgment. As he told his mother, Belloc's "word is worth more than the whole of Fleet Street" (Alexander, *Campbell*, p. 181). Belloc would have recognized in Campbell's poem clear echoes of his own analysis of what he called "the Jewish question" and Spain.

111. Quoted in Valentine Cunningham, *British Writers of the Thirties* (New York, 1988), p. 458.

112. Wall, *Headlong into Change,* p. 181. Wall and Campbell were fast friends during the civil war days. Wall, claimed Campbell, wrote the one favorable review that *Flowering Rifle* received. Campbell was angered by the fact that Wall became more liberal in his mature years. Roy, wrote Wall, never got out of his Spanish civil war mind-set (*Headlong into Change,* p. 180).

113. Many January Club members were supportive of Sir Oswald Mosley's British Union of Fascists, and eventually the BUF took over the association. In fact, Colin Cross has argued that the January Club served as a "front organization" for Mosley's group (Colin Cross, *The Fascists in Britain* [London, 1961], pp. 100–101). Douglas Jerrold and Francis Yeats-Brown of the January Club were also members of the Anglo-German Fellowship, a post-Nazi creation which replaced the former Anglo-German Society. The latter was dissolved because the Nazis disliked it and because many of its members were anti-Hitler. (Lord Reading had been president and members included such people as H. G. Wells, H. A. L. Fisher, and Lord Jellicoe.) The Anglo-German Fellowship was designed by the Nazis to create a better image of the Third Reich by encouraging social contacts between eminent Nazis and influential Englishmen. (See Haxey, *England's Money Lords,* pp. 199, 214–215.) However, there were many charter members of the January Club (they later left) who were adamantly anti-Hitler and opposed to Mosley. These would include Yeats-Brown, John Squire, Charles Petrie, and Muriel Curry, among others. As Richard Griffiths has shown, there was a correlation on the British Right between support for Franco and Mussolini but not between Spanish Nationalist sympathy and Hitler. This was especially the case with Catholics who, like Belloc, identified Nazism with the Protestant tradition. (See Griffiths, *Fellow Travellers of the Right.*)

114. Francis Yeats-Brown, for example, as the newly appointed editor of *Everyman* (Autumn 1933), vowed to use the journal as a vehicle for converting the English political system into Mussolini-style corporatism. (For background on Yeats-Brown see John Evelyn Wrench, *Francis Yeats-Brown, 1886–1994* [London, 1948], and the writer's own works: *European Jungle* [London, 1939], and the autobiographical books, *Bengal Lancer* [London, 1930] and *Golden Horn* [London, 1932].)

Yeats-Brown's fascistic tendencies were revealed in the essay "Why I Believe in War," published in the *Spectator,* 30 December 1932. "Patriotism," he wrote, is a very real thing, the flower of which "has been watered by the blood of heroic men and women, whereas the weedy hothouse plant of Geneva has been nourished chiefly by talk and self-interest. . . . Perfect and perpetual peace seems to me to lead to stagnation, sterility and psychic suicide" (as quoted in Wrench, *Yeats-Brown,* p. 175). Yeats-Brown was close friend of both Douglas Jerrold and Belloc's sister, Mrs. Belloc-Lowndes.

115. For example, compare Belloc's analysis of Europe's political scene with Charles Petrie's "Fascism and the Nazis," *Saturday Review,* 20 May 1933.

116. Charles Petrie, *The Story of Government* (Boston, 1929), pp. 200–201. "Once one is convinced of the need for authority in matters spiritual," wrote Petrie, "it is but the logical sequence to believe that it is necessary in matters temporal" (p. 212).

117. "For a long while the seed which they were sowing appeared to be falling on but stony ground, yet when it was reinforced by the lessons of the Great War and by the growing influence of the Roman Church it began to grow rapidly." Barrès and other French Catholic writers were to the twentieth century what the Encyclopaedists represented to the eighteenth century: "the harbingers of a fresh dawn" (Ibid., p. 214).

118. See Charles Petrie, *Monarchy in the Twentieth Century* (London, 1952). This of course was Belloc's opinion as well.

119. Charles Petrie, *Lords of the Inland Sea: A Study of the Mediterranean Powers* (London, 1937), p. 68. See also Petrie's *Mussolini* (London, 1931). The Italian dictator, in Petrie's mind, represented the evolution of "civilized Europe." He is not like Napoleon, a child of revolution, he is rather the revolution itself. Mussolini is the incarnation of Italy (p. 37).

120. Petrie, *Lords of the Inland Sea,* pp. 48–49.

121. Bolín, *Spain: The Vital Years,* p. 122.

122. John Whitaker claimed Bolín's office allowed no correspondents into Nationalist territory unless he was certain they were fascists. Whitaker, who was in fact anti-Franco, was allowed in because the Italians during the Ethiopian War had decorated him with the *Croce di Guerra* and Bolín simply assumed he was a fascist sympathizer (*We Cannot Escape History,* p. 109).

123. For details see Koestler's *Spanish Testament,* pp. 27–28, 219–231. For Bolín's account, see his *Spain: The Vital Years,* pp. 248–249. Koestler at the time of his arrest was a house guest of Sir Peter Chalmers Mitchell, an English citizen who was neutral in the Civil War, being engaged neither in politics nor in armed conflict. Mitchell had taken into his home Luis Bolín's relatives, the family of Don Tomás Bolín, who were his neighbors, and gave them protection during the Loyalist occupation of Málaga; after several months he helped them escape the city for safety in Gibraltar. When the Insurgents entered Málaga Mitchell sadly discovered that

the Bolíns were not prepared to repay the favor. Don Tomás, who had returned to Málaga at that point, seems to have done nothing to prevent Mitchell's arrest by Luis Bolín. Mitchell believes that he might have been shot except for the intervention of the acting British consul in Málaga and the British naval commander of HMS *Basilik*. (See Mitchell, *My House in Málaga*, pp. 293–296.)

124. Bolín had been an ardent servant of Franco's. For example, it was his mission to Rome for a meeting with Count Galeazzo Ciano in July 1936 that arranged for the first shipment of Italian airplanes to Spain. See his *Spain: The Vital Years*, pp. 167–172. Jerrold, for his part, took great pride in having undertaken a mission to obtain fifty machine guns and half a million rounds of S.A. ammunition for anti-Republican groups before the outbreak of the Civil War.

125. See Bolín, *Spain: The Vital Years*, pp. 122–123; Haxey, *England's Money Lords*, pp. 210–220; and Griffiths, *Fellow Travellers of the Right*, pp. 260–264.

126. Arnold Lunn, *Memory to Memory*, p. 141, as cited in Kevin L. Morris, "Fascism and British Catholic Writers 1924–1939," *The Chesterton Review*, vol. 25, nos. 1 and 2 (February/May 1999): 42.

127. The authorship of this book is a bit confusing. Jerrold, then director of Eyre and Spottiswoode, the firm that published *The Spanish Republic*, claimed a "tactical victory" with the appearance of the book, which he described as the result of collaboration between Bolín, the Marquis del Moral, and himself (Douglas Jerrold, *Georgian Adventure* [London, 1937], p. 361). Bolín, however, declared in his memoirs of the Civil War that he was the author, the book having been signed "anonymous" since his association with the enterprise would have been too risky (Bolín, *Spain: The Vital Years*, p. 123). In fact the book is frequently referenced with "anon." as the author.

128. Greene, "The English Catholic Press and the Spanish Republic," p. 76.

129. Jerrold, *Georgian Adventure*, p. 362.

130. See Southworth, *Guernica!*, note 23, p. 435.

131. See Southworth, *Guernica!*, p. 433, and his *Le mythe de la croisade de Franco* (Paris, 1964), pp. 163–176. The British historian K. W. Watkins also has studied these documents and rejects their authenticity. (See his *Britain Divided*, pp. 39–45.) Watkins provides a full text of Loveday's translation of these documents in the appendix of his book. Loveday's translations were published with "the permission and full authority of the nationalist government." Douglas Jerrold also reproduced portions of these "secret" texts in his widely-circulated defense of Franco, "Spain:

Impressions and Reflections" (reprint from *The Nineteenth Century and After*, April 1937, pp. 470–492).

132. McGuire claimed that he had "documents" from the government in Salamanca that conclusively proved that the Bolsheviks planned to turn Spain into a Soviet satellite (Owen B. McGuire, "Spain Transformed," *The Sign*, May 1938, p. 603). The same argument was given by Sir Robert Hodgson, who was sent to Spain by Clement Attlee to open diplomatic relations prior to Britain's recognition of Franco's government. When the Nationalist revolt broke out, wrote Hodgson, "it was undoubtedly the case that the 'Red' Spain at war was completely permeated by Communist infiltration" (Hodgson, *Spain Resurgent*, p. 29).

The story of a Red plot is the core argument used by Franco's regime to justify their rebellion, and it has been accepted by most Catholic writers outside of Spain. However, highly respected historians of the Spanish Civil War have rejected the existence of such a plot. See Jackson, *The Spanish Republic and the Civil War*, pp. 514–517, and David T. Cattell, *Communism and the Spanish Civil War* (Berkeley, Calif., 1955), pp. 42–43.

133. Croft continued to praise Franco as a gentleman in the greatest Christian tradition even after World War II when the outside world was finally told the truth about the tens of thousands executed by Franco after the Nationalist victory. Croft claimed he had no brief for Franco, but could write that "rarely in any war did any general show such wisdom, chivalry and mercy as the conqueror of Red Spain." Franco, he continued, always resisted the temptation of completely routing his enemy and was "determined to spare innocent people. . . ." See *My Life of Strife* (London, 1954), p. 275–276. This depiction of Franco as a benevolent, paternalistic dictator who always offered clemency to his enemies was a typical feature of pro-Nationalist British and American Catholic writing. Representative of the style are McGuire's articles in *The Sign*, Francis X. Talbot, S.J., and his associates writing for *America*, Cardinal William O'Connell's friends at the *Boston Pilot*, and Hodgson's *Spain Resurgent*.

134. Phillimore to Belloc, 15 February 1939; Belloc to Phillimore, 17 March 1939; Belloc to Phillimore, 22 March 1939, Box 374–F, Hilaire Belloc Papers, Burns Library. Belloc took ill before the meeting and had to have his speech read to the gathering.

135. Belloc drew up two lists, one including those who could pay their own way and another of people who would require "some measure of hospitality." After each name Belloc provided advice on how best one might appeal to the individual's political sympathies. For instance, attached to the name of Somers Somerset, Esq., heir presumptive to the Duke of Beaufort, was written: "He has a strong dislike of the Jewish influence in

Europe," suggesting an angle a recruiter might take to enlist his support for the cause. Non-Catholics, like Belloc's friend Hoffman Nickerson, were identified as "having Catholic sympathies," thus a natural tendency to support the Friends of Nationalist Spain. The wealthy Nickerson, noted Belloc, might even bring his own automobile to Spain ("Articles on Spain," Box 371, Hilaire Belloc Papers, Burns Library).

136. When Woodruff became editor in April 1936 he attracted some of the best-known Catholic conservative intellectuals to write for the magazine, including Chrisopher Dawson, Arnold Lunn, and Christopher Hollis.

137. "The New Despair," *Colosseum*, June 1934. Chesterton welcomed Wall's journalistic venture and thought the first issue an excellent number (Barbara Wall, "Bernard Wall and the *Colosseum* [1934–1939]," *The Chesterton Review*, August 1981, p. 211). Father Victor White, the Dominican editor of *Blackfriars*, also offered his congratulations on the first number. Wall and White were close friends but soon had a falling-out over differing opinions on the Spanish Civil War.

138. Wall, *Headlong into Change*, p. 19.

139. The Renaissance, wrote Lunn, represented a rebirth of "pagan pride," the pride of the humanist in conflict with the humility of the Christian (Arnold Lunn, *Now I See* [London, 1956], p. 56). Lunn, Hollis, and Douglas Jerrold as college students were obsessed with the intrinsic sinfulness of man and saw the necessity of authoritarian moral and political standards in a modern world of ethical chaos. This collective longing is what brought them to Chesterton and Belloc.

140. Ramiro de Maeztu was a seminal thinker who had a major impact on pre–World War I British intellectual life before going to Spain. In 1934 he published the highly influential *Defensa de la hispanidad*, in which he argued (like Belloc) that all of Spanish culture and history were defined by its close association with and service to the Catholic faith. De Maeztu soon became a lead writer for *Acción Española* (a monthly journal named after the *Action française*) in support of Franco. By this point de Maeztu, a close friend of Luis Bolín, had become increasingly authoritarian and pro-fascist. He perhaps represented the purest example of native Spanish fascism during the civil war. No contemporary Spanish writer, claimed Bolín, surpassed de Maeztu's insight and clarity in analyzing the problems of modern Spain (*Spain: The Vital Years*, p. 142). Wall greatly admired de Maeztu: his "ideas are in some ways a Spanish version of what *Colosseum* often tries to put forward" ("Editorial," *Colosseum*, December 1937). Ramiro de Maeztu was shot by the Loyalists four months after the civil war broke out.

486 Notes to Pages 327–330

141. Compare this with Wyndham Lewis's comments on romantics and neo-classicism. Wall certainly thought highly of Lewis's pro-fascist analysis of European politics. (See his "Three Comments," *Colosseum*, September 1937.)

A good discussion of Lewis's political ideas can be found in Geoffrey Wagner, *Wyndham Lewis* (London, 1957). For T. E. Hulme's influence on Lewis and other reactionary intellectuals see John R. Harrison, *The Reactionaries* (London, 1966). Some excellent sources on the ideas of Hulme and Ramiro de Maeztu are Martin Wallace, *The New Age under Orage* (New York, 1967); T. E. Hulme, *Speculations,* ed. Herbert Read (London, 1924); and A. R. Jones, *The Life and Opinions of T.E. Hulme* (Boston, 1960).

142. "The End of Revolution," *Colosseum*, June 1934.

143. "A Comment," *Colosseum*, January 1937. Even British diplomats of the likes of Sir Robert Hodgson, writing after World War II, had difficulty finding too much at fault with fascism. In his view the Falange, with all its blemishes, had unquestionable virtues. Hodgson was "most favorably impressed . . . by the keenness with which boys of from four upwards joined up and the sense of discipline it engendered in them." The Falange, he wrote, provided a most valuable propaganda machine which did much to popularize "The Cause" (Hodgson, *Spain Resurgent*, p. 93).

144. "Editorial," *Colosseum*, December 1936. Wall contended here that Italy's Abyssinian adventure was also good for Europe's health, since it marked a victory over the League of Nations.

145. "Tradition and Social Justice," *Dublin Review*, April 1937, p. 258.

146. Ibid., p. 261.

147. Unlike most of his right-wing Catholic confederates, Wall welcomed criticism of his own political views. Despite its endorsement of fascism for Spain, *Colosseum* was open to writers of varying, often conflicting positions on the politics of the civil war. The September 1937 issue, for instance, was devoted to presenting different views that Catholic writers took on Spain.

148. "Germany and Racism," *Colosseum*, January 1939.

149. "Pen Points after the Crisis," *Colosseum*, October 1938. Curiously, Wall later in his autobiographical account of the 1930s claimed that he had not been interested in fascism, a statement that does not square with what he wrote as editor of *Colosseum*. (See *Headlong into Change,* p. 63.) Wall's reminiscences on the subject may have been influenced by his political apotheosis after World War II. By this juncture he had become openly critical of conservative Catholicism, in particular of the policies of Pope Pius XII. Looking back on the 1930s, Wall seemed genuinely

ashamed of his views, admitting that his callow political commentaries had fallen victim to the passions of the times and, like those on the extreme left, were hysterical and absurd. By the 1950s Wall's views had evolved to the point that they converged with those of Stephen Spender, the left-leaning anti-Nationalist he and Roy Campbell so loathed in the 1930s. Along with Spender, Wall became a member of the Society of Cultural Freedom, which published the anticommunist magazine *Encounter*.

Wall also came to recognize the folly of his uncompromising views on Franco (Barbara Wall, "Wall and *Colosseum*," p. 218). The same cannot be said for many others on the Catholic Right. Douglas Woodruff, for instance, whose propaganda for Franco in the *Tablet* was certainly as strident as Wall's, told Frank Sheed in 1975 that Sheed should not be the least apologetic for having supported Franco so vigorously: "What was at stake was nothing less than the religious future for the next generations' young Spaniards." Sheed admitted that his own response had been largely emotional, conditioned by the murder of priests. The real issue, wrote Woodruff to Sheed, was the future of Spain and the freedom of the Catholic Church, "and this may well erupt again" (Douglas Woodruff to Frank Sheed, 8 April 1975, Box 6, Folder 34, Douglas Woodruff Papers, Georgetown University Special Collections). It is important to point out in this context that even the Spanish Church has apologized for its role in the Civil War: "We humbly recognize, and ask pardon for it, that we failed at the proper time to be ministers of reconciliation in the midst of our people, divided by a war between brothers" (*New York Times*, 17 September 1971, p. 3, as cited in Guenter Lewy, *Religion and Revolution* [New York, 1974], p. 429).

Several of those hostile to fascism who wrote propaganda during the interwar years later came forth to confess their disingenuous deeds (George Lowther Steer on Ethiopia, Arthur Koestler and Claud Cockburn on Spain, for example), but few who served the Right have found a way to do the same. The editors of the *Tablet*, noted Herbert Southworth, who "wrote untruths about Guernica . . . have not yet informed their faithful readers of the misinformation they gave them during the war." (*Guernica!*, p. 304). After leaving the *Tablet* Woodruff became distressed at the journal's increasing turn toward more liberal positions. From the vantage of the 1970s and the turn taken by his magazine, it was depressing for Woodruff to reflect back on his hard work to keep English Catholics correctly informed about the "grim realities" of politics during the interwar years (Douglas Woodruff to Frank Sheed, 8 April 1975, Box 6, Folder 34, Douglas Woodruff Papers, Georgetown University Special Collections).

Roy Campbell in his autobiography (1951) also gave no indication that he regretted anything he wrote during the 1930s on France, fascism, and anti-Semitism. Such are the ways of the true believer.

Chapter 13. Against the Tide: The Catholic Critics of Franco

1. Jacques Maritain, *Questions de conscience* (Paris, 1938), p. 278. Quoted in Herbert Rutledge Southworth, *Guernica! Guernica!: A Study of Journalism, Diplomacy, Propaganda, and History* (Berkeley, Calif., 1977), p. 160.

2. Bernard Doering, *Jacques Maritain and the French Catholic Intellectuals* (Notre Dame, Ind., 1983), p. 71.

3. For more on Maritain's thinking about the relationship between religion and politics see *The Things That Are Not Caesar's* (New York, 1931); *Scholasticism and Politics* (New York, 1940); "Church and State," in Joseph W. Evans and Leo Ward, eds., *Jacques Maritain: Challenges and Renewals* (Cleveland, Ohio, 1968); and *Humanisme intégral* (Paris, 1936). Maritain's position on Catholic political action complemented the Vatican's thinking on the subject. Rome preferred that Catholics not form confessional parties since it could limit Church independence and encourage anticlerical reaction. Instead, the Vatican favored strategies that transcended narrow partisan politics and would contribute to the reconstruction of a Christian cultural ethic for a modern social order.

4. Hélène Iswolsky, *Light before Dusk* (New York, 1942), p. 187.

5. Ibid., p. 189.

6. Quoted in Doering, *Jacques Maritain and the French Catholic Intellectuals,* p. 78.

7. Mounier's philosophy had much appeal to those in the American liturgical movement, in particular Virgil Michel and H. A. Reinhold. Personalism had a significant impact on the thinking of Peter Maurin, who with Dorothy Day was a founder of the Catholic Worker Movement. Maurin introduced Mounier to an American audience by arranging for the translation and publication of his *Personalist Manifesto.* (See Arthur Sheehan, *Peter Maurin: Gay Believer* [Garden City, N.Y., 1959], p. 191; Neil Betten, *Catholic Activism and the Industrial Worker* [Gainesville, Fla, 1976], pp. 55–57; and Mel Piehl, *Breaking Bread: The Catholic Worker and the Origin of Catholic Radicalism in America* [Philadelphia, 1982], pp. 70–71.) There was also an obvious resonance between personalism and the ideas of G. K. Chesterton. For details on Mounier's ideas and career see John Hellman,

Emmanuel Mounier and the New Catholic Left, 1930–50 (Toronto, 1981), Emmanuel Mounier, *The Character of Man* (New York, 1956), and Thomas Bokenkotter, *Church and Revolution: Catholics in the Struggle for Democracy and Social Justice* (New York, 1998), chapter 11: "Maritain (1882–1973) and Mounier (1882–1975)."

8. Iswolsky, *Light before Dusk*, p. 110.

9. See Stanley G. Payne, *Spanish Catholicism: An Historical Overview* (Madison, Wis., 1984), pp. 171–172.

10. Ibid., p. 176.

11. Ibid., p. 179.

12. Maritain's position on the Spanish Civil War was first articulated in the preface he wrote for his friend Alfred Mendizabal's book, *Aux origines d'une tragédie: la politique espagnole de 1923 à 1936*, later published separately as "De la guerre sainte," in *La Nouvelle Revue Française* (1 July 1937). See also "War and the Bombardment of Cities," *Commonweal*, 2 September 1938.

13. Franco's government even censored the Pope's radio broadcast of 15 April 1939 congratulating the Nationalists on victory. A passage urging kindness and good will toward the vanquished was eliminated by Spanish radio (Payne, *Spanish Catholicism*, p. 180).

14. Arnold Lunn, *Spain and the Christian Front: Ubi Crux Ibi Patria* (New York, 1937), p. 21.

15. As José Sánchez has argued, irrespective of the Basque's abhorrence of military dictatorship and fascist politics, the dominant issue was security. In order to protect their property and religious and cultural freedoms, the Basques had to support the Republic. An alliance with conservative Spanish Catholicism would have been suicidal (*The Spanish Civil War as a Religious Tragedy* [Notre Dame, Ind., 1987], pp. 75–76).

16. Gabriel Jackson, *The Spanish Republic and the Civil War, 1931–1939* (Princeton, N.J., 1965), p. 376.

17. Hugh Thomas, *The Spanish Civil War* (New York, 1961), p. 449.

18. Basque Christian syndicates encompassed fifty-three thousand industrial laborers and more than nine thousand peasant households. Rightists in the whole of Spain could claim no more than forty thousand workers affiliated with their Catholic syndicates, and almost all of these were exclusively political in orientation. See J. de Hiriartia, *The Case of the Basque Catholics* (The Basque Archives, New York, 1939), pp. 14–15.

19. For example, the American historian William A. Christian, Jr., noted that the town of Zeanuri, with 2,500 inhabitants, was the birthplace of fifty-three living priests, 106 male members of religious orders, and

109 nuns (*Visionaries: The Spanish Republic and the Reign of Christ* [Berkeley, Calif., 1996], p. 218).

20. Matxin de Ondartzaphe, *The Basques and the Communists* (London, 1939), p. 15.

21. Norman B. Cooper, *Catholicism and the Franco Regime* (London, 1975), p. 12.

22. Ibid. p. 14.

23. The Collective Letters of the Spanish Episcopate read in part: "The Church never fails to inculcate due respect and obedience to the legal government, even in times when its officials and representatives abuse and misuse their powers to the injury of the Church itself. . . ." Furthermore, "to assist by our own actions in the destruction of the social order, in the hope that out of such catastrophe might be born a better condition of things, would be almost treason both to our Religion and to our native-land." Quoted in Hiriartia, *The Case of the Basque Catholics*, p. 21.

24. "A Declaration by the Basque Nationalist Catholic Youth on the Spanish Civil War," published by the Press Department of the Spanish Embassy in London, 1936?, Abraham Lincoln Brigade Archives, Special Collections, Brandeis University. For a further discussion of Basque Nationalist Party goals and aspirations see G. L. Steer, *The Tree of Gernika* (London, 1938), p. 66 ff.

25. There was widespread violence against soldiers and civilians on both sides during the civil war. However, the terror of the Nationalists was different from that of the Loyalists. The outburst of violence against the Church when the military rebellion began was spontaneous, well beyond the control of the Republican government. Once the government got control of the situation (and it took six months to do so), the fury stopped. Contrary to Nationalist propaganda, it was never a policy of the Republican government to employ systematic violence against civilians or the clergy. This was not the case with the Insurgents. Franco's forces pursued a calculated program of terror against unfriendly populations in order to subdue potential resistance to Nationalist rule in the future.

Mass executions were carried out by Franco's troops in the territories they conquered, and the systematic employment of death squads accounts for the far greater numbers killed in Insurgent areas of occupation than in the Republican zone. Estimates of the actual numbers killed vary. Hugh Thomas, for example, has estimated that about forty thousand were killed outside the battle zone by Nationalist forces (*Civil War*, p. 631). Gabriel Jackson, on the other hand, gives a far higher figure of some two hundred thousand and concludes that "Nationalist political executions during and after the war constituted the largest single category of deaths attributable to the Civil War (*The Spanish Republic and the Civil War,* p. 538). Most recent estimates of the executions in Nationalist Spain after the war put the number between eighty thousand and a hundred thousand (from José Sánchez as expressed to author, 15 July 1996).

26. Paul Preston, *Franco: A Biography* (New York, 1994), p. 242. Franco had resisted efforts to reach a negotiated peace settlement through the offices of Great Britain, the Vatican, and Italy in the spring of 1937, since he wanted total victory. He also had no desire that the war end quickly. Much to the dismay of the Germans and Italians, Franco wanted to wage a long, drawn-out war of attrition for political reasons. The annihilation of large numbers of Republicans and the total humiliation and terroriza- tion of the surviving population would make it much easier to create a new order when the conflict ended (Preston, *Franco,* p. 176).

27. Ibid., p. 49. These tactics were even shocking to the Germans who aided Franco. Captain Roland von Strunk, Hitler's special agent in Spain, told the American journalist John T. Whitaker that he had twice inter- vened with Franco to stop shooting prisoners on grounds that it was stiff- ening Republican resistance. Apparently his injunctions made no difference. Whitaker observed that there was a division of labor in the killing: civilians behind the lines were executed by Falangists; prisoners of war were killed by Franco's soldiery and on his express orders (John T. Whitaker, *We Cannot Escape History* [New York, 1943], p. 113).

28. Hiriartia, *The Case of the Basque Catholics,* p. 31. Hugh Thomas gives the number of executed priests as sixteen but possibly as high as twenty (*The Spanish Civil War,* p. 484). The most eminent among the victims were Joaquin Arin, archpriest of the parish of Mondragón, and Father Aris- timuño, a famous scholar of Basque culture. Senior Italian officers were shocked by the viciousness of these repressions. Efforts to decrease the number of shootings through personal appeals to Franco himself were of little avail. Franco responded to his own brother-in-law's request to adopt more juridically sound procedures for dealing with prisoners by telling him to "keep out of this. Soldiers don't like civilians intervening in affairs connected with the application of their code of justice" (Ramón Serrano Suñer, *Entre el silencio y la propaganda, la Historia como fue. Memorias* [Bar- celona, 1977], quoted in Preston, *Franco,* p. 227).

29. See "Spanish Catholic and Protestant Priests, Freemasons and Liberals Shot by the Rebels" (Press Department of the Spanish Embassy, London), p. 4, Abraham Lincoln Brigade Archives, Special Collections, Brandeis University.

30. Mateo Múgica, the bishop of Vitoria, wrote to Cardinal Gomá, primate of Spain, protesting the Nationalists' policy of killing Basque priests. He was later especially upset that Gomá, in an open letter to Basque President Aguirre, failed to give the reason for such Nationalist policy. In a private reply to Múgica's protest Gomá admitted that the Nationalists had abused their authority in ordering the assassinations but stated, "How could I pick a quarrel with those in a position of power? It would be most imprudent." Gomá asked Múgica to keep this confession an absolute secret. (See Sánchez, *The Spanish Civil War as a Religious Tragedy*, p. 83.)

The Basques also got little support from the Vatican over the Guernica affair. Secretary of State Eugenio Pacelli only reluctantly received Basque priests who came to Rome with a letter from eyewitnesses contradicting Nationalist claims that Guernica was destroyed by Reds. When Pacelli finally agreed to see the Basque delegates he coldly remarked, "The Church is persecuted in Barcelona," and showed them the door (Thomas, *The Spanish Civil War*, p. 420).

31. See Jackson, *The Spanish Republic and the Civil War*, p. 391. Mussolini wrote Franco to urge moderation at the surrender of the Basques and to refrain from reprisals against the civilian population, for he feared another round of atrocities would be a public relations disaster in the Catholic world. Franco gave his promise, but in an act of duplicity initiated massive executions of prisoners. The Italians were shocked at Franco's deception and cruelty. Even Himmler protested in vain to Franco about his senseless slaughter of prisoners. See Preston, *Franco*, pp. 225–228; 284–285.

32. The Republicans pointed out that this pattern was not replicated in Nationalist territory, where many clergy were in fact active members of the political organizations of the Right.

33. Cooper, *Catholicism and the Franco Regime*, pp. 9–11.

34. Such is the view of George Steiner. See his "Murder Will Out," *New Yorker*, 6 March 1978, p. 114.

35. From the *Times* of London, 27 April 1937.

36. "La significance de Guernica," *L'Aube*, 2 June 1937, as quoted in Southworth, *Guernica!*, pp. 31–32.

37. Jackson, *Spanish Republic*, p. 382. Father Onaindia reported that he had arrived at Guernica on 26 April at 4:40 p.m. Just after having left his car the bombing began and lasted until 7:45 p.m. During this time, he wrote, "five minutes did not elapse without the sky's being black with German planes." The planes attacked very low, tearing up the woods into splinters with machine gun fire. "Screams of lamentation were heard everywhere, and the people, filled with terror, knelt, lifting their hands to

heaven as if to implore divine protection" (quoted in Claude G. Bowers, *My Mission to Spain* [London, 1954], p. 345).

38. See Thomas, *Spanish Civil War,* p. 420.

39. So argues Francis McCullagh, *In Franco's Spain* (London, 1937), pp. 106–107.

40. John T. Whitaker, *We Cannot Escape History* (New York, 1943), pp. 109–110. Although reporters on the Nationalist side were closely watched, tightly restricted in their movements, and obliged to print only what the authorities permitted, correspondents on the Republican side had virtually no restrictions on movement, and censorship was relatively mild. (See Herbert L. Matthews, *A World in Revolution: A Newspaperman's Memoir* [New York, 1971], p. 21.) This is corroborated by journalists and soldiers who were supportive of the Nationalists as well. For example, see McCullagh, *In Franco's Spain,* and Peter Kemp, *Mine Were of Trouble* (London, 1957).

Bolín looms large in the memoirs of Captain Francis McCullagh, an Irish war correspondent who traveled with Eoin O'Duffy's Irish Brigade and was deeply devoted to the Nationalist cause. As director of the Nationalist Press Bureau, Bolín was known as Captain Bustamente. McCullagh saw "Busty" (as he was called derisively by reporters) as representative of an unfortunate style in the New Spain, a stern, uncompromising Torquemada type who gave Franco's cause a bad name. McCullagh and other pro-Franco newsmen rued the fact that the Nationalists were losing the propaganda war to the Reds, a setback resulting largely from people like Bolín, whose authoritarian, censorious policies gave the correct impression that Franco had something to hide. His modus operandi was so odious, lamented McCullagh, that no English or American newspaper would send its star reporter to the Nationalist side until Bustamente was removed. Yet, in the end, despite the personal anguish that Bolín caused him, McCullagh thanked "Busty," since the disillusionment with Bolín caused McCullagh to look at the Nationalists with a more impartial eye, thereby tempering a callow idealism (*in Franco's Spain,* p. 320).

Yet another friend of Nationalist Spain who also had the misfortune of encountering Bolín during the war was Captain E. C. Lance, D.S.O. Known as the "Spanish Pimpernel" for his daring exploits smuggling well-connected Nationalists out of Madrid, Lance claimed that Bolín was "Quite the most unpleasant creature I've ever met" (E. C. Lucas Phillips, *The Spanish Pimpernel* [London, 1960], p. 78).

41. Those who did paid a high price. For example, René Brue, cameraman for the *Pathé Gazette,* was jailed by Bolín for having filmed the

Badajoz massacres. Of course, Bolín, as was his habit, also threatened to have Brue shot. The threat made Brue's prison interlude an unusually anxious experience. Bolín had also expelled a good number of conservative and Francophile British press correspondants from Nationalist territory for having made the egregious indiscretion of referring to Franco's army as "insurgents." See Arthur Koestler, *Spanish Testament* (London, 1937), pp. 28 and 220.

42. Francis McCullagh, who sympathized with the Insurgents (he believed their cause to be a "holy" one), wrote that "there are, today in London, English journalists, home on holiday from Franco's army, who dare not open their lips on certain subjects" (*In Franco's Spain*, p. 322).

Douglas Jerrold and Arnold Lunn at no time during the Civil War ever mentioned in their voluminous writings the existence of German airplanes or pilots. Jerrold went even further on the subject: "There are no German fighting troops and never have been." He also stated that "it was fantastic" to claim that Italian troops were fighting for Franco ("The Issues in Spain," *American Review*, April 1937, p. 16). The British historian K. W. Watkins found it almost incredible that Jerrold could write this, since he had personally toured Nationalist Spain in the previous month just before Italian troops were used in Franco's attack on Madrid (K. W. Watkins, *Britain Divided: The Effect of the Spanish Civil War on British Political Opinion* [London, 1963], p. 98). It did not serve Jerrold's purpose to tell the whole story, and in this he was simply following the dictates of his friend, Luis Bolín. Captain Francis McCullagh, on the other hand, who attempted to be objective in reporting about the Nationalist struggle he so whole heartedly supported, was less compliant. McCullagh became "somewhat ruffled" to discover upon arriving in Lisbon that all articles that he had written mentioning the "Irish Brigade" had been detained. Bolín, he was told, did not wish it known abroad that Franco had foreigners in his army. "Worse still," wrote McCullagh, "I had not been told at the time of these detentions" (*In Franco's Spain*, pp. 320–321).

43. Herbert Rutledge Southworth's careful study of the affair led him to this conclusion. See his *Guernica!*, p. 33. Southworth may have had the last word on the Guernica affair. Although his book rings with indignation over the systematic lying of Franco's propagandists and the support given it by journalists and politicians, he documents every falsehood perpetrated by Franco's supporters with rare professional diligence. The evidence Southworth provides to unmask the deceit is overwhelming.

44. In fact, this was the case for 27 April, but not on the previous day when Guernica was attacked.

45. Luis Bolín, *Spain: The Vital Years* (New York, 1967), p. 281.

46. Southworth, *Guernica!*, p. 90.

47. George Lowther Steer, *The Tree of Gernika* (London, 1938), p. 246. Steer's most indefatigable critic was Douglas Jerrold, whose writings on Nationalist Spain, examined with the benefit of historical perspective, were notoriously unreliable. Jerrold wrote, for example, that both friend and foe could travel freely without any restrictions in Bolín's territory: "If the National government errs, it errs on the side of informality, of clemency and casualness. . . . Go where you like; say what you like. . . . No one asks who you are and what is your business. No one is inaccessible; no one has anything to conceal" ("Spain: Impressions and Reflections," from *The Nineteenth Century and After* [April 1937], p. 479).

48. "The Truth about Guernica," *The Tablet*, 5 June 1937, pp. 801–802. Jerrold repeated the argument with a few emendations for an American audience in the pro-fascist monthly, the *American Review* (Summer 1937). Essentially the same explanation was given in Arnold Lunn's *The Spanish Rehearsal*, pp. 266–269. In fact Lunn here quoted Jerrold's judgment on Guernica. Luis Bolín then completed the circle which he himself began. In his memoirs of the war Bolín recapitulated Jerrold's analysis of the Guernica myth as the truth. Jerrold, in Bolín's assessment, was an unimpeachable source: he "is a writer gifted with the technique of sifting evidence" (Luis Bolín, *Spain: The Vital Years*, p. 276).

49. For details on this and the contradictions that soon engulfed Jerrold's testimony, see Southworth, *Guernica!*, pp. 96–106; Steer, *Tree of Gernika;* and the *Spectator*, 30 July 1937, where Steer challenges Jerrold's account of the affair.

50. Father Thorning, a professor of sociology at Mount St. Mary's College in Maryland and a regular contributor to *Spain*, a propaganda front for Franco secretly financed by the Nationalist government, was one of America's most prolific critics of what he called the distorted, propagandistic news reporting on Spain that came from such "liberal" sources as the *New York Times* and the *Washington Post*. Thorning conducted a relentless campaign against the *New York Times*, and despite its publisher's personal efforts to assuage him and other Catholic readers by pursuing a policy of giving equal space to both sides (the paper had reporters in each war zone), Thorning was not placated. He called the paper's Madrid correspondent, Herbert L. Matthews, the "Walter Duranty of Red Spain" and continued his personal attacks until Matthews retired from the *New York Times* in October 1967. In fact, Matthew's reporting on Spain was some of the very best to come out of the war. (See his dispatches in carbon

copy at the Journalism Library of Columbia University. Matthews kept copies of everything he wrote from Spain for the historical record, since his editor censored much of what he sent to New York.) On the other hand, William P. Carney, the paper's correspondent in Franco's zone, whose reporting was unreliable, one-sided, and at times even fabricated (see George Seldes, *The Catholic Crisis* [New York, 1939], pp. 196–197, and *Tell the Truth and Run* [New York, 1953], p. 243, and Herbert L. Matthews, *A World in Revolution,* pp. 21, 29, 39), was praised by Thorning as the most objective and responsible reporter in Spain. (See "Why the Press Failed on Spain!," pamphlet published by the International Catholic Truth Society, Brooklyn, N.Y., p. 4.) Thorning insisted that Guernica was indeed fire-bombed by the Reds from the ground, and that the secular editors and publishers would "do themselves and their readers a favor by a close acquaintanceship with the Catholic National magazines, reviews, and weekly newspapers," the only reliable sources concerning what was really going on in Spain (ibid., p. 19).

Father Joseph Code in his writing not only denied the bombing of Guernica but went so far as to claim that there never had been any human rights violations carried out by the Nationalists. Stories of Nationalist atrocities, he claimed, owed much to the machinations of international Jewry. Apparently unfamiliar with the heavy-handed censorship policies of Luis Bolín, Code pointed out that one of his special eyewitness sources informed him that "in all his travels in Nationalist Spain" there was "no evidence of any actual atrocities committed by the troops of General Franco" (Joseph B. Code, "The Spanish War and Lying Propaganda," pamphlet published by the Paulist Press, 1938, p. 43).

The appearance of *Guernica: The Official Report,* published by Jerrold's firm, Eyre and Spottiswoode, in 1938, one year after the bombing, was the Nationalist assessment of the event. The document reveals how the sympathizers of Franco contradicted one another in their attempts to find a credible explanation for the Guernica disaster.

51. *Guernica! Guernica!,* p. 118. Yet the myth of Guernica endures. In 1973 Jeffrey Hart, professor of English at Dartmouth College, in an article entitled "The Great Guernica Fraud," in the *National Review,* 5 January 1973, rehashed the explanations of Bolín—drawing on the publication of his memoirs, *Spain: The Vital Years*—along with unidentified quotations by Lunn and Jerrold, essentially arguing that Guernica was never bombed. As for those eyewitnesses who observed Guernica burning (including the highly-regarded Canon Alberto de Onaindia), their testimony, in the view of Hart, suggested fabricated "propaganda" engineered by the Comintern.

Steer had actually collected fragments of the incendiary bombs marked "made in Germany," and included photographs of them in his book *The Tree of Gernika*. Hart dismissed such evidence as yet another example of the clever work of Willi Muenzenberg, the German director of the Paris-based Propaganda Department of the Comintern and the main source, it seems, for what Hart and Bolín call the "myth" of Guernica. Muenzenberg, wrote Hart, was an even greater artist than Picasso. "Picasso painted the picture; but Muenzenberg invented the episode out of the whole cloth" ("The Great Guernica Fraud," p. 29).

The denial of what actually happened at Guernica appeared again, this time as late as 1991, when the Australian journalist Brian Crozier, drawing on the Bolín thesis, wrote in the *Guardian* (27 May 1991) that German planes had not bombed Guernica.

Hart's and Crozier's arguments, however, are no longer accepted even in Spain. In 1970 a group of younger scholars, the neo-Franquista historians, revised the Spanish government's official version of the Guernica legend. These scholars admit that Guernica was destroyed by air bombardment, but assert that it was done by order of the Germans without the knowledge or consent of Franco. Some of these new books on Guernica could not have been published in Spain until after the death of Luis Bolín or until there had been a change in the Franco regime. (See Southworth, *Guernica! Guernica!*, p. 297. For a discussion of this see Southworth, pp. 249–314.)

Southworth's exhaustive examination of all the documentary, eyewitness, and journalistic evidence on the Guernica controversy concludes that the town was destroyed in an air raid carried out by the German Condor Legion on the request of the Spanish Nationalist command. The German air group was directly subordinate to Franco (*Guernica! Guernica!*, p. 376). Southworth's conclusions are supported by Franco's most recent biographer. (See Preston, *Franco*, p. 247.) As to why Guernica was destroyed with such brutality, Southworth admits that he himself cannot say for certain (*Guernica! Guernica!*, p. 386).

52. Jacques Maritain, *Scholasticism and Politics* (New York, 1960), p. 28. In fact, Maritain went so far as to call capitalism evil. Capitalism, he wrote, was "propelled by a sin," which little by little inflicts temporal death on the social body: the cult of earthly enrichment becoming the form of civilization (Jacques Maritain, *Integral Humanism* [New York, 1968], pp. 114–115).

53. In Maritain's case the attack was led by Paul Claudel, who was outraged by Maritain's having called into question the ethical foundation of the capitalist system and seemingly blaming it for the evils of poverty

and destitution. Claudel's anger here was tied up with the implications of Maritain's critique for Franco's rebellion, an event, much like capitalism itself, which Claudel defended on religious grounds. (See *Le Figaro,* 24 June 1939 and 8 July 1939.)

54. The signers included such well-known Catholics as Maritain, Hélène Iswolsky, Gabriel Marcel, Emmanuel Mounier, and Luigi Sturzo, among many others.

55. "Maritain Looks at Franco," *Commonweal,* 4 February 1938.

56. Catholic theologians today dismiss the legitimacy of holy wars. The concept of the crusade celebrates war as a positive moral good in that it advances God's will and cleanses the world of sin. This notion, writes theologian George Weigel, is a medieval aberration and a direct contradiction of essential Christian values. Unfortunately, he notes, crusading has not become a mercifully forgotten dimension of Church history, for it appears to be reasserting itself again as a Christian blessing in liberation theology: "'wars of liberation' bear the marks of a crusade mentality: absolute certainty in the justice of the cause; the division of contending forces into good and evil; the rejection of a neutral position; the willingness to take great risks and to 'make a final sacrifice,' the unwillingness to make compromises. In brief, the transormation of political action into a religious cause, a holy war" (George Weigel citing the words of James Finn in *Peace and Freedom: Christian Faith, Democracy and the Problem of War* [Washington, D.C., 1983], pp. 38–39).

Weigel believes that the rebirth of the crusade idea is a moral disaster for the Christian Church. Its development must be resisted because it is fundamentally at odds with the Gospel.

57. Luigi Sturzo, *Church and State* (New York, 1939), pp. 511–512.

58. There were occasional parish priests who pleaded for the lives of particular individuals, noted Gabriel Jackson, "but none questioned the principle and the general extent of the purge itself" (Jackson, *The Spanish Republic,* p. 306).

59. Isidro Gomá y Tomás, *Por Dios y por España* (Barcelona, 1940), pp. 312–313, as cited in Guenter Lewy, *Religion and Revolution* (New York, 1974), p. 421.

60. Bernanos had formerly been an implacable enemy of Maritain, whom he had not forgiven for turning against *Action Française.* Bernanos's outrage at the behavior of Nationalist forces in the Spanish conflict led him to join the Committee for Civil and Religious Peace. This was the first time he publicly gave his support to one of Maritain's projects. A good overview of the life and works of Georges Bernanos can be found in

William Bush, *Georges Bernanos* (New York, 1971) and Thomas Molnar, *Bernanos: His Political Thought and Prophecy* (New York, 1960).

61. At the age of eighteen Bernanos had joined the *Action Française* and was active in the movement's study group, the "*Cercle Proudhon,*" and the "*Camelots du roi.*" The latter distributed Charles Maurras' newspaper and fought with canes and clubs against his political opponents. During those years, wrote Bernanos, "at an age when abstract ideas and feelings make an explosive mixture," I was "permeated to the marrow of my bones" with the ideas of the *Action Française.* (Quoted in John Hellman, "From the Radical Right to Resistance: De Gaulle, Maritain, and Bernanos," *The Chesterton Review,* November 1989, p. 514.)

62. Quoted in Josep Massot i Muntaner, "Bernanos and the Spanish Civil War: *Diary of My Times,*" *The Chesterton Review,* November 1989, p. 510.

63. Georges Bernanos, *A Diary of My Times* (New York, 1938), p. 86.

64. See William Bush, "Bernanos—One Hundred Years Later," *The Chesterton Review,* November 1989, pp. 461–462.

65. Bernanos, *Diary of My Times,* pp. 66–67.

66. Ibid., p. 113.

67. Quoted from Molnar, *Bernanos: His Political Thought and Prophecy,* p. 102.

68. Bernanos, *Diary of My Times,* p. 120.

69. One of the most virulent critics of Maritain in the United States was the *Brooklyn Tablet.* Because of his stand on Spain Maritain had been accused of being a Jew, a Freemason, and a Marxist. Dr. Harry McNeill, a professor at Fordham University, came to Maritain's defense in this paper; he was in turn attacked by Dr. Edward Fenlon, a professor of philosophy at Brooklyn College, who wrote that there was nothing "offensive" in Fascist philosophy. In any case, wrote Fenlon (betraying his own political ignorance and directly contradicting Mussolini himself), Fascism was not totalitarian. Father Henry Palmer, a diocesan priest from Long Island, entered the fray on Maritain's side and was buried in an avalanche of letters from irate *Brooklyn Tablet* readers. (See the *Brooklyn Tablet* for 25 February, 4 March, 11 March, and 18 March 1939).

70. Doering, *Jacques Maritain,* p. 76. The Catholic Right associated *Sept* and its collaborators, some of the most influential and respected Catholic intellectuals in France, with communism. The journal's position on the Spanish conflict was also causing a great deal of bitter and divisive conflict within the Dominican order. This may have contributed to the decision to close the magazine down. The writer Robert Speaight had yet

another take on the fate of *Sept:* it was said at the time that the journal was suppressed on the orders of Mussolini in return for the restoration of Santa Sabina (*The Property Basket: Recollections of a Divided Life* [London, 1970], p. 242).

71. Raissa Maritain and her sister were Jewish and were born in Russia. Maritain's enemies tried to use this family heritage to cast doubt on his religious credibility. Perhaps the most flagrant example of this smear campaign came from the pen of the Nazi sympathizer Luis Serrano Suñer, Franco's father-in-law and minister of the interior in the Nationalist government. Serrano attacked the philosopher in a slanderous article entitled "Maritain, Judío convertido." Maritain's friend, François Mauriac, came to his defense in *Le Figaro.* Maritain was not Jewish, wrote Mauriac; but he was certainly an exemplary Christian who, like Christ himself, "makes no distinction of persons, but venerated in each single person a redeemed soul, and on the faces of all races, recognizes the features of the same Father" (quoted in Doering, *Maritain,* p. 117). Serrano's philo-Nazism was hardly subtle. He told the American ambassador to Spain, for example, that he "believed in, desired, and worked for German victory" (John T. Whitaker, *We Cannot Escape History* [New York, 1943], p. 122).

72. Reginald Dingle, "Two Years of Spain's War," *The Month,* August 1938.

73. See Thomas, *Spanish Civil War,* p. 450. The joint letter was published in *Sept* on 13 August 1937 and widely circulated throughout France in pamphlet form. It was published in London by the Catholic Truth Society.

74. Luigi Sturzo, *Church and State,* p. 514. The Bishop of Vitoria refused to sign the document because it stated at least three falsehoods: that the Church in Franco's territory was free; that justice was fairly administered in Nationalist territory; and that the city of Bilbao was a "blasphemous town." The last statement was considered a calumny. Besides the Bishop of Vitoria and Cardinal Vidal i Barraquer of Tarragona, the Bishop of Orihuela also refused to sign the letter. (See Hiriantia, "The Case of the Basque Catholics," p. 38.)

The joint letter of the Spanish bishops also brought much critical response from non-Catholics. Some 150 American Protestant clergymen, educators, and laymen drafted a manifesto asserting that the Spanish bishops were "apologists for reaction and fascism." This in turn brought American Catholics to the defense of their religion, and in some cases even those who were neutral on the issue now felt they had to take sides. This was the case with Professor Carleton Hayes, for example. Hayes became one of the 175 signatories of *America's* letter supporting the Spanish hierarchy. The *Brooklyn Tablet*, on the other hand, responded in its own fashion, calling the signers of the Protestant manifesto "Reds" or at best "Parlor Pinks." (See issue of 9 October 1937.)

75. Jackson, *The Spanish Republic*, p. 386.

76. It is important to point out that the collective letter of 1937 did not have doctrinal authority. It was rather a historical testimony of what the signatory bishops believed had happened in Spain. In this respect it must be seen as a historical document open to analysis and criticism and therefore certainly not binding on all Spaniards. Compare this, for example, with the collective letters of 1931 and 1933, which were addressed to the Spanish people regarding matters that the bishops believed were bindig on the faithful in Spain. The 1937 document was not addressed to the faithful of Spain; it was rather directed to the bishops of the world.

77. Reginald Dingle, "Two Years of Spain's War," *The Month*, August 1938.

78. Reginald Dingle, "French Catholics and Spain," *The Tablet*, 21 August 1937.

79. *The Tablet*, 24 July 1937.

80. "Editorial Comments," *The Month*, December 1938.

81. "Editorial Comments," *The Month*, May 1938.

82. Reginald Dingle, "French Catholics and Politics," *The Month*, February 1938. Father Keating saw Maritain's Committee for Civil and Religious Peace in Spain to be a sort of Trojan horse pushing for a compromise between "Christ and Belial." The Basques and other such groups in Catalonia which supported the Republic had "sinned grievously against the light" ("Editorial Comments," *The Month*, November 1938).

83. This is the story of Robert Speaight, who at the time assisted Dawson in editing the *Dublin Review*. After Dawson was forced out, Speaight served as acting editor until T. S. Gregory was given the job (Speaight, *The Property Basket*, pp. 220–221).

84. Neither *Commonweal* nor *America* said anything about Bernanos's work even after it had caused a major stir on the continent. The *New Republic* noted this fact and suggested that the book was certainly significant and perhaps had even prepared the shift in *Commonweal* from defending Franco to recommending impartiality. The *New Republic* claimed that Catholic papers in the United States had a moral obligation to discuss Bernanos's observations, since only a few months prior to this both *Commonweal* and *America* had praised Bernanos as a model and courageous Catholic writer. (See "Questions for Catholics," *New Republic*, 27 July 1938.)

85. See "Editorial Comments," *The Month*, June 1938.

86. "French Catholics and Franco," *The Tablet,* 7 August 1937.

87. "Tertullian in Majorca," *The Month,* November 1938.

88. There were a few smaller, less well-known journals that also opposed the crusade idea, notably *Pax* and the *Sower,* the latter a publication devoted to Catholic education and popular with Catholic trade unionists. Its editors were highly criticial of the reactionary political posturing of the English Catholic press. The *Sower* denounced what it called the anti-democratic diatribes of "our Fascist journalists" and feared that such attitudes would drive the working classes from the Church. This was also a major concern of liberal Catholics in the United States. For a discussion of the *Sower's* stand on the Spanish question see James Flint, "Must God Go Fascist?: English Catholic Opinion and the Spanish Civil War," *Church History* 56 (September 1987): 364–374. This article also discusses *Blackfriar's* criticism of the reductionist editorializing of *The Tablet* and *The Month.*

89. The Catholic Right's reductionist views on the Spanish Civil War were also criticized by Dorothy Day's *Catholic Worker* and the Chicago-based *New World.*

90. See "Editorial," *Blackfriars,* October 1936.

91. Ibid.

92. "A Comment," *Colosseum,* January 1937.

93. Quoted in "Extracts and Comments," *Blackfriars,* November 1936.

94. *The Tablet,* 22 January 1938, p. 100.

95. In 1947 at the age of 84 Crawford wrote a book on the life of Ozanam which praised his pioneering intellectual leadership of social Catholicism.

96. The work of this group is discussed in Don Luigi Sturzo's *Nationalism and Internationalism* (New York, 1946), pp. 124–127.

Crawford had been deeply influenced by an association with Cardinal Manning, who befriended her after the infamous Dilke divorce case in which she was involved. Manning played a crucial role in Crawford's conversion to Catholicism and helped launch her on a career in Catholic social work. Crawford was one of the founders of the Catholic Social Guild, dedicated to furthering the teachings of *Rerum Novarum.* She was also an astute observer of international affairs and became an early critic of fascism. Crawford recognized the charlatanism of Mussolini from the outset, much to the consternation of the dictator, who forbad her from visiting Italy. (See Francis Bywater, "Cardinal Manning and the Dilke Divorce Case," *The Chesterton Review,* vol. 18, no. 4 [November 1992]: 550.)

97. See Gerald Vann, "Jews, Reds, and Imbeciles," *Catholic World,* April 1939.

98. Don Luigi Sturzo, *Church and State* (New York, 1939), p. 544.

99. See Don Luigi Sturzo, "Rome and Anti-Rome," *Dublin Review,* January 1937.

100. Initially, Franco seems to have been unaware of the importance of the Church's support of the uprising, but he quickly cultivated the deportment and vocabulary of a religious warrior to suit his assigned role. See Cooper, *Catholicism and the Franco Regime,* p. 6.

101. Sturzo, *Church and State,* p. 511.

102. Quoting St. Thomas's *Summa Theologica* II-II, q. 42, a. 2, Arnold Lunn wrote: "A tyrannical regime is never just, because it is ordained, not to the good of the people, but to that of the ruler himself. And, therefore, to disturb a regime of this kind is not sedition" (*Spain and the Christian Front,* p. 29).

103. Quoted in Don Luigi Sturzo, "The Right to Rebel," *Dublin Review,* July 1937, p. 31.

104. See Sturzo, ibid., pp. 35–37. The principle of "proportionality" comes from Thomas Aquinas, the rule being that the damage caused by conflict should be no worse than the evils rebellion seeks to eliminate. As to such issues applying to Spain, see Sánchez, *Spanish Civil War as Religious Tragedy,* pp. 145–156.

105. For Sturzo's views on Catholic morality and war see *The International Community and the Right of War* (New York, 1930), *Les Guerres Modernes et la Pensée Catholique* (Montreal, 1942), and *The Inner Laws of Soceity* (New York, 1944). For a broader discussion of the question of a "just war" see Esther Josephine MacCarthy, "The Catholic Periodical Press and Issues of War and Peace: 1914–1946," Ph.D. diss., Stanford University, 1977.

Sturzo was consistently critical of the Church's failure to adhere to Christian ethical principles in its attitude toward war. Regarding the Holy See's position on wars of nineteenth-century Europe, Sturzo noted that the supposed lesser evil generally involved supporting governments in power rather than rebels, the right over the left, and liberal rather than socialist, but that this choice was calibrated more to Catholic political interests than to ethics. The Church's position was driven by the fact that change would have brought an alteration in the status of its own possessions. Unfortunately, he noted, this pattern had persisted among Catholics in the twentieth century. Why had so many Catholics of neutral countries favored Austria at the beginning of World War I when she attacked Serbia, and later Germany when France and neutral Belgium were attacked? Catholic responses to Italy's Abyssinian invasion, Franco's

504 Notes to Pages 361–364

rebellion, and Hitler's annexation of Austria (few Catholic journals opposed it—Austrians were Germans anyway!) were part of this continuing tendency to place political expediency above ethical evaluations. (See Luigi Sturzo, "Wars and Catholic Thought," *Review of Politics*, vol. 3 (April 1941): 164–171.)

106. Sturzo, *Church and State* (New York, 1939), p. 506.

107. Ibid., p. 554.

108. "Interview with Jacques Maritain," *Commonweal*, 3 February 1939.

109. See George Shuster, "Some Reflections on Spain," *Commonweal*, 12 April 1937.

110. In France alone the journals *L'Aube, Esprit, La Vie Catholique, Sept,* and *La Vie Intellectualle* waged regular campaigns against the identification of Franco's cause with religion. "Our justice," wrote Francisque Gay in *L'Aube*, 22 October 1936, "cannot have two weights and two measures. We have no more regard for the rebelliousness of workingmen than for the militiamen who kill nuns or burn churches" (quoted in Barbara Barclay Carter, "European Catholics and Spain," *Commonweal*, 5 March 1937, p. 517).

111. *Boston Globe*, 4 November 1994, p. 7.

112. Don Luigi Sturzo, *Nationalism and Internationalism* (New York, 1946), p. 40.

113. Personal interview with Shuster, in John David Valaik, "American Catholics and the Spanish Civil War, 1931," Ph.D. diss., University of Rochester, 1964, p. 75.

114. George Shuster, "The Spanish Civil War and American Catholics," speech delivered at a conference on the Spanish Civil War, Massachusetts Institute of Technology, 21 May 1969. Cited in Vincent P. Lannie, ed., *On the Side of Truth; George N. Shuster: An Evaluation with Readings* (Notre Dame, Ind., 1974), p. 224.

115. "The Spanish Crisis," *America*, 6 June 1936, pp. 194–195.

116. See *America*, 8 August 1936.

117. "Murder in Madrid," *Commonweal*, 28 August 1936, p. 414. Shuster viewed Franco as the leader of an "anti-worker invasion" with strong fascist underpinnings (John David Valaik, "American Catholic Dissenters and the Spanish Civil War," *Catholic Historical Review*, vol. 53, no. 4 (January 1968): 541). One of Shuster's major concerns was a repetition of what happened to the Catholic Church in the French Revolution. The Spanish clergy's alliance with the forces of reaction would further alienate the Catholic masses from the Church.

118. See Barbara Barclay Carter, "European Catholics and Spain," *Commonweal*, 5 March 1937.

119. Shuster's first study tour in 1930 was funded by a grant from the *Vereinigung Carl Schurz,* a German foundation encouraging wider American interest in German cultural life. He studied at the Hochschule für Politik and took classes with the Catholic theologian Romano Guardini at the University of Berlin. Guardini had been a major influence on H. A. Reinhold's liturgical thinking. Considered one of the most important and popular theologians of the twentieth century, Guardini has been seen as a precursor of Vatican Council II. As opposed to his conservative co-religionists, Guardini insisted that Catholics had to break out of their siege mentality and forcefully encounter the modern world. His voluminous writings were virtually unknown in Canada and the United States until the mid-1950s. Shuster led the way in introducing the great theologian to an American audience, writing the first article in English on Guardini's thought in 1930. Several American Catholics were later influenced profoundly by Guardini, most notably Flannery O'Connor, Dorothy Day, and Thomas Merton. (See Robert A. Krieg, C.S.C., "North American Catholics' Reception of Romano Guardini's Writings," in Robert A. Krieg, ed., *Romano Guardini: Proclaiming the Sacred in a Modern World* [Chicago, 1995].)

Shuster also met Heinrich Bruening on this study tour. A second tour took place in 1933, funded by the Oberlaender Trust of Philadelphia. Shuster's main objective was to gather information on the decline of Bruening's Center Party (he was obliged to meet clandestinely with Bruening at this point—see George Shuster, *The Ground I Walked On* [New York, 1961], p. 146) and on the rise of the National Socialists. During this trip Shuster began to arrange for Bruening's emigration to America. On his return to the United States Shuster published two books on Germany, *Strong Man Rules* (1934) and *Like a Mighty Army* (1935), the latter of which revealed the extent of Hitler's war against the Protestant, Catholic, and Jewish religions. (For a biographical account of Shuster's experiences in Germany and his views on religious and political issues in that country see Thomas E. Blantz, C.S.C., *George N. Shuster: On the Side of Truth* [Notre Dame, Ind., 1993], pp. 89–120.)

120. See Shuster's "Germany under the Concordat," *Commonweal,* 1 September 1933, pp. 420–422; "Days in Beuron," *Commonweal,* 10 November 1933, pp. 43–45; and "Catholic Resistance in Nazi Germany," *Thought,* March 1947, pp. 12–15.

121. See Shuster's "General Sherill and the Olympics," *Commonweal,* 8 November 1935, pp. 40–42.

122. Bruening entered the United States incognito, under the name of "Harry Anderson," a family name of friends in London. He managed

to escape Germany just before the Nazi-directed political murders during the summer of 1934. He kept his assumed name in America because he feared that if Berlin knew of his anti-Nazism there would be an increase in violence against its domestic critics. Bruening stayed for a time under the jurisdiction of the bishop of Brooklyn, a man, wrote Shuster, of marked liberality and notable generosity. Refugee priests and laymen fleeing fascist persecution could find shelter in this bishop's diocese, even though the gates of the neighboring archdiocese of New York were locked against them. See George N. Shuster, "Dr. Brüning's Sejourn [*sic*] in the United States (1935–1945)," in Ferdinand Hermens and Theodor Schieder, *Staat, Wirtschaft und Politik in der Weimarer Republik* (Berlin, 1967), pp. 449–466.

123. See Blantz, *George N. Shuster*, pp. 112–113, and H. A. Reinhold, *H.A.R.; the Autobiography of Father Reinhold* (New York, 1968), pp. 108–109.

124. Muckermann looms large in the correspondence between Reinhold and Waldemar Gurian. See "Gurian, Waldemar," and "Correspondence L-R," Reinhold Papers, Special Collections, Burns Library, Boston College.

125. George Shuster, "Some Reflections on Spain," *Commonweal*, 12 April 1937, p. 626.

126. This phrase Shuster had drawn from a letter written by one of Talbot's fellow Jesuits at the Vatican (Roger Van Allen, *The Commonweal and American Catholicism* [Philadelphia, 1974], p. 65).

127. George Shuster, "Spanish Civil War and American Catholics," in Lannie, *On the Side of Truth*, p. 223.

128. Ibid., p. 224. The *Brooklyn Tablet*, a weekly diocesan paper, had a circulation of nearly fifty thousand. *Commonweal's* audience was considerably smaller, approaching only about twenty thousand. It was, however, far more influential among better-informed Americans and represented the most intelligent lay Catholic opinion. The *Brooklyn Tablet* was one of the most philo-fascist of all American Catholic journals. It presented more material on Germany than any other Catholic publication, and much of this was given a pro-Nazi slant. As opposed to *Commonweal* it had no pretensions to intellectualism. The paper's audience was the Brooklyn Irish Catholic working-class community, which it effectively influenced through the use of bold and strident headlines, sweeping, unsubstantiated accusations, and heavy-handed cartoons thrashing out repetitive anti-liberal themes. See F. K. Wentz, "American Catholic Periodicals React to Nazism," *Church History* 31 (December 1962): 400–420.

129. "In Answer to Some Reflections on the Spanish Situation," Editor, *America*, 10 April 1937, pp. 9–10.

130. "Some Further Reflections," *Commonweal*, 23 April 1937, p. 716. Shuster claimed loyalty to the political positions of Senator William Edgar Borah, Republican senator from Idaho (1907-1940), who was noted for his personal integrity and political independence.

131. Ibid.

132. From Virgina Price's personal interview with Edward Skillin, who at the time was a junior editor at *Commonweal* (Virginia Price, "*Commonweal* Magazine and the Spanish Civil War," unpublished manuscript, 29 May 1971, Abraham Lincoln Brigade Archives, Special Collections, Brandeis University).

133. "Further Reflections on the Spanish Situation: A Brief Finale on the Position of Catholics," *America*, 1 May 1937, pp. 76–77. This was essentially the same position assumed by *America*'s English Jesuit counterpart, *The Month*, as well as Woodruff's *The Tablet*.

134. Major General William N. Haskell, commander of the New York National Guard, resigned from the executive committee of Williams's association because he claimed relief was limited to rebel territory. The Spanish Embassy in Washington wanted Americans to be aware of the fact that the Committee for Spanish Relief favored Franco's cause. Many were also convinced that the rally was designed to raise funds for political and military purposes. (See the *New York Times*, 30 May 1937, p. 12.) Such fears were justified. Cardinal Gomá, for example, in 1937 had transferred money raised by Irish fundraisers for clerical relief organizations in Republican Spain to the Nationalist army. (See Sánchez, *Spanish Civil War as a Religious Tragedy*, pp. 109–110.)

135. Williams's behavior by this point was becoming increasingly erratic and extreme. As John David Valaik has written, Williams's infatuation for the "Gallegan *caudillo*" was such that he could be found at pro-Franco rallies exuberantly chanting prayers of St. Teresa in the aisles (interview with John LaFarge, S.J., in Valaik, "American Catholic Dissenters and the Spanish Civil War," p. 549).

136. "Broun's Page," *Nation*, 29 May 1937, p. 620.

137. See ibid., p. 620, and the *New York Times*, 20 May 1937, p. 8.

138. Hayes was representative of a position held by several members of the Calvert Associates who had been unhappy with the way in which Williams had launched his campaign for Franco. Hayes himself did not want his name associated with a militant religious campaign. Other, more conservative Wall Street Catholic associates disapproved of Williams's outspoken support of the New Deal. Since the steady hand of Shuster was no longer available, and Williams was battling poor health and bouts of

alcoholism, the Calvert Associates determined that there had to be more balanced editorial direction. (See Roger Van Allen, *The Commonweal and American Catholicism* [Philadelphia, 1974], pp. 73–74).

For the issues involved in Williams's removal as editor of *Commonweal,* see John A. Ryan Papers, letters from Ryan to R. Danna Skinner, 17 June 1937; Skinner to Ryan, 18 June 1937; Michael Williams to Calvert Associates, 28 June 1937; Ryan to Williams, 25 June 1937; and Carleton Hayes to Williams, 29 June 1937, "Michael Williams Folder," Box "Ryan Correspondences, 1936–37, R–Z," Department of Archives and Manuscripts, the Catholic University of America.

139. "Civil War in Spain and the United States," *Commonweal,* 24 June 1938, pp. 229–230. It had been arranged that Michael Williams, as founder of the magazine, would continue to write a column in *Commonweal* called "News and Views." Not surprisingly, he strongly objected in his essay to the editors' neutrality on Spain.

140. Van Allen, *The Commonweal and American Catholicism,* p. 79.

141. Owen B. McGuire, "So Catholics Should Be Neutral!" *The Sign,* September 1938, p. 76.

142. The American episcopate's uncompromising stand effectively dampened critical Catholic thinking on the issue of Spain. Donald F. Crosby, S.J., who studied the reaction of Boston Catholics to the Spanish Civil War, has shown how the power of Cardinal William O'Connell and his mouthpiece, the conservative diocesan newspaper the *Boston Pilot,* micro-managed the debate. The *Pilot* mounted a furious attack on the communist plot to use Spain as a springboard for destroying Christian civilization. Like most other Catholic diocesan papers, the *Pilot* continued to publish lurid atrocity stories long after the persecution of the Spanish Church had subsided by the autumn of 1936 and systematically denied any similar wrongdoing on Franco's side. Once the Boston Catholic hierarchy and politicians firmed up their support of the Nationalists, the city's Catholic clubs and associations quickly fell into line. Crosby's interviews with Boston Catholics who still remembered the Civil War revealed that many privately disagreed with and even felt disgraced by the official line but not one dared speak out or form an organized movement of oppostion. Such was the power of the Catholic establishment and the reach of its propaganda. See Donald F. Crosby, "Boston Catholics and the Spanish Civil War: 1936–1939," *New England Quarterly* 44 (March 1971): 82–100.

143. Valaik, "American Catholic Dissenters and the Spanish Civil War," p. 551.

144. Van Allen, *The Commonweal and American Catholicism*, p. 82. It was not unusual during the Depression years for Catholics to disassociate their religion from capitalism, which was in their eyes primarily an outgrowth of the Protestant ethic. The *Catholic Mind, Catholic World*, and even *America* had frequently highlighted the connections between capitalism and Protestantism. Catholicism, on the other hand, was seen as more oriented toward cooperative communitarianism than toward competition and individualism.

145. See E. Skillin to V. Michel, 1 July 1938, "Skillin Correspondences," Virgil Michel Papers, Z-27, St. John's University, Collegeville, Minn., and Paul Marx, *The Life and Works of Virgil Michel* (Washington, D.C., 1957), p. 32.

146. Virgil Michel, "Catholics and the Catholic Spirit," p. 21, unpublished manuscript, Box Z-32, Virgil Michel Papers, St. John's University. Michel blamed both sides but claimed that the Francoists "did the greater sinning" (p. 23). This essay was submitted to the *Atlantic Monthly* but was turned down because the journal had recently published a paper on the same subject, Prince Hubertus Loewenstein's "Catholicism at the Crossroads," in September 1938. (See letter to Michel from managing editor of the *Atlantic Monthly*, 18 July 1938, Box Z-32.) Loewenstein's essay caused much controversy in England and the United States. He asserted that the Catholic hierarchy had generally been sympathetic to and supportive of right-wing dictators, blamed the corruption of the Spanish Church for alienating the masses from their religion, and urged the Church to lead a popular front against fascism.

147. "The Mystical Body and Spain," *Catholic Worker*, September 1936, p. 4.

148. When the *Catholic Worker* first published this letter the author's name was not given. In a follow-up piece, in which the translator of the article, Stephen Johnson, was called upon to answer the critics, the writer was only identified as a well-known Catholic journalist and as the Spanish correspondent for the widely-read French Catholic weekly newspaper *Sept*.

149. "Spanish Catholic Flays Both Sides," *Catholic Worker*, December 1936, p. 1.

150. Ibid., p. 8.

151. This activity was under the direction of "The Friends of Catholic Germany," organized by William Callahan and the Campion Propaganda Committee, a group of young Catholic Workers who wished to take practical measures against the abuses of capitalism, fascism, and

communism. The Campions were tired of talking and wanted direct action. They studied the papal labor encyclicals closely, sold the *Catholic Worker* on the street, and debated with communists. After learning about Nazi anti-religious programs they lobbied for a general boycott of German goods. (See "Catholic Pickets Protest German Fascist Terror," *Catholic Worker*, September 1935, p. 1.)

The Campion Committee drew on both Reinhold's and Sturzo's writings to condemn Germany's war against religion. Quoting the latter, the Campions wrote: "For Christ there is neither Jew nor Gentile—all are equal before God" ("Campion Group Pickets with Pictures," *Catholic Worker*, October 1935, p. 8).

152. See Cyril Echele, "Fascism Revealed in German Persecution," *Catholic Worker*, November 1936, pp. 1–2. Along these lines see also "The Prince of this World," by a German Catholic exile, parts I, II, and III, March, April, and May 1937, which discusses the Church in totalitarian states.

153. The West Side News Agency in Chicago, for example, notified the editors that they would no longer accept the *Catholic Worker* for distribution. The manager claimed that "there is no such thing as working class neutrality where the Spanish people are involved" (Stanley Vishnewski, "Catholic Worker History: Days of Action," unpublished manuscript, p. 142, W-123, Box 1, Dorothy Day/Catholic Worker Papers, Marquette University).

154. Stanley Vishnewski, "Catholic Worker History," unpublished manuscript, p. 5, W-123, Box 2, Dorothy Day/Catholic Worker Papers, Marquette University.

155. Those given the label "Commonweal Catholic" aspired to be free from what they considered the largely self-imposed ghettoization of the American Catholic community. Conservative critics, however, considered them "outside the pale." John Cogley wrote that the designation was inspired by political considerations rather than religious observance. Reflecting back on his experiences as an editor of *Commonweal* in the 1950s, Cogley recalled:

> . . . the idea was spread abroad that any group which consistently criticized Senator Joe McCarthy, gave unfavorable reviews to Cardinal Spellman's novel, and took a dim view of the Legion of Decency's moralistic simplicity, might be Catholic in name and orthodox in faith, but certainly was not Catholic 'enough.' Popular Catholicism in those days was not seriously bigoted, but it did represent a tight, cohesive group and demanded the kind of loyalty we were not

prepared to offer. (*A Canterbury Tale, Experiences and Reflections: 1916–1976* [New York, 1976], p. 51)

156. Maritain was president of the Committee for Civil and Religious Peace in Spain which worked in cooperation with a Spanish branch under the presidency of Salvador de Madariaga and Alfredo Mendizábal and a British committee led by Wickham Steed. Along with help from the Vatican, Maritain's allies had been able to save many lives in Spain. They also had been responsible for making arrangements abroad for taking in Basque children, and with the help of Cardinal Archbishop Jean Verdier of Paris, supplied food and medicine to the starving children of Catalonia.

157. See "An Interview with Jacques Maritain," *Commonweal*, 3 February 1939, pp. 398–402.

158. Maritain, *Integral Humanism*, p. 164.

Chapter 14. Completing the Circle

1. Translation by J. M. Cameron, citing de Tocqueville in support of his own assessment of American political culture as he experienced it while a visiting scholar at the University of Notre Dame. At a deep level, commented Cameron, setting aside the "irrelevant political attitudes of European Catholicism," there is in principle "a striking affinity between Catholicism and egalitarian democracy" ("Catholicism in America," *Blackfriars*, January 1963, pp. 5–6).

2. The historian Gabriel Jackson has written that for a majority of the Spanish bishops Catholicism was consubstantial with monarchy. "A republic was by definition the child of the impious French Revolution, surreptitiously imposed upon Catholic Spain by the Masons" (*The Spanish Republic and the Civil War: 1931–1939* [Princeton, N.J., 1965], p. 106).

3. As the Catholic scholar Gordon C. Zahn has observed, the unanticipated extension of papal social thought made possible by *Rerum Novarum* has been the encyclical's major and most lasting contribution: it legitimized and even invited open criticism of the established order, thereby encouraging activity that allowed for continuing reform and social betterment ("Social Movements and Catholic Social Thought," in John A. Coleman, S.J., ed., *One Hundred Years of Catholic Social Thought: Celebration and Challenge* [Maryknoll, N.Y., 1991], p. 50).

4. This assertion is based on a broad generalization that takes into account the myriad of differences among the social reformers in the Catholic tradition. For a more detailed discussion of such groups see

Paul Misner, *Social Catholicism in Europe: From the Onset of Industrialization to the First World War* (New York, 1991).

5. For a discussion of anti-modernist sentiment as a catalyst for philo-fascism among Catholic intellectuals see Peter C. Grosvenor, "The British Anti-Moderns and the Medievalist Appeal of European Fascism," *The Chesterton Review*, vol. 25, nos. 1 and 2 (February/May 1999): 103–115.

6. From *Restoration* (1934), Hoffman's religious biography, as quoted in William M. Halsey, *The Survival of American Innocence: Catholicism in an Era of Disillusionment* (Notre Dame, Ind., 1980), p. 68. Hoffman claimed that he took the title of his biography from his realization of "the need of a restoration, of subduing the anarchy of the world, the mind, and the soul with principles of order, value, and integration" (*Restoration* [New York, 1934], p. 181).

7. Hoffman, *Restoration*, pp. 139–140.

8. From Richard Kralik, "Martin Spahn und Anton Orel," *Das Neu Reich* IV (1921–1922), p. 372, quoted in Alfred Diamant, *Austrian Catholics and the First Republic: Democracy, Capitalism, and the Social Order, 1918–1934* (Princeton, N.J., 1960), pp. 142–143.

9. *The Tablet*, 22 January 1938, pp. 100–101.

10. Christopher Dawson, *Religion and the Modern State* (London, 1935), p. 51.

11. Ibid., p. 133.

12. Belloc's reach as a journalist was also compromised by his extremist ideas. He was asked to give up his editorship of the *Illustrated Review*, for example, because his presence made it difficult for the paper to attract advertisers (Belloc to Hoffman Nickerson, 29 October 1923, Belloc/Nickerson Correspondence, Burns Library).

13. H.A.R. to Cushing, 11 January 1937, Box 6: "Cushing, September 29, 1936–January 14, 1937," Reinhold Papers, Burns Library, Boston College.

14. Hilaire Belloc, of course, is a paragon of the type. He could claim in his day to be the most influential Catholic intellectual in the English-speaking world. Of course Belloc's influence went well beyond Britain. Another example is the conservative historian Ross J. S. Hoffman, who converted to the faith in 1934 largely under the influence of Belloc and was regarded as America's leading spokesman for Roman Catholicism. No American historian, wrote Lawrence H. Gibson, "is more justly entitled to the accolade 'Defender of the Catholic Faith'" (Gaetarro L. Vincitorio, ed., *Crisis in the 'Great Republic': Essays Presented to Ross J.S. Hoffman* [New York, 1969], p. xviii).

15. Christopher Dawson, *Religion and the Modern State*, pp. 135–136.

16. Ibid., p. 48.

17. In particular see Luigi Sturzo, "The Roman Question before and after Fascism," *Review of Politics* 5 (October 1943): 488–507, and D. A. Binchy, *Church and State in Fascist Italy* (New York, 1942).

18. Sturzo, "The Roman Question," pp. 502–504. *Civiltà Cattolica* made a distinction between what Catholic theologians called "thesis" and "hypothesis." The "thesis" represents the ethical and religious principles upon which the ideal Christian society should be established. The "hypothesis" constitutes the various practical and historical ways ("realization") in which Christians have been able to construct society. Thus the living reality is always a hypothesis, a limited and imperfect attempt to "realize" the ideal. Since humankind is by nature flawed, the ideal (thesis) can never be fully achieved, yet it remains the standard by which all human efforts to create a good society are to be measured. The Church always proclaimed that it was indifferent to political forms (in other words, to what could be realized—hypothesis), provided morality and religion were respected.

Sturzo's argument was that in modern society the political system of democracy (hypothesis) represents an advancement of the evolutionary process, the closest historical effort to achieve perfection according to Christian standards. This constituted historical progress, since in premodern times Catholic theologians saw secular perfection in the practice of monarchy.

For a more contemporary discussion of Sturzo's argument see Eugene C. Bianchi and Rosemary Radford Ruether, eds., *A Democratic Catholic Church: The Reconstruction of Roman Catholicism* (New York, 1992), and J. Michael Miller, *The Divine Right of the Papacy in Recent Ecumenical Theology* (Rome, 1980).

19. This line of argument was given high public profile in America by the writings of Paul Blanshard. See his *Communism, Democracy, and Catholic Power* (Boston, 1951). Blanshard depicted the Catholic Church as a bitter enemy of freedom and democracy and thus incompatible with American pluralistic values. His views were challenged by the Jesuit John Courtney Murray, who argued that Catholic teachings complemented the American democratic tradition. Matters were not helped, however, when conservatives in the Vatican pressured Murray to back off on his liberal interpretation of church-state relations. For more on this see Donald E. Pellottee, S.S.S., *John Courtney Murray: Theologian in Conflict* (New York, 1976).

One of the best recent discussions of Catholicism and its institutional biases toward authoritarianism can be found in Kevin L. Morris, "Fascism and British Catholic Writers 1924–1939," *The Chesterton Review*, vol. 25, nos. 1 and 2 (February/May 1999): 21–51. Morris also offers some compelling cultural and historical explanations for the Catholic Church's failure to vigorously oppose fascism.

20. See Douglas Seaton, *Catholics and Radicals: The Association of Catholic Trade Unionists and the American Labor Movement from Depression to Cold War* (Lewisburg, Pa., 1981).

An examination of Catholic influence on the American labor movement can also be found in the work of Donald F. Crosby, S.J. Crosby, however, argues that the bulk of the conservative inspiration came not from Church teachings (liberal Catholics looked to the social encyclicals, conservative Catholics limited themselves to the Church's anticommunist polemics) but from American politics. (See his "American Catholics and the Anti-Communist Impulse," in Robert Griffith and Athan Theohonis, eds., *The Specter: Original Essays on the Cold War and the Origins of McCarthyism* [New York, 1974].)

21. Bernard C. Cronin, *Father Yorke and the Labor Movement in San Francisco 1900–1910* (Washington, D.C., 1943), p. 221, as cited in Jay P. Dolan, *The American Catholic Experience: A History from Colonial Times to the Present* (Garden City, N.Y., 1987), p. 339. For an excellent discussion of the activity of the Catholic clergy and the American labor movement see Dolan, chapter 12, "Toward a Social Gospel," *The American Catholic Experience*.

22. Richard Gribble has referred to Father Yorke as the "Martin Luther King, Jr. of the San Francisco labor movement." See his *Catholicism and the San Francisco Labor Movement, 1896–1921* (San Francisco, Calif., 1993). Gribble shows here that the American progressive movement on the Pacific coast, unlike the Social Gospel movement in the East which was dominated by Protestants, had at its forefront Catholic Church leaders. These clergymen attempted to deal with the problems of industrial society by acting as a Catholic conscience for the benefit of all impoverished workers irrespective of their religious persuasion. In addition to his focus on Father Yorke as the "firebrand advocate" of labor, Gribble has much to say about the progressive labor work of Archbishop Edward Hanna.

23. Orthodox economic theory, on the other hand, posits the autonomy of these institutions, thereby separating economic activity from political, social, and cultural dynamics. Rather than recognizing labor itself as central to economic activity, orthodox theory stresses buying and sell-

ing. The essence of economic activity is the market which regulates production and consumption.

24. For a further treatment of the relationship between radical theory and Catholic social teaching see Gregory Baum, *Catholics and Canadian Socialism* (Toronto, 1980). Baum argues that the Church has been afraid of the radical conclusions to which its own principles and socioeconomic analyses have led (p. 83). Perhaps the fullest discussion of the radical affinities between Catholic social theory and Marxism can be found in Mary E. Hobgood's *Catholic Social Teaching and Economic Theory: Paradigms in Conflict* (Philadelphia, 1991). Hobgood elaborates on Baum's observation: the organic social theory upon which Catholic social thinking rested conflicted with its own analysis of the capitalist system, a critique, she asserts, that was essentially the same as Marx's (p. 123).

Radical Catholic social and economic thinking in Great Britain could be found among intellectuals associated with the Slant group. Using a name taken from the magazine they published, these Catholics searched for ways to fuse Christian social principles with reformed Marxism. The Slant group was highly critical of both liberalism and capitalist practice and was convinced that the Kingdom of God must necessarily be socialist. See Brian Wicker, *First the Political Kingdom* (Notre Dame, Ind., 1967) and *The Slant Manifesto: Catholics and the Left* (London, 1966).

None of this should suggest that Marx alone pioneered radical theory. As I have noted in chapter 1 of this book, the radical economic critique of capitalism developed by Frédéric Ozanam, upon which much of Catholic social teaching was built, actually preceeded the work of Karl Marx.

25. For instance, Lewy notes, at the 1931 Fulda Bishop's Conference only Preysing of Eichstätt showed any insight into the totalitarian aspirations of Nazism. Most other members of the episcopate had a limited understanding of such matters, or were so conservative (being ardent monarchists) and antagonistic to liberalism, democracy, and socialism that they welcomed a reactionary political regime. Once the Catholic Center Party and the Fulda Conference were given assurances that confessional prerogatives would be guaranteed by the state, they were prepared to work with Hitler's government.

It is instructive to read Lewy's study in conjuction with Gordon Zahn's *German Catholics and Hitler's Wars* (New York, 1962). Lewy and Zahn were Fulbright scholars whose periods of study in Germany briefly overlapped. Zahn suggested some of the more important Catholic leaders for Lewy, a non-Catholic, to seek out for his research. (interview with author, September 1996).

26. There is also the troubling history of the little-known encyclical commissioned by Pius XI condemning anti-Semitism. The encyclical was prepared by the American Jesuit John LaFarge but was suppressed by reactionaries within the curia. Pope Pius XII was informed of the document but declined to publish it.

27. Guenter Lewy, *The Catholic Church and Nazi Germany* (New York, 1964), p. 99.

28. Ibid., p. 326.

29. This lapse in moral leadership was illustrated all too clearly in the Vatican's response to the Spanish hierarchy and the Basque separatists during the Spanish Civil War. The Spanish hierarchy argued that the rising against the Republic was not merely a moral duty but a holy calling, since its rule was illegitimate, unjust, and tyrannical. The Basques, in direct opposition, argued that the Madrid government was legitimate and democratically elected. They insisted that the *pronunciamiento* was untenable given the Church's imperatives for justified rebellion. A rising by a totalitarian movement with the support of Nazis and soldiers who were Moslem by faith (a reference to Franco's command of Moorish troops known as the "Army of Africa") could not possibly meet the standards for resistance established by medieval scholastics.

Throughout the Civil War the papacy failed to adjudicate the fratricidal carnage framed by these contradictory doctrinal positions. The Vatican gave mixed messages on the question; although cautiously endorsing the hierarchy's support of Franco as a means of protecting Catholic freedom, it never formally repudiated the Basque position. (See Lewy, *Religion and Revolution*, pp. 436–440.)

30. John F. Noll, "German Bishops Most Anti-Nazi of All," CNOL Box 10, 10/16, John F. Noll Papers, Special Collections, University of Notre Dame. This is part of a collection of undated papers which appeared in the bishop's columns in *Our Sunday Visitor.*

31. Noll to Adolf Hitler, 18 July 1938, "*Our Sunday Visitor,* Noll Correspondence," File 1935–1938, Box 1 1/2, Special Collections, University of Notre Dame. Bishop Noll sent a similar letter to Mussolini.

32. Pope John XXIII's two major encyclicals, *Mater et Magistra* (1961) and *Pacem in Terris,* drew on the legacy of the Leonine encyclicals but specifically emphasized the importance of upholding human rights (civil and religious), welfare state social reforms, and popular participation in government. These positions had long been supported by liberal Catholics, and the eventual acceptance of them reflects the normal institutional lag between advanced thinking and official sanction. The tendency was

also revealed in the papal attitude toward socialism, which remained rigidly hostile along doctrinaire lines long after many individual Catholics had recognized that some socialist ideas complemented the social teachings of their religion. In fact, the Vatican did not officially recognize the transformation of certain types of socialism from Marxism to democracy until the reign of John XXIII. (For the evolution of papal social thought see Richard L. Camp, *The Papal Ideology of Social Reform: A Study in Historical Development, 1878–1967* [Leiden, 1969].)

33. The history of *Rerum Novarum* is a good example of this tendency. Leo XIII drew on the writings of Ozanam, Ketteler, Manning, and others, community leaders who had already staked out claims for Catholic social and political action based on their own personal experiences. It was, as Michael P. Fogarty has noted, "the summing up of a certain stage of thought and discussion about social problems among Catholics" (*Christian Democracy in Western Europe, 1820–1953* [Notre Dame, Ind., 1957], p. 342). In this respect individual Catholics pioneered the way; the Vatican followed. All this demonstrates that the governance of Church affairs has generally reflected the prevailing political norms of historical circumstances. (This is the view of Eugene C. Bianchi, "A Democratic Church: Task for the Twenty-first Century," in Bianchi and Ruether, *A Democratic Catholic Church*, p. 41).

34. Robert Nowell, "Authority in the Church," *New Blackfriars*, July 1967, pp. 510–511.

35. Gosling to Douglas Woodruff, 16 August 1942, Box 26, Folder 1, Douglas Woodruff Papers, Georgetown University Special Collections.

36. Christopher Dawson, *Religion and the Modern Age*, p. 40.

37. Unlike many other pundits, an astute observer like George Shuster did not make the mistake of hitching Chesterton and Belloc to the same political horse. Shuster searched far and wide for the voices of liberal European Catholics while at the *Commonweal* but despaired of finding any in Britain. Writing to Donald Powell Shuster said: "I simply will not turn to the English—excepting that I would take Chesterton if we could get him. Those Belloc articles seem to me partly absurd, and I for my part am delighted that Collins and not 'us' published them" (Shuster to Donald Powell, 18 October 1934, Box 1, Folder 15, Donald Powell Papers, Georgetown University Special Collections).

38. Binchy, *The Church in the World*, p. 716.

39. The following were well-known Catholic converts (with dates of conversion) who at various times were either fascist apologists or reactionary in their politics:

Roy Campbell (1934)
Georges Bernanos (?)
Paul Claudel (1886)
Christopher Dawson (1914)
Cecil Chesterton (?)
Ross Hoffman (1931)
Christopher Hollis (1924)
Stanley James (1923)
Hugh de Blacam (?)
Ronald Knox (1917)
D. B. Wyndham Lewis (1921)
Arnold Lunn (1933)
Evelyn Waugh (1930)
Douglas Woodruff (1910)

40. This was a criticism frequently voiced by Jacques Maritain, Virgil Michel and others: "It is easy to see the affinity which this dangerous divergence has with the error we have called *Imperialism in spiritualibus* and which consists in confounding the Catholic religion with the culture of Catholic peoples; in treating the Kingdom of God as if it were a terrestrial city or a terrestrial civilization and then claiming for it and for divine truth the same kinds of triumph as we do for a city or a civilization of the purely temporal order" (Jacques Maritain, *Freedom in the Modern World* [New York, 1935], p. 99, as quoted in Virgil Michel, "Timely Tracts: Political Catholicism," *Orate Fratres,* 25 December 1938, pp. 80–81).

41. For a good overview of Gosling's liberal social, political, and religious views see his "Liberty and Some Modern Theories of State," *Dublin Review,* October 1938, pp. 229–241.

42. Gosling to Woodruff, 26 February 1942, Box 26, Folder 1, Douglas Woodruff Papers, Georgetown University Special Collections.

43. Gosling to Woodruff, 16 August 1942, Box 26, Folder 1, Douglas Woodruff Papers, Georgetown University Special Collections.

44. Woodruff's phrase probably refers to Catholic and Protestant clergy with liberal leanings.

45. Gosling to Woodruff, 5 March 1942, Box 26, Folder 1, Douglas Woodruff Papers, Georgetown University Special Collections.

46. Francis X. Talbot, S.J., for example, exhibited the tendency during preparations for the creation of the Catholic Social Action Institute. He insisted that its board of directors be under the chairmanship of *America's* editor. Talbot did not want the Institute to initiate economic and sociological reforms independent of American Jesuit control. "If some of

these young Harvard economists got involved they would lean over too much in the Ryan way." (See Talbot to Blakes [Paul Blakes, S.J.], 21 November 1938, Box 5, 1938, and 5 May 1939, Box 5, 1939, January–May, *America/* Talbot Papers, Georgetown University Special Collections.)

This authoritarian bias can be seen in the political realm in the writings of the Catholic convert journalist Stanley B. James. It was necessary, wrote James, that Catholics adjust to the demands of dictatorship. Their religious background, he asserted, should make this transition easier than for other people. Democracies were losing out, claimed James, because they bred factiousness and were inefficient (see "Democracy in the New Age," *Catholic World,* August 1933). Michael Kenny, S.J., gave the impression that James's views had the Vatican's blessing. He applauded the authoritarian corporative schemes of Mussolini, Franco, and Salazar because they were "perfectly in accord with papal encyclicals" ("A Model Republic Reviewed by Its Molder," *Catholic World,* April 1938, p. 44).

47. Part of the fear was that Catholics who might experiment with the liturgy and other such practices that were best wedded to the past would lose their organic ties to the Church and simply drift into Protestantism. James Hitchcock has noted, for instance, that post-conciliar Catholic radicals have gotten along best with Protestant ecumenists who show little respect for or understanding of Catholic traditions (*The Decline and Fall of Radical Catholicism* [New York, 1971], p. 20). Hitchcock believes that the effort of progressive Catholics to find harmony with the secular world has led to the loss of anything authentically Catholic in their religion.

48. Gosling to Woodruff, 6 August 1942, Box 26, Folder 1, Douglas Woodruff Papers, Georgetown University Special Collections.

49. Gosling to Woodruff, 16 October 1942, Box 26, Folder 1, Douglas Woodruff Papers, Georgetown University Special Collections.

50. As opposed to Orwell, G. K. Chesterton was the best known British anti-socialist who assailed the evils of his day through the dogma of orthodox Christianity. These two writers selected different paths to engage the troubles of their times—hence their contrasting politics—but what has not been adequately appreciated is the similarity in worldview from which they arrived at their opposing political positions. A careful reading of Chesterton's and Orwell's cultural criticisms reveals that their political commitments conceal a shared social vision that is perhaps greater and more significant than their political differences.

51. Sonia Orwell and Ian Angus, eds., *The Collected Essays, Journalism and Letters of George Orwell,* vol. 2 (New York, 1968), p. 229.

52. Orwell, *Collected Essays,* vol. 3, p. 364.

53. Orwell, *Collected Essays,* vol. 3, p. 365.

54. Orwell, *Collected Essays,* vol. 3, p. 366.

55. See Chesterton's "A Socratic Symposium—III," *G.K.'s Weekly,* 25 July 1935.

56. Orwell, *Collected Essays,* vol. 4, p. 412.

57. See Julien Benda, *La Trahison des Clercs (The Treason of the Intellectuals),* trans. Richard Aldrington (New York, 1928).

58. Maritain's transcendence of political dogma and religious tribalism is illustrated in his thirty-year relationship with Saul Alinsky, the Jewish agnostic community organizer. George Shuster had introduced the two during World War II. Maritain admired Alinsky's anarchistic vision of citizen-empowered neighborhood associations as "mediating structures" bridging the gap between families and government. Maritain tried to interest Charles De Gaulle in Alinsky's democratic ideas as an approach for rebuilding French society after World War II. (See Bernard Doering, ed., *The Philosopher and the Provocateur: the Correspondence of Jacques Maritain and Saul Alinsky* [Notre Dame, Ind., 1994].)

59. Orwell, *Collected Essays,* vol. 4, pp. 412–413.

60. Orwell, *Collected Essays,* vol. 2, p. 515.

61. William Steinhoff, *George Orwell and the Origins of 1984* (Ann Arbor, Mich., 1975), p. 116.

62. Orwell, *Collected Essays,* vol. 3, p. 236.

63. The anti-God dimension of communism was good reason for the Catholic Church to target the creed as its major nemesis. The problem, however, was that the enemy enticed Catholics into alliances with untrustworthy allies and tended to blind Church leadership to other issues that needed attention for the promotion of social and political justice. As I have argued, this became a problem in the interwar years with fascism. Unfortunately, this trajectory continued during the Cold War, as is demonstrated in the wide Catholic support given Senator Joseph McCarthy's demagogic anticommunist crusade. All this is placed in interesting historical perspective by Robert L. Frank's "Prelude to Cold War: American Catholics and Communism," *Journal of Church and State* 34 (Winter 1992): 39–56.

64. The historian Ernst-Wolfgang Böckenförde, for example, has argued that the leaders of German Catholicism had already prepared the ground for a natural, logical alliance with the National Socialist system through their widely circulated views on the superiority of an "organic" authoritarian order over a liberal democratic society. (See "German Catholicism in 1933," *Cross Currents,* vol. 2, no. 3 [Summer 1961]: 300–303.)

65. Morris, "Fascism and British Catholic Writers," p. 48.

66. For example, see *One Hundred Years of Catholic Social Thought: Celebration and Change* (Maryknoll, N.Y., 1991), ed. John A. Coleman, S.J. The contributors admit a bias toward Catholic progressivism and the Catholic Left. They regard *Rerum Novarum* as the "Magna Carta" of modern social Catholicism, inaugurating a tradition of imaginative social, economic, and political thinking that has always offered rational yet Christian alternatives to the excesses of industrial-technological society. Their sense of social deaconry and respect for pluralistic political forms complement the central values of those Catholics associated with the Distributist, Personalist, and liturgical movements of the 1930s.

One Hundred Years of Catholic Social Thought singles out the interconnection of the above associations. For an excellent discussion of their differences in methodologies and objectives, as well as respective strengths and weaknesses, see Jonathan Boswell, "Catholic Communitarianism and Advanced Economic Systems: Problems of Middle-level Thinking since 1891," in Paul Furlong and David Curtis, eds., *The Church Faces the Modern World: Rerum Novarum and Its Impact* (Hull, England, 1994).

67. Jonathan Boswell, for example, points out that Distributist-Personalist-Corporativist contributions to Catholic social reformism (the legacies of Ketteler and company) have been vastly underestimated. They were very important, he argues, for stimulating thinking about the redistributive and cooperative features of an ethical sociopolitical system in the Catholic tradition. They failed, however, to explore how to actually bring about such needed humane priorities (Boswell, "Catholic Communitarianism," p. 63).

68. The well-known Catholic advocate of ecumenism, Gustav Weigel, for example, noted fundamental methodological differences between Protestantism and Catholicism regarding religious truth. The former believed that God's purpose could be known through scriptures illuminated by the guidance of the Holy Spirit. In this case the individual "judges" the divine message on the basis of one's experience and assumptions about God. Catholics do not "judge" the divine message but "receive" it as interpreted by the "ever-living magisterium" (from Margaret Mary Reher, *Catholic Intellectual Life in America: A Historical Profile of Persons and Movements* [New York, 1989], pp. 130–131).

69. *Dublin Review*, October 1939, pp. 325–326.

Select Bibliography

I. Journals and Periodicals Extensively Consulted

Action
America
The American Review
The Aylesford Review
Blackfriars
Blackshirt
Brooklyn Tablet
The Catholic Digest
The Catholic Worker
Catholic World
The Chesterton Review
Christendom
Christian Democracy
The Christian Front
Church Socialist
The Church Socialist Quarterly
Colosseum
Commonweal
The Commonwealth
The Cross and the Plough
Daily Herald
The Daily Mail
Daily News
Downside Review
Dublin Review
The English Review
The Eye-Witness
G.K.'s Weekly
The Month

The New Age
New Republic
The New Witness
The New York Times
Orate Fratres
Our Sunday Visitor
PAX
The Sign
The Speaker
Spectator
The Syndicalist
The Tablet
Thought
The Weekly Review
Worship

II. Archival Sources

Abraham Lincoln Brigade Archives, Special Collections, Brandeis University

America Papers, Special Collections, Georgetown University

America/Wilfrid Parsons Papers, Special Collections, Georgetown University

America/Francis X. Talbot Papers, Special Collections, Georgetown University

Hilaire Belloc Papers, Burns Library, Boston College

G. K. Chesterton Papers, Marion E. Wade Center, Special Collections, Wheaton College, Wheaton, Illinois

Dorothy Day/Catholic Worker Papers, Special Collections, Marquette University

Lyle Dorsett Oral History Project, Marion E. Wade Center, Special Collections, Wheaton College, Wheaton, Illinois

Arnold Lunn Papers, Special Collections, Georgetown University

Gregory Macdonald Papers, Marion E. Wade Center, Special Collections, Wheaton College, Wheaton, Illinois

Virgil Michel Papers, St. John's University, Collegeville, Minnesota

William Montovan Papers, Department of Archives and Manuscripts, Catholic University of America

Hoffman Nickerson Collection, Burns Library, Boston College

Bishop John F. Noll Papers, Special Collections, University of Notre Dame
Wilfrid Parsons Papers, Special Collections, Georgetown University
Donald Powell Papers, Special Collections, Georgetown University
H. A. Reinhold Papers, Burns Library, Boston College
John A. Ryan Papers, Department of Archives and Manuscripts, Catholic University of America
George Shuster Archives, Special Collections, University of Notre Dame
Douglas Woodruff Papers, Special Collections, Georgetown University

III. Unpublished Sources

Darrow, Robert Morton. "Catholic Political Power: A Study of the Activities of the American Catholic Church on Behalf of Franco during the Spanish Civil War, 1936–1939." Ph.D. diss., Columbia University, 1953.
Herbold, A. "Chesterton and *G. K.'s Weekly*." Ph.D. diss., University of Michigan, 1963.
Holton, R. J. "Syndicalism and Its Impact in Britain with Particular Reference to Merseyside, 1910–1914." Ph.D. diss., Sussex University, 1973.
MacCarthy, Esther J. "The Catholic Periodical Press and Issues of War and Peace: 1914–1946." Ph.D. diss., Stanford University, 1977.
Rolfs, Richard. "The Role of Adolf Cardinal Bertram. . . in the Church's Struggle in the Third Reich." Ph.D. diss., University of California, Santa Barbara, 1976.
Valaik, John David. "American Catholics and the Spanish Civil War, 1931." Ph.D. diss., University of Rochester, 1964.
Voshchynin, I. "Solidarism and Economics." n.d. Translated from Russian by Joseph Curran.
Weiss, Carlo Francesco. "Corporatism and the Italian Catholic Movement." Ph.D. diss., Yale University, 1955.

IV. Selected Primary and Secondary Sources

Abell, A. I. "Monsignor John A. Ryan: An Historical Appreciation." *Review of Politics*, January 1946.
———. "The Reception of Leo XIII's Labor Encyclical." *Review of Politics*, October 1945.

Abell, Aaron. *American Catholicism and Social Action: A Search for Social Justice*. Notre Dame, Ind., 1963.

Adolph, Walter. *Geheime Auszeichnungen aus dem Nationalsozialistischen Kirchen Kampf 1935–1945*. Mainz, 1979.

———. *Sie sind nicht Vergessen*. Berlin, 1972.

Alexander, Peter. *Roy Campbell: A Critical Biography*. Oxford, England, 1982.

Allitt, Patrick. *Catholic Intellectuals and Conservative Politics in America, 1950–1985*. Ithaca, N.Y., 1993.

Allmayer-Beck, Johann. *Vogelsang: Vom feudalismus zur Volksbewegung*. Vienna, 1952.

Arendt, Hannah. "The Personality of Waldemar Gurian." *Review of Politics*, January 1955.

Arnot, R. P. *The Miners: Years of Struggle*. London, 1948.

Askwith, G. R. *Industrial Problems and Disputes*. London, 1920.

Barker, Dudley. *G. K. Chesterton*. London, 1973.

Barker, E. *Political Thought in England*. London, 1915.

Barnes, James Strachey. *Fascism*. London, 1931.

———. *Half a Life Left*. London, 1937.

Baum, Gregory. *Catholics and Canadian Socialism*. Toronto, 1980.

Bechofer, C., and Maurice Reckitt. *The Meaning of the National Guilds*. London, 1918.

Beevor, Antony. *The Spanish Civil War*. London, 1982.

Belloc, Hilaire. *A Companion to Mr. Wells' 'Outline of History'*. San Francisco, Calif., 1927.

———. *The Crisis of Our Civilization*. New York, 1937.

———. *The Cruise of the Nona*. London, 1925.

———. *Danton*. London, 1910.

———. *An Essay on the Restoration of Property*. London, 1936.

———. *The French Revolution*. London, 1911.

———. *The House of Commons and Monarchy*. London, 1920.

———. *The Jews*. Boston, 1922.

———. *Napoleon*. London, 1932.

———. *The Place of Peasantry in Modern Civilization*. Manchester, England, 1910.

———. *Robespierre*. London, 1927.

———. *The Servile State*. New York, 1946.

———. *A Shorter History of England*. London, 1934.

Hilaire, Belloc, et al. *Essays in Liberalism*. London, 1897.

Bernanos, Georges. *A Diary of My Times*. New York, 1938.

Betten, Neil. *Catholic Activism and the Industrial Worker*. Gainesville, Fla., 1976.

Bianchi, Eugene C., and Rosemary Radford Ruether, eds. *A Democratic Catholic Church: The Reconstruction of Roman Catholicism*. New York, 1992.

Binchy, D. A. *Church and State in Fascist Italy*. London, 1941.

Blanshard, Paul. *Communism, Democracy and Catholic Power*. Boston, 1951.

Blantz, Thomas E., C.S.C. *George Shuster: On the Side of Truth*. Notre Dame, Ind., 1993.

Bökenförde, Ernst-Wolfgang. "German Catholicism in 1933." Translated by Raymond Schmandt. *Cross Currents,* Summer 1961.

Bokenkotter, Thomas. *Church and Revolution: Catholics in the Struggle for Democracy and Social Justice*. New York, 1998.

Bolín, Luis. *Spain: The Vital Years*. New York, 1967.

Bolloten, Burnett. *The Spanish Civil War: Revolution and Counterrevolution*. Chapel Hill, N.C., 1991.

———. *The Spanish Revolution*. Chapel Hill, N.C., 1979.

Borkenau, Franz. *The Spanish Cockpit*. Ann Arbor, Mich., 1971.

Bovee, Warren G. "H.A.R., Front Line Fighter." *Today,* December 1954.

Bowers, Claude G. *My Mission to Spain*. London, 1954.

Boyd, Ian. *The Novels of G. K. Chesterton: A Study in Art and Propaganda*. London, 1975.

Boyea, Earl. "The Reverend Charles Coughlin and the Church: The Gallagher Years, 1930–1937." *The Catholic Historical Review,* April 1995.

Brand, Mary Vivian. *The Social Catholic Movement in England*. New York, 1963.

Braybrooke, Patrick. *Some Thoughts on Hilaire Belloc*. London, 1923.

Brenan, Gerald. *The Spanish Labyrinth: An Account of the Social and Political Background of the Spanish Civil War*. Cambridge, England, 1943.

Brinkley, Alan. *Voices of Protest: Huey Long, Father Coughlin, and the Great Depression*. New York, 1982.

Broderick, Francis L. *Right Reverend New Dealer: John A. Ryan*. New York, 1963.

Brown, Kenneth D., ed. *Essay in Anti-Labour History*. London, 1975.

Browne, Henry, S.J. *The Catholic Evidence Movement*. London, 1921.

Burgess, Keith. *The Challenge of Labour: Shaping British Society, 1850–1930*. New York, 1980.

Bush, William. *Georges Bernanos*. New York, 1971.

Camp, Richard. *The Papal Ideology of Social Reform: A Study in Historical Development, 1878–1967*. Leiden, 1969.

Campbell, Roy. *Flowering Rifle*. London, 1939.

————. *Light on a Dark Horse. An Autobiography (1901–1935)*. Chicago, 1952.

Cannistrano, Philip V., and Theodore P. Kovaleff. "Father Coughlin and Mussolini: Impossible Allies." *Journal of Church and State* 13 (1971).

Canovan, Margaret. *G.K. Chesterton*. New York, 1977.

Carpender, L. P. *G.D.H. Cole: An Intellectual Biography*. Cambridge, England, 1973.

Carr, Raymond. *The Spanish Tragedy: The Civil War in Perspective*. London, 1977.

Cattell, David T. *Communism and the Spanish Civil War*. Berkeley, Calif., 1955.

Celier, L. *Ozanam*. Paris, 1956.

Chesterton, Cecil. *Gladstonian Ghosts*. London, 1905.

————. *Party and People*. London, 1910.

Chesterton, Cecil, and Hilaire Belloc. *The Party System*. London, 1911.

Chesterton, G. K. *The Autobiography of G. K. Chesterton*. New York, 1936.

————. *Avowals and Denials*. London, 1934.

————. *The Everlasting Man*. New York, 1925.

————. *George Bernard Shaw*. New York, 1950.

————. *Heretics*. London, 1905.

————. *Orthodoxy*. London, 1908.

————. *The Outline of Sanity*. New York, 1927.

————. *The Resurrection of Rome*. London, 1930.

————. *The Well and the Shallows*. New York, 1935.

Chesterton, Mrs. Cecil. *The Chestertons*. London, 1941.

Christian, William A., Jr. *Visionaries: The Spanish Republic and the Reign of Christ*. Berkeley, Calif., 1996.

Clark, G. Kitson. *The Making of Victorian England*. New York, 1969.

Clay, Sir Arthur. *Syndicalism and Labour*. London, 1912.

Coates, John D. *Chesterton and the Edwardian Cultural Crisis*. Hull, England, 1984.

Code, Joseph B. "The Spanish War and Lying Propaganda." Pamphlet published by the Paulist Press, 1938.

Cogley, John. *A Canterbury Tale, Experiences and Reflections: 1916–1976*. New York, 1976.

Cole, G. D. H. *The World of Labour*. London, 1913.

Cole, Margaret, ed.. *The Webbs and Their Work*. New York, 1974.

Coleman, John A., S.J., ed. *One Hundred Years of Catholic Social Thought: Celebration and Change*. New York, 1991.

Conlon, D. J., ed. *G. K. Chesterton: A Half Century of Views.* New York, 1987.

Cooper, Norman B. *Catholicism and the Franco Regime.* Beverly Hills, Calif., 1975.

Corrigan, Raymond, S.J. *The Church and the Nineteenth Century.* Milwaukee, Wis., 1938.

Corrin, Jay P. *G. K. Chesterton and Hilaire Belloc: The Battle against Modernity.* Athens, Ohio, 1981.

———. "The Neo-Distributism of Friedrich A. Hayek and Wilhelm Röpke." *Thought,* December 1988.

Cox, James. "Father Cox Has a Closeup View of Mussolini." *Christian Century,* 27 July 1932.

Crick, Bernard. *George Orwell.* Boston, 1980.

Croft, Henry Page. *My Life of Strife.* London, 1954.

Cronin, Bernard C. *Father Yorke and the Labor Movement in San Francisco 1900–1910.* Washington, D.C., 1943.

Crosby, Donald F. "Boston Catholics and the Spanish Civil War: 1936–1939." *New England Quarterly,* March 1971.

Cross, Colin. *The Fascists in Britain.* London, 1961.

Cross, Robert. *The Emergence of Liberal Catholicism.* Cambridge, Mass., 1967.

Cunningham, Adrian. "Aspects of Distributism." *The Newman,* January 1969.

Cunningham, Adrian, Terry Eagleton, et al., eds. *'Slant Manifesto': Catholics and the Left.* Springfield, Ill., 1966.

Cunningham, Valentine. *British Writers of the Thirties.* New York, 1988.

Curran, Edward Lodge. *Franco: Who Is He? What Does He Fight For?* New York, 1937.

Dale, Alzina Stone. *The Outline of Sanity: A Life of G. K. Chesterton.* Grand Rapids, Mich., 1982.

Dawson, Christopher. *Religion and the Modern State.* New York, 1936.

Delzell, Charles F., ed. *The Papacy and Totalitarianism between the Two World Wars.* New York, 1974.

Derum, James Patrick. *Apostle in a Top Hat: The Life of Frederic Ozanam.* New York, 1960.

Diamant, Alfred. *Austrian Catholics and the First Republic: Democracy, Capitalism, and the Social Order, 1918–1934.* Princeton, N.J., 1960.

Diggins, John P. "American Catholics and Italian Fascism." *Journal of Contemporary History,* vol. 2, no. 4 (1967).

———. *Mussolini and Fascism: The View from America.* Cambridge, Mass., 1972.

Doering, Bernard. *Jacques Maritain and the French Catholic Intellectuals.* Notre Dame, Ind., 1983.

Dolan, Jay P. *The American Catholic Experience: A History from Colonial Times to the Present.* Garden City, N.Y., 1987.

Donaldson, Frances. *The Marconi Scandal.* London, 1962.

Evans, Joseph W., and Leo Ward, eds. *Jacques Maritain: Challenges and Renewals.* Cleveland, Ohio, 1968.

Evans, Maurice. *G. K. Chesterton.* Cambridge, England, 1939.

Farr, Barbara Storm. *The Development and Impact of Right-Wing Politics in Britain, 1903–1932.* New York, 1987.

Ffinch, Michael. *G. K. Chesterton: A Biography.* New York, 1986.

Figgis, John Neville. *Churches in the Modern State.* London, 1913.

Finley, James F. *James Gillis, Paulist.* Garden City, N.Y., 1958.

Fisher, James Terence. *The Catholic Countercultre in America, 1933–1962.* Chapel Hill, N.C., 1989.

Fitzsimmons, M. A. "Die DeutschenBrief: Gurian and the German Crisis." *Review of Politics,* January 1955.

Flint, James. "Must God Go Fascist? English Catholic Opinion and the Spanish Civil War." *Church History,* September 1987.

Flynn, George Q. *Roosevelt and Romanism: Catholics and American Diplomacy, 1937–1945.* Westport, Conn., 1976.

Fogarty, Michael Patrick. *Christian Democracy in Western Europe, 1820–1953.* Notre Dame, Ind., 1969.

Frank, Robert L. "Prelude to Cold War: American Catholics and Communism." *Journal of Church and State,* Winter 1992.

Franklin, R. W., and Robert L. Spaeth. *Virgil Michel: American Catholic.* Collegeville, Minn., 1988.

Furet, Francois, and Mona Ozouf. *A Critical Dictionary of the French Revolution.* Cambridge, Mass., 1989.

Furlong, Paul, and David Curtis, eds. *The Church Faces the Modern World: Rerum Novarum and Its Impact.* Hull, England, 1994.

Gallin, Mary Alice. *German Resistance to Hitler: Ethical and Religious Factors.* Washington, D.C., 1961.

Galopin, E. *Essai de bibliographie chronologique sur Antoine-Frédéric Ozanam.* Paris, 1933.

Gargan, Edward T., ed. *Leo XIII and the Modern World.* New York, 1961.

Gerhart, Walter (Waldemar Gurian). *Um des Reiches Zukunft.* Freiburg, 1932.

Gill, Eric. *Eric Gill: Autobiography.* New York, 1971.

———. *It All Goes Together.* London, 1944.

———. *Money and Morals.* London, 1934.

Gilley, Sheridon. *Newman and His Age*. London, 1990.

Gilson, Etienne., ed. *The Church Speaks to the Modern World: The Social Teachings of Leo XIII*. Garden City, N.Y., 1954.

Gironella, José Maria. *The Cypresses Believe in God*. Translated from Spanish by Harriet de Onis. New York, 1955.

Glass, S. T. *The Responsible Society: The Ideas of the English Guild Socialists*. London, 1966.

Gleason, Philip. *The Conservative Reformers: German-American Catholics and the Social Order*. Notre Dame, Ind., 1968.

Goyau, G. *Ozanam*. Paris, 1925.

Grasso, Kenneth L., Gerard V. Bradley, and Robert P. Hunt, eds. *Catholicism, Liberalism, and Communitarianism: The Catholic Intellectual Tradition and the Moral Foundations of Democracy*. Lanham, Md., 1995.

Gray, Robert. *Cardinal Manning: A Biography*. London, 1985.

Greene, Thomas R. "The English Catholic Press and the Spanish Republic, 1931–1936." *Church History*, March 1976.

Gribble, Richard. *Catholicism and the San Francisco Labor Movement, 1896–1921*. San Francisco, Calif., 1993.

———. *Guardian of America: The Life of James Martin Gillis, C.S.P.* New York, 1998.

Griffin, Leslie, ed. *Religion and Politics in the American Milieu*. Notre Dame, Ind., 1986.

Griffith, Robert, and Athan Theohonis, eds. *The Specter: Original Essays and the Cold War and the Origins of McCarthyism*. New York, 1974.

Griffiths, Richard. *Fellow Travellers of the Right: British Enthusiasts for Nazi Germany, 1933–1939*. London, 1983.

———. *The Reactionary Right*. London, 1966.

Grisewood, Harmon, et al., eds. *Ideas and Beliefs of the Victorians*. New York, 1966.

Guernica: The Official Report. London, 1938.

Gurian, Waldemar. "Bolshevism and Anti-Bolshevism." *Colosseum*, June 1937.

———. *Bolshevism as a World Danger*. New York, 1935.

———. *Um des Reiches Zukunft*. Freiburg, 1932.

Guttman, Allen. *The Wound in the Heart: America and the Spanish Civil War*. New York, 1962.

Gwynn, Denis Rolleston. *A Hundred Years of Catholic Emancipation (1829–1929)*. London, 1929.

Halsey, William M. *The Survival of American Innocence: Catholics in an Era of Disillusionment, 1920–1940*. Notre Dame, Ind., 1980.

Hamilton, Alastair. *The Appeal of Fascism*. New York, 1971.

Harrison, John R. *The Reactionaries*. London, 1966.

Hart, Jeffrey. "The Great Guernica Fraud." *National Review*, 5 January 1973.

Haxey, Simon (pseud.). *England's Money Lords; Tory M.P.* New York, 1939.

Hayek, F. A. *The Road to Serfdom*. Chicago, 1944.

Hearley, John. *Pope or Mussolini*. New York, 1929.

Heineman, Kenneth J. "A Catholic New Deal: Religion and Labor in 1930s Pittsburgh." *Pennslyvania Magazine of History and Biography* 118 (1994).

Hellman, John. *Emmanuel Mounier and the New Catholic Left, 1930–50*. Toronto, 1981.

Hiriartia, J. de. *The Case of the Basque Catholics*. New York, 1939.

Hitchcock, James. *The Decline and Fall of Radical Catholicism*. New York, 1971.

Hobgood, Mary E. *Catholic Social Teaching and Economic Theory: Paradigms in Conflict*. Philadelphia, Pa., 1991.

Hobsbawm, E. J. *The Age of Extremes*. New York, 1994.

Hobson, S. G. *Pilgrim to the Left: Memoirs of a Modern Revolutionist*. London, 1938.

Hodgson, Sir Robert. *Spain Resurgent*. London, 1953.

Hoffman, Ross. *Restoration*. New York, 1934.

Hogan, William E. *The Development of William Emmanuel von Kettler's Interpretation of the Social Problem*. Washington, D.C., 1946.

Hollis, Christopher. *The Mind of G. K. Chesterton*. Coral Gables, Fla., 1970.

Holmes, Colin. *Anti-Semitism in British Society, 1876–1939*. New York, 1979.

Holton, R. J. *British Syndicalism 1900–1914: Myths and Realities*. London, 1976.

———. "*Daily Herald* vs. *Daily Citizen*, 1912–1915." *International Review of Social History*, 1974.

Hoskins, Katherine Bail. *Today the Struggle: Literature and Politics in England during the Spanish Civil War*. London, 1969.

Hughes, H. L. *Frederick Ozanam*. London, 1933.

Hughes, Kathleen. *The Monk's Tale: A Biography of Godfrey Diekmann, O.S.B.* Collegeville, Minn., 1991.

Hughes, Philip. "Mr. Belloc's Reviewer Replies." *Clergy Review*, April 1935.

Hulme, T. E. *Speculations*. London, 1924.

Humphries, H. E. *Liberty and Property: An Intorduction to Distributism*. London, 1928.

Hunter, Lynette. *G. K. Chesterton: Explorations in Allegory*. New York, 1979.

Husslein, Joseph, S.J. *Social Wellsprings: Fourteen Epochal Documents by Pope Leo XIII*. Milwaukee, Wis., 1940.

Inglis, K. S. *Churches and the Working Classes in Victorian England*. London, 1963.

Iswolsky, Hélène. *Light before Dusk*. New York, 1942.

Jackson, Gabriel. *The Spanish Republic and the Civil War, 1931–1939*. Princeton, N.J., 1965.

Jenkins, Philip. *Hoods and Shirts: The Extreme Right in Pennsylvania, 1925–1950*. Chapel Hill, N.C., 1997.

Jerrold, Douglas. *Georgian Adventure*. London, 1937.

———. *The Necessity of Freedom*. London, 1938.

———. "Spain: Impressions and Reflections." *The Nineteenth Century and After*, April 1937.

Joll, James. *The Anarchists*. New York, 1964.

Jones, A. R. *The Life and Opinions of T. E. Hulme*. Boston, 1960.

Jones, Peter d'A. *The Christian Socialist Revival, 1877–1914*. Princeton, N.J., 1968.

Kelly, George A. *Battle for the American Church Revisited*. San Francisco, Calif., 1995.

Kemp, Peter. *Mine Were of Trouble*. London, 1957.

Kendall, Walter. *The Revolutionary Movement in Britain, 1900–1921*. London, 1969.

Ker, Ian. *John Henry Newman: A Biography*. Oxford, England, 1988.

Ketteler, Bishop Wilhelm Emmanuel von. "Freedom, Authority, and the Church." Translated by Rupert F. Ederer. *Social Justice Review*, April 1976.

———. "The Relationship of the Labor Movement to Religion and Morality." Translated by Rupert F. Ederer. *Social Justice Review*, May 1975.

Klemperer, Klemns von. *The German Resistance against Hitler*. Oxford, England, 1992.

Koestler, Arthur. *Spanish Testament*. London, 1937.

Kraus, Andreas, ed. *Acten Kardinal Michael von Faulhabers*, vol. 1: *1917–1945*. Mainz, 1978.

Kreig, Robert Anthony, C.S.C. *Karl Adam: Catholicism in German Culture*. Notre Dame, Ind., 1992.

———. *Romano Guardini: Proclaiming the Sacred in a Modern World*. Chicago, 1995.

Lannie, Vincent P., ed. *On the Side of Truth; George N. Shuster: An Evaluation of His Writings*. Notre Dame, Ind., 1974.

Lea, Frank A. *The White Knight of Battersea: G. K. Chesterton.* London, 1946.

Leslie, Shane. *Cardinal Manning: His Life and Labours.* New York, 1954.

Leventhal, F. M. *Respectable Radical: George Howell and Victorian Working Class Politics.* Cambridge, Mass., 1971.

Lewy, Guenter. *The Catholic Church in Nazi Germany.* New York, 1964.

———. *Religion and Revolution.* New York, 1974.

Lowndes, Marie Belloc. *Where Love and Friendship Dwelt.* New York, 1943.

Lunn, Arnold. *And Yet So New.* New York, 1958.

———. *Come What May.* London, 1940.

———. *Memory to Memory.* London, 1956.

———. *Now I See.* London, 1956.

———. *Spain and the Christian Front: Ubi Crux Ibi Patria.* New York, 1937.

———. *Spanish Rehearsal.* New York, 1937.

Lunn, Kenneth, and Richard Thurlow, eds. *British Fascism: Essays on the Radical Right in Inter-War Britain.* London, 1980.

MacDonald, James Ramsay. *The Social Unrest: Its Causes and Solution.* London, 1913.

Maier, Hans. *Revolution and Church: The Early History of Christian Democracy.* Translated by Emily M. Schossberger. Notre Dame, Ind., 1965.

Mandell, C. Creighton, and Edward Shanks. *Hilaire Belloc: The Man and His Work.* London, 1916.

Mann, Tom. *Memoirs.* London, 1923.

Manning, Cardinal Henry E. *The Dignity and Rights of Labour.* London, 1934.

———. *Miscellanies.* Vol. 3, London, 1877.

Maritain, Jacques. *Integral Humanism: Temporal and Spiritual Problems of a New Christendom.* Translated by Joseph W. Evans. New York, 1968.

———. *Scholasticism and Politics.* New York, 1960.

———. *The Things That Are Not Caesar's.* New York, 1931.

Marwick, Arthur. *Clifford Allen, The Open Conspirator.* Edinburgh, 1964.

Marx, Paul. *The Life and Works of Virgil Michel.* Washington, D.C., 1957.

Matthews, Herbert L. *Half of Spain Died: A Reappraisal of the Spanish Civil War.* New York, 1973.

———. *A World in Revolution: A Newspaperman's Memoir.* New York, 1971.

Maurois, André. *Prophets and Poets.* New York, 1935.

McCarthy, John P. *Hilaire Belloc: Edwardian Radical.* Indianapolis, Ind., 1978.

———. "Hilaire Belloc: Jacobite and Jacobin." *The Chesterton Review,* May 1986.

McCarthy, Terry. *The Great Dock Strike of 1889: The Story of the Labour Movement's First Great Victory.* London, 1988.

McClelland, Vincent Alan. *Cardinal Manning: His Public Life and Influence 1865–1892*. London, 1962.

McCullagh, Francis. *In Franco's Spain*. London, 1937.

McDonough, Peter. *Men Astutely Trained: A History of the Jesuits in the American Century*. New York, 1992.

McEntee, Georgiana Putnam. *The Social Catholic Movement in Great Britain*. New York, 1927.

McGeever, Patrick J. *Rev. Charles Owen Rice: Apostle of Contradiction*. Pittsburgh, Pa., 1989.

McGrath, Patrick. "Catholic Historians and the Reformation—II." *Blackfriars*, April 1963.

McManners, John. *Church and State in France, 1870–1914*. London, 1972.

McShane, Joseph M., S.J. *Sufficiently Radical: Catholicism, Progressivism, and the Bishops Program of 1919*. Washington, D.C., 1986.

Metlake, George (pen-name for J. J. Laux). *Christian Social Reform: Program Outlined by Its Pioneer W. E. Baron von Ketteler, Bishop of Mainz*. Philadelphia, Pa., 1923.

Michel, Virgil. *Christian Social Reconstruction*. Milwaukee, Wis., 1937.

Middlemas, Keith. *Politics in Industrial Society: The Experience of the British System since 1911*. London, 1979.

Miliband, Ralph. *Parliamentary Socialism: A Study in the Politics of Labour*. London, 1961.

Miller, Michael. *The Divine Right of the Papacy in Recent Ecumenical Theology*. Rome, 1980.

Minnich, Nelson H., Robert B. Eno, S. J., and Robert F. Trisco, eds. *Studies in Catholic History in Honor of John Tracy Ellis*. Wilmington, Del., 1985.

Misner, Paul. *Social Catholicism in Europe from the Onset of Industrialization to the First World War*. London, 1991.

Mitchell, Sir Peter Chalmers. *My House in Málaga*. London, 1938.

Molnar, Thomas. *Bernanos: His Political Thought and Prophecy*. New York, 1960.

Molony, John N. *The Emergence of Political Catholicism in Italy*. Totowa, N.J., 1977.

Moody, Joseph N., ed. *Church and Society: Catholic Social and Political Thought and Movements 1789–1950*. New York, 1953.

Moon, Parker. *The Social Catholic Movement*. New York, 1921.

Moore, Roger. *The Emergence of the Labour Party 1800–1924*. London, 1978.

Moos, Malcolm. "Don Luigi Sturzo: Christian Democrat." *American Political Science Review*, April 1945.

Moreno, Don Enrique. *Catholics and the Spanish State.* London, 1937.

Morris, Kevin L. "Fascism and British Catholic Writers 1924–1939." *The Chesterton Review,* February/May 1999.

Mounier, Emmanuel. *The Character of Man.* New York, 1956.

Muckermann, Friedrich, S.J. *Der deutsche Weg.* Zurich, 1946.

Murray, John Courtney, S.J. "The Church and Totalitarian Democracy." *Theological Studies* 13 (1952).

———. "Contemporary Orientations of Catholic Thought on Church and State in Light of History." *Theological Studies* 10 (1949).

———. "Leo XIII on Church and State: The General Structure of the Controversy." *Theological Studies* 14 (1953).

———. "The Problem of State Religion." *Theological Studies* 12 (1951).

———. "On Religious Freedom." *Theological Studies* 10 (1949).

Nell-Breuning, Oswald von, S.J. *Reorganization of Social Economy: The Social Encyclical Developed and Explained.* New York, 1936.

Nicholls, David. *The Pluralist State.* New York, 1975.

———. *Three Varieties of Pluralism.* New York, 1974.

Nitti, Francesco S. *Catholic Socialism.* London, 1895.

Noel, Conrad. *Autobiography.* London, 1945.

———. *Socialism in Church History.* London, 1910.

Norman, Edward R. *Church and Society in England, 1770–1970.* Oxford, England, 1976.

———. *The English Catholic Church in the Nineteenth Century.* Oxford, England, 1964.

Novak, Michael. *Freedom with Justice: Catholic Social Thought and Liberal Institutions.* New York, 1984.

O'Brien, David. *American Catholics and Social Reform.* New York, 1968.

———. *Public Catholicism.* Maryknoll, N.Y., 1996.

Oliveria, A. Ramos. *Politics, Economics and Men of Modern Spain, 1808–1946.* London, 1946.

O'Meara, Kathleen (Grace Ramsay). *Frederic Ozanam: His Life and Works.* Preface by Cardinal Manning. New York, n.d.

Ondartzaphe, Matxin de. *The Basques and the Communists.* London, 1939.

Orage, A. R., ed. *The National Guilds.* London, 1919.

Orwell, George. *The Road to Wigan Pier.* London, 1937.

Orwell, Sonia, and Ian Angus, eds. *The Collected Essays, Journalism, and Letters of George Orwell.* Vols. 1, 2, 3, and 4. New York, 1968.

Parsons, Wilfrid, S.J. *Which Way, Democracy?* New York, 1939.

Payne, Stanley G. *Falange: A History of Spanish Fascism.* Stanford, Calif., 1961.

————. *Politics and the Military in Modern Spain*. Stanford, Calif., 1967.

————. *Spain's First Democracy: The Second Republic, 1931–1936*. Madison, Wis., 1993.

————. *Spanish Catholicism: An Historical Overview*. Madison, Wis., 1984.

Pearce, Joseph. *Wisdom and Innocence: A Life of G. K. Chesterton*. San Francisco, 1996.

Pelling, Henry, ed. *Popular Politics and Society in Late Victorian England*. London, 1968.

Pellottee, Donald E., S.S.S. *John Courtney Murray: Theologian in Conflict*. New York, 1976.

Penty, A. J. *Distributism: A Manifesto*. London, 1937.

————. *Old Worlds for New*. London, 1917.

————. *Post-Industrialism*. London, 1922.

————. *Towards a Christian Sociology*. London, 1923.

Petri, Barbara P. *Churches and the Working Classes in Victorian England*. London, 1963.

Petrie, Charles. *Chapters of Life*. London, 1950.

————. "Fascism and the Nazis." *Saturday Review*, 20 May 1933.

————. *Lords of the Inland Sea*. London, 1937.

————. *Monarchy in the Twentieth Century*. London, 1933.

————. *Mussolini*. London, 1931.

————. *The Story of Government*. London, 1929.

Piehl, Mel. *Breaking Bread: The Catholic Worker and the Origin of Catholic Radicalism in America*. Philadelphia, Pa., 1982.

Pierson, Stanley. *British Socialists: The Journey from Fantasy to Politics*. Cambridge, Mass., 1979.

Pinson, Koppel, ed. *Essays on Anti-Semitism*. New York, 1946.

Postgate, R. W. *The Builders' History*. London, 1923.

————. *The Life of George Lansbury*. London, 1951.

Preston, Paul, ed. *Franco: A Biography*. New York, 1994.

————. *Revolution and War in Spain, 1931–1939*. New York, 1984.

Quinn, Dermot. *Patronage and Piety: English Roman Catholicism and Politics, 1850–1900*. Stanford, Calif., 1993.

Read, Herbert. *Poetry and Anarchism*. London, 1939.

Reckitt, Maurice. "Anglo-Catholic Aspects." *Colosseum*, December 1937.

————. *As It Happened*. London, 1941.

————. *G. K. Chesterton: A Christian Prophet for England Today*. London, 1950.

————. *Maurice to Temple*. London, 1947.

————. *The World and the Faith*. London, 1954.

Rees, Richard. *George Orwell: Fugitive from the Camp of Victory*. London, 1962.

Reher, Margaret Mary. *Catholic Intellectul Life in America: A Historical Profile of Persons and Movements*. New York, 1989.

Reinhold, Hans Ansgar. *H. A. R.; The Autobiography of Father Reinhold*. New York, 1968.

Rendel, Sir George. *The Sword and the Olive*. London, 1957.

Ritter, Gerhard. *The German Resistance: Carl Goerdeler's Struggle against Tyranny*. London, 1958.

Rogers, F. *Labour, Life and Literature: Some Memories of Sixty Years*. London, 1913.

Rogger, Hans, and Eugen Weber, eds. *The European Right: A Historical Profile*. Berkeley, Calif., 1966.

Röpke, William. "Fascist Economics." *Economica*, February 1935.

Rosswurm, Steve, ed. *CIO's Left-led Unions*. New Brunswick, N.J., 1992.

Rothfels, Hans. *The German Opposition to Hitler: An Assessment*. London, 1961.

Rotvand, George. *Franco Means Business*. Translated by Reginald Dingle. New York, n.d.

Ryan, Alvan S. "The Development of Newman's Political Thought." *Review of Politics*, April 1945.

Ryan, John A. *Declining Liberty*. New York, 1927.

Ryan, John A., and Joseph Husslein. *The Church and Labor*. New York, 1920.

Sanchez, José M. *Reform and Reaction; the Political-Religious Background of the Spanish Civil War*. Chapel Hill, N.C., 1964.

———."The Spanish Church and the Revolutionary Republican Movement, 1930–1931." *Church History*, December 1962.

———. "The Spanish Church and the Second Republic and Civil War, 1931–1939." *The Catholic Historical Review*, October 1996.

———. *The Spanish Civil War as a Religious Tragedy*. Notre Dame, Ind., 1987.

Schimberg, Albert Paul. *Frederick Ozanam*. Milwaukee, Wis., 1966.

Schmidt, Carl T. *The Corporate State in Action: Italy under Fascism*. London, 1939.

Scott, Christina. *A Historian and His World: A Life of Christopher Dawson*. New Brunswick, N.J., 1992.

Seaton, Douglas. *Catholics and Radicals: The Association of Catholic Trade Unionists and the American Labor Movement from Depression to Cold War*. Lewisburg, Pa., 1981.

Seldes, George. *The Catholic Crisis*. New York, 1939.

————. *Sawdust Caesar.* New York, 1935.

————. *Tell the Truth and Run.* New York, 1953.

Sheed, Frank. *The Church and I.* New York, 1974.

Sheed, Wilfrid. *The Morning After: Essays and Reviews.* New York, 1972.

Sheehan, Arthur. *Peter Maurin: Gay Believer.* Garden City, N.Y., 1959.

Shuster, George N. *The Catholic Spirit in Modern English Literature.* New York, 1922.

————. *The Ground I Walked On: Recollections by the Former President of Hunter College.* Notre Dame, Ind., 1969.

————. *Like a Mighty Army: Hitler versus Established Religion.* New York, 1935.

————. *Strong Man Rules.* New York, 1934.

Skidelsky, Robert. *Oswald Mosley.* New York, 1975.

Smith, Rowland. "The Spanish Civil War and the British Literary Right." *The Dalhousie Review,* Spring 1971.

Snead-Cox, J. G. *The Life of Cardinal Vaughan.* Vol. 1. London, 1910.

Snowden, Philip. *Socialism and Syndicalism.* London, 1913.

Somerville, Henry. *The Catholic Social Movement.* London, 1933.

Southworth, Herbert R. *Guernica! Guernica!: A Study of Journalism, Propaganda, and History.* Berkeley, Calif., 1977.

Sparr, Arnold. *To Promote, Defend, and Redeem: Literary Revival in American Catholicism, 1920–1960.* Westport, Conn., 1990.

Speaight, Robert. "The European Mind: Hilaire Belloc's Thought and Writings." *Times Literary Supplement,* 21 May 1954.

————. *Letters from Hilaire Belloc.* London, 1928.

————. *The Life of Eric Gill.* New York, 1966.

————. *The Life of Hilaire Belloc.* New York, 1957.

————. *The Property Basket: Recollections of a Divided Life.* London, 1970.

Spender, Stephen. *The Thirties and After: Poetry, Politics, People, 1933–1970.* New York, 1978.

Steer, George L. *The Tree of Gernika.* London, 1938.

Stehlin, Stewart A. *Weimar and the Vatican 1919–1933: German-Vatican Diplomatic Relations in the Interwar Years.* Princeton, N.J., 1983.

Steinhoff, William. *George Orwell and the Origins of 1984.* Ann Arbor, Mich., 1975.

Sturzo, Luigi. *Church and State.* New York, 1939.

————. *Les Guerres Modernes et la Pensée Catholique.* Montreal, 1942.

————. *The Inner Laws of Society: A New Sociology.* New York, 1943.

————. *The International Community and the Right of War.* New York, 1930.

————. *Italy and Fascism*. New York, 1967.

————. *Nationalism and Internationalism*. New York, 1946.

————. "The Roman Question before and after Fascism." *Review of Politics*, October 1943.

Taylor, A. J. P. *Beaverbrook*. New York, 1972.

Telling, William. *The Pope in Politics*. London, 1937.

Thatcher, Donald. *Nietzsche in England 1890–1914: The Growth of a Republican*. Toronto, 1970.

Thomas, Hugh. *The Spanish Civil War*. Revised and enlarged edition. New York, 1977.

Thurlow, Richard. *Fascism in Britain: A History 1918–1945*. London, 1987.

Timasheff, Nicholas S. *The Sociology of Luigi Sturzo*. Baltimore, Md., 1962.

Toke, Leslie. *Some Methods of Social Study*. London, 1908.

Toynbee, Philip, ed. *The Distant Drum: Reflections on the Spanish Civil War*. London, 1976.

Tull, Charles J. *Father Coughlin and the New Deal*. Syracuse, N.Y., 1965.

Turner, Henry A. "Fascism and Modernization." *World Politics*, June 1972.

Ullman, Joan Connelly. *The Tragic Week: A Study of Anti-Clericalism in Spain, 1875–1912*. Cambridge, Mass., 1968.

Valaik, J. David. "American Catholic Dissenters and the Spanish Civil War." *The Catholic Historical Review*, January 1968.

Valentine, Ferdinand. *Father Vincent McNabb, O.P.* Westminster, Md., 1955.

Van Allen, Roger. *The Commonweal and American Catholicism*. Philadelphia, Pa., 1974.

Vanacalli, Joseph A. *Toward the Establishment of Liberal Catholicism in America*. Washington, D.C., 1983.

Vigener, Fritz. *Kettler. Ein deutsches Bischofsleben aus dem 19. Jahrhundert*. Munich, 1924.

Vincitorio, Gaetarro L., ed. *Crisis in the 'Great Republic': Essays Presented to Ross J. S. Hoffman*. New York, 1969.

Volk, Ludwig. *Katholische Kirche und Nationalsozialismus*. Mainz, 1987.

Wagner, Geoffrey. *Wyndham Lewis*. London, 1957.

Wall, Bernard. *Headlong into Change: An Autobiography and Memoir of Ideas since the Thirties*. London, 1969.

Wallace, Lillian Parker. *Leo XIII and the Rise of Socialism*. Durham, N.C., 1966.

Wallace, Martin. *The New Age under Orage*. New York, 1967.

Ward, Maisie. *G. K. Chesterton*. New York, 1943.

Wasserstein, Bernard. *Herbert Samuel: A Political Life*. Oxford, England, 1992.

Watkins, K. W. *Britain Divided: The Effects of the Spanish Civil War on British Political Opinion.* London, 1963.

Waugh, Evelyn. *Waugh in Abyssinia.* London, 1936.

Weaver, Mary Jo, and R. Scott Appleby. *Being Right: Conservative Catholics in America.* Bloomington, Ind., 1995.

Webb, Sidney. *Fabian Essays.* London, 1889.

Weber, Eugen. *Action Française: Royalism and Reaction in Twentieth-Century France.* Stanford, Calif., 1962.

Weigel, George. *Catholicism and the Renewal of American Democracy.* New York, 1989.

———. *Freedom and Its Discontents: Catholicism Confronts Modernity.* Washington, D.C., 1991.

———. *Peace and Freedom: Christian Faith, Democracy, and the Problem of War.* Washington, D.C., 1983.

Weintraub, Stanley. *The Last Great Cause: The Intellectuals and the Spanish Civil War.* New York, 1968.

Wentz, F. K. "American Catholic Periodicals React to Nazism." *Church History,* December 1962.

Whitaker, John T. *We Cannot Escape History.* New York, 1943.

Wicker, Brian. *First the Political Kingdom.* Notre Dame, Ind., 1967.

Wills, Garry. *Chesterton, Man and Mask.* New York, 1961.

Wilson, A. N. *Hilaire Belloc: A Biography.* New York, 1984.

Woodruff, Douglas. "Hilaire Belloc: His Life and Work, an Outline of Activities and Achievements." *The Tablet,* 25 July 1953.

———. ed. *For Hilaire Belloc: Essays in Honor of His 71st Birthday.* New York, 1942.

Wrench, John Evelyn. *Francis Yeats-Brown, 1886–1944.* London, 1948.

Wright, Anthony W. "Fabianism and Guild Socialism: Two Views of Democracy." *International Review of Social History,* vol. 43, part 2 (1978).

———. *G. D. H. Cole and Socialist Democracy.* Oxford, England, 1979.

———. "Guild Socialism Revisited." *Journal of Contemporary History* 9 (1974).

Wright, David. *Roy Campbell.* London, 1961.

Yeats-Brown, Francis. *Bengal Lancer.* London, 1939.

———. *European Jungle.* London, 1939.

———. *Golden Horn.* London, 1932.

Zahn, Gordon. *German Catholics and Hitler's Wars.* New York, 1962.

———. "The Unpublished Encyclical—An Opportunity Missed." *National Catholic Reporter,* 15 December 1972.

Zwerdling, Alex. *Orwell and the Left.* New Haven, Conn., 1974.

Index